ADVANCED PROGRAMMING USING VISUAL BASIC 2008

Julia Case Bradley
Mt. San Antonio College

Anita C. Millspaugh
Mt. San Antonio College

Higher Education

Boston   Burr Ridge, IL   Dubuque, IA   New York   San Francisco   St. Louis
Bangkok   Bogotá   Caracas   Kuala Lumpur   Lisbon   London   Madrid   Mexico City
Milan   Montreal   New Delhi   Santiago   Seoul   Singapore   Sydney   Taipei   Toronto

 **Higher Education**

ADVANCED PROGRAMMING USING VISUAL BASIC 2008
Published by McGraw-Hill, a business unit of The McGraw-Hill Companies, Inc., 1221 Avenue of the
Americas, New York, NY, 10020. Copyright © 2010 by The McGraw-Hill Companies, Inc. All rights
reserved. Previous editions © 2001, 2003, and 2007. No part of this publication may be reproduced or
distributed in any form or by any means, or stored in a database or retrieval system, without the prior
written consent of The McGraw-Hill Companies, Inc., including, but not limited to, in any network or
other electronic storage or transmission, or broadcast for distance learning.

Some ancillaries, including electronic and print components, may not be available to customers outside
the United States.

This book is printed on acid-free paper.

1 2 3 4 5 6 7 8 9 0 CUS/CUS 0 9

ISBN 978-0-07-351722-3
MHID 0-07-351722-4

Vice president/Editor in chief: *Elizabeth Haefele*
Vice president/Director of marketing: *John E. Biernat*
Senior sponsoring editor: *Scott Davidson*
Developmental editor II: *Alaina Grayson*
Marketing manager: *Tiffany Wendt*
Lead media producer: *Damian Moshak*
Director, Editing/Design/Production: *Jess Ann Kosic*
Project manager: *Marlena Pechan*
Senior production supervisor: *Janean A. Utley*
Senior designer: *Srdjan Savanovic*
Media developmental editor: *William Mulford*
Media project manager: *Mark A. S. Dierker*
Cover design: *Jessica Lazar*
Typeface: *11/13 Bodoni*
Compositor: *Aptara, Inc.*
Printer: *R. R. Donnelley*

Library of Congress Cataloging-in-Publication Data

Bradley, Julia Case.
   Advanced programming using Visual Basic 2008 / Julia Case Bradley, Anita C.
   Millspaugh.—4th ed.
   p. cm.
   Includes index.
   ISBN-13: 978-0-07-351722-3 (alk. paper)
   ISBN-10: 0-07-351722-4 (alk. paper)
   1. Microsoft Visual BASIC. 2. BASIC (Computer program language) 3. Application
   software—Development. 4. Web site development. I. Millspaugh, A. C. (Anita C.) II. Title.

QA76.73.B3B6955 2010
005.2'768—dc22
                                                                                      2008038156

www.mhhe.com

PREFACE

Visual Basic (VB) has become the most popular programming language for several reasons. VB is easy to learn, which makes it an excellent tool for understanding programming concepts. In addition, it has evolved into such a powerful and popular product that skilled Visual Basic programmers are in demand in the job market.

Visual Basic 2008, the latest version of VB, has many new features, especially in queries and Web application development. Visual Basic is designed to allow the programmer to develop applications that run under Windows and/or in a Web browser without the complexity generally associated with programming.

This edition of the text is updated to Visual Studio 2008, .NET 3.5, and ASP.NET 3.5. The screen captures are based on Windows Vista, but all programs can be run in Windows XP, although the special effects of WPF cannot be seen in XP.

About This Text

This textbook is intended for use in an advanced programming course, which assumes completion of an introductory course. The text incorporates the basic concepts of programming, problem solving, programming logic, as well as the design techniques of an object-oriented language.

Appendix B contains a summary of topics normally covered in an introductory text, as a tool for review.

Approach

Chapter topics are presented in a sequence that allows the programmer to learn how to deal with a visual interface while acquiring important programming skills such as accessing and updating data in a relational database, developing applications for the Web and for mobile devices, and adding browser-based Help files to an application.

The chapters may be used in various sequences to accommodate the needs of the course, as well as a shorter quarter system or a semester-long course.

Changes in This Edition

This edition presents material in a sequence designed for teaching students and does not attempt to cover all topics for certification exams.

FEATURES OF THIS TEXT

Hands-On Programming Examples

These complete programming exercises guide students through the process of planning, writing, and executing Visual Basic programs.

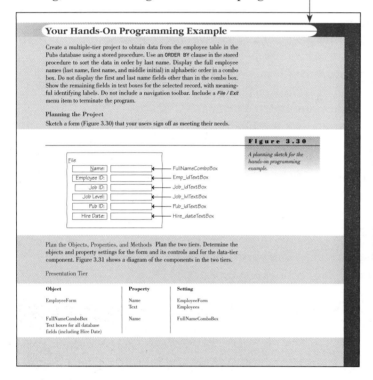

Your Hands-On Programming Example

Create a multiple-tier project to obtain data from the employee table in the Pubs database using a stored procedure. Use an ORDER BY clause in the stored procedure to sort the data in order by last name. Display the full employee names (last name, first name, and middle initial) in alphabetic order in a combo box. Do not display the first and last name fields other than in the combo box. Show the remaining fields in text boxes for the selected record, with meaningful identifying labels. Do not include a navigation toolbar. Include a *File / Exit* menu item to terminate the program.

Planning the Project
Sketch a form (Figure 3.30) that your users sign off as meeting their needs.

Figure 3.30

A planning sketch for the hands-on programming example.

Plan the Objects, Properties, and Methods Plan the two tiers. Determine the objects and property settings for the form and its controls and for the data-tier component. Figure 3.31 shows a diagram of the components in the two tiers.

Presentation Tier

Object	Property	Setting
EmployeeForm	Name	EmployeeForm
	Text	Employees
FullNameComboBox	Name	FullNameComboBox
Text boxes for all database fields (including Hire Date)		

CHAPTER

4

Windows Database Using Related Tables

at the completion of this chapter, you will be able to . . .

1. Explain the types of table relationships.
2. Display master/detail records.
3. Display a field from a second table using a lookup.
4. Create a search using a parameterized query and write a filter to retrieve specific data.
5. Assign data values to unbound controls.
6. Retrieve and display the parent row for a selected child row.
7. Retrieve and display an array of child rows for a selected parent row.
8. Create an application that displays data from a many-to-many relationship.
9. Select the correct locations for handling and formatting data in a multitier application.

Learning Objectives

Specific objectives tell students what will be covered in the chapter and what they will be able to do after completing the chapter.

Feedback 4.2

1. What Fill method statements are created for a relationship for Customers and Orders? Assume that the project contains two TableAdapters called CustomersTableAdapter and OrdersTableAdapter as well as a DataSet called NorthwindDataSet.
2. How can you view the relationship between two tables?
3. Describe the necessary steps to display the job description from the jobs table rather than the job id when displaying the employee table.

Feedback Questions

Feedback questions encourage students to reflect on the topics covered and evaluate their understanding of details relating to that topic.

 TIP

If the drop-down arrows do not appear in the Data Sources window, make sure that you have a form displaying in the designer. ■

TIPs

Tips, found in the margins throughout the text, help students avoid potential trouble spots in their programs and encourage them to develop good programming habits.

Case Studies

Case Studies provide continuing-theme exercises that may be used throughout the course.

Security Issue

Any coverage that discusses security concerns is pointed out with a Security Issue icon.

Case Studies

Claytor's Cottages

Modify your Claytor's Cottages case study project to display the room information. The Room form should display for the *Edit / Rooms* menu item.

On the Room form, include a combo box that holds the room name. Use check boxes to indicate if the room has a Jacuzzi, Private access, and/or Fireplace. Display the Bed type and the room rates from the Beds table.

Hint: You can bind the checked property of a check box to a Boolean data field.

Christian's Car Rentals

Modify your case study application to display the vehicle information. Display a combo box that contains the car sizes. When the user selects a size, display the price and mileage rate in text boxes. The related models and manufacturer should display in a grid.

---

files have the same name, you are prompted to select the file to keep. A check box allows you to show the deleted files since the last copy operation.

See *"How to: Copy Web Site Files with the Copy Web Site Tool"* in MSDN for steps to copy all files at once, copy files individually, or synchronize files.

Publishing a Web Site

The Publish Web Site utility precompiles the Web pages and code content. The compilation process removes the source code from the files and leaves only stub files and compiled assemblies for the pages. You can specify the output location as either a directory or a server location.

Precompiling the Web pages offers a couple of advantages over just copying the pages. One advantage is response speed. When pages are just copied to a site, they must compile when a request is made for the page. Not having the source code on the site also provides some security. During the publish process, you have the option of having markup protection, which does not allow for later updates to the pages. If you opt to not have the files updatable, the code in single-file pages is deployed as source code rather than being compiled into an assembly.

Online Learning Center

Visit the Advanced Programming Using Visual Basic 2008 Web site at http://www.mhhe.com/AdvVB2008/ for instructor and student resources.

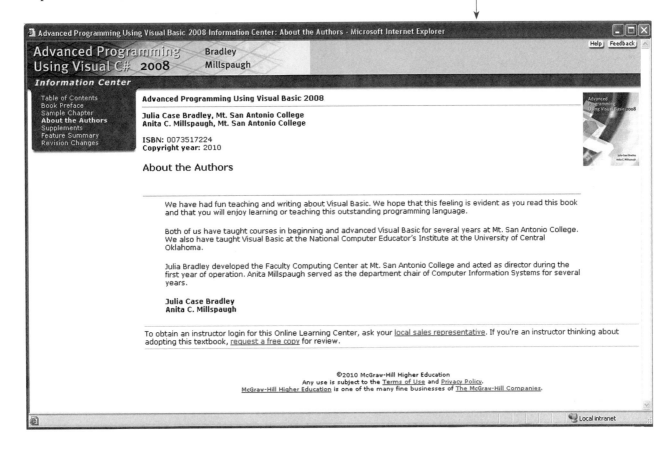

Many topics from the introductory course are presented in greater detail and demand more from the students. Many other advanced topics are presented, including displaying and updating relational databases, WCF Services, data structures, user controls, Help files, and mobile application development for Windows devices, along with expanded coverage of cascading style sheets and AJAX for Web development.

This edition now includes coverage of the many new features in Visual Studio including LINQ, WPF, and WCF. Both LINQ and WPF have been placed in Chapter 13, the "Additional Topics" chapter, allowing you to cover them at any point in the course.

The layout for Web pages uses the preferred method of incorporating <div> for sections and all formatting with styles. Tables are only used within a <div>.

Major Revisions and Additional Topics in This Edition

With the exception of small, concept-demonstrating programs, all programs are written as multitier applications. WCF Services are covered prior to Web applications, and the middle-tier components are written as services.

The text covers the new features of Visual Studio 2008 and many useful existing features, including

- Windows Presentation Foundation (WPF).

- Windows Communication Foundation (WCF).

- Language-Integrated Queries (LINQ).

- Creation of DataContext objects from database tables for use with LINQ.

- AJAX.

- Cascading style sheets.

- Adding of validation code to the DataSet object.

- Crystal Reports using local databases for both Windows and Web applications.

- Partial classes.

- The singleton design pattern for a class that should be instantiated only once.

- Validation of user input using `TryParse`.

- ClickOnce deployment.

- Generics and generic collections.

- Master pages.

- SQL Server Express, which provides the advantage of local database files for development and testing.

- TableAdapter, BindingSource, TableAdapterManager (new), and Binding-Navigator objects.

- Table lookups for populating a combo box from a related table.

- Use of properties and methods of the BindingSource to filter, navigate, and update database tables.

- Use of named table relationships.

- Use of related tables in a Web service.

- The Login controls for Web applications.

- Display and updating of data using the Web DataSource objects and data components: GridView, DetailsView, and FormView.

- The built-in Web server, which allows development of Web applications without the necessity of running IIS. This feature also allows development on the home editions of Windows XP and Vista, and does not require administrative rights for all Web development.

- Smart Device applications, including the new device emulators.

- Use of My.Application for changing culture settings.

- The BackgroundWorker component for executing more than one thread.

New features of the Visual Studio IDE that are covered in the text include

- The Object Relational O/R Designer.

- XAML split windows.

- The TableAdapterManager.

- CSS Properties window, Manage Styles window, and Apply Styles window.

Chapter Organization

Each chapter begins with identifiable objectives and a brief overview. Numerous coding examples as well as hands-on projects with guidance for the coding appear throughout. Thought-provoking feedback questions give students time to reflect on the current topic and to evaluate their understanding of the details. The end-of-chapter items include key terms, a chapter review, questions, programming exercises, and two case studies. The case studies provide a continuing-theme exercise that may be used throughout the course. The in-chapter programs are included on the student Web site, allowing the student to test and modify existing code. Of course, it is also important to develop a complete application from scratch to really learn the programming techniques.

> ***Chapter 1, "Visual Studio and the .NET Framework,"*** discusses the features of the Visual Studio IDE and the .NET Framework. Applications demonstrate how to display data from the AssemblyInfo.vb file using the My object. MDI projects, toolbars, and status bars are reviewed.

> ***Chapter 2, "Building Multitier Programs with Classes,"*** reviews object-oriented terminology, creating classes, and instantiating objects. Creating and throwing exceptions from the business services tier is introduced. The ErrorProvider and TryParse are demonstrated to improve the efficiency of validation in the presentation tier.

> ***Chapter 3, "Windows Database Applications,"*** explains the relationship of datasets, tables, rows, and constraints. Database applications use SQL Server databases to display information in grids, combo boxes, labels, and the database display controls.

Chapter 4, "Windows Database Using Related Tables," explores the types of table relationships and covers the display of related tables on Windows forms. The chapter discusses how to retrieve and display the parent row for a selected child row and also an array of child rows for a selected parent row.

Chapter 5, "Windows Database Updates," performs updates on data in a grid, in bound controls on a form, and in unbound controls. Updating related tables also is covered. Both a combo box selection and the form's binding navigator are used to navigate records.

Chapter 6, "Services," discusses the concepts of WCF Services. Examples for services include calculations and database access.

Chapter 7, "Web Applications," discusses the concepts of Web-based applications and the files that make up a Web project. Hyperlinks and link buttons allow navigation from one Web page to another while maintaining the state (data values). The Validator controls test user input. Master pages and cascading style sheets assist in designing the layout for the Web site.

Chapter 8, "Web Database Applications," covers the techniques for accessing data using data source controls. The chapter discusses displaying data from related tables and updating databases from a Web page. Multitier development uses a service for database access and updates.

Chapter 9, "Reports," uses advanced reporting features, such as numeric functions, grouping, sorting, and special fields. Both Windows applications and Web applications are covered.

Chapter 10, "Collections," discusses types of collections including stacks, queues, dictionaries, hash tables, sorted lists, and array lists. The chapter demonstrates adding objects to the Items collection of a list box. The chapter also demonstrates implementing the generics and generic collections.

Chapter 11, "User Controls," creates Windows user controls and Web controls. The techniques for raising an event and writing code in the form to handle the event are discussed.

Chapter 12, "Help Files," creates the necessary files to set up HTML Help and uses HTML Help Workshop to create a Help file.

Chapter 13, "Additional Topics in Visual Basic," demonstrates how to develop applications for mobile devices, how to create interfaces with WPF and use the WPF controls in a Windows Form Application, how to localize an application, and how to use the BackgroundWorker class to run processes in a separate thread. LINQ is introduced with arrays, LINQ to SQL, and LINQ to XML.

The appendices offer important additional material. Appendix A holds the answers to all Feedback questions. Appendix B is an extensive review of VB topics generally covered in an introductory course. Appendix C covers deployment using ClickOnce and Appendix D contains many helpful tips and shortcuts for mastering the Visual Studio environment.

Resources for Instructors

The **Online Learning Center (OLC)** available at www.mhhe.com/AdvVB2008 contains the following supplemental materials:

Instructor's Manual

- Objectives with built-in summaries for each chapter.

- Teaching suggestions.

- Answers to the Review Questions from the end-of-chapter material.

- Chapter topics covered in the Programming Exercises.

   Testbank offers over 500 questions covering key terms and concepts found in each chapter. The test questions appear in the form of true-false and multiple-choice questions. Text page references have been provided for all questions, including level-of-difficulty rating. A computerized version of the **testbank in EZTest** is also available.

   PowerPoint Presentation, authored by Brenda Nielsen of Mesa Community College–Red Mountain, follows the outline of the Instructor's Manual and gives instructors a resource for presenting the text material to a classroom.

   Text figures are available electronically for use in presentations, transparencies, or handouts. These include all the illustrations, screenshots, and tables featured throughout the book.

   An **Online Learning Center (OLC)** is also available for students and instructors. The OLC can be found at www.mhhe.com/AdvVB2008 and offers a wide variety of learning opportunities for students, including additional case studies, self-quizzes, and downloadable data files. Instructors also will find the OLC a useful resource.

Acknowledgments

We would like to express our appreciation to the many people who have contributed to the successful completion of this text. Most especially, we thank the students at Mt. San Antonio College who helped class-test the material and who greatly influenced the manuscript.

   Many people have worked very hard to design and produce this text. We would like to thank our editors Liz Haefele, Scott Davidson, and Alaina Grayson. Our thanks also to the many people who produced this text including Marlena Pechan, and Betsy Blumenthal.

   We greatly appreciate John Blyzka, Peter van der Goes, and Robert Price for their thorough technical reviews, constructive criticism, and many valuable suggestions. And most importantly, we are grateful to Dennis and Richard for their support and understanding through the long days and busy phone lines.

TO THE STUDENT

Welcome to the exciting new features of Visual Basic 2008. You have probably already learned that the best way to learn how to program is to actually sit at a computer and write code, change things, and test it again. Stepping through existing code is also a great tool in learning new techniques. With that in mind, we have included all of the code from the examples within the chapters on your student text Web site. Please feel free to load the programs, change things, and test it again.

But . . . if you really want to learn how it works, it is critical that you create a blank project and try the techniques yourself. If you run into a problem, take a look at the sample and compare properties and code.

There are several tools in this text to help you on your way.

- Each chapter begins with a list of topics and ends with a summary. Combine these for a thumbnail review of the chapter. Understanding the terminology is an important part of learning any new language, which is also true with programming languages.

- A list of key terms is at the end of each chapter. Each of those terms is in boldface within the chapter. There is also a glossary at the end of the text where you can look up the definition of the terms.

- Test yourself with the Feedback questions as you work through each section of a chapter. The review questions at the end of the chapter can test your understanding of the topics.

- Tips are included to give suggestions in situations where you may run into problems caused by the version of software installed/not installed or with settings.

- Make sure to check out the appendixes, which hold a wealth of support material.

J.C.B.
A.C.M.

The Authors

We have had fun teaching and writing about Visual Basic. We hope that this feeling is evident as you read this book and that you will enjoy learning or teaching this outstanding programming language.

Both of us have taught courses in beginning and advanced Visual Basic for several years at Mt. San Antonio College. We also have taught Visual Basic at the National Computer Educator's Institute at the University of Central Oklahoma.

Julia Bradley developed the Faculty Computing Center at Mt. San Antonio College and acted as director during the first year of operation. Anita Millspaugh served as the department chair of Computer Information Systems for several years.

Julia Case Bradley
Anita C. Millspaugh

BRIEF CONTENTS

Chapter 1
Visual Studio and the .NET
Framework   1

Chapter 2
Building Multitier Programs
with Classes   49

Chapter 3
Windows Database
Applications   105

Chapter 4
Windows Database Using Related
Tables   149

Chapter 5
Windows Database Updates   187

Chapter 6
Services   249

Chapter 7
Web Applications   275

Chapter 8
Web Database Applications   351

Chapter 9
Reports   403

Chapter 10
Collections   431

Chapter 11
User Controls   465

Chapter 12
Help Files   491

Chapter 13
Additional Topics in Visual
Basic   507

Appendix A
Answers to Feedback
Questions   541

Appendix B
Review of Introductory
VB Concepts   553

Appendix C
Deployment   599

Appendix D
Tips and Shortcuts for Mastering
the Environment   607

Glossary   625

Index   634

CONTENTS

Visual Studio and the .NET Framework   1

The .NET Framework   2

The Common Language Runtime   2
The Class Library   2
Compiling to Intermediate Language   4
Assemblies   5
The References Collection   5
ASP.NET   6

Visual Studio   6

Temporary Projects   6
Setting Environment Options   7
The Solution Explorer   8
Partial Classes   11
The Project Designer   12
Deploying Windows Applications   13

The VB My Objects   13

Using Assembly Information   14

Setting the Assembly Information   14
Retrieving the Assembly Information   16
Viewing a Program's Attributes   17

Menus, Toolbars, and Status Bars   18

Creating Menus with MenuStrips   18
Creating Context Menus with ContextMenuStrips   21
CreatingToolbars with ToolStrips   22
Creating Status Bars with StatusStrips   23

MDI Applications   25

Multiple Document Interface   25
Creating an MDI Project   26
Adding a Window Menu   26
The Singleton Design Pattern   28
Splash Screen Forms   29
About Box Forms   31

Class Diagrams   31
Creating a Class Diagram   31
Customizing a Class Diagram   32

Your Hands-On Programming Example   34

Building Multitier Programs with Classes   49

Object-Oriented Programming   50
OOP Terminology   50
Reusable Objects   53
Multitier Applications   53

Creating Classes   54
Designing Your Own Class   54
Creating Properties in a Class   54
Constructors and Destructors   56
A Basic Business Class   58
Throwing and Catching Exceptions   60
Alternatives to Exception Handling   62
Modifying the User Interface to Validate at the Field Level   63
Modifying the Business Class   68
Displaying the Summary Data   72

Namespaces, Scope, and Accessibility   74
Namespaces   74
Scope   74
Lifetime   76
Accessibility Domains   76

Creating Classes that Inherit   77
Adding a New Class File   77
Creating a Constructor   78
Inheriting Variables and Methods   78
Using Properties and Methods of the Base Class   79

**Passing Control Properties
to a Component**   80
  Creating an Enumeration   81

Garbage Collection   83

**Your Hands-On
Programming Example**   84

3 Windows Database Applications   105

**Visual Studio and Database
Applications**   106
  ADO.NET   106
  *Accessing Data in the .NET
Framework*   107
  XML Data   109
  The Visual Studio IDE   110

**Creating a Database
Application**   111
  Local Database Files   112
  *Creating a Windows Database
Application—Step-by-Step*   112
  *Displaying Data in Individual
Fields—Step-by-Step*   117
  *Selecting the Control Type
for Details View*   118
  *Setting the Captions for
Database Fields*   119
  Formatting Bound Data   120

**Selecting a Record from
a List**   123
  *Populating Combo Boxes
with Data*   123
  *Adding a Combo Box for
Selection—Step-by-Step*   124
  *Adding an Expression to
Concatenate Fields*   125
  *Adding a Concatenated
Field—Step-by-Step*   126

**Sorting the Data for the
ListBox**   127
  Sorting with the BindingSource   127
  *Modifying the SQL Select
Statement*   127
  *Eliminating Unnecessary SQL
Queries*   130

Using a Stored Procedure   131
  *Creating a Stored Procedure
in the VS IDE*   131
  *Retrieving Data by Using a
Stored Procedure*   132

Multiple Tiers   133
  *Creating a Data-Tier
Component*   133
  *Coding the Form's Database
Objects*   134
  *Binding Data Fields to
Form Controls*   135
  *Creating a Data Tier—
Step-by-Step*   137

**Your Hands-On
Programming Example**   141

4 Windows Database Using Related Tables   149

Data Relationships   150
  One-to-Many Relationships   150
  Many-to-Many Relationships   150
  One-to-One Relationships   151
  Constraints   152

Related Tables   153
  *Creating a DataSet with More
Than One Table*   153
  *Displaying Master/Detail
Records—Step-by-Step*   153
  *Viewing or Setting a
Relationship*   157
  *Creating a Table Lookup—
Step-by-Step*   157

Queries and Filters   159
  Using a Parameterized Query   160
  *Creating a Parameterized
Query—Step-by-Step*   160
  Filtering a DataSet   162
  *Filtering a DataSet—
Step-by-Step*   164

Unbound Data Fields   166
  Referring to Records and Fields   167
  *Retrieving a Related
Parent Row*   168
  Retrieving Related Child Rows   170

Many-to-Many Relationships   172
  Retrieving Matching Rows   173
  *The Titles Authors
M:N Program*   175

Multitier Considerations   178
  Formatting a Grid at Run Time   178

**Your Hands-On Programming
Example**   179

5 Windows Database Updates   187

A Simple Update in a Grid   188
Updating a DataSet   188
Database Handling in the
Visual Studio IDE   189

The Data Objects, Methods,
and Properties   191
The TableAdapter and
TableAdapterManager   194

The BindingSource Object   195
Binding Source Properties and
Methods   196
Binding Source Update Methods   197
Binding Source Events   198

DataSet Updating   198
SQL Statements for Updates   198
Concurrency   199
Testing Update Programs   199

Updating a DataSet in Bound
Controls   199
The Logic of an Update Program   200
User Options during an Update   201
The Add and Save Logic   202
The Delete and Cancel Logic   204
The Edit Logic   205
A Complete Update Program   206
Navigating from a Combo Box
Selection   210

Validating User Input Data   212
Checking for Nulls   212
Adding Validation to a Details
View Program   213
Adding Validation to the DataSet
for a DataGridView Program   215

Handling Data Exceptions   217
The DataGridView DataError
Event   217
The BindingSource DataError
Event   218

Updating Related Tables   218
Parent and Child Relationships   219
Hierarchical Updates   220
A Related Table Update
Program—Step-by-Step   220

Security Considerations   232

Your Hands-On Programming
Example   232

6 Services   249

Concepts and Terminology   250

Window Communication
Foundation (WCF)   251
XML   251
SOAP   252
WSDL   252
More Acronyms   252

Creating a WCF Service   252
Create a Hello World Service—
Step-by-Step   252
Testing a Service—
Step-by-Step   255

Consuming a WCF Service   256
Create a Project to Consume
the Service—Step-by-Step   256

Performing Calculations in a
WCF Service   259

Accessing Data through a
WCF Service   261
Creating a Data WCF
Service—Step-by-Step   261
The DataSet Merge Method   266
Placing Validation and Access
Code in the Data-Tier Projects   266
Writing Validation Code   267
Setting Properties of the
Dataset Fields   268

Working with Related Tables   268

Your Hands-On
Programming Example   268

7 Web Applications   275

Web Applications   276
Client/Server Web Applications   276

Types of Web Sites   278
File System Web Sites   278
IIS Web Sites   279
Remote Sites and FTP Sites   279

Creating Web Sites   279
Web Page Files   280
Web Forms in the Visual
Studio IDE   281
Control Types   282
Event Handling   284
Button Controls   285
Debugging   286

The Hyperlink Control 287
Including Images on Web
Pages 288
The Calendar Control 289

**Layout and Design of
Web Forms** **290**

Current Standards for
Page Layout 291
Cascading Style Sheets 291
Using DIV Elements to Lay
Out a Web Page 295
Creating a Page Layout—
Step-by-Step 295
Master Pages and Content
Pages 304
Creating a Master Page—
Step-by-Step 305
Setting the Tab Order 311

Using the Validation Controls **312**

Displaying Asterisks 314
Testing for Validity 314

**The Web Application
Objects** **315**

State Management **315**

Overview of State Management
Techniques 316
Application and Session
Objects 317
Cookies 318
The ViewState 319
Retaining the Values of Variables 319

Login Features **321**

The Login Controls 321
Adding Login Controls
to an Application 324
Using the Web Site
Administration Tool 324
Setting Up a Login Application 325

AJAX **327**

AJAX Control Toolkit 328
Download and Use AJAX
Controls—Step-by-Step 328
Use a SlideShow Extender
Control—Step-by-Step 330
Partial Page Updates 333
Other AJAX Notes 334

ASP.NET Page Life Cycle **334**

Managing Web Projects **335**

Location of Files 335
Opening a Saved Web Site 335
Moving and Renaming a
Web Project 335

Copying and Publishing
Web Sites 336

**Your Hands-On Programming
Example** **336**

**Web Database
Applications** **351**

Data Access in ASP.NET **352**

Data Source Controls 352
Displaying Data on a Form
with a Data Source 355
Creating a Parameterized
Query—Step-by-Step 359
Displaying Data from Related
Tables 362
Adding Related Tables—
Step-by-Step 363
Displaying Related Data on
Multiple Pages 364
Creating Multiple Pages—
Step-by-Step 365
Selecting Data in a GridView 366
Data Readers versus Datasets 368
Caching 368

Updating a Database **368**

Updating with a Data Source
Control 369
Exception Handling 378
Validating Input Data 379

Multiple Tiers **381**

Using an ObjectDataSource 381
Creating a Service for Database
Updating—Step-by-Step 381

**Maintaining the State of
List Boxes** **387**

Maintaining the Selection of a
Drop-Down List 387
Maintaining the List in a
Dynamic List Box 387

Unbound Controls **388**

Using Unbound Controls with
a SqlDataSource 388
Using Unbound Controls with
an ObjectDataSource 390
Adding a Table from the IDE 391

Creating Custom Error Pages **392**

Using Validation Controls **393**

**Your Hands-On Programming
Example** **394**

Reports   403

Writing Reports   404

Creating and Displaying a Crystal Report   404

Creating a Grouped Report—
Step-by-Step   404
Displaying a Report from a
Windows Form—Step-by-Step   410
Using the Report Designer   412
Modifying the Products
Report—Step-by-Step   413
Displaying a Report from a
Web Form   419
Selecting from Multiple
Reports   420

Your Hands-On Programming Example   421

Collections   431

Referencing Collection Items   432

System.Collections Namespace   432

Using Stacks   434
Using Queues   434
Using Hash Tables   435
Sorted Lists   436
Using the Example Program   437
Using Array Lists   440

Creating a Collection of Objects   441

A Collection of Student
Objects   441
Declaring a Collection   441
Adding Objects to a Collection   442
Removing an Element from a
Collection   442
Retrieving an Element from a
Collection   442
Using For Each/Next   442
The Completed Program   443

Using an Items Collection   446

Generics   449

Generic Classes   450
Generic Collections   452

Your Hands-On Programming Example   456

User Controls   465

Windows User Controls   466

The Control Author versus
the Developer   466
Creating a New Control   466
Inheriting from an Existing
Control   467
Creating an Inherited User
Control—Step-by-Step   467
Adding Properties to a Control   471
Adding Events to a Control   472
Putting It All Together   474
Creating a Composite User
Control   475

Web User Controls   480

Creating a Web User Control—
Step-by-Step   480

Your Hands-On Programming Example   483

Help Files   491

HTML Help Workshop   492

Setting Up Help   492
A Help Facility   492
File Types   494
Creating the Files   494

Creating a Help Facility   495

Creating a Help Facility—
Step-by-Step   495

Connecting the HTML Help File to an Application   500

Continuing the Step-by-Step
Exercise   501
Adding Help to a Menu   501
Modifying Help Files   502
Connecting Context-Sensitive
Help Topics to Controls   503
Adding a Help Button to a
Message Box   503
The Help Button   503

Other Forms of User Assistance   504

Additional Topics in Visual Basic   507

Device Applications   508

Using Emulators   508
Smart Device Applications   508

*A First Smart Device
Application—Step-by-Step*   *510*
A Database Application   *514*

**Windows Presentation
Foundation (WPF)**   **517**

*The Roles of Designer and
Programmer*   *517*
WPF Features   *518*
Creating a WPPF Project   *518*
A WPF Calculation Example   *520*
A Multiple-Window Example   *521*
Interoperability   *521*

LINQ   **522**

LINQ Keywords   *522*
A First Look at LINQ   *523*
Additional LINQ Keywords   *524*
LINQ to SQL   *524*
LINQ to XML   *528*

World-Ready Programs   **531**

*Globalization, Localizability,
and Localization*   *531*
*Writing a Localized Hello
World—Step-by-Step*   *533*

Threading   **534**

Background Workers   *534*

**Your Hands-On Programming
Example**   **537**

**Answers to
Feedback
Questions**   **541**

**Review of
Introductory
VB Concepts**   **553**

Deployment   **599**

**Tips and Shortcuts
for Mastering the
Environment**   **607**

Glossary   **625**

Index   **634**

1

Visual Studio and the .NET Framework

at the completion of this chapter, you will be able to . . .

1. Distinguish the features of the Visual Studio IDE and the .NET Framework.

2. Identify and understand the purpose of each of the files listed in the Solution Explorer.

3. Understand what happens at compile time.

4. Set and display data from the application's assembly attributes.

5. Create an MDI project with a parent form, child forms, a toolbar, status bar, context menus, and ToolTips.

6. Use the singleton design pattern to create a class that should be instantiated only once.

Microsoft revolutionized the programming for Windows applications and became a bigger player in the development of Web applications with the introduction of the .NET Framework and Visual Studio (VS). These products introduced significant changes into program development for Visual Basic (VB). Not only did .NET bring true object orientation to the language; it also provided great advances in the ease of developing projects for cross-platform compatibility.

The two major parts of .NET are the Microsoft .NET Framework and the Visual Studio integrated development environment (IDE). The IDE is used to develop programs and the Framework runs the programs.

The .NET Framework

The **.NET Framework** provides a platform for developing and running applications and Windows Communications Foundation (WCF) services written in multiple languages on multiple platforms. The Framework is composed of the common language runtime, class libraries, and ASP.NET—a component-based version of active server pages (ASP).

The Common Language Runtime

The **common language runtime (CLR)** is an environment that manages execution of code. It provides services for tasks such as integrating components developed in different languages, handling errors across languages, providing security, and managing the storage and destruction of objects.

Any code that is compiled to run in the CLR is called *managed code*. The managed code automatically contains **metadata**, which means *data that describe data*. A common language runtime portable executable (PE) file contains the metadata along with the code. The metadata include data types, members, references, and information needed to load classes and to call methods from a class.

The CLR also manages memory used by .NET applications. Objects that are no longer being used are automatically removed from memory by the garbage collector component of the CLR. When you allow the runtime to handle the garbage collection of objects, the data are referred to as *managed data*. Although you can manage application memory yourself, it is usually better and more secure to let the runtime handle it.

Your code can be integrated with classes and methods of managed code written in other programming languages. The CLR has standards for data types that allow you to pass an instance of one of your classes to a method created in a different language. Although we will not be doing any cross-language programming in this text, you should be aware of this powerful feature. Note that it is also possible to integrate methods and components created in unmanaged code, but beware of calling unmanaged code such as C++ functions or COM components as they may introduce security risks to your program.

The Class Library

All of the .NET classes and interfaces are stored in a library known as the **.NET Framework class library**. The library is organized into sections or groups known as *namespaces*. You should be familiar with some of the common namespaces such as *System* and *System.Drawing*. Each namespace contains classes, structures, enumerations, delegates, and/or interfaces that you can use in your programs. Table 1.1 shows some of the namespaces in the .NET Framework class library.

Selected Namespaces from the .NET Class Library   **Table 1.1**

Namespace	Contents
System	Base classes and fundamental classes for data types, events, and event handlers.
System.Collections	Definitions of collections of objects such as lists, queues, and dictionaries.
System.Data	ADO.NET architecture used to access databases.
System.Drawing	GDI+ graphics for drawing on the screen, printer, or any other graphic device.
System.IO	Types for reading and writing data streams and files.
System.Linq	Supports queries for Language-Integerated Queries
System.Security	Base classes for permissions.
System.Threading	Classes for multithreaded programming.
System.Web.Services	Classes for building and using Web Services.
System.Windows.Forms	Classes for creating graphical components for programs that execute in the Windows operating environment.
System.XML	Support for XML processing. XML is a standard for transferring data.

The classes in the library comply with published standards known as the **Common Language Specification (CLS)**. The CLS specifies how a language that interacts with the CLR should behave. If you want a program to interact with programs and components written in other languages, you should make sure that it is CLS compliant. The rules for CLS compliance can be found in the .NET Framework Developer's Guide under the heading "Writing CLS-Compliant Code." Note that all VB programs that you write using the VS IDE will be CLS compliant automatically.

Types

The .NET documentation uses the general term *types* to refer to the classes, structures, enumerations, delegates, interfaces, and data types in the library, as well as any that you define. You can think of a type as any element that you can use in the As clause of a declaration:

```
Dim AnyName As SomeType
```

Value Types versus Reference Types

When you declare a variable, it may be considered a **value type** or a **reference type**. The difference between the two determines how the runtime will treat the variables when you assign one variable to another. For example, if you assign one integer variable to another, you have two memory locations with the same value:

```
SecondValueInteger = FirstValueInteger
```

However, if you assign one reference type to another, you have two variables that point to the same object in memory:

```
SecondForm = FirstForm     ' Assign reference for first form to second form.
```

Any changes that you make to either variable are made to the one object in memory to which both variables refer. In some previous versions of VB, reference types were called *object variables*. However, VB reference types include more types than the more restrictive object variables.

```
' Value types.
Dim FirstValueInteger As Integer = 10
Dim SecondValueInteger As Integer
SecondValueInteger = FirstValueInteger
FirstValueInteger = 5
' What is the value in each of the variables?
Debug.WriteLine("FirstValueInteger = " & FirstValueInteger.ToString() & _
   "; SecondValueInteger = " & SecondValueInteger.ToString())

' Reference types.
Dim FirstForm As New Form1()
Dim SecondForm As Form1
SecondForm = FirstForm      ' Assign reference for first form to second form.
SecondForm.Text = "Second Form Caption"
FirstForm.Text = "New Caption for First Form"
' What is the Text property of FirstForm? Of SecondForm?
Debug.WriteLine("FirstForm = " & FirstForm.Text & _
   "; SecondForm = " & SecondForm.Text)
```

Can you predict the debug output from the two groups of statements above? Follow the logic and write down your answer; then look back here to check your understanding.

```
FirstValueInteger = 5; SecondValueInteger = 10
FirstForm = New Caption for First Form; SecondForm = New Caption for First Form
```

All numeric data types are value types. Reference types include class types, arrays (even if the individual elements are numeric), and strings. A value type always holds a value; when you declare a new variable of a value type, the variable is always initialized, either to a value that you supply or to the default value. A reference type may or may not hold a value; you can use the IsNot Nothing condition to determine whether the variable refers to an instance of an object.

Compiling to Intermediate Language

The program code that you write is referred to as *source code*. The compiler translates your code into **Microsoft intermediate language (MSIL)** or sometimes referred to as just *IL*. MSIL is a platform-independent set of instructions that is combined with the metadata to form a file called a *portable executable* (PE) file, which has an .exe or .dll extension. When your program runs, the MSIL is converted to the native code of the specific machine only as it is needed, using a just-in-time (JIT) compiler, which is part of the CLR (Figure 1.1).

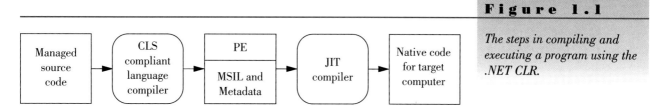

Assemblies

An **assembly** is a basic unit of code that may be a single PE file or multiple files. Each of your applications will be contained in a single assembly, which is the smallest deployable piece of code. An assembly has an **assembly manifest** that contains metadata about the version, a table describing all of the files needed by the assembly, and an "assembly reference list" that specifies all of the external files needed, such as DLLs created by someone else. An assembly is similar to an .exe or a .dll file written in earlier versions of Visual Basic—it contains all of the necessary information to run the application or component.

Recall that the .NET Framework class library is not one big file but rather a collection of files. The classes are stored in many files with the extension .dll and referred to as *DLLs* (for dynamic link libraries). Each of the DLLs in the class library is one assembly. As your program begins execution, only the needed assemblies are loaded into memory. When you want to use a type that is not already referenced, you must add a reference to the DLL (assembly).

Attributes

Attributes are tags containing information about parts of a program such as types or methods. The system defines many attributes of your assembly, such as the name, version, culture, and security. The attributes are part of the metadata in a .NET assembly. The process of examining the metadata in an assembly's attributes is called *reflection*.

Later in this chapter, you will learn to retrieve and use the custom attributes in a project's assembly information, which is stored in the AssemblyInfo.vb file.

The References Collection

A **reference object** is used to connect a Visual Basic project to external components. The two types of reference objects are assemblies and COM objects. A reference to another project is an assembly reference and is called a *project-to-project reference*. COM objects are components written in versions of VB prior to .NET, or other non-CLS-compliant languages.

ASP.NET

Another big part of the .NET world is the improvement in Web development. ASP.NET 3.5 is the newest version of **Active Server Pages (ASP)**. It is a Web development environment that can compile applications written in any .NET-compatible language including Visual Basic. This means that the benefits of the common language runtime and managed code are available for developing Web applications. ASP.NET makes Web development easier by providing the same debugging support for Web Forms and Web Services as for Windows applications.

You will begin working with ASP.NET in Chapter 7. Chapters 8 and 9 cover accessing databases from ASP.NET, which is a common technique for displaying data on a Web site.

Feedback 1.1

1. What is meant by the term *.NET Framework*?
2. What are the meaning and function of each of these terms?
   a. CLR
   b. CLS
   c. MSIL
   d. PE
3. What is the difference between a reference type and a value type? Why is it important to know the difference?

Visual Studio

Although you could write your programs in any editor and then use the VB compiler to compile them, Visual Studio provides an environment to make your development task easier. You should already be familiar with the various windows in the environment as well as the basic debugging capabilities. For a review of the VS IDE, as well as tips and shortcuts, see Appendix D. This section introduces you to more details about the parts of a project and changes to the VS environment.

Note: This chapter introduces writing Windows applications. You also have the option of writing Windows Presentation Foundation (WPF) applications. Although WPF applications are introduced in Chapter 13, you might prefer to begin there and write all of your programs using WPF.

Temporary Projects

You can create temporary projects for testing, without saving them. This can be both good and bad: You don't have to clutter your drive with small projects that you create just to test something, but you may forget to save a project that you wanted to keep.

When you create a new project, by default it is a temporary project, which VS stores in a temporary folder on the hard drive. So even when you compile and run the project, the compiler saves the files in the temporary folder. When you exit VS or choose to begin another project, you are presented with the option to save or discard the project (Figure 1.2).

If you want to always save new projects, you can select that option in the *Options* dialog box. Choose *Tools / Options / Projects and Solutions* and select *Save new projects when created*.

Figure 1.2

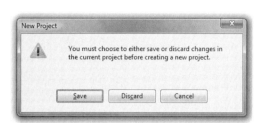

Setting Environment Options

The *Options* dialog box provides several useful features. Select *Tools / Options* and select the check box for *Show all settings* (Figure 1.3). By default, for a VB developer profile, the *Options* dialog box shows a limited subset of the options you can set. You may want to spend some time exploring the various options.

Figure 1.3

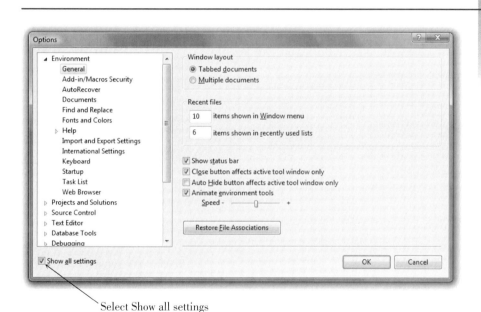

Select Show all settings

Selecting the Visual Basic Development Settings

When you install VS 2008, you are prompted to specify the profile for the default settings. This text is based on choosing the Visual Basic Development settings. If you are sharing a computer with someone developing in a different language, or the proper settings were not chosen, you may need to reset the defaults. Choose *Tools / Import and Export Settings*. In the wizard, specify *Reset all settings*. Next you can choose to save the current settings or just overwrite them (likely the best choice), and then select *Visual Basic Development Settings*.

Setting the Location of Project Files

You can change the default folder that VS uses to store and retrieve project files. Select *Tools / Options*; in the *Options* dialog box, select *Projects and Solutions* and change the entry for *Visual Studio projects location*.

Setting Option Explicit and Option Strict Defaults

It's best to set the Option Strict default for all projects, rather than set it in every project. Select *Projects and Solutions / VB Defaults* in the *Options* dialog box and set both *Option Explicit* and *Option Strict* on.

Displaying the Grid on Windows Forms

The Windows Form Designer includes snap lines, which is a great feature that can help you to align controls. Blue snap lines appear when the edges of controls are aligned; red snap lines appear when the text baselines of controls are aligned; and dotted lines appear when two controls are the recommended distance apart. The visible grid does not appear on a Windows Form by default, but you can make the grid dots appear to match early versions of VB. In the *Windows Forms Designer* section of the *Options* dialog box, select *SnapToGrid* for *LayoutMode* and *True* for *ShowGrid*. Before setting this option, however, make sure to try using snap lines, which make form design much easier than the old snap-to-grid method.

The Solution Explorer

Take a look at the files in the Solution Explorer for a new Windows application (Figure 1.4). When you click on the *Show All Files* button, you can see the

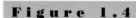

TIP

Set the default for Option Strict to On now so that you don't have to be concerned about it in the future. ∎

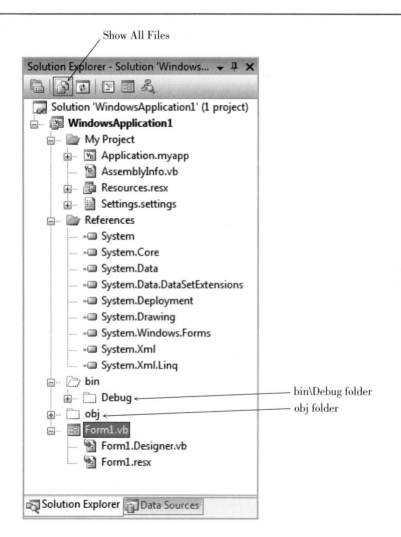

Show All Files

bin\Debug folder
obj folder

Figure 1.4

Click the Show All Files button to see all of the files and folders in the Solution Explorer.

hidden files and folders. The My Project folder holds several files for project configuration, including AssemblyInfo.vb. You will learn to view and set configuration options in the Project Designer, which is discussed in the "The Project Designer" section later in this chapter.

In Figure 1.4, you can see the expanded References collection, the bin and obj folders, and the form files for Form1.vb. You can expand each of the nodes to see more details. Note that the solution name does not display by default. To show the solution name, as in Figure 1.4, select *Tools / Options / Projects and Solutions* and check *Always show solution*. You will want to always show solutions so that you can edit solution names.

References

In the References folder, you can see a list of System libraries (DLLs), such as System, System.Deployment, System.Drawing, and System.Windows.Forms. These are the references included by default for a new Windows application. You can add a reference by right-clicking on the References folder and selecting *Add Reference* from the context menu. You also can add references in the Project Designer, which is discussed a little later. You may need to add a reference if you want to refer to objects in another assembly or components written in a different language.

The Bin and Obj Folders

Notice the organization of the bin and obj folders:

bin
    Debug
    Release
obj
    Debug
    Release

When you compile and run a project using the debugger, you are running the program stored in the bin\Debug folder. The debug versions of the compiled project are not optimized for release. If you compile a program for release, the compiled versions are placed in the Release folders. Notice the files in the bin\Debug folder in Figure 1.5, which shows the Solution Explorer after compiling a project.

Figure 1.5

*After compiling a project and clicking the **Refresh** button, the bin\Debug folder holds the files needed to run the program in the debugger.*

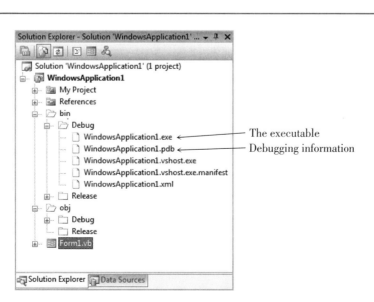

The executable
Debugging information

The project's .exe file is the executable, which is used to run the program; the .pdb file holds debugging information. If you are distributing your application, you only need to distribute the .exe file, not the .pdb file. The *ProjectName.*vshost.exe file is a small application that runs the project in the environment.

Project Resources

The Resources folder holds resources that you add to your project. Figure 1.6 shows a graphic file stored in the Resources folder; you can also add sound files and text strings to the resources.

Figure 1.6

The Resources folder holds the project resources, such as graphic and sound files, and text strings.

Visual Studio provides several ways to add resources to the folder and to access those resources. You can add resources in the Project Designer, discussed later in this chapter. You also can add resources from the Properties window, such as when you set the Image property of a PictureBox control. At design time, you can assign properties of controls to resources that are in the Resources folder, and you can retrieve resources at run time using the My.Resources object, which also is discussed later in this chapter.

Each form in your project also has a resource file, which has a .resx extension. For example, Form1.vb has a Form1.resx file, which you can see in the Solution Explorer when you click on the *Show All Files* button and expand the form's node.

The .resx file is mostly text in XML format, which you can open and view in the IDE. The .resx file holds pointers to the files in your Resources folder and supplies the resources to the form at compile time. Any graphic elements that you add to the form, such as a PictureBox's Image property or a form's Icon property, also are stored in the .resx file in text that represents the binary graphic file.

If you rename your form file in the Solution Explorer, the .resx file is automatically renamed to match. At times you may find extra .resx files in the project's folder; you can safely delete any extra .resx files if their names do not match any forms in the project.

Image Files in Visual Studio 2008 Microsoft is including many graphic files with Visual Studio 2008. The graphics are those used in Windows so that you can make your applications use the standard images. The default location for the graphics is C:\Program Files\Microsoft Visual Studio 9.0\Common7\ VS2008ImageLibrary\1033\VS2008ImageLibrary.zip. You may have to unzip the files to use them.

Partial Classes

Partial classes, also called ***partial types***, is a feature that was added in the 2005 version of Visual Studio. In its simplest form, partial classes allow you to split a class into two or more separate files.

The Form's Designer-Generated Code

A big advantage of partial classes is that the VB Form Designer can split the form's class into two parts, separating the designer-generated code from the developer-written code. In Figure 1.7, you can see that Form1 consists of two files, plus the .resx file. Form1.vb holds the VB code that you write; Form1. Designer.vb holds the designer-generated code. You don't generally see these extra files unless you select *Show All Files* in the Solution Explorer. You can double-click a filename to see the contents of the file.

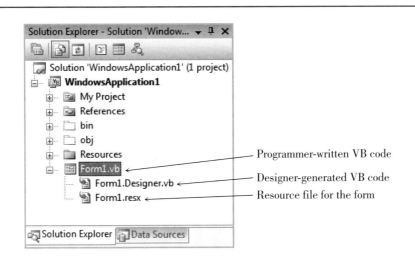

Programmer-written VB code
Designer-generated VB code
Resource file for the form

Figure 1.7

Form1.vb holds your VB code; Form1.Designer.vb holds the code automatically generated by the Windows Form Designer. Click on Show All Files to see these normally hidden files.

The file that holds the designer-generated code includes the class inheritance information:

```
Partial Class Form1
    Inherits System.Windows.Forms.Form
```

The partial class instantiates the form and the visual components for the form as well as stores property settings.

The form's class file that holds the programmer-written code begins with this line:

```
Public Class Form1
```

The compiler uses the statements in both files to create the compiled class. Note that you can create multiple partial class files and one single file without the "Partial" designation.

The Project Designer

The **Project Designer** is sometimes called the *Project Properties* dialog box. You can open the Project Designer by double-clicking on the My Project folder in the Solution Explorer or by selecting *Project / ProjectName Properties*. The Project Designer includes tabs for *Application, Compile, Debug, References, Resources, Services, Settings, Signing, My Extensions, Security,* and *Publish* (Figure 1.8).

Figure 1.8

Display the Project Designer by double-clicking on the My Project folder in the Solution Explorer.

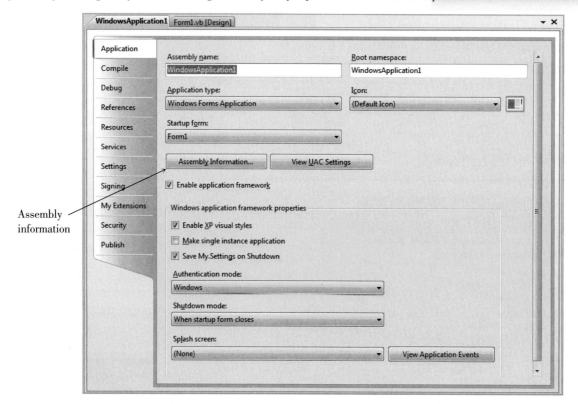

The Application Tab The *Application* tab is the default tab that appears on top when you open the Project Designer. On the *Application* tab, you can set the application type, the startup form, the icon, and the splash screen. You also can display and set the application's assembly information from this dialog. Later in this chapter, we will use many of these options.

The Compile Tab On the *Compile* tab, you can set the path for the compiler output. You also can alter the settings for Option Explicit and Option Strict and specify which errors should be flagged by the compiler and which should be ignored.

The References Tab The *References* tab displays the names and paths for the project references. You can add and remove references to Windows or Web library components, as well as external components, in this dialog.

The Resources Tab The *Resources* tab allows you to easily add and remove the graphic files that you use for picture boxes and toolbars, any sound files, and text strings in various languages to use for localization.

The Signing, Security, and Publish Tabs The settings on the *Signing*, *Security*, and *Publish* tabs are used for ClickOnce deployment. Using ClickOnce deployment, you can set up applications to be deployed and updated on multiple sites via the Web. This technique is primarily used by large organizations to facilitate deploying applications to many users.

Deploying Windows Applications

Most of this text is devoted to writing and testing applications using the Visual Studio IDE. However, once you get an application tested and ready for use, you will want to deploy it and run it on another computer. To run a .NET Windows application, the target computer must have the .NET Framework or the .NET Framework Redistributable installed. The Redistributable file is available for free download on Microsoft's Web site and is available for Windows XP and Vista.

You can choose from several methods for deploying your Windows applications: (1) XCopy deployment, (2) Windows Installer technology, (3) ClickOnce deployment, or (4) third-party installer products.

XCopy deployment gets its name from the old DOS XCOPY command, which copied all files in the current folder and all subfolders. Although you *can* use the XCOPY command for copying files, XCopy deployment simply means that you copy the necessary files from the development machine to the target machine.

Deploying a compiled Windows application can be as easy as copying the .exe file from the bin folder to another computer. This technique is not very robust but can work for a simple installation. However, deploying a Web application is a little more complicated because more than one file is needed to run an application.

Microsoft Windows Installer is a separate application that ships with Windows. The installer creates .msi files that contain the application and any support files needed for deployment. Deployment is covered in Appendix C.

The VB My Objects

The Visual Basic **My** object provides several objects and properties. My gives you easy access to information about your application and its resources, the computer on which the application is executing, and the current user.

It is easy to discover the available objects using IntelliSense (Figure 1.9): Application, Computer, Forms, Resources, Settings, User, and Web Services.

Figure 1.9

Type "My." to see the available My objects in IntelliSense.

You can retrieve information about the user's computer, operating system, and amount of memory with My.Computer.Info (Figure 1.10).

If you want to know the name of the user, you can use

```
UserNameString = My.User.Name
```

In the following section, you will use My.Application to retrieve the assembly information about an application.

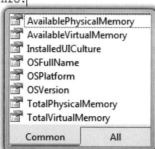

My.Computer.Info.

Using Assembly Information

You can set an application's **assembly information**, also called the *assembly attributes*, and retrieve the information at run time.

Setting the Assembly Information

You can view and set an application's assembly information in the *Assembly Information* dialog box. Double-click on My Project in the Solution Explorer to display the Project Designer's *Application* tab (refer to Figure 1.8); then click on the *Assembly Information* button, which displays the dialog box. Figure 1.11 shows the default information for an application called WindowsApplication1.

☑TIP

Always give the new project a name when you create it, which sets the root namespace, assembly name, and project name. ■

Figure 1.11

The Assembly Information dialog box with the values supplied by default. You can edit the entries to the values of your choice.

Figure 1.12

The assembly information for the chapter hands-on programming example.

Type appropriate entries for your applications. Figure 1.12 shows the assembly information for the chapter hands-on example program.

Another way to modify a project's assembly information is to edit the AssemblyInfo.vb file directly. You can see the file in the Solution Explorer beneath the My Project folder when *Show All Files* is selected (Figure 1.13). Double-click the filename to display the file in the editor.

Figure 1.13

You can modify the assembly information by editing the AssemblyInfo.vb file.

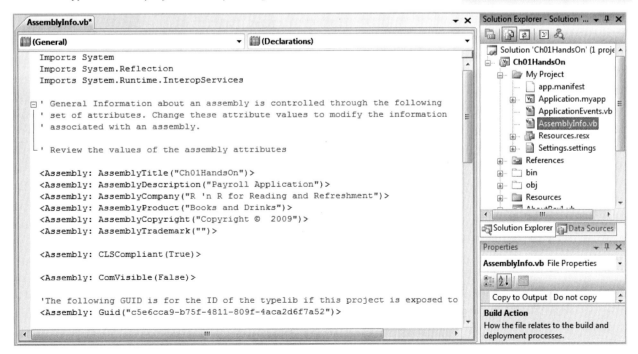

Retrieving the Assembly Information

You can retrieve assembly attributes in a VB program using the My.Application.
Info object. The properties of the object include many items that describe the
application, including

- AssemblyName

- CompanyName

- Description

- DirectoryPath

- Copyright

- Trademark

- Name

- ProductName

- Title

- Version

You can display the Title attribute in a label using the following statement:

```
TitleLabel.Text = My.Application.Info.Title
```

The following program displays the assembly attributes in labels on a form.

Write a Test Program

Begin a new project in VB and double-click on the My Project folder in the Solution Explorer to open the Project Designer. Click on the *Assembly Information*
button to open the *Assembly Information* dialog box and enter the information
(Figure 1.14).

On the form, add labels for Name, Title, Description, Company, Product,
Version, and Copyright.

Figure 1.14

*Enter the assembly information
for the demonstration program.*

Write the code to assign values to the labels in the Form_Load event procedure. The code uses the My.Application.Info object to retrieve the attributes.

```
Private Sub MainForm_Load(ByVal sender As System.Object, _
    ByVal e As System.EventArgs) Handles MyBase.Load
    ' Retrieve the assembly information.

    With My.Application.Info
        NameLabel.Text = .AssemblyName
        TitleLabel.Text = .Title
        DescriptionLabel.Text = .Description
        CompanyLabel.Text = .CompanyName
        ProductLabel.Text = .ProductName
        VersionLabel.Text = "Version: " & .Version.ToString
        CopyrightLabel.Text = .Copyright
    End With
End Sub
```

Run the Test Program

Run the program. Your output should be similar to Figure 1.15.

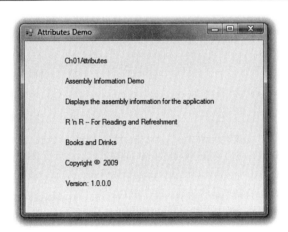

Figure 1.15

The assembly information displays in labels in the example program's output.

Viewing a Program's Attributes

After you enter assembly information and compile your project, you can view the attributes in Windows Explorer. Point to the filename in the project's bin\ Debug folder, either an .exe or .dll file, and pause; the attributes pop up automatically (Figure 1.16).

Figure 1.16

The application's attributes display when you pause the mouse pointer over the filename in Windows Explorer.

Feedback 1.2

Write the statements necessary to retrieve and display the copyright attribute in CopyrightLabel.

Menus, Toolbars, and Status Bars

To create menus, context menus, toolbars, and status bars, use the components in the *Menus & Toolbars* section of the toolbox (Figure 1.17). The components are **MenuStrip**, **ContextMenuStrip**, **ToolStrip**, and **StatusStrip**.

Visual Studio also includes designers that simplify creating menus, toolbars, and status bars. The designers are pretty smart; they give each element a meaningful name so that you don't have to rename your menu items. You also can use the controls' smart tags, which simplify setting properties.

Figure 1.17

The MenuStrip, ContextMenuStrip, ToolStrip, and StatusStrip components are grouped together in the Menus & Toolbars section of the toolbox.

Creating Menus with MenuStrips

When you add a MenuStrip to a form, the component appears in the component tray and the words "Type Here" appear in the new menu bar. Notice in Figure 1.18 that when you point to the new menu item, a drop-down arrow appears, which you can use to add different controls to the menu bar. The selected menu bar also shows a smart tag arrow, which you can use to set some of the properties of the menu bar.

Figure 1.18

The MenuStrip component appears in the component tray. Type your first menu item where the words "Type Here" appear.

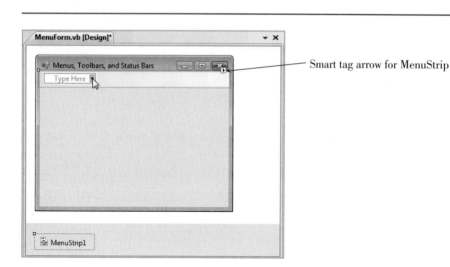

Smart tag arrow for MenuStrip

The MenuStrip and ContextMenuStrip components allow you to select a control or separator bar for each menu item. Drop down the list for a menu item to see the choices (Figure 1.19). You can easily add a new item or a separator bar in the menu.

Figure 1.19

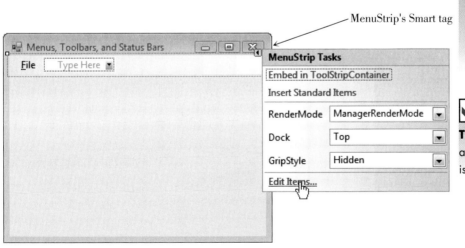

Drop down the list for a new menu item and make a selection from the list.

You can use the MenuStrip's smart tag (Figure 1.20) to set some properties of the menu bar. Select *Edit Items* to open the Items Collection Editor (Figure 1.21), where you can set properties of the menu items, and add, remove, and rearrange the items.

When you use the visual menu designer to create menus and menu items, each item is automatically given a meaningful name. But if you add a menu item in the Items Collection Editor, you must name the item yourself.

Figure 1.20

Open the MenuStrip's smart tag to set properties of the menu bar; select Edit Items to edit the individual menu items.

✓**TIP**

The keyboard shortcut for opening a smart tag when its arrow appears is Alt + Shift + F10. ■

Menus and Menu Items

Each MenuStrip and ContextMenuStrip component is a container, which holds a collection of menu items. Both top-level menus and the items below the menu names are considered menu items. A menu item also can contain a collection of items. For example, the *File* menu is a menu item, called FileToolStripMenu-Item by default; the FileToolStripMenuItem contains a collection of the menu items that appear in the *File* menu, such as ExitToolStripMenuItem.

Referring to Figure 1.21, notice that at the top-right side, the collection is MenuStrip1, the MenuStrip itself. The items listed in the *Members* list are the top-level menus.

Figure 1.21

In the Items Collection Editor, you can add and remove menu items, reorder items, and set properties of the items.

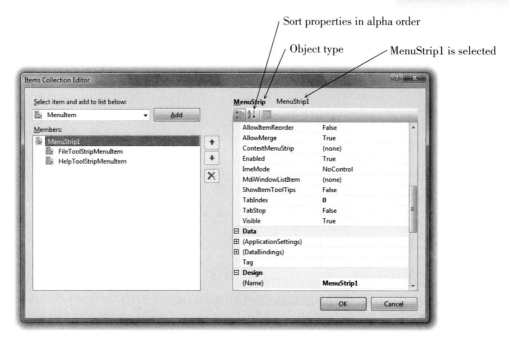

You can edit any of the items by selecting it in the *Members* list. Figure 1.22 shows the FileToolStripMenuItem selected. Notice that the top right now indicates the selected item and that one of the properties of the FileToolStripMenuItem is a DropDownItems collection. If you select that collection, the Items Collection

Figure 1.22

Edit the properties of the individual menu items in the Items Collection Editor. Notice that the FileToolStripMenuItem has a DropDownItems property, which is a collection of the menu items that appear below the File menu.

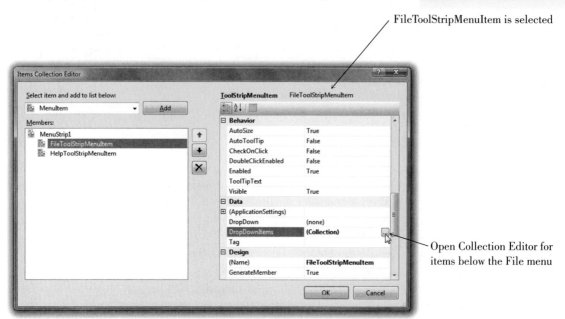

Editor displays the items beneath the *File* menu. Also notice in Figure 1.22 that the right side of the Items Collection Editor is similar to the Properties window in the IDE. You can click on the buttons to display the properties in alphabetic order or categorized view.

Creating Context Menus with ContextMenuStrips

Context menus are the shortcut menus that you display by pointing to an item and right-clicking. You should plan your applications to include context menus for all operations that the user might want to perform.

You create context menus in nearly the same way that you create menus. Add a ContextMenuStrip to a form and add menu items using the visual menu designer (Figure 1.23).

Figure 1.23

The ContextMenuStrip component appears in the component tray. When it is selected, the visual menu designer appears to allow you to enter menu items.

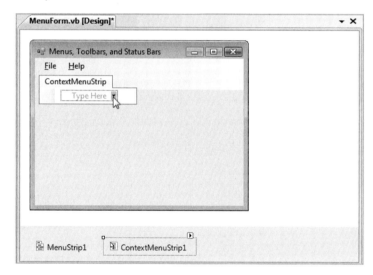

A context menu does not include a top-level menu name; instead each of the items belongs to the Items collection of the ContextMenuStrip. Notice that the smart tag arrow appears on the component in the component tray, rather than on the menu in the designer. You can select *Edit Items* from the smart tag or select the Items property in the Properties window to edit the individual menu items.

The form and each of the controls that you add to the form has a Context-MenuStrip property. You assign the context menu to the form or control by selecting its name in the Properties window. Note that you can add multiple context menus to the component tray and assign each to a different control.

If you assign a context menu to a form, it becomes the default context menu for the form and most controls on the form. However, controls that allow text entry, such as text boxes and combo boxes, have a default context menu that contains the editing items *Cut, Copy,* and *Paste.* If you assign your own context menu to a text control, you will lose the items on the default context menu.

You can easily assign a single event handler to both a menu item and a context menu item. Add the second item to the `Handles` clause of the event handler. In the following example, the event handler is executed for the Click event of both the menu item and context menu item. Note that the menu designer named the context menu item with the same name as the menu item, with the addition of the numeral "1".

```
Private Sub ExitToolStripMenuItem_Click(ByVal sender As System.Object, _
  ByVal e As System.EventArgs)_
  Handles ExitToolStripMenuItem.Click, ExitToolStripMenuItem1.Click
    ' Exit the program.

    Me.Close()
End Sub
```

Creating Toolbars with ToolStrips

Toolbars typically hold buttons that are shortcuts to menu items. You will use ToolStrip components to create toolbars.

ToolStrips are very closely related to MenuStrips. In fact, the MenuStrip class inherits from the ToolStrip class and shares many of the same properties and behaviors.

You have many choices for the types of controls to add to a ToolStrip (Figure 1.24).

TIP

Beware of using Application.Exit() as any code in the FormClosing event will not execute. ∎

Figure 1.24

The ToolStrip component appears in the component tray. You can drop down the list for the types of buttons and controls that you can add to the ToolStrip.

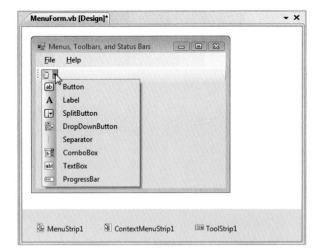

After you add the buttons to the ToolStrip container, you can set the properties of each button in the Properties window or in the Items Collection Editor, which you display from the smart tag. You will need to give the toolbar buttons meaningful names; the visual designer assigns names like ToolStripButton1.

Your buttons can hold an image, text, or both. Generally you will want to place an image on the button and set the ToolTip text to indicate the purpose of

TIP

Set the ToolTipText property of each toolbar button to aid the user, in case the meaning of each graphic is not perfectly clear. ∎

Figure 1.25

Set the Name, Image, and ToolTipText properties for each ToolStripButton.

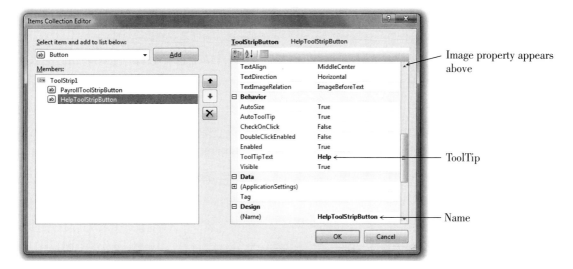

the button. Figure 1.25 shows a ToolStripButton's properties with an image, ToolTip text, and a meaningful name.

Creating Status Bars with StatusStrips

Status bars generally appear at the bottom of a form and supply information to the user. Some applications display error messages in status bars; often a status bar holds the system date and time.

VB uses StatusStrip components to create status bars. StatusStrip components, like MenuStrips and ContextMenuStrips, inherit from ToolStrips and share many of the same characteristics. Figure 1.26 shows the controls that you can add to a StatusStrip.

To display text on a status bar, add a StatusLabel to the StatusStrip. You will want to give StatusLabel objects meaningful names since you will refer to the labels in code. You can control whether labels appear at the right or left end of the status bar by setting the StatusStrip's RightToLeft property to Yes or No. By default, the property is set to No and labels appear at the left end of the status bar. You also can set a StatusLabel to appear at the left end of a status bar and fill the status bar, even though RightToLeft is set to Yes and some labels appear at the right end: Set the StatusLabel's Spring property to *true*.

You can display the date and time in status labels in the Form_Load event handler.

```
Private Sub MenuForm_Load(ByVal sender As System.Object, _
   ByVal e As System.EventArgs) Handles MyBase.Load
      ' Set the date and time in the status bar.

   DateToolStripStatusLabel.Text = Today.ToShortDateString
   TimeToolStripStatusLabel.Text = Now.ToLongTimeString
End Sub
```

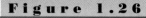
Figure 1.26

Drop down the list to add a control to a StatusStrip.

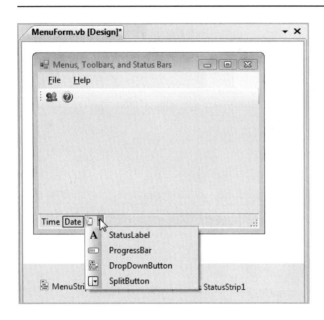

Displaying the Date and Time

You use the properties and methods of the **DateTime structure** to retrieve and format the current date and time. The **Now property** holds the system date and time in a numeric format that can be used for calculations. You can format the date and/or time for display using one of the following methods: `ToShortDateString`, `ToLongDateString`, `ToShortTimeString`, or `ToLongTimeString`. The actual display format of each method depends on the local system settings.

You can set the display value of StatusStripLabels in any procedure; however, the display does not update automatically. Generally, you will set initial values in the Form_Load event procedure and use a Timer component to update the time.

Using a Timer Component

To use a **Timer component**, you add the component to the form, set some properties, and write code in the Timer's Tick event handler. Add the Timer component from the *Components* section of the toolbox. Then in the Properties window, set the Enabled property to *true* and set the Interval property. The Interval is measured in milliseconds; set the Interval to 1000 to make the Timer's Tick event fire every second.

```
Private Sub Timer1_Tick(ByVal sender As System.Object, _
   ByVal e As System.EventArgs) Handles Timer1.Tick
      ' Update the time in the status bar.

      DateToolStripStatusLabel.Text = Today.ToShortDateString
      TimeToolStripStatusLabel.Text = Now.ToLongTimeString
End Sub
```

> ## Feedback 1.3

What steps are necessary to display the current time in a StatusStrip label called CurrentTimeStatusStripLabel?

MDI Applications

In this section, you will create a multiple document application with parent and child forms, a menu bar, context menus, a toolbar, and a status bar.

Multiple Document Interface

You can create forms as a **single document interface (SDI)** or **multiple document interface (MDI)**. Using SDI, each form in the project acts independently from the other forms. However, VB also allows you to create a multiple document interface. For an example of MDI, consider an application such as Microsoft Word 2003, which has a **parent form** (the main window) and **child forms** (each document window). You can open multiple child windows, and you can maximize, minimize, restore, or close each child window, which always stays within the boundaries of the parent window. When you close the parent window, all child windows close automatically. Figure 1.27 shows an MDI parent window with two open child windows.

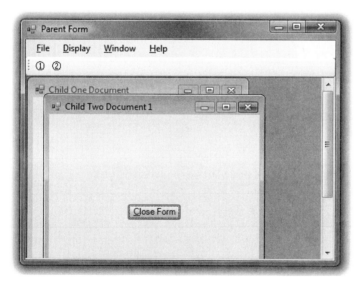

Figure 1.27

The main form is the parent and the smaller forms are the child forms in an MDI application.

With MDI, a parent and child relationship exists between the main form and the child forms. One of the rules for MDI is that if a parent form closes, all of its children leave with it—a pretty good rule. Another rule is that children cannot wander out of the parent's area; the child form always appears inside the parent's area.

VB allows you to have forms that act independently from each other. You may have a parent form and several child forms *and* some forms that operate independently. For example, a splash form likely should remain SDI.

One feature of MDI is that you can have several child windows open at the same time. The menu bar generally contains a *Window* menu that allows you to display a list of open windows and move from one active window to another.

Creating an MDI Project

You can make any form a parent. In fact, a form can be both a parent and a child form (just as a person can be both a parent and a child). To make a form into a parent, simply change its **IsMdiContainer property** to *true* in the Properties window of the designer. In a single project, you can have multiple child forms and multiple parents.

Creating a child is almost as easy. Of course, your project must contain more than one form. You make a form into a child window in code at run time. Before displaying the child form from the parent, set the child's **MdiParent property** to the current (parent) form.

```
Private Sub DisplayChildTwoMenuItem_Click(ByVal sender As System.Object, _
    ByVal e As System.EventArgs) Handles DisplayChildTwoMenuItem.Click
        ' Display Child Two form.

        Dim AChildTwoForm As New ChildTwoForm
        AChildTwoForm.MdiParent = Me
        AChildTwoForm.Show()
End Sub
```

Our example application allows the user to display multiple child windows. Therefore, the title bar of each child window should be unique. We can accomplish this by appending a number to the title bar before displaying the form. This is very much like Microsoft Word, with its Document1, Document2, and so forth.

```
' Module-level declarations.
Private ChildTwoCountInteger As Integer

Private Sub DisplayChildTwoMenuItem_Click(ByVal sender As System.Object, _
    ByVal e As System.EventArgs) Handles DisplayChildTwoMenuItem.Click
        ' Display Child Two form.

        Dim AChildTwoForm As New ChildTwoForm
        ChildTwoCountInteger += 1
        With AChildTwoForm
            .MdiParent = Me
            .Text = "Child Two Document" & ChildTwoCountInteger.ToString()
            .Show()
        End With
End Sub
```

Adding a Window Menu

A parent form should have a *Window* menu (Figure 1.28). The *Window* menu lists the open child windows and allows the user to switch between windows

Figure 1.28

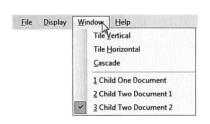

The Window menu in an MDI application lists the open child windows and allows the user to select the arrangement of the windows.

and arrange multiple child windows. Take a look at the *Window* menu in an application such as Word or Excel. You will see a list of the open documents as well as options for arranging the windows. Typically, a separator bar separates the two groups.

To designate a menu item as the *Window* menu, select the MenuStrip component. In the Properties window, set the MDIWindowListItem property to the desired menu item; generally, that's WindowToolStripMenuItem (Figure 1.29).

Figure 1.29

Select the menu item to be the Window menu from the MenuStrip's MDIWindowList-Item property drop-down list.

Layout Options

When several child windows are open, the windows may be arranged in several different layouts: tiled vertically, tiled horizontally, or cascaded. You set the type of layout in code by using an argument of the **LayoutMdi method**.

```
Me.LayoutMdi(MdiLayout.TileHorizontal)
```

You can use one of the three constants: TileHorizontal, TileVertical, and Cascade.

```
Private Sub TileVerticalToolStripMenuItem_Click(ByVal sender _
  As System.Object, ByVal e As System.EventArgs) _
  Handles TileVerticalToolStripMenuItem.Click
    ' Display open windows tiled vertically.

    Me.LayoutMdi(MdiLayout.TileVertical)
End Sub

Private Sub TileHorizontalToolStripMenuItem_Click(ByVal sender As Object, _
  ByVal e As System.EventArgs) Handles TileHorizontalToolStripMenuItem.Click
    ' Display open windows tiled horizontally.

    Me.LayoutMdi(MdiLayout.TileHorizontal)
End Sub

Private Sub CascadeToolStripMenuItem_Click(ByVal sender As Object, _
  ByVal e As System.EventArgs) Handles CascadeToolStripMenuItem.Click
    ' Cascade open windows.

    Me.LayoutMdi(MdiLayout.Cascade)
End Sub
```

The Singleton Design Pattern

In some applications, such as a word processor, you may allow the user to open multiple child windows of the same type. In other applications, you want to allow only one child window of a particular type. For example, if your application has a Summary window that the user can display by selecting a menu item, he or she may select the option multiple times. If you want to allow only a single instance of a form, you need to write code to make that happen.

Although there are several techniques that can prevent multiple instances of a class, the recommended technique for OOP is a design pattern called a **singleton pattern**.

You may be wondering, "What is a **design pattern**?" Basically, it is the design logic to solve a specific problem. It isn't necessary to reinvent the wheel every time we need a solution to a problem. Experienced programmers have developed and published design patterns and practices that other programmers can use. Sometimes we refer to it as adding to your programmer "bag of tricks."

You can find a good article about design patterns and the singleton design pattern at www.codeguru.com/columns/VB/article.php/c6563/.

To create the singleton pattern, you define a property in the child form that returns an instance of the class. Declare a shared private variable to hold an instance of the class. The first time an object is instantiated, the instance is assigned to the variable; before that, the variable is "Is Nothing".

Note: If you are unfamiliar with creating new properties, see "Creating Properties in a Class" in Chapter 2.

```
'Project:      Ch01MDIApplication
'Programmer:   Bradley/Millspaugh
'Date:         June 2009
'Form:         ChildOneForm
'Description:  Demonstrates the singleton design pattern to allow only one
'              instance of the form.

Public Class ChildOneForm

    Private Shared AnInstance As ChildOneForm

    Public Shared ReadOnly Property Instance() As ChildOneForm
        Get
            If AnInstance Is Nothing Then
                AnInstance = New ChildOneForm
            End If
            Return AnInstance
        End Get
    End Property
End Class
```

The singleton class also must dispose of the instance in the form's Form-Closing event handler.

```
Private Sub ChildOneForm_FormClosing(ByVal sender as Object, ByVal e As _
    System.Windows.Forms.FormClosingEventArgs) Handles Me.FormClosing
        ' Delete the object when the form is closed.

    AnInstance = Nothing
End Sub
```

When you want to display a form that was created as a singleton, you reference the Instance property of the form rather than use the New keyword.

```
Dim AChildOneform As ChildOneForm = ChildOneForm.Instance()
```

To display the form, use the Show method prior to the Focus method.

```
Private Sub ChildOneToolStripMenuItem_Click(ByVal sender As System.Object, _
    ByVal e As System.EventArgs) _
    Handles ChildOneToolStripMenuItem.Click, ChildOneToolStripButton.Click, _
    ChildOneToolStripMenuItem1.Click
        ' Create an instance of Child One.

    Dim AChildOneForm As ChildOneForm = ChildOneForm.Instance()
    With AChildOneForm
        .MdiParent = Me
        .Show()
        .Focus()
    End With
End Sub
```

In the Ch01MDIApplication project on your student CD, ChildOneForm follows a singleton pattern but ChildTwoForm does not. Notice that you can create multiple copies of ChildTwoForm but only one ChildOneForm.

► **Feedback 1.4**

Write the statements to display AboutForm as a child form.

Splash Screen Forms

An initial screen normally displays while a program is loading. This initial form is called a **splash screen**. Professional applications use splash screens to tell the user that the program is loading and starting. It can make a large application appear to load and run faster since something appears on the screen while the rest of the application loads. Even though our programs are relatively small and will load quickly, a splash screen adds a professional touch. You can set form properties and add images and labels to a standard Windows Form or use the Splash Screen template.

Creating Your Own Splash Screen

To create your own splash screen, add a new Windows Form to an existing project. Set the properties to remove the title bar, to make the form nonresizable, and to remain on top of any other forms. Notice that you must set four properties to hide the form's title bar: ControlBox, MaximizeBox, MinimizeBox, and Text.

Property	Setting	Description
Name	SplashForm	Name the file SplashForm.vb and the class SplashForm.
ControlBox	False	Hide the close button and Control menu icon; needed to hide the title bar.
FormBorderStyle	FixedDialog	Select a nonresizable style; also can be FixedSingle or Fixed3D.
StartPosition	CenterScreen	Center the splash form on the screen.
Text	(blank)	Needed to hide the title bar.
TopMost	True	Make the splash form remain on top of the main form until it closes.

Setting the Splash Screen

After you create your splash screen form, open the Project Designer by double-clicking on My Project in the Solution Explorer. Set the Splash Screen to your splash screen form (Figure 1.30).

Figure 1.30

Select the splash screen form in the Project Designer.

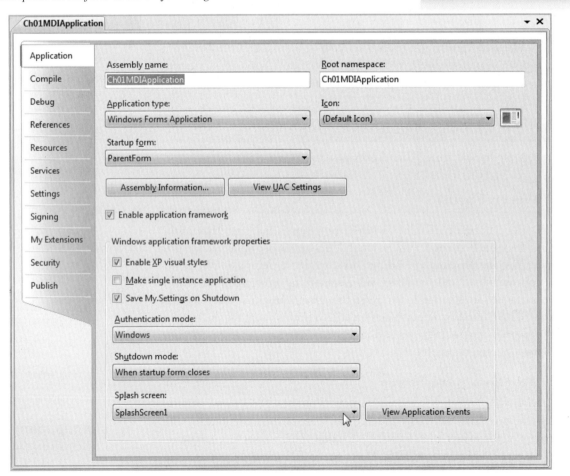

Holding the Splash Screen Display

The splash screen should display for as long as it takes for the rest of the application to load. But our applications are so small that the splash screen disappears before the user can read it. You can write code to make the splash screen appear longer using **threads**, which allow multiple processes to execute simultaneously. Use the `Thread.Sleep` method in the form's FormClosing event handler. The FormClosing event occurs just before the form actually closes.

```
Private Sub SplashScreen1_FormClosing(ByVal sender As Object, _
  ByVal e As System.Windows.Forms.FormClosingEventArgs) _
  Handles Me.FormClosing
    ' Hold the form on the screen approximately 5 seconds before closing.

    System.Threading.Thread.Sleep(5000) ' Sleep 5000 milliseconds.
End Sub
```

Note: You will learn more about threading in Chapter 13.

Using the Splash Screen Template

You can use the Splash Screen template for your splash screen. When you choose to add a new Windows Form to a project, you will see the template in the *Add New Item* dialog box. You will want to clear the standard graphic from the form or add your own. The graphic is set in the MainLayoutPanel's BackgroundImage property. To clear the image, select the property and click the property's Builder button (the button with the ellipsis). In the *Select Resource* dialog box, you can select *Clear*, select a graphic from the project resources, or import a new graphic into the resources to use for the image.

The labels on the template are set up to display the attributes from the assembly information. You can keep the labels, delete them, change their properties, or add your own.

Make sure to examine the code for coding suggestions. Also, add the code in the FormClosing event handler to hold the form on the screen.

About Box Forms

You can add a standard Windows Form and create your own About box, or use the About Box template. The template form has labels and code to place the project's assembly information attributes on the form. Of course, you can modify the labels and the code as much as you wish.

The graphic on the About Box form is displayed in a PictureBox's Image property. You can clear the image or add your own.

Class Diagrams

Visual Studio includes a tool that you can use to create **class diagrams**, which help you to visualize the classes in your projects. Note that the class diagram designer is not available in the Express Edition of Visual Basic.

Creating a Class Diagram

To create a class diagram of the complete project, select the project name in the Solution Explorer and click on the *View Class Diagram* button at the top of the window. The class diagram will be generated and displayed in the main Document window (Figure 1.31). If one class is selected in the Solution Explorer, only that class will appear in the class diagram. You also can add a class diagram in the *Add New Item* dialog box, selected from the *Project / Add New Item* menu item.

Figure 1.31

Select the project name and click on the View Class Diagram button in the Solution Explorer to create or view a class diagram. Not available in the Express Edition.

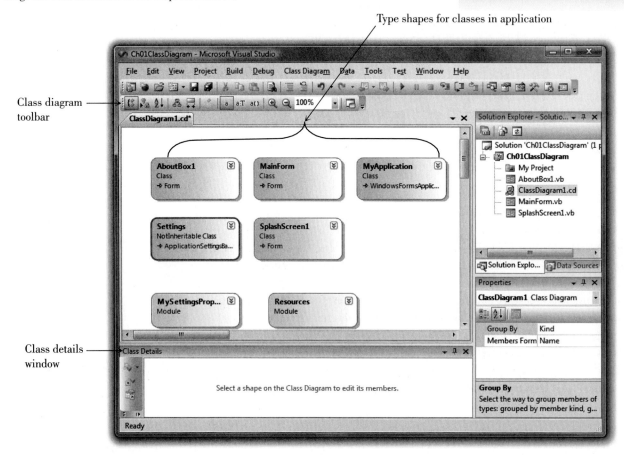

You can create more than one class diagram for a project; each is stored in its own file with a .cd extension. The diagrams are saved with the project and can be redisplayed at any time. Each diagram can show a customized view of the complete application or a particular view of the application.

Notice in Figure 1.31 that a new *Class Diagram* menu and a Class Details toolbar appear in the IDE when a class diagram is displaying (Figure 1.32). When you switch to a different window, the *Class Diagram* menu and Class Details window disappear. The toolbox also contains tools for working with class diagrams when a class diagram displays.

Customizing a Class Diagram

The default class diagram shows many type shapes for the classes that you created and many automatically generated types. You may find it easier to visualize the organization of the application without those extra type shapes. You can click on any of the shapes and press the Delete key, which removes the shape

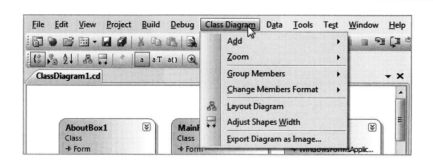

Figure 1.32

The Class Diagram menu appears when a class diagram displays in the main Document window. Notice the many options for editing and displaying class diagrams. Most of these same options are also available on the context menus and the toolbar.

from the diagram but does not remove the class from the project. You also can move the shapes around and resize them.

Looking at Figure 1.31, notice the down-pointing chevron in the upper-right corner of each shape. The chevron is called a *rolldown* button (or *rollup* button when pointed upward). Click on the rolldown button to expand the compartments in the shape, or you can select a shape and select *Expand* from the *Class Diagram* menu.

Each of the sections in a type shape is called a *compartment*. The compartments that display can vary, depending on the type and grouping selected. You can expand or collapse each compartment individually, using the menu, the context menu, or the plus or minus sign by the compartment name.

You can clarify the class diagram by hiding some members. In the Class Details window, which appears automatically when a class diagram displays, click in the *Hide* box for any members that you don't want to display (Figure 1.33). You also can click on members inside the type shapes, right-click, and select *Hide* from the context menu. You can select multiple members by using Shift + click or

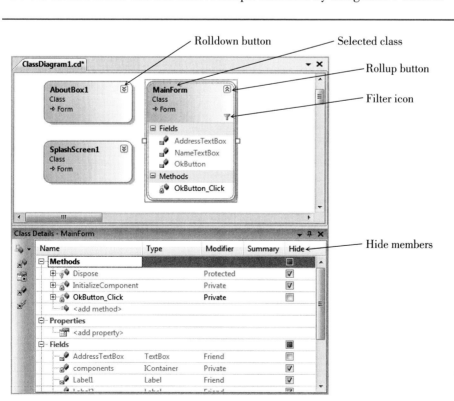

Figure 1.33

Hide some members to view only those that you want to see. In the Class Details window, click the Hide box or right-click a member name and select Hide from the context menu. Hover your mouse over the Filter icon to pop up a list of the hidden objects.

Ctrl + click. Notice the small filter icon in the top section of MainForm in Figure 1.33; the icon indicates that some members are hidden.

The Class Details window is also handy for navigation. You can point to any member, right-click, and choose *View Code* from the context menu, which displays the definition of the member in code.

Your Hands-On Programming Example

Write an MDI project for R 'n R—For Reading and Refreshment. The project should have five forms: the Main form, the About form, the Payroll form, the Summary form, and the Splash form. The Payroll and Summary forms should allow only a single instance and have only a *Close* button. You will write code for the Payroll and Summary forms in Chapter 2.

The About form should display the company name and the copyright information from the assembly attributes.

You can use the Splash Screen and About Box templates or create your own Splash form and About form.

The Main form menu

File	*View*	*Window*	*Help*
Exit	*Payroll*	*Tile Vertical*	*About*
	Summary	*Tile Horizontal*	
		Cascade	

Include a toolbar with buttons to display each of the forms: Payroll, Summary, and About. Each button should display an appropriate ToolTip. Also allow the user to display any of the forms from a context menu.

Display the current date and time in the status bar.

Planning the Project

Sketch the five forms for the application (Figure 1.34). Your users must sign off the sketches as meeting their needs before you begin programming.

Figure 1.34

Sketch the forms for the R 'n R Payroll project; a. Main form (parent), b. Payroll form; c. Summary form; d. About form; and e. Splash form.

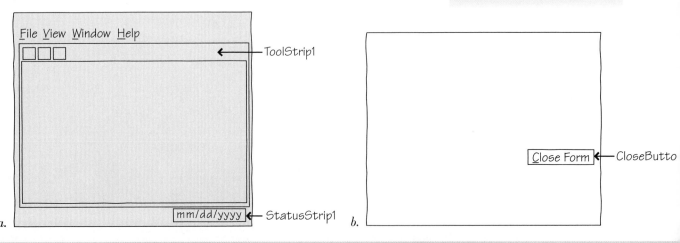

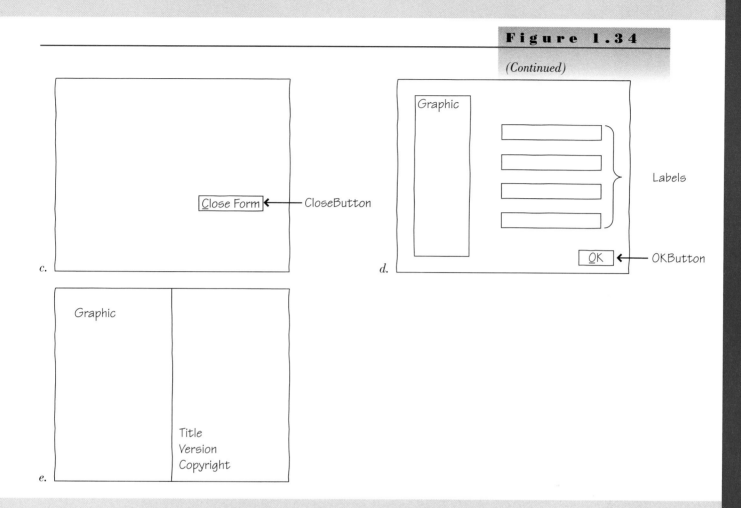

Figure 1.34

(Continued)

Plan the Objects, Properties, and Methods Determine the objects and property settings for the forms and controls. Figure 1.35 shows the diagram of the program classes.

MainForm

Object	Property	Setting
MainForm	Text	R 'n R For Reading and Refreshment
	IsMdiContainer	True
	ContextMenuStrip	ContextMenuStrip1
MenuStrip1	MdiWindowListItem	WindowToolStripMenuItem
FileToolStripMenuItem	Text	&File
ExitToolStripMenuItem	Text	E&xit
ViewToolStripMenuItem	Text	&View
PayrollToolStripMenuItem	Text	&Payroll Form
SummaryToolStripMenuItem	Text	&Summary
WindowToolStripMenuItem	Text	&Window

Figure 1.35

The class diagram for the hands-on programming example.

Object	Property	Setting
TileVerticalToolStripMenuItem	Text	Tile &Vertical
TileHorizontalToolStripMenuItem	Text	Tile &Horizontal
CascadeToolStripMenuItem	Text	&Cascade
HelpToolStripMenuItem	Text	&Help
AboutToolStripMenuItem	Text	&About
ToolStrip1	Items collection	Payroll Summary Help
StatusStrip1	Items collection	Add 2 labels for the date and time
ContextMenu	Items collection	Payroll Summary Help

Procedure	Actions—Pseudocode
MainForm_Load	Retrieve the date and time for the StatusStrip.
ExitToolStripMenuItem_Click	Close the form.
AboutToolStripMenuItem_Click	Show the AboutBox form.
PayrollFormToolStripMenuItem_Click	Create an instance of the Payroll form. Set the MdiParent property. Show the form.
SummaryToolStripMenuItem_Click	Create an instance of the Summary form. Set the MdiParent property. Show the form.

PayrollForm

Object	Property	Setting
PayrollForm	Text	Payroll
CloseButton	Text	&Close Form

Procedure	Actions—Pseudocode
CloseButton_Click	Close the form.

Property	
Instance	Read Only If an instance does not exist Create a new instance.

Summary Form

Object	Property	Setting
SummaryForm	Text	Payroll Summary
CloseButton	Text	&Close Form

Procedure	Actions—Pseudocode
CloseButton_Click	Close the form.

Property	
Instance	Read Only If an instance does not exist Create a new instance.

AboutBox

Object	Property	Setting
AboutBox1	FormBorderStyle	FixedDialog
Labels to display information about the company and application.		
OKButton	Text	&OK

Procedure	Actions—Pseudocode
AboutBox_Load	Retrieve the attributes and set up the labels. (Code already in template file.)
OKButton_Click	Close the form.

Splash Screen Form Include a graphic and labels identifying the company and application. You can use the Splash Screen template and replace the graphic. Add code to hold the form on the screen for a few seconds.

Assembly Information Modify the assembly information:

Property	Setting
Title	Payroll Application
Company	R 'n R for Reading and Refreshment
Product	Books and Drinks
Copyright	Copyright © 2009

Write the Project Following the sketches in Figure 1.34, create the forms. Figure 1.36 shows the completed forms.

- Set the properties of each of the objects, as you have planned. Don't forget to set the tab order on all forms.

- Write the code for the forms. Working from the pseudocode, write each procedure.

- Modify the assembly information in the Project Designer to hold the company attributes.

- When you complete the code, test each of the options. Make sure that all menu items work, the context menus work, and ToolTips appear for each button.

Figure 1.36

The forms for the R 'n R Payroll project; a. Main form (parent); b. Payroll form; c. Summary form; d. About box; and e. Splash form.

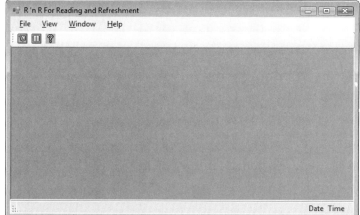

a.

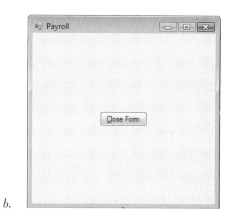

b.

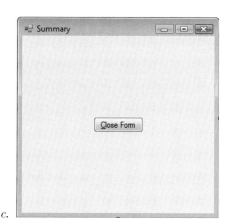

c.

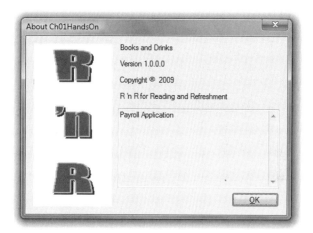

d.

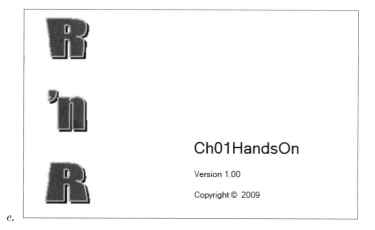

e.

The Project Coding Solution
Main Form

```
'Program:      Ch01HandsOn
'Programmer:   Bradley/Millspaugh
'Form:         MainForm
'Date:         June 2009
'Description:  MDI parent form; contains the menu and displays
'              the various forms.

Public Class MainForm

    Private Sub MainForm_Load(ByVal sender As System.Object, _
      ByVal e As System.EventArgs) Handles MyBase.Load
        ' Display the date in the status bar.

        DateToolStripStatusLabel.Text = Now.ToShortDateString
        TimeToolStripStatusLabel.Text = Now.ToLongTimeString
    End Sub

    Private Sub TileVerticalToolStripMenuItem_Click( _
      ByVal sender As System.Object, ByVal e As System.EventArgs) _
      Handles TileVerticalToolStripMenuItem.Click
        ' Display the open windows tiled vertically.

        Me.LayoutMdi(MdiLayout.TileVertical)
    End Sub

    Private Sub TileHorizontalToolStripMenuItem_Click( _
      ByVal sender As Object, ByVal e As System.EventArgs) _
      Handles TileHorizontalToolStripMenuItem.Click
        ' Display the open windows tiled horizontally.

        Me.LayoutMdi(MdiLayout.TileHorizontal)
    End Sub

    Private Sub CascadeToolStripMenuItem_Click(ByVal sender As Object, _
      ByVal e As System.EventArgs) Handles CascadeToolStripMenuItem.Click
        ' Cascade the open windows.

        Me.LayoutMdi(MdiLayout.Cascade)
    End Sub

    Private Sub PayrollFormToolStripMenuItem_Click( _
      ByVal sender As System.Object, ByVal e As System.EventArgs) _
      Handles PayrollFormToolStripMenuItem.Click, _
      PayrollToolStripButton.Click, PayrollToolStripMenuItem.Click
        ' Create an instance of the payroll form.
        Dim APayrollForm As PayrollForm = PayrollForm.Instance

        With APayrollForm
            .MdiParent = Me
            .Show()
            .Focus()
        End With
    End Sub
```

```vb
    Private Sub SummaryToolStripMenuItem_Click(ByVal sender As System.Object, _
        ByVal e As System.EventArgs) _
        Handles SummaryToolStripMenuItem.Click, SummaryToolStripButton.Click, _
        SummaryFormToolStripMenuItem.Click
            ' Create an instance of the summary form.
            Dim ASummaryForm As SummaryForm = SummaryForm.Instance

            With ASummaryForm
                .MdiParent = Me
                .Show()
                .Focus()
            End With
    End Sub

    Private Sub ExitToolStripMenuItem_Click(ByVal sender As System.Object, _
        ByVal e As System.EventArgs) Handles ExitToolStripMenuItem.Click
            ' Terminate the program.
            ' Closing the startup form ends the program.

            Me.Close()
    End Sub

    Private Sub AboutToolStripMenuItem_Click(ByVal sender As System.Object, _
        ByVal e As System.EventArgs) _
        Handles AboutToolStripMenuItem.Click, AboutToolStripButton.Click
            ' Display the About Box form with attribute information.

            Dim AnAboutBox As New AboutBox1
            AnAboutBox.ShowDialog()
    End Sub

    Private Sub ClockTimer_Tick(ByVal sender As System.Object, _
        ByVal e As System.EventArgs) Handles Timer1.Tick
            ' Update the date and time on the status bar.
            ' Interval = 1000 milliseconds (one second).

            DateToolStripStatusLabel.Text = Now.ToShortDateString()
            TimeToolStripStatusLabel.Text = Now.ToLongTimeString()
    End Sub
End Class
```

Payroll Form

```vb
'Program:        Ch01HandsOn
'Programmer:     Bradley/Millspaugh
'Form:           PayrollForm
'Date:           June 2009
'Description:    The Payroll form for the MDI application.
'                Uses the singleton design pattern to ensure that only one
'                instance of the form can be created.
'                Note: This form will be used for calculations in
'                Chapter 2.

Public Class PayrollForm
    Private Shared AnInstance As PayrollForm
```

```vbnet
Public Shared ReadOnly Property Instance() As PayrollForm
    Get
        If AnInstance Is Nothing Then
            AnInstance = New PayrollForm
        End If
        Return AnInstance
    End Get
End Property

Private Sub CloseButton_Click(ByVal sender As System.Object, _
  ByVal e As System.EventArgs) Handles closeButton.Click
    ' Close the form.

    Me.Close()
End Sub

Private Sub PayrollForm_FormClosing(ByVal sender As Object, _
  ByVal e As System.Windows.Forms.FormClosingEventArgs) _
  Handles Me.FormClosing
    ' Release the instance of this form.

    AnInstance = Nothing
End Sub
End Class
```

Summary Form

```vbnet
'Program:       Ch01HandsOn
'Programmer:    Bradley/Millspaugh
'Form:          SummaryForm
'Date:          June 2009
'Description:   Summary form for an MDI application.
'               Uses the singleton design pattern to ensure that only one
'               instance of the form can be created.
'               Note: This form will be used to display the result of
'               calculations in Chapter 2.

Public Class SummaryForm
    Private Shared AnInstance As SummaryForm

    Public Shared ReadOnly Property Instance() As SummaryForm
        Get
            If AnInstance Is Nothing Then
                AnInstance = New SummaryForm
            End If
            Return AnInstance
        End Get
    End Property

    Private Sub CloseButton_Click(ByVal sender As System.Object, _
      ByVal e As System.EventArgs) Handles CloseButton.Click
        ' Close the form.

        Me.Close()
    End Sub
```

```vb
    Private Sub SummaryForm_FormClosing(ByVal sender As Object, _
      ByVal e As System.Windows.Forms.FormClosingEventArgs) _
      Handles Me.FormClosing
         ' Release the instance of this form.

         AnInstance = Nothing
    End Sub
End Class
```

AboutBox

If you use the AboutBox template, you don't have to write any code at all.

SplashScreen

If you use the Splash Screen template, add one event handler to hold the form on the screen for a few seconds.

```vb
Private Sub SplashScreen1_FormClosing(ByVal sender As Object, _
  ByVal e As System.Windows.Forms.FormClosingEventArgs) _
  Handles Me.FormClosing
     ' Hold the form on the screen for about 5 seconds before closing.

     System.Threading.Thread.Sleep(5000)
End Sub
```

Summary

1. The .NET Framework contains the class libraries, the common language runtime, and ASP.NET.
2. Managed code is compiled to run in the common language runtime (CLR).
3. A portable executable (PE) file contains intermediate language (managed code) and metadata.
4. Metadata store information about the methods, classes, and types for the runtime.
5. The .NET Framework is composed of a set of classes stored in the class library. The classes are organized into a hierarchy of namespaces.
6. The CLR treats value types and reference types differently. Each value type variable has the value stored in the variable's memory location and is always initialized. A reference type variable holds a pointer to an actual object and may be equal to Nothing if not assigned.
7. The compiler produces MSIL (Microsoft intermediate language), a platform-independent set of instructions.
8. An assembly is the smallest deployable unit of code, which contains one or more .exe or .dll files and a manifest that describes the assembly.
9. The AssemblyInfo.vb file holds attributes, which are tags that contain information about the assembly.
10. A Reference object connects Visual Basic to external components, either assemblies or COM objects.

11. Web development is done using ASP.NET.

12. The Visual Studio (VS) integrated development environment (IDE) is used to develop and debug projects. Two helpful features of the IDE are temporary projects, which don't have to be saved, and profiles, which customize the IDE for a particular type of developer. This text uses the VB development profile.

13. The *Options* dialog box can be used to set the defaults for Option Explicit and Option Strict for all projects, default project file locations, and the grid in the Form Designer.

14. The My Project folder, which appears in the Solution Explorer, holds configuration files, including AssemblyInfo.vb. You can double-click on My Project to display the new Project Designer.

15. A compiled program becomes an .exe or .dll file in the bin\Debug folder of the project. The .resx file holds an XML representation of the resources for the form, including any graphics.

16. The VS IDE uses the partial classes feature to store a form class in two separate files. The programmer-written code is in a different file from the designer-written code.

17. The Project Designer can be used to set many options for the project, including the assembly information in AssemblyInfo.vb and the project resources.

18. You can deploy a Windows application by copying the .exe file to another location.

19. The My feature includes several objects that provide access to the application, resources, the user, and the user's computer.

20. You can modify the application's assembly information attributes in the *Assembly Information* dialog box or by editing the AssemblyInfo.vb file directly. To retrieve the attributes at run time, use the My.Application.Info object.

21. Toolbars and status bars improve the ease of operation for users. Menus are created with the MenuStrip and ContextMenuStrip components, a toolbar is created with a ToolStrip, and a status bar is created with a StatusStrip.

22. A form and each control have a ContextMenuStrip property, which you can set to a context menu that you create. Text controls have an automatic context menu with items for text editing.

23. An event handler can respond to events of multiple controls by adding the events to the `Handles` clause. Use this technique to use the same event handler for a menu item, context menu item, and toolbar button.

24. To display the date and/or time in a status bar, use the Now property of the DateTime structure. Typically, the date and time are set in the Form_Load event handler and in the Tick event handler for a Timer component, so that the time remains current.

25. When using multiple forms, the forms may be single document interface (SDI) or multiple document interface (MDI). An MDI application has parent and child forms. To create a parent, set a form's IsMdiContainer property to *true*. A child form must be set in code by setting the form's MdiParent property to the parent form.

26. An MDI application generally has a Window menu that displays the open child windows and options for arranging the child windows. Designate the *Window* menu by setting the MDIWindowListItem property of the Menu-Strip on the parent form.

27. A singleton design pattern is used to ensure that only one instance of a class can be created.

28. A splash screen displays as an application loads. You can create a splash screen by setting properties of a standard Windows Form or by using the Splash Screen template. Set the splash screen in the Project Designer.

29. Use the `Sleep` method of a Thread object in the splash screen's Form-Closing event handler to hold the form on the screen long enough for the user to read it.

30. The VS IDE can automatically generate class diagrams, which show a visual representation of the classes in an application. You have many options for expanding, collapsing, rearranging, showing, and hiding elements in the class diagram.

Key Terms

Active Server Pages (ASP) *6*
assembly *5*
assembly information *14*
assembly manifest *5*
attributes *5*
child form *25*
class diagram *31*
common language runtime
   (CLR) *2*
Common Language Specification
   (CLS) *3*
ContextMenuStrip component *18*
DateTime structure *24*
design pattern *28*
IsMdiContainer property *26*
`LayoutMdi` method *27*
managed code *2*
managed data *2*
MdiParent property *26*
MenuStrip component *18*
metadata *2*
Microsoft intermediate
   language (MSIL) *4*

multiple document
   interface (MDI) *25*
My *13*
.NET Framework *2*
.NET Framework class
   library *2*
Now property *24*
parent form *25*
partial class *11*
partial type *11*
Project Designer *12*
reference object *5*
reference type *3*
single document
   interface (SDI) *25*
singleton pattern *28*
splash screen *29*
StatusStrip component *18*
thread *31*
Timer component *24*
ToolStrip component *18*
value type *3*

Review Questions

1. Differentiate between the .NET Framework and Visual Studio.
2. Explain the following
   a. CLR
   b. CLS
   c. PE
   d. MSIL
   e. ASP.NET
3. Explain the relationship between the common language runtime and managed code.
4. What is the purpose of compiling to an intermediate language?
5. What is the difference between a value type and a reference type?
6. What is an assembly? What does an assembly contain?
7. What are attributes? Give three examples.
8. What is ASP.NET and what is its purpose?
9. Where can you find a project's compiled version? What else might you find in that same location?
10. What is the Project Designer? How is it displayed? How is it used?
11. How can you deploy Windows applications?
12. What is the VB My feature? Name at least one use for My.
13. Explain how to display the attributes in AssemblyInfo.vb on a form at run time.
14. What components does VS provide for creating menus, context menus, toolbars, and status bars?
15. Describe the steps necessary to make the current time appear in a status bar.
16. What is an MDI application? How many parent forms can be in a single MDI application?
17. What is a design pattern?
18. How is the singleton pattern implemented?
19. Explain how to create a splash screen, how to display it as the application loads, and how to hold it on the screen for several seconds.
20. What is a class diagram? How can you create and customize a class diagram using the VS IDE?

Programming Exercises

Note: If you prefer to write Windows Presentation Foundation (WPF) applications, rather than Windows applications, see "Windows Presentation Foundation (WPF)" in Chapter 13.

1.1 Create a Windows application that displays the company, title, and copyright information from the assembly information attributes. Make sure to modify the assembly information.

1.2 Create a multiple form project for Tricia's Travels that contains a splash screen, a Main form, a Specials form, a Summary form, and an About form. On the Specials form, display specials for dream vacations; include destinations of your choice for a weekend, a cruise, and a week-long trip. The main form will have a menu that contains the following:

_F_ile	_T_ravels	_H_elp
E_x_it	Specials	About
	Summary	

Case Studies

Claytor's Cottages

Create a project for Claytor's Cottages, a small bed and breakfast. Use an MDI form with a menu, a context menu, a toolbar, and a status bar.

The About form should not be a child form. Use the My object to display the description, title, version number, and copyright attributes.

Include a splash screen with information about your program.

Create child forms for each option (Guests, Rooms, and Reservations) that simply have the title bar text indicating the form purpose and a *Close* button to return to the main form.

Note: These forms will be modified in later chapters.

Menus

_F_ile	_E_dit	_W_indow	_H_elp
E_x_it	_G_uests	Tile _H_orizontal	_A_bout
	Roo_m_s	Tile _V_ertical	
	_R_eservations	_C_ascade	

Set up the menus so that the open child forms display on the *Window* menu.

Toolbar

Include three buttons to open each of the child forms. Place ToolTips on each button.

Guests
Rooms
Reservations

Status Bar

Include the date and the time of day at the right side of the status bar. Leave a panel for text messages to the left side.

Hint: Add three labels and set the Spring property of the first label to *true*.

Context Menu

Create a context menu on the parent form that has options to display the Guests, Rooms, and Reservations forms.

Standards

- Follow naming standards for all variables, objects, and procedures.

- Menu items and controls must have keyboard access. Use standard selections when appropriate.

- Set the parent form's Icon property to an appropriate icon.

Note: The parent form icon displays in the task bar when the application is minimized.

Christian's Car Rentals

Create a project for Christian's Car Rentals. The project should contain an MDI main form with a menu, a context menu, a toolbar, and a status bar.

The About form should be a child form and contain at least your name and the date. Use the My object to display the description, title, version number, and copyright attributes.

Include a splash screen with information about your program.

Create child forms for each option (Customers, Vehicles, and Rentals) that simply have the title bar text indicating the form purpose and a *Close* button to return to the main form.

Note: These forms will be modified in later chapters.

Menu

File	Edit	Window	Help
Exit	Customers	Tile Horizontal	About
	Vehicles	Tile Vertical	
	Rentals	Cascade	

Include keyboard shortcuts for all menu options, following standards where applicable.

Set up the menus so that the open child forms display on the *Window* menu.

Toolbar

Place three buttons on the toolbar, one to display each of the child forms. Use any icon that you wish for each of the buttons and include ToolTips for each.

Customers
Vehicles
Rentals

Status Bar

Include the date and the time of day at the right end of the status bar. Leave a label for text messages at the left end.

Hint: Add three labels and set the Spring property of the first label to *true*.

Context Menu

Create a context menu on the parent form that has options to display the Customers, Vehicles, and Rentals forms.

Standards

- Follow naming standards for all variables, objects, and procedures.

- Menu items and controls must have keyboard access. Use standard selections when appropriate.

- Set the parent form's Icon property to an appropriate icon.

Note: The parent form icon displays in the task bar when the application is minimized.

2

Building Multitier Programs with Classes

at the completion of this chapter, you will be able to . . .

1. Discuss object-oriented terminology.

2. Create your own class and instantiate objects based on the class.

3. Create a new class based on an existing class.

4. Divide an application into multiple tiers.

5. Throw and catch exceptions.

6. Choose the proper scope for variables.

7. Validate user input using the `TryParse` and display messages using an ErrorProvider component.

At this point in your programming career, you should be comfortable with using objects, methods, and properties. You have already learned most of the basics of programming including decisions, loops, and arrays. You must now start writing your programs in styles appropriate for larger production projects.

Most programming tasks are done in teams. Many developers may work on different portions of the code and all of the code must work together. One of the key concepts of object-oriented programming (OOP) is that of using building blocks. You will now break your programs into blocks, or, using the proper term, classes.

This chapter reviews object-oriented programming concepts and techniques for breaking your program into multiple tiers with multiple classes. Depending on how much of your first course was spent on OOP, you may find that much of this chapter is review.

Object-Oriented Programming

Visual Basic is an object-oriented language and all programming uses the OOP approach. You have *used* objects but were likely shielded from most of the nitty-gritty of *creating* objects. In VB you will find that everything you do is based on classes. Each form is a class, which must be instantiated before it can be used. Even variables of the basic data types are objects, with properties and methods.

OOP Terminology

The key features of object-oriented programming are abstraction, encapsulation, inheritance, and polymorphism.

Abstraction

Abstraction means to create a model of an object, for the purpose of determining the characteristics (properties) and the behaviors (methods) of the object. For example, a Customer class is an abstract representation of a real customer, and a Product class is an abstract version of a real product. You need to use abstraction when planning an object-oriented program, to determine the classes that you need and the necessary properties and methods. It is helpful to think of objects generically; that is, what are the characteristics of a typical product, rather than a specific product.

Encapsulation

Encapsulation refers to the combination of characteristics of an object along with its behaviors. You have one "package" that holds the definition of all properties, methods, and events.

Encapsulation makes it possible to accomplish data hiding. Each object keeps its data (properties) and procedures (methods) hidden. Through use of the `Public` and `Private` keywords, an object can "expose" only those data elements and procedures that it wishes to allow the outside world to see.

You can witness encapsulation by looking at any Windows program. The form is actually a class. All of the methods and events that you code are enclosed within the `Class` and `End Class` statements. The variables that you place in your code are actually properties of that specific form class.

Inheritance

Inheritance is the ability to create a new class from an existing class. You can add enhancements to an existing class without modifying the original. By creating a new class that inherits from an existing class, you can add or change class variables and methods. For example, each of the forms that you create is inherited from, or derived from, the existing Form class. The original class is known as the **base class**, **superclass**, or **parent class**. The inherited class is called a **subclass**, a **derived class**, or a **child class**. Of course, a new class can inherit from a subclass—that subclass becomes a superclass as well as a subclass.

You can see the inheritance for a form, which is declared in the form's designer.vb file. Show all files in the Solution Explorer, expand the files for a form, and open the form's designer.vb file. Look closely at the first line of code:

```
Partial Public Class MainForm
    Inherits System.Windows.Forms.Form
```

Inherited classes should always have an "is a" relationship with the base class. In the form example, the new MainForm "is a" Form (Figure 2.1). You could create a new Customer class that inherits from a Person class; a customer "is a" person. But you should not create a new SalesOrder class that inherits from Person; a sales order is *not* a person.

The real purpose of inheritance is **reusability**. You may need to reuse or obtain the functionality from one class when you have another similar situation. The new MainForm class that you create has all of the characteristics and actions of the base class, System.Windows.Forms.Form. From there you can add the functionality for your own new form.

You can create your own hierarchy of classes. You place the code you want to be common in a base class. You then create other classes, the derived classes or subclasses, which can call the shared functions. This concept is very helpful if you have features that are similar in two classes. Rather than writing two classes that are almost identical, you can create a base class that contains the similar procedures.

Sometimes you create a class specifically to use it as a base for derived classes. You can create a class strictly for inheritance; such a class is called an **abstract class** and is declared with `MustInherit` in the class header. You

Figure 2.1

A derived or inherited class has an "is a" relationship with its base class.

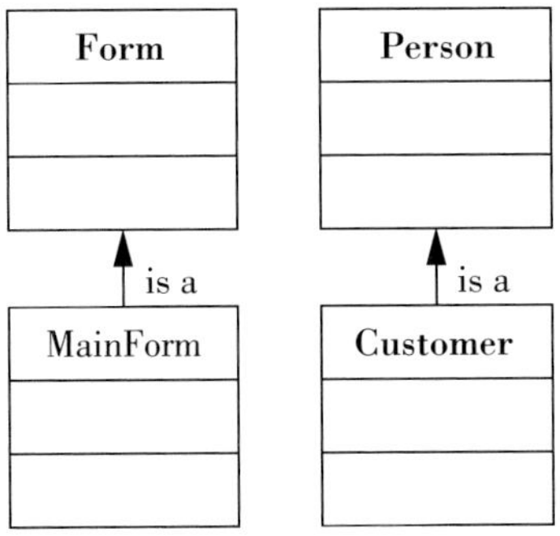

cannot instantiate objects from an abstract class, only inherit new classes from it. Some of the methods in the base class may not even contain any code but are there as placeholders, forcing any derived classes to have methods with the defined names. A derived class with a method named the same as a method in the base class is said to **override** the method in the base class. Overriding allows an inherited class to take different actions from the identically named method in the base class.

An example of reusing classes could be a Person class, where you might have properties for name, address, and phone number. The Person class can be a base class, from which you derive an Employee class, a Customer class, or a Student class (Figure 2.2). The derived classes could call procedures from the base class and contain any additional procedures that are unique to the derived class. In inheritance, typically the classes go from the general to the more specific. You can add functionality to an inherited class. You also can change a function by overriding a method from the base class.

Figure 2.2

Multiple subclasses can inherit from a single base class.

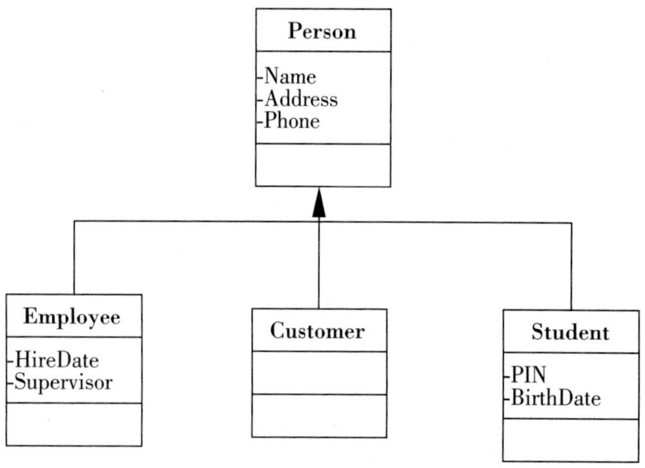

Polymorphism

The term *polymorphism* actually means the ability to take on many shapes or forms. As applied to OOP, polymorphism refers to method names that have identical names but different implementations, depending on the situation. For example, radio buttons, check boxes, and list boxes each has a `Select` method. In each case, the `Select` method operates appropriately for its class.

When a derived class overrides a method of its base class, both methods have the same signature (name plus parameter list). But in each case, the actions performed are appropriate for the class. For example, a Person class might have a `Print` method that prints an address label with name and address information. But the `Print` method of the Employee class, which overrides the `Print` method of the Person class, might display the employee's information, including hire date and supervisor name, on the screen.

Polymorphism also allows a single class to have more than one method with the same name but a different argument list. The method is said to be *overloaded*. When an overloaded method is called, the argument type determines which version of the method to use. Each of the identically named methods performs its tasks in a slightly different way from the other methods.

Reusable Objects

A big advantage of object-oriented programming over traditional programming is the ability to reuse objects. When you create a new class by writing a class module, you can then use that class in multiple projects. Each object that you create from the class has its own set of properties. This process works just like the built-in VB controls you have been using all along. For example, you can create two PictureBox objects: imageOnePictureBox and imageTwoPictureBox. Each has its own Visible property and Image property, which will probably be set differently for each one.

The building-block concept can streamline programming. Consider a large corporation such as Microsoft, with many different programming teams. Perhaps one team develops the Word product and another team works on Excel. What happened when the Word team decided to incorporate formulas in tables? Do you think they wrote all new code to process the formulas? Likewise, there was a point when the Excel team added spell checking to worksheets. Do you think that they had to rewrite the spell-checking code? Obviously, it makes more sense to have a spell-checking object that can be used by any application and a calculation object that processes formulas in any application where needed.

Developing applications should be like building objects with Lego blocks. The blocks all fit together and can be used to build many different things.

Multitier Applications

A common use of classes is to create applications in multiple "tiers" or layers. Each of the functions of a **multitier application** can be coded in a separate component and the components may be stored and run on different machines.

One of the most popular approaches is a three-tier application. The tiers in this model are the presentation (or user interface) tier, business services tier, and data tier (Figure 2.3). You also may hear the term "*n*-tier" application, which is an expansion of the three-tier model. The middle tier, which contains all of the business logic or **business rules**, may be written in multiple classes that can be stored and run from multiple locations.

In a multitier application, the goal is to create components that can be combined and replaced. If one part of an application needs to change, such as a redesign of the user interface or a new database format, the other components do not need to be replaced. A developer can simply "plug in" a new user interface and continue using the rest of the components of the application.

The **presentation tier** refers to the user interface, which in a Windows application is the form. Consider that, in the future, the user interface could be completely redesigned or even converted to a Web page.

Figure 2.3

The three-tier model for application design.

Presentation Tier	Business Services Tier	Data Tier
User Interface Forms, controls, menus	Business Objects Validation Calculations Business logic Business rules	Data Retrieval Data storage

The **business services tier** is a class or classes that manipulate the data. This layer can include validation to enforce business rules as well as the calculations. If the validation and calculations are built into the form, then modifying the user interface may require a complete rewrite of a working application.

The **data tier** includes retrieving and storing the data in a database or other data store. Occasionally an organization will decide to change database vendors or need to retrieve data from several different sources. The data tier retrieves the data and passes the results to the business services tier, or takes data from the business services tier and writes them in the appropriate location.

Programmers must plan ahead for reusability in today's environment. You may develop the business services tier for a Windows application. Later the company may decide to deliver the application via the Web or a mobile device, such as a cell phone or palm device. The user interface must change, but the processing shouldn't have to change. If you develop your application with classes that perform the business logic, you can develop an application for one interface and easily move it to another platform.

Feedback 2.1

1. Name at least three types of operations that belong in the business services tier.
2. List as many operations that you can think of that belong in the presentation tier.

Creating Classes

You most likely learned to create classes in your introductory course. It's time to review the techniques and to delve deeper into the concepts. If you are comfortable with creating new classes, writing property procedures including read-only properties, and using a parameterized constructor, you may want to skip over the next few sections and begin with "A Basic Business Class."

Designing Your Own Class

To design your own class, you need to analyze the characteristics and behaviors that your object needs. The characteristics or properties are defined as variables, and the behaviors (methods) are sub procedures or function procedures.

Creating Properties in a Class

Inside your class you define private variables, which contain the values for the properties of the class. Theoretically, you could declare all variables as `Public` so that all other classes could set and retrieve their values. However, this approach violates the rules of encapsulation that require each object to be in charge of its own data. Remember that you use encapsulation to implement data hiding. To accomplish encapsulation, you will declare all variables in a class as `Private`. As a private variable, the value is available only to the procedures within the class, the same way that private module-level variables in a form are available only to procedures within the form's class.

When your program creates objects from your class, you will need to assign values to the properties. Because the properties are private variables, you will use special property procedures to pass the values to the class module and to return values from the class module.

Property Procedures

The way that your class allows its properties to be accessed is through **property procedures**. A property procedure may contain a Get to retrieve a property value and/or a Set to assign a value to the property. The name that you use for the Property procedure becomes the name of the property to the outside world. Create "friendly" property names that describe the property without using a data type, such as LastName or EmployeeNumber.

The Property Procedure—General Form

General Form

```
Private ClassVariable As DataType   ' Declared at the module level.

[Public] Property PropertyName() As DataType
    Get
        PropertyName = ClassVariable
      or
        Return ClassVariable
    End Get

    Set(ByVal Value As DataType)

        [Statements, such as validation]
        ClassVariable = Value
    End Set
End Property
```

The Set statement uses the **Value keyword** to refer to the incoming value for the property. Property procedures are public by default, so you can omit the optional Public keyword. Get blocks are similar to function procedures in at least one respect: Somewhere inside the procedure, before the End Get, you must assign a return value to the procedure name or use a Return statement. The data type of the incoming value for a Set must match the type of the return value of the corresponding Get.

The Property Procedure—Example

Example

```
Private LastNameString As String   ' Declared at the module level.

Public Property LastName() As String
    Get
        Return LastNameString
        ' Alternate version:
        ' LastName = LastNameString
    End Get

    Set(ByVal Value As String)
        LastNameString = Value
    End Set
End Property
```

Remember, the private module-level variable holds the value of the property. The `Property Get` and `Set` retrieve the current value and assign a new value to the property.

Read-Only and Write-Only Properties

In some instances, you may wish to set a value for a property that can only be retrieved by an object but not changed. To create a read-only property, use the **ReadOnly** modifier and write only the `Get` portion of the property procedure. Security recommendations are to not include a `Set` procedure unless one is needed for your application or for class inheritance.

```
Private PayDecimal As Decimal      ' Declared at the module level

Public ReadOnly Property Pay() As Decimal      ' Make the property read-only.
    Get
        Return PayDecimal
    End Get
End Property
```

A write-only property is one that can be set but not returned. Use the **WriteOnly** modifier and write only the `Set` portion of the property procedure:

```
Private PasswordString As String      ' Declared at the module level.

Public WriteOnly Property Password() As String ' Make it write-only.
    Set(ByVal Value As String)
        PasswordString = Value
    End Set
End Property
```

Constructors and Destructors

A **constructor** is a method that automatically executes when a class is instantiated. A **destructor** is a method that automatically executes when an object is destroyed. In VB, the constructor must be a procedure named `New`. The destructor must be named `Dispose` and must override the `Dispose` method of the base class. You will generally write constructors for your classes, but usually not destructors. Most of the time the `Dispose` method of the base class handles the class destruction very well.

You create a constructor for your class by writing a `Sub New` procedure. The constructor executes automatically when you instantiate an object of the class. Because the constructor method executes before any other code in the class, the constructor is an ideal location for any initialization tasks that you need to do, such as opening a database connection.

The `Sub New` procedure must be `Public` or `Protected` because the objects that you create must execute this method. Remember that the default is `Public`.

```
Sub New()
    ' Constructor for class.

    ' Initialization statements.
End Sub
```

Overloading the Constructor

Recall that ***overloading*** means that two methods have the same name but a different list of arguments (the signature). You can create overloaded methods in your class by giving the same name to multiple procedures, each with a different argument list. The following example shows an empty constructor (one without arguments) and a constructor that passes arguments to the class.

```
' Constructors in the Payroll class.

Sub New()
    ' Constructor with empty argument list.
End Sub

Sub New(ByVal HoursInDecimal As Decimal, ByVal RateInDecimal As Decimal)
    ' Constructor that passes arguments.

    ' Assign incoming values to private variables.
    HoursDecimal = HoursInDecimal
    RateDecimal = RateInDecimal
End Sub
```

Note: It isn't necessary to include the `ByVal` modifier to arguments since `ByVal` is the default. The editor adds `ByVal` to the arguments if you leave it out.

A Parameterized Constructor

The term ***parameterized constructor*** refers to a constructor that requires arguments. This popular technique allows you to pass arguments/properties as you create the new object. In the preceding example, the Payroll class requires two decimal arguments: the hours and the rate. By instantiating the Payroll object in a `Try` / `Catch` block, you can catch any missing input value as well as any nonnumeric input.

```
' Code in the Form class to instantiate an object of the Payroll class.

Try
    Dim APayroll As New Payroll( _
        Decimal.Parse(HoursTextBox.Text), Decimal.Parse(RateTextBox.Text))

Catch Err As Exception
    MessageBox.Show("Enter the hours and rate.", "Payroll")
End Try
```

Assigning Arguments to Properties

As a further improvement to the Payroll parameterized constructor, we will use the property procedures to assign initial property values. Within the class module, use the `Me` keyword to refer to the current class. So `Me.Hours` refers to the Hours property of the current class. `HoursInDecimal` refers to the class-level variable. Assigning the passed argument to the property name is preferable to just assigning the passed argument to the module-level property variable since validation is performed in the `Property Set` procedures.

```
' Improved constructor for the Payroll class.
Sub New(ByVal HoursInDecimal As Decimal, ByVal RateInDecimal As Decimal)
    ' Assign arguments to properties.
```

```
    With Me
        .Hours = HoursInDecimal
        .Rate = RateInDecimal
    End With
End Sub
```

When your class has both an empty constructor and a parameterized constructor, the program that creates the object can choose which method to use.

A Basic Business Class

The following example creates a very simplistic payroll application in two tiers (Figure 2.4). The application does not have a data tier since it doesn't have any database element.

Figure 2.4

Create a nondatabase project in two tiers.

Presentation Tier	Business Services Tier

User Interface
    PayrollForm
    Controls
    Menus
	Business Objects
	    Validation
	    Calculations
	    Business logic
	    Business rules

This first version of the payroll application inputs hours and rate from the user, validates for numeric data and some business rules, calculates the pay, and displays the pay on the form. We must analyze the tasks that belong in the presentation tier and those that belong in the business services tier (Figure 2.5).

The Presentation Tier

The presentation tier, also called the *user interface*, must handle all communication with the user. The user enters input data and clicks the *Calculate* button. The result of the calculation and any error messages to the user must come from the presentation tier. Generally, validation for numeric input is handled in the form, but validation for business rules is handled in the business services tier.

The Business Services Tier

Looking at Figure 2.5, you can see what should go in the class for the business services tier. The class needs private property variables for Hours, Rate, and

Figure 2.5

The form is the user interface; the validation and calculations are performed in the Payroll class, which is the business services tier.

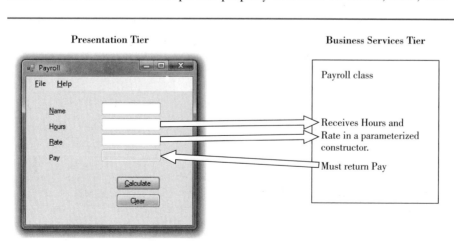

Pay. It also needs a parameterized constructor to pass the arguments, property procedures to validate and set the Hours and Rate, and a read-only property to allow a Payroll object to retrieve the calculated pay.

The property procedures will include code to validate the input Hours and Rate for business rules. At this point, company policy is that the number of hours must be in the range 0–60 and the pay rate must be at least 6.25 and no more than 50. If the input values for Hours or Rate are outside of the acceptable range, the class will throw an exception that can be caught in the form's code. Remember that all user interaction, including any error messages, should occur in the presentation tier (the form).

Note: Throwing exceptions is covered in the section that follows the class code.

The Payroll Class

```
'Project:       Ch02PayrollApplication
'Module:        Payroll Class
'Programmer:    Bradley/Millspaugh
'Date:          June 2009
'Description:   Business services tier for payroll calculation: validates
                input data and calculates the pay.

Public Class Payroll

    ' Private class variables.
    Private HoursDecimal As Decimal   ' Hold the Hours property.
    Private RateDecimal As Decimal    ' Hold the Rate property.
    Private PayDecimal As Decimal     ' Hold the Pay property.

    ' Constants.
    Private Const MINIMUM_WAGE_Decimal As Decimal = 6.25D
    Private Const MAXIMUM_WAGE_Decimal As Decimal = 50D
    Private Const MINIMUM_HOURS_Decimal As Decimal = 0D
    Private Const MAXIMUM_HOURS_Decimal As Decimal = 60D
    Private Const REGULAR_HOURS_Decimal As Decimal = 40D
    Private Const OVERTIME_RATE_Decimal As Decimal = 1.5D

    ' Constructor.
    Sub New(ByVal HoursInDecimal As Decimal, ByVal RateInDecimal As Decimal)
        ' Assign properties and calculate the pay.

        Hours = HoursInDecimal
        Rate = RateInDecimal
        FindPay()
    End Sub

    Private Sub FindPay()
        ' Calculate the pay.
        Dim OvertimeHoursDecimal As Decimal

        If HoursDecimal <= REGULAR_HOURS_Decimal Then   ' No overtime.
            PayDecimal = HoursDecimal * RateDecimal
            OvertimeHoursDecimal = 0D
        Else                                            ' Overtime.
            OvertimeHoursDecimal = HoursDecimal - REGULAR_HOURS_Decimal
            PayDecimal = (REGULAR_HOURS_Decimal * RateDecimal) + _
                (OvertimeHoursDecimal * OVERTIME_RATE_Decimal * RateDecimal)
        End If
    End Sub
```

```
' Property procedures.
Public Property Hours() As Decimal
    Get
        Return HoursDecimal
    End Get
    Set(ByVal Value As Decimal)
        If Value >= MINIMUM_HOURS_Decimal And _
           Value <= MAXIMUM_HOURS_Decimal Then
            HoursDecimal = Value
        Else
            Dim Ex As New ApplicationException( _
                "Hours are outside of the acceptable range.")
            Ex.Source = "Hours"
            Throw Ex
        End If
    End Set
End Property

Public Property Rate() As Decimal
    Get
        Return RateDecimal
    End Get
    Set(ByVal Value As Decimal)
        If Value >= MINIMUM_WAGE_Decimal And _
           Value <= MAXIMUM_WAGE_Decimal Then
            RateDecimal = Value
        Else
            Throw New ApplicationException( _
                "Pay rate is outside of the acceptable range.")
        End If
    End Set
End Property

Public ReadOnly Property Pay() As Decimal
    Get
        Return PayDecimal
    End Get
End Property
End Class
```

Throwing and Catching Exceptions

The system throws an exception when an error occurs. Your program can catch
the exception and take some action, or even ignore the exception. Your own class
also can **throw an exception** to indicate that an error occurred, which generally is the best way to pass an error message back to the user interface. You can
enclose any code that could cause an exception in a Try / Catch block.

```
' Code in the form's class.
Try
    Dim APayroll As New Payroll( _
        Decimal.Parse(HoursTextBox.Text), Decimal.Parse(RateTextBox.Text))
Catch Err As ApplicationException
    ' Display a message to the user.
    MessageBox.Show(Err.Message)
End Try
```

Note: If you are not familiar with structured exception handling using a `Try / Catch` block, see Appendix B.

What Exception to Throw?

The .NET Framework has several exception classes that you can use, or you can create your own new exception class that inherits from one of the existing classes. However, the system-defined exception classes can handle most every type of exception.

Microsoft recommends that you use the System.ApplicationException class when you throw your own exceptions from application code. System.ApplicationException has the same properties and methods as the System.Exception class, which is the generic system exception. All specific exceptions generated by the CLR inherit from System.Exception.

When you want to throw a generic application exception, use the **Throw statement** in this format:

```
Throw New ApplicationException("Error message to display.")
```

The message that you include becomes the Message property of the exception, which you can display when you catch the exception.

Passing Additional Information in an Exception

The constructor for the ApplicationException class takes only the error message as a parameter. But the class has additional properties that you can set and check. For example, you can set the Source property and the Data property, which can hold sets of key/value pairs.

In our Payroll class, we want to be able to indicate which field is in error, so that the code in the form can set the focus and select the text in the field in error. For this, we will use the exception's Source property. We must instantiate a new exception object, set the Source property, and then throw the exception:

```
Public Property Hours() As Decimal
    Get
        Return HoursDecimal
    End Get
    Set(ByVal Value As Decimal)
        If Value >= MINIMUM_HOURS_Decimal And _
          Value <= MAXIMUM_HOURS_Decimal Then
            HoursDecimal = Value
        Else
            Dim Ex As New ApplicationException( _
              "Hours are outside of the acceptable range.")
            Ex.Source = "Hours"
            Throw Ex
        End If
    End Set
End Property

Public Property Rate() As Decimal
    Get
        Return RateDecimal
    End Get
```

```
        Set(ByVal Value As Decimal)
            If Value >= MINIMUM_WAGE_Decimal And _
              Value <= MAXIMUM_WAGE_Decimal Then
                RateDecimal = Value
            Else
                Dim Ex As New ApplicationException( _
                  "Pay rate is outside of the acceptable range.")
                Ex.Source = "Rate"
                Throw Ex
            End If
        End Set
End Property
```

Throwing Exceptions Up a Level

You should show messages to the user only in the user interface. At times, you may have several levels of components. For example, the form creates an object that calls code in another class. If an exception occurs in a class that does not have a user interface, you should pass the exception up to the next higher level—the component that called the current code. Use the Throw keyword to pass an exception to the form or other component that invoked the class.

```
Try
    ' Code that might cause an exception.
Catch Err As Exception
    Throw Err
End Try
```

Guidelines for Throwing Exceptions

When you throw exceptions, you should always include an error message. The message should be

- Descriptive.

- Grammatically correct, in a complete sentence with punctuation at the end.

Alternatives to Exception Handling

It takes considerable system resources to handle exceptions. You should use exception handling for situations that are errors and truly out of the ordinary. If an error occurs fairly often, you should look for another technique to handle it. However, Microsoft recommends throwing exceptions from components rather than returning an error code.

You can use another tool to help avoid generating parsing exceptions for invalid user input. You can use the **TryParse method** of the numeric classes instead of using Parse. The TryParse method sets the variable to zero and returns Boolean *false* if the parse fails, rather than throwing an exception.

The TryParse Method—General Form

General Form

```
DataType.TryParse(ValueToParse, NumericVariableToHoldResult)
```

The `TryParse` method converts the ValueToParse into an expression of the named data type, returns *true*, and places the result into the numeric variable, which should be declared before this statement. If the conversion fails, the numeric variable is set to zero and the method returns Boolean *false*.

The TryParse Method—Example

```
Dim HoursDecimal As Decimal

Decimal.TryParse(HoursTextBox.Text, HoursDecimal)
If HoursDecimal > 0 Then
    ' Passed the conversion; perform calculations.
Else
    MessageBox.Show("Invalid data entered.")
End If

If Decimal.TryParse(HoursTextBox.Text, HoursDecimal Then
    ' HoursDecimal contains the converted value.
Else
    MessageBox.Show("Invalid data entered.")
End If
```

As you can see, this technique is preferable for numeric validation of user input since it does not throw an exception for nonnumeric data. Instead, bad input data are handled by the `Else` clause.

Modifying the User Interface to Validate at the Field Level

You can further improve the user interface in the payroll application by performing field-level validation. This technique displays a message directly on the form, next to the field in error, before the user moves to the next control. You can use an ErrorProvider component for the message, rather than a message box, which is a more up-to-date approach. You perform field-level validation for numeric data in the **Validating event** of each text box.

The Validating Event

As the user enters data in a text box and moves to another control, the events of the text box occur in this order:

Enter
GotFocus
Leave
Validating
Validated
LostFocus

Each control on the form has a CausesValidation property that is set to *true* by default. When the user finishes an entry and presses Tab or clicks on another control, the Validating event occurs for the control just left. That is, the event occurs if the CausesValidation property of the *new* control is *true*. You can leave the CausesValidation property of most controls set to *true* so that validation occurs. Set CausesValidation to *false* on a control such as *Cancel* or *Exit* to give the user a way to bypass the validation when canceling the transaction. *Note:* The Validating event occurs only for a control that receives the focus; you also may need to perform form-level validation to determine that the user skipped a field entirely.

The Validating event handler is the preferred location for field-level validation. Here is the procedure header for a Validating event handler:

```
Private Sub RateTextBox_Validating(ByVal sender As Object, _
    ByVal e As System.ComponentModel.CancelEventArgs) _
    Handles RateTextBox.Validating
```

Canceling the Validating Event You can use the CancelEventArgs argument of the Validating event handler to cancel the Validating event and return focus to the control that is being validated.

```
e.Cancel = True
```

Canceling the event returns the focus to the text box, making the text box "sticky." The user is not allowed to leave the control until the input passes validation.

One note of caution: If you use the validating event on the field that receives focus when the form is displayed, and the validation requires an entry, the user will be unable to close the form without making a valid entry in the text box. To get around this problem, write an event handler for the form's FormClosing event and set e.Cancel = False.

```
Private Sub PayrollForm_FormClosing(ByVal sender As Object, _
    ByVal e As System.Windows.Forms.FormClosingEventArgs) _
    Handles Me.FormClosing
        ' Do not allow validation to cancel the form's closing.

    e.Cancel = False
End Sub
```

Controlling Validating Events You can get into trouble if you generate Validating events when you don't want them. For example, after an input value has passed the numeric checking, it may fail a business rule, such as not falling within an acceptable range of values. To display a message to the user, you will probably execute the Focus method of the text box in error. But the Focus method triggers a Validating event on the control most recently left, which is likely not the result that you want. You can suppress extra Validating events by temporarily turning off CausesValidation. You will see this technique used in the form's code in the "The Code for the Modified Form" section.

```
With .RateTextBox
    .SelectAll()
    .CausesValidation = False
    .Focus()
    .CausesValidation = True
End With
```

The ErrorProvider Component

Using an **ErrorProvider component**, you can make an error indicator appear next to the field in error, rather than pop up a message box. Generally, you use one ErrorProvider for all controls on a form. You add the ErrorProvider to the form's component tray at design time and set its properties in code. If the input data value is invalid, the ErrorProvider component can display a blinking icon next to the field in error and display a message in a popup, similar to a ToolTip (Figure 2.6).

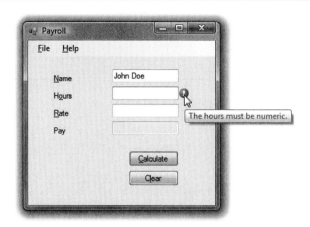

Figure 2.6

The ErrorProvider displays a blinking icon next to the field in error. When the user points to the icon, the error message appears in a popup.

The ErrorProvider SetError Method—General Form

You turn on the blinking error indicator and error message with the ErrorProvider's `SetError` method.

```
ErrorProviderObject.SetError(ControlName, MessageString)
```

The ErrorProvider SetError Method—Examples

```
ErrorProvider1.SetError(QuantityTextBox, "Quantity must be numeric.")
ErrorProvider1.SetError(CreditCardTextBox, "Required field.")
```

You can replace message boxes with ErrorProviders in most any program without changing the logic of the program.

Turning Off the Error Indicator You must clear the ErrorProvider after the error is corrected. Use the ErrorProvider's `Clear` method to turn off the error indicator.

```
ErrorProvider1.Clear()
```

In a button's Click event handler, the best approach is to clear the ErrorProvider at the top of the procedure and turn it on anywhere that a value fails validation.

```vb
Private Sub CalcuateButton_Click(ByVal sender As System.Object, _
  ByVal e As System.EventArgs) Handles CalculateButton.Click
    ' Validate and perform calculations.
    Dim HoursDecimal As Decimal

    ' Check for valid input data.
    ErrorProvider1.Clear()
    If Decimal.TryParse(HoursTextBox.Text, HoursDecimal) Then
        ' Perform any calculations with good data.
    Else
        ' Hours did not pass validation.
        ErrorProvider1.SetError(HoursTextBox, _
           "The hours must be numeric.")
    End If
End Sub
```

In a Validating event handler, the most common technique is to use an `If` statement and turn the ErrorProvider on or off.

```vb
Private Sub HoursTextBox_Validating(ByVal sender As Object, _
  ByVal e As System.ComponentModel.CancelEventArgs) _
  Handles HoursTextBox.Validating
    ' Test hours for numeric.
    Dim HoursDecimal As Decimal

    If Decimal.TryParse(HoursTextBox.Text, HoursDecimal) Then
        ErrorProvider1.Clear()
    Else
        ErrorProvider1.SetError(HoursTextBox, _
           "The hours must be numeric.")
        HoursTextBox.SelectAll()
        e.Cancel = True
    End If
End Sub
```

The Code for the Modified Form

Here is the code for the modified form, using the `TryParse` and field-level validation in the Validating event handlers of the text boxes.

```vb
'Project:      Ch02PayrollApplication
'Module:       Payroll Form
'Programmer:   Bradley/Millspaugh
'Date:         June 2009
'Description:  User interface for payroll application.
'              Provides data entry and validates for nonnumeric data.

Public Class PayrollForm
    Private Sub CalcuateButton_Click(ByVal sender As System.Object, _
      ByVal e As System.EventArgs) Handles CalculateButton.Click
        ' Create a Payroll object to connect to the business services tier.
        Dim HoursDecimal As Decimal
        Dim RateDecimal As Decimal

        ' Check for valid input data.
        ErrorProvider1.Clear()
```

```vb
            If Decimal.TryParse(HoursTextBox.Text, HoursDecimal) Then
                If Decimal.TryParse(RateTextBox.Text, RateDecimal) Then
                    ' Both values converted successfully.
                    Try
                        Dim APayroll As New Payroll(HoursDecimal, RateDecimal)
                        PayTextBox.Text = APayroll.Pay.ToString("C")

                    Catch Err As ApplicationException
                        ' Catch exceptions from the Payroll class.
                        Select Case Err.Source
                            Case "Hours"
                                ErrorProvider1.SetError(HoursTextBox, _
                                    Err.Message)
                                With HoursTextBox
                                    .SelectAll()
                                    .Focus()
                                End With
                            Case "Rate"
                                ErrorProvider1.SetError(RateTextBox, _
                                    Err.Message)
                                With RateTextBox
                                    .SelectAll()
                                    .Focus()
                                End With
                        End Select
                    End Try
                Else
                    ' Rate did not pass validation.
                    ErrorProvider1.SetError(RateTextBox, _
                        "The rate must be numeric.")
                End If
            Else
                ' Hours did not pass validation.
                ErrorProvider1.SetError(HoursTextBox, _
                    "The hours must be numeric.")
            End If
End Sub

Private Sub ClearButton_Click(ByVal sender As System.Object, _
  ByVal e As System.EventArgs) Handles ClearButton.Click
    ' Clear the screen fields.

    ErrorProvider1.Clear()
    With NameTextBox
        .Clear()
        .Focus()
    End With
    HoursTextBox.Clear()
    RateTextBox.Clear()
    PayTextBox.Clear()
End Sub

Private Sub HoursTextBox_Validating(ByVal sender As Object, _
  ByVal e As System.ComponentModel.CancelEventArgs) _
  Handles HoursTextBox.Validating
    ' Test hours for numeric.
    Dim HoursDecimal As Decimal
```

```
            If Decimal.TryParse(HoursTextBox.Text, HoursDecimal) Then
                ErrorProvider1.Clear()
            Else
                ErrorProvider1.SetError(HoursTextBox, _
                  "The hours must be numeric.")
                HoursTextBox.SelectAll()
                e.Cancel = True
            End If
        End Sub

        Private Sub RateTextBox_Validating(ByVal sender As Object, _
          ByVal e As System.ComponentModel.CancelEventArgs) _
          Handles RateTextBox.Validating
            ' Test pay rate for numeric.
            Dim RateDecimal As Decimal

            If Decimal.TryParse(RateTextBox.Text, RateDecimal) Then
                ErrorProvider1.Clear()
            Else
                ErrorProvider1.SetError(RateTextBox, _
                  "The hours must be numeric.")
                RateTextBox.SelectAll()
                e.Cancel = True
            End If
        End Sub

        Private Sub ExitToolStripMenuItem_Click(ByVal sender As System.Object, _
          ByVal e As System.EventArgs) Handles ExitToolStripMenuItem.Click
            ' Close the program.

            Me.Close()
        End Sub

        Private Sub AboutToolStripMenuItem_Click(ByVal sender As System.Object, _
          ByVal e As System.EventArgs) Handles AboutToolStripMenuItem.Click
            ' Show the About box.

            Dim AnAboutBox As New AboutBox1
            AnAboutBox.ShowDialog()
        End Sub

        Private Sub PayrollForm_FormClosing(ByVal sender As Object, _
          ByVal e As System.Windows.Forms.FormClosingEventArgs) _
          Handles Me.FormClosing
            ' Do not allow validation to prevent the form closing.

            e.Cancel = False
        End Sub
    End Class
```

Modifying the Business Class

As business rules change, you can modify the business class or create a new class that inherits from the original class. You can usually add properties and methods to an existing class without harming any application that uses the class, but you should not change the behavior of existing properties and methods if any applications use the class.

In our Payroll example, we will expand the user interface to display a summary form. The summary form displays the number of employees processed, the total amount of pay, and the number of overtime hours. We must modify the Payroll class to calculate these values and return the values in read-only properties (Figure 2.7).

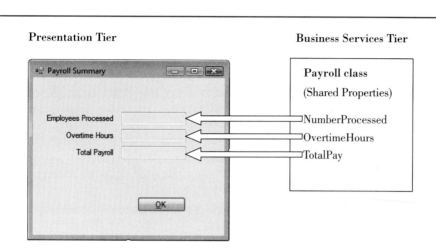

Presentation Tier   Business Services Tier

Figure 2.7

The new summary form displays summary information. The Payroll class must accumulate the summary figures in shared properties.

Instance Variables versus Shared Variables

Each new instance of the Payroll object has its own values for the hours, pay rate, and pay. These properties are called *instance properties*, *instance variables*, or *instance members*. But the properties we are adding now, such as the number of employees processed and the total pay amount, must accumulate totals for all instances of the class. These properties are called *shared properties*, *shared variables*, or *shared members*. Recall that properties are just the variables of a class, so the terms *properties* and *variables* can be used interchangeably.

The Payroll class requires three shared variables, one for each of the summary fields. As each instance of the Payroll class is created, the values are accumulated in the shared variables. In this way, the values for employee two are added to the values for employee one, and so on.

```
' Payroll Class.
' Shared properties declared at the module level.

' Hold the NumberProcessed shared property.
Private Shared NumberEmployeesInteger As Integer
' Hold the TotalPay shared property.
Private Shared TotalPayDecimal As Decimal
' Hold the OvertimeHours shared property.
Private Shared TotalOvertimeHoursDecimal As Decimal
```

Since these variables are Private to the class, public `Get` methods are required to make the properties accessible. You retrieve shared properties by using the class name such as Payroll.NumberProcessed or Payroll.OvertimeHours. This is the same concept that you use when converting input values: `Decimal.Parse()` calls the `Parse` method of the Decimal class.

```
Public Shared ReadOnly Property NumberProcessed() As Integer
    Get
        Return NumberEmployeesInteger
    End Get
End Property

Public Shared ReadOnly Property TotalPay() As Decimal
    Get
        Return TotalPayDecimal
    End Get
End Property

Public Shared ReadOnly Property OvertimeHours() As Decimal
    Get
        Return TotalOvertimeHoursDecimal
    End Get
End Property
```

The FindPay method must be modified to add to the summary fields:

```
' Payroll class.
' Additional module-level named constants.
Private Const REGULAR_HOURS_Decimal As Decimal = 40D
Private Const OVERTIME_RATE_Decimal As Decimal = 1.5D

Private Sub FindPay()
    ' Calculate the Pay.
    Dim OvertimeHoursDecimal As Decimal

    If HoursDecimal <= REGULAR_HOURS_Decimal Then        ' No overtime.
        PayDecimal = HoursDecimal * RateDecimal
        OvertimeHoursDecimal = 0D
    Else            ' Overtime.
        OvertimeHoursDecimal = HoursDecimal — REGULAR_HOURS_Decimal
        PayDecimal = (REGULAR_HOURS_Decimal * RateDecimal) + _
            (OvertimeHoursDecimal * OVERTIME_RATE_Decimal * RateDecimal)
    End If
    TotalOvertimeHoursDecimal += OvertimeHoursDecimal
    TotalPayDecimal += PayDecimal
    NumberEmployeesInteger += 1
End Sub
```

Following is the completed Payroll class that calculates and returns the shared properties:

```
'Project:      Ch02PayrollWithSummary
'Module:       Payroll Class
'Programmer:   Bradley/Millspaugh
'Date:         June 2009
'Description:  Business services tier for payroll calculation: validates input
'                  data and calculates the pay, with overtime, regular, and
'                  summary data.

Public Class Payroll

    ' Instance variables.
    Private HoursDecimal As Decimal     ' Hold the Hours property.
    Private RateDecimal As Decimal      ' Hold the Rate property.
    Private PayDecimal As Decimal       ' Hold the Pay property.
```

```vb
' Shared variables.
' Hold the NumberProcessed shared property.
Private Shared NumberEmployeesInteger As Integer
' Hold the TotalPay shared property.
Private Shared TotalPayDecimal As Decimal
' Hold the OvertimeHours shared property.
Private Shared TotalOvertimeHoursDecimal As Decimal

' Constants.
Private Const MINIMUM_WAGE_Decimal As Decimal = 6.25D
Private Const MAXIMUM_WAGE_Decimal As Decimal = 50D
Private Const MINIMUM_HOURS_Decimal As Decimal = 0D
Private Const MAXIMUM_HOURS_Decimal As Decimal = 60D
Private Const REGULAR_HOURS_Decimal As Decimal = 40D
Private Const OVERTIME_RATE_Decimal As Decimal = 1.5D

' Constructor.
Sub New(ByVal HoursInDecimal As Decimal, ByVal RateInDecimal As Decimal)
    ' Assign properties and calculate the pay.

    Me.Hours = HoursInDecimal
    Me.Rate = RateInDecimal
    FindPay()
End Sub

Private Sub FindPay()
    ' Calculate the pay.
    Dim OvertimeHoursDecimal As Decimal

    If HoursDecimal <= REGULAR_HOURS_Decimal Then    ' No overtime.
        PayDecimal = HoursDecimal * RateDecimal
        OvertimeHoursDecimal = 0D
    Else                                             ' Overtime.
        OvertimeHoursDecimal = HoursDecimal — REGULAR_HOURS_Decimal
        PayDecimal = (REGULAR_HOURS_Decimal * RateDecimal) + _
          (OvertimeHoursDecimal * OVERTIME_RATE_Decimal * RateDecimal)
    End If
    TotalOvertimeHoursDecimal += OvertimeHoursDecimal
    TotalPayDecimal += PayDecimal
    NumberEmployeesInteger += 1
End Sub

' Property procedures.
Public Property Hours() As Decimal
    Get
        Return HoursDecimal
    End Get
    Set(ByVal Value As Decimal)
        If Value >= MINIMUM_HOURS_Decimal And _
          Value <= MAXIMUM_HOURS_Decimal Then
            HoursDecimal = Value
        Else
            Dim Ex As New ApplicationException( _
              "Hours are outside of the acceptable range.")
            Ex.Source = "Hours"
            Throw Ex
        End If
    End Set
End Property
```

```
    Public Property Rate() As Decimal
        Get
            Return RateDecimal
        End Get
        Set(ByVal Value As Decimal)
            If Value >= MINIMUM_WAGE_Decimal And _
               Value <= MAXIMUM_WAGE_Decimal Then
                RateDecimal = Value
            Else
                Dim Ex As New ApplicationException( _
                   "Pay rate is outside of the acceptable range.")
                Ex.Source = "Rate"
                Throw Ex
            End If
        End Set
    End Property

    Public ReadOnly Property Pay() As Decimal
        Get
            Return PayDecimal
        End Get
    End Property

    Public Shared ReadOnly Property NumberProcessed() As Decimal
        Get
            Return NumberEmployeesInteger
        End Get
    End Property

    Public Shared ReadOnly Property TotalPay() As Decimal
        Get
            Return TotalPayDecimal
        End Get
    End Property

    Public Shared ReadOnly Property OvertimeHours() As Decimal
        Get
            Return TotalOvertimeHoursDecimal
        End Get
    End Property
End Class
```

Displaying the Summary Data

To display a second form from the main form, you can declare an instance of
the form's class and show the form.

```
Dim ASummaryForm As New SummaryForm()
ASummaryForm.ShowDialog()
```

You also can take advantage of the default instance of a form and just show
the default instance:

```
SummaryForm.ShowDialog()
```

You can choose from two techniques for filling the screen fields with the summary data:

1. Set the summary output from the Payroll form using the `Shared` methods of the Payroll class before showing the Summary form:

```
' In PayrollForm:
Private Sub SummaryButton_Click(ByVal sender As System.Object, _
  ByVal e As System.EventArgs) Handles SummaryButton.Click
    ' Show the summary form.

    Dim ASummaryForm As New SummaryForm()

    With ASummaryForm
        .CountLabel.Text = Payroll.NumberProcessed.ToString()
        .OvertimeLabel.Text = Payroll.OvertimeHours.ToString("N1")
        .TotalPayLabel.Text = Payroll.TotalPay.ToString("C")
        .ShowDialog()
    End With
End Sub
```

2. Use the shared properties from the Payroll class in the Form_Load procedure of the Summary form and fill the labels there.

```
' In SummaryForm.
Private Sub SummaryForm_Load(ByVal sender As Object, _
  ByVal e As System.EventArgs) Handles MyBase.Load
    ' Retrieve the summary values.

    CountLabel.Text = Payroll.NumberProcessed.ToString()
    OvertimeLabel.Text = Payroll.OvertimeHours.ToString("N1")
    TotalPayLabel.Text = Payroll.TotalPay.ToString("C")
End Sub
```

Although both of these techniques work perfectly well, the second method is preferable for encapsulating the forms' data. Each of the forms in the project can access the shared properties, which is preferable to having PayrollForm access the controls on SummaryForm.

Feedback 2.2

1. What is the purpose of property procedures?
2. Why should the variables for the properties of a class be declared as `Private`?
3. You want to create a new class called Student that inherits from Person. Properties required to create an instance of the class are LastName, FirstName, and BirthDate. Write a parameterized constructor for the class.
4. Write the statement(s) to create an instance of the Student class defined in the previous question. Supply the arguments for the parameterized constructor.
5. An error occurs in a class written for the business services tier. Explain how to handle the error condition and how the user should be notified.

Namespaces, Scope, and Accessibility

This section is intended as a review of the topics of scope and visibility of variables, constants, and classes. You may want to skip this section if you feel comfortable with declaring and using namespaces, scope, lifetime, and accessibility domains such as Public, Private, Protected, and Friend.

Namespaces

Namespaces are used for grouping and referring to classes and structures. A class or structure name must be unique in any one namespace. You can think of namespaces like telephone area codes; a given phone number can exist only once in a single area, but that number may appear in many different area codes.

The classes in a namespace do not have to be in a single file. In fact, most of the classes in the .NET Framework are in the System namespace, which is stored in many files.

You can declare namespaces in your VB projects. In fact, by default each project has a namespace that matches the project name. If you display the Project Designer for any project, you will see an entry titled *Root Namespace*. However, if you change the project name in the Solution Explorer, the root namespace does not change automatically. Declare namespaces within your project using the `Namespace / End Namespace` construct:

```
Namespace RnRApplications
    ' Classes and structures in the namespace can appear here.
End Namespace
```

You can place the same `Namespace` statement in more than one project.

For most projects, there is no advantage in declaring a namespace. A company might choose to group applications by using namespaces.

Scope

The **scope** of a variable or constant refers to the area of the program that can "see" and reference it. For simplicity and clarity, we use the term *variable*, but each of the following examples applies to named constants as well as variables.

You determine the scope of a variable by the location of the declaration and the accessibility modifier (`Public` or `Private`). The choices for scope, from the widest to the narrowest, are namespace, module level, procedure level, and block level.

Namespace

Any variable, constant, class, or structure declared with the `Public` modifier has **namespace scope**. You can refer to the identifier anywhere within the namespace. Because each project is in its own namespace by default, generally *namespace scope* also means *project scope*. However, as you know, you can structure your own namespaces to contain multiple projects.

You usually need to declare classes and structures as Public, but not variables and constants. It is considered poor OOP programming to declare variables with namespace scope because it violates the rules of encapsulation.

Each class should be in charge of its own data and share variables only by using `Property Set` and `Get` procedures.

Note: Earlier versions of VB, as well as many other programming languages, refer to variables that can be referenced from any location in a project as *global variables*. VB has dropped this terminology.

Module Level

Module-level scope is sometimes also called *class-level* scope. A module-level variable is a Private variable that is declared inside any class, structure, or module but outside of any sub procedure or function. By convention, you should declare module-level variables at the top of the class, but the variables can actually be declared anywhere inside the class that is outside of a procedure or function.

```
Private TotalDecimal As Decimal
```

Note: If you leave off the accessibility modifier (`Public` or `Private`), the variable is Private by default.

In some previous versions of Visual Basic, each file was called a module, so any variable declared as Private at the top of the file (not inside a sub procedure or function) was a module-level variable. The terminology carries through to the current version of VB, even though the language now has a `Module / End Module` construct, which can contain miscellaneous procedures and functions that are not included in a class.

Procedure Level

Any variable that you declare inside a procedure or function, but not within a block, has **procedure-level scope**, also called *local scope*. You can reference the variable anywhere inside the procedure but not in other procedures. Note that the `Public` keyword is not legal inside a procedure; all procedure-level variables are private and are declared with the `Dim` keyword.

Block Level

If you declare a variable inside a code block, the variable has **block-level scope**. That is, the variable can be referenced only inside that block. Code blocks include

```
If / End If
Do / Loop
For / Next
Select Case / End Select
Try / Catch / Finally / End Try
```

The blocks that are likely to cause confusion are the `Try / Catch / Finally / End Try`. The `Try` is one block; each `Catch` is a separate block; and the `Finally` is a separate block. This means that you cannot declare a variable in the `Try` and reference it in the `Catch` or the `Finally` blocks. It also means that you can declare the same variable name for each `Catch` since the scope of each is only that `Catch` block.

```
Try
    ' Declare a block-level variable.
    ' Bad idea, since it cannot be referenced outside of this Try block.
    Dim AmountDecimal As Decimal = Decimal.Parse(AmountTextBox.Text)
Catch Err As InvalidCastException
    ' Err is a block-level variable valid only inside this Catch block.
    MessageBox.Show(Err.Message, "Invalid Input Data.")
Catch Err As Exception
    ' Err is a block-level variable valid only inside this Catch block.
    MessageBox.Show(Err.Message, "Unknown Error.")
Finally
    ' Any variable declared here is valid only inside this Finally block.
End Try
```

When you instantiate objects, if there is any chance the creation will fail, you should create the new object inside a `Try/Catch` block. But if you declare the variable inside the `Try` block, the variable goes out of scope when the `Try` block completes. Therefore, most of the time you will declare the object variable at the module level or procedure level and instantiate the object inside the `Try` block.

```
' Declare the object variable at the module level.
Private APayroll As Payroll

Private Sub CalculateButton_Click(ByVal sender As System.Object, _
    ByVal e As System.EventArgs) Handles CalculateButton.Click
    ' Create a Payroll object to connect to the business services tier.

    Try
        ' Instantiate the object in the Try block.
        APayroll = New Payroll(Decimal.Parse(Me.HoursTextBox.Text), _
            Decimal.Parse(Me.RateTextBox.Text))
    Catch . . .
```

Lifetime

The **lifetime** of a variable, including object variables, is as long as the variable remains in scope. The lifetime of a namespace-level variable is as long as the program is running. The lifetime of a module-level variable is as long as any reference to the class remains, which is generally as long as the program runs.

The lifetime of a procedure-level variable is one execution of the procedure. Each time the procedure is executed, a new variable is established and initialized. For this reason, you cannot use procedure-level variables to maintain running totals or counts unless you declare them with the `Static` keyword, which changes the lifetime of a procedure-level variable to the life of the class or module.

Accessibility Domains

You have already declared variables and classes with the `Public` and `Private` keywords. You also can use `Protected`, `Friend`, and `Protected Friend` (Table 2.1). Each of these keywords defines the **accessibility** of the variable or class.

Keywords to Declare Accessibility Domains

Table 2.1

Keyword	Description
Public	Accessible from anywhere in the project or from any other project that references this one.
Private	Accessible from anywhere inside this class.
Protected	Accessible from anywhere inside this class or in any class that inherits from this class.
Friend	Accessible from anywhere inside this project/assembly.
Protected Friend	A combination of Protected and Friend. Accessible from anywhere inside this project/assembly and in any class that inherits from this class, even though the derived class is in a different project/assembly.

Creating Classes That Inherit

To create a class that inherits, you should first add a new class to the project. Although a single file can hold multiple class definitions, the recommended approach is to create a new file for each Public class and make the name of the file match the class name. The only exceptions are small "helper classes" that would never be used by any other application. These helper classes should be declared with the Friend keyword because they are used only in the current project.

Adding a New Class File

Add a new file for a class by selecting *Project / Add Class*, which creates a new file with the extension .vb. Make sure to give the class the name that you want to use; the file will be named correctly and the solution and project will be set up with the correct name.

The newly added class will have the first and last lines of code:

```
Public Class ClassName
End Class
```

Add the Inherits clause on the first line following the Class declaration and add comments above the Class statement.

```
'Project:       Ch02PayrollInheritance
'Module:        PayrollSalaried Class
'Programmer:    Bradley/Millspaugh
'Date:          June 2009
'Description:   A class in the business services tier for payroll calculation:
'               validates input data and calculates the pay for
'               salaried employees.

Public Class PayrollSalaried
    Inherits Payroll
End Class
```

Creating a Constructor

A subclass must have its own constructor because constructors are not inherited. However, if you do not create a constructor (a Sub New), VS creates an implicit empty constructor.

The first statement in a constructor of an inherited class should call the constructor of the base class using the `MyBase` keyword:

```
MyBase.New()
```

If the base class has only a parameterized constructor, you must pass arguments to the constructor.

```
MyBase.New(HoursDecimal, RateDecimal)
```

And just like the base class, you can have several overloaded New constructors, one for each signature that the base class has.

Inheriting Variables and Methods

As you know, when you derive a new class from an existing class, all Public and Protected variables and methods are inherited, with the exception of the base class's constructors.

Shadowing and Overriding Methods

An inherited class can have a method with the same name as a method in its base class. Depending on how it is declared, the new method may shadow or override the base class method.

Overriding To override a method in the base class, the method must be declared as **overridable**:

```
' Base Class.
Public|Protected Overridable Sub DoSomething()
```

In the derived class, you must use the `Overrides` keyword and have the same accessibility (`Public|Private`) the base class has:

```
' Derived Class.
Public|Protected Overrides Sub DoSomething()
```

If the base-class method has more than one signature (overloaded methods), the override applies only to the base-class method with the identical signature. You must write separate methods to override each version (signature) of the base-class method.

Shadowing A method in a derived class can **shadow** a method in the base class. The new (shadowing) method replaces the base-class method in the derived class but not in any new classes derived from that class. The shadowing method "hides" all signatures (overloaded methods) with the same name in the base class.

```
' Base Class.
Public|Protected [Overridable] Sub DoSomething()
```

In the derived class, you can use the Shadows keyword:

```
' Derived Class.
Public|Protected Shadows Sub DoSomething()
```

If you do not use either the Overrides or Shadows keyword, Shadows is
assumed. And if you use the Overrides or Shadows keyword for one method
of a group, you must include the keyword for all overridden or shadowed
methods.

Using Properties and Methods of the Base Class

You can reference any Public property or method of the base class from the
subclass. If the base-class method has not been overridden or shadowed in the
subclass, you can call the method directly:

```
' Base class.
Public Function FindPay()
    ' Code to calculate the pay.
End Function

' Sub class.
' Call the FindPay function from the base class.
FindPay()
```

If the subclass also has a FindPay function, you can call the function in the
base class by including the MyBase keyword:

```
MyBase.FindPay()
```

It is legal to use the MyBase keyword even when it isn't required, which
can make your program more understandable. For example, assuming that the
subclass does not have a FindPay function, you can still call the base-class
function with

```
MyBase.FindPay()
```

You can use the same rules for accessing Public properties of the base
class. You can reference the property directly or add the MyBase keyword,
which aids in readability.

```
' Assign a value to a read/write Public property of the base class.
Hours = HoursDecimal
```

or

```
MyBase.Hours = HoursDecimal
```

You can use the Me keyword to refer to a property or method of the current class to clarify the code.

```
' Sub class.

Sub New(ByVal LevelInteger As Integer)
    ' Constructor of the sub class.

    MyBase.New()
    Me.SalaryLevel = LevelInteger
    Me.FindPay()
    MyBase.AddEmployee()
End Sub
```

Note: You can find the complete inheritance example on the text Web site (www.mhhe.com/AdvVB2008/) as Ch02PayrollWithInheritance.

Passing Control Properties to a Component

So far in this chapter, all examples pass the Text property of text boxes to the business services tier component. But often you need to pass data from check boxes, radio buttons, or list boxes. How you pass the data depends on how the properties are declared in the business class.

The examples in this section are based on a two-tier application to calculate prices for theater tickets (Figure 2.8). Seat prices vary by the section: General, Balcony, or Box Seats. Seniors and students receive a $5.00 discount from the ticket price.

Figure 2.8

In the user interface, the user makes selections in radio buttons and a check box, which must be used to set properties in the business-services-tier component.

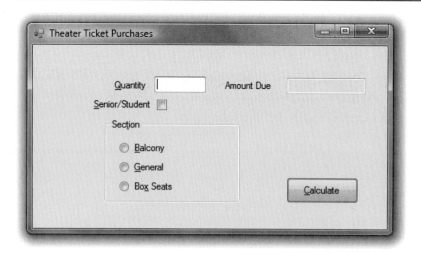

The business services tier needs to know the section, the number of tickets, and whether a discount is to be given. Therefore, the constructor will receive three values:

```
Sub New(ByVal QuantityInteger As Integer, ByVal SectionInteger As Integer, _
    ByVal DiscountBoolean As Boolean)
```

Notice that there are three values: the quantity, the section, and a Boolean value for the discount. Passing the quantity is straightforward; you can convert the text box value to integer: `Integer.Parse(QuantityTextBox.Text)`. And you can easily pass the Checked property of a check box to a Boolean property:

```
Dim ATicketPrice As New TicketPrice(Integer.Parse(Me.QuantityTextBox.Text), _
    SectionInteger, DiscountCheckBox.Checked)
```

Setting a property based on a selection in radio buttons or a list box presents an additional challenge, both in determining the best way to set up the property in the business-services-tier component and in setting the correct value in the user interface. Notice that the Section property is declared as integer. Although you could set up the property as string, there is a real advantage in using integer—you can create an enumeration for the available choices.

Creating an Enumeration

Whenever you have a list of choices for a property, it's because someone set up an **enumeration** that lists the choices. For example, selecting `Color.Red`, `Color.Blue`, or `Color.Yellow` is choosing one of the elements from the Color enumeration. When you choose one of the elements of the Color enumeration, the VB compiler actually substitutes the numeric value of the element. This saves you, the developer, from having to remember either the color names or the color numbers. You just type the name of the enumeration and a period, and the possible choices pop up in IntelliSense.

You can create your own enumeration, which is called an *enum* ("E-noom"). An enum is a list of named constants. The data type of the constants must be one of the integer types (integer, short, long, or byte). Whenever you create a reusable component class that has a list of possible choices for a property, consider setting up an enum.

The Enum Statement—General Form

```
Enum EnumName
    ConstantName1 [ConstantValue]
    ConstantName2 [ConstantValue]
    . . .
End Enum
```

The `Enum` statement belongs at the namespace level or class level, which means that it cannot appear inside a procedure. By default, an `Enum` is public, but you can declare it to be private, friend, or protected, if you wish.

The Enum Statement—Examples

```vb
Public Enum SectionType
    General
    Balcony
    Box
End Enum

Enum ReportType
    BooksBySubject   10
    BooksByAuthor
End Enum

Enum EvenNumbers
    Two     2
    Four    4
    Six     6
    Eight   8
End Enum
```

When you don't assign a constant value to the element, VB automatically assigns the first element a value of zero, and each following element one greater than the last. So, in the first of the examples above, *General* has a constant value of 0, *Balcony* has a value of 1, and *Box* has a value of 2. If you assign one element, as in the second example above for ReportType, each following element is assigned one greater than the last. So, in the ReportType example, BooksBySubject has a constant value of 10, which you assigned, and Books-ByAuthor has a value of 11.

In the business-services-tier component for the program example, which you can see in Ch02EnumRadioButtons, the Section property is set up as an integer with an enum. In the CalculatePrice procedure, use the enum values in a `Select Case` to determine the correct constant to use for the price.

```vb
' Enum declared at the namespace level, above the class declaration.
Public Enum SectionType
    General
    Balcony
    Box
End Enum

Public Class TicketPrice

' Private variable for Section property.
Private SectionInteger As Integer
' Alternate declaration:
' Private SectionInteger As SectionType

' . . .Omitted code for class.

    Private Sub CalculatePrice()
        ' Determine the amount due.
        Dim PriceDecimal As Decimal
        Select Case SectionInteger
            Case SectionType.General
                PriceDecimal = GENERAL_Decimal
```

```
        Case SectionType.Balcony
            PriceDecimal = BALCONY_Decimal
        Case SectionType.Box
            PriceDecimal = BOX_Decimal
    End Select
    If DiscountBoolean Then
        PriceDecimal -= DISCOUNT_Decimal
    End If
    AmountDueDecimal = PriceDecimal * QuantityInteger
End Sub
End Class
```

Use the following code in the form's CalculateButton_Click event handler to use the enum. Note that if you declare the enum inside the class in the business-services-tier component, you also must specify the class name when using the enum (TicketPrice.SectionType.General).

```
Private Sub CalculateButton_Click(ByVal sender As System.Object, _
  ByVal e As System.EventArgs) Handles CalculateButton.Click
    ' Find price by passing data input in the presentation tier
    ' to the business services tier using a TicketPrice object.
    Dim SectionInteger As Integer

    ' Determine the section from radio buttons.
    If BalconyRadioButton.Checked Then
        SectionInteger = SectionType.Balcony
    ElseIf BoxRadioButton.Checked Then
        SectionInteger = SectionType.Box
    Else
        SectionInteger = SectionType.General     ' Default to General.
    End If

    Try
        Dim ATicketPrice As New TicketPrice( _
          Integer.Parse(QuantityTextBox.Text), SectionInteger, _
          DiscountCheckBox.Checked)
        AmountTextBox.Text = ATicketPrice.AmountDue.ToString("C")
        ErrorProvider1.Clear()
    Catch
        ErrorProvider1.SetError(QuantityTextBox, _
          "Quantity must be numeric.")
    End Try
End Sub
```

This example comes from Ch02EnumRadioButtons. To see an example of selecting from a combo box rather than radio buttons, see Ch02EnumComboBox.

Garbage Collection

The .NET Framework destroys unused objects and reclaims memory in a process called **garbage collection**. The garbage collector runs periodically and destroys any objects and variables that no longer have any active reference. You have no way of knowing when the garbage collection will occur. In earlier versions of VB, you were advised to set object variables to Nothing and to write

Finalize procedures for your classes. For current versions of VB, Microsoft recommends that you just allow object variables to go out of scope when you are finished with them.

Feedback 2.3

Use this declaration to answer questions 1–4.

```
Private VariableInteger As Integer
```

1. What is the scope of VariableInteger if it is declared inside a class but not inside a procedure?
2. What is its lifetime?
3. What is its accessibility?
4. If the class in which VariableInteger is declared is used as a base class for inheritance, will the derived class have access to the variable?

Your Hands-On Programming Example

R 'n R—For Reading and Refreshment needs an application to calculate payroll. Create a multiple-form project that includes an MDI parent form, a Payroll form, a Summary form, an About form, and a Splash form. The Payroll form, Summary form, and About form should be child forms of the parent form. If you completed the hands-on project for Chapter 1, you will now complete the Payroll and Summary forms.

The parent form should have the following menu:

File	View	Window	Help
Exit	Payroll	Tile Vertical	About
	Summary	Tile Horizontal	
		Cascade	

This should be a multitier project, with the business rules and calculations in a class separate from the user interface.

Use attributes to display the company name and copyright information on the About form.

Make sure to validate the input data. Display a meaningful message to the user and select the field in error when the user enters bad data.

Include a toolbar and a status bar on the main form.

Planning the Project

Sketch the five forms for the application (Figure 2.9). Your users must sign off the sketches as meeting their needs before you begin programming.

Plan the Objects, Properties, and Methods Plan the classes for the two tiers. Determine the objects and property settings for the forms and controls and for the business services tier. Figure 2.10 shows the diagram of the program classes.

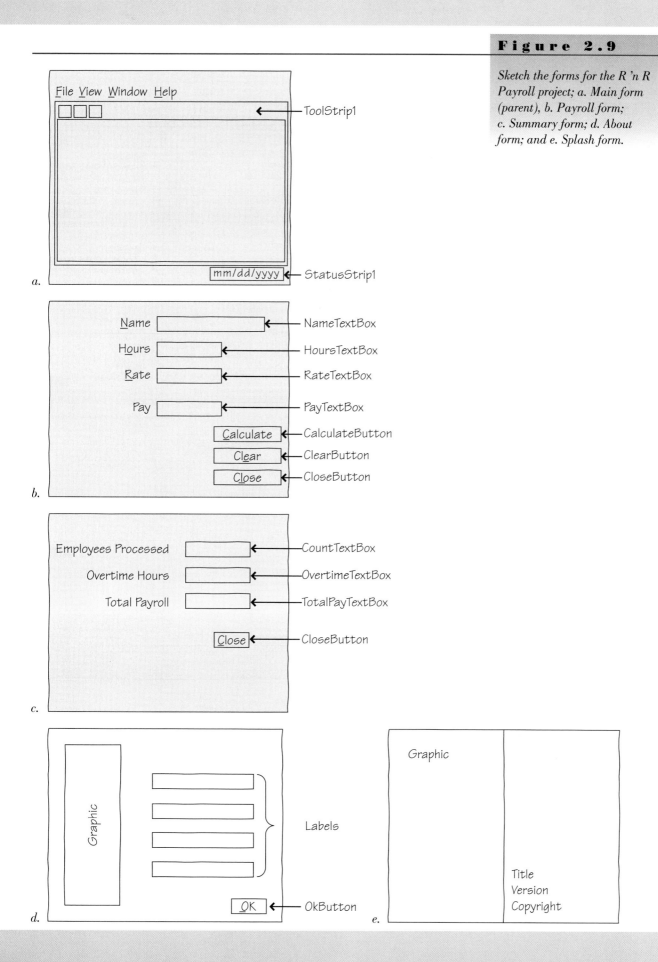

Figure 2.10

The class diagram for the hands-on programming example.

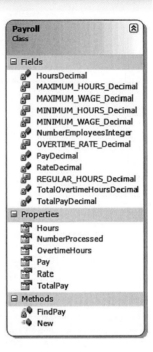

Presentation Tier

MainForm

Object	Property	Setting
MainForm	Text	R 'n R For Reading and Refreshment
	IsMdiContainer	True
MenuStrip1	Items Collection	(drop-down items)
	FileToolStripMenuItem	ExitToolStripMenuItem
	ViewToolStripMenuItem	PayrollFormToolStripMenuItem
		SummaryToolStripMenuItem
	WindowToolStripMenuItem	TileHorizontalToolStripMenuItem
		TileVerticalToolStripMenuItem
		CascadeToolStripMenuItem
	HelpToolStripMenuItem	AboutToolStripMenuItem

Object	Property	Setting
ContextMenuStrip1	ItemsCollection	PayrollToolStripMenuItem
		SummaryToolStripMenuItem1
ToolStrip1	Items collection	PayrollToolStripButton
		SummaryToolStripButton
		AboutToolStripButton
StatusStrip1	Items collection	Add labels for the date and time.

Procedure	Actions—Pseudocode
MainForm_Load	Retrieve the date and time for the status bar.
ExitToolStripMenuItem_Click	Close the form.
AboutToolStripMenuItem_Click	Create an instance of the About form.
AboutToolStripButton_Click	Set the MdiParent property.
	Show the form.
PayrollFormToolStripMenuItem_Click	Create an instance of the Payroll form.
PayrollToolStripButton_Click	Set the MdiParent property.
PayrollToolStripMenuItem_Click	Show the form.
	Set the focus on the form.
SummaryToolStripMenuItem_Click	Create an instance of the Summary form.
SummaryToolStripButton_Click	Set the MdiParent property.
SummaryToolStripMenuItem1_Click	Show the form.
	Set the focus on the form.
CascadeToolStripMenuItem_Click	Set MDI layout to Cascade.
TileHorizontalToolStripMenuItem_Click	Set MDI layout to Tile Horizontal.
TileVerticalToolStripMenuItem_Click	Set MDI layout to Tile Vertical.
ClockTimer_Tick	Update the date and time.

PayrollForm

Object	Property	Setting
PayrollForm	AcceptButton	CalculateButton
	CancelButton	ClearButton
	Text	Payroll
	WindowState	Maximized
Label1	Text	&Name
NameTextBox	Text	(blank)
Label2	Text	H&ours
HoursTextBox	Text	(blank)
Label3	Text	&Rate
RateTextBox	Text	(blank)

Object	Property	Setting
Label4	Text	Pay
PayTextBox	Text	(blank)
	ReadOnly	True
CalculateButton	Text	&Calculate
ClearButton	Text	Cl&ear
CloseButton	Text	C&lose

Procedure	Actions—Pseudocode
Instance property Get	If an instance doesn't exist Declare a new instance.

CalculateButton_Click	Clear the error provider.
	Convert the hours to decimal.
	If hours convert successfully
	  Convert the rate to decimal.
	  If rate converts successfully
	    Try
	      Instantiate a Payroll object, passing the input values.
	      Display the pay formatted in a label.
	    Catch
	      Display the error message.
	      Select the control in error.
	    Else
	      Display error for rate.
	      Select the control in error.
	  Else
	    Display error for hours.
	    Select the control in error.

ClearButton_Click	Clear all input fields on the screen. Set the focus in NameTextBox.
CloseButton_Click	Close the form.

HoursTextBox_Validating	If not valid
	  Display the error message.
	  Cancel the Validating event handler.
	  Select the control in error.
	Else
	  Clear the error message.

RateTextBox_Validating	If not valid
	  Display the error message.
	  Cancel the Validating event handler.
	  Select the control in error.
	Else
	  Clear the error message.

PayrollForm_FormClosing	Set e.Cancel = False. Set AnInstance = Nothing.
SelectControlInError(ControlName)	Select text. Set the focus.

SummaryForm

Object	Property	Setting
SummaryForm	AcceptButton	CloseButton
	WindowState	Maximized
	Text	Payroll Summary
Label1	Text	Employees Processed
EmployeeCountTextBox	Text	(blank)
	ReadOnly	True
Label2	Text	Overtime Hours
OvertimeHoursTextBox	Text	(blank)
	ReadOnly	True
Label3	Text	Total Payroll
TotalPayrollTextBox	Text	(blank)
	ReadOnly	True
CloseButton	Text	&Close

Procedure	Actions—Pseudocode
Instance propertyGet	If an instance doesn't exist Declare a new instance.
SummaryForm_Activated	Format and display the 3 summary properties in labels.
CloseButton_Click	Close the form.
SummaryForm_FormClosing	Set AnInstance = Nothing.

AboutBox

Object	Property	Setting
AboutBox1	FormBorderStyle	FixedDialog
	StartPosition	CenterParent
	Text	About This Application (Changes at run time.)
	AcceptButton	OkButton
OkButton	Text	&OK

Procedure	Actions—Pseudocode
AboutBox1_Load	Retrieve the attributes and set up the labels. (Code already in template file.)

SplashScreen Include a graphic and labels identifying the company and application. You can use the Splash Screen template and replace the graphic. Add code to hold the form on the screen for a few seconds.

The Business Services Tier

Payroll Class

Properties	Data Type	Property Type	Accessibility
Hours	Decimal	Instance	Read / Write
Rate	Decimal	Instance	Read / Write
Pay	Decimal	Instance	Read Only
NumberProcessed	Decimal	Shared	Read Only
TotalPay	Decimal	Shared	Read Only
OvertimeHours	Decimal	Shared	Read Only

Constants	Data Type	Initial Value
MINIMUM_WAGE_Decimal	Decimal	6.25D
MAXIMUM_WAGE_Decimal	Decimal	50D
MINIMUM_HOURS_Decimal	Decimal	0D
MAXIMUM_HOURS_Decimal	Decimal	60D
REGULAR_HOURS_Decimal	Decimal	40D
OVERTIME_RATE_Decimal	Decimal	1.5D

Methods

New(ByVal HoursInDecimal As Decimal, ByVal RateInDecimal As Decimal) (Parameterized constructor)
    Assign parameters to properties.
    Call FindPay.

FindPay
  If hours <= regular hours
    pay = hours * rate
      overtime hours = 0
  Else
    overtime hours = hours − regular hours
    pay = (hours * rate) + (overtime hours * overtime rate)
  Add overtime hours to total.
  Add pay to total.
  Add 1 to number processed.

Write the Project Following the sketches in Figure 2.9, create the forms. Figure 2.11 shows the completed forms.

- Set the properties of each of the objects, as you have planned.

- Write the code for the business services tier class, referring to your planning document.

- Write the code for the forms. Working from the pseudocode, write each procedure.

- When you complete the code, use a variety of test data to thoroughly test the project.

Figure 2.11

The forms for the R 'n R Payroll project; a. Main form (parent), b. Payroll form; c. Summary form; d. About form; and e. Splash form.

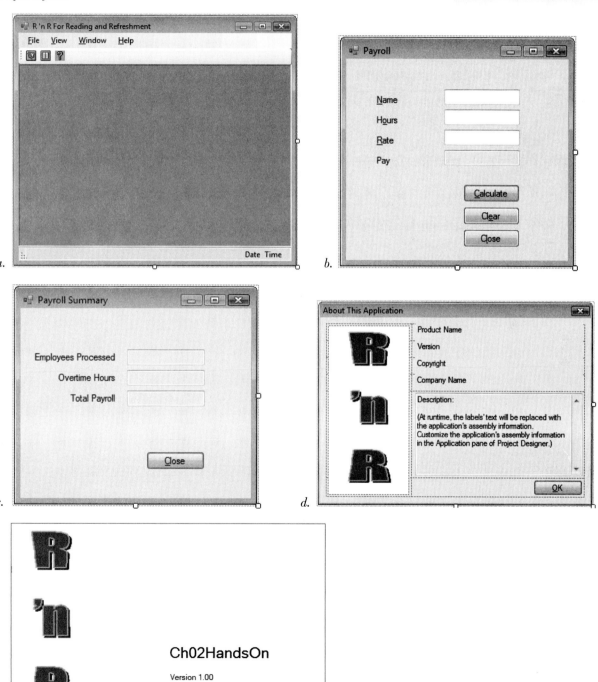

The Project Coding Solution

MainForm

```
'Program:      Ch02HandsOn
'Programmer:   Bradley/Millspaugh
'Form:         MainForm
'Date:         June 2009
'Description:  MDI parent form; contains the menu and displays
'              the various forms for the R 'n R Payroll application.

Public Class MainForm

    Private Sub MainForm_Load(ByVal sender As System.Object, _
      ByVal e As System.EventArgs) Handles MyBase.Load
        ' Display the date and time in the status bar.

        DateToolStripStatusLabel.Text = Now.ToShortDateString()
        TimeToolStripStatusLabel.Text = Now.ToLongTimeString()
    End Sub

    Private Sub TileVerticalToolStripMenuItem_Click( _
      ByVal sender As System.Object, ByVal e As System.EventArgs) _
      Handles TileVerticalToolStripMenuItem.Click
        ' Display the open windows tiled vertically.

        Me.LayoutMdi(MdiLayout.TileVertical)
    End Sub

    Private Sub TileHorizontalToolStripMenuItem_Click( _
      ByVal sender As Object, ByVal e As System.EventArgs) _
      Handles TileHorizontalToolStripMenuItem.Click
        ' Display the open windows tiled horizontally.

        Me.LayoutMdi(MdiLayout.TileHorizontal)
    End Sub

    Private Sub CascadeToolStripMenuItem_Click(ByVal sender As Object, _
      ByVal e As System.EventArgs) Handles CascadeToolStripMenuItem.Click
        ' Cascade the open windows.

        Me.LayoutMdi(MdiLayout.Cascade)
    End Sub

    Private Sub PayrollFormToolStripMenuItem_Click( _
      ByVal sender As System.Object, ByVal e As System.EventArgs) _
      Handles PayrollFormToolStripMenuItem.Click, _
      PayrollToolStripButton.Click, PayrollToolStripMenuItem.Click
        ' Create an instance of the payroll form.
        Dim APayrollForm As PayrollForm = PayrollForm.Instance

        With APayrollForm
            .MdiParent = Me
            .Show()
            .Focus()
        End With
    End Sub

    Private Sub SummaryToolStripMenuItem_Click(ByVal sender As System.Object, _
      ByVal e As System.EventArgs) _
      Handles SummaryToolStripMenuItem.Click, SummaryToolStripButton.Click, _
      SummaryFormToolStripMenuItem.Click
```

```vb
        ' Create an instance of the summary form.
        Dim ASummaryForm As SummaryForm = SummaryForm.Instance

        With ASummaryForm
            .MdiParent = Me
            .Show()
            .Focus()
        End With
    End Sub

    Private Sub ExitToolStripMenuItem_Click(ByVal sender As System.Object, _
      ByVal e As System.EventArgs) Handles ExitToolStripMenuItem.Click
        ' Terminate the program.
        ' Closing the startup form ends the program.

        Me.Close()
    End Sub

    Private Sub AboutToolStripMenuItem_Click(ByVal sender As System.Object, _
      ByVal e As System.EventArgs) _
      Handles AboutToolStripMenuItem.Click, AboutToolStripButton.Click
        ' Display the About Box form with attribute information.

        Dim AnAboutBox As New AboutBox1
        AnAboutBox.ShowDialog()
    End Sub

    Private Sub ClockTimer_Tick(ByVal sender As System.Object, _
      ByVal e As System.EventArgs) Handles Timer1.Tick
        ' Update the date and time in the status bar.
        ' Interval = 1000 milliseconds (one second).

        DateToolStripStatusLabel.Text = Now.ToShortDateString
        TimeToolStripStatusLabel.Text = Now.ToLongTimeString()
    End Sub
End Class
```

PayrollForm

```vb
'Project:      Ch02HandsOn
'Module:       PayrollForm
'Programmer:   Bradley/Millspaugh
'Date:         June 2009
'Description:  User interface for payroll application.
'              Provides data entry and validates for nonnumeric data.
'              Uses the singleton design pattern to ensure that only one
'              instance of the form can be created.


Public Class PayrollForm
    Private Shared AnInstance As PayrollForm

    Public Shared ReadOnly Property Instance() As PayrollForm
        Get
            If AnInstance Is Nothing Then
                AnInstance = New PayrollForm
            End If
            Return AnInstance
        End Get
    End Property
```

```vb
Private Sub CalculateButton_Click(ByVal sender As System.Object, _
  ByVal e As System.EventArgs) Handles CalculateButton.Click
    ' Create a Payroll object to connect to the business services tier.
    Dim HoursDecimal As Decimal
    Dim RateDecimal As Decimal

    ' Check for valid input data.
    ErrorProvider1.Clear()
    If Decimal.TryParse(HoursTextBox.Text, HoursDecimal) Then
        If Decimal.TryParse(RateTextBox.Text, RateDecimal) Then
            ' Both values converted successfully.
            Try
                Dim APayroll As New Payroll(HoursDecimal, RateDecimal)
                PayTextBox.Text = APayroll.Pay.ToString("C")

            Catch Err As ApplicationException
                ' Catch exceptions from the Payroll class.
                Select Case Err.Source
                    Case "Hours"
                        ErrorProvider1.SetError(HoursTextBox, _
                          Err.Message)
                        SelectControlInError(HoursTextBox)
                    Case "Rate"
                        ErrorProvider1.SetError(RateTextBox, _
                          Err.Message)
                        SelectControlInError(RateTextBox)
                End Select
            End Try
        Else
            ' Rate did not pass validation.
            ErrorProvider1.SetError(RateTextBox, _
              "The rate must be numeric.")
            SelectControlInError(RateTextBox)
        End If
    Else
        ' Hours did not pass validation.
        ErrorProvider1.SetError(HoursTextBox, _
          "The hours must be numeric.")
        SelectControlInError(HoursTextBox)
    End If
End Sub

Private Sub ClearButton_Click(ByVal sender As System.Object, _
  ByVal e As System.EventArgs) Handles ClearButton.Click
    ' Clear the screen fields.

    ErrorProvider1.Clear()
    With NameTextBox
        .Clear()
        .Focus()
    End With
    HoursTextBox.Clear()
    RateTextBox.Clear()
    PayTextBox.Clear()
End Sub
```

```vb
    Private Sub CloseButton_Click(ByVal sender As System.Object, _
      ByVal e As System.EventArgs) Handles CloseButton.Click
        ' Close this form.

        Me.Close()
    End Sub

    Private Sub HoursTextBox_Validating(ByVal sender As Object, _
      ByVal e As System.ComponentModel.CancelEventArgs) _
      Handles HoursTextBox.Validating
        ' Test the hours for numeric.
        Dim HoursDecimal As Decimal

        If Decimal.TryParse(HoursTextBox.Text, HoursDecimal) Then
            ErrorProvider1.Clear()
        Else
            ErrorProvider1.SetError(HoursTextBox, _
              "The hours must be numeric.")
            HoursTextBox.SelectAll()
            e.Cancel = True
        End If
    End Sub

    Private Sub RateTextBox_Validating(ByVal sender As Object, _
      ByVal e As System.ComponentModel.CancelEventArgs) _
      Handles RateTextBox.Validating
        ' Test pay rate for numeric.
        Dim RateDecimal As Decimal

        If Decimal.TryParse(RateTextBox.Text, RateDecimal) Then
            ErrorProvider1.Clear()
        Else
            ErrorProvider1.SetError(RateTextBox, _
              "The hours must be numeric.")
            RateTextBox.SelectAll()
            e.Cancel = True
        End If
    End Sub

    Private Sub PayrollForm_FormClosing(ByVal sender As Object, _
      ByVal e As System.Windows.Forms.FormClosingEventArgs) _
      Handles Me.FormClosing
        ' Do not allow validation to cancel the form's closing.

        e.Cancel = False
        ' Release the instance of this form.
        AnInstance = Nothing
    End Sub

    Private Sub SelectControlInError(ByVal ErrorTextBox As TextBox)
        ' Select the control in error.

        With ErrorTextBox
            .SelectAll()
            .Focus()
        End With
    End Sub
End Class
```

SummaryForm

```
'Program:       Ch02HandsOn
'Programmer:    Bradley/Millspaugh
'Form:          SummaryForm
'Date:          June 2009
'Description:   Summary form for the chapter hands-on MDI application.
'               Displays summary information for multiple transactions.
'               Uses the singleton design pattern to ensure that only one
'               instance of the form can be created.


Public Class SummaryForm
    Private Shared AnInstance As SummaryForm

    Public Shared ReadOnly Property Instance() As SummaryForm
        Get
            If AnInstance Is Nothing Then
                AnInstance = New SummaryForm
            End If
            Return AnInstance
        End Get
    End Property

    Private Sub SummaryForm_Activated(ByVal sender As Object, _
      ByVal e As System.EventArgs) Handles Me.Activated
        ' Retrieve and display the summary values.

        EmployeeCountTextBox.Text = Payroll.NumberProcessed.ToString()
        OvertimeHoursTextBox.Text = Payroll.OvertimeHours.ToString("N1")
        TotalPayrollTextBox.Text = Payroll.TotalPay.ToString("C")
    End Sub

    Private Sub CloseButton_Click(ByVal sender As System.Object, _
      ByVal e As System.EventArgs) Handles CloseButton.Click
        ' Close this form.

        Me.Close()
    End Sub

    Private Sub SummaryForm_FormClosing(ByVal sender As Object, _
      ByVal e As System.Windows.Forms.FormClosingEventArgs) _
      Handles Me.FormClosing
        ' Release the form's instance.

        AnInstance = Nothing
    End Sub
End Class
```

Payroll Class

```
'Project:       Ch02HandsOn
'Module:        Payroll Class
'Programmer:    Bradley/Millspaugh
'Date:          June 2009
'Description:   Business services tier for payroll calculation: validates input
'               data and calculates the pay, with overtime, regular, and
'               summary data.
```

```
Public Class Payroll

    ' Instance variables.
    Private HoursDecimal As Decimal      ' Hold the Hours property.
    Private RateDecimal As Decimal       ' Hold the Rate property.
    Private PayDecimal As Decimal        ' Hold the Pay property.

    ' Shared variables.
    ' Hold the NumberProcessed shared property.
    Private Shared NumberEmployeesInteger As Integer
    ' Hold the TotalPay shared property.
    Private Shared TotalPayDecimal As Decimal
    ' Hold the OvertimeHours shared property.
    Private Shared TotalOvertimeHoursDecimal As Decimal

    ' Constants.
    Private Const MINIMUM_WAGE_Decimal As Decimal = 6.25D
    Private Const MAXIMUM_WAGE_Decimal As Decimal = 50D
    Private Const MINIMUM_HOURS_Decimal As Decimal = 0D
    Private Const MAXIMUM_HOURS_Decimal As Decimal = 60D
    Private Const REGULAR_HOURS_Decimal As Decimal = 40D
    Private Const OVERTIME_RATE_Decimal As Decimal = 1.5D

    ' Constructor.
    Sub New(ByVal HoursDecimal As Decimal, ByVal RateDecimal As Decimal)
        ' Assign properties and calculate the pay.

        Me.Hours = HoursDecimal
        Me.Rate = RateDecimal
        FindPay()
    End Sub

    Private Sub FindPay()
        ' Calculate the pay.
        Dim OvertimeHoursDecimal As Decimal

        If HoursDecimal <= REGULAR_HOURS_Decimal Then    ' No overtime.
            PayDecimal = HoursDecimal * RateDecimal
            OvertimeHoursDecimal = 0D
        Else                                             ' Overtime.
            OvertimeHoursDecimal = HoursDecimal - REGULAR_HOURS_Decimal
            PayDecimal = (REGULAR_HOURS_Decimal * RateDecimal) + _
                (OvertimeHoursDecimal * OVERTIME_RATE_Decimal * RateDecimal)
        End If
        TotalOvertimeHoursDecimal += OvertimeHoursDecimal
        TotalPayDecimal += PayDecimal
        NumberEmployeesInteger += 1
    End Sub

    ' Property procedures.
    Public Property Hours() As Decimal
        Get
            Return HoursDecimal
        End Get
        Set(ByVal Value As Decimal)
            If Value >= MINIMUM_HOURS_Decimal And _
                Value <= MAXIMUM_HOURS_Decimal Then
                    HoursDecimal = Value
```

```vb
            Else
                Dim Ex As New ApplicationException( _
                  "Hours are outside of the acceptable range.")
                Ex.Source = "Hours"
                Throw Ex
            End If
        End Set
    End Property

    Public Property Rate() As Decimal
        Get
            Return RateDecimal
        End Get
        Set(ByVal Value As Decimal)
            If Value >= MINIMUM_WAGE_Decimal And _
              Value <= MAXIMUM_WAGE_Decimal Then
                RateDecimal = Value
            Else
                Dim Ex As New ApplicationException( _
                  "Pay rate is outside of the acceptable range.")
                Ex.Source = "Rate"
                Throw Ex
            End If
        End Set
    End Property

    Public ReadOnly Property Pay() As Decimal
        Get
            Return PayDecimal
        End Get
    End Property

    Public Shared ReadOnly Property NumberProcessed() As Decimal
        Get
            Return NumberEmployeesInteger
        End Get
    End Property

    Public Shared ReadOnly Property TotalPay() As Decimal
        Get
            Return TotalPayDecimal
        End Get
    End Property

    Public Shared ReadOnly Property OvertimeHours() As Decimal
        Get
            Return TotalOvertimeHoursDecimal
        End Get
    End Property
End Class
```

Summary

1. In VB, all programming is based on classes, which consist of properties, methods, and events.
2. You can create a new class and use the class to create new objects.
3. Creating a new object is called *instantiating* the class; the object is called an *instance* of the class.

4. In OOP terminology, abstraction means to create a model of an object.

5. Encapsulation refers to the combination of the characteristics and behaviors of an item into a single class definition.

6. Inheritance provides a means to derive a new class based on an existing class. The existing class is called a *base class*, *superclass*, or *parent class*. The inherited class is called a *subclass*, *derived class*, or *child class*.

7. An abstract class is a class designed strictly for inheritance; you cannot instantiate an object of the class but must derive new classes from the class.

8. Polymorphism allows classes that inherit to have methods that behave differently than the identically named methods in the base class.

9. One of biggest advantages of object-oriented programming is that classes that you create for one application may be reused in other applications.

10. Multitier applications separate program functions into the presentation tier (the user interface), the business services tier (the logic of calculations and validation), and the data tier (access to stored data).

11. One advantage of using multitier development is that the business rules can be changed without changing the interface or the interface can be changed without changing the business services tier.

12. The variables inside a class used to store the properties should be declared as Private so that data values are accessible only by procedures within the class.

13. The way to make the properties of a class available to code outside the class is to use property procedures. The Get portion returns the value of the property and the Set portion assigns a value to the property. Validation is often performed in the Set portion.

14. You can create read-only and write-only properties.

15. A constructor is a method that executes automatically when an object is created. In VB, the constructor must be named New and must be Public or Protected.

16. You can overload the New sub procedure to have more than one signature. A New sub procedure that requires arguments is called a *parameterized constructor*.

17. The public functions and sub procedures of a class module are its methods.

18. To instantiate an object of a class, you must use the New keyword on either the declaration statement or an assignment statement. The location of the New keyword determines when the object is created.

19. Your classes can throw an ApplicationException to indicate an error condition.

20. A class can pass an exception up to the calling code by using the Throw keyword.

21. Exceptions require substantial system resources and should be avoided for situations that occur frequently, such as invalid user input.

22. The TryParse method of the numeric classes can convert strings to numeric without throwing an exception for invalid data. Instead, the numeric variable is set to zero for an invalid conversion.

23. The Validating event of a text box occurs as the user attempts to move to another control that has its CausesValidation property set to *true*. The Validating event handler is the preferred location to perform field-level validation. The Validating event can be canceled for invalid data, which holds the focus in the field in error.

24. You can use an ErrorProvider component to display an error indicator and message on a form, rather than use a message box.

25. Shared members (properties and methods) have one copy that can be used by all objects of the class, generally used for totals and counts. Instance members have one copy for each instance of the object. Declare shared members with the `Shared` keyword. You can reference Public shared members of a class without creating an instance of the class.
26. A namespace is an area used for grouping and referring to classes and structures.
27. The scope of variables, constants, and objects, from the greatest to the smallest: namespace, module level, procedure level, and block level.
28. The lifetime of a variable, constant, or object corresponds to its scope.
29. You can declare the accessibility of entities using the keywords `Public`, `Private`, `Protected`, `Friend`, and `Protected Friend`.
30. A subclass inherits all public and protected properties and methods of its base class, except for the constructor. An identically named method in a subclass will override or shadow the base-class method. Shadow is the default.
31. To override a method from a base class, the original method must be declared as overridable, and the new method must use the `Overrides` keyword.
32. A class that has a predefined set of possible values for a property should define the values in an enum. The enum structure can appear at the namespace or class level and must define integer values.
33. The garbage collection feature periodically checks for unreferenced objects, destroys the object references, and releases resources.

Key Terms

abstract class *51*	namespace scope *74*
abstraction *50*	overloading *57*
accessibility *76*	overridable *78*
base class *51*	override *52*
block-level scope *75*	parameterized constructor *57*
business rules *53*	parent class *51*
business services tier *54*	polymorphism *52*
child class *51*	presentation tier *53*
constructor *56*	procedure-level scope *75*
data tier *54*	property procedure *55*
derived class *51*	`ReadOnly` *56*
destructor *56*	reusability *51*
encapsulation *50*	scope *74*
enum *81*	shadow *78*
enumeration *81*	shared member *69*
ErrorProvider component *64*	shared property *69*
garbage collection *83*	shared variable *69*
inheritance *51*	subclass *51*
instance member *69*	superclass *51*
instance property *69*	throw an exception *60*
instance variable *69*	`Throw` statement *61*
lifetime *76*	`TryParse` method *62*
module-level scope *75*	Validating event *63*
multitier application *53*	`Value` keyword *55*
namespace *74*	`WriteOnly` *56*

R e v i e w   Q u e s t i o n s

1. Define abstraction, encapsulation, inheritance, and polymorphism.
2. What is an abstract class and how is it used?
3. Why should property variables in a class be declared as private?
4. What are property procedures and what is their purpose?
5. Explain how to create a new class and instantiate an object from that class.
6. What is a constructor, how is it created, and when is it triggered?
7. What is a parameterized constructor?
8. How can you write methods for a new class?
9. What is a shared member? What is its purpose? How is it created?
10. Explain the steps necessary to inherit a class from another class.
11. Differentiate between overriding and overloading.
12. What are the advantages of developing applications using multiple tiers?
13. Describe the steps necessary to perform validation in the business services tier but display the message to the user in the presentation tier.
14. Explain the differences between a namespace-level variable and a module-level variable. How is each created and how is it used?
15. Explain the differences between a procedure-level variable and a block-level variable. How is each created and how is it used?
16. What is the lifetime of a procedure-level variable? a block-level variable? a module-level variable?
17. Explain the difference between overriding and shadowing methods.
18. What is the effect of using the `Protected` accessibility modifier? the `Friend` modifier?
19. What is an advantage of using the `TryParse` methods rather than `Parse`?
20. What is an advantage of using an ErrorProvider component rather than a message box?
21. What is the purpose of an enum? How is one created?
22. What is garbage collection? What does it do and when does it run?

P r o g r a m m i n g   E x e r c i s e s

2.1 Tricia's Travels: You can add to your Exercise 1.2 or just create the main form.

Presentation Tier

Main Form

Include text boxes for the customer name, phone number, number traveling, departure date, and credit card number. Include a list box for the destinations: Caribbean, Mediterranean, and Alaska. Include radio buttons for 7-day or 14-day packages and a check box for first class. Validate that the user has made an entry for all fields.

Summary Form

Display the total billing amount, the total number traveling, the number for each destination, and the number of first-class fares.

Business Services Tier

Calculate the amount due based on the following schedule:

Days	Destination	Standard price	First-class price
7	Caribbean	3250	5000
14	Caribbean	6000	9000
7	Mediterranean	4250	7999
14	Mediterranean	7999	11999
7	Alaska	3300	5250
14	Alaska	7200	10500

2.2   Kenna's Kandles offers candles in various shapes, scents, and colors. Write an MDI project that contains a Main form, an About form, and a Summary form using a separate tier for the business rules.

Presentation Tier

Main Form

- Text boxes for customer information (name and credit card number).

- Text box for quantity.

- Radio buttons or list box for candle style (tea light, votive, or pillar).

- Radio buttons or list box for color (Federal Blue, Sunflower Yellow, Christmas Red, and Lily White).

- Check box for Scented.

- Label for the price of the item.

Summary Form

Display the subtotal for all candles, the tax of 8 percent, a shipping fee of 3 percent, and the total due.

Business Services Tier

Calculate the price for each candle based on the options selected. The business services tier also should accumulate the information for the total.

Style	Base price	Scented price (additional)
Tea lights	5.75	0.75
Votives	7.50	1.25
Pillar	12.25	1.75

2.3   Create a project for maintaining a checkbook using multiple tiers.

Presentation Tier

Main Form

Use radio buttons or a drop-down list to indicate the transaction type: check, deposit, interest, or service charge. Allow the user to enter the amount in a text box for the amount and display the account balance in a label or read-only text box. Display a message box for insufficient funds, based on an appropriate exception generated by the business services tier.

Summary Form

Display the total number and the total dollar amounts for deposits, checks, interest, and service charges.

Business Services Tier

Validate that the balance can cover a check. If not, throw an exception and deduct a service charge of $10; do not process the check. Process interest and deposits by adding to the balance and checks and service charges by reducing the balance.

Optional Extra

Create an MDI application that includes an About form, a toolbar, and a status bar.

2.4 Piecework workers are paid by the piece. Workers who produce a greater quantity of output are often paid at a higher rate.

Presentation Tier

The program should input the name and number of pieces and calculate the pay. Include a *Calculate* button and a *Clear* button. You can include either a *Summary* button or menu item. The *Summary* option displays the total number of pieces, the total pay, and the average pay per person on a Summary form.

The name and number of pieces are required fields.

Business Services Tier

The number of pieces must be a positive number; throw an exception for negative numbers. Calculate the pay using this schedule:

Pieces completed	Price paid per piece for all pieces
1–199	.50
200–399	.55
400–599	.60
600 or more	.65

Accumulate and return the summary totals for number of pieces, pay, and average pay per person. Notice that you also must accumulate the number of persons to calculate the average.

2.5 Add an inherited class to Exercise 2.4. This class calculates pay for senior workers, who are paid on a different scale. You must add a check box to the form for senior workers and use the inherited class for those workers.

Senior workers receive a base pay of $300 plus a per-piece pay using this schedule:

Pieces completed	Price paid per piece for all pieces
1–199	.20
200–399	.25
400–599	.30
600–799	.35
800 or more	.40

Case Studies

Claytor's Cottages

Modify your Claytor's Cottages case study project from Chapter 1. Complete the Reservations option using a presentation tier and a business services tier.

Presentation Tier

The form should have radio buttons for King, Queen, or Double. Include text boxes for entering the customer's name, address, and phone number; the number of nights stayed; credit card type (use a list box or combo box for Visa, Mastercard, and American Express); and credit card number. Name, nights stayed, and credit card number are required fields. Use a check box for weekend or weekday rate and a check box for AARP or AAA members. Display the price in a label or Read-Only text box.

Business Services Tier

Throw an exception if the number of days is not greater than 0. Calculate the price using this table. Add a room tax of 7 percent. AAA and AARP customers receive a 10 percent discount rate, which is calculated before the tax.

Beds	Sunday through Thursday rate	Weekend rate (Friday and Saturday)
King	95.00	105.00
Queen	85.00	95.00
Double	69.95	79.95

Optional extra: Enter the date of arrival and date of departure instead of the check boxes. You can use a calendar object or text boxes to obtain the dates. Use the methods of the DateTime structure to determine if the check-in dates are weekdays or weekend. Increase the rates by 25 percent in May through September.

Hint: Determine the number of days by using the Subtract method of the DateTime structure:

```
NumberDaysInteger = _
    EndDate.Subtract(StartDate).Days
```

Christian's Car Rentals

Modify your Christian's Car Rentals project from Chapter 1. Code the Rentals form using a presentation tier and a business services tier.

Presentation Tier

The presentation tier should include data entry for the size of car: Compact, Mid size, or Luxury. Include text boxes for entering the renter's name, address, phone number, license, credit card type, and credit card number. A group box should include the number of days rented, the beginning odometer reading, and the ending odometer reading.

Validate that the ending odometer reading is greater than the beginning odometer reading before allowing the data to be sent to the business services tier. Make sure that an entry has been made for license and number of days rented.

Business Services Tier

Validate that the number of days rented is greater than 0. There is no mileage charge if the number of miles does not exceed an average of 100 miles per day rented. Use the following rates:

Car size	Daily rate	Mileage rate
Compact	26.95	.12
Mid size	32.95	.15
Luxury	50.95	.20

Corporate and Insurance Accounts (Inheritance)

Corporate accounts waive the mileage rate and have a 5 percent discount; insurance accounts have a 10 percent discount on the daily rate.

CHAPTER

3

Windows Database Applications

at the completion of this chapter, you will be able to . . .

1. Retrieve and display data from a SQL Server database on Windows Forms.

2. Use the ADO.NET data components: TableAdapters, DataSets, and DataConnectors.

3. Display database fields in a grid and in details view.

4. Sort database data using a method and an SQL query.

5. Concatenate data fields using SQL or the DataSet Designer.

6. Access data using a stored procedure.

7. Write a multitier application that separates the data tier from the presentation tier.

8. Declare and instantiate DataSet and TableAdapter objects in code and write the code to bind data to form controls.

In this chapter, you learn to access and display database data on a Windows form. You will follow good OOP principles and perform the database access in a data-tier component. You will learn to use table adapters and DataSets to display data from a database file. This chapter looks at the underlying SQL statements that retrieve the data and also introduces stored procedures. In Chapter 4 you will work with multiple related tables and in Chapter 5 you will learn to update a database.

Visual Studio and Database Applications

Professional VB programmers spend the majority of their time on applications that involve databases. To be a good programmer, you will want to concentrate on the various methods of displaying and updating database information.

With VB you can create very simple database applications that require virtually no coding, all the way up to very powerful distributed applications that access and modify data on multiple large-scale servers. You can create programs that display and/or update data on a single stand-alone computer as well as multiuser networked databases. Although this text concentrates on SQL Server Express databases, the techniques that you learn also extend to larger-scale databases, such as SQL Server, Oracle, Sybase, and DB2. You also can apply most of the techniques in this chapter to an Access database.

The managed providers that ship with the .NET Framework are

- Microsoft Access Database File.

- Microsoft ODBC Data Source.

- Microsoft SQL Server Compact 3.5.

- Microsoft SQL Server Database File.

- Oracle Database (other database formats).

ADO.NET

ActiveX Data Objects (ADO) .NET 3.5 is Microsoft's latest database object model. The goal of ADO.NET is to allow programmers to use a standard set of objects to refer to data from any source.

The trend toward accessing data from the Web and multiple platforms has changed the techniques that we use for data handling. In the past, it was common to connect to a database in a client/server format. The connection was kept open while the user browsed and/or updated the data, and data typing was not much of a concern. But now, using the .NET approach, we use disconnected DataSets with common data representation (data types) from multiple sources. The .NET Framework is also tightly integrated with Extensible Markup Language (XML), an industry-standard format for storing and transferring data over multiple platforms.

A well-written multitier application that uses disconnected DataSets provides for **flexibility** and **scalability**. A flexible application can adapt to changes in the database (the back end or data tier) or to the user interface (the front end or presentation tier). And a scalable application can handle increases in the number of users and the number of servers.

Accessing Data in the .NET Framework

You will find a new world of terminology for working with data: data sources, data designers, datasets, binding sources, table adapters, and more. In addition, you will use many of the standard terms for data elements.

Database Terminology

A **data table** can be viewed like a spreadsheet—with rows and columns. Each **row** in a table represents the data for one item, person, or transaction and is called a **record**. Each **column** in a table is used to store a different element of data, such as an account number, a name, address, or numeric amount. The elements represented in columns are called **fields**. You can think of the table in Figure 3.1 as consisting of rows and columns or of records and fields.

F i g u r e   3 . 1

A table consists of rows (records) and columns (fields).

Most **tables** use a **primary key field** (or combination of fields) to uniquely identify each record. The primary key field is often a number, such as employee number, account number, identification number, or social security number; or it may be a text field, such as last name, or a combination, such as last name and first name.

Data Sources

Your application obtains data from a **data source**. You can create a data source from a large-scale database, a local database file, a Web service, or other types of objects. For local database files, which reside on the developer's computer, .NET currently supports Access .mdb and .accdb files and SQL Server Express .mdf files. SQL Server Express .mdf files are the recommended choice for Visual Basic. The Visual Studio environment allows you to create and edit SQL Server Express data sources.

When you create a data source from a database, a typed DataSet is added to your project. Each typed DataSet has a schema, which describes the fields and their data types. Although .NET provides for several kinds of data sources, we will concentrate on typed DataSets, which are the recommended approach for handling data in most situations.

DataSet Objects

A **DataSet object** holds a copy of the data in memory, disconnected from the data source. You can consider a DataSet to be a temporary cache, rather than the actual database data.

A DataSet object can hold one or more tables. A relational database generally contains multiple tables and relationships between the tables. For example, an Employee table may have an Employee ID field and the Payroll table also will have an Employee ID field. The two tables are related by Employee ID. You can find the employee information for one payroll record by retrieving the record for the corresponding Employee ID. In the example in Figure 3.2, Employee ID is the primary key for the Employee table. The Employee ID field in the Payroll table is considered a **foreign key**—the field that links a Payroll record to its corresponding Employee record. So to retrieve the Employee's name for a given Payroll record, for example, the foreign key is used to look up the corresponding record in the Employee table.

Figure 3.2

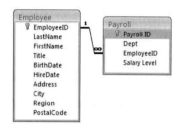

The Employee table and Payroll table are related by Employee ID, which is the primary key in the Employee table and the foreign key in the Payroll table.

The DataSet Object Model

Each DataSet object contains a DataTable collection, which is made up of individual DataTable objects. The DataTable object has both DataRow and DataColumn collections. A single DataRow holds the actual data for one record. The DataRow object maintains the original values and any changed values. This information is used to determine which rows have changed during program execution.

A DataRelation object stores information about related tables, including which columns contain the primary keys and foreign keys that link the tables.

The Constraints collection, which belongs to the DataTable object, holds two types of Constraint objects: Unique constraints and ForeignKey constraints. Unique constraints enforce the requirement that values in the specified field be unique, which is usually required for primary key fields. ForeignKey constraints require that any foreign key value that appears in a secondary table match a primary key value in the primary table.

Figure 3.3 shows the object model of the DataSet object.

Note: See "Datasets in Visual Studio Overview" in Visual Studio Help.

TableAdapters

A **TableAdapter** object provides the communication between your program and the database, sometimes called the "data access layer." A TableAdapter connects to the database and handles SQL queries and stored procedures, fills the DataSets, and handles writing any changes back in the data source.

One of the features of a TableAdapter is that it can hold multiple queries. You can retrieve the data by calling a specific query or by getting all of the data for the table. These TableAdapter objects have more functionality than the DataAdapters used in earlier editions of this text. (DataAdapters are still available in VB 2008.) The visual designers in the Visual Studio IDE automatically generate TableAdapters for you when you add a typed DataSet.

Figure 3.3

The DataSet object model.

BindingSource Objects

A **BindingSource object** facilitates binding the controls on a Windows Form to the data source. The BindingSource keeps all of the form's controls displaying data from the same record (called *currency*), as well as handling the navigation, sorting, filtering, and updating of the data. In Chapter 5, you will work with methods of the BindingSource object for updating your data.

XML Data

XML is an industry-standard format for storing and transferring data. You can find the specifications for XML at www.w3.org/XML, which is the site for the World Wide Web Consortium (W3C). Although you don't need to know any XML to write database applications in VB, a few facts about XML can help you understand what is happening in your programs.

Most proprietary database formats store data in binary, which cannot be accessed by other systems or pass through Internet firewalls. Data stored in XML is all text, identified by tags, similar to HTML tags. An XML file can be edited by any text editor program, such as Notepad.

If you have seen or written any HTML, you know that opening and closing tags define elements and attributes. For example, any text between `<b>` and `</b>` is rendered in bold by the browser.

```
<b>This text is bold.</b> <i>This is italic.</i>
```

The tags in XML are not predefined as they are in HTML. The tags can identify fields by name. For example, following are the first two records of a DataSet called AuthorsDataSet (refer to Figure 3.1), based on the Authors table in the Pubs SQL Server database, represented in XML. (Later in this chapter, you will use the Pubs database for VB projects.)

```xml
<?xml version="1.0" standalone="yes"?>
<AuthorsDataSet xmlns="AuthorsDataSet.xsd">
  <authors>
    <au_id>172-32-1176</au_id>
    <au_lname>White</au_lname>
    <au_fname>Johnson</au_fname>
    <phone>408 496-7223</phone>
    <address>10932 Bigge Rd.</address>
    <city>Menlo Park</city>
    <state>CA</state>
    <zip>94025</zip>
    <contract>true</contract>
  </authors>
  <authors>
    <au_id>213-46-8915</au_id>
    <au_lname>Green</au_lname>
    <au_fname>Marjorie</au_fname>
    <phone>415 986-7020</phone>
    <address>309 63rd St. #411</address>
    <city>Oakland</city>
    <state>CA</state>
    <zip>94618</zip>
    <contract>true</contract>
  </authors>
</AuthorsDataSet>
```

Each typed DataSet has a schema, which defines the fields, data types, and any constraints, such as required fields. ADO.NET validates the data against the schema and checks for constraint violations.

The format of XML data offers several advantages for programming. Because the schema provides for strong data typing, the various data types can be handled properly. ADO.NET can treat the XML data as objects, allowing the IntelliSense feature of the Visual Studio environment to provide information for the programmer. In addition, data handling in XML and ADO.NET executes faster than in earlier forms of ADO.

The Visual Studio IDE

The VS IDE provides tools to help you develop database applications. You will use the Data Sources window to set up the data sources for your applications, as well as the Server Explorer (called the Database Explorer in the Express Edition), which replaces some of the functions of the Server Explorer of previous editions.

The Data Sources Window

The **Data Sources window** provides an easy way to set up the data sources for an application. Using the Data Sources window, you can easily create data-bound controls on a form. After you set up the data source, you can add grids or individual fields by dragging a table or fields from the Data Sources window to the form. Or you can make an existing control display database data by dragging a field from the Data Sources window and dropping it on the control, which causes data binding to be set up automatically.

When you drag database tables or fields to a form, several things happen: New data controls are added to the form; an .xsd file with the schema is added to the Solution Explorer window; and DataSet, BindingSource, TableAdapter, and BindingNavigator objects are added to the form's component tray.

The Data Sources window (Figure 3.4) allows you to add and view the DataSets that are used in a project. It also provides access to the DataSet Designer, which can visually display the DataSets and the relationships of the data tables.

Figure 3.4

Set up the data sources and binding in the Data Sources window.

Feedback 3.1

1. Assume that you have a data table that contains the names and phone numbers of your friends. Describe how the terms *row*, *column*, *record*, *field*, and *primary key field* apply to your table.
2. What is an advantage of transferring data as XML, rather than a proprietary format, such as Access or SQL Server?

Creating a Database Application

In this section, you will create a simple database application to display a table in a grid.

Microsoft supports several products for designing and maintaining database files:

- SQL Server. Designed for large-scale databases, which can handle the needs of large enterprises. Can support many users and provides robust security and reliability.

- Access. Designed for single-user databases or small networked databases with five or fewer users. Uses the Microsoft Jet Engine. Until a few years ago, Access was the preferred database format for a single-user database.

- **SQL Server 2008 Express Edition**. The scaled-down desktop or personal version of SQL Server, designed for a single-user database and for development and testing for larger-scale applications. Uses the same SQL statements and the same .mdf file format as the full SQL Server product.

The exercises in this text are based on SQL Server Express Edition. Even if you have the full SQL Server product available, you can use the SQL Server Express that comes with Visual Studio and is usually installed as a setup option.

Local Database Files

When you create a project based on a database, Visual Studio offers an option to make a copy of the database file into the project. This option places a duplicate of the original file into your project, which has some advantages and some disadvantages.

Although you would never place a copy of the database into the project for a production situation, for development and testing it can be a definite advantage. You can move the project from one folder to another, or from one computer to another, and the database file is still in the project and available. You don't have to be concerned about security of a company database, and you can test updating the data without altering the original file. So for a learning environment, it is best to always select the option to include the file in the project. But recognize that this scenario would not be reasonable for a company's entire database.

Creating a Windows Database Application—Step-by-Step

This step-by-step exercise creates a Windows application that displays a data table in a grid.

Begin a New Project

STEP 1: Begin a new Windows application called *Ch03SBS* (for step-by-step). Make sure that the option *Create directory for solution* is not selected, or you will create two folders, one inside the other. Click the *Save All* button to save the project.

STEP 2: In the Solution Explorer, change the form's filename to Employee-Form.vb and answer *Yes* to the dialog box. This step also renames the form's class.

STEP 3: Change the form's Text property to *Employees*.

Add a Data Source

STEP 1: If the Data Sources window is not visible, check for its tab docked with the toolbox. If it is there, click on it; if not, select *Show Data Sources* from the *Data* menu.

STEP 2: Click on *Add New Data Source* in the Data Sources window and the Data Source Configuration Wizard appears. Choose *Database* for the Data Source type and click *Next*.

STEP 3: Click on the *New Connection* button, select *Microsoft SQL Server Database File (SqlClient)* for *Data Source*, and browse to find the Pubs.mdf database file. (You can find this file in the StudentData folder from the text Web site (www.mhhe.com/AdvVB2008/).) Click *OK* on the dialog box and *Next* in the wizard.

   Note: If you are using files downloaded from Microsoft, the filename is lowercase. Just keep the name lowercase and realize that your names will not quite match those in the figures. Alternately, you can rename the file (and its accompanying pubs_log.ldf, if present) using Windows Explorer before you select the database in the project. Do not attempt to rename the database after adding it to the project.

STEP 4: A message appears indicating that the connection you selected uses a local data file that is not in the current project and asks if you would like to copy it. Select *Yes*.

STEP 5: Next you have the option to save the connection string. Click *Next* with *Yes* selected (the default).

STEP 6: Expand the *Tables* node from the list of database objects. Then expand the node for the employee table. Note that you can expand the table and use the check boxes to select the fields that you want. Select emp_id, fname, lname, and hire_date.

STEP 7: The default name is PubsDataSet, which is just fine. Click *Finish*.

Notice the icon in front of the table (Figure 3.5). The icon indicates that the table is set to DataGridView. The drop-down arrow at the end of the name allows you to select different views. Later you will work with the details view.

Figure 3.5

The PubsDataSet in the Data Sources window.

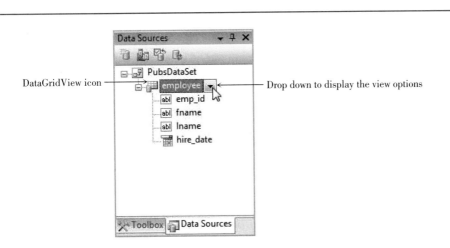

DataGridView icon ————   ———— Drop down to display the view options

Display Data in a Grid

STEP 1: Select the employee table from the Data Sources window and drag it to your form.

STEP 2: Take a look at the component tray. It should contain PubsDataSet, EmployeeBindingSource, EmployeeTableAdapter, TableAdapterManager, and EmployeeBindingNavigator.

STEP 3: You will want to resize the form and reposition and size the grid as you wish them to appear (Figure 3.6).

STEP 4: Start the program; the data automatically display (Figure 3.7). How much code did you have to write to display the data?

STEP 5: Click on the form's Close button to stop the program. Resize the grid, if necessary.

Notice the bar across the top of the form; this is a BindingNavigator bar, created from the BindingNavigator component in the component tray. The bar allows you to reposition to any record in the table and use the buttons to add a record, delete a record, or save the data. Recall that changes are made to the in-memory DataSet, which is disconnected from the original data file.

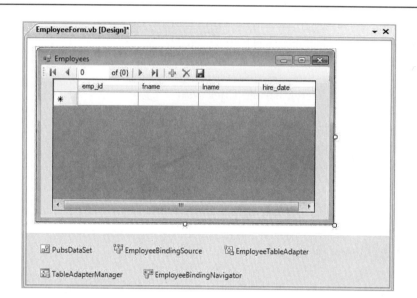

Figure 3.6

The DataGridView control on the form, with the database components in the form's component tray.

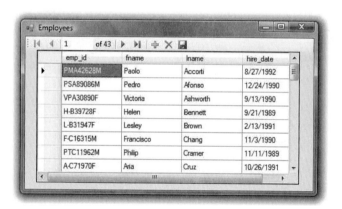

Figure 3.7

Display the DataSet in the DataGridView.

Examine the Code

After stopping execution, take a look at the automatically generated code. The EmployeeForm_Load event handler contains the code to fill the DataSet from the table adapter:

```
Me.EmployeeTableAdapter.Fill(Me.PubsDataSet.employee)
```

You also can see a SaveItem event handler for the BindingNavigator. You will learn more about saving changes in Chapter 5, where you learn to handle updating the database.

Change the Column Headings

You can improve the readability of the grid by changing the column headings. Follow these steps to set each column's HeaderText property to the desired value.

STEP 1: Click on the grid's smart tag arrow and select *Edit Columns*.
STEP 2: In the *Edit Columns* dialog (Figure 3.8), notice that the fields (columns) appear in the left pane and the properties for the selected column display in the *Bound Column Properties* pane on the right. The Header-Text property determines the heading displayed on the grid.

Click on a column header in a grid at run time to sort the data by the selected column. ■

Figure 3.8

Change the HeaderText property for the selected column.

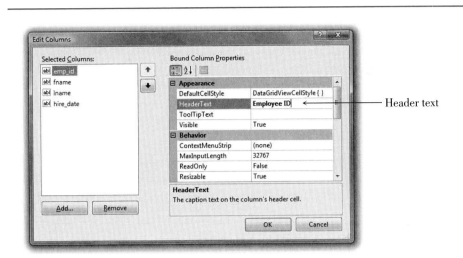

Header text

STEP 3: Change the HeaderText for emp_id to *Employee ID*, fname to *First Name*, lname to *Last Name*, and hire_date to *Hire Date*. Make sure that you are changing the HeaderText and not the Name property.

STEP 4: Click *OK* and run the program again to see the changes.

Grid Properties

The DataGridView control has many properties that allow you to specify how the user can interact with the grid. Following are some useful properties:

Property	Default setting
AllowUserToAddRows	True
AllowUserToDeleteRows	True
AllowUserToOrderColumns	False
AllowUserToResizeColumns	True
AllowUserToResizeRows	True
MultiSelect	True
RowHeadersVisible	True

The DataSet Designer

After you add a new data source to your project, a file with the extension .xsd is added to the files in the Solution Explorer. The .xsd file contains the schema definition. When you double-click on the .xsd file, you see the **DataSet Designer** (Figure 3.9).

The DataSet Designer is a visual tool that you can use to view and modify the definition of a DataSet. In the DataSet Designer, you can add fields, tables, and relationships. You also can view the data in the database using the designer. The visual display shows a key icon in front of the primary keys for each table.

Figure 3.9

You can use the DataSet Designer to modify the properties of the DataSet.

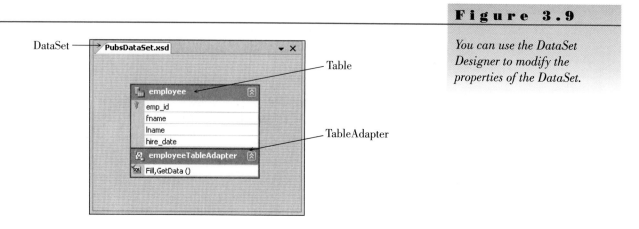

Notice the TableAdapter for each table, which handles the `Fill` and `GetData` methods for the table. Right-click on the `Fill,GetData()` row under the TableAdapter and select *Configure* to see the SQL statement used to select the data for the DataSet. Click *Cancel* to close the dialog box when finished looking at it.

Note: There are several other techniques for showing and editing the TableAdapter's SQL statement in the Query Builder. You will see these techniques later in this chapter in the section "SQL."

Preview the Dataset Data

STEP 1: In the Solution Explorer, double-click on the PubsDataSet.xsd file to view the DataSet Designer.

STEP 2: Right-click on the table name and select *Preview Data*.

STEP 3: Click on the *Preview* button (Figure 3.10).

Figure 3.10

Right-click on the table name in the DataSet Designer and select **Preview Data** *to preview the DataSet's data.*

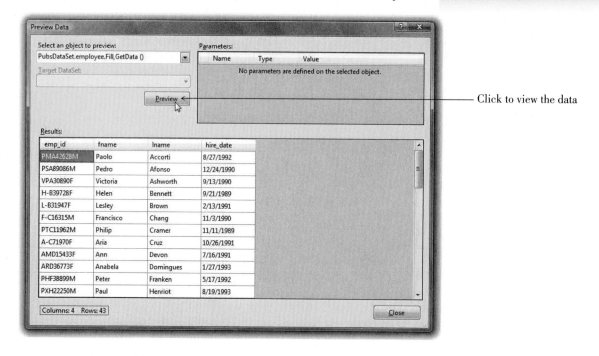

View the Designer's Code

You can view the code generated by the designer in a couple of ways. You can display the code in the DatasetName.Designer.vb file, which appears in the Solution Explorer when you select *Show All Files*. To see the code as it executes, place a breakpoint in your program on the line of code containing the `Fill` method (in the Form_Load event handler). Run the program and step into the code using the *Step Into* command (F8 or F11, depending on the keyboard setting).

Displaying Data in Individual Fields—Step-by-Step

You can easily display individual fields in text boxes, labels, or other types of controls. Next you will modify the step-by-step program to display the data in text boxes. When you select a table from the Data Sources window, a drop-down arrow appears on the right. From the drop-down menu, you can select the *DataGridView*, which is the default, or *Details*. The default control for displaying details is the text box.

Note: A form must be open in the designer for the drop-down arrows to appear in the Data Sources window.

Convert from a Grid to Details View

STEP 1: Delete the data grid from your form.

STEP 2: Click on the down arrow next to the employee table in the Data Sources window; select *Details* (Figure 3.11). Notice that the icon for the table changes to match the view.

Figure 3.11

Drop down the list of choices for the employee table and select Details, rather than the default DataGridView.

Note: If the down arrow does not appear, click on the form in the Document window, and then click on the table name in the Data Sources window again.

STEP 3: Drag the table to a spot near the upper-left corner of the form.

STEP 4: Change the text on the labels as desired.

STEP 5: Run the project.

Each of the fields displays in a text box (Figure 3.12), except the date, which uses a DateTimePicker control by default. In the next section, you will learn how to select the type of control for each field.

Figure 3.12

Display the employee table in details view.

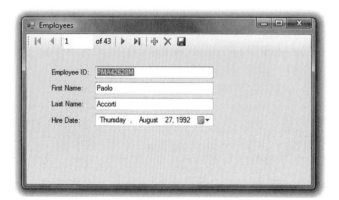

Selecting the Control Type for Details View

You can choose the type of control that will be used for each database field in details view. You also can change the defaults; for example, you can set the default for text fields to always use labels instead of text boxes. Note that you must make the selection *before* dragging the table to the form; you cannot change the type of control after placing it on the form without deleting the control and starting over.

To change the control type for a field in the current project, select the database field in the Data Sources window. Then drop down the list for an individual field (Figure 3.13) and make a selection. You can change the control type for one or as many fields as you wish. Then make sure that the table's selection is *Details View* and drag the table to the form.

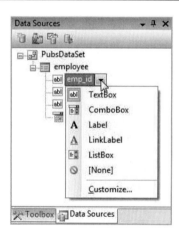

To choose a control type that is not on the list, select *Customize* and place a check mark in the box for the desired control. For example, you may wish to add a masked text box, a check box, or a picture box to the list of control types. If your application displays a specially formatted field, such as a social security number, phone number, or date, you can use the masked text box and then set the Mask property to handle the formatting of the display.

You can change the default control type in the *Options* dialog box. Select *Tools / Options*, expand the *Windows Forms Designer* node, and select *Data UI Customization*. Figure 3.14 shows the selections for string data type. Notice that you can select from the list of controls and set the default control. You also can make selections for other data types, such as DateTime, Decimal, and Integer.

Figure 3.14

Change the default control type for each database data type in the Options dialog box.

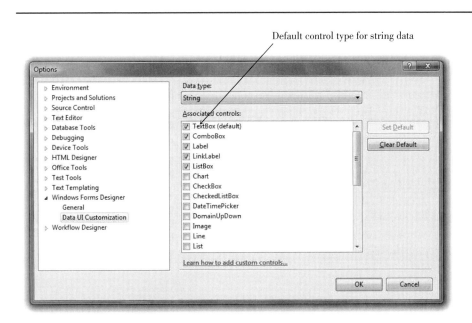

Default control type for string data

Caution: The list of control types includes TextBox and Textbox (lowercase "b"). Make sure to select TextBox, as Textbox is an old version that does not have all of the capabilities of the current version.

Setting the Captions for Database Fields

The VS database design tools are pretty smart when it comes to setting the captions for individual fields. The captions display as identifying labels in details view. If database fields are named with camel casing (camelCasing) or Pascal casing (PascalCasing), the designer separates the words to make meaningful captions. For example, a field called *EmployeeNumber* has a caption of "Employee Number".

Unfortunately, the fields in the Pubs database that we are using in the chapter examples were named using abbreviations and underscores, which the designer cannot parse. Of course, you can wait until the controls are on the form and change the column headings or identifying labels, but there's a better way. You can change the caption assigned to each field in a DataSet, which has a distinct advantage over changing the controls on a form. Often a DataSet is used multiple times in one application, or the user interface must be modified, and the captions always go with the field.

You can change field captions in the DataSet Designer. Click on a field name in the DataSet and then go to the Caption property in the Properties window. You can change the caption to a meaningful string, with multiple words, if you wish.

Formatting Bound Data

You can easily control the formatting of data items both in details view and in a data grid view. Most likely you will want to format dates and currency, but many other options are also available.

Formatting a DateTimePicker Control

By default, the date in a DateTimePicker control is displayed in Long date format (refer to Figure 3.12). You can choose a different date format by setting the Format property of the control. You can select Long, Short, Time, or Custom. Although the actual formats are determined by the system settings, the default U.S. Short format displays as mm/dd/yyyy.

Other useful properties for a DateTimePicker, when allowing the user to make updates, are the MinDate and MaxDate properties, which cause the picker to display only the specified years.

Formatting Data in a TextBox

You can control the format of bound data in a text box, which is the default control for displaying most data types. To choose the display format of a bound text box, select the control and scroll to the top of the Properties window to choose *(DataBindings)* and *(Advanced)*. Click on the build (ellipsis) button to display the *Formatting and Advanced Binding* dialog box (Figure 3.15) and make

Figure 3.15

*View or set the formatting of a bound text box in the **Formatting and Advanced Binding** dialog box. Select **Currency** and set the number of decimal positions.*

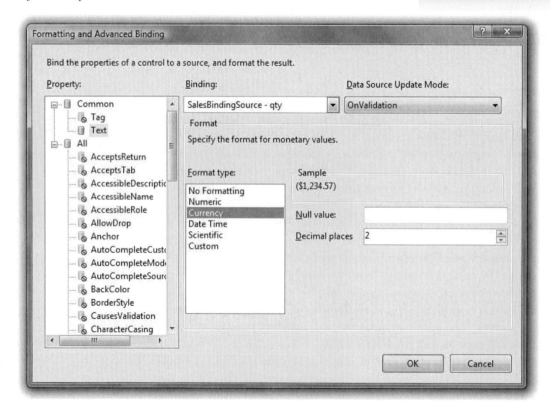

a selection for *Format type.* For Currency, you have a choice of the number of decimal positions, and for Date Time you can choose from among the various date and time formats (Figure 3.16).

Figure 3.16

Select any of the Date Time formats for a bound control.

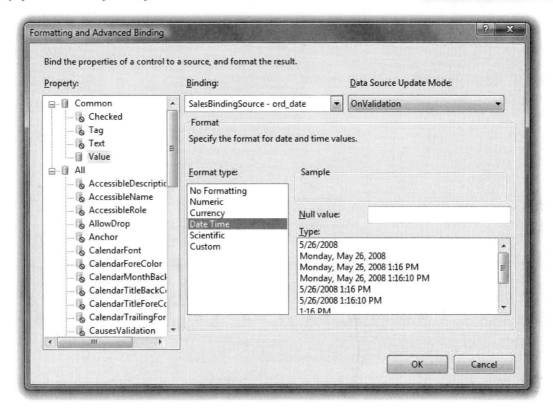

Formatting a DataGridView

For a DataGridView, you can choose the cell type and formatting for individual cells in the *Edit Columns* dialog box. The easiest way to display the dialog box is to select *Edit Columns* from the grid's smart tag or from the bottom of the Properties window. Change the type of "control" by using the *ColumnType* property under the *Design* category (Figure 3.17). To change the display format, scroll to the *Appearance* category and click on the build button for *DefaultCell-Style*; the *Cell Style Builder* dialog box appears (Figure 3.18), where you can set many properties of the cell style. Click on the build button for *Format* to display the *Format String Dialog* and select the desired formatting (Figure 3.19).

Feedback 3.2

1. Describe the function of each of the following: TableAdapter, DataSet, BindingSource, and BindingNavigator.
2. What steps are needed to place text boxes or a grid on a form from the Data Sources window?

Figure 3.17

Select the type of cell for a DataGridView column in the Edit Columns dialog box.

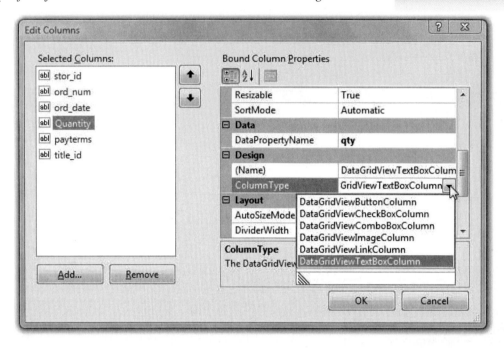

Figure 3.18

Set display properties of a DataGridView column in the CellStyle Builder dialog box. Click on the build button for Format to change the column's formatting.

Figure 3.19

Select the column's formatting in the Format String Dialog.

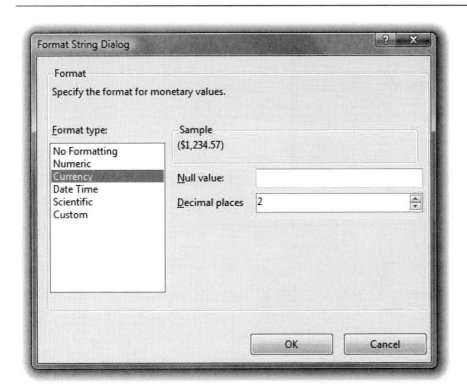

Selecting a Record from a List

One of the most common ways to display data from any data source is to allow the user to select the desired record from a list. The list may hold a record's key field or some other value, such as a person's name. Once the user has made a selection, you can retrieve the corresponding record and display the detail data on the form.

Populating Combo Boxes with Data

You can fill a list box or combo box with values from a database. List controls have the necessary properties to bind to a data source. To fill a list box or combo box with data from a DataSet object (Figure 3.20), you must set two properties: the **DataSource** and **DisplayMember properties**. The Data-Source connects to the DataSet. The DisplayMember specifies the field name of the data that you want to display in the list.

Before you drag a table name or field name to a form, you can select the type of control for each field. For the field that you want to display in a combo box, drop down the list for that field in the Data Sources window and select *ComboBox*. After you drag the field to the form, you set the DataSource and DisplayMember properties of the combo box using either the control's smart tag or the Properties window.

Figure 3.20

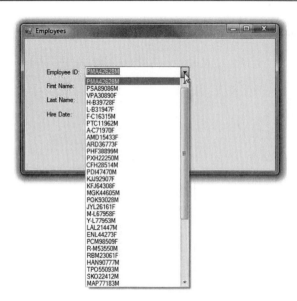

Allow users to select a value from a list. You can automatically fill the list by binding it to a field in a DataSet.

Adding a Combo Box for Selection—Step-by-Step

In this continuation of the chapter step-by-step exercise, you will change the text box for Employee ID to a combo box, to allow the user to select the record to display.

Prepare the Form

STEP 1: Open your Ch03SBS project, if necessary. It should still contain labels, text boxes, and a date-time picker for the data.

STEP 2: Delete the navigation bar from the top of the form; or you can delete the BindingNavigator component from the component tray. Both actions have the same effect.

Convert the Text Box to a Combo Box

STEP 1: Delete the text box for Employee ID. (The label may say "emp_id" if you didn't change it earlier.)

STEP 2: In the Data Sources window, click on the emp_id field to display the down arrow.

STEP 3: Drop down the list and select *ComboBox*. Notice that the icon next to the field changes to indicate a combo box.

STEP 4: Drag the emp_id field to the form. Delete the extra identifying label and move and resize the combo box, as necessary, to align it with the other controls.

Set the Combo Box Properties

STEP 1: At this point, you can choose to use the control's smart tag or the Properties window to set properties. To use the smart tag, you must display it and select *Use data bound items*.

STEP 2: Set the DataSource to EmployeeBindingSource when the *Data Binding Mode* appears in the *ComboBox Tasks* smart tag.

STEP 3: Set the DisplayMember to emp_id.

Figure 3.21

*Set the combo box data bindings
to not update the DataSet when
the combo box selection changes.*

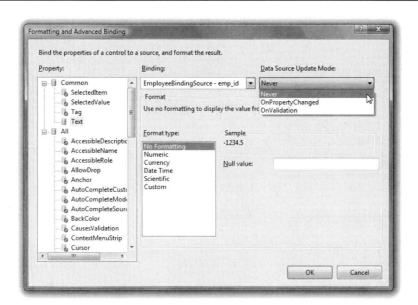

STEP 4: In the Properties window for the combo box, expand the DataBindings at the top of the list. Select the *Advanced* option, click on the build (ellipsis) button, and set the *Data Source Update Mode* to *Never* (Figure 3.21). This option is required so that new selections from the combo box are not saved in the DataSet. You will learn to change this setting in Chapter 5 when you update a database.

STEP 5: Set the tab order for the form so that the combo box is at the correct location in the tab sequence.

Try It

STEP 1: Run the program. The combo box should fill with all of the field values for employee ID.

STEP 2: Select a new employee from the combo box. The other controls on the form change to display the fields from the selected record.

Adding an Expression to Concatenate Fields

Sometimes you need to use information from a database in a format other than the way it is stored. You may need a calculated expression, such as a unit cost multiplied by a quantity. Or you may wish to concatenate fields together, such as first and last names. In fact, sometimes you need first name and then last name and other applications need last name followed by a comma and then the first name. If you create a new expression based on the fields in the table, you can bind the expression to one of the form's controls.

You create new expressions in the DataSet Designer. Double-click the DataSet's filename (.xsd file) in the Solution Explorer, or use the Data Sources window and select *Edit DataSet with Designer*. Either technique displays the DataSet Designer.

You want to add a new column to the table and then set the Expression property to specify the contents of the new column. Right-click on the table's title bar and select *Add / Column*, or right-click on an existing column and select *Insert Column*. A new row is added to the field list. You can select the name and change the name in the table or change the Name property in the Properties window.

Set the Expression property to specify what the new field contains. To concatenate the last and first names separated by a comma and space, you use the expression `lname + ', ' + fname`. (These are the field names for the employee table. If you are using a different database, substitute the correct field names.)

Note that SQL Server uses a plus sign for concatenation, rather than the ampersand used by VB, and single quotes around string literals, rather than double quotes.

After you create a new column in the DataSet, you can display the new column's data in the combo box. The Data Source is still the same DataSet, but the DisplayMember should be set to the new column.

Adding a Concatenated Field—Step-by-Step

In this continuation of the chapter step-by-step exercise, the combo box is modified to display the full name.

Open the Project

STEP 1: Open the Ch03SBS project, if necessary.

Add the New Expression

STEP 1: Open the DataSet Designer by double-clicking on the .xsd file in the Solution Explorer or by selecting *Edit DataSet with Designer* in the Data Sources window.

STEP 2: Right-click on the title bar of the employee table and select *Add / Column*.

   Trouble? If you receive an error message, close and reopen the DataSet Designer.

STEP 3: Type in "FullName" in place of "DataColumn1" as the name of the column.

STEP 4: In the Properties window, set the Expression property to "`lname + ', ' + fname`". Do not include the outer double quotes and make sure to include the space inside the single quotes after the comma.

Set the Combo Box Properties

STEP 1: Return to the Form Designer and select the combo box.
STEP 2: Change the DisplayMember to FullName.

Note: When you use multiple tables in Chapter 4, you will have to work with the SelectedValue and ValueMember properties.

Run the Program

STEP 1: Run the program. The full name should appear in the combo box. Make additional selections to see the records change.

   Trouble? If you receive an error at this point, return to the Form Designer and reset each of the properties of the combo box. Set them back to the same values as before; the process of resetting regenerates the necessary code.

You may want to add the Employee ID field to the form as a text box or a label since the combo box no longer displays the ID.

Sorting the Data for the ListBox

You can sort the items in the ComboBox in a couple of ways. Your first reaction might be, "Why not just set the Sorted property of the ComboBox?" Although that seems like an easy solution, it does not work when the items are coming from a data source. The sorting must be done on the data, which you can accomplish by using the binding source or by sorting the data using SQL. The next sections present both of these alternatives.

Sorting with the BindingSource

The BindingSource class automatically contains a Sort method. You can sort the data for any BindingSource object by simply supplying the field name for the sort process. The field can even be a calculated field.

```
JobBindingSource.Sort = "job_desc"
EmployeeBindingSource.Sort = "FullName"
```

Modifying the SQL Select Statement

When you create a DataSet from a database, the resulting table data are produced by a query written in **Structured Query Language (SQL)**. Each table in the DataSet has an associated TableAdapter component, which has a Fill method. It is the Fill method that retrieves the data from the data source. Recall that the form's code contains a call to the Fill method by default. Notice the format of the statement:

```
Me.EmployeeTableAdapter.Fill(Me.PubsDataSet.employee)
```

The above code tells the table adapter to call its Fill method and put the data in the employee table of the PubsDataSet. The Fill method that executes is actually an SQL query to the database.

Displaying the Query Builder

You can view and modify the SQL statement directly or by using the **Query Builder** (the recommended practice). Display the Query Builder by using one of these techniques:

- Double-click the .xsd file in the Solution Explorer to open the DataSet Designer (Figure 3.22). Click on the TableAdapter's Fill,GetData() line; click on the CommandText property in the Properties window to display the build (ellipsis) button; and click to display the Query Builder. In Figure 3.22, you can see the SQL SELECT command; you can type a new command there, if you wish.

- In the Data Sources window, either click the *Edit Data Source with Designer* button at the top of the window or right-click and select *Edit Data Source with Designer* from the context menu. Then follow the rest of the steps in the previous instructions to click the build button for the Fill command's CommandText property.

- Click on the *Query Builder* button in the TableAdapter Configuration Wizard.

Figure 3.22

Display the Query Builder from the DataSet Designer. Click on the TableAdapter's `Fill,GetData()` *command, select the CommandText property, and click on the build (ellipsis) button.*

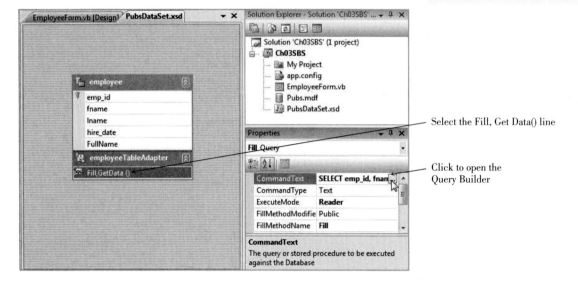

Select the Fill, Get Data() line

Click to open the Query Builder

Using the Query Builder

If you have done any development with Access, the Visual Studio Query Builder (Figure 3.23) will look familiar. You can add and remove tables, select the fields to include, and specify sort and selection criteria. The Query Builder creates the SQL statement to match the selection criteria that you enter. You also can type the SQL statement yourself and test the statement using the *Execute Query* button.

The Query Builder and the DataSet Designer are a part of what is referred to as the Microsoft Visual Database Tools.

Figure 3.23

Select fields and enter sort and filter criteria in the Query Builder, which builds the SQL statement to match the criteria that you enter.

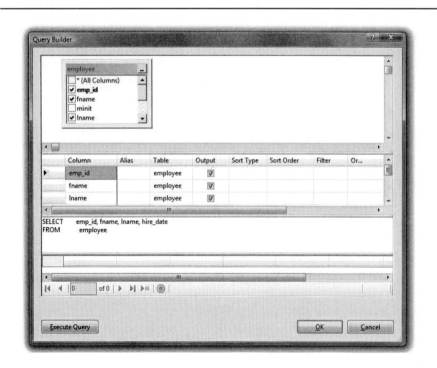

Sorting the Data for the ComboBox

To sort by last name, you would set the Sort Type to Ascending for the lname row in the list. When you press Enter, the query will be updated with an ORDER BY clause containing the field or fields that you selected.

```
SELECT  emp_id, fname, lname, hire_date
FROM    employee
ORDER BY lname
```

Note: When asked whether you want to update the query, select *Yes*.

Adding Expression Fields

Earlier in this chapter, you added a new expression in the DataSet Designer to create a concatenated field. You added a row to the table definition and set the Expression property. You also can create an expression in the SQL statement using the Query Builder.

Display the Query Builder and move to a new row below the last existing field. In the column labeled Column, type the expression "lname + ', ' + fname" (without the outer double quotes). The name *Expr1* will automatically appear in the Alias column. Change the Alias to something meaningful, such as FullName. Figure 3.24 shows the completed query with sample data produced by clicking the *Execute Query* button.

You also can use an alias to create calculated fields from numeric data.

You can use the new field that you create in the SQL statement on the form, either at design time in the Properties window or in code:

```
NameLabel.DataBindings.Add("text", PubsDataSet.employee, "FullName")
```

or

```
NameComboBox.DisplayMember = "FullName"
```

> **✓ TIP**
>
> **T**est your modified query in the Query Designer before running the program. ■

Figure 3.24

The Query Builder with a sort and an added expression. The sample data appear when you click the Execute Query button.

Eliminating Unnecessary SQL Queries

When you generate a TableAdapter, the Visual Studio designer automatically generates the SQL SELECT statement for retrieving data. The designer also generates SQL INSERT, DELETE, and UPDATE statements, which you will use in Chapter 5 when you write applications that update the database. For programs that only display data, such as those in this chapter, the extra statements serve no purpose and should be eliminated.

To eliminate the extra code for updates, display the DataSet in the designer and click on the TableAdapter name. Then you can either select *Configure* from the *Data* menu or right-click on the TableAdapter name and select *Configure* from the context menu. The TableAdapter Configuration Wizard opens, where you can see the SQL SELECT statement (Figure 3.25). Click on the *Advanced Options* button to display the dialog (Figure 3.26). By default, all of the options are initially selected. Deselect the option *Generate Insert, Update and Delete statements* and the other two options automatically become deselected and disabled. You will learn to use those options in Chapter 5.

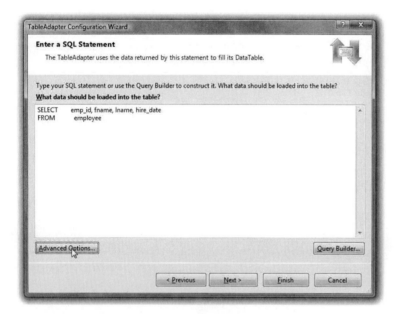

Figure 3.25

Display the TableAdapter Configuration Wizard from the DataSet Designer. Click on the Advanced Options button to display the options for additional SQL statements.

Figure 3.26

When the Advanced Options dialog first appears, all three check boxes are selected. Deselect the option to Generate Insert, Update and Delete statements and the other two options are deselected automatically.

Using a Stored Procedure

In this section, you will create a DataSet using a stored procedure. A SQL Server **stored procedure** (SPROC) is a block of SQL code that is stored with the database for use as needed. Stored procedures are more secure than the query code generated by default for a TableAdapter and often run faster. Hackers can sometimes penetrate applications that contain SQL queries by entering SQL code into an input field of a running application. This technique, called *SQL injection*, can allow a person to gain unintended access to a database. SQL injections are not possible using stored procedures, because the code is contained inside the SQL Server environment rather than the application code.

A stored procedure can usually run faster than a query in your program because the stored procedure is stored in compiled form. A query that is sent to the database as source must be compiled each time it is sent.

Creating a Stored Procedure in the VS IDE

You can create a SQL Server stored procedure directly inside the Visual Studio IDE by using the Server Explorer. The Server Explorer generally docks with the toolbox; you can display it by selecting *View / Server Explorer*.

You can view and add connections in the Server Explorer, in addition to the Data Sources window. The Server Explorer shows all connections that you have defined, with all of the available objects in each database. You cannot drag tables and fields from the Server Explorer to a form as you can from the Data Sources window. But to create a new stored procedure, you must use the Server Explorer.

You can expand each connection in the Server Explorer to display tables, views, and stored procedures. If you have installed any of Microsoft's sample databases, they all have stored procedures, which you can view, if you wish. The Pubs database already has some stored procedures (Figure 3.27); in the next section, you will add a new one.

To create a new stored procedure, right-click on the Stored Procedures folder for a database and select *Add New Stored Procedure*. A new procedure with the default name of StoredProcedure1 is created, with comments that help you to create the procedure. In the listing of a new procedure in the next section,

Figure 3.27

The Server Explorer shows database connections. You can expand each of the nodes to see tables, views, and stored procedures that are already stored in the database.

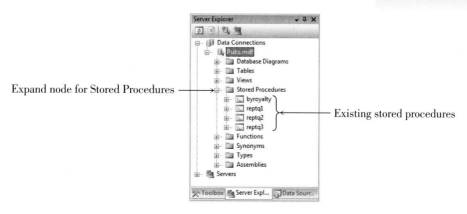

the comments follow C# format: /* begins a block of comments and */ ends the block. So in the empty procedure, the only lines that are not comments are

```
CREATE PROCEDURE
AS
RETURN
```

An Empty Stored Procedure

Here is a new empty stored procedure, which you will modify for your purposes.

```
CREATE PROCEDURE dbo.StoredProcedure1
  /*
  (
  @parameter1 int = 5,
  @parameter2 datatype OUTPUT
  )
  */
AS
  /* SET NOCOUNT ON */
  RETURN
```

Place your SQL statements between the AS and RETURN and name your procedure as you wish:

```
CREATE PROCEDURE GetEmployees
AS
  SELECT emp_id, fname, lname, hire_date
   FROM employee
   ORDER BY lname
  RETURN
```

Retrieving Data by Using a Stored Procedure

Adding a grid or details to a form from a stored procedure is almost the same as using a table. From the Data Sources window, select *Add a New Data Source* to display the Data Source Configuration Wizard. Follow the steps as you would for any connection but expand the Stored Procedures item under Database objects and check the procedure that you created. The name following the CREATE PROCEDURE clause appears on the list.

Assuming that you create a data source using a stored procedure called GetEmployees, the TableAdapter becomes GetEmployeesTableAdapter and the DataSet is PubsDataSet. The Fill method that is automatically generated in the Form_Load event handler would be

```
Me.GetEmployeesTableAdapter.Fill(Me.PubsDataSet.GetEmployees)
```

Feedback 3.3

1. What are two techniques for arranging database data in order by ZIP code?
2. List the steps to create an expression field that combines the City, State, and ZIP fields.

Multiple Tiers

Now that you have worked with a DataSet object, a TableAdapter, and SQL, it's time to separate the project into multiple tiers. When possible, you should separate the database access from the user interface. For a multitier application, we will create a data component as a separate tier. The data component will contain the DataSet and its TableAdapter, as well as methods to return the data to the presentation tier (Figure 3.28). When you have a well-constructed data tier, you can use the component in multiple projects with various user interfaces.

Until now you have used the VS visual designers to create the objects for database access. The visual designers automatically create all of the necessary code when you drag objects to a form. In this section, you will learn to declare and instantiate DataSet and TableAdapter objects and also to bind database objects to form controls in code.

You will find that most professional applications perform database access in code rather than use the visual designers. And when you create a separate class for database access, you must write code for binding the controls.

Creating a Data-Tier Component

To create a data-tier component, you will add a new class to a project and write code to create and fill a DataSet. You also will need at least one method to allow the form to retrieve the DataSet. In later chapters, you will add methods for updating the DataSet.

For a Windows application, you will begin a new application and add a new data source, using the Data Sources window. This step creates the schema classes for a DataSet and TableAdapter but does not create the actual DataSet or TableAdapter objects. (In earlier projects, the DataSet and TableAdapter objects were created when you dragged data to the form.)

After you have declared the DataSet as a data source, you can write code in your new class to declare, instantiate, fill, and return the DataSet. Take a look at the code before looking at the explanation in the section that follows.

Figure 3.28

Good applications generally separate the user interface from the data access.

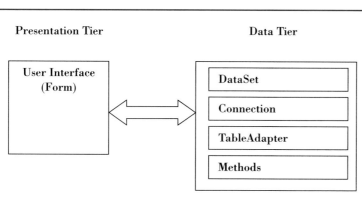

Presentation Tier   Data Tier

The Code

```
Public Class PubsEmployeeData

    ' Declare class-level variables.
    Private AnEmployeeTableAdapter _
      As PubsDataSetTableAdapters.employeeTableAdapter
```

```
    Private APubsDataSet As PubsDataSet

    Public Function GetEmployeeDataset() As PubsDataSet
        ' Fill and return the DataSet.

        Try
            ' Instantiate the TableAdapter and DataSet.
            AnEmployeeTableAdapter = _
                New PubsDataSetTableAdapters.employeeTableAdapter
            APubsDataSet = New PubsDataSet

            ' Fill the DataSet.
            AnEmployeeTableAdapter.Fill(APubsDataSet.employee)
            ' Return the DataSet.
            Return APubsDataSet
        Catch ex As Exception
            Throw ex
        End Try
    End Function

End Class
```

Notes about the Code

We chose to declare the TableAdapter and DataSet at the class level, even though they are used in only one procedure and could be declared as local. In later chapters, you will add more procedures to the data-tier class and will need to have the TableAdapter and DataSet objects available at the class level.

If the declarations for the DataSet and TableAdapter puzzle you, you might like to examine the code that was automatically generated by the DataSet Designer. If you select *Show All Files* in the Solution Explorer, you can see and open the PubsDataSet.Designer.vb file for the PubsDataSet.xsd file. The designer-generated file holds multiple classes for dealing with the DataSet, as well as a new namespace called *PubsDataSetTableAdapters* and a class called *employeeTableAdapter*. It is this class that you instantiate with the statements

```
Private AnEmployeeTableAdapter _
    As PubsDataSetTableAdapters.employeeTableAdapter

AnEmployeeTableAdapter = New PubsDataSetTableAdapters.employeeTableAdapter
```

The `Throw ex` statement will pass any exception back up to the calling procedure so that the exception can be handled from the form.

Coding the Form's Database Objects

In the form for a database application, you must write code to instantiate the data-tier component, retrieve the DataSet, and bind the form's controls. The code to instantiate the data-tier component is similar to the code you used to instantiate the business class in Chapter 2.

```
' Create an instance of the data-tier component.
Dim APubsEmployeeData As New PubsEmployeeData
' Retrieve the dataset from the data tier.
Dim APubsDataSet As PubsDataSet
APubsDataSet = APubsEmployeeData.GetEmployeeDataset()
```

Of course, you will include the above code in a `Try` / `Catch` block. You will see the exception handling in the complete code example later.

Binding Data Fields to Form Controls

Since the DataSet is created at run time, you cannot bind the form's controls at design time. But you can bind the fields from the DataSet to form controls after you have retrieved the DataSet.

The best way to bind form controls is to use the BindingSource object. You declare and instantiate a new BindingSource object in code and set its Data-Source and DataMember properties. You can then bind form controls to the BindingSource object.

```
' Set up the binding source.
Dim ABindingSource As New BindingSource
With ABindingSource
    .DataSource = APubsDataSet
    .DataMember = "employee"
    .Sort = "emp_id" ' Optionally sort the data.
End With
```

Note: It isn't necessary to sort the data using the BindingSource if your `SELECT` statement includes an `ORDER BY` clause.

Binding to a DataGridView

To bind a DataGridView to a DataSet that you instantiate in code, you can set the grid's DataSource to the BindingSource. After you set up the binding source, as shown in the preceding example, set the grid's DataSource property to the new BindingSource object.

```
' Bind the grid.
EmployeeDataGridView.DataSource = ABindingSource
```

You can use a handy technique to set the properties of the grid, such as selecting and ordering the columns and modifying the column headings. In the Form Designer, drag the grid from the Data Sources window, which sets up all of the components for data binding. Use the smart tag and Properties window to set up the grid columns as you want them. Then you can delete the visual components from the component tray and write code to fill the grid (or you can leave them there but just not use them, but bind to the data-tier DataSet in code).

One word of caution: If you delete the DataSet and BindingSource components, you won't be able to make modifications to the DataGridView columns in the designer.

Binding Table Data to a List Box or Combo Box

For a list box or combo box, you can set the control's DataSource to the Bind-ingSource object and set the DisplayMember to one of the table fields. Notice in the following code that you must specify the field name of an existing field in quotes.

```
' Bind a combo box.
With Emp_idComboBox
    .DataSource = ABindingSource
    .DisplayMember = "emp_id"
    .DataBindings.Add("text", ABindingSource, "emp_id", _
      False, DataSourceUpdateMode.Never)
End With
```

To bind labels, text boxes, the Text property of a combo box, and the date-time picker, you must use the **DataBindings.Add method** in code to bind to a field from a DataSet.

The DataBindings.Add Method—General Form

```
Object.DataBindings.Add("property", DataSource, "FieldName")
```

Overloaded format; to format the data field:

```
Object.DataBindings.Add("property", DataSource, "FieldName", True,
    DataSourceUpdateMode.Never, Nothing, "FormatString")
```

Note that the property and field name must be enclosed in quotes and the data source is not. Also, be aware that the property name must be lowercase; the field name is not case-sensitive.

Use the overloaded format if you need to format the data. You can use the same codes that you use in the `ToString` method for formatting, such as `"C"` for currency and `"d"` for a short date. The `True` argument specifies that formatting is enabled; the `DataSourceUpdateMode` argument specifies that each time a new value is assigned, either from a database field or user input, the formatting occurs. The `Nothing` argument specifies that if the field is empty, it should be allowed to have a value of Nothing. And the `FormatString` is the formatting code. See Help for a complete list of codes.

The DataBindings.Add Method—Example

```
LastNameTextBox.DataBindings.Add("text", ABindingSource, "lname")

HireDateTextBox.DataBindings.Add("text", EmployeeBindingSource, "hire_date",
    True, DataSourceUpdateMode.Never, Nothing, "d")
```

Here is the complete Form_Load event handler that instantiates the data tier, retrieves the DataSet, sets up the BindingSource, and binds to the form fields.

```
Private Sub EmployeeForm_Load(ByVal sender As Object, _
    ByVal e As System.EventArgs) Handles Me.Load
    ' Retrieve the data and bind the form's controls.

    Try
        ' Create an instance of the data-tier component.
        Dim EmployeeData As New PubsEmployeeData
```

```
        ' Retrieve the dataset from the data tier.
        Dim APubsDataSet As PubsDataSet
        APubsDataSet = EmployeeData.GetEmployeeDataset()

        ' Set up the binding source.
        Dim ABindingSource As New BindingSource
        With ABindingSource
            .DataSource = APubsDataSet
            .DataMember = "employee"
            .Sort = "emp_id"
        End With

        ' Fill the combo box.
        With Emp_idComboBox
            .DataSource = ABindingSource
            .DisplayMember = "emp_id"
            .DataBindings.Add("text", ABindingSource, "emp_id", _
                False, DataSourceUpdateMode.Never)
        End With

        ' Bind the other controls.
        FullNameTextBox.DataBindings.Add("text", _
            ABindingSource, "FullName")
        Hire_dateDateTimePicker.DataBindings.Add("text", _
            ABindingSource, "hire_date")
    Catch ex As Exception
        MessageBox.Show(ex.Message)
    End Try
End Sub
```

Binding Data from a Stored Procedure

The previous examples of data binding illustrated using fields from a table. If you are using a stored procedure, you must specify the name of the stored procedure in place of the table name. Here is the binding from the previous code example, but using a GetEmployeeData stored procedure instead of the employee table.

```
' Set up the binding source.
Dim ABindingSource As New BindingSource
With ABindingSource
    .DataSource = APubsDataSet
    .DataMember = "GetEmployeeData" ' Stored procedure name.
End With
```

Notice that the Sort property of the BindingSource is not set in this example because the GetEmployeeData stored procedure includes an ORDER BY clause that sorts the data.

Creating a Data Tier—Step-by-Step

The following step-by-step tutorial re-creates the Employee project using a presentation tier and a data tier.

Create a New Project

STEP 1: Begin a new Windows Application project. Name the project Ch03EmployeeTiers.

STEP 2: Name the form EmployeesForm and change the Text property to Employees.

Add a Data Source

STEP 1: From the Data Sources window, add a Pubs database data source. Include the emp_id, fname, lname, and hire_date fields from the employee table.

STEP 2: In the DataSet Designer, add a new column called FullName to the employee table using the expression "fname + ' ' + lname" (without the outer double quotes). Notice that the order is reversed from the earlier examples.

> *Trouble?* If you receive a message that the column could not be added, close and reopen the DataSet Designer and repeat the step, which should now work.

STEP 3: In the DataSet Designer, right-click on employeeTableAdapter and select *Configure*. In the TableAdapter Configuration Wizard, select *Advanced Options*.

STEP 4: In the *Advanced Options* dialog box, deselect the check box for generating the extra statements. All three check boxes should be deselected. Click *OK*. Click *Finish* in the TableAdapter Configuration Wizard.

STEP 5: In the DataSet Designer, modify the Caption property for each field to be a "user-friendly" string.

STEP 6: Save all.

Add a Class for the Data Tier

You need to add a new class for the data tier. Although you could use the Component class, which has a visual designer, for this example we will not need the visual designer.

STEP 1: From the *Project* menu, choose *Add Class*. (Alternate method: Right-click the project name in the Solution Explorer and select *Add / Class*.)

STEP 2: Name the new class PubsEmployeeData.vb.

Code the Component

STEP 1: Display the code for your new class. Notice that the design template generated the lines

```
Public Class PubsEmployeeData

End Class
```

STEP 2: Code the class-level variables. Although these variables could be coded as local in this program, in future programs you will need class-level variables for the DataSet and TableAdapter.

```
' Declare class-level variables.
Private AnEmployeeTableAdapter _
   As PubsDataSetTableAdapters.employeeTableAdapter
Private APubsDataSet As PubsDataSet
```

STEP 3: Write the `GetEmployeeDataset` method in the data-tier class. Notice that this method returns a DataSet object.

```
Public Function GetEmployeeDataset() As PubsDataSet
    ' Fill and return the DataSet.

    Try
        ' Instantiate the TableAdapter and DataSet.
        AnEmployeeTableAdapter = _
            New PubsDataSetTableAdapters.employeeTableAdapter
        APubsDataSet = New PubsDataSet

        ' Fill the DataSet.
        AnEmployeeTableAdapter.Fill(APubsDataSet.employee)
        ' Return the DataSet.
        Return APubsDataSet
    Catch ex As Exception
        Throw ex
    End Try
End Function
```

STEP 4: Write comments at the top of the class.
STEP 5: Save all.

Add Controls to the Form

Although you can create the user interface by adding individual controls from the toolbox, we are going to take a shortcut. We will use the drag-and-drop feature from the Data Sources window and then delete the extra components.

STEP 1: Display the form in the designer.
STEP 2: In the Data Sources window, set the employee table to *Details*.
STEP 3: Change the emp_id field to a ComboBox.
STEP 4: Drag the table to the form.
STEP 5: Delete all of the objects in the component tray. We cannot use these components because we will get the data from the data tier.
STEP 6: Display the form's code and delete the automatically generated code. All error messages should disappear.
STEP 7: Delete the text boxes and identifying labels for the first name and last name fields. (Keep the controls for Employee ID, Full Name, and Hire Date.)
STEP 8: Rearrange the controls and change the labels, if necessary, to Employee ID, Name, and Hire Date. Figure 3.29 shows the form at this point.

Figure 3.29

Rearrange the controls for the step-by-step exercise.

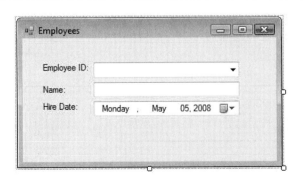

Code the Form

In the form, you must write code to retrieve the DataSet and bind to the data fields. You cannot do this at design time since the DataSet is declared in the data-tier component. You must declare an instance of the DataTier component and a DataSet object. Then you can call the GetEmployeeDataset method to retrieve the DataSet from the data tier and bind the data to a BindingSource object.

STEP 1: Switch to the form's code and delete all automatically generated procedures.

STEP 2: Write the code for the form's Load event handler.

```vb
Private Sub EmployeeForm_Load(ByVal sender As Object, _
  ByVal e As System.EventArgs) Handles Me.Load
    ' Retrieve the data and bind the form's controls.

    Try
        ' Create an instance of the data-tier component.
        Dim EmployeeData As New PubsEmployeeData
        ' Retrieve the dataset from the data tier.
        Dim APubsDataSet As PubsDataSet
        APubsDataSet = EmployeeData.GetEmployeeDataset()

        ' Set up the binding source.
        Dim ABindingSource As New BindingSource
        With ABindingSource
            .DataSource = APubsDataSet
            .DataMember = "employee"
            .Sort = "emp_id"
        End With

        ' Fill the combo box.
        With Emp_idComboBox
            .DataSource = ABindingSource
            .DisplayMember = "emp_id"
            .DataBindings.Add("text", ABindingSource, "emp_id", _
                False, DataSourceUpdateMode.Never)
        End With

        ' Bind the other controls.
        FullNameTextBox.DataBindings.Add("text", _
            ABindingSource, "FullName")
        Hire_dateDateTimePicker.DataBindings.Add("text", _
            ABindingSource, "hire_date")
    Catch ex As Exception
        MessageBox.Show(ex.Message)
    End Try
End Sub
```

STEP 3: Write remarks at the top of the form class.

Test the Project

STEP 1: Test the project. The fields should fill with data, just as they did when the data components were in the form. Select various records using the combo box.

► **Feedback 3.4**

1. Where do you place the binding source and TableAdapter for a multi-tier project?
2. What return type is necessary for a function in the class that fills a DataSet from a TableAdapter?
3. Write the code to bind a first name label to a DataSet called Customers-DataSet. The form uses CustomersBindingSource. Display the First-Name field from the Customer table.

Your Hands-On Programming Example

Create a multiple-tier project to obtain data from the employee table in the Pubs database using a stored procedure. Use an ORDER BY clause in the stored procedure to sort the data in order by last name. Display the full employee names (last name, first name, and middle initial) in alphabetic order in a combo box. Do not display the first and last name fields other than in the combo box. Show the remaining fields in text boxes for the selected record, with meaningful identifying labels. Do not include a navigation toolbar. Include a *File / Exit* menu item to terminate the program.

Planning the Project

Sketch a form (Figure 3.30) that your users sign off as meeting their needs.

Figure 3.30

A planning sketch for the hands-on programming example.

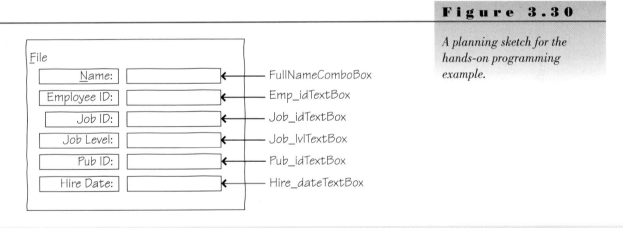

Plan the Objects, Properties, and Methods Plan the two tiers. Determine the objects and property settings for the form and its controls and for the data-tier component. Figure 3.31 shows a diagram of the components in the two tiers.

Presentation Tier

Object	Property	Setting
EmployeeForm	Name	EmployeeForm
	Text	Employees
FullNameComboBox	Name	FullNameComboBox
Text boxes for all database fields (including Hire Date)		

Event Handlers/Methods	Actions—Pseudocode
ExitToolStripMenuItem_Click	Exit the project.
Form_Load	Instantiate the data tier. Retrieve the DataSet. Bind the controls. Format the date in its binding.

Presentation Tier   Data Tier

Figure 3.31

A diagram of the components in each tier for the hands-on programming example.

Data Tier

Methods	Actions—Pseudocode
GetEmployeeData	Instantiate the DataSet and TableAdapter. Fill the DataSet. Return the DataSet.

Write the Project Following the sketch in Figure 3.30, create the form. Figure 3.32 shows the completed form.

- Add a copy of Pubs.mdf to your project and set a connection to the file using the Server Explorer. Then create a stored procedure to retrieve and sort the data and create the new concatenated FullName field.

- Using the Data Sources window, set up the data source and DataSet.

- Create the data-tier component, writing the method according to the pseudocode.

- Set up the user interface according to the plans.

- Write the code for the form. Working from the pseudocode, write each event handler.

- When you complete the code, test the operation several times. Compare the screen output to the data tables to make sure that you are displaying the correct information.

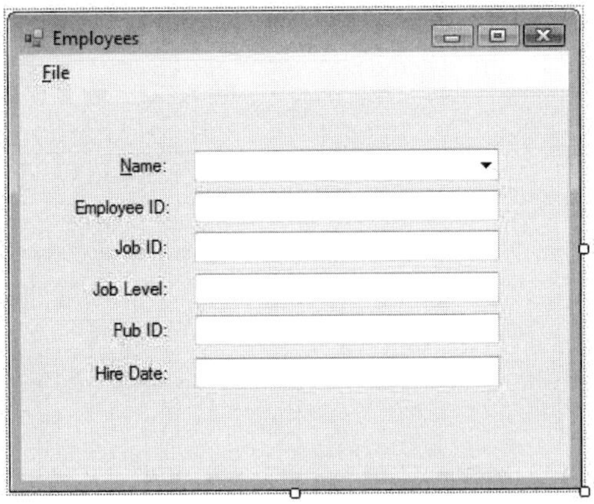

Figure 3.32

The completed form for the hands-on programming example.

The Project Coding Solution

The Form

```vb
'Project:       Ch03HandsOn
'Programmer:    Bradley/Millspaugh
'Date:          June 2009
'Class:         EmployeeForm
'Description:   Presentation tier to display the employee information.

Public Class EmployeeForm

    Private Sub EmployeeForm_Load(ByVal sender As System.Object, _
        ByVal e As System.EventArgs) Handles MyBase.Load
        ' Retrieve data from data tier and bind controls.

        Try
            Dim EmployeeData As New EmployeeDataTier
            Dim EmployeeDataSet As PubsDataSet

            EmployeeDataSet = EmployeeData.GetEmployeeData()

            ' Set up the BindingSouce.
            Dim ABindingSource As New BindingSource
            With ABindingSource
                .DataSource = EmployeeDataSet
                .DataMember = "getEmployees"
            End With

            ' Bind the controls.
            With FullNameComboBox
                .DataSource = ABindingSource
                .DisplayMember = "fullname"
                .DataBindings.Add("text", ABindingSource, "FullName", _
                    False, DataSourceUpdateMode.Never)
            End With
            Emp_idTextBox.DataBindings.Add("text", _
                ABindingSource, "emp_id")
            Job_idTextBox.DataBindings.Add("text", _
                ABindingSource, "job_id")
            Job_lvlTextBox.DataBindings.Add("text", _
                ABindingSource, "job_lvl")
```

```vb
            Pub_idTextBox.DataBindings.Add("text", _
                ABindingSource, "pub_id")
            Hire_dateTextBox.DataBindings.Add("text", _
                ABindingSource, "hire_date", True, _
                DataSourceUpdateMode.OnValidation, Nothing, "d")
        Catch ex As Exception
            MessageBox.Show(ex.Message)
        End Try
    End Sub

    Private Sub ExitToolStripMenuItem_Click(ByVal sender As System.Object, _
        ByVal e As System.EventArgs) Handles ExitToolStripMenuItem.Click
            ' End the program.

        Me.Close()
    End Sub
End Class
```

The Data-Tier Component

```vb
'Project:       Ch03HandsOn
'Programmer:    Bradley/Millspaugh
'Date:          June 2009
'Class:         EmployeeDataTier
'Description:   The data-tier component for the Ch03HandsOn program.
'               Includes the code for the database access.

Public Class EmployeeDataTier

    ' Class-level declarations.
    Private EmployeeDataSet As PubsDataSet
    Private EmployeeTableAdapter As PubsDataSetTableAdapters.getEmployeesTableAdapter

    Public Function GetEmployeeData() As PubsDataSet
        ' Fill and return the DataSet.

        EmployeeDataSet = New PubsDataSet
        EmployeeTableAdapter = New PubsDataSetTableAdapters.getEmployeesTableAdapter

        EmployeeTableAdapter.Fill(EmployeeDataSet.getEmployees)
        Return EmployeeDataSet
    End Function
End Class
```

The Stored Procedure

```sql
CREATE PROCEDURE getEmployees
    /*
    Procedure to retrieve and sort the Employee table.
    */
AS
    Select *, lname+', '+fname+' '+minit as FullName
    from Employee
    order by lname
    RETURN
```

Summary

1. Data are accessible from many sources including databases, files, e-mail, and spreadsheets.
2. ADO.NET is the object model for referencing data in a VB application program.
3. Database tables contain rows (records) and columns (fields).
4. A primary key uniquely identifies a record. When a primary key is included in a second table for linking purposes, it is called a foreign key in the second table.
5. A typed DataSet can contain multiple tables, as well as relationships and constraints. The data in a DataSet are a temporary copy in memory, which are disconnected from the file from which they come.
6. A DataSet object has a DataTable collection, which can hold multiple DataTable objects. Each DataTable has a DataRow collection, a DataColumn collection, and a Constraints collection. The DataSet also can contain DataRelation objects.
7. A TableAdapter object connects to the database and handles SQL queries.
8. The objects used for database handling include the BindingSource, TableAdapter, and DataSet components.
9. XML is an industrywide standard for storing and transferring data in a text-based format with tags that identify the data fields. An XML file also may have a schema file that defines field names, data types, and constraints.
10. The Data Sources window provides the ability to add data sources to a project and drag tables to a form to create data-bound controls.
11. SQL Server 2008 Express Edition, which allows programming against SQL Server databases, is included with Visual Studio and is considered the "native" database format for a single-user database in VB.
12. By dragging a table name from the Data Sources window to the form, you can automatically display data in a DataGridView control. Set the HeaderText property of each column to modify the column headings.
13. The DataSet Designer is a visual tool for working with a DataSet. You can add fields, tables, and relationships in the DataSet Designer, as well as preview the data.
14. In the Data Sources window, you can select the control to use for each database field and whether to display the table in a grid or details view.
15. In the DataSet Designer, you can set the caption for each field in the DataSet, which is used for the identifying labels for detail controls. You also can add a field with an expression, which can be concatenated strings or calculated values.
16. A common way to allow the user to access data is to display a list box with a field for the user to select. You must set the list's DataSource and DisplayMember properties to automatically fill the list.

17. You can sort database data by using the Sort method of the TableAdapter.

18. You also can sort data by modifying the SQL SELECT statement generated by the TableAdapter to include an ORDERBY clause. The Query Builder can assist you in creating and modifying SQL queries.

19. Fields may be combined or calculated as expressions by using an Alias field in the SQL SELECT statement of the TableAdapter.

20. The TableAdapter automatically creates SQL statements for updating the data; you can choose to not create those extra statements in the TableAdapter Configuration Wizard.

21. Stored procedures provide a more secure method for accessing data than SQL queries in your application. You can create stored procedures from within the VS IDE.

22. OOP principles suggest that separating data access from the user interface is the preferred solution. You can create a separate data tier by adding a new class to the project. In the new class, write code to declare and instantiate the DataSet and TableAdapter and fill the DataSet. The DataSet can be passed to the user interface (presentation tier) as needed. The presentation tier must explicitly bind the fields from the data-tier component.

23. You must explicitly bind form controls to the data fields from the data tier. For a ComboBox, set the DataSource and DisplayMember properties; for TextBoxes and DateTimePickers, use the DataBindings.Add method of each control.

Key Terms

ActiveX Data Objects
  (ADO) .NET   *106*
BindingSource object   *109*
column   *107*
data source   *107*
Data Sources window   *110*
data table   *107*
DataBindings.Add method   *136*
DataSet Designer   *115*
DataSet object   *107*
DataSource property   *123*
DisplayMember property   *123*
field   *107*
flexibility   106

foreign key   *108*
primary key field   *107*
Query Builder   *127*
record   *107*
row   *107*
scalability   *106*
SQL Server 2008 Express
  Edition   *111*
stored procedure   *131*
Structured Query
  Language (SQL)   *127*
table   *107*
TableAdapter   *108*
XML   *109*

Review Questions

1. What is referred to by the following acronyms?
   a. ADO.NET
   b. XML
   c. SQL
2. Define the following terms: table, row, record, column, and field.
3. What is a primary key field? Why must it be unique? What is a foreign key?
4. What is SQL Server Express Edition? How is it used?
5. List and describe the steps to set up an application for accessing data and displaying the data in a grid.
6. How can you sort database data for a list box?
7. Describe how to combine the city, state, and ZIP code fields into a single field. Where would this step appear?
8. Explain how to add a data tier to a project.
9. What types of items should be added to the data tier?

Programming Exercises

For each of these exercises, create a multitier application if so specified by your instructor.

3.1   Use a grid control to display customer information from the Customers table of the Northwind database. Include the CustomerID, Company-Name, ContactName, Region, Phone, and Fax fields.

3.2   Display information from the Employees table in the Northwind database. Populate a drop-down list with the concatenated first and last names sorted in alphabetic order by last name. When a name is selected from the list, display the title, region, and extension on the form.

3.3   Create a project that displays information from the Products table in the Northwind database. Fill a drop-down list with the product names. When the user selects a product, display these fields: ProductID, UnitPrice, and UnitsInStock.

3.4   Display all of the fields in the Publishers table in the Pubs database. You may display all of the fields in a grid or use a list box for pub_name in alphabetic order and display the rest of the fields in text boxes or labels.

3.5   Create a stored procedure that returns the CompanyName, Address, City, and PostalCode from the Customers table in the Northwind database. Use the stored procedure to display the information on a form.

Case Studies

Claytor's Cottages

Modify your Claytor's Cottages case study project to add the guest information on the Guest form. Use a data tier for passing the dataset back to a Binding-Source object on the presentation tier. Display the guest names in a combo box sorted in alphabetic order.

When the user selects a guest name, display the fields from the Guest table in text boxes with the ReadOnly property set to *true*. You may use a DateTimePicker for the date field, if you wish.

Christian's Car Rentals

Modify your Christian's Car Rentals project to implement the *Edit / Customers* menu item. Use a data tier for passing the dataset back to a BindingSource object on the presentation tier. Display the customer names in a combo box sorted in alphabetic order on the Customer form. When the user selects a name, display the fields from the Customer table in text boxes with the ReadOnly property set to *true*. You may use a DateTimePicker for the date field, if you wish.

4

Windows Database Using Related Tables

at the completion of this chapter, you will be able to . . .

1. Explain the types of table relationships.

2. Display master/detail records.

3. Display a field from a second table using a lookup.

4. Create a search using a parameterized query and write a filter to retrieve specific data.

5. Assign data values to unbound controls.

6. Retrieve and display the parent row for a selected child row.

7. Retrieve and display an array of child rows for a selected parent row.

8. Create an application that displays data from a many-to-many relationship.

9. Select the correct locations for handling and formatting data in a multitier application.

Now that you know some basics about data access, it's time to consider multiple tables and/or multiple queries in a DataSet. This chapter examines techniques for establishing relationships among tables and extracting data from the tables.

Data Relationships

In relational databases, the data items are generally stored in multiple related tables. The primary table is called the **parent** or **master table** and the second table is the **child** or **detail table**. The relationship between two tables may be one-to-one (1:1), one-to-many (1:M), or many-to-many (M:N). Each table usually has a field or fields, called the primary key, that uniquely identify each record. When the primary key of one table is included as a field in a related table to link the two tables, that field is called a *foreign key*. The foreign key is common to both tables.

One-to-Many Relationships

The most common type of relationship is **one-to-many**: one record in the parent table relates to one or more records in the child table. Examples include a customer with multiple orders, a department with multiple employees, or a student with multiple courses. In a one-to-many relationship, a row in the parent table can have many matching rows in the child table, but a row in the child table has only one matching record in the parent.

Figure 4.1 shows a database diagram of a 1:M relationship, using the stores and sales tables of the Pubs database. Figure 4.2 shows some sample data from the two tables. You can see that one store can have many sales, but each sale has only one store.

Many-to-Many Relationships

Another possible relationship is **many-to-many**. An example in the Pubs database is titles and authors. One author can write many books and one book can have many authors. Most database management systems, including SQL Server and Access, cannot directly handle many-to-many relationships. Instead, a third table is needed to join the two tables. In the third table, called a *junction table*, the primary key consists of the foreign keys from both tables. In Pubs, the junction table is called titleauthors and contains title_id and au_id columns.

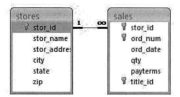

Figure 4.1

A database diagram of a 1:M relationship.

Figure 4.2

A 1:M relationship exists between the stores and sales tables. One store may have many sales.

stores					
stor_id	**stor_name**	**stor_address**	**city**	**state**	**zip**
6380	Eric the Read Books	788 Catamaugus Ave.	Seattle	WA	98056
7066	Barnum's	567 Pasadena Ave.	Tustin	CA	92789
7067	News & Brews	577 First St.	Los Gatos	CA	96745
7131	Doc-U-Mat:Quality Laundry	24-A Avogadro Way	Remulade	WA	98014
7896	Fricative Bookshop	89 Madison St.	Fremont	CA	90019
8042	Bookbeat	679 Carson St.	Portland	OR	89076

sales					
stor_id	**ord_num**	**ord_date**	**qty**	**payterms**	**title_id**
6380	6871	9/14/1994	5	Net 60	BU1032
6380	722a	9/13/1994	3	Net 60	PS2091
7066	A2976	5/24/1993	50	Net 30	PC8888
7066	QA7442.3	9/13/1994	75	ON invoice	PS2091
7067	D4482	9/14/1994	10	Net 60	PS2091
7067	P2121	6/15/1992	40	Net 30	TC3218
7067	P2121	6/15/1992	20	Net 30	TC4203
7067	P2121	6/15/1992	20	Net 30	TC7777

Figure 4.3 shows the database diagram of a many-to-many relationship and Figure 4.4 shows some sample data from the three related tables. Verify from the figures that one author can have more than one book and one book can have more than one author. Notice that book BU1111 has two authors and that Stearns MacFeather wrote two books.

One-to-One Relationships

A **one-to-one relationship** is the least common. This type of relationship has one record in the parent matching one record in the child table. Usually the two tables can be combined but may be kept separate for security reasons, or because the child table contains short-term information, or the data in the child table are more volatile and updates are more efficient with the separation. In the case of the publishers and pubs_info tables, the pubs_info table holds graphics that could complicate and slow down access to the publishers table. Figure 4.5 shows the database diagram of a 1:1 relationship.

Figure 4.3

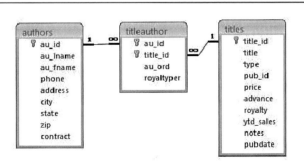

A database diagram of an M:N relationship. The diagram was created in Access.

Figure 4.4

An M:N relationship. The titleauthor table joins the titles and authors tables.

titles

title_id	title	type
BU1111	Cooking with Computers: Surreptitious Balance Sheets	business
PS1372	Computer Phobic AND Non-Phobic Individuals: Behavior Variations	psychology
TC7777	Sushi, Anyone?	trad_cook

titleauthor

au_id	title_id	au_ord
267-41-2394	BU1111	2
267-41-2394	TC7777	2
472-27-2349	TC7777	3
672-71-3249	TC7777	1
724-80-9391	BU1111	1
724-80-9391	PS1372	2
756-30-7391	PS1372	1

authors

au_id	au_iname	au_fname	phone
267-41-2394	O'Leary	Michael	408 286-2428
472-27-2349	Gringlesby	Burt	707 938-6445
672-71-3249	Yokomoto	Akiko	415 935-4228
724-80-9391	MacFeather	Stearns	415 354-7128
756-30-7391	Karsen	Livia	415 534-9219

Figure 4.5

A database diagram of a 1:1 relationship.

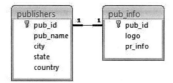

Constraints

Relationships also may require the use of constraints. A **unique constraint** specifies that no duplicate entries are allowed in a column. **Foreign-key constraints** ensure that parent and child tables remain synchronized when records are deleted or changed. As an example, in the Pubs database, if an author's ID is changed, the ID must be changed for all books written by that author. This concept, called *referential integrity*, can be enforced by the database management system by setting foreign-key constraints.

Feedback 4.1

1. Give one example each of an appropriate situation to use 1:1, 1:M, and M:N relationships. Do not use the examples already given in the text.

Use this diagram from the Northwind database to answer the following questions:

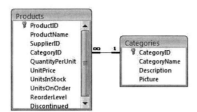

2. In this 1:M relationship, which table is the one and which is the many? Which field is used as the primary key and which is the foreign key in the relationship?
3. Which table is the parent and which is the child?

Related Tables

As you know, a DataSet can hold multiple tables and their relationships. The next section shows you how to set up the master/details display that shows information from two tables. The master table will display information in individual controls and the details will be shown in a grid.

Creating a DataSet with More Than One Table

One of the big advantages of the DataSet object in ADO.NET is that it can hold more than one table and the relationships between the tables. Before ADO. NET and DataSets, you had to use a SQL JOIN statement to join multiple tables, which produces one row in the result set for every matching record; the columns in the parent table are repeated for every matching record in the child table. Using a DataSet, each record appears only once and the data can be displayed hierarchically. To generate a DataSet with multiple tables, check the boxes for both tables in the Data Source Configuration Wizard (Figure 4.6).

Displaying Master/Detail Records—Step-by-Step

The following step-by-step exercise creates a DataSet that holds the stores and sales tables. The information from the master or parent record is displayed in individual controls. The child or detail information from the sales table displays in a grid. Figure 4.7 shows the completed form.

Begin a New Project
STEP 1: Begin a new Windows Application project called Ch04DataGridView.
STEP 2: Rename the form to *StoreSaleForm* and set its Text property to *Store Sales*.

Create the Data Source and View the Relationship
STEP 1: Add a new data source connected to the Pubs database; select both the stores and sales tables. (Refer to Figure 4.6.) Complete the wizard.

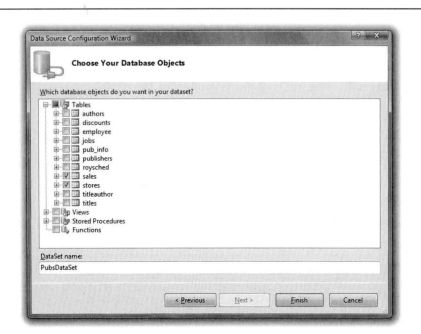

Figure 4.6

To generate a DataSet with multiple tables, check the boxes for both tables in the Data Source Configuration Wizard.

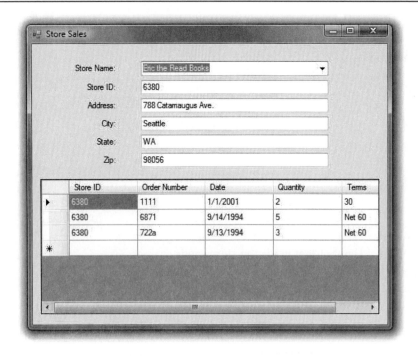

Figure 4.7

The completed step-by-step exercise with master/detail records.

STEP 2: Double-click on PubsDataSet.xsd in the Solution Explorer to open the DataSet Designer.

STEP 3: Right-click on the line connecting the two tables (Figure 4.8), which represents the already-established relationship from the database.

STEP 4: Select *Edit Relation* from the context menu to view the relationship (Figure 4.9). After you have examined the relationship, click *OK*.

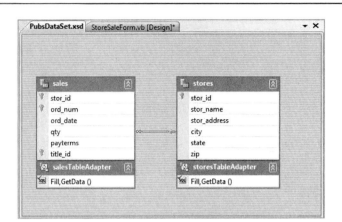

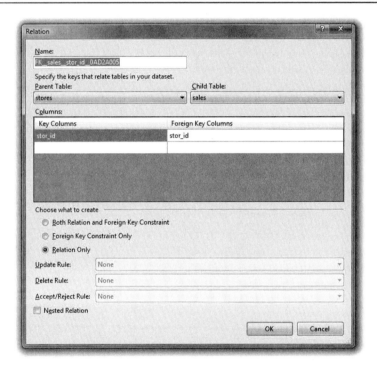

STEP 5: In the DataSet Designer, right-click the storesTableAdapter and select *Configure*. Click the *Advanced Options* button and deselect the check box to *Generate Insert, Update and Delete statements*. This application only displays data and does not require the updating commands. Click *OK* and *Finish*.

STEP 6: Repeat Step 5 for the salesTableAdapter and close the DataSet Designer.

Set Up the Form

STEP 1: In the Data Sources window, set the stores table to display as *Details* and set the store name field to a combo box.

STEP 2: Drag the stores table to the form, rearrange the controls, edit the identifying labels, and reset the tab order. (Refer to Figure 4.7.)

TIP

If the drop-down arrows do not appear in the Data Sources window, make sure that you have a form displaying in the designer. ■

STEP 3: Using the smart tag on the combo box, select *Use Databound Items*, set the DataSource property to StoresBindingSource, and set the DisplayMember to stor_name.

    Note: If you prefer to use the Properties window instead of the smart tag, scroll to the top of the properties and expand the DataBindings property to find these properties.

STEP 4: In the Properties window for the combo box, expand the DataBindings property and select *(Advanced)*. Change the *Data Source Update Mode* to *Never*.

STEP 5: Also in the Properties window for the combo box, set the CausesValidation property to False. If CausesValidation is set to True (the default setting) the validation prevents the form from closing.

STEP 6: Delete the navigation bar; we will use the combo box for selecting records.

STEP 7: Expand the stores table in the Data Sources window and select the last item, which is an expandable sales table (the related table). Drag the DataGridView to the form for the sales table. Notice that additional BindingSource and TableAdapter objects are added to the component tray for the sales table.

Examine the Code

STEP 1: Display the form's code. If a procedure for the BindingNavigator appears, delete it.

STEP 2: The only code required is to fill the DataSet. There is a `Fill` method for each TableAdapter, naming the same DataSet. These `Fill` methods retrieve the data for both tables into the single DataSet. You can remove the `TODO` comments to clean up the code.

```
Private Sub StoreSaleForm_Load(ByVal sender As System.Object, _
    ByVal e As System.EventArgs) Handles MyBase.Load
    ' Fill the DataSet.

    Me.SalesTableAdapter.Fill(Me.PubsDataSet.sales)
    Me.StoresTableAdapter.Fill(Me.PubsDataSet.stores)
End Sub
```

Run the Program

STEP 1: Run the program. The store information (the parent row) should show in the individual controls and the sales for that store (the child rows) should display in the grid.

STEP 2: Select another store from the drop-down list and the sales for that store appear in the grid.

STEP 3: Stop program execution

Clean Up the Grid

In these optional steps, you will make the grid look more professional.

STEP 1: Select the grid and click on the Columns Collection in the Properties window. Click on the build button to display the *Edit Columns* dialog box.

    Alternate technique: Display the grid's smart tag and select *Edit Columns*.

STEP 2: Select the title_id column on the left of the dialog box and click the *Remove* button.

STEP 3: Change the HeaderText property for each column to a meaningful name. Click *OK* when finished.

STEP 4: Resize the grid on the form for the new layout.

STEP 5: Run the program again. Look over the layout and make any more changes that you think will improve the look.

Viewing or Setting a Relationship

A **DataRelation object** describes the relationship between the tables. You can view or create a relationship using the DataSet Designer. Open the Designer (.xsd) file for the DataSet. Right-click on the line connecting two tables and select *Edit Relation*, which displays the default name of the relationship that links the two tables. Remember that the parent is always the "one side" of the one-to-many relationship.

If you open the DataSet Designer and find that a relationship does not already exist, you can add one. You can either right-click on the designer and select *Add / Relation* or drag a Relation object from the toolbox. Either action opens the *Relation* dialog box, where you can set the fields to relate and name the relation.

Specifying the Parent, Child, and Foreign Key

When you add a relationship to a DataSet's schema, it's important to get the parent/child relationship right. No matter how you think of the parent/child or master/detail relationship of the data you are working with, you must determine which table is the "one side" and which is the "many side" in a one-to-many relationship. The "one side" should always be the parent and the "many side" should always be the child.

Creating a Table Lookup—Step-by-Step

Sometimes a field in a table holds a code that is an ID number or a foreign key to another table. You would prefer to display the value from the second table instead of the code. For example, if the table has a publisher ID field, you may prefer to display the publisher name, or in the sales table that has a store ID field, you may want to display the store name. You can accomplish this **lookup** operation very easily using the visual database tools and ADO.NET.

Begin a New Project

STEP 1: Begin a new Windows Application project called Ch04TableLookup.

STEP 2: Rename the form to *SalesForm* and set its Text property to *Sales*.

Create the Data Source

STEP 1: Add a new data source connected to the Pubs database. Select both the stores and sales tables.

STEP 2: Open the DataSet Designer and configure the two TableAdapters to not generate `Insert`, `Update`, and `Delete` statements.

STEP 3: In the DataSet Designer, set the Caption property for each field in the sales table to a value that will make a good identifying label on a form. You can close the DataSet Designer when you are finished with this step.

Set Up the Form Controls

STEP 1: In the Data Sources window, change the sales table to Details and set the stor_id field to a combo box.

STEP 2: Drag the sales table to the form. Notice that the component tray now holds a DataSet, SalesTableAdapter, SalesBindingSource, SalesBindingNavigator, and TableAdapterManager.

STEP 3: Drag the stores node from the Data Sources window and drop it on top of the stor_id combo box. This will set up the combo box bindings so that the store name from the stores table displays, instead of the stor_id. Two new components are added to the component tray: StoresTableAdapter and StoresBindingSource.

STEP 4: Change the DropDownStyle property of the combo box to Simple and resize the box, if necessary, to make it match the text boxes. This step removes the drop-down arrow from the combo box to eliminate the possibility of the user navigating from the store name.

STEP 5: Run the program. Using the navigation bar, step through the sales records. The store names should display for each sale. Stop program execution.

What Happened?

It's time to examine what happened behind the scenes. When you dropped the stores table on top of the combo box, the combo box properties were modified automatically. The DataSource property is set to the BindingSource of the table that contains the value to display (StoreBindingSource to display the store name). The DisplayMember is set to the column name, stor_name, and the ValueMember property is the primary key from the original table.

Although the bindings for the combo box changed, the bindings for the rest of the form's controls are unchanged. You can verify that by expanding the DataBindings property from another control; the binding is still set to the SalesBindingSource.

The properties of the combo box are set according to the following table:

Property	Setting	Purpose	Example
DataSource	BindingSource of the related table.	Determines the table from which to select the data.	StoresBindingSource
DisplayMember	Field name for the value from the related table.	The field value that you want to display.	stor_name
ValueMember	The primary key from the original table.	The link to connect the code in the primary table with the key in the secondary table.	stor_id

Look Up a Second Field

Notice that the sales data still hold a code for the title. The sales table holds a title_id field, and the database has a titles table that has a title_id primary key and title field. You can use most of the same steps that you used above to display the full title for each sale. Figure 4.10 shows the completed exercise; the steps to accomplish the task appear in the following step-by-step exercise.

Figure 4.10

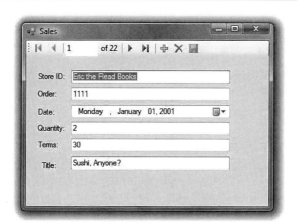

STEP 1: In the Data Sources window, click the *Configure DataSet with Wizard* button.

STEP 2: Expand the Tables node and the titles table. Select the title_id and title fields and click *Finish*.

STEP 3: In the Form Designer, delete the text box and label for title_id. In the Data Sources window, for the sales table, change the control type for title_id to a combo box and drag only that field to the form. Fix the spacing of the controls and change the identifying label to "Title".

STEP 4: Drag the titles table from the Data Sources window and drop it on top of the title_id combo box. This should set the bindings for the combo box.

STEP 5: Change the DropDownStyle property of the combo box to Simple and resize the box to match the text boxes. This step removes the drop-down arrow from the combo box to eliminate the possibility of the user navigating from the title.

STEP 6: Test it. Does it work?

Feedback 4.2

1. What `Fill` method statements are created for a relationship for Customers and Orders? Assume that the project contains two TableAdapters called CustomersTableAdapter and OrdersTableAdapter as well as a DataSet called NorthwindDataSet.
2. How can you view the relationship between two tables?
3. Describe the necessary steps to display the job description from the jobs table rather than the job id when displaying the employee table.

Queries and Filters

If you want to retrieve the records that match a specific value, you can use a parameterized query or a filter. A parameterized query creates a new DataSet; a filter selects records from an existing DataSet. When you already have the complete DataSet, the best choice is to use a filter, rather than return to the original data source and create a new DataSet.

You will choose a filter or a parameterized query depending on the needs of the specific application. To use a filter, you select records from an existing DataSet. For a parameterized query, you send a new request (query) to the database. You may have a huge database and do not want the entire database loaded in memory. On the other hand, your needs may require you to limit the number of requests to the database, therefore limiting the number of queries. You need to be able to write an application either way, depending on the situation.

Using a Parameterized Query

A **parameterized query** is a SQL statement that retrieves selected record(s) from the database based on a value that the user enters at run time. The fact that the user supplies the value, called the *parameter*, is the basis for the term *parameterized query*.

You have seen that a TableAdapter property holds the query for selecting a DataSet's data. Actually, a TableAdapter can hold multiple queries, so we can add queries for various purposes. In the step-by-step exercise in this section, you will create an application that allows the user to enter a job_id. You will then execute a parameterized query that selects only the records that match that job_id from the database and creates a new DataSet from the result.

Selecting Specific Records

When you want your DataSet to contain only selected record(s), you can modify the SQL SELECT statement used by the TableAdapter. Use a WHERE clause in a SQL query to specify which records to select, called the ***criteria***.

Here are some example SELECT statements with WHERE clauses:

```
SELECT Title, Author, ISBN FROM Books
    WHERE Title = 'Romeo and Juliette'

SELECT Name, AmountDue FROM OverdueAccounts
    WHERE AmountDue > 100

SELECT emp_id, lname, fname FROM employee
    WHERE lname = 'Jones'
```

However, you usually don't know until run time the value that you want to include in the WHERE clause. In that case, you can use a wildcard in place of the actual value and supply the value as a parameter in code:

```
SELECT emp_id, lname, fname FROM employee
    WHERE lname = @lname
```

You can type the SQL SELECT statements yourself, or use the Query Builder, which generates the correct SQL when you enter a value in the Filter column. The exercise that follows uses the Query Builder.

In the SQL version used by Access, the WHERE clause should read: WHERE lname = ? ■

Creating a Parameterized Query—Step-by-Step

In this program, the user enters a job id. The program displays a grid of matching employees.

Begin a New Project

STEP 1: Begin a new Windows Application project called Ch04Query.

STEP 2: Rename the form to *EmployeesForm* and set its Text property to *Employees*.

Create the Data Source

STEP 1: Add a new data source connected to the Pubs database. Select the employee table.

STEP 2: In the DataSet Designer, configure the TableAdapter to not generate `Insert`, `Update`, and `Delete` statements.

Set Up the Form

STEP 1: Drag the employee table from the Data Sources window to the form. It should appear in a DataGridView.

STEP 2: Edit the grid's column headings.

STEP 3: In the DataGridView's smart tag, deselect *Enable Adding*, *Enable Editing*, and *Enable Deleting*.

Create the Query

STEP 1: From the smart tag on the DataGridView, select *Add Query*.

STEP 2: On the *Search Criteria Builder* dialog box, give your new query the name *FillByJobID*.

STEP 3: At this point, you could type your new SQL query into the box. Instead, click on the *Query Builder* button.

STEP 4: In the *Filter* column of the job_id row, type "= @job_id" (without the quotes). Press Enter. Notice the `WHERE` clause added to the query (Figure 4.11). Click *OK*. Click *OK* again to return to the form.

Figure 4.11

Enter the parameter in the Filter column; the designer adds the WHERE *clause to the query.*

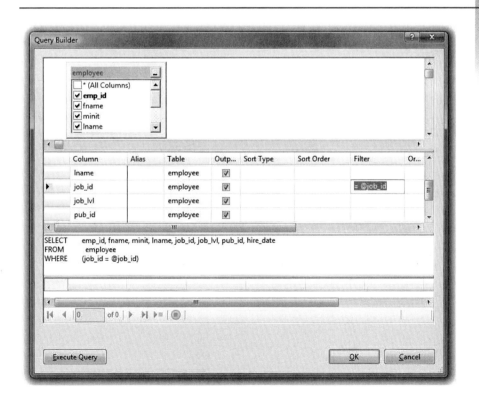

STEP 5: A FillByJobID toolstrip is added to your form. Move the grid, if necessary, to see both toolbars.

Run the Program

STEP 1: Run the program.

STEP 2: Type "5" in the text box on the search toolstrip.

STEP 3: Click on the *FillByJobID* button on the toolstrip. The grid should fill with all of the employees with 5 for the Job ID (Figure 4.12). Try some other values; the Job IDs range from 2 to 14.

Figure 4.12

Enter "5" for the job_id and click the FillByJobID button; the grid fills with matching employee records.

Employee ID	First Name	Initial	Last Name	Job ID	Job Level	Publis
PXH22250M	Paul	X	Henriot	5	159	0877
CFH28514M	Carlos	F	Hemadez	5	211	9999
JYL26161F	Janine	Y	Labrune	5	172	9901
LAL21447M	Laurence	A	Lebihan	5	175	0736
RBM23061F	Rita	B	Muller	5	198	1622
SKO22412M	Sven	K	Ottlieb	5	150	1389
MJP25939M	Maria	J	Pontes	5	246	1756

Make Modifications

STEP 1: You can make the form look more professional. You might change the text on the toolstrip buttons, set the grid's column widths, dock the grid to the form, remove the editing buttons from the navigation toolbar, or even remove the navigation toolbar entirely.

TIP

You can undock both toolbars and align them to be side-by-side. ∎

Examine the Code

Display the form's code: The FillByJobIDToolStripButton has a click event handler. A `FillByJobID` method for the EmployeeTableAdapter is enclosed in a `Try / Catch` block. And still another program with all of its code has been generated automatically!

Every time the user clicks the *FillByJobID* button, a new DataSet is created, holding only the records that match the selection criteria.

Filtering a DataSet

You can select rows from an existing DataSet by using a **filter**. In Chapter 3, you used the `Sort` method of a BindingSource; here you will learn to use the BindingSource's `Filter` method.

```
' Filter an existing DataSet based on a combo box selection.
SelectionString = JobComboBox.SelectedValue.ToString
With BindingSource1
    .DataMember = "employee"
    .Filter = "job_id = " & SelectionString
    .Sort = "Name"
End With
```

Writing a Filter

The rules for creating a filter are the same as for a `WHERE` clause of a SQL statement. Specify the field, a comparison operator (usually the equal sign), and the value to match.

```
"LastName = Jones"
"SalesAmount = 1000"
"Quantity > 0"
```

The tricky part comes when you want to filter on a string that may contain spaces. The value to match must be enclosed in single quotes.

```
"Title = 'A Great Book'"
```

If you are matching a value stored in a variable, you must concatenate the elements to create a filter string in the correct format. For string data, you must concatenate the single quotes around the data values:

```
"Title = '" & TitleString & "'"
"Title = '" & TitleComboBox.SelectedValue.ToString & "'"
```

In the second statement, assume that TitleComboBox.SelectedValue = "Great Expectations". After the concatenation, the entire string would be "`Title = 'Great Expectations'`", which is exactly what is needed for the filter.

For numeric values, you create a filter string without the quotes:

```
"SalesAmount = " & AmountDecimal.ToString
"Quantity > " & QuantityTextBox.Text
```

Here is a list of the most useful operators. You can find a complete listing of operators on the "Comparison Operators" page in MSDN.

Operator	Meaning	Examples
=	equal to	`"Subject = 'Business'"` `"Subject = '" & SubjectTextBox.Text & "'"`
>	greater than	`"Sales > 1000"` `"Sales > " & SalesTextBox.Text`
<	less than	`"Sales < 1000"` `"Sales < " & SalesTextBox.Text`
Like	pattern match	`"Subject Like ('B%')"` (For SQL Server databases) `"Subject Like 'B*'"` (For Access databases)

Binding a List at Run Time

When you display filtered data in a list, usually you want the list to appear empty until a selection is made. In that case, you must bind the control in code, rather than at design time.

```
' Bind the list box with the filtered data.
With EmployeeListBox
    .DataSource = BindingSource1
    .DisplayMember = "Name"
End With
```

When you set the DataSource, the list fills with the data from the Binding-Source.

Filtering a DataSet—Step-by-Step

In this step-by-step exercise, you will again allow the user to select a job and display the employees that match. However, this time, the job description will appear in a combo box for selection, and you will display the employees by full name in a list box. Figure 4.13 shows the completed application.

This exercise uses a different technique to create data-bound controls: You will first add the controls from the toolbox to the form and then set up the data binding.

Figure 4.13

The completed filter exercise. The user selects a job description from the combo box. The corresponding job_id is used to filter the data, which is displayed in the list box.

Begin a New Project

STEP 1: Begin a new Windows Application project called Ch04RowFilter.

STEP 2: Rename the form to *EmployeesForm* and set its Text property to *Employees By Job*.

Create the Data Source

STEP 1: Add a new data source connected to the Pubs database. Select both the employee and jobs tables.

STEP 2: Drag a BindingSource object from the Data section of the toolbox to the form.

STEP 3: In the Properties window, set the DataSource of BindingSource1 to PubsDataSet and the DataMember to employee. Notice that a Pubs-DataSet component and an EmployeeTableAdapter component are added to the component tray.

STEP 4: In the DataSet Designer, add a column to the employee table. Name the column *Name* and set the Expression property to concatenate the first name and last name fields. You can preview the data to test the new column.

STEP 5: Configure both TableAdapters to not generate `Insert`, `Update`, and `Delete` statements.

Set Up the Form

STEP 1: Add a combo box and a list box from the toolbox to the form. (Refer to Figure 4.13.) Name the list box *EmployeeListBox* and the combo box *JobComboBox*.

STEP 2: Drag the jobs table from the Data Sources window and drop it on the combo box. Use the smart tag to confirm that the control is now bound to the JobsBindingSource and the display member is set to the job description. Also notice that the ValueMember is set to job_id, the primary key of the jobs table.

Reviewing Combo Box Properties

Combo boxes and list boxes have several properties that you should know how to use. As you know, the DisplayMember determines the items that appear to the user. The ValueMember can hold a key that identifies the item that displays. For the JobComboBox, the DisplayMember holds the job description and the ValueMember holds the job_id (Figure 4.14). When the user makes a selection from a combo box, the control's SelectedIndexChanged and SelectionChangeCommitted events fire and the SelectedValue property is set to the ValueMember of the selected item. You will use the SelectedValue property to create the filter to find the matching employees.

Write the Code

STEP 1: Select the combo box and click on the *Events* button in the Properties window. Locate SelectionChangeCommitted and double-click to open

Figure 4.14

The user selects from the DisplayMember. Use the ValueMember to find matching values.

DisplayMember	ValueMember
job_desc	job_id
New Hire - Job not specified	1
Chief Executive Officer	2
Business Operations Manager	3
Chief Financial Officer	4
Publisher	5
Managing Editor	6
Marketing Manager	7
Public Relations Manager	8
Acquisitions Manager	9
Productions Manager	10
Operations Manager	11
Editor	12
Sales Representative	13
Designer	14

that event handler in the Code Editor window. The SelectionChange-Committed event is preferable to the SelectedIndexChanged event, which occurs several times during loading the form and binding the controls.

STEP 2: Write the code:

```
Private Sub JobComboBox_SelectionChangeCommitted(ByVal sender As Object, _
    ByVal e As System.EventArgs) Handles JobComboBox.SelectionChangeCommitted
    ' Filter the matching employees in the DataSet.
    Dim SelectionString As String

    SelectionString = JobComboBox.SelectedValue.ToString
    With BindingSource1
        .DataMember = "employee"
        .Filter = "job_id = '" & SelectionString & "'"
        .Sort = "Name"
    End With
    With EmployeeListBox
        .DataSource = BindingSource1
        .DisplayMember = "Name"
    End With
End Sub
```

Run the Program

STEP 1: Run the program. Select a job title from the combo box and the employees that match appear in the list.

Unbound Data Fields

Although it's easy and handy to bind data fields to controls, many applications require that you work with data fields that are not bound to controls. You need to be able to retrieve rows of data and reference the individual records and fields. In this section, you will use DataRelation objects that relate parent and child records, retrieve a selected parent row, retrieve an array of matching child rows, and refer to the individual fields in the selected rows. You also will assign the data values to the Text property or the List.Items property of **unbound controls**; that is, controls that do not have any data bindings established.

The following example uses the employee and jobs tables of the Pubs database, which are related by the job_id field. The jobs table is considered the parent and the employee table is the child. Although that might not seem intuitive, remember the rule: The one side of a one-to-many relation is the parent; the many side is the child. In the case of jobs and employees, each job title appears only once in the jobs table, and many employees may have the same job. Figure 4.15 shows the jobs and employee tables in the Visual Studio Data-Set Designer. Notice that the relation line shows a key at the "one" side and an infinity symbol (∞) at the "many" side. The relation line connects the tables but does not point directly to the related fields.

In the programs in this section, you will have to refer to the relations between tables by name. It's best to give the relation a meaningful name: point to

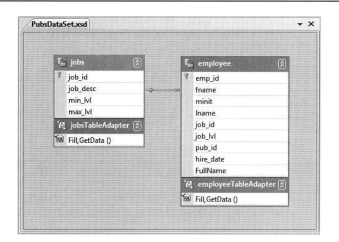

The jobs and employee tables in the DataSet Designer. The jobs table is the one side of the one-to-many relationship.

the relation line, right-click, and select *Edit Relation*. In the *Relation* dialog box (Figure 4.16), you can view and modify the relationship. The default name for a relation is rather cryptic: "FK__employee__job_id__1BFD2C07" in this example. Change the name to something more meaningful, such as "EmployeeTo-JobsRelation," before you write any code that refers to the relation.

Change the name of the relation to something more meaningful than the default name, such as Employee-ToJobsRelation.

Referring to Records and Fields

When you are working with data from a DataSet, you often want to refer to an individual field from a selected record. The actual data values are held in **DataRow objects**. Each Table object in a DataSet has a DataRows collection made up of DataRow objects (Figure 4.17).

```
DataTable
    DataRows Collection
        DataRow(0)
        DataRow(1)
        DataRow(n)
```

The data values are held in the DataRow.Items collection. You can refer to the individual fields by index position (the first field is index 0), by field name enclosed in quotes, or with an exclamation mark (called the "bang"). For example, you can use any of these three statements to retrieve the fname field of this employee DataRow object:

```
FirstNameString = EmployeeDataRow.Item(1).ToString
```

or

```
FirstNameString = EmployeeDataRow.Item("fname").ToString
```

or

```
FirstNameString = EmployeeDataRow!fname.ToString
```

Unless you want to look up the index position of each field in a record, you'll find that using field names is much preferred. You can find the field names in the DataSet Designer and the Data Sources window.

Retrieving a Related Parent Row

The following example allows the user to select an employee name from a bond combo box and then displays the hire date from the employee table and the job description from the jobs table (Figure 4.18). The data fields are displayed in unbound text boxes; that is, no data bindings exist for the text boxes. Each field is assigned to the Text property of a text box.

Note: This application could easily be written using bound controls. The point of the exercise is to learn to use unbound controls and to refer to

F i g u r e   4 . 1 8

From the selected employee name, the program retrieves the correct employee DataRow and the matching jobs parent DataRow to display the job description.

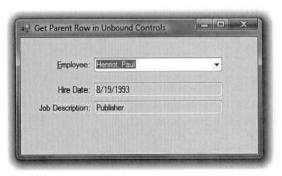

individual database fields, because many professional applications use that approach.

When you allow the user to select a value from a bound combo box, you write the code to retrieve the data in the SelectionChangeCommitted event handler. There are basically three steps in the process:

1. Find the row in the employee table that matches the combo box selection.
2. Use the **GetParentRow method** to retrieve the matching row from the jobs table.
3. Retrieve the specific data item and assign it to the Text property of a text box.

Find the Employee (Child) Row

Declare a DataRow object for the employee table and another one for the jobs table.

```
Dim EmployeeDataRow As DataRow
Dim JobDataRow As DataRow
```

Use the SelectedValue from the employee combo box to find the complete employee record. Each table in the DataSet contains a method to find records by the key field. Since the primary key in the employee table is emp_id, the FindByemp_id method is automatically generated for the table object.

The format for the find is

```
DataRow = DataSetName.TableName.FindByMethod(PrimaryKeyValue)
```

If you set up the combo box ValueMember property as emp_id, then you can use this code to retrieve the correct employee record by its key field.

```
' Save the Employee ID for the selected employee.
EmployeeIDString = EmployeeComboBox.SelectedValue.ToString
' Find the data row for this employee.
EmployeeDataRow = PubsDataSet.employee.FindByemp_id(EmployeeIDString)
```

Get the Parent Row

Now that you know the row in the employee (child) table that matches the combo box entry, you must get the parent row from the jobs table.

```
' Find the matching row from the parent (jobs) table.
JobDataRow = EmployeeDataRow.GetParentRow("EmployeeToJobsRelation")
```

Note that "EmployeeToJobsRelation" in the GetParentRow method argument is the name of the relation that we discussed setting up in Figure 4.16.

Retrieve a Specific Field

The final step is to get the field from the data row.

```
' Display a field from the matching row.
JobTitleTextBox.Text = JobDataRow!job_desc.ToString
```

TIP

Add Imports System.Data before the Class statement; then you can omit the "Data." namespace on all declarations for data objects in code. ∎

The Complete Find Parent Program

```
'Program:      Ch04FindParentUnbound
'Programmer:   Bradley/Millspaugh
'Date:         June 2009
'Description:  Allow the user to select the employee name from a combo box
'              and display the corresponding hire date from the same table
'              and the job description from the jobs table.
'              Demonstrates finding a parent row for a selected child row,
'              referring to individual fields in a DataRow object, and
'              assigning database fields to unbound controls.

Imports System.Data

Public Class EmployeeForm

    Private Sub EmployeeForm_Load(ByVal sender As System.Object, _
      ByVal e As System.EventArgs) Handles MyBase.Load
        ' Fill the DataSet.

        JobsTableAdapter.Fill(PubsDataSet.jobs)
        EmployeeTableAdapter.Fill(PubsDataSet.employee)
    End Sub

    Private Sub EmployeeComboBox_SelectionChangeCommitted( _
      ByVal sender As Object, ByVal e As System.EventArgs) _
      Handles EmployeeComboBox.SelectionChangeCommitted
        ' Find and display the selected record.
        Dim EmployeeIDString As String
        Dim EmployeeDataRow As DataRow
        Dim JobDataRow As DataRow

        ' Find the data row for the selected name.
        EmployeeIDString = EmployeeComboBox.SelectedValue.ToString
        EmployeeDataRow = PubsDataSet.employee.FindByemp_id( _
          EmployeeIDString)

        ' Display a field from the selected row.
        HireDateTextBox.Text = EmployeeDataRow!hire_date.ToString
        ' Use this alternate statement to format the date.
        HireDateTextBox.Text = Convert.ToDateTime( _
          EmployeeDataRow!hire_date).ToString("d")

        ' Find the matching row from the parent (jobs) table.
        JobDataRow = EmployeeDataRow.GetParentRow( _
          "EmployeeToJobsRelation")

        ' Display a field from the matching row.
        JobTitleTextBox.Text = JobDataRow!job_desc.ToString
    End Sub
End Class
```

Retrieving Related Child Rows

Retrieving related child rows is similar to retrieving a related parent row. The primary difference is that the **GetChildRows method** returns an array of rows rather than a single row. In this variation on the previous program, the user selects a job title from the combo box. The program retrieves the correct data row for the job and displays the array of matching employees in a list box

(Figure 4.19). Note that the DataSet and relationship in this program are exactly the same as in the preceding example.

Figure 4.19

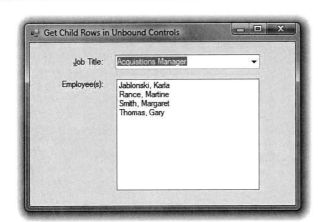

When the user selects the job title (the parent), the program retrieves and displays an array of the matching employee (child) records.

The Complete Find Children Program

```
'Program:      Ch04FindChildrenUnbound
'Programmer:   Bradley/Millspaugh
'Date:         June 2009
'Description:  Allow the user to select the job description from a
'              combo box and display the corresponding employees
'              (child rows) from the employee table.
'              Demonstrates finding child rows for a selected parent row,
'              referring to individual fields in a DataRow object, and
'              assigning database fields to unbound controls.

Imports System.Data

Public Class EmployeeForm

    Private Sub EmployeeForm_Load(ByVal sender As System.Object, _
      ByVal e As System.EventArgs) Handles MyBase.Load
        'This line of code loads data into the 'PubsDataSet.jobs' table.
        Me.JobsTableAdapter.Fill(Me.PubsDataSet.jobs)
        'This line of code loads data into the 'PubsDataSet.employee' table.
        Me.EmployeeTableAdapter.Fill(Me.PubsDataSet.employee)
    End Sub

    Private Sub JobComboBox_SelectionChangeCommitted(ByVal sender As Object, _
      ByVal e As System.EventArgs) Handles JobComboBox.SelectionChangeCommitted
        ' Find and display employees for the selected job.

        Dim JobIDShort As Short
        Dim JobDataRow As DataRow
        Dim EmployeeDataRow As DataRow
        Dim EmployeeDataRows As DataRow()

        Try
            ' Get the job_id of the selected job.
            JobIDShort = Convert.ToInt16(JobComboBox.SelectedValue)

            ' Find the row from the job table for the selected job_id.
            JobDataRow = PubsDataSet.jobs.FindByjob_id(JobIDShort)
```

```
                    ' Retrieve an array of employee rows.
                    EmployeeDataRows = JobDataRow.GetChildRows( _
                        "EmployeeToJobsRelation")

                    ' Fill the list with the array of employee rows.
                    EmployeeListBox.Items.Clear()
                    For Each EmployeeDataRow In EmployeeDataRows
                        EmployeeListBox.Items.Add( _
                            EmployeeDataRow!FullName.ToString)
                    Next
            Catch ex As Exception
                MessageBox.Show(ex.Message)
            End Try
        End Sub
End Class
```

Feedback 4.3

1. Assume that a combo box displays store names and uses the stor_id property as a ValueMember. Write the statement(s) to filter the stores table using StoresBindingSource, selecting the record(s) that match a store selected from the list.

Use the following diagram for questions 2 and 3. Assume that a proper 1:M relationship, called ProductsToCategoriesRelation, has been set up between the categories and products tables. The DataSet is called ProductsDataSet and the data type of CategoryID and ProductID is Integer (Int32).

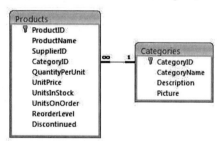

2. The user selects a product name from a list box and you want to retrieve the category name. Write the statements to retrieve the category name and display it in a label.
3. Assuming the same proper relationship, write the statements to retrieve an array of all of the products in a selected category. Fill a list box with the array of products.

Many-to-Many Relationships

Recall that a many-to-many relationship requires a third table, called a *junction table*. Figure 4.20 shows the relationships for the titles table and authors table, which are joined by the titleauthor table. Notice that au_id is the primary key in the authors table; a given au_id can appear only once. Similarly, title_id is the primary key of the titles table and any one title_id can appear only once. But in the junction table, titleauthor, any one au_id and any one title_id can appear any number of times. The combination of au_id and title_id

F i g u r e   4 . 2 0

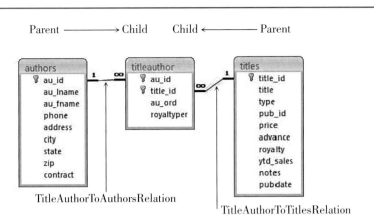

In an M:N relationship, two 1:M relationships must be set up. The junction table is the child table in each of the two 1:M relationships.

makes up the primary key, so any one combination must be unique. As you set up the relationships, the junction table is the child table in the relationships with each of the parent tables.

Retrieving Matching Rows

The following example finds all titles for a selected author. Recall that titles and authors are M:N tables; a single title may have multiple authors and an author may have multiple titles.

    To join the records from the titles and authors tables requires two steps:

- For a selected author, find the child records in the junction table.

- Then, for each child record in the junction table, you must find the parent in the titles table.

    For example, if you have the au_id of a selected author and want to find the titles written by that author, you must first get the child rows from the junction table, which produces an array of rows. Then you step through the array of rows and get the parent row of each from the titles table. You likely will store these parent rows in an array or display them in a list box or combo box. The example program that follows allows the user to select an author from a bound combo box and displays the titles in an unbound list box (Figure 4.21).

F i g u r e   4 . 2 1

When the user selects an author from the list, the program finds the matching titles from the titles table.

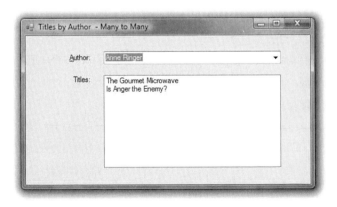

When you allow the user to select a value from a bound combo box, you write the code to retrieve the data in the SelectionChangeCommitted event handler. You follow these three steps:

- Find the row in the authors table that matches the combo box.

- Use the `GetChildRows` method to retrieve the matching rows from the titleauthor (junction) table.

- Use the `GetParentRow` method to retrieve the parent row (the title) that matches each of the rows retrieved in the previous step (the rows from the titleauthor table).

Find the Child Rows

Use the SelectedValue from the combo box to find the author record. Use the `FindByau_id` method for the authors table. If you set up the combo box Value-Member property as au_id, then you can use this code to retrieve the correct record by its key field.

```
' Find the row to match the selection.
Dim AuthorDataRow As DataRow = _
  PubsDataSet.authors.FindByau_id(Au_idComboBox.SelectedValue.ToString)
```

Note that the `GetChildRows` method uses the name of the relation between the authors and titleauthor tables. You should give the relations meaningful names in the DataSet Designer, as described earlier. Notice the names of the two relations in Figure 4.20.

```
' Get an array of matching child rows from the junction table.
Dim TitleAuthorDataRows As DataRow()
TitleAuthorDataRows = _
  AuthorDataRow.GetChildRows("TitleAuthorToAuthorsRelation")
```

Find the Parent Rows

Once you get the child rows from the junction table, you can iterate through the child rows to perform any needed processing. This example gets the title column from the parent row and adds it to a list box.

```
' Get each title and add to the array of titles.
For Each TitleAuthorDataRow As DataRow In TitleAuthorDataRows
    ' Retrieve the parent row and title field from the title table.
    TitleString = TitleAuthorDataRow.GetParentRow( _
      "TitleAuthorToTitlesRelation")!title.ToString

    ' Add the title to the array of titles.
    TitleStrings(IndexInteger) = TitleString

    ' Increment the index for the next title.
    IndexInteger += 1
Next
```

The Titles Authors M:N Program

This M:N program is written as a multitier application. Figure 4.20 shows the data relationships and Figure 4.21 shows the user interface. The data tier fills the DataSet, returns the authors used to fill the combo box, and finds and returns the titles for an author that is passed as a parameter. Note that both classes have an `Imports System.Data` statement above the Class declaration.

The Presentation Tier

☑**TIP**

If you get a Null Exception error when accessing the data, make sure that you have filled all of the tables in the DataSet. ■

```vb
'Program:       Ch04ManyToManyMultitier
'Date:          June 2009
'Programmer:    Bradley/Millspaugh
'Class:         TitlesByAuthorForm
'Description:   A multitier application to display data from related
'               tables. The user selects an author name from the
'               authors table and the program displays the books
'               for that author from the titles table.

Imports System.Data

Public Class TitlesByAuthorForm

    Private APubsDataTier As PubsDataTier

    Private Sub TitlesByAuthorForm_Load(ByVal sender As Object, _
      ByVal e As System.EventArgs) Handles Me.Load
        ' Load the combo box.

        Try
            ' Get data from the data tier.
            APubsDataTier = New PubsDataTier
            Dim AuthorsDataTable As New DataTable
            AuthorsDataTable = APubsDataTier.GetAuthorNames

            ' Bind the table to the combo box.
            With AuthorComboBox
                .DataSource = AuthorsDataTable
                .DisplayMember = "FullName"
                .ValueMember = "au_id"
                .SelectedIndex = -1
            End With
        Catch ex As Exception
            MessageBox.Show(ex.Message)
        End Try

    End Sub

    Private Sub AuthorComboBox_SelectionChangeCommitted( _
      ByVal sender As Object, ByVal e As System.EventArgs) _
      Handles AuthorComboBox.SelectionChangeCommitted
        ' Find the titles for the selected author.
        Dim AuthorIDString As String
        Dim TitlesStrings(10) As String

        Try
            ' Save the ID of the selected author.
            AuthorIDString = AuthorComboBox.SelectedValue.ToString
```

```
            ' Retrieve the array of matching titles.
            TitlesStrings = _
              APubsDataTier.GetTitlesByAuthor(AuthorIDString)

            ' Fill the list with the titles.
            TitleListBox.Items.Clear()
            ' Iterate through the array.
            For Each TitleString As String In TitlesStrings
                If TitleString <> Nothing Then
                    ' Add the title to the list.
                    TitleListBox.Items.Add(TitleString)
                End If
            Next
        Catch ex As Exception
            MessageBox.Show(ex.Message)
        End Try
    End Sub
End Class
```

The Data-Tier Class

```
'Program:     Ch04ManyToManyMultitier
'Date:        June 2009
'Programmer:  Bradley/Millspaugh
'Class:       PubsDataTier
'Description: Provides the data for a many-to-many application
'             for authors and titles in the Pubs database.

Imports System.Data

Public Class PubsDataTier

    Private ADataSet As PubsDataSet
    Private AnAuthorsTableAdapter _
      As PubsDataSetTableAdapters.authorsTableAdapter
    Private ATitlesTableAdapter _
      As PubsDataSetTableAdapters.titlesTableAdapter
    Private ATitleAuthorTableAdapter _
      As PubsDataSetTableAdapters.titleauthorTableAdapter

    Public Sub New()
        ' Fill the dataset.

        Try
            ADataSet = New PubsDataSet
            AnAuthorsTableAdapter = _
              New PubsDataSetTableAdapters.authorsTableAdapter
            ATitlesTableAdapter = _
              New PubsDataSetTableAdapters.titlesTableAdapter
            ATitleAuthorTableAdapter = _
              New PubsDataSetTableAdapters.titleauthorTableAdapter

            AnAuthorsTableAdapter.Fill(ADataSet.authors)
            ATitlesTableAdapter.Fill(ADataSet.titles)
            ATitleAuthorTableAdapter.Fill(ADataSet.titleauthor)
        Catch ex As Exception
            Throw ex
        End Try
    End Sub
```

```
Public Function GetTitlesByAuthor(ByVal AuIDString As String) As String()
    ' Find and return the titles for the selected author.
    Dim AuthorDataRow As DataRow
    Dim TitleAuthorDataRows As DataRow()
    Dim TitleString As String
    Dim TitleStrings(10) As String
    Dim IndexInteger As Integer

    ' Find the row for the selected author (the passed parameter).
    AuthorDataRow = ADataSet.authors.FindByau_id(AuIDString)

    ' Retrieve the array of matching rows from the junction table.
    TitleAuthorDataRows = _
      AuthorDataRow.GetChildRows("TitleAuthorToAuthorsRelation")

    ' Get each title and add to the array of titles.
    For Each TitleAuthorDataRow As DataRow In TitleAuthorDataRows
        ' Retrieve the parent row and title field from the titles table.
        TitleString = TitleAuthorDataRow.GetParentRow( _
          "TitleAuthorToTitlesRelation")!title.ToString

        ' Add the title to the array of titles.
        TitleStrings(IndexInteger) = TitleString

        ' Increment the index for the next title.
        IndexInteger += 1
    Next
    Return TitleStrings    ' Return the array of titles.
End Function

Public Function GetAuthorNames() As DataTable
    ' Return the author names from the dataset.

    Return ADataSet.authors
End Function
End Class
```

Feedback 4.4

Use this data diagram from the Northwind database to answer the following questions:

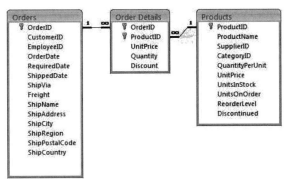

1. Name the parent table(s) and child table(s) and describe each of the relationships with the terms 1:1, 1:M, or M:N.
2. Assume that you have the OrderID for a selected order. Describe in words how to retrieve a list of the product names for that order.

Multitier Considerations

When you separate an application into multiple classes, make sure to think through the goals of OOP. Specifically, the presentation tier should provide only the user interface. All user input and output formatting belongs in the form. The data retrieval and any processing should be handled in other classes. When you finish, you should be able to completely change the user interface without having to modify the other classes. You also can change the filtering or data retrieval method without affecting the interface.

Formatting a Grid at Run Time

In Chapter 3, you formatted the columns of a DataGridView at design time by adding a DataSet to the form. This technique has some drawbacks, since the DataSet actually comes from the data tier, and if you remove the form's Data-Set, you can no longer modify the column formatting.

    You can format the columns of a DataGridView at run time, but be aware that binding the grid resets all properties. So if your program performs binding, place the statements to format the columns *after* the binding is complete.

Formatting code for the data grid should follow the code for binding. ∎

```vb
Private Sub StoreNameComboBox_SelectionChangeCommitted( _
   ByVal sender As Object, ByVal e As System.EventArgs) _
   Handles StoreNameComboBox.SelectionChangeCommitted
      ' Retrieve the sales information for the grid.
      Dim StoreIDString As String

      ' Retrieve the ID of the selected store.
      StoreIDString = StoreNameComboBox.SelectedValue.ToString

      ' Initialize the grid's binding.
      If Not GridInitializedBoolean Then
          ' Bind and format the grid.
          SalesDataGridView.DataSource = SalesBindingSource
          SetUpGridColumns()
          GridInitializedBoolean = True
      End If

      ' Filter the grid's data.
      SalesBindingSource.Filter = "stor_id = '" & StoreIDString & "'"
End Sub

Private Sub SetUpGridColumns()
    ' Set up the columns for the grid.

    Try
        With SalesDataGridView
            .Columns!stor_id.Visible = False
            .Columns!ord_num.HeaderText = "Order Number"
            .Columns!ord_date.HeaderText = "Date"
            .Columns!qty.HeaderText = "Quantity"
            .Columns!payterms.HeaderText = "Terms"
            .Columns!title_id.HeaderText = "Title ID"
        End With
    Catch ex As Exception
        MessageBox.Show("Error setting up the grid. " & ex.Message)
    End Try
End Sub
```

Your Hands-On Programming Example

Create a program to display the sales for a selected store using a multitier application. Allow the user to select the store name from a combo box. Display the selected store's sales in a grid.

Planning the Project

Sketch a form (Figure 4.22) that your users sign off as meeting their needs.

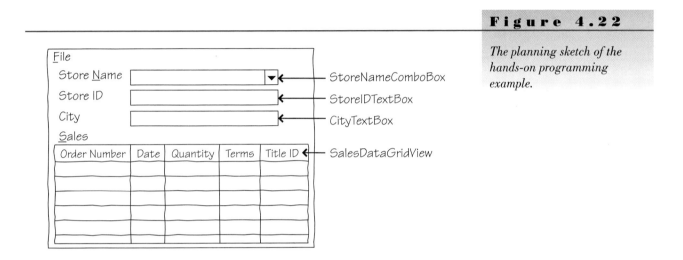

Figure 4.22

The planning sketch of the hands-on programming example.

Plan the Objects, Properties, and Methods Plan the two tiers. Determine the objects and property settings for the form and its controls and for the data tier class. Figure 4.23 shows the diagram of the program components.

Figure 4.23

The components for the hands-on programming example.

Presentation Tier

Object	Property	Setting
StoreSalesForm	Name	StoreSalesForm
	Text	Store Sales
StoreNameComboBox	Name	StoreNameComboBox
StoreIDTextBox	Name	StoreIDTextBox
CityTextBox	Name	CityTextBox
SalesDataGridView	Name	SalesDataGridView
ExitToolStripMenuItem	Text	E&xit

Event handlers/methods	Actions—Pseudocode
ExitToolStripMenuItem	Exit the project.
Form_Load	Instantiate the data tier.
	Retrieve the DataSet table to fill the combo box.
	Set up the binding source.
	Set the combo box properties.
	Bind the other controls.
	Clear the initial values in the controls.
	Set listLoadedBoolean = True.
StoreComboBox_SelectionChangeCommitted	If listLoadedBoolean = True
	Retrieve the data for the selected list item.
	Set up the binding source for the data grid.
	Bind the data grid.
	SetUpGridColumns.
SetUpGridColumns	Hide the first column (the store ID).
	Set the column headings for the remaining columns.

Data Tier

Object	Property	Setting
Class	Name	PubsDataTier

Methods	Actions—Pseudocode
New (constructor)	Instantiate the two TableAdapters and the DataSet.
	Fill the DataSet.
GetDataSet	Return the DataSet.

Private module-level variables

ASalesTableAdapter
AStoresTableAdapter
APubsDataSet

Write the Project Following the sketch in Figure 4.22, create the form. Figure 4.24 shows the completed form.

- Set the properties of each of the form objects, according to your plans.

- Create the data-tier component and write the methods, following the pseudocode.

- Write the code for the form. Working from the pseudocode, write each procedure.

- When you complete the code, test the operation several times. Compare the screen output to the data tables to make sure that you are displaying the correct information.

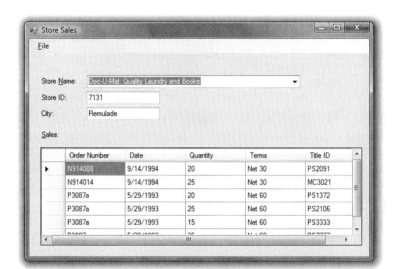

Figure 4.24

The completed form for the hands-on programming example.

The Project Coding Solution
The Form

```
'Program:      Ch04HandsOn
'Programmer:   Bradley/Millspaugh
'Date:         June 2009
'Class:        StoreSalesForm
'Description:  Display store information and sales for a selected
'              store. This is the presentation tier, which uses
'              the services of the data tier.

Imports System.Data

Public Class StoreSalesForm

    ' Module-level variables.
    Private APubsDataTier As PubsDataTier
    Private APubsDataSet As PubsDataSet
    Private StoresBindingSource As BindingSource
    Private SalesBindingSource As BindingSource
```

```vbnet
Private Sub StoreForm_Load(ByVal sender As System.Object, _
  ByVal e As System.EventArgs) Handles MyBase.Load
    ' Set up the data for the combo box and text boxes.

    Try
        APubsDataTier = New PubsDataTier
        APubsDataSet = APubsDataTier.GetDataSet

        ' Set up stores binding source.
        StoresBindingSource = New BindingSource
        With StoresBindingSource
            .DataSource = APubsDataSet
            .DataMember = "stores"
            .Sort = "stor_name"
        End With

        ' Bind the form controls.
        With StoreNameComboBox
            .DataSource = StoresBindingSource
            .DisplayMember = "stor_name"
            .ValueMember = "stor_id"
            .DataBindings.Add("text", StoresBindingSource, _
              "stor_name", False, DataSourceUpdateMode.Never)
            .SelectedIndex = -1
        End With
        StoreIDTextBox.DataBindings.Add("text", _
          StoresBindingSource, "stor_id", False, _
          DataSourceUpdateMode.Never)
        CityTextBox.DataBindings.Add("text", _
          StoresBindingSource, "city", False, _
          DataSourceUpdateMode.Never)
        ' Clear initial contents.
        StoreIDTextBox.Clear()
        CityTextBox.Clear()

        ' Set up the sales binding source.
        SalesBindingSource = New BindingSource
        With SalesBindingSource
            .DataSource = APubsDataSet
            .DataMember = "sales"
        End With
    Catch ex As Exception
        MessageBox.Show("Error: " & ex.Message)
    End Try
End Sub

Private Sub ExitToolStripMenuItem_Click(ByVal sender As System.Object, _
  ByVal e As System.EventArgs) Handles ExitToolStripMenuItem.Click
    ' End the program.

    Me.Close()
End Sub

Private Sub StoreNameComboBox_SelectionChangeCommitted( _
  ByVal sender As Object, ByVal e As System.EventArgs) _
  Handles StoreNameComboBox.SelectionChangeCommitted
    ' Retrieve the sales information for the grid.
    Dim StoreIDString As String
    Static GridInitializedBoolean As Boolean = False
```

```vb
            ' Retrieve the ID of the selected store.
            StoreIDString = StoreNameComboBox.SelectedValue.ToString

            ' Initialize the grid's binding.
            If Not GridInitializedBoolean Then
                ' Bind and format the grid.
                SalesDataGridView.DataSource = SalesBindingSource
                SetUpGridColumns()
                GridInitializedBoolean = True
            End If

            ' Filter the grid's data.
            SalesBindingSource.Filter = "stor_id = '" & StoreIDString & "'"
        End Sub

    Private Sub SetUpGridColumns()
        ' Set up the columns for the grid.

        Try
            With SalesDataGridView
                .Columns!stor_id.Visible = False
                .Columns!ord_num.HeaderText = "Order Number"
                .Columns!ord_date.HeaderText = "Date"
                .Columns!qty.HeaderText = "Quantity"
                .Columns!payterms.HeaderText = "Terms"
                .Columns!title_id.HeaderText = "Title ID"
            End With
        Catch ex As Exception
            MessageBox.Show("Error setting up the grid. " & ex.Message)
        End Try
    End Sub
End Class
```

The Data-Tier Class

```vb
'Program:      Ch04HandsOn
'Programmer:   Bradley/Millspaugh
'Date:         June 2009
'Class:        PubsDataTier
'Description:  Data tier for the store sales application.
'              Fills and returns the DataSet with stores and sales.

Imports System.Data

Public Class PubsDataTier

    ' Module-level variables.
    Private ASalesTableAdapter _
      As PubsDataSetTableAdapters.salesTableAdapter
    Private AStoresTableAdapter _
      As PubsDataSetTableAdapters.storesTableAdapter
    Private APubsDataSet As PubsDataSet

    Public Sub New()
        Try
            ' Instantiate the TableAdapters and DataSet.
            AStoresTableAdapter = New _
              PubsDataSetTableAdapters.storesTableAdapter()
```

```
                    ASalesTableAdapter = New _
                        PubsDataSetTableAdapters.salesTableAdapter()
                    APubsDataSet = New PubsDataSet
                    ' Fill the DataSet.
                    AStoresTableAdapter.Fill(APubsDataSet.stores)
                    ASalesTableAdapter.Fill(APubsDataSet.sales)
            Catch ex As Exception
                    Throw ex
            End Try
        End Sub

        Public Function GetDataSet() As PubsDataSet
            ' Return the DataSet.

            Return APubsDataSet
        End Function
End Class
```

Summary

1. Data in a relational database are stored in multiple related tables. The primary table is the parent or master and the second table is referred to as the child or detail table.
2. The primary key of a table uniquely identifies each record. When the primary key of one table is included in a second table to link the tables together, the key included in the second table is called a *foreign key.*
3. Relationships may be one-to-many (1:M), many-to-many (M:N), or one-to-one (1:1). An M:N relationship requires a third table, called a *junction table*, to join the tables.
4. Constraints may be *unique contraints* or *foreign-key constraints.* Enforcing constraints is handled by the database management system to maintain referential integrity.
5. A DataSet with related tables needs one table adapter for each table. A `Fill` is required for each adapter.
6. In a 1:M relationship, the one is the parent table and the many is the child.
7. To set up master/detail records, use the node in the Data Sources window that shows the child table beneath the parent table.
8. Relationships can be viewed or edited in the DataSet Designer.
9. You can create bound controls on a form either by dragging tables and/or fields to a form or by dragging to an existing control, which sets up the binding for that control.
10. A parameterized query creates a new DataSet based on the parameter that you supply. A filter selects records from an existing DataSet according to the criteria that you specify.
11. The actual data in a DataSet are held in DataRow objects in the DataRows collection of the table. You can assign a record to a DataRow object and retrieve the data items from each field.

12. You can assign the value of a field to a control, which is referred to as an *unbound control.*

13. You can retrieve the parent row of a given child row by using the `GetParentRow` method, which returns a DataRow object. You can retrieve the child rows of a given parent by using the `GetChildRows` method, which returns an array of DataRow objects.

14. When working with an M:N relationship, each of the tables has a 1:M relationship with the junction table, which is considered a child to both of the other tables. To retrieve related records from the two master tables, get the child records for a row in one master and then get the parent rows from the second master table.

15. In a multitier database application, all data access should be performed in the data tier and all output formatting should be in the form.

Key Terms

child table   *150*

criteria   *160*

DataRelation object   *157*

DataRow object   *167*

detail table   *150*

filter   *162*

foreign key   *150*

foreign-key constraint   *152*

`GetChildRows` method   *170*

`GetParentRow` method   *169*

junction table   *150*

lookup   *157*

many-to-many relationship
  (M:N)   *150*

master table   *150*

one-to-many relationship (1:M)   *150*

one-to-one relationship (1:1)   *151*

parameterized query   *160*

parent table   *150*

referential integrity   *152*

unbound controls   *166*

unique constraint   *152*

Review Questions

1. Name the three types of table relationships and give an example of each.
2. What is a constraint? Give some examples.
3. Explain how to create a DataSet that holds multiple tables.
4. Describe the steps necessary to establish a relationship in the IDE.
5. Can a relationship be edited or deleted? How?
6. Explain the differences between a parameterized query and a filter. How is each created and what is the result?
7. What is meant by the term *unbound control*? How can you display database data in an unbound control?
8. Explain how to retrieve and display all matching child rows for a given parent row.
9. Explain the steps necessary to retrieve records from tables related by a many-to-many relationship.

Programming Exercises

For each of these exercises, create a multitier application with the database access in a separate component.

4.1 (Master/Detail) Use the Northwind database to display customer and order information. Populate a combo box with the CompanyName sorted in alphabetic order. Display the customer information in bound labels and the order information in a grid. For customers, display the CustomerID, ContactName, ContactTitle, and Phone. For orders, display the OrderID, OrderDate, RequiredDate, and ShippedDate.

4.2 (Two grids) Use the Northwind database to display customer and order information. Populate a list box with the CompanyName sorted in alphabetic order. Display customer information in the top grid and the order information in a second grid. For customers, display the CustomerID, Address, City, Region, PostalCode, and Country. For orders, display the OrderID, OrderDate, RequiredDate, and ShippedDate.

4.3 (M:N) Use the Employees, Territories, and EmployeeTerritories tables in the Northwind database to display related information. Populate a combo box with the employee names (concatenated) in alphabetic order by last name. Use the EmployeeID as the ValueMember. Display a list of the territories for that employee, using the TerritoryDescription field from the Territories table.

Note: The EmployeeID field is Integer; the TerritoryID field is String. You can see the data types in the Data Sources window.

Case Studies

Claytor's Cottages

Modify your Claytor's Cottages case study project to display the room information. The Room form should display for the *Edit / Rooms* menu item.

On the Room form, include a combo box that holds the room name. Use check boxes to indicate if the room has a Jacuzzi, Private access, and/or Fireplace. Display the Bed type and the room rates from the Beds table.

Hint: You can bind the checked property of a check box to a Boolean data field.

Christian's Car Rentals

Modify your case study application to display the vehicle information. Display a combo box that contains the car sizes. When the user selects a size, display the price and mileage rate in text boxes. The related models and manufacturer should display in a grid.

C H A P T E R

5

Windows Database Updates

at the completion of this chapter, you will be able to . . .

1. Update a database table in a grid and in individual controls.

2. Use the BindingSource properties for navigation and for determining the current record number.

3. Update the original data source by saving the values from a dataset.

4. Validate user input in an update program.

5. Update related tables.

In the preceding chapters, you displayed data from datasets and related tables. In this chapter, you will update the data.

When you bind data to controls in Visual Basic, updating a dataset is somewhat automatic. When the user makes any change in a data-bound control and moves to another control, the changes are saved in the in-memory dataset. In a grid, the user can add a new row at the end, delete a row, or make changes to existing data. In details view, if the BindingNavigator's navigation bar is displaying, the user can click the *Add* button to add a new record, click the *Delete* button to remove a record, or make changes in any of the text boxes and the changes are saved in the dataset when the user moves to another record.

In an application that displays and allows updates to the data, do you really want to allow the user to make changes to any piece of data while viewing the file? Just because updating a dataset *can be* automatic does not mean that's the best way to structure an update application. Most well-structured applications allow the user to view *or* edit, but not both at the same time. And generally you must perform validation on adds and edits. In this chapter, you will learn to control navigation, validate data, and allow updates, which includes adding records, deleting records, and making changes to existing records.

The first two-thirds of this chapter shows various techniques for updating single tables. In the last third and in the chapter hands-on project, you learn to update multiple related tables.

A Simple Update in a Grid

For a first look at updates, we'll use a single table in a DataGridView (Figure 5.1). The navigation bar automatically includes buttons for adding a record, deleting a record, and saving changes.

Figure 5.1

The navigation bar created by the BindingNavigator class has buttons for updating data.

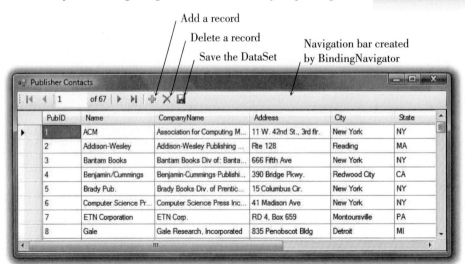

Updating a DataSet

A DataGridView object includes features that allow the user to update the dataset. To add a new record, the user can click on the *Add* button (the yellow plus sign), which moves the selection to a new row at the end of the grid. To delete a record, a user selects a row and presses the Delete key or clicks the *Delete* button in the navigation bar. The user also can modify data in any row in the grid. All changes are made in the dataset (the in-memory copy of the data). When the user clicks the *Save* button, the BindingNavigator's SaveItem event is fired and an attempt is made to save the data back to the original data source. Here is the code that is automatically generated by the designer when a BindingNavigator is added to a form:

```
Private Sub PublishersBindingNavigatorSaveItem_Click( _
  ByVal sender As System.Object, ByVal e As System.EventArgs) _
  Handles PublishersBindingNavigatorSaveItem.Click
    ' Save any changes in response to the Save toolbar button.
    ' Code generated by the designer.
    Me.Validate()
    Me.PublishersBindingSource.EndEdit()
    Me.PublishersTableAdapterManager.UpdateAll(Me.ContactsDataSet)
End Sub
```

Notice that the code includes a method call from the BindingSource object and a method from the TableAdapterManager object. The EndEdit saves any changes on the current row and the UpdateAll method sends the data back to the original data source. Later in this chapter, you will see several other methods for data objects.

Remember that a dataset is a temporary set of data in memory, disconnected from the original data source. The user can make changes to the rows of data in the dataset, but those changes are not automatically sent back to the original data source. The TableAdapter is the go-between for the data source and the dataset (Figure 5.2). You execute the Update method of the TableAdapter or the UpdateAll method of the TableAdapterManager to send any changes back to the original data source.

Figure 5.2

The TableAdapter retrieves data from the data source to create the dataset and sends back changes from the dataset to the data source.

Database Handling in the Visual Studio IDE

When you write and debug database update programs in the Visual Studio IDE, you should be aware of how the database file is handled. Assuming that you select the option to include the database file in the project when you set up the data source, you see the file in the project's folder in the Solution Explorer. But the file that you see is not the one that is used when the program runs. The first time you run your program in the debugger, the database file is copied into the bin\Debug folder. The copy in the bin\Debug folder is the one used by the program.

The decision whether to copy the database file from the project folder to the bin\Debug folder when the application runs is based on a setting for the database file. By default, the file's *Copy to Output Directory* property is set to *Copy always* (Figure 5.3). For a program that allows updates to the database, *Copy always* is not the correct setting. If you want database updates to show up from one run to the next, you must select the filename in the Solution Explorer and change the setting for *Copy to Output Directory* to *Copy if newer*.

Figure 5.3

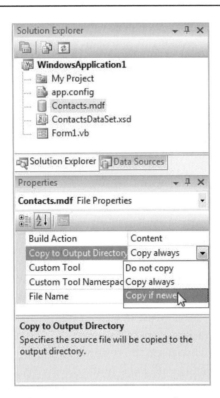

To set the copy behavior of the database file, select the filename in the Solution Explorer and set the Copy to Output Directory to Copy if newer.

When you set the file to *Copy if newer*, on each program run the debugger checks the file versions: If the file in the bin\Debug folder has a later date than the one in the project folder, no copy is performed. But if the file in the project folder is newer, or no file exists in the bin\Debug folder, the file is copied.

You can take advantage of the file-copying behavior when you test update programs, so that you can return the file to its original state after testing. Display all files in the Solution Explorer and expand the node for bin\Debug. If you don't see

Figure 5.4

The database file appears in the project folder and in the bin\Debug folder. Delete the copy in bin\Debug to work with a fresh copy of the original file when the file is set to Copy if newer.

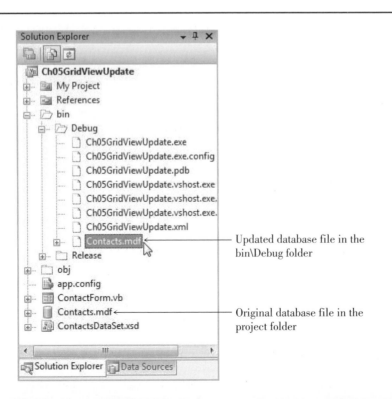

Updated database file in the bin\Debug folder

Original database file in the project folder

the database file, click the *Refresh* button. Then delete the file in the bin\Debug folder, either by right-clicking and choosing *Delete* or by pressing the Delete key. The next time you run the program, a fresh copy of the original file will appear in the folder. Figure 5.4 shows the files in the Solution Explorer. Note that when you delete the .mdf file, the .ldf file also is deleted automatically. If you delete the file using My Computer or Windows Explorer, make sure to delete both files.

The Data Objects, Methods, and Properties

You need to understand the various methods and properties of the data objects to write more sophisticated update programs. Table 5.1 shows an overview of many of the useful methods and properties of the data components.

Overview of Useful Data Methods and Properties   **Table 5.1**

Data class	Property/method	Purpose
DataSet	RowState property	Enumeration to indicate the status of each row.
	HasChanges method	Queries if there are changes; can check for a specific type of change.
DataSet, DataTable	GetChanges method	Returns the changes made to a dataset; can return a specific type of change.
DataSet, DataTable, DataRow	AcceptChanges method	Resets row enumerations to Unchanged.
	RejectChanges method	Rolls back all changes made since the object was created or the last time AcceptChanges was called.
	HasErrors property	Returns a value that indicates whether there are errors in the row(s) of the object.
TableAdapter	Fill method	Retrieves values from a data source.
	Update method	Submits the changes to the original data source.
TableAdapterManager	UpdateAll method	Performs a hierarchical update for related tables.
BindingSource	CancelEdit method	Ends an edit, throws away any changes, and leaves the row state Unchanged.
	EndEdit method	Changes values and changes the row state.
	AddNew method	Adds a new record at the end of the dataset.
	Insert method	Adds a new record at the specified index.
	CancelNew method	Discards a pending added object.
	Current property	Retrieves the current record.
	RemoveCurrent method	Deletes the current record.
	MoveFirst method	Moves to the first row.
	MoveNext method	Moves to the next row.
	MoveLast method	Moves to the last row.
	MovePrevious method	Moves to the previous row.
	Position property	Index of the current record.
	Count property	Number of rows in the table.
	IndexOf method	Returns the index of the row.

Recall that a DataSet object can consist of multiple tables and each table can consist of multiple data rows, where the actual data *values* are stored (Figure 5.5). Each row of data has a **RowState property**, which indicates whether any changes have been made to the row. Table 5.2 shows the values of the DataRowState enumeration for the possible values of the RowState property.

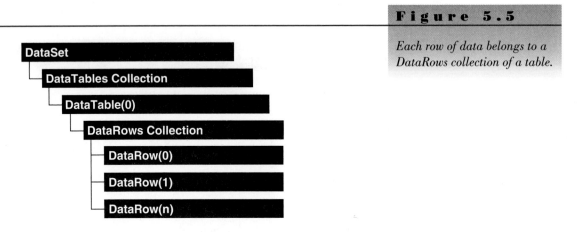

The DataRowState Enumeration Values That Are Used for the RowState Property of a DataRow, Which Indicate Whether Any Changes Have Been Made to the Row

Table 5.2

DataRowState enumeration	Purpose
Added	Indicates that this is a new row.
Deleted	The row is marked for deletion.
Detached	The row is not a part of a collection. A row has the detached value before it is added or after it has been removed.
Modified	Changes have been made to the row.
Unchanged	No changes have been made to the row.

The HasChanges Method

You can determine if any changes have been made to a dataset by calling the **HasChanges method**, which returns a Boolean value.

```
If PubsDataSet.HasChanges() Then
    ' Ask the user to save the changes.
End If
```

One of the overloaded versions of the HasChanges method allows you to check for specific types of changes, using the values for DataRowState shown in Table 5.2.

```
If PubsDataSet.HasChanges(DataRowState.Deleted) Then
    ' Code to handle the deletion(s).
End If
```

The GetChanges Method

You can use the **GetChanges method** of a dataset or a data table to retrieve the rows that have changes. Use an empty argument to retrieve all changed rows, or specify the type of changes that you want using the DataRowState enumeration values.

Create a new dataset that holds all changed rows:

```
Dim EmployeeChangesDataSet As DataSet
EmployeeChangesDataSet = PubsDataSet.GetChanges()
```

Create a dataset that holds all of the rows that are marked for deletion:

```
Dim EmployeeDeletesDataSet As DataSet
EmployeeDeletesDataSet = PubsDataSet.GetChanges(DataRowState.Deleted)
```

The Edit Methods

When the user modifies a row of data, the row must be in edit mode. If the data are displayed in bound controls, the edit methods are called automatically. When an edit begins, the **BeginEdit method** executes; when the edit terminates, the **EndEdit method** executes. Any time before the EndEdit method executes, you can call the **CancelEdit method** to return the field values to their original values.

DataRow Versions

The DataRow object maintains several versions of its data: the Current, Original, and Default versions. If no changes have been made, the Current and Original versions are the same. While an edit is in progress—between the BeginEdit and EndEdit—one more version exists: the Proposed version. When EndEdit executes, the Current version is replaced by the Proposed version.

The EndEdit method confirms the changes, but the changes are not actually made in the dataset until the AcceptChanges method executes.

The AcceptChanges Method

The **AcceptChanges method**

- Removes all rows marked for deletion.

- Makes the adds and edits indicated for the table.

- Sets the Original version of each changed row to the Current version.

- Sets the RowState of each row to Unchanged.

- Clears any RowError information and sets the HasErrors property to false.

The AcceptChanges method commits all of the changes to the dataset. The **RejectChanges method** rolls back all changes that have been made by replacing the Current versions with the Original versions. After either the AcceptChanges or RejectChanges method executes, all RowState properties are reset to Unchanged.

Remember that the dataset is disconnected, so the changes are made to the dataset, not to the original data source. To send the changes back to the data source, you must execute the TableAdapter's Update method or the TableAdapterManager's UpdateAll method before calling the AcceptChanges method.

both of which call

The TableAdapter and TableAdapterManager

Although the user can make changes to the dataset in memory, no changes are made to the original data source until you execute the **Update method** of the TableAdapter or the **UpdateAll method** of the TableAdapterManager. You can choose to perform updates after every change, or once when the program terminates.

The TableAdapterManager, which is new for Visual Studio 2008, manages updates to multiple related tables. For single tables, such as we are updating first, a TableAdapter is all that is needed. If you use the Update Wizard to update a database application created in an earlier version of Visual Basic, you do not generate a TableAdapterManager and updates are performed with the `TableAdapter.Update` method. By default, in new database applications that you create with Visual Studio 2008, creating a TableAdapter also creates a TableAdapterManager.

Later in this chapter in the section "Updating Related Tables," you will learn about hierarchical updates performed with a TableAdapterManager. You can prevent the automatic addition of a TableAdapterManager in a single-table application by setting the dataset's HierarchicalUpdate property to *false* before dragging any tables or fields to a form.

Both the `TableAdapter.Update` and `TableAdapter.UpdateAll` methods save the changes from the dataset to the original data source.

The Update and UpdateAll Methods—General Form

```
TableAdapter.Update(DataSet.table)
TableAdapterManager.UpdateAll(DataSet)
```

Notice that the `TableAdapterManager.UpdateAll` method specifies only the dataset name; the `TableAdapter.Update` method can specify only the dataset name if it has only one table; otherwise you must supply DataSetName.TableName.

The Update and UpdateAll Methods—Examples

```
PublishersTableAdapter.Update(ContactsDataSet.Publishers)
PublishersTableAdapter.Update(ContactsDataSet)
TableAdapterManager.UpdateAll(ContactsDataSet)
```

You can decide when to execute an update method. You can save the change every time an add, edit, or delete occurs, or you can wait until the program terminates. Or combine the two techniques by providing a *Save* option on a menu or button and then prompting for unsaved changes when the program terminates. This technique matches Office applications: You can save a document any time you want, but if you try to close without saving the changes, a dialog box displays.

The `Update` and `UpdateAll` methods cause communication from the table adapter to the data source. If the data source is stored on the same system as the application, updating is no problem. However, if the data source is else-where, such as on an intranet or the Internet, saving each change may require substantial network traffic. You must consider where the application and data reside, how many users can make changes, and whether it's important that the data source be up-to-date at all times.

It may be best to wait and save all changes when the program terminates. (However, a loss of power could lose all changes.) To prompt for unsaved changes, place the update method in the form's FormClosing event handler. The FormClosing event occurs when Me.Close executes, which should happen when the user selects *Exit* from a menu or button, or when the user clicks the form's Close button or even exits Windows.

To ask the user whether to save the dataset when changes have been made, check the return value for the HasChanges method. If changes have been made, display the message "Do you want to save the changes?" The following code belongs in the form's FormClosing event handler:

```
Private Sub ContactForm_FormClosing(ByVal sender As Object, _
  ByVal e As System.Windows.Forms.FormClosingEventArgs) _
  Handles Me.FormClosing
    ' Check for unsaved changes.
    Dim AnswerDialogResult As DialogResult

    If ContactsDataSet.HasChanges() Then
        ' Query the user to save the changes.
        AnswerDialogResult = MessageBox.Show( _
          "Do you want to save the changes?", "Unsaved Changes", _
          MessageBoxButtons.YesNoCancel, MessageBoxIcon.Question, _
          MessageBoxDefaultButton.Button2)
        Select Case AnswerDialogResult
            Case Windows.Forms.DialogResult.Yes
                ' Save the DataSet.
                PublishersBindingSource.EndEdit()
                PublishersTableAdapter.Update(ContactsDataSet)
            Case Windows.Forms.DialogResult.Cancel
                ' Cancel the closing.
                e.Cancel = True
        End Select
    End If
End Sub
```

▶ **Feedback 5.1**

Write the statements to save all of the changes to CustomerDataSet using NorthwindTableAdapter.

The BindingSource Object

When you are working with bound controls, such as a grid, list, text box, or label, the bound table data are managed by the **BindingSource object**. The binding source controls the record position within a table and is responsible for assuring that all bound controls on a form display data from the same record. You can use properties of the binding source to determine the current record and to navigate from one record to the next.

Binding Source Properties and Methods

You can use properties and methods of the BindingSource object to display the record number and to navigate.

Displaying the Record Number

The **Position property** of the BindingSource holds the current row number (zero based) and the **Count property** indicates the number of records in a table.

```
PublishersBindingSource.Position
PublishersBindingSource.Count
```

Using these properties, you can display the record number in a label or a status bar on the form: "Record 5 of 200".

Notice that you must add 1 to the Position property, since it is zero based.

```
With PublishersBindingSource
    RecordPositionLabel.Text = "Record " & _
        (.Position + 1).ToString() & " of " & .Count.ToString()
End With
```

Table 5.3 shows some useful properties and methods of the BindingSource class.

Useful Properties and Methods of the BindingSource Class   **Table 5.3**

Property/method	Purpose
Current property	Retrieves the current row.
Position property	Index of the current row.
Count property	Number of rows in the table.

Navigating Using BindingSource Methods

You can use the binding source for record navigation. For example, you might have buttons for *Next Record*, *Previous Record*, *First Record*, and *Last Record*. Modifying the Position property changes the record position; and if you have bound fields or a grid, the new current record displays. Table 5.4 shows the navigation methods.

Navigation Methods of the BindingSource Class   **Table 5.4**

Method	Purpose
MoveFirst	Moves to the first row.
MoveNext	Moves to the next row.
MoveLast	Moves to the last row.
MovePrevious	Moves to the previous row.

You should check to make sure that you don't try to move to a record beyond the last record or before the first record. Remember that the record position or index begins with 0, making the last record a position of Count minus one.

```
' Move to the next record.
With PublishersBindingSource
    If .Position = .Count - 1 Then
        .MoveFirst()
    Else
        .MoveNext()
    End If
End With

' Move to the previous record.
With PublishersBindingSource
    If .Position = 0 Then
        .MoveLast()
    Else
        .MovePrevious()
    End If
End With

' Move to the first record.
PublishersBindingSource.MoveFirst()

' Move to the last record.
PublishersBindingSource.MoveLast()
```

Binding Source Update Methods

You can use the methods of the binding source to maintain table data (Table 5.5). Use the **AddNew method** to begin the operation to add a new record to the dataset. When you execute the AddNew method for data displayed in a grid, the last line in the grid (the one with the asterisk) is activated so the user can enter a new row. If you execute AddNew for individually bound fields, the field contents are cleared so that the user can enter the new record. When the user moves off of the new record, the EndEdit method is executed automatically; or you can explicitly execute the method, perhaps in response to a button click. If the user wishes to cancel the add or edit, you can call the CancelEdit method. You also can use CancelNew for an add in progress, which has the same effect as CancelEdit. But always remember that the dataset is disconnected, so any new records are added to the dataset in memory and not saved to the original data source until you execute the Update or UpdateAll method.

Editing Methods of the BindingSource Object　　　　　　　　　　　**Table 5.5**

Method	Purpose
AddNew	Clears bound fields to allow new data to be entered. Adds a new row to the table.
Insert	Adds a record at the specified index.
CancelNew	Cancels the record being added.
CancelEdit	Cancels the edit currently being processed.
EndEdit	Completes the current edit and saves the changes in the dataset.
RemoveAt	Deletes the row at the specified index from the table.
RemoveCurrent	Deletes the current record.

Use the **RemoveCurrent method** to delete the current record:

```
PublishersBindingSource.RemoveCurrent()
```

Binding Source Events

Two useful events for the BindingSource class are the CurrentChanged event and the PositionChanged event. The **CurrentChanged event** occurs when a bound value is changed. When a user navigates to another record, the **PositionChanged event** occurs. The PositionChanged event handler is a good place to display the current record number in a label or status bar.

Displaying the Record Number and Record Count

This procedure executes automatically every time the record number changes.

```
Private Sub PublishersBindingSource_PositionChanged( _
  ByVal sender As Object, ByVal e As System.EventArgs) _
  Handles PublishersBindingSource.PositionChanged
    ' Display the position and record number.

  With PublishersBindingSource
      ToolStripStatusLabel1.Text = "Record " & _
        (.Position + 1).ToString() & " of " & .Count.ToString()
  End With
End Sub
```

Feedback 5.2

For each of these questions, assume that the table's binding source is CustomersBindingSource.

1. Write the code to navigate to the previous record in the customers table.
2. Write the statement(s) to display the current record number in the status bar.

DataSet Updating

ADO.NET handles the complicated process of updating the original data source based on the changes made to a disconnected dataset. Recall that each row in a table has a RowState property that may be set to Unchanged, Modified, Added, or Deleted. When you execute the Update method, the indicated changes from the dataset are made in the original data source for all rows that have a RowState other than Unchanged.

SQL Statements for Updates

When you add a data source, several SQL statements are generated. In addition to the SELECT statement that you are familiar with, an INSERT statement, DELETE statement, and UPDATE statement also are created by default. You can see those SQL statements by examining the CommandText properties of the DeleteCommand, InsertCommand, and UpdateCommand properties of the

TableAdapter. In the Dataset Designer, click on the TableAdapter header and examine the Properties window. The syntax of the statements is affected by the concurrency setting (described in the next section).

When the `Update` or `UpdateAll` method executes, ADO.NET sends the `DELETE` SQL command for each record with a RowState of Deleted, the `INSERT` SQL command for each record with a RowState of Added, and the `UPDATE` SQL command for all rows with a RowState of Modified.

Concurrency

If more than one user can update a file at the same time, **concurrency** problems can occur. **Concurrency control** is the process of handling conflicts in updates by multiple users. There are three types of concurrency control in ADO.NET:

1. Pessimistic concurrency control: A row is unavailable to other users from the time the record is retrieved until the update is complete.
2. Optimistic concurrency control: A row is unavailable only while an update is in progress. If an update has been made between the time a record is retrieved and an attempt is made to save changes, a currency violation occurs.
3. "Last in wins": A row is unavailable only when the update is being made. No checks are made for multiple changes to the same record.

Pessimistic concurrency control is not an option with a disconnected dataset. Using a DataReader, which you will learn about in Chapter 8, you can retrieve and update individual records; then you can specify pessimistic concurrency.

The default is optimistic concurrency. If you want to change the setting to "last in wins," run the TableAdapter Configuration Wizard by selecting *Configure* from the context menu in the DataSet Designer. Click on *Advanced Options* and you can choose the option to remove the check for concurrency. You might want to do this if you are making multiple changes to the same record during testing.

Testing Update Programs

You may encounter many types of errors when testing an Add or Update in an update program if you are not familiar with the database. First, you must have the proper rights to the database to allow you to write to the data source. Second, be aware of constraints—which fields can contain nulls, which are required fields, which must contain specific values. You should include exception handling for all statements that access the database. Display the exception message, which will help you determine the cause of the problem.

Updating a DataSet in Bound Controls

You can allow the user to update records using bound individual controls, which is more common than using a grid. You will need to display the dataset fields in bound text boxes so that the user can type in changes. However, you will keep the text boxes set to Read Only unless an Add or Edit is in progress.

The following sections demonstrate the logic and code to update data in individual bound controls. The sample programs available for download from the text Web site include update programs that use buttons for navigation and that use a combo box for navigation. There are applications that save every update as it occurs and one that saves updates when the user selects a menu option and when the program terminates. Table 5.6 shows a summary of the sample update programs with their features. Figure 5.6 shows a form for an update program with navigation buttons and Figure 5.7 shows a form that uses a combo box to select the record.

All of the techniques for updating a dataset apply equally to an Access database and a SQL Server database.

Details View Database Update Programs Included on the Text Web Site (www.mhhe.com/AdvVB2008/)

Table 5.6

Program	Update timing	Navigation
Ch05DetailsViewUpdate	On each change	Combo box
Ch05DetailsViewUpdateNavigation	On each change	Buttons
Ch05DetailsViewUpdateValidate (Validation included)	On each change	Combo box
Ch05HierarchicalUpdate	User option and on form closing	Combo box

Figure 5.6

The form for a details view update program that uses buttons for navigation.

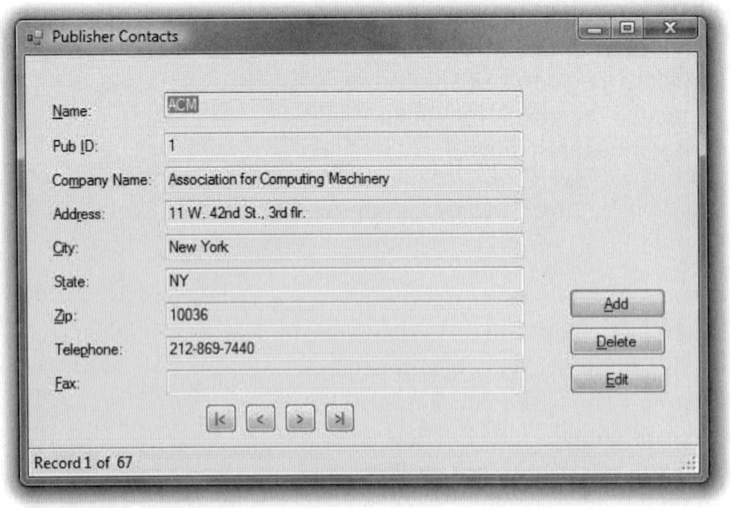

The Logic of an Update Program

An update program needs procedures to modify existing records (called *editing records*), delete records, and add new records. For this example, we will call the Update method after every change so that the data source is up-to-date for every change.

Make sure to enclose all statements that access the dataset in Try / Catch blocks. You don't want to allow the program to cancel with an exception.

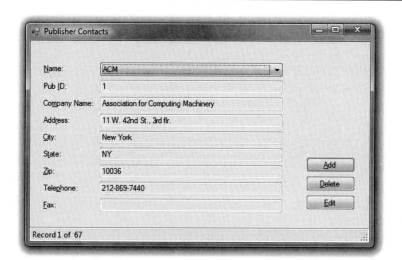

Figure 5.7

The form for a details view update program that allows the user to select records using a combo box.

User Options during an Update

You must carefully control the options available to a user during an update. While an Add or Edit is in progress, the only available options should be Save or Cancel. And while the user is navigating from one record to another, do not allow any changes to be made to the data. If you allow the user to make changes to data and navigate to another record, those changes are automatically saved in the dataset.

The example database update program in the next section provides buttons for the update selections. Following a widely used technique, the buttons change, depending on the current operation. During navigation, the form displays buttons for *Add*, *Delete*, and *Edit*. When the user clicks on *Add* or *Edit*, the Text property of the *Add* button changes to "Save", the Text of the *Delete* button changes to "Cancel", and the *Edit* button is disabled, which provides only *Save* and *Cancel* options. After the user selects either *Save* or *Cancel*, the Text properties of the *Add* and *Delete* buttons are restored to their original state and the *Edit* button is again enabled. Refer to Figure 5.7 to see the buttons during navigation. Figure 5.8 shows the buttons during an Add or Edit operation.

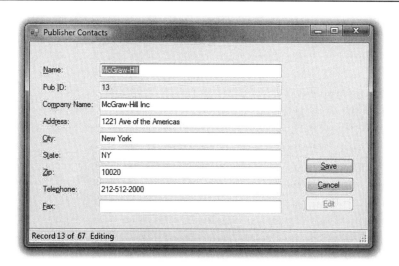

Figure 5.8

*During an Add or Edit, the **Add** button becomes the **Save** button and the **Delete** button becomes the **Cancel** button. The Edit button must be disabled during an Add or Edit operation.*

The Add and Save Logic

The *Add* button becomes the *Save* button during an Add or Edit operation.

Adding a Record

The logic of an Add operation is somewhat more complicated than the other operations. The user must click an *Add* button to begin an Add operation. The program must clear the text boxes, unlock them, and allow the user to enter the data for the new record. During the Add operation, the user should have only the choices *Save* and *Cancel* and record navigation must be disabled.

Note that all records are added to the end of the table. After the application is closed and reopened, the records are arranged according to their keys or the sort order requested.

Pseudocode for an Add Operation
Call the BindingSource's `AddNew` method, which begins the Add and clears the
   text boxes.
Set AddingBoolean to True
Set the focus to the first text box.
Disable navigation.
Set the text boxes' ReadOnly property to False.
Set up the buttons for an Add:
   Set up the *Save* and *Cancel* buttons.
   Disable the *Edit* button.
   Display "Adding" in the status bar.

Saving an Added or Edited Record

After the user finishes entering the data for a new record and clicks the *Save* button, you must save the new data.

The *Save* button is available for both Adds and Edits.

Pseudocode for the Save Operation
' Save both Adds and Edits.
End the current edit.
Update the data source.
Display "Record Saved" in the status bar.
Enable navigation.
Set the text boxes' ReadOnly property to True.
Reset the buttons for normal operation.

The Code for the Add and Save Buttons

```
Private Sub AddSaveButton_Click(ByVal sender As System.Object, _
   ByVal e As System.EventArgs) Handles AddSaveButton.Click
      ' Begin an Add operation or cancel the current operation.

   If AddSaveButton.Text = "&Add" Then
      With APublishersBindingSource
          .EndEdit()
          .AddNew()
      End With
```

```
            AddingBoolean = True
            SetComboBoxBinding()
            NameComboBox.Focus()
            SetControlsReadOnly(False)
            SetButtonsForEdit()
            If NameComboBox.SelectedIndex <> -1 Then
                ' Save the index of the new record for later navigation.
                PreviousSelectedIndex = NameComboBox.Items.Count - 1
            Else
                PreviousSelectedIndex = 0
            End If
        Else
            ' Save button clicked.
            Try
                APublishersBindingSource.EndEdit()
                APublishersTableAdapter.Update(AContactsDataSet.Publishers)
                ToolStripStatusLabel2.Text = "Record Saved"
                AddingBoolean = False
                EditingBoolean = False
                SetControlsReadOnly(True)
                ResetButtonsAfterEdit()
                SetComboBoxBinding()
                NameComboBox.SelectedIndex = PreviousSelectedIndex
            Catch ex As Exception
                ' Catch duplicate records and constraint violations.
                MessageBox.Show(ex.Message)
            End Try
        End If
End Sub
```

Setting Navigation and Read Only

You need to be able to disable and enable navigation from several locations, so you should place the code in a separate sub procedure. You can pass a Boolean value that specifies whether navigation is to be turned on or off.

```
Private Sub SetNavigation(ByVal ValueBoolean As Boolean)
    ' Set the Enabled property of the navigation buttons.

    FirstRecordButton.Enabled = ValueBoolean
    LastRecordButton.Enabled = ValueBoolean
    NextRecordButton.Enabled = ValueBoolean
    PreviousRecordButton.Enabled = ValueBoolean
End Sub
```

When you call the procedure, pass the Boolean value that specifies whether you want to enable or disable navigation:

```
' Disable navigation.
SetNavigation(False)
```

or

```
' Enable navigation.
SetNavigation(True)
```

You can use the same technique for setting the text boxes' ReadOnly property:

```
Private Sub SetControlsReadOnly(ByVal ValueBoolean As Boolean)
    ' Lock or unlock the controls.

    NameTextBox.ReadOnly = ValueBoolean
    CompanyNameTextBox.ReadOnly = ValueBoolean
    AddressTextBox.ReadOnly = ValueBoolean
    CityTextBox.ReadOnly = ValueBoolean
    StateTextBox.ReadOnly = ValueBoolean
    ZipTextBox.ReadOnly = ValueBoolean
    TelephoneTextBox.ReadOnly = ValueBoolean
    FaxTextBox.ReadOnly = ValueBoolean
End Sub
```

The Delete and Cancel Logic

When an Add or Edit is in progress, the *Delete* button becomes the *Cancel* button.

Deleting a Record

Pseudocode for a Delete Operation
Confirm if record is to be deleted.
If yes,
   Display "Record deleted" in the status bar.
   Execute the RemoveCurrent method of the binding source to delete a record
      from the dataset.

Canceling an Operation

Pseudocode for a Cancel Operation
Cancel the edit (replace the text boxes with their previous contents).
Set AddingBoolean and EditingBoolean to False.
Enable navigation.
Set the text boxes' ReadOnly property to True.
Reset the buttons for normal operation:
   Reset the Text property of the *Add* and *Delete* buttons.
   Set the Text of the *Add* button back to "Add".
   Enable the *Edit* button.
   Clear the message in the status bar.

The Code for the Delete and Cancel Buttons

```
Private Sub DeleteCancelButton_Click(ByVal sender As System.Object, _
  ByVal e As System.EventArgs) Handles DeleteCancelButton.Click
    ' Delete the current record after confirming or cancel an Add or Edit.
    Dim DeleteDialogResult As DialogResult

    Try
        If DeleteCancelButton.Text = "&Delete" Then
            DeleteDialogResult = MessageBox.Show("Delete this record?", _
              "Confirm Delete", MessageBoxButtons.YesNo, _
              MessageBoxIcon.Question)
```

```
            If DeleteDialogResult = Windows.Forms.DialogResult.Yes Then
                APublishersBindingSource.RemoveCurrent()
                APublishersTableAdapter.Update( _
                  AContactsDataSet.Publishers)
                ToolStripStatusLabel2.Text = "Record deleted"
            End If
        Else
            ' Cancel button clicked.
            APublishersBindingSource.CancelEdit()
            AddingBoolean = False
            EditingBoolean = False
            SetNavigation(True)
            SetControlsReadOnly(True)
            ResetButtonsAfterEdit()
        End If
    Catch ex As Exception
        Dim MessageString As String
        MessageString = _
          "Unable to complete the delete/cancel operation: " _
          & ex.Message
        MessageBox.Show(MessageString, "Delete/Cancel", _
          MessageBoxButtons.OK, MessageBoxIcon.Exclamation)
    End Try
End Sub
```

The Edit Logic

You display data fields in bound text boxes. An easy way to allow changes to the data would be to just allow the user to type in changes in the text boxes. Any changes made to bound fields are automatically saved in the dataset. However, this is considered a dangerous practice. Instead, set the ReadOnly property of each text box to *true*, which locks the text box. For bound check boxes, lists, and grids, you can set the Enabled property to *false*; these controls don't have a ReadOnly property.

When the user clicks the *Edit* button, set the ReadOnly property of each text box to *false*. You also should disable navigation so that the user cannot move off the record and automatically save any changes. The only choices the user should have during an Edit should be *Save* or *Cancel*.

If the user clicks *Save*, you will execute the same procedure that you saw earlier for saving an Add.

Pseudocode to Begin an Edit
Set EditingBoolean to True.
Disable navigation.
Set the text boxes' ReadOnly property to False.
Set up the buttons for an Edit:
   Set up the *Save* and *Cancel* buttons.
   Disable the *Edit* button.
   Display "Editing" in the status bar.

The Code for the Edit Button

```vb
Private Sub EditButton_Click(ByVal sender As Object, _
  ByVal e As System.EventArgs) Handles EditButton.Click
    ' Allow editing to the current record.

    EditingBoolean = True
    SetNavigation(False)
    SetControlsReadOnly(False)
    SetButtonsForEdit()
End Sub
```

A Complete Update Program

Here is the code for the complete update program that uses navigation buttons and updates the data source after each change (Ch05DetailsViewUpdateNavigation). Refer to Figure 5.6 for the form.

```vb
'Program:      Ch05DetailsViewUpdateNavigation
'Date:         June 2009
'Programmer:   Bradley/Millspaugh
'Class:        ContactForm
'Description:  Update a single table in a details view in a single-
'              tier application. Uses buttons for navigation.
'              Saves each change back to the original data source as
'              it occurs.

Imports System.Data

Public Class ContactForm

    ' Module-level variables.
    Private AContactsDataSet As ContactsDataSet
    Private APublishersTableAdapter _
      As ContactsDataSetTableAdapters.PublishersTableAdapter
    Private WithEvents APublishersBindingSource As BindingSource

    Private AddingBoolean As Boolean = False
    Private EditingBoolean As Boolean = False

    Private Sub ContactForm_Load(ByVal sender As System.Object, _
      ByVal e As System.EventArgs) Handles MyBase.Load
        ' Load the DataSet.

        Try
            ' Set up and fill the DataSet.
            AContactsDataSet = New ContactsDataSet
            APublishersTableAdapter = _
              New ContactsDataSetTableAdapters.PublishersTableAdapter
            APublishersTableAdapter.Fill(AContactsDataSet.Publishers)

            ' Set up the binding source.
            APublishersBindingSource = New BindingSource
            With APublishersBindingSource
                .DataSource = Me.AContactsDataSet
                .DataMember = "Publishers"
```

```vbnet
                    ' Get the correct count of the rows in the DataSet.
                    .MoveLast()
                    .MoveFirst()
                End With

                ' Bind the controls.
                NameTextBox.DataBindings.Add("text", _
                  APublishersBindingSource, "Name")
                PubIDTextBox.DataBindings.Add("text", _
                  APublishersBindingSource, "PubID")
                CompanyNameTextBox.DataBindings.Add("text", _
                  APublishersBindingSource, "CompanyName")
                AddressTextBox.DataBindings.Add("text", _
                  APublishersBindingSource, "Address")
                CityTextBox.DataBindings.Add("text", _
                  APublishersBindingSource, "City")
                StateTextBox.DataBindings.Add("text", _
                  APublishersBindingSource, "State")
                ZipTextBox.DataBindings.Add("text", _
                  APublishersBindingSource, "Zip")
                TelephoneTextBox.DataBindings.Add("text", _
                  APublishersBindingSource, "Telephone")
                FaxTextBox.DataBindings.Add("text", _
                  APublishersBindingSource, "Fax")
                SetControlsReadOnly(True)

        Catch ex As Exception
            MessageBox.Show("Data Error: " & ex.Message)
        End Try
    End Sub

    Private Sub APublishersBindingSource_PositionChanged( _
      ByVal sender As Object, ByVal e As System.EventArgs) _
      Handles APublishersBindingSource.PositionChanged
        ' Display the position and record number.

        With APublishersBindingSource
            ToolStripStatusLabel1.Text = "Record " & _
              (.Position + 1).ToString() & " of  " & .Count.ToString()
        End With
    End Sub

    Private Sub AddSaveButton_Click(ByVal sender As System.Object, _
      ByVal e As System.EventArgs) Handles AddSaveButton.Click
        ' Begin an Add operation or cancel the current operation.

        If AddSaveButton.Text = "&Add" Then
            With APublishersBindingSource
                .EndEdit()
                .AddNew()
            End With
            AddingBoolean = True
            NameTextBox.Focus()
            SetNavigation(False)
            SetControlsReadOnly(False)
            SetButtonsForEdit()
        Else
            ' Save button clicked.
            Try
                APublishersBindingSource.EndEdit()
                APublishersTableAdapter.Update(AContactsDataSet.Publishers)
```

```vb
                    ToolStripStatusLabel2.Text = "Record Saved"
                    AddingBoolean = False
                    EditingBoolean = False
                    SetNavigation(True)
                    SetControlsReadOnly(True)
                    ResetButtonsAfterEdit()
                Catch ex As Exception
                    ' Catch duplicate records and constraint violations.
                    MessageBox.Show(ex.Message)
                End Try
            End If
        End Sub

        Private Sub DeleteCancelButton_Click(ByVal sender As System.Object, _
          ByVal e As System.EventArgs) Handles DeleteCancelButton.Click
            ' Delete the current record after confirming or cancel an Add or Edit.
            Dim DeleteDialogResult As DialogResult

            Try
                If DeleteCancelButton.Text = "&Delete" Then
                    DeleteDialogResult = MessageBox.Show("Delete this record?", _
                        "Confirm Delete", MessageBoxButtons.YesNo, _
                        MessageBoxIcon.Question)
                    If DeleteDialogResult = Windows.Forms.DialogResult.Yes Then
                        APublishersBindingSource.RemoveCurrent()
                        APublishersTableAdapter.Update( _
                          AContactsDataSet.Publishers)
                        ToolStripStatusLabel2.Text = "Record deleted"
                    End If
                Else
                    ' Cancel button clicked.
                    APublishersBindingSource.CancelEdit()
                    AddingBoolean = False
                    EditingBoolean = False
                    SetNavigation(True)
                    SetControlsReadOnly(True)
                    ResetButtonsAfterEdit()
                End If
            Catch ex As Exception
                Dim MessageString As String
                MessageString = _
                    "Unable to complete the delete/cancel operation: " _
                    & ex.Message
                MessageBox.Show(MessageString, "Delete/Cancel", _
                    MessageBoxButtons.OK, MessageBoxIcon.Exclamation)
            End Try
        End Sub

        Private Sub EditButton_Click(ByVal sender As Object, _
          ByVal e As System.EventArgs) Handles EditButton.Click
            ' Allow editing to the current record.

            EditingBoolean = True
            SetNavigation(False)
            SetControlsReadOnly(False)
            SetButtonsForEdit()
        End Sub

        Private Sub SetControlsReadOnly(ByVal ValueBoolean As Boolean)
            ' Lock or unlock the controls.
```

```vb
        NameTextBox.ReadOnly = ValueBoolean
        CompanyNameTextBox.ReadOnly = ValueBoolean
        AddressTextBox.ReadOnly = ValueBoolean
        CityTextBox.ReadOnly = ValueBoolean
        StateTextBox.ReadOnly = ValueBoolean
        ZipTextBox.ReadOnly = ValueBoolean
        TelephoneTextBox.ReadOnly = ValueBoolean
        FaxTextBox.ReadOnly = ValueBoolean
    End Sub

    Private Sub SetButtonsForEdit()
        ' Set up the buttons for an Add or Edit operation.

        AddSaveButton.Text = "&Save"
        DeleteCancelButton.Text = "&Cancel"
        EditButton.Enabled = False
        If AddingBoolean Then
            ToolStripStatusLabel2.Text = "Adding"
        Else
            ToolStripStatusLabel2.Text = "Editing"
        End If
    End Sub

    Private Sub ResetButtonsAfterEdit()
        ' Reset the buttons after an Add or Edit operation.

        AddSaveButton.Text = "&Add"
        DeleteCancelButton.Text = "&Delete"
        EditButton.Enabled = True
        ToolStripStatusLabel2.Text = String.Empty
    End Sub

    Private Sub SetNavigation(ByVal ValueBoolean As Boolean)
        ' Set the Enabled property of the navigation buttons.

        FirstRecordButton.Enabled = ValueBoolean
        LastRecordButton.Enabled = ValueBoolean
        NextRecordButton.Enabled = ValueBoolean
        PreviousRecordButton.Enabled = ValueBoolean
    End Sub

    Private Sub FirstRecordButton_Click(ByVal sender As System.Object, _
      ByVal e As System.EventArgs) Handles FirstRecordButton.Click
        ' Move to the first record.

        APublishersBindingSource.MoveFirst()
    End Sub

    Private Sub PreviousRecordButton_Click(ByVal sender As System.Object, _
      ByVal e As System.EventArgs) Handles PreviousRecordButton.Click
        ' Move to the previous record.

        With APublishersBindingSource
            If .Position = 0 Then
                .MoveLast()
            Else
                .MovePrevious()
            End If
        End With
    End Sub
```

```
Private Sub NextRecordButton_Click(ByVal sender As System.Object, _
    ByVal e As System.EventArgs) Handles NextRecordButton.Click
        ' Move to the next record.

    With APublishersBindingSource
        If .Position = .Count - 1 Then
            .MoveFirst()
        Else
            .MoveNext()
        End If
    End With
End Sub

Private Sub LastRecordButton_Click(ByVal sender As System.Object, _
    ByVal e As System.EventArgs) Handles LastRecordButton.Click
        ' Move to the last record.

    APublishersBindingSource.MoveLast()
End Sub
End Class
```

Navigating from a Combo Box Selection

The update program must change somewhat for a program that allows the user to select a record from a combo box, rather than navigate using buttons. The logic of an add, delete, or update is essentially the same, but the combo box introduces additional complications. Refer to Figures 5.7 and 5.8 for the form. You can see the complete program in Ch05DetailsViewUpdate.

During Navigation

When the user is navigating using the combo box, the text box portion of the combo box must not allow the user to enter any keystrokes that would change the displayed value. Also, the combo box text binding should be set to `Data-SourceUpdateMode.Never`.

You can change the DataSourceUpdateMode for the combo box using the DataBindings collection. Recall that you set the initial mode in the `DataBindings.Add` method:

```
NameComboBox.DataBindings.Add("text", ABindingSource, "Name", _
    False, DataSourceUpdateMode.Never)
```

The `DataBindings.Add` statement adds the text binding to the DataBindings collection. You can change the binding at run time using the bang (!) notation to refer to the text element in the DataBindings collection:

```
NameComboBox.DataBindings!text.DataSourceUpdateMode = _
    DataSourceUpdateMode.OnValidation
```

During an Add or Edit

The state of the combo box must change during an Add or Edit in regards to navigation. The user must not be allowed to make a new selection from the combo box, but instead be able to type text into the text portion of the box. You can prevent the user from dropping down the combo box by setting its

DropDownStyle to Simple during an Add or Edit. After the user has completed the Add or Edit by selecting *Save* or *Cancel*, you must change the combo box's DropDownStyle back to DropDownList.

```
NameComboBox.DropDownStyle = ComboBoxStyle.Simple
```

or

```
NameComboBox.DropDownStyle = ComboBoxStyle.DropDownList
```

The Combo Box Code

Write the code to handle the combo box binding and drop-down behavior in a general procedure and call it from the Add, Edit, Save, and Cancel routines.

```
Private Sub SetComboBoxBinding()
    ' Set the combo box to save changes.
    ' Saves for Add or Edit; does not save during navigation.
    ' Sets the combo box to not allow drop-down during an Add or an Edit.

    With NameComboBox
        If (AddingBoolean Or EditingBoolean) Then
            .DataBindings!text.DataSourceUpdateMode = _
            DataSourceUpdateMode.OnValidation
            .DropDownStyle = ComboBoxStyle.Simple
        Else
            .DataBindings!text.DataSourceUpdateMode = _
            DataSourceUpdateMode.Never
            .DropDownStyle = ComboBoxStyle.DropDownList
        End If
    End With
End Sub
```

Additional Requirements for Combo Box Navigation

You must guard against another potential problem. During an Add or Edit, if the focus is on the combo box and the user presses the Escape key, the keystroke is lost. So you must handle the Escape key yourself.

```
Private Sub NameComboBox_KeyDown(ByVal sender As Object, _
  ByVal e As System.Windows.Forms.KeyEventArgs) _
  Handles NameComboBox.KeyDown
    ' Cancel the Add or Edit if the Escape key is pressed.

    If (AddingBoolean Or EditingBoolean) And _
            e.KeyData = Keys.Escape Then
        DeleteCancelButton_Click(sender, e)
    End If
End Sub
```

> ### Feedback 5.3

1. You want to delete a record from a dataset and the original data source. Are these statements in the correct order?

   ```
   AuthorsBindingSource.RemoveCurrent()
   AuthorsTableAdapter.Update(NorthwindDataSet)
   ```

2. What steps are required to set up the form to allow a record to be added?

Validating User Input Data

As your user enters data, some fields need to be validated. You may need to check constraints, such as required fields or the data type. Your application also may contain business rules for validating the data. Validating the data before sending it back to the database can reduce the number of round trips between your application and the database. You can perform field-level or record-level validation in the code for the form or for the dataset. The recommended practice is to place validation code in the dataset.

Checking for Nulls

A common problem for programming database updates relates to null fields. What should happen if the user does not enter data in a required field? When and how should the validation occur? If the user does not enter data in a field that does not permit nulls and you send the record to the database, an exception occurs, which probably is not the desired behavior.

You can check to see which fields allow nulls in two ways in the VS IDE. If you display the DataSet Designer, you can click on each individual field and view its AllowDBNull property, which is a Boolean value. Or you can view the settings for an entire table by using the Server Explorer (or the Database Explorer in the VB Express Edition). Select *View / Server Explorer* (or *Database Explorer*) to see the window, which generally docks with the Toolbox window. Expand the node for your connection and its Tables collection to find the name of the table. Right-click on the table name and select *Open Table Definition*, which displays the column names, data types, and whether nulls are allowed for each field. In Figure 5.9, you can see that for the Publishers table, nulls are

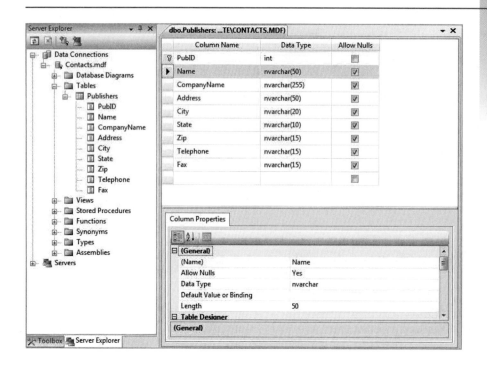

Figure 5.9

View and modify the table definition by selecting Open Table Definition *from the table's context menu in the Server Explorer or Database Explorer.*

allowed in all but the PubID field, which is the primary key. Notice that you can see more properties of each column in the lower portion of the window. You also can modify the table definition in this window.

Now look at the same table definition in the DataSet Designer (Figure 5.10) and notice the properties for the PubID field. The DefaultValue property is set to <DBNull>, which means that if the user doesn't make an entry, the field will be set to DBNull; the NullValue property is set to (Throw exception). You can see that this table is set up to throw an exception when the user does not enter data.

Figure 5.10

View and modify the table definition in the DataSet Designer and Properties Window.

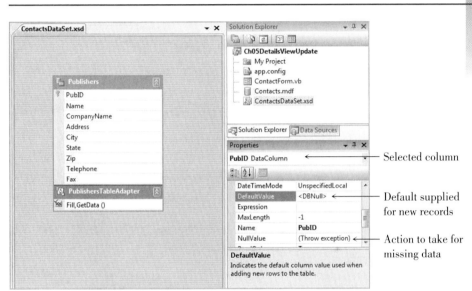

You can simplify the programming and catch errors by changing the DefaultValue property of a field to an empty string (just delete the existing value). Then you can perform validation when the user leaves a row that has changed, to check for an empty string.

Note that an empty string is not the same value as DBNull.

Adding Validation to a Details View Program

You can use the Validating event of bound controls to validate data entered by the user. The Validating event is fired when the user attempts to leave a control, depending on the setting of the CausesValidation property of the control to which the user moves. You want to keep the CausesValidation property of most controls set to their default value of *true*, but change the *Cancel* button's setting to *false*, so that the user can choose to cancel the edit.

In a control's Validating event handler, set `e.Cancel = True` for bad data. This action holds the input focus on the control in error, effectively making the control "sticky." You also will set the error message for an ErrorProvider control to display a message to the user (Figure 5.11). Don't forget to clear the message when the control passes validation.

Note: You can see the entire validation program in Ch05DetailsView-UpdateValidate.

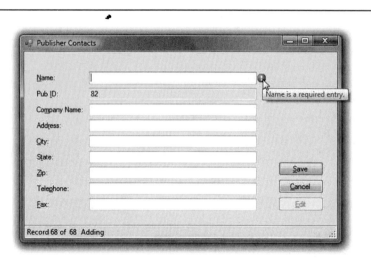

```
Private Sub NameComboBox_Validating(ByVal sender As Object, _
    ByVal e As System.ComponentModel.CancelEventArgs) _
    Handles NameComboBox.Validating
        ' Check for a required entry.
        ' Note: The CausesValidation property of the Delete/Cancel button must be
        '       set to False to allow the user to cancel the operation. Also, the
        '       user must be allowed to exit the program when an error occurs.

        If Not ClosingBoolean Then   ' Allow the user to exit the program.
            If NameComboBox.Text = String.Empty Then
                ErrorProvider1.SetError(NameComboBox, _
                    "Name is a required entry.")
                e.Cancel = True
            Else
                ErrorProvider1.Clear()
            End If
        End If
End Sub
```

Consider what actions a user should be able to take while adding or editing data. If the correct data are not available, the user must be able to back out of the operation, by clicking the *Cancel* button, pressing the Escape key, or exiting the program. You can take care of the *Cancel* button by setting the button's CausesValidation property to *false*. For the Escape key, we wrote code earlier in the combo box KeyDown event handler.

You must allow the user to close the application, even when a validation error is holding the focus in a control. One possibility is to code `e.Cancel` in the FormClosing event handler if an error is in effect. A better approach is to set a module-level Boolean variable in the FormClosing event handler and check it in the Validating event handler.

```
Private Sub ContactForm_FormClosing(ByVal sender As Object, _
    ByVal e As System.Windows.Forms.FormClosingEventArgs) _
    Handles Me.FormClosing
        ' Set switch to indicate that the user is attempting to close the form.

        ClosingBoolean = True
End Sub
```

The test for the ClosingBoolean variable appears in the Validating event handler for the combo box, which was shown earlier:

```
If Not ClosingBoolean Then ' Allow the user to exit the program.
```

Earlier, we had code in the *Cancel* button to cancel the current operation. Since the same steps are necessary for the Escape key, the best approach is to write those steps in a separate procedure and call it from the two locations.

```
Private Sub CancelOperation()
    ' Cancel the current Add or Edit operation.
    ' Called from the Cancel button and the Escape key.

    APublishersBindingSource.CancelEdit()
    ErrorProvider1.Clear()
    AddingBoolean = False
    EditingBoolean = False
    SetControlsReadOnly(True)
    ResetButtonsAfterEdit()
    SetComboBoxBinding()
    ToolStripStatusLabel2.Text = String.Empty
    If AddingBoolean Then
        PreviousSelectedIndex -= 1
    End If
End Sub
```

Adding Validation to the DataSet for a DataGridView Program

You can write validation code inside the dataset class, which is the preferred approach. As with other multitier programming, the purpose of the presentation tier is to display the data, not to process them. Writing the validation inside the dataset keeps the validation logic separate from the form's logic.

To view and modify the dataset class code, open the DataSet Designer, right-click on the table name, and select *View Code*. You can write event handlers for many events of the data table, including the ColumnChanged and TableNewRow events. The ColumnChanged event occurs when the user enters or changes the value for a single field; the TableNewRow event occurs when the user starts to add a new record.

As mentioned earlier, a required field may not contain either an empty string or a null value. The following code checks the CompanyName field in the publishers table of the Contacts dataset.

```
' Check for a null or empty string.
If PublisherRow.IsCompanyNameNull OrElse _
    PublisherRow.CompanyName = "" Then
        ' Bad data, set the error.
        PublisherRow.SetColumnError("CompanyName", _
            "CompanyName is a required field.")
Else
        ' Entry OK, remove any previous error.
        PublisherRow.SetColumnError("CompanyName", "")
End If
```

The IsCompanyNull property appears in IntelliSense for the row. You also can write the expression as `PublisherRow.IsNull("CompanyName")`.

You will want to check the CompanyName field in two different locations—from the ColumnChanged event handler and the TableNewRow event handler—so the best approach is to create a general sub procedure and call it when either a row is changed or a row is added.

```vb
Private Sub PublishersDataTable_TableNewRow(ByVal sender As Object, _
  ByVal e As System.Data.DataTableNewRowEventArgs) Handles Me.TableNewRow
    ' Check for errors when a new row is added.
    Dim TheRow As PublishersRow = CType(e.Row, PublishersRow)

    CheckCompanyName(TheRow)
    ' Code here to check other fields.
End Sub
```

In the ColumnChanged event handler, check to see which column is being changed:

```vb
Private Sub PublishersDataTable_ColumnChanged(ByVal sender As Object, _
  ByVal e As System.Data.DataColumnChangeEventArgs) Handles Me.ColumnChanged
    ' Check for errors when an existing row is edited.
    Dim TheRow As PublishersRow = CType(e.Row, PublishersRow)

    ' CompanyName.
    If (e.Column.ColumnName = Me.CompanyNameColumn.ColumnName) Then
        CheckCompanyName(TheRow)
    End If

    ' Code here to check for each of the fields.
End Sub
```

The CheckCompanyName general procedure:

```vb
Private Sub CheckCompanyName(ByVal PublisherRow As ContactsDataSet.PublishersRow)
    ' Check for a null or empty string.
    If PublisherRow.IsCompanyNameNull OrElse _
      PublisherRow.CompanyName = "" Then
        ' Bad data, set the error.
        PublisherRow.SetColumnError("CompanyName", _
          "CompanyName is a required field.")
    Else
        ' Entry OK, remove any previous error.
        PublisherRow.SetColumnError("CompanyName", "")
    End If
End Sub
```

The column errors in the dataset work well with a DataGridView. When the column error is turned on for a field, an error icon appears in the grid cell (Figure 5.12). And when the user enters good data, any error icon is turned off.

Figure 5.12

An error icon displays in the cell in error. It has an associated error message that pops up when the mouse points to the icon.

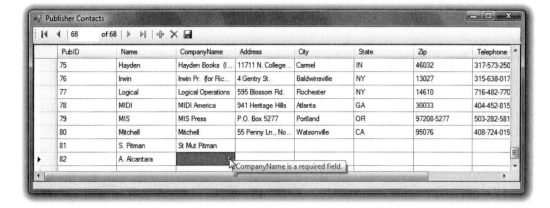

You can see the complete listing in Ch05GridViewUpdateValidate. And you can follow the step-by-step exercise in the section "Updating Related Tables," which takes you through creating these events and adding the code to the dataset's VB code file.

When you have validation in an application, you also must handle the Escape key. For the grid, you should cancel the current edit in the grid's KeyUp event handler.

```
Private Sub PublishersDataGridView_KeyUp (ByVal sender As Object, _
  ByVal e As System.Windows.Forms.KeyEventArgs) _
  Handles PublishersDataGridView.KeyUp
    ' Check for ESC key pressed in grid.
    ' Required to quit an Add operation when validation is in effect.

    If e.KeyData = Keys.Escape Then
        PublishersBindingSource.CancelEdit()
    End If
End Sub
```

Handling Data Exceptions

It is never a good idea to allow a program to cancel with a data exception. You can prevent some data input errors with validation; other errors you must catch with exception handling. The BindingSource for each table has a DataError event that is fired when an attempt is made to save bad data, and a DataGridView has a DataError event to help you identify errors in the data in the grid.

The DataGridView DataError Event

You can catch an error in the data for a DataGridView and display a message and icon in the current row. The EventArgs for the DataError event handler includes a RowIndex property, which identifies the row in error. Set `e.Cancel = True` to hold the user on the current row.

```
Private Sub PublishersDataGridView_DataError(ByVal sender As Object, _
  ByVal e As System.Windows.Forms.DataGridViewDataErrorEventArgs) _
  Handles PublishersDataGridView.DataError
    ' Handle data entry error.

    Dim CurrentRow As DataGridViewRow = PublishersDataGridView.Rows(e.RowIndex)
    CurrentRow.ErrorText = "Error in the data. Unable to save."
    e.Cancel = True
End Sub
```

The BindingSource DataError Event

To catch an error in data displayed in details view, write code for the Binding-Source's DataError event. This event does not give specific information about the location of the error, so you will have to write a generalized message, either in a message box or using an error provider.

```
Private Sub PublishersBindingSource_DataError(ByVal sender As Object, _
  ByVal e As System.Windows.Forms.BindingManagerDataErrorEventArgs) _
  Handles PublishersBindingSource.DataError
    ' Handle a data entry error.

    MessageBox.Show("Error in the data. " & e.Exception.Message.ToString)
End Sub
```

Updating Related Tables

When you execute the TableAdapter.Update method for a single table, you don't have to be concerned with how the records are updated. The TableAdapter. Update method issues the proper INSERT, DELETE, and UPDATE SQL commands. But if you are updating multiple tables with parent and child relationships, you must make sure that the commands are executed in the correct sequence.

The new TableAdapterManager component greatly simplifies updating related tables. By default, a TableAdapterManager is generated automatically when you drag a table or a field to a form to create a new BindingSource. You can change the default behavior by setting the dataset's HierarchicalUpdate property to *false*.

To view or change the HierarchicalUpdate property of the dataset, double-click the .xsd filename in the Solution Explorer to open the DataSet Designer. Then click anywhere in the blank area of the designer and the Properties window displays the properties of the dataset (Figure 5.13). By default, the HierarchicalUpdate property is set to *true* for new projects created in VB 2008, and *false* in any project created in any earlier version. You should consider changing the property to *false* for single-table applications; change the property before dragging any data elements to the form.

Figure 5.13

Click in a blank area of the DataSet Designer to display the dataset's properties in the Properties window. When the HierarchicalUpdate property is set to true *(the default), a TableAdapterManager is created for any new BindingSource added to a form.*

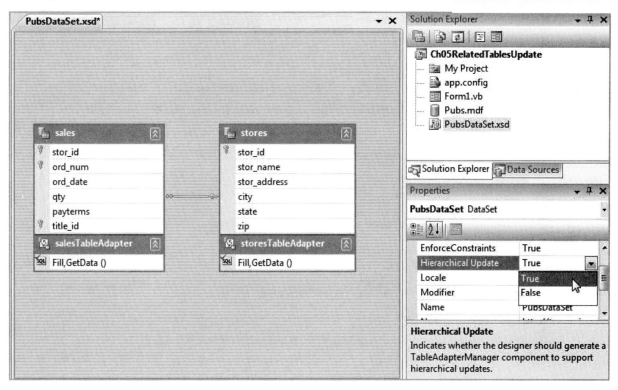

Parent and Child Relationships

If you add a new child and a new parent record, you must add the parent first or there will be no relationship for the child record. However, if you are deleting a parent record, all of the child records must be deleted first.

You cannot delete a parent or master if there are still associated child records. For example, you cannot eliminate a customer if there are still orders for the customer. First, all orders for the customer must be deleted; then the customer record can be deleted. Similarly, you cannot add child records for a parent record that has not yet been created. How could you add orders for a customer that is not on file?

Cascading Deletes and Updates

When you edit the relationship for related tables, you can specify **cascading deletes** and **cascading updates** (Figure 5.14). Cascading deletes and updates help to maintain referential integrity. When you delete a parent record, all child records for that parent are automatically deleted; and if you change the primary key field of a parent record, all child records that relate to that parent change to the new value. (However, allowing changes to the key field is not a good idea for most database applications.)

The update and delete rules determine how records are deleted and updated in the disconnected dataset, not the original data source. The `UpdateAll` method makes the changes in the original data source.

Figure 5.14

Set the relationship for cascading updates and deletes in the Relation dialog box, which you can display by right-clicking on the relationship in the DataSet Designer.

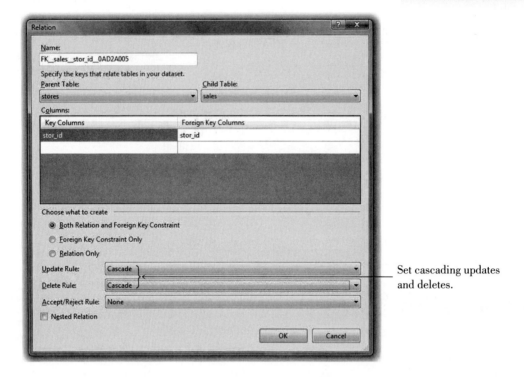

Set cascading updates and deletes.

Hierarchical Updates

The `TableAdapterManager.UpdateAll` method issues the correct updates to the original data source in the correct order. It first sends all inserts (parent, then child), all updates (parent, then child), and then all deletes (child, then parent).

A Related-Table Update Program—Step-by-Step

This example program uses the stores and sales tables of the Pubs database. The user can add, delete, and edit store records (the parents) and add, delete, and edit sales records (the child records). The data source is not updated for each change; instead, the user can click the *Save* toolbar button at any time, and in the form's FormClosing event handler, if there are unsaved changes, a message box asks whether to save the changes.

To illustrate the concept of a hierarchical update, the user is allowed to use the default navigation bar to navigate, add, delete, and save parent records, and use the grid to navigate, add, and delete child records. The completed form is shown in Figure 5.15.

Begin a New Project

STEP 1: Create a new Windows Forms project; name the project Ch05Hierar-chicalUpdate.

STEP 2: Add a new data source connected to Pubs.mdf. In the wizard, select the option to add the file to the project.

Figure 5.15

The completed step-by-step hierarchical update program. The stores table is the parent and the sales table is the child. In a related-table update program, the user can make changes to records in both tables.

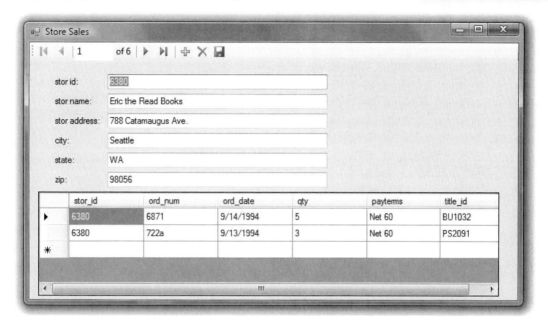

STEP 3: Select the stores and sales tables and finish the wizard.

STEP 4: In the Solution Explorer, click on the Pubs.mdf file. Change the file's CopyToOutputDirectory property to *Copy if newer*, so that any changes made to the database will be visible for the next program run.

STEP 5: Change the form name to StoreSalesForm and the form's Text property to "Store Sales". Widen the form to make room for the controls.

Modify the Tables' Relationship

STEP 1: Open the DataSet Designer by double-clicking on PubsDataSet.xsd in the Solution Explorer.

STEP 2: In the DataSet Designer, right-click on the line between the two tables and select *Edit Relation* from the context menu.

STEP 3: Referring to Figure 5.14, select the radio button for *Both Relation and Foreign Key Constraint*, which will enforce that any sales records have a matching store record. Then set the *Update Rule* and *Delete Rule* both to *Cascade*.

STEP 4: Click on an empty spot in the DataSet Designer and check the dataset's properties in the Properties window. EnforceConstraints and HierarchicalUpdate should both be set to *true*.

Create the Data-Bound Controls

STEP 1: Display the Form Designer and the Data Sources window.

STEP 2: In the Data Sources window, expand the stores node (the parent table). Drop down the list for the stores table and set its display mode to *Details*.

STEP 3: Drag the stores table to the form, approximately ½ inch down from the top of the form. While the controls are still selected, widen them.

Take a look at the components added to the component tray: Pubs-DataSet, StoresBindingSource, StoresTableAdapter, StoresBinding-Navigator, and TableAdapterManager.

STEP 4: Notice in the Data Sources window that the sales table appears twice—once at the same level as the stores table and again below the stores table (a child of the stores table). See Figure 5.16.

Figure 5.16

The sales table appears at the same level as the stores table and a second time as a child of the stores table. Make sure to select the child table, beneath the parent table, so that only the sales for the selected store will display in the grid.

STEP 5: Point to the child sales table, beneath the stores table, and drag the table to the form below the details controls. While the grid is still selected, widen it.

Notice that two new components were added to the component tray: SalesBindingSource and SalesTableAdapter.

STEP 6: With the grid still selected, set its Anchor property to anchor in all four directions: *Top*, *Bottom*, *Left*, and *Right*. This property setting makes the grid resize when the form is resized.

STEP 7: Save all

Modify the Generated Code

The designer automatically added code to the Form_Load event and the Click event for the *Save* button, but you must modify the code in both locations.

STEP 1: In the StoreSalesForm_Load event handler, check the order of the two `Fill` methods. You must fill the parent table before the child table, or you will generate constraint violations when a child record has no matching parent on the `Fill`.

STEP 2: Move the `Fill` for StoresTableAdapter before the `Fill` for SalesTableAdapter, if necessary.

STEP 3: Examine the code in the StoresBindingNavigatorSaveItem_Click event handler. The `StoresBindingSource.EndEdit` completes any pending edit in the stores table and commits it to the dataset.

STEP 4: Add another statement to also commit any unfinished edits for the sales table. Place the new statement before the `UpdateAll`.

```
Me.Validate() ' Causes validation of the control losing focus.
Me.StoresBindingSource.EndEdit()
Me.SalesBindingSource.EndEdit()
Me.TableAdapterManager.UpdateAll(Me.PubsDataSet)
```

STEP 5: Run the project just to make sure that the form's controls all fill correctly. You can step through the store records, but don't make any changes yet. You have some work to do first.

Commit Added Parent Records before Adding Child Records

If a user adds a new parent record (a new store) and then wants to add a sale for the new store, a constraint violation could occur since the dataset would not yet hold the store record. You can commit the store record when the user switches to the sales grid.

STEP 1: In the Code Editor, drop down the *Class Name* list and select *Sales-DataGridView*. Drop down the *Method Name* list and select *GotFocus*.

STEP 2: In the SalesDataGridView_GotFocus event procedure, add this code, which will commit any unfinished edit in the store record and reset the Stor_id text box to be ReadOnly:

```
Private Sub SalesDataGridView_GotFocus(ByVal sender As Object, _
   ByVal e As System.EventArgs) Handles SalesDataGridView.GotFocus
      ' Make sure that a new store is committed to the dataset before
      '   allowing a new sale to be added.

   Try
       StoresBindingSource.EndEdit()
       Stor_idTextBox.ReadOnly = True
   Catch Ex As Exception
       MessageBox.Show("Unable to save the changes. " _
         & Ex.Message, "Data Error")
   End Try
End Sub
```

Add the Save Query for Exit

The user can click the *Save* button to save the in-memory copy of the dataset to the original data source. We also want to check for unsaved changes when the user closes the application.

STEP 1: Create a new event handler for the form's FormClosing event and add the following code. If the user chooses to save the changes, we will call the *Save* button's event handler.

```
' Check for unsaved changes.

If PubsDataSet.HasChanges Then
    Dim ResponseDialogResult As DialogResult
    ResponseDialogResult = MessageBox.Show("Save the database changes?", _
      "Unsaved Changes", MessageBoxButtons.YesNoCancel, _
      MessageBoxIcon.Question)
    Select Case ResponseDialogResult
        Case Windows.Forms.DialogResult.Yes
            StoresBindingNavigatorSaveItem_Click(sender, e)
```

```
                  Case Windows.Forms.DialogResult.Cancel
                     e.Cancel = True
            End Select
       End If
```

Run the Application

STEP 1: Very cautiously, run the application. We want to try editing existing records and adding new sales and stores, but the Pubs database has many constraints and we have not yet added validation and exception handling.

STEP 2: Make a change to the information of an existing store and move to another record. When you move back to the changed record, the change should still be showing.

STEP 3: Add a new sale for an existing store. Be aware that all fields are required for a sale record, so you must enter something in every cell. You must add a title_id for a title that exists in the titles table, so for now use "BU1032" for testing. We will take care of this problem shortly.

Unless you are very careful, you will likely generate constraint violations. We will add validation and exception handling soon.

STEP 4: Click the *Save* button on the navigation bar. If you didn't violate any of the database constraints, the database should save.

STEP 5: Assuming that you were able to save the database successfully, close the application and run it again. Check for your changes.

If you were unable to save, try making less drastic changes and save again.

If you have made unwanted changes to the database, you can delete the file in the bin\Debug folder. On the next program run, a fresh copy of the database will be copied to the folder.

Help the User Enter Valid Data

You can take some simple steps to help the user enter valid data.

STEP 1: In the Form Designer, set the Stor_idTextBox to ReadOnly. This will prevent the user from changing the store's primary key field. Later we will set it back for adding a new store.

STEP 2: Open the DataSet Designer and check the MaxLength property of each of the text fields in both tables. Note that the date and quantity fields in the sales table do not have a MaxLength. Take notes for each field so you can set the MaxLength properties of all of the controls.

STEP 3: Switch back to the Form Designer and set the MaxLength property of each of the text boxes for the store table. You want to set the Stor_id-TextBox also, as the user will be entering a stor_id for any new stores. Make these settings for the text boxes:

stor_id	4
stor_name	40
stor_address	40
city	20
state	2
zip	5

STEP 4: Select the grid and choose *Edit Columns* from the smart tag, from the bottom of the Properties window, or from Columns property.

STEP 5: Select each grid column, with the exception of the date and quantity, and set the MaximumInputLength property of each:

stor_id	4
ord_num	20
payterms	12
title_id	6

STEP 6: Set the stor-id column to ReadOnly.

STEP 7: In the form's code, set the Stor_idTextBox to allow changes when the user clicks the *Add* button on the navigation bar.

```
Private Sub BindingNavigatorAddNewItem_Click(ByVal sender As System.Object, _
    ByVal e As System.EventArgs) Handles BindingNavigatorAddNewItem.Click
    ' Begin a store add; allow entry of Store ID.

    Stor_idTextBox.ReadOnly = False
End Sub
```

Add Exception Handling

STEP 1: In the form's code, add a Try/Catch in the *Save* button's event handler. Only save the database if there are unsaved changes.

```
Private Sub StoresBindingNavigatorSaveItem_Click(ByVal sender _
    As System.Object, ByVal e As System.EventArgs) _
    Handles StoresBindingNavigatorSaveItem.Click
    ' Save the dataset to the original data source.

    Try
        Me.Validate()  ' Causes validation of the control losing focus.
        Me.StoresBindingSource.EndEdit()
        Me.SalesBindingSource.EndEdit()
        If PubsDataSet.HasChanges Then
            Me.TableAdapterManager.UpdateAll(Me.PubsDataSet)
        End If
    Catch Ex As Exception
        MessageBox.Show("Unable to save the changes. " _
            & Ex.Message, "Data Error")
    End Try
End Sub
```

STEP 2: Handle the grid's DataError event so that bad data will display an error message and not cancel the program.

```
Private Sub SalesDataGridView_DataError(ByVal sender As Object, _
   ByVal e As System.Windows.Forms.DataGridViewDataErrorEventArgs) _
   Handles SalesDataGridView.DataError
      ' Handle an error in the grid.

      Dim CurrentRow As DataGridViewRow = SalesDataGridView.Rows(e.RowIndex)
      ' Display an error icon and message.
      CurrentRow.ErrorText = "Error in the data. Unable to save."
      ' Keep the data in the row.
      e.Cancel = True
End Sub
```

STEP 3: Handle the DataError event for the StoresBindingSource, to take care of any error in the stores data.

```
Private Sub StoresBindingSource_DataError(ByVal sender As Object, _
   ByVal e As System.Windows.Forms.BindingManagerDataErrorEventArgs) _
   Handles StoresBindingSource.DataError
      ' Handle error in Stores data entry.

      MessageBox.Show("Error in Sales data. " & e.Exception.ToString)
End Sub
```

STEP 4: Turn off any leftover error messages in the grid. If an error is corrected and the user moves to a new row, we must turn off the error indicator.

```
Private Sub SalesDataGridView_RowLeave(ByVal sender As Object, _
   ByVal e As System.Windows.Forms.DataGridViewCellEventArgs) _
   Handles SalesDataGridView.RowLeave
      ' Reset any error messages for an accepted row.

      Dim CurrentRow As DataGridViewRow = SalesDataGridView.Rows(e.RowIndex)
      CurrentRow.ErrorText = ""
End Sub
```

Add a Table Lookup Column for the Titles

When the user enters a title in the sales grid, the title must already be in the titles table. You can add a drop-down list of the titles to aid the user and allow only selections from the list (Figure 5.17)

STEP 1: In the Data Sources window, select the button at the top to *Configure DataSet with Wizard.*

STEP 2: Expand the *Tables* node, then expand the node for the titles table and select only the title_id and title fields. Click *Finish* and view the third table in the DataSet Designer.

STEP 3: In the Form Designer, select *Edit Columns* for the grid.

STEP 4: Click *Add* to add a new column, select *Unbound column,* enter a name and header text for the new column, select *DataGridViewComboBox* for *Type* (Figure 5.18), and click the *Add* button and then the *Close* button to close the *Add Column* dialog box. Use the down arrow to move the column to the bottom of the list.

Figure 5.17

Allow the user to select a title from a drop-down list.

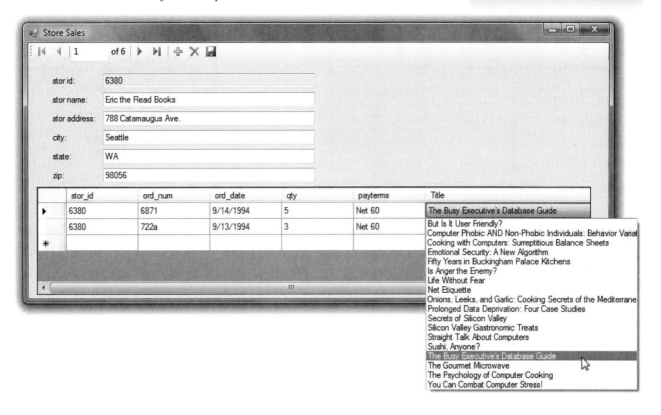

Figure 5.18

Add a new column to hold a combo box with a list of choices for the title.

STEP 5:   Next you will set some properties of the new column, still using the *Edit Columns* dialog box. Set the DataSource property to the titles table (Figure 5.19). *Note*: To find the titles table, you must expand the nodes for *Other Data Sources*, *Project Data Sources*, and *PubsDataSet*.

Figure 5.19

Set the new column's DataSource property to the titles table. You will have to expand the nodes for Other Data Sources, Project Data Sources, *and* PubsDataSet *to find the titles table.*

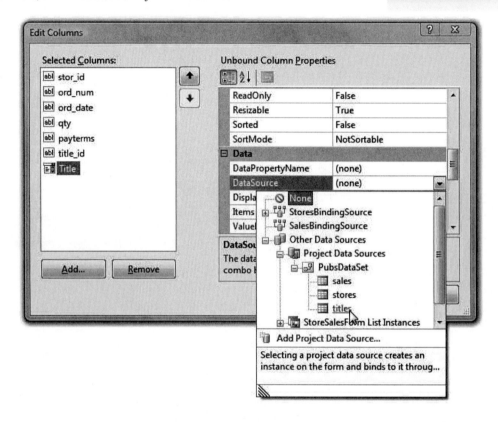

STEP 6:   Set the DisplayMember to title, the field that you want to display in the list.

STEP 7:   Set the DataPropertyName to the title_id field from the sales table, which is the field on which to perform the lookup.

STEP 8:   Set the ValueMember to the title_id from the titles table, which is the field from the lookup table to return when a selection is made.

STEP 9:   Set the DisplayStyle to *Nothing*. The result of this setting is that the cell looks like a text box unless an edit is in progress; then it looks like a combo box.

STEP 10:   Set the MinimumWidth to 100 and the Width to 300.

STEP 11:   Set the Visible property of the title_id column to *false* and close the *Edit Columns* dialog box.

STEP 12:   Test the application again. Test the titles lookup table, but remember that we still haven't added validation for empty cells in the grid.

Add Validation to the Dataset

For multitier programming, you should plan to add validation rules to the dataset (the data tier) rather than in the form (the presentation tier). Then you can change the user interface and the validation goes with the dataset.

Each of the fields in the sales table requires an entry. You can determine this fact by displaying the DataSet Designer and clicking on each field name. In the Properties window, you can view the AllowDBNull property; an entry of *false* means that the field must have a value.

We will write code in the PubsDataSet.vb file for two events of the SalesDataTable: the ColumnChanged (for changes to existing rows) and the TableNewRow (for the addition of a new row). In each event, we must check the name of the column being changed and test that column for an empty value, which is DBNull in a database field. For any error that we find, we call the SetColumnError method, which causes the error message to display in the presentation tier.

STEP 1: In the DataSet Designer, double-click on the ord_num field in the sales table. This will open the PubsDataSet.vb file in the salesDataTable_ColumnChanging event handler. We prefer to validate in the ColumnChanged event, rather than the ColumnChanging event, so the field value that is available in the EventArgs is the new value, rather than the previous value.

STEP 2: Drop down the *Class Name* list and select *salesDataTable Events*. Then drop down the *Methods* list and select *ColumnChanged* to open an event handler for the table's ColumnChanged event.

We plan to write code to check each field for DBNull, and we need to be able to call that code from the ColumnChanged event handler and the TableNewRow event handler.

STEP 3: In the ColumnChanged event handler, write this code to see if the current column is the ord_num column:

```
' Cast the current row to a salesRow type.
Dim TheRow As salesRow = CType(e.Row, salesRow)

' Ord_num column.
' If the name of the current column matches the name of the ord_num column:
If (e.Column.ColumnName = Me.ord_numColumn.ColumnName) Then
    ' Call the CheckOrder_Num sub, passing it the current row.
    CheckOrder_Num(TheRow)
End If
```

STEP 4: Write the CheckOrder_Num sub procedure. Notice the use of OrElse, which short circuits the compound expression. If the field is null and the first condition is *true*, you don't want to allow it to test for an empty string, which would cause an exception. Place the new sub below the last sub but before the two End Class statements.

```
Private Sub CheckOrder_Num(ByVal ASalesRow As PubsDataSet.salesRow)
    ' Validate the ord_num field.

    If ASalesRow.IsNull("ord_num") OrElse ASalesRow.ord_num = "" Then
        ASalesRow.SetColumnError("ord_num", _
            "Order number is a required entry.")
```

```
            Else
                ' Reset any previous error messages.
                ASalesRow.SetColumnError("ord_num", "")
            End If
    End Sub
```

STEP 5: Now write the code in the TableNewRow event handler. Drop down the *Class Name* list and select *salesDataTable Events* and select *Table-NewRow* from the *Methods* list.

STEP 6: Write the code to call the sub that you wrote in the previous step.

```
    ' Cast the current row to a salesRow type.
    Dim TheRow As salesRow = CType(e.Row, salesRow)

    ' Check for errors in the Order_Num field.
    CheckOrder_Num(TheRow)
```

STEP 7: Now that you can see how to write the check for one column of the table, here is the code to check all of the columns.

```
'Program:           Ch05HierarchicalUpdate
'Date:              June 2009
'Programmer:        Bradley/Millspaugh
'Class:             PubsDataSet
'Description:       Perform validation in the DataSet class.

Partial Public Class PubsDataSet

    Partial Class salesDataTable

        Private Sub salesDataTable_ColumnChanged(ByVal sender As Object, _
            ByVal e As System.Data.DataColumnChangeEventArgs) _
            Handles Me.ColumnChanged
            ' Check for errors when an existing row is edited.
            Dim TheRow As salesRow = CType(e.Row, salesRow)

            Select Case e.Column.ColumnName
                Case ord_numColumn.ColumnName
                    CheckOrder_Num(TheRow)
                Case ord_dateColumn.ColumnName
                    CheckOrderDate(TheRow)
                Case qtyColumn.ColumnName
                    CheckQuantity(TheRow)
                Case paytermsColumn.ColumnName
                    CheckPayTerms(TheRow)
            End Select
        End Sub
```

```vb
        Private Sub salesDataTable_TableNewRow(ByVal sender As Object, _
          ByVal e As System.Data.DataTableNewRowEventArgs) _
          Handles Me.TableNewRow
            ' Check for errors when a new row is added.
            Dim TheRow As salesRow = CType(e.Row, salesRow)

            CheckOrder_Num(TheRow)
            CheckOrderDate(TheRow)
            CheckQuantity(TheRow)
            CheckPayTerms(TheRow)
        End Sub

        Private Sub CheckOrder_Num(ByVal ASalesRow As PubsDataSet.salesRow)
            ' Validate the ord_num field.

            If ASalesRow.IsNull("ord_num") OrElse ASalesRow.ord_num = "" Then
                ASalesRow.SetColumnError("ord_num", _
                  "Order number is a required entry.")
            Else
                ASalesRow.SetColumnError("ord_num", "")
            End If
        End Sub

        Private Sub CheckOrderDate(ByVal ASalesRow As salesRow)

            If ASalesRow.IsNull("ord_date") OrElse _
              ASalesRow.ord_date.ToString = "" Then
                ASalesRow.SetColumnError("ord_date", _
                  "Order date is a required entry.")
            Else
                ASalesRow.SetColumnError("ord_date", "")
            End If
        End Sub

        Private Sub CheckQuantity(ByVal ASalesRow As salesRow)

            If ASalesRow.IsNull("qty") OrElse ASalesRow.qty.ToString = "" Then
                ASalesRow.SetColumnError("qty", "Quantity is a required entry.")
            Else
                ASalesRow.SetColumnError("qty", "")
            End If
        End Sub

        Private Sub CheckPayTerms(ByVal ASalesRow As salesRow)
            If ASalesRow.IsNull("payterms") OrElse ASalesRow.payterms = "" Then
                ASalesRow.SetColumnError("payterms", _
                  "Pay Terms is a required entry.")
            Else
                ASalesRow.SetColumnError("payterms", "")
            End If
        End Sub
    End Class
End Class
```

Run the Application

STEP 1: Run the application. Test adding new stores, adding new sales, modifying store data, and modifying sales data.

STEP 2: Consider improving the application by fixing the identifying labels for the text boxes and the header text for the grid columns.

STEP 3: Consider removing the navigation bar and navigating the stores table with a combo box. Add buttons or menu items for adding a new store, editing an existing store, deleting a store, and saving the file.

Security Considerations

You should take care to not provide a user with information that could be used to violate database security. For example, you should not use actual field names in your error messages, but instead use descriptive, friendly names for the data items. The practice of displaying `ex.Message` in a `Catch` clause is useful for testing and debugging a program but should not appear in a production program because often the actual field names are included in the message.

Your Hands-On Programming Example

Create an application to update the stores and sales tables in the Pubs database. Display the store names in a combo box for user selection and navigation and display the related sales for the selected store in a grid. The grid should display the full title, rather than the title_id, and allow the user to select a new title from a combo box while adding or editing a sale record.

Allow the user to add, edit, and delete store records. During an Add or Edit, the only choices should be Cancel or Commit; do not allow the user to click a menu choice or select from the combo box until the Add or Edit is complete. Keep the text boxes locked (ReadOnly) unless an Add or Edit is in progress. Display a message box to confirm a Delete.

Display the record number and record count in a status bar. Also, display the current status information, such as "Adding", "Editing", and "Record deleted".

The Pubs database is a sample database from Microsoft. It contains many constraints of which you must be aware. Set the MaxLength properties of text boxes to prevent a too-long entry and perform validation so that the user will not cancel the program with an exception.

Note that this program performs the same functions as the related-table update in the chapter. The major differences are that this program does not use a navigation bar but has menu choices for editing, adding, and deleting store records. When an Edit or Add is in progress, the only choices to the user are *Commit* and *Cancel.*

Planning the Project

Sketch a form (Figure 5.20) that your users sign off as meeting their needs.

Figure 5.20

The planning sketch for the hands-on programming example.

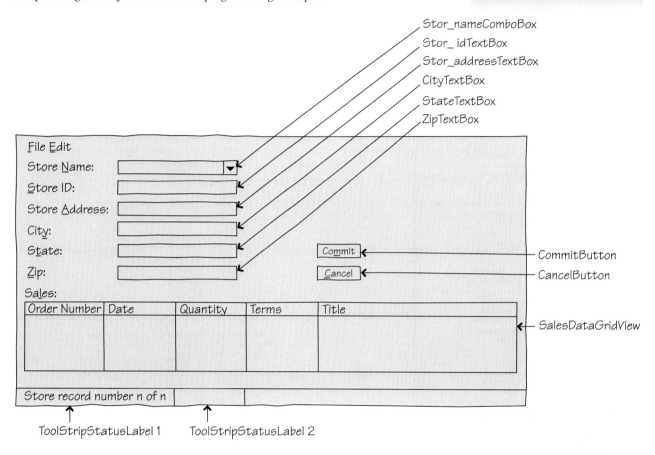

Plan the Objects, Properties, and Methods Determine the objects and property settings for the form and its controls and for the data-tier component. Figure 5.21 shows the diagram of the program components.

Presentation Tier

Object	Property	Setting
StoreSalesForm	Text	Store Sales
Stor_nameComboBox	Text	(blank)
	MaxLength	40
Stor_idTextBox	Text	(blank)
	MaxLength	4
Stor_addressTextBox	Text	(blank)
	MaxLength	40
CityTextBox	Text	(blank)
	MaxLength	40

(continued)

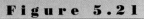

Figure 5.21

The components for the hands-on programming example.

StoreSalesForm
Class
→ Form

Fields
- AddingBoolean
- AddNewStoreToolStripMenuItem
- CancelEditButton
- CityTextBox
- CommitEditButton
- DeleteSelectedStoreToolStripMenuItem...
- EditingBoolean
- EditSelectedStoreToolStripMenuItem
- EditToolStripMenuItem
- ExitToolStripMenuItem
- FileToolStripMenuItem
- PreviousSelectedIndex
- PubsDataSet
- SalesBindingSource
- SalesDataGridView
- SalesTableAdapter
- SaveDatabaseToolStripMenuItem
- SetupCompleteBoolean
- StatusStrip1
- Stor_addressTextBox
- Stor_idTextBox
- Stor_nameComboBox
- StoresBindingSource
- StoresTableAdapter
- TableAdapterManager
- Title
- TitlesBindingSource
- TitlesTableAdapter
- ToolStripStatusLabel1
- ToolStripStatusLabel2
- ZipTextBox

Methods
- AddNewStoreToolStripMenuItem_Click
- CancelAddOrEdit
- CancelEditButton_Click
- CommitEditButton_Click
- DeleteSelectedStoreToolStripMenuItem...
- EditSelectedStoreToolStripMenuItem...
- ExitToolStripMenuItem_Click
- ResetButtonsAfterEdit
- SalesDataGridView_DataError
- SalesDataGridView_RowLeave
- SaveDatabaseToolStripMenuItem_Cli...
- SaveDataSet
- SetButtonsForEdit
- SetComboBoxBinding
- SetControlsReadOnly
- Stor_nameComboBox_KeyDown
- StoreSales_Load
- StoreSalesForm_FormClosing
- StoresBindingSource_DataError
- StoresBindingSource_PositionChanged

PubsDataSet
Class
→ DataSet

- Fields
- Properties
- Methods
- Nested Types

Object	Property	Setting
StateTextBox	Text	(blank)
	MaxLength	2
ZipTextBox	Text	(blank)
	MaxLength	5
SalesDataGridView	Name	SalesDataGridView
SaveDatabaseToolStripMenuItem	Text	&Save Database
ExitToolStripMenuItem	Text	E&xit
AddNewStoreToolStripMenuItem	Text	&Add New Store

DeleteSelectedStoreToolStripMenuItem	Text	&Delete Selected Store
EditSelectedStoreToolStripMenuItem	Text	&Edit Selected Store
CommitEditButton	Text	Co&mmit
	Enabled	False
CancelEditButton	Text	&Cancel
	Enabled	False
ToolStripStatusLabel1	Text	(blank)
ToolStripStatusLabel2	Text	(blank)

Event handlers/methods	**Actions—Pseudocode**
Form Load event	Fill all three tables. Set the combo box binding. Set the text boxes to read only. Set SetupCompleteBoolean to True.

Form
FormClosing event
	If the dataset has changes
	    Query the user for save.
	        Select Case on the result.
	            Case Yes
	                SaveDataSet.
	            Case Cancel
	                Set e.Cancel = True
	        End Select

AddNewStoreToolStripMenuItem Click event	End any edit in progress. Execute **AddNew** method to clear fields. Set AddingBoolean = True Set the combo box to allow keyboard entry. Set the focus to the combo box. Unlock the text boxes (ReadOnly = False). Set buttons for add or edit. Save the current index of the combo box. Disable the sales grid.

DeleteSelectedStoreToolStripMenuItem
Click event.
	Confirm delete in message box.
	If Yes
	    Delete the record from the dataset.
	    Set the status label to "Deleted".
	Else
	    Clear the status label.

EditSelectedStoreToolStripMenuItem Click event	Set EditingBoolean to True. Set text boxes' ReadOnly to False. Set buttons for edit. Save the current index of the combo box. Set the combo box to allow keyboard entry.
SaveDatabaseToolStripMenuItem Click event	SaveDataSet.
ExitToolStripMenuItem Click event	Close the form.

(continued)

Event handlers/methods	Actions—Pseudocode
CommitEditButton Click event	End the current edit. Set the status label to "Record Saved". Set AddingBoolean and EditingBoolean to False. Set text boxes to ReadOnly. Reset the buttons for normal operation. Set the combo box to not save changes. Reset the combo box index to its previous value.
CancelEditButton Click event	If adding or editing CancelAddOrEdit.
SalesDataGridView RowLeave event	Reset any grid error messages.
StoresBindingSource PositionChanged event	Display the record number in the status bar label.

Stor_nameComboBox
   KeyDown
	If adding or editing and Escape key pressed
	    Call CancelAddOrEdit.

CancelAddOrEdit	If adding Subtract 1 from previous selected index. Cancel the edit. Set AddingBoolean and EditingBoolean = False Set the text boxes to read only. Reset the buttons for normal operation. Set the combo box to not save changes. Reset the combo box's selected index to the previous value. Clear the status label.
ResetButtonsAfterEdit	Disable the *Commit* and *Cancel* buttons. Enable the *Add*, *Edit*, and *Delete* menu items. Enable the sales grid.

SaveDataSet	If the dataset has changes
	    End any edits in both tables.
	    Execute the `UpdateAll` method of the TableAdapterManager.

SetButtonsForEdit	Enable the *Commit* and *Cancel* buttons.
	Disable the *Add*, *Edit*, and *Delete* menu items.
	If adding
	    Set the status label to "Adding".
	Else
	    Set the status label to "Editing".

SetComboBoxBinding	If adding or editing
	    Set the data binding to save changes.
	    Set DropDownStyle to Simple.
	Else
	    Set the data binding to not save changes.
	    Set DropDownStyle to DropDownList.

SetControlsReadOnly(Boolean)	Set text boxes' ReadOnly property to Boolean value.
SalesDataGridView DataError event	Set the ErrorText to an error message. Set e.Cancel = True
StoresBindingSource DataError event	If setup complete Display an error message.

Data Tier—PubsDataSet

Event handlers/methods	Actions—Pseudocode
salesDataTable ColumnChanged event	Check each column for a null or blank entry. Set the ColumnError message for any missing data.
salesDataTable TableNewRow event	Check each column for a null or blank entry. Set the ColumnError message for any missing data.

Write the Project Following the sketch in Figure 5.20, create the form. Figure 5.22 shows the completed form.

- Add the data source to the project, including the stores and sales tables, and the title_id and title field from the titles table.

- Set the properties of each of the form objects, according to your plans.

- Write the validation methods in the DataSet component.

- Write the code for the form. Working from the pseudocode, write each event handler and general procedure.

- When you complete the code, test the operation many times. Compare the screen output to the data tables to make sure that you are displaying the correct information. Make sure to test every option, including the validation routines.

Note: Make sure to set the *Copy to Output Directory* property of the database file to *Copy if newer* in order to test the updating.

Figure 5.22

The form for the hands-on programming example.

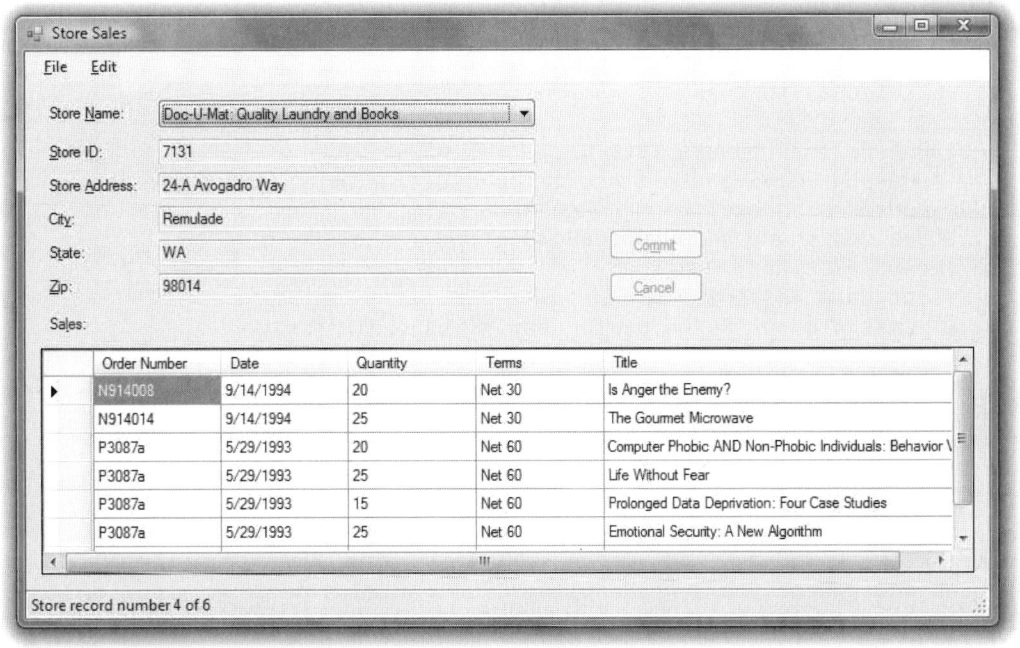

The Project Coding Solution
The Form

```
'Program:          Ch05HandsOn
'Date:             June 2009
'Programmer:       Bradley/Millspaugh
'Class:            StoreSalesForm
'Description:      Allow the user to display and update data for stores and
'                  their related sales. Uses a combo box for navigation.

Public Class StoreSalesForm

    ' Module-level declarations.
    Private AddingBoolean As Boolean = False
    Private EditingBoolean As Boolean = False
    Private PreviousSelectedIndex As Integer
    Private SetupCompleteBoolean As Boolean = False

    Private Sub StoreSales_Load(ByVal sender As System.Object, _
      ByVal e As System.EventArgs) Handles MyBase.Load
        ' Fill the parent and child tables, in that order.

        Try
            StoresTableAdapter.Fill(PubsDataSet.stores)
            SalesTableAdapter.Fill(PubsDataSet.sales)
            TitlesTableAdapter.Fill(PubsDataSet.titles)
            SetComboBoxBinding()
            SetControlsReadOnly(True)
            SetupCompleteBoolean = True
        Catch ex As Exception
            MessageBox.Show("Unable to retrieve the data." & ex.Message, _
                "Data Error", MessageBoxButtons.OK, MessageBoxIcon.Exclamation)
            Me.Close()
        End Try
    End Sub

    Private Sub StoreSalesForm_FormClosing(ByVal sender As Object, _
      ByVal e As System.Windows.Forms.FormClosingEventArgs) _
      Handles Me.FormClosing
        ' Check for unsaved changes.

        If PubsDataSet.HasChanges Then
            Dim ResponseDialogResult As DialogResult
            ResponseDialogResult = MessageBox.Show("Save the database changes?", _
                "Unsaved Changes", MessageBoxButtons.YesNoCancel, _
                MessageBoxIcon.Question)
            Select Case ResponseDialogResult
                Case Windows.Forms.DialogResult.Yes
                    SaveDataSet()
                Case Windows.Forms.DialogResult.Cancel
                    e.Cancel = True
            End Select
        End If
    End Sub

    ' MenuItem event handlers.
    Private Sub AddNewStoreToolStripMenuItem_Click(ByVal sender _
      As System.Object, ByVal e As System.EventArgs) _
      Handles AddNewStoreToolStripMenuItem.Click
        ' Begin an Add operation.
```

```vbnet
        Try
            With StoresBindingSource
                .EndEdit()
                .AddNew()
            End With

            AddingBoolean = True
            SetComboBoxBinding()
            Stor_nameComboBox.Focus()
            SetControlsReadOnly(False)
            SetButtonsForEdit()
            If Stor_nameComboBox.SelectedIndex <> -1 Then
                ' Save the index of the new record for later navigation.
                PreviousSelectedIndex = Stor_nameComboBox.Items.Count - 1
            Else
                PreviousSelectedIndex = 0
            End If
            SalesDataGridView.Enabled = False
        Catch ex As Exception
            MessageBox.Show("Error on AddNew: " & ex.Message)
        End Try
    End Sub

    Private Sub DeleteSelectedStoreToolStripMenuItem_Click( _
      ByVal sender As System.Object, ByVal e As System.EventArgs) _
      Handles DeleteSelectedStoreToolStripMenuItem.Click
        ' Delete the current store record after confirming.
        Dim DeleteDialogResult As DialogResult

        Try
            DeleteDialogResult = MessageBox.Show( _
              "Delete this store and all sales for the store?", _
              "Confirm Delete", MessageBoxButtons.YesNo, _
              MessageBoxIcon.Question)
            If DeleteDialogResult = Windows.Forms.DialogResult.Yes Then
                StoresBindingSource.RemoveCurrent()
                ToolStripStatusLabel2.Text = "Store record deleted."
            Else
                ToolStripStatusLabel2.Text = String.Empty
            End If
        Catch ex As Exception
            Dim MessageString As String
            MessageString = "Unable to complete the delete operation: " _
              & ex.Message
            MessageBox.Show(MessageString, "Delete", MessageBoxButtons.OK, _
              MessageBoxIcon.Exclamation)
            ToolStripStatusLabel2.Text = String.Empty
        End Try
    End Sub

    Private Sub EditSelectedStoreToolStripMenuItem_Click( _
      ByVal sender As System.Object, ByVal e As System.EventArgs) _
      Handles EditSelectedStoreToolStripMenuItem.Click
        ' Allow editing to the current store record.

        EditingBoolean = True
        SetControlsReadOnly(False)
```

```vb
            SetButtonsForEdit()
            PreviousSelectedIndex = Stor_nameComboBox.SelectedIndex
            SetComboBoxBinding()
    End Sub

    Private Sub SaveDatabaseToolStripMenuItem_Click(ByVal sender _
      As System.Object, ByVal e As System.EventArgs) _
      Handles SaveDatabaseToolStripMenuItem.Click
        ' Save the DataSet.

        SaveDataSet()
    End Sub

    Private Sub ExitToolStripMenuItem_Click(ByVal sender As System.Object, _
      ByVal e As System.EventArgs) Handles ExitToolStripMenuItem.Click
        ' Close the application.

        Me.Close()
    End Sub

    ' Button event handlers.
    Private Sub CommitEditButton_Click(ByVal sender As System.Object, _
      ByVal e As System.EventArgs) Handles CommitEditButton.Click
        ' Save Updates and Adds to the DataSet.

        Try
            StoresBindingSource.EndEdit()
            ToolStripStatusLabel2.Text = "Record Saved"
            AddingBoolean = False
            EditingBoolean = False
            SetControlsReadOnly(True)
            ResetButtonsAfterEdit()
            SetComboBoxBinding()
            Stor_nameComboBox.SelectedIndex = PreviousSelectedIndex
        Catch ex As Exception
            ' Catch duplicate records and constraint violations.
            MessageBox.Show("Database error. Duplicate or missing Store ID: " _
              & ex.Message, "Data Error", MessageBoxButtons.OK, _
              MessageBoxIcon.Exclamation)
        End Try
    End Sub

    Private Sub CancelEditButton_Click(ByVal sender As System.Object, _
      ByVal e As System.EventArgs) Handles CancelEditButton.Click
        ' Cancel an Add or Edit operation.
        '  Note that this button is the form's Cancel button, so could
        '    possibly come here when there isn't an Add or Edit in
        '    progress.

        If AddingBoolean Or EditingBoolean Then
            CancelAddOrEdit()
        End If
    End Sub

    ' Control event handlers.
    Private Sub SalesDataGridView_RowLeave(ByVal sender As Object, _
      ByVal e As System.Windows.Forms.DataGridViewCellEventArgs) _
      Handles SalesDataGridView.RowLeave
        ' Reset any error messages for an accepted row.
```

```
        Dim CurrentRow As DataGridViewRow = SalesDataGridView.Rows(e.RowIndex)
        CurrentRow.ErrorText = ""
End Sub

Private Sub StoresBindingSource_PositionChanged(ByVal sender As Object, _
    ByVal e As System.EventArgs) _
    Handles StoresBindingSource.PositionChanged
        ' Display the record number in the status bar.

        With StoresBindingSource
            ToolStripStatusLabel1.Text = "Store record number " & _
                (.Position + 1).ToString & " of " & .Count.ToString
        End With
End Sub

Private Sub Stor_nameComboBox_KeyDown(ByVal sender As Object, _
    ByVal e As System.Windows.Forms.KeyEventArgs) _
    Handles Stor_nameComboBox.KeyDown
        ' Handle the Escape key while adding and editing.

        If (AddingBoolean Or EditingBoolean) And _
            e.KeyData = Keys.Escape Then
            CancelAddOrEdit()
        End If
End Sub

' General procecedures.
Private Sub CancelAddOrEdit()
        ' Cancel an Add or Edit.
        '  Called from the Cancel button.

        If AddingBoolean Then
            PreviousSelectedIndex -= 1
        End If
        StoresBindingSource.CancelEdit()
        AddingBoolean = False
        EditingBoolean = False
        SetControlsReadOnly(True)
        ResetButtonsAfterEdit()
        SetComboBoxBinding()
        Stor_nameComboBox.SelectedIndex = PreviousSelectedIndex
        ToolStripStatusLabel2.Text = String.Empty
End Sub

Private Sub ResetButtonsAfterEdit()
        ' Reset the buttons and menu items after an Add or Edit operation.

        CancelEditButton.Enabled = False
        CommitEditButton.Enabled = False
        AddNewStoreToolStripMenuItem.Enabled = True
        DeleteSelectedStoreToolStripMenuItem.Enabled = True
        EditSelectedStoreToolStripMenuItem.Enabled = True
        SalesDataGridView.Enabled = True
End Sub

Private Sub SaveDataSet()
        ' Save the DataSet to the original data source.
```

```
        If PubsDataSet.HasChanges Then
            Try
                Validate()
                StoresBindingSource.EndEdit()
                SalesBindingSource.EndEdit()
                TableAdapterManager.UpdateAll(PubsDataSet)
            Catch ex As Exception
                MessageBox.Show("Unable to save the changes: " & _
                    ex.Message, "Save", _
                    MessageBoxButtons.OK, MessageBoxIcon.Warning)
            End Try
        End If
    End Sub

    Private Sub SetButtonsForEdit()
        ' Set up the buttons and menu items for an Add or Edit operation.

        CancelEditButton.Enabled = True
        CommitEditButton.Enabled = True
        AddNewStoreToolStripMenuItem.Enabled = False
        DeleteSelectedStoreToolStripMenuItem.Enabled = False
        EditSelectedStoreToolStripMenuItem.Enabled = False
        If AddingBoolean Then
            ToolStripStatusLabel2.Text = "Adding"
        Else
            ToolStripStatusLabel2.Text = "Editing"
        End If
    End Sub

    Private Sub SetComboBoxBinding()
        ' Set the combo box to save any changes.
        ' Saves for Add or Edit; does not save during navigation.
        '  Sets the combo box to not allow drop-down during an Add or an Edit.

        With Stor_nameComboBox
            If (AddingBoolean Or EditingBoolean) Then
                .DataBindings!text.DataSourceUpdateMode = _
                    DataSourceUpdateMode.OnValidation
                .DropDownStyle = ComboBoxStyle.Simple
            Else
                .DataBindings!text.DataSourceUpdateMode = _
                    DataSourceUpdateMode.Never
                .DropDownStyle = ComboBoxStyle.DropDownList
            End If
        End With
    End Sub

    Private Sub SetControlsReadOnly(ByVal ValueBoolean As Boolean)
        ' Lock or unlock the controls.

        Stor_idTextBox.ReadOnly = ValueBoolean
        Stor_addressTextBox.ReadOnly = ValueBoolean
        CityTextBox.ReadOnly = ValueBoolean
        StateTextBox.ReadOnly = ValueBoolean
        ZipTextBox.ReadOnly = ValueBoolean
    End Sub

    Private Sub SalesDataGridView_DataError(ByVal sender As Object, _
      ByVal e As System.Windows.Forms.DataGridViewDataErrorEventArgs) _
      Handles SalesDataGridView.DataError
        ' Handle an error in the grid.
```

```vb
            Dim CurrentRow As DataGridViewRow = SalesDataGridView.Rows(e.RowIndex)
            CurrentRow.ErrorText = "Error in the data. Unable to save."
            e.Cancel = True
        End Sub

        Private Sub StoresBindingSource_DataError(ByVal sender As Object, _
          ByVal e As System.Windows.Forms.BindingManagerDataErrorEventArgs) _
          Handles StoresBindingSource.DataError
            ' Handle error in Stores data entry.

            If SetupCompleteBoolean Then
                MessageBox.Show("Error in Sales data. " & e.Exception.ToString, _
                    "Data Error", MessageBoxButtons.OK, MessageBoxIcon.Warning)
            End If
        End Sub

End Class
```

The Data Tier—PubsDataSet

```vb
'Program:           Ch05HierarchicalUpdate
'Date:              June 2009
'Programmer:        Bradley/Millspaugh
'Class:             PubsDataSet
'Description:       Perform validation in the DataSet class.

Partial Public Class PubsDataSet

    Partial Class salesDataTable

        Private Sub salesDataTable_ColumnChanged(ByVal sender As Object, _
          ByVal e As System.Data.DataColumnChangeEventArgs) _
          Handles Me.ColumnChanged
            ' Check for errors when an existing row is edited.
            Dim TheRow As salesRow = CType(e.Row, salesRow)

            Select Case e.Column.ColumnName
                Case ord_numColumn.ColumnName
                    CheckOrder_Num(TheRow)
                Case ord_dateColumn.ColumnName
                    CheckOrderDate(TheRow)
                Case qtyColumn.ColumnName
                    CheckQuantity(TheRow)
                Case paytermsColumn.ColumnName
                    CheckPayTerms(TheRow)
            End Select
        End Sub
```

```vb
Private Sub salesDataTable_TableNewRow(ByVal sender As Object, _
  ByVal e As System.Data.DataTableNewRowEventArgs) _
  Handles Me.TableNewRow
    ' Check for errors when a new row is added.
    Dim TheRow As salesRow = CType(e.Row, salesRow)

    CheckOrder_Num(TheRow)
    CheckOrderDate(TheRow)
    CheckQuantity(TheRow)
    CheckPayTerms(TheRow)
End Sub

Private Sub CheckOrder_Num(ByVal ASalesRow As PubsDataSet.salesRow)
    ' Validate the ord_num field.

    If ASalesRow.IsNull("ord_num") OrElse ASalesRow.ord_num = "" Then
        ASalesRow.SetColumnError("ord_num", _
          "Order number is a required entry.")
    Else
        ASalesRow.SetColumnError("ord_num", "")
    End If
End Sub

Private Sub CheckOrderDate(ByVal ASalesRow As salesRow)

    If ASalesRow.IsNull("ord_date") OrElse _
      ASalesRow.ord_date.ToString = "" Then
        ASalesRow.SetColumnError("ord_date", _
          "Order date is a required entry.")
    Else
        ASalesRow.SetColumnError("ord_date", "")
    End If
End Sub

Private Sub CheckQuantity(ByVal ASalesRow As salesRow)

    If ASalesRow.IsNull("qty") OrElse ASalesRow.qty.ToString = "" Then
        ASalesRow.SetColumnError("qty", _
          "Quantity is a required entry.")
    Else
        ASalesRow.SetColumnError("qty", "")
    End If
End Sub

Private Sub CheckPayTerms(ByVal ASalesRow As salesRow)
    If ASalesRow.IsNull("payterms") OrElse _
      ASalesRow.payterms = "" Then
        ASalesRow.SetColumnError("payterms", _
          "Pay Terms is a required entry.")
    Else
        ASalesRow.SetColumnError("payterms", "")
    End If
End Sub
    End Class
End Class
```

Summary

1. A dataset remains disconnected from the data source. Any changes to the dataset must be sent back to the data source. The TableAdapter handles saving changes as well as creating the dataset.

2. If you choose the option to store your database in the project folder, make the selection to copy the file to the bin\Debug folder when you run the project. You can delete the copy in the bin\Debug folder to get an unchanged version of the file.

3. The RowState property of each row in the dataset or table reflects any changes. The value can be Added, Deleted, Modified, or Unchanged.

4. Use the DataSet's `HasChanges` method to determine if there are any changes in the dataset since it was created or the `AcceptChanges` method last executed. You also can specify the type of changes to look for using the RowState as an argument.

5. The `GetChanges` method of a DataSet or DataTable can return only the changes for a specific value in RowState.

6. The `BeginEdit` method starts an edit operation, which can be terminated with either `EndEdit` or `CancelEdit`.

7. Several versions of a DataRow are maintained: Current, Original, Default, and, during an edit, Proposed.

8. The `AcceptChanges` method commits the changes in the table. The Original version is set to the Current version and all RowState properties are set to Unchanged. The `RejectChanges` rolls back all of the changes.

9. The `Update` method of the TableAdapter calls SQL statements to make the changes in the dataset to the original data source. You can either execute the `Update` method for every change or hold the changes and update only when the user selects a Save option or when the program ends.

10. A TableAdapterManager component coordinates multiple TableAdapters for a project with multiple tables. The `TableAdapterManager.UpdateAll` method sends the updated dataset to the original data source.

11. The BindingSource object tracks the position and count of rows in a table within a dataset. Setting all controls on a form to the same binding source ensures that all bound controls display fields from the same record. Use the binding source's Position property to view or change the current record number; the Count property returns the number of records in the table.

12. The `AddNew`, `Insert`, `RemoveCurrent`, `RemoveAt`, `CancelEdit`, and `EndEdit` methods of the BindingSource object are used to update rows in a table.

13. The Binding Source's PositionChanged event occurs each time the record number changes. You can write an event handler to display the record number. If you are writing a multitier application, declare the BindingSource object `WithEvents` in order to respond to its events.

14. To begin an Add, use the Binding Source's `AddNew` method, which clears the bound fields for the new record.

15. Use the Binding Source's `RemoveCurrent` method to remove a record.

16. When multiple users can update a database at the same time, the concurrency control settings determine how the changes are saved.

17. When the user is adding or editing, the only choices should be to save or cancel. Navigation should not be an option.

18. When the user is navigating, the controls should be set to ReadOnly. No changes should be allowed unless an add or edit is selected.

19. When using a combo box for navigation, the DataSourceUpdateMode of the data bindings must change, depending on the operation. If navigating, no changes should be saved; if an Add or Edit is in progress, the user should be allowed to make changes and the changes should be saved.

20. You should always check the constraints of database tables and make sure that you validate for those constraints, rather than allow the user to see exceptions.

21. You can use the Validating event handlers of controls to perform validation and set the `e.Cancel` argument to *true* to cancel the operation and keep the user in the control in error. Use an ErrorProvider component to display the error message.

22. A DataGridView has both a CellValidating event and a RowValidating event. The CellValidating event occurs when the user leaves a cell and moves across the row to a new cell; the RowValidating event occurs when the user moves off the current row. You can set the cell or row ErrorText property to an error message and set ShowCellErrors and ShowRowErrors to *true* or *false*.

23. When updating related tables, the sequence of the updates is important. The TableAdapterManager saves all inserts (parent first, then child), next it saves all updates (parent first, then child), and then it saves all deletes (child first, then parent).

24. In a relationship between tables, you can specify cascading deletes and cascading updates, which helps to maintain referential integrity in the tables.

25. You can allow the user to select values from a combo box in a table lookup cell of a DataGridView.

26. It is preferable to write the validation code in the dataset's code, rather than in the form itself.

Key Terms

AcceptChanges method *193*
AddNew method *197*
BeginEdit method *193*
BindingSource object *195*
CancelEdit method *193*
cascading deletes *219*
cascading updates *219*
concurrency *199*
concurrency control *199*
Count property *196*
CurrentChanged event *198*

EndEdit method *193*
GetChanges method *193*
HasChanges method *192*
Position property *196*
PositionChanged event *198*
RejectChanges method *193*
RemoveCurrent method *198*
RowState property *192*
Update method *194*
UpdateAll method *194*

Review Questions

1. What is the purpose of the RowState property and what values can it hold?
2. Differentiate between the `GetChanges` method and the `HasChanges` method. Explain when each would be used.
3. List and explain each of the properties, methods, and events of the BindingSource class.
4. How can you navigate from one record to the next using the Binding Source?
5. Explain how you perform each of the following updates:
   a. Add a record.
   b. Delete a record.
   c. Modify a record.
   d. Save changes.
6. Explain how to prompt the user to save changes when the application closes.
7. Explain the steps necessary to use a combo box for navigation in an update program.
8. Discuss the sequence of updates for related tables to ensure referential integrity.

Programming Exercises

Note: For each of these exercises, allow the user to add, edit, or delete a record. Do not allow the user to make changes to fields on the screen unless an Add or Edit is in progress. Make sure to query for any unsaved changes when the program closes.

5.1 Write an application to update the subjects table from RnRBooks.mdf in details view. Display the current record and number of records in a label or a status bar. Use a combo box for navigation.

5.2 Write an application that uses a DataGridView to update the publishers table from the Pubs.mdf database. Test your application to make sure that all fields that might throw an exception are being validated.

5.3 Write an application to update the authors table in the Pubs.mdf database. Use individual text boxes for display and data entry but make sure that the user can enter data only in Edit or Add mode. The project should include navigation buttons or a combo box for navigation.

5.4 Write an application to update the stores table in the Pubs.mdf database. Use individual text boxes for display and data entry but make sure that the user can enter data only in Edit or Add mode. The project should include navigation buttons or a combo box for navigation.

Case Studies

Claytor's Cottages

Modify the *Guest* option to allow update (add, delete, and edit) capability for the guest information. Display the current record number and the number of records in the status bar.

Christian's Car Rentals

Modify the *Customer* menu option to display and allow editing of customer information. The fields are

First Name
Last Name
Street
City
State
Zip
Vehicle ID
Drivers License Number
Rental Date

Use detail fields and make sure that all changes have been made before the Customer form closes. Include the current record number and number of records in the status bar.

C H A P T E R

6

Services

at the completion of this chapter, you will be able to . . .

1. Discuss the concepts of Windows Communication Foundation (WCF) Services and understand the terminology.

2. Create a WCF Service.

3. Add a service reference to a Windows project.

4. Consume a WCF Service from a Windows project.

5. Perform calculations in a WCF Service.

6. Access data through a WCF Service.

7. Consume a third-party WCF Service.

An important feature of programming is the ability to send messages between tiers or between clients and services. Previous versions of Visual Studio used XML Web Services for creating services. Although XML Web Services are still supported, a newer, broader, and more powerful technology was introduced in ASP. NET 3.5. This new technology, **Windows Communication Foundation (WCF)**, is Microsoft's technology used for communicating between applications on the same computer system, on a network, or across the Internet. The authors' previous edition of this text covered XML Web Services; this edition focuses on WCF.

Concepts and Terminology

The communication starts with a **client** application. The **service** application waits for a client to send a message and then responds to the communication. It is possible for a single application to be both a client and a service.

WCF uses Web Service specifications (WS-*) such as WS-Security and WS-ReliableMessaging, which were developed by many vendors working together. Web Service specifications are handled by the World Wide Web Consortium (W3C) or the Organization for the Advancement of Structure Information Standards (OASIS). You can learn more about OASIS at www.oasis-open.org/committees/tc_cat.php?cat=ws.

WCF can communicate with other platforms that support the SOAP protocol such as J2EE-based (Java 2) application servers. In addition, it also can work with simple XML formats such as RSS that are not based on SOAP.

A few terms that you should understand before we get started are *endpoint* and *contracts*. An **endpoint** indicates where messages can be sent (address), how they will be sent (binding), and a contract that defines the service provided. These are referred to as the "abc" of the service—address, binding, and contract. The endpoints are handled by VB when we use a service by adding a service reference in the client application.

The following code is added to the Web.config file.

```
<system.serviceModel>
  <services>
    <service name="Service" behaviorConfiguration="ServiceBehavior">
      <!-- Service Endpoints -->
      <endpoint address="" binding="wsHttpBinding" contract="IService">
```

When the project is deployed, the next section of the Web.config file indicates the appropriate address and binding. For now, our address will be localhost because we are using the Visual Studio web server.

The **WCF Service** has two files; by default they are IService.vb and Service.vb (Figure 6.1). The "I" in IService tells us that it is an interface. An interface is similar to a class but it contains contracts that specify what must be defined in the Service.vb class. The ServiceContract and OperationContract attributes distinguish a WCF interface from a standard interface. Notice that the attribute names are enclosed in brackets <>.

```
<ServiceContract()> _
Public Interface IService

    <OperationContract()> _
    Function HelloWorld() As String

End Interface
```

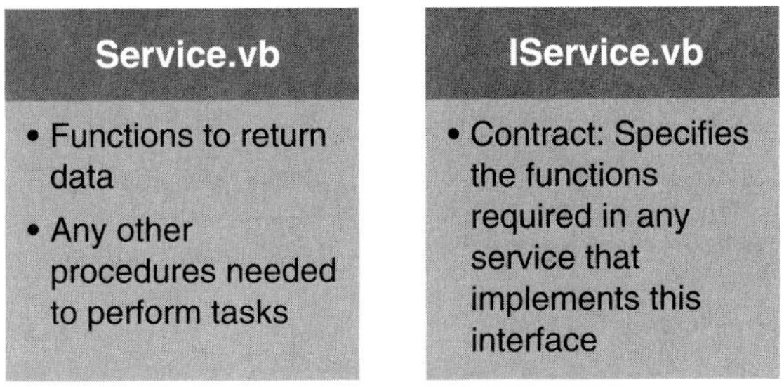

Figure 6.1

The Service.vb and IService.vb files make up a WCF Service.

Service.vb

- Functions to return data
- Any other procedures needed to perform tasks

IService.vb

- Contract: Specifies the functions required in any service that implements this interface

An **operation contract** shows a function or sub procedure header listing the parameters and the return type. In this example, there are no parameters and the return value is of type String. Each operation contract requires the method to be written in the Service.vb file.

```
Public Function HelloWorld() As String Implements IService.HelloWorld
    Return "Hello"
End Function
```

Service.vb and IService.vb are the default filenames; we will change those to reflect the purpose of the service.

After you create a service, it may be used or **consumed** from another application. In our examples, we will use Windows Forms applications, but the service may be consumed by other types of applications as well.

Windows Communication Foundation (WCF)

When you create a Windows component and use it in a Windows application, each element of the project conforms to Windows specifications. But when you create a component as a WCF Service, many other types of services and technologies are used. These services may include XML, SOAP, WSDL, and HTTP. Although this may look like alphabet soup or appear rather intimidating, VS handles most of the details so you don't need to study each of these technologies. However, you should understand the purpose of each.

You can think of each of the following technologies as protocols, or "rules" that both sides understand, to store, locate, and use WCF Services.

XML

As you already know, XML is a standard method for storing data that can be transferred easily from one machine or platform to another. One of the key advantages of using XML for Web services is that data are transmitted in a text format rather than in binary format. This feature allows data to pass through many firewalls that binary data cannot penetrate. You have been using XML since your first days of creating Visual Basic applications. You don't need to learn any more concepts about XML for Web services because the .NET Framework takes care of the details.

SOAP

Once data are in a format that can be sent (XML), you need a protocol for sending the data. **Simple Object Access Protocol (SOAP)** is a popular standard. SOAP includes a set of rules for handling requests and responses including class names, method names, and parameters. SOAP works with XML but does not include a specific protocol for transporting the response and request packets. The transport protocol is most frequently HTTP.

WSDL

Some Web services are controlled by a description specified in **Web Services Description Language (WSDL)**. WSDL contains information about the names of the methods, the parameters that can be passed, and the values that are returned from the functions.

More Acronyms

You should know a few additional acronyms before beginning a Web service example. A **uniform resource identifier (URI)** uniquely identifies a resource on the Web and is somewhat more generic than the older term, *URL*. For technical specifications, the industry standard term *URI* is preferred to *URL*. For more information on URIs and URLs, see www.w3.org/Addressing/.

TIP

Always end your URI (or URL) with a slash such as "http:/MySite/" to avoid an extra trip to the server to determine that it is a site rather than a directory. ■

Feedback 6.1

1. Name two protocols that transport data.
2. To what does the acronym WS refer?
3. Describe the "abc" of WCF Services.

Creating a WCF Service

In this section, you will create a simple service that returns a string: "Hello World", naturally. Although the project doesn't do much, it gives you an opportunity to associate names to some of the parts of the project.

Create a Hello World Service—Step-by-Step

Create a Solution and the Consumer Application

STEP 1: Create a new Windows Forms application project and name it Ch06Wcf-HelloWorld.

> *Note*: If the Solution Explorer does not display the name of the solution, select *Tools / Options / Projects and Solutions / General* and select *Always show solution*.

STEP 2: Save your project using *File / Save All*. Make sure you check the box for *Create directory for solution*. Keep the solution name as Ch06Wcf-HelloWorld and change the *Name* entry to ConsumeServiceApplication (Figure 6.2). (You may have to retype the solution name.)

Figure 6.2

Save the project and solution, keeping the solution files in a separate directory.

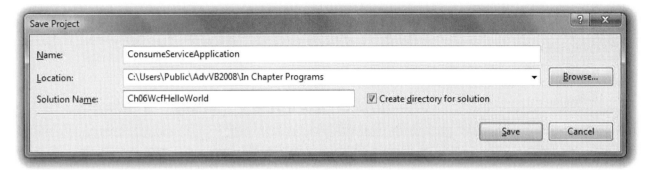

Note: In the past we have unchecked the *Create directory for solution box*, but when creating solutions with multiple projects, the option can be a big help. In the solution folder, you will have only the .sln and .suo files and one folder for each project.

Add a WCF Service

STEP 1: Select the solution name (Ch06WcfHelloWorld) in the Solution Explorer and select *Add / New Web Site* from the *File* menu or right-click on the Solution name in Solution Explorer.

STEP 2: Select the WCF Service template.

STEP 3: Click *OK*, keeping the default name of "WCFService1".

Rename the WCF Service

STEP 1: In the Solution Explorer, rename the Service.vb file to "HelloWorld-Service.vb".

To complete renaming the service, you must change the name in several more locations, as described in the following steps.

STEP 2: Open the HelloWorldService.vb file and change the name of the service's class to HelloWorldService.

```
Public Class HelloWorldService
```

STEP 3: Open the Service.svc file and change the service attribute to:

```
service="HelloWorldService"
```

STEP 4: Open the Web.config file and scroll down to near the bottom and find the `<system.serviceModel>` tag. Under `<services>` change to:

```
<service name="HelloWorldService" behaviorConfiguration="ServiceBehavior">
```

STEP 5: In the Solution Explorer, rename the IService.vb file to IHelloWorld-Service.vb.

STEP 6: Open the IHelloWorldService.vb file and change the name to IHello-WorldService:

```
Public Interface IHelloWorldService
```

STEP 7: Open the HelloWorldService.vb code file and change the `Implements` statement:

```
Public Class HelloWorldService
    Implements IHelloWorldService
```

STEP 8: Open the Web.config file and change the contract name in the endpoint tag:

```
<endpoint address="" binding="wsHttBinding" contract="IHelloWorldService">
```

Create the Operation Contract

STEP 1: Open the IHelloWorldService.vb file and add your operation contract in the service contract attribute where it says `' TODO`.

```
<OperationContract()> _
Function HelloWorld() As String
```

It's a good idea to delete the other operation contracts (the `GetData` and `GetDataUsingDataContract` functions). You can do so if you wish.

For now, you can ignore the error messages.

STEP 2: Add your comments to the top of the IHelloWorldService.vb file.

Code the WCF Service

STEP 1: Open the HelloWorldService.vb file. You will notice the blue squiggly "error" under the IService that states "Class 'HelloWorldService' must implement 'Function HelloWorld() As String' for interface 'IHello-WorldService'".

STEP 2: You need to add a public function procedure. Try this little-known trick: Place your cursor at the end of the squiggly line and press Enter; the editor will create the function block for you at the bottom of the file.

Note: If you deleted the extra operation contracts in the IHello-WorldService.vb file, you must also delete the corresponding functions in the HelloWorldService.vb file.

```
Public Class HelloWorldService
    Implements IHelloWorldService

    Public Sub New()
    End Sub

    Public Function HelloWorld() As String _
      Implements IHelloWorldService.HelloWorld
        ' Return a "Hello" string.

        Return "Hello World"
    End Function
End Class
```

STEP 3: Add your comments to the top of the class file.
STEP 4: Build your solution. At this point you should have no error messages.

Testing a Service—Step-by-Step

It's time to test this WCF Service.

Test the Service

STEP 1: Set the service as the startup project by right-clicking on WcfService1 in the Solution Explorer and selecting *Set as StartUp Project*.

STEP 2: Run the program without debugging (Ctrl + F5).

STEP 3: Select the link for Service.svc (Figure 6.3).

Figure 6.3

Select Service.svc to test the service.

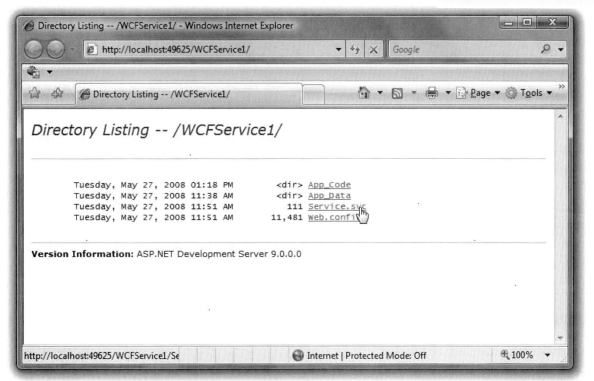

STEP 4: The service is now created. As the execution message indicates, you now need to "create a client and use it to call the service" (Figure 6.4).

STEP 5: Notice the address generated for svcutil.exe. You can click on this link, if you wish, to open the wsdl and take a look at the WCF Service definition.

STEP 6: Close the browser window.

Feedback 6.2

1. Give an example of an attribute tag.
2. Distinguish between the purpose of an IService.vb file and a Service.vb file.

Figure 6.4

The service is created.

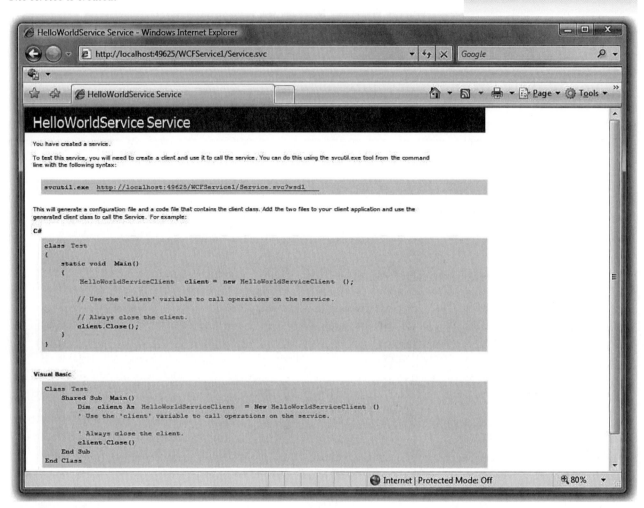

Consuming a WCF Service

Next we will create a Windows application to consume (use) the `HelloWorld` method from the WCF Service. We are going to continue the Ch06WcfHello-World and implement the ConsumeServiceApplication.

Create a Project to Consume the Service—Step-by-Step

Although you can place the project to consume the service anywhere, it's best to keep the projects together in the same solution during testing.

Create a Project with a Service Reference

STEP 1: Set the ConsumeServiceApplication project in Ch06WcfHelloWorld as the startup project. Notice that the startup project appears in bold text.

STEP 2: Rename the form to HelloForm.

TIP

When you add a new project to a WCF Service solution, the projects are saved independently. Make sure you know where your project is being saved. ■

STEP 3: Set the Text property of the form to WCF Service Client.

STEP 4: Place a label on the form; name it WelcomeLabel and delete the Text property.

STEP 5: Place a button on the form; name it DisplayButton; and set the Text property to "&Display".

Add a Service Reference

STEP 1: Select *Add Service Reference* from the *Project* menu or by right-clicking on the project name in Solution Explorer.

STEP 2: Click on the *Discover* button.

STEP 3: Expand WCFService1 and open HelloWorldService.

STEP 4: Select IHelloWorldService and HelloWorld will appear in the *Operations* list.

STEP 5: Change the *Namespace* entry from ServiceReference1 to HelloService (Figure 6.5).

Figure 6.5

Add a reference to your service in the **Add Service Reference** dialog box.

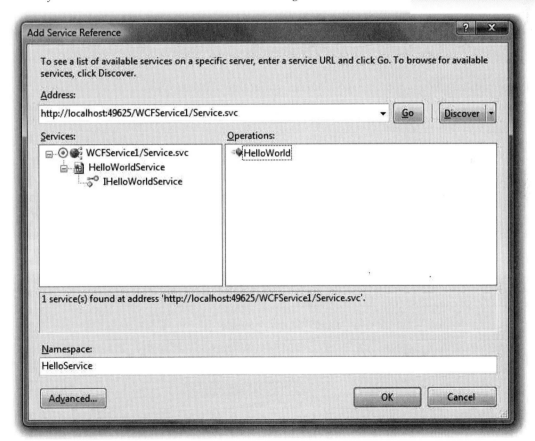

STEP 6: Click *OK*. A Service References folder is added to the ConsumeServiceApplication project (Figure 6.6).

Write the Code

Once you have added a reference to a service, you can instantiate an object of the class and call its methods, in the same way that you access methods of any other class.

Figure 6.6

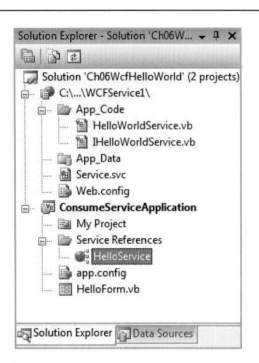

The HelloService reference appears in the Solution Explorer beneath the ConsumeServiceApplication project.

IntelliSense will help you select the method name when you write the code (Figure 6.7). Remember that the method returns a string, which you can assign to a label.

Figure 6.7

IntelliSense displays the methods in your service.

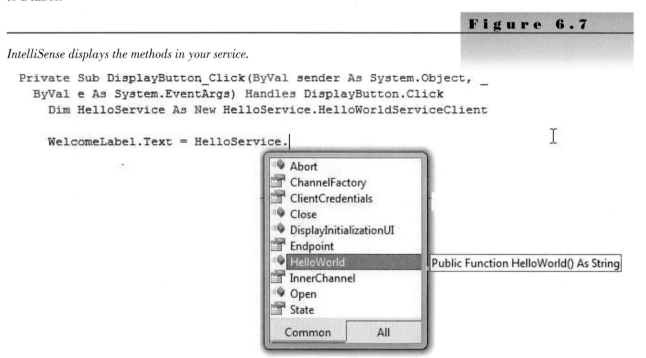

```
Private Sub DisplayButton_Click(ByVal sender As System.Object, _
   ByVal e As System.EventArgs) Handles DisplayButton.Click
   Dim HelloService As New HelloService.HelloWorldServiceClient

   WelcomeLabel.Text = HelloService.
```

STEP 1: In the DisplayButton_Click event handler, write the code to access the service and assign the string to the label.

```
Private Sub DisplayButton_Click(ByVal sender As System.Object, _
    ByVal e As System.EventArgs) Handles DisplayButton.Click
    ' Display the Hello World message from the service.

    Dim HelloService As New HelloService.HelloWorldServiceClient

    WelcomeLabel.Text = HelloService.HelloWorld
End Sub
```

STEP 2: Add comments to the form class.

Run the Completed Application

STEP 1: Run the program without debugging (Ctrl + F5). Unless you allowed the WCF Service project to add debugging support, you will receive an error message here if you run with debugging (F5). The completed form is shown in Figure 6.8.

Note: Have patience. You may think that nothing is happening; it takes a while for this to run. If you are running additional firewall software, you may need to reply to a message to allow Visual Studio access to the local network.

TIP

If you get an error while running your service, change to debug = true in the Web.config file for the service. ■

Figure   6.8

The completed form that consumes the HelloWorld service.

▶ Feedback 6.3

Write the code to instantiate a service object from InventoryService.

Performing Calculations in a WCF Service

This next example service performs a calculation. We will pass the Extended-Price method two arguments (price and quantity) and the method will calculate and return the extended price.

The first step is to add the ExtendedPrice contract to IHelloWorldService, then add the following ExtendedPrice method to the HelloWorldService class.

```
Public Function ExtendedPrice(ByVal Price As Decimal, _
   ByVal Quantity As Integer) As Decimal _
   Implements ICalculationService.ExtendedPrice
      ' Multiply the price by the quantity.

      Return Price * Quantity
End Function
```

The next step is to create a client or consumer application. Add a service reference to the project and add controls to the form. You will want text boxes to enter the price and quantity and to display the result and a button to calculate the result. Figure 6.9 shows the completed form.

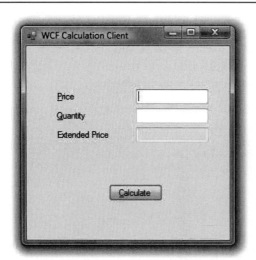

Figure   6.9

The completed form that uses the WCF Service.

```
Private Sub CalculateButton_Click(ByVal sender As System.Object, _
   ByVal e As System.EventArgs) _
   Handles CalculateButton.Click
      ' Call the Service to calculate the result.

      Dim PriceDecimal As Decimal
      Dim QuantityInteger As Integer
      Dim CalculationService As New _
         CalculationServiceReference.CalculationServiceClient()

      Try
          PriceDecimal = Decimal.Parse(PriceTextBox.Text)
          QuantityInteger = Integer.Parse(QuantityTextBox.Text)

          ExtendedPriceTextBox.Text = _
             CalculationService.ExtendedPrice(PriceDecimal, _
             QuantityInteger).ToString("C")
      Catch ex As Exception
          MessageBox.Show(ex.Message)
      End Try
End Sub
```

Accessing Data through a WCF Service

You can easily create a service that returns a dataset. The technique that you use is similar to the data tier in a multitier data project. The component fills a DataSet and returns it to the calling program from a WCF Service function.

New for Visual Studio 2008, you can separate the TableAdapter from the DataSet using the Data Designer. This feature assists for true multitier development and also as an extra security measure since the SQL statements from the TableAdapter are not available to the client application.

Creating a Data WCF Service—Step-by-Step

In the following step-by-step exercise, you will create a WCF Service Library project to access data. The data are in a data tier, as you have done in previous chapters. However, this chapter also will demonstrate how to divide the data tier into two separate projects: one will hold the definitions for the data access (**data access tier**) and the second one will hold the actual data (**data entity tier**). Figure 6.10 shows a diagram of the various components of the project and Figure 6.11 shows the Solution Explorer for the completed application.

Figure 6.10

The components for data access in a service application.

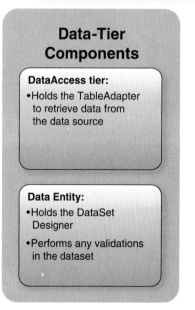

Create the Solution

STEP 1: Create a new Windows Forms application project called DataClient.

STEP 2: Save the project and solution, setting the solution name to Ch06-WcfData and keeping the project name as DataClient. Make sure to keep *Create directory for solution* checked.

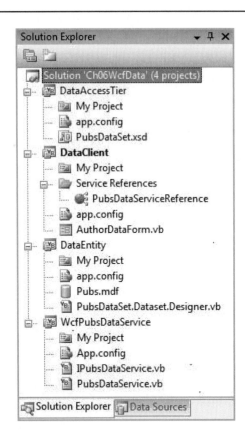

Create the WCF Service

STEP 1: Add a new project to the solution. Under *Visual Basic*, select *WCF* and use the *WCF Service Library* template (Figure 6.12). Set the name to WcfPubsDataService.

Add the Data-Tier Components

STEP 1: Add two new projects to the Solution using the *Windows Class Library* template. Call the two projects *DataAccessTier* and *DataEntity*. You can refer to Figure 6.10 to see where these two projects fit into the application.

STEP 2: Delete Class1.vb from both projects.

Add the Data Source

STEP 1: Click on the DataAccessTier in the Solution Explorer to select it.

STEP 2: Go to the Data Sources window and add a new data source.

STEP 3: Add the Pubs database, selecting the authors table.

STEP 4: Double-click on the PubsDataSet.xsd file in Solution Explorer to open the DataSet Designer.

STEP 5: In the Properties window for the DataSet, set the DataSet Project property to *DataEntity*.

STEP 6: Build the solution.

Figure 6.12

Add a WCF Service Library project to the solution.

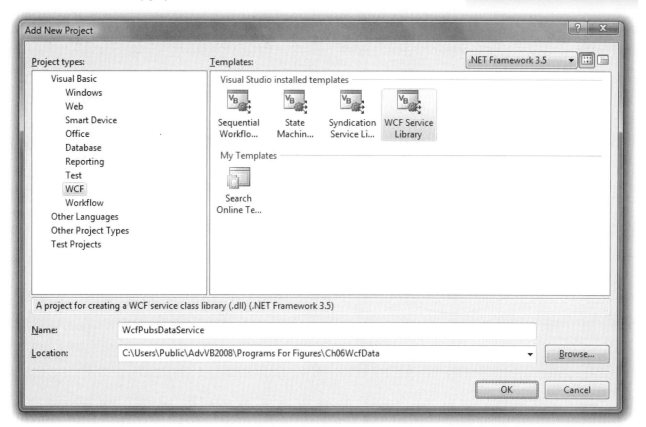

Step 5 puts the structure of the dataset in the DataEntity project but leaves the TableAdapter in the DataAccessTier. Validation code is placed in the DataEntity project. This new feature for VB 2008 separating the data access layer and the dataset adds greater security and scalability to a project by allowing the data to be separated into multiple tiers. The client will have access to the data but not to the structure of the data.

Configure the DataSource

STEP 1: Open the DataSet Designer for PubsDataSet.xsd.

STEP 2: Right-click on the authorsTableAdapter row and select *Add / Query*.

STEP 3: Click *Next*, leaving the query type as *Use SQL statements*.

STEP 4: Click *Next* for a *SELECT statement which returns rows of data*.

STEP 5: Click *Next*, keeping the default query.

STEP 6: Deselect the check box for *Fill a DataTable* and select *Return a DataTable*. Name your method "GetAuthorData".

STEP 7: Click *Finish*.

Code the WCF Service

STEP 1: Rename the Service and IService to PubsDataService and IPubsDataService respectively. Also be sure to change the names in the App. config file.

```
<service name="WcfPubsDataService.PubsDataService"...
<endpoint address ="" binding="wsHttpBinding"
contract="WcfPubsDataService.IPubsDataService">
```

STEP 2: Add a reference to connect the service to the data tiers. Right-click on the data service project (WcfPubsDataService) and select *Add Reference*. From the *Projects* tab, select *DataAccessTier* and *DataEntity*.

STEP 3: Write the operation contract in the IPubsDataService.vb file as

```
<OperationContract()> _
    Function GetAuthors() As DataEntity.PubsDataSet.authorsDataTable
```

STEP 4: Delete the unused OperationContracts in the file and delete or comment out the entire DataContract class.

STEP 5: Write the function in the PubsDataService class as

```
Public Function GetAuthors() As DataEntity.PubsDataSet.authorsDataTable _
    Implements IPubsDataService.GetAuthors
        ' Declare an object for the pubs data manager in the
        ' DataAccessTier and return the authors table.

    Dim AuthorsTableAdapter As New _
      DataAccessTier.PubsDataSetTableAdapters.authorsTableAdapter

    Return AuthorsTableAdapter.GetAuthorData()
End Function
```

STEP 6: Build the solution.

Everything is now in place for us to access the data from a client. We have already created the Windows client project. We can now add the controls to view the data and the connection to the service.

Set Up the Client User Interface

STEP 1: In the DataClient project, rename Form1.vb to AuthorDataForm.vb and set the Text property as Display Author Data.

STEP 2: Add a service reference to PubsDataService in the DataClient project. In the *Namespace* text box, type in PubsDataServiceReference (Figure 6.13).

STEP 3: Open the Data Sources window and expand the PubsDataSet to view the authors table.

STEP 4: Drag the authors table to the form.

STEP 5: Using the AuthorsDataGridView smart tag, dock the grid in the parent container.

STEP 6: Adjust the size of the form to display the data columns.

Write the Client Code

STEP 1: In the Form_Load event handler, instantiate the data service:

If the service does not appear in the service reference list, make sure you have a successful build of the solution. ∎

Rather than selecting *Add a Service*, you may add a new data source and select *Service*. You will get the same *Discover* dialog for a reference. ∎

```
Dim ADataService As New PubsDataServiceReference.PubsDataServiceClient
```

Figure 6.13

Add a service reference to the PubsDataService in the DataClient project.

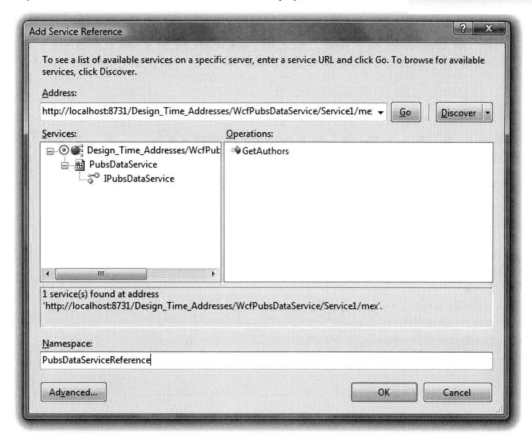

STEP 2: Merge the data from the WCF Service into the PubsDataSet.

```
PubsDataSet.Merge(ADataService.GetAuthors)
```

STEP 3: Run the application. Figure 6.14 shows the completed application.

Figure 6.14

The completed data service application.

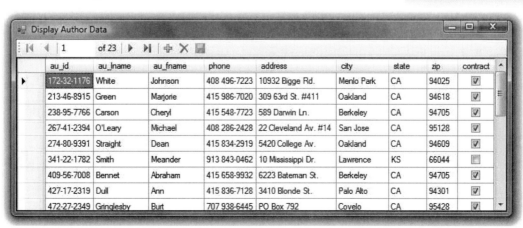

The DataSet Merge Method

The DataSet class contains a `Merge` method that may be used to merge rows, tables, or datasets that have a similar schema. A client or consumer application is one situation that calls for a `Merge` method.

When we create a service that defines a dataset, there must be a point where the `Fill` or `Get` method from the table adapter gets called. In the previous example, the code

```
PubsDataSet.Merge(ADataService.GetAuthors)
```

calls the `GetAuthors` method from the TableAdapter and merges the resulting data set into the PubsDataSet defined by the service.

Placing Validation and Access Code in the Data-Tier Projects

Before we move on to related tables, let's take another look at the multiple data tiers in Ch06WcfData. You probably have already noticed that the DataSet.xsd file is in the DataAccessTier project, but the Dataset.Designer.vb code file lives in the DataEntity project. This is a result of the setting we made for the DataSet Project property in the PubsDataSet properties. To review the property settings, open the DataSet Designer and select the dataset in the Properties window (Figure 6.15).

Figure 6.15

Click on any empty spot of the DataSet Designer to view the dataset's properties. The DataSet Project property determines where the Dataset.Designer.vb code file resides.

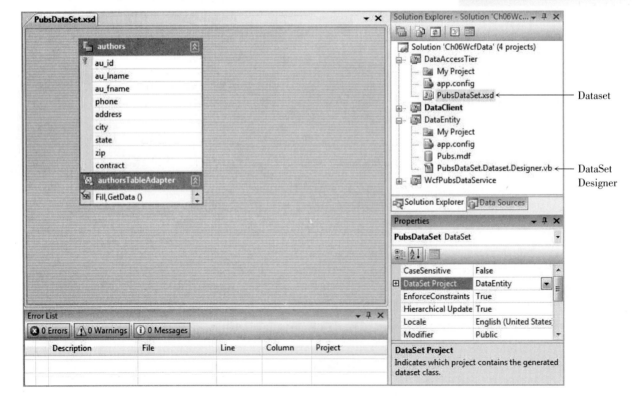

Splitting the data access and the dataset into different projects also has some interesting impact on the code that we can write. If you want to write code for the data access tier, you would add a class library item to the project (recall that we deleted it). This class is often referred to as the DataManager. The Ch06WcfData project on the text Web site shows the following code in the PubsDataManager file.

```
' Program:      Ch06WcfData
' Programmer:   Bradley/Millspaugh
' Date:         June 2009
' Class         PubsDataManager
' Description:  Retrieves the data.

Public Class PubsDataManager
    ' Can be used as an alternate if you want to code the data access.
    ' This project just calls the table adapter queries directly.

    Public Function GetAuthors() As DataEntity.PubsDataSet
        ' Use the table adapter in the data access tier to fill
        ' the dataset in the data entity.

        Dim PubsTableAdapter As New _
            DataAccessTier.PubsDataSetTableAdapters.authorsTableAdapter
        Dim AuthorsDataSet As New DataEntity.PubsDataSet

        PubsTableAdapter.FillAuthors(AuthorsDataSet.authors)
        Return AuthorsDataSet
    End Function
End Class
```

If you want to write the `Fill` and `Update` methods yourself for data access, write them in the Data Manager file of the data access tier.

Writing Validation Code

In Chapter 5 you learned about writing validation code for updates. To perform the same type of activity with a service, the validation code belongs in the Data-Entity tier. From the DataSet Designer, you can double-click on the table and the class is added to the DataEntity project. You can write the dataset validation procedures in the file.

```
Partial Class PubsDataSet
    Partial Class authorsDataTable

        Private Sub authorsDataTable_authorsRowChanging(ByVal sender _
            As System.Object, ByVal e As authorsRowChangeEvent) _
            Handles Me.authorsRowChanging

        End Sub

    End Class
End Class
```

Setting Properties of the Dataset Fields

To set properties of the fields in the dataset, such as the Caption and Default-Value properties, double-click on the Dataset.xsd file in the Solution Explorer. You can select each field name and view or set its properties.

Working with Related Tables

The hands-on project for this chapter uses related tables. The steps are essentially the same as creating a single-table application. Because two tables must be filled with data, the form must contain two dataset `Merge` methods. Also notice that you specify the table name as well as the dataset name.

```
Private Sub StoreSalesForm_Load(ByVal sender As System.Object, _
   ByVal e As System.EventArgs) Handles MyBase.Load
      ' Call the service to retrieve the data.
   Dim ADataService As New PubsServiceReference.PubsDataServiceClient

   PubsDataSet.stores.Merge(ADataService.GetStores)
   PubsDataSet.sales.Merge(ADataService.GetSales)
End Sub
```

You will need to add a query for each table in the DataSet Designer window, just as we created a GetAuthors query for the single-table application. When working with multiple tables, you should add a query for each data table that you wish to return.

Your Hands-On Programming Example

Write a project to display store and sales information from the Pubs database. The data should be supplied by a WCF Service.

Display the store data as details and the sales data in a grid.

Planning the Project

Sketch a form (Figure 6.16) that your users sign off as meeting their needs.

Plan the Objects, Properties, and Methods The solution contains projects for data access class library, data entity class library, client Windows Form application, and a WCF Service Library. Figure 6.17 shows the diagram of the program components and Figure 6.18 shows the completed form.

Data Access Tier

- Create a Pubs DataSet that contains the stores and sales tables.

- Add queries to return the stores table and the sales table.

- Set the DataSet Project property to the DataEntity project.

Figure 6.16

The planning sketch of the hands-on programming example.

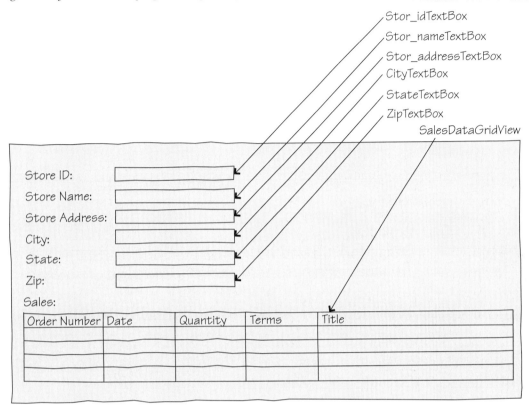

Stor_idTextBox
Stor_nameTextBox
Stor_addressTextBox
CityTextBox
StateTextBox
ZipTextBox
SalesDataGridView

Store ID:
Store Name:
Store Address:
City:
State:
Zip:
Sales:

Order Number	Date	Quantity	Terms	Title

Figure 6.17

The components for the hands-on programming example.

StoreSalesForm
Class
→ Form

Fields
- CityTextBox
- PubsDataSet
- SalesBindingSource
- SalesDataGridView
- StateTextBox
- Stor_addressTextBox
- Stor_idTextBox
- Stor_nameTextBox
- StoresBindingNavigator
- StoresBindingNavigatorSaveItem
- StoresBindingSource
- ZipTextBox

Methods
- StoreSalesForm_Load

IPubsDataService
Interface

Methods
- GetSales
- GetStores

PubsDataServiceClient
Class
→ ClientBase(Of IPubsDataService)

Methods
- GetSales
- GetStores
- New (+ 4 overloads)

Figure 6.18

The form for the hands-on programming example.

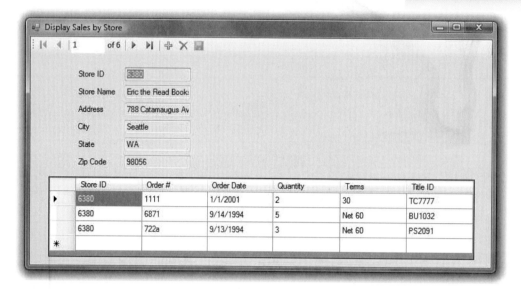

Functions	Actions—Pseudocode
StoreData	Return the stores table.
SalesData	Return the sales table.

Presentation Tier

Object	Property	Setting
StoreSalesForm	Name Text	StoreSalesForm Display Sales by Store
Store_idTextBox	Text ReadOnly	(blank) True
Store_nameTextBox	Name ReadOnly	StoreNameComboBox True
Store_addressTextBox	Text ReadOnly	(blank) True
CityTextBox	Text ReadOnly	(blank) True
StateTextBox	Text ReadOnly	(blank) True
ZipTextBox	Text ReadOnly	(blank) True
SalesDataGridView	Name ReadOnly	SalesDataGridView True

Event handlers/methods	Actions—Pseudocode
Form_Load	Instantiate the WCF Service. Merge the tables from the service.

The Project Coding Solution

The WCF Service

```
' Program:       Ch06HandsOn
' Programmer:    Bradley/Millspaugh
' Date:          June 2009
' Class          IPubsDataService
' Description:   Identifies the contracts.

<ServiceContract()> _
Public Interface IPubsDataService

    <OperationContract()> _
    Function GetStores() As DataEntities.PubsDataSet.storesDataTable

    <OperationContract()> _
    Function GetSales() As DataEntities.PubsDataSet.salesDataTable

End Interface
```

```
' Program:       Ch06HandsOn
' Programmer:    Bradley/Millspaugh
' Date:          June 2009
' Class          PubsDataService
' Description:   Retrieves the store and sale data.

Public Class PubsDataService
    Implements IPubsDataService

    Public Function GetStores() As DataEntities.PubsDataSet.storesDataTable _
        Implements IPubsDataService.GetStores
        ' Retrieve the stores table.
        Dim StoresTableAdapter As New _
          DataAccessTier.PubsDataSetTableAdapters.storesTableAdapter()

        Return StoresTableAdapter.GetStores
    End Function

    Public Function GetSales() As DataEntities.PubsDataSet.salesDataTable _
        Implements IPubsDataService.GetSales
        ' Retrieve the sales table.
        Dim SalesTableAdapter As New _
          DataAccessTier.PubsDataSetTableAdapters.salesTableAdapter()

        Return SalesTableAdapter.GetSales
    End Function
End Class
```

Form

```
' Program:       Ch06HandsOn
' Programmer:    Bradley/Millspaugh
' Date:          June 2009
' Class          StoreSalesForm
' Description:   Consumes the store and sales data from a service.

Public Class StoreSalesForm

    Private Sub StoreSalesForm_Load(ByVal sender As System.Object, _
        ByVal e As System.EventArgs) Handles MyBase.Load
        ' Call the service to retrieve the data.
        Dim ADataService As New PubsServiceReference.PubsDataServiceClient

        PubsDataSet.stores.Merge(ADataService.GetStores)
        PubsDataSet.sales.Merge(ADataService.GetSales)
    End Sub
End Class
```

S u m m a r y

1. A WCF Service is a code component that can be used by other applications. WCF Services require standard protocols for data, message formats, and transmissions. The .NET Framework accomplishes these with XML, SOAP, and WSDL.
2. A URI uniquely identifies a resource on the Web.
3. A WCF Service contains an interface to define contracts for the functions and a Service class to define the functions.
4. The abc of a WCF Service refers to the address, the binding, and the contract.
5. To make use of a WCF Service in another application, called the *consumer* or *client* application, you must add a service reference to the project in the Solution Explorer. Then you can declare and instantiate an object of the service class and call its methods.
6. A service function returns a value to the client or consumer application when the service method is called. The return value can be an object such as a dataset or a specific value such as a String or the Decimal result of a calculation.
7. Use a multitier approach when using data with a service. The data access tier contains the table adapter and the data entity tier has the dataset and the validation code.

K e y   T e r m s

client   *250*

consumed   *251*

data access tier   *261*

data entity   *261*

endpoint   *250*

operation contract   *251*

service *250*

Simple Object Access Protocol
  (SOAP) *252*

uniform resource identifier
  (URI) *252*

WCF Service *250*

Web Services Description Language
  (WSDL) *252*

Windows Communication
  Foundation (WCF) *250*

Review Questions

1. Describe the purpose of each of the following:
   a. XML
   b. WSDL
   c. SOAP
2. Explain the steps required to create a WCF Service.
3. What tag is required to allow exposure of the WCF Service and its functions?
4. What types of applications have access to the services provided by a WCF Service?
5. What code is needed in a consumer application to access a Web method?
6. What steps are necessary to add a data source to a WCF Service project?

Programming Exercises

6.1 Modify any multitier project to use a WCF Service instead of a component.

6.2 Use a WCF Service to access the data in the titles table in the Pubs database. Write a Windows application that consumes the service and displays the data in a grid.

6.3 Create a WCF Service to return a dataset that contains the employee table from the Pubs database. In a Windows application, use the service to display the full name in the combo box, concatenated as "LastName, FirstName MiddleInitial". When the user selects a name from the list, display the Employee ID, Hire Date, First Name, Middle Initial, and Last Name in labels or text boxes for the selected record.

6.4 A local recording studio rents its facilities for $200 per hour. Management charges only for the number of minutes used. Create a Windows project in which the input is the name of the group and the number of minutes it used the studio. Use a WCF Service to calculate the appropriate charges. Make sure to validate input data.

6.5 Create a Windows project that determines the future value of an investment at a given interest rate for a given number of years. Use a WCF Service for the calculations. The formula for the calculation is

$$\text{Future value} = \text{Investment amount} * (1 + \text{Interest rate}) \char94 \text{Years}$$

Make sure to validate input data.

Case Studies

Claytor's Cottages

Modify the Reservations option of the Claytor's Cottages case study project from Chapter 2 to use a WCF Service for the calculations.

Presentation Tier

The form should have a drop-down list or radio buttons for King, Queen, or Double. Include text boxes for entering the customer's name, phone number, the number of nights stayed, credit card type (use a combo box for Visa, Mastercard, and American Express), and credit card number. Name, nights stayed, and credit card number are required fields. Use a check box for weekend or weekday rate and a check box for AARP or AAA members. Display the price on the form.

Note: If you prefer, use a calendar control, in which case you do not need the text box for number of nights or the check boxes for weekend/weekday.

WCF Service Tier

Calculate the price using the following table, which also appears in the Chapter 2 case study. Add a room tax of 7 percent. AAA and AARP customers receive a 10 percent discount rate.

Beds	Sunday through Thursday rate	Weekend rate (Friday and Saturday)
King	95.00	105.00
Queen	85.00	95.00
Double	69.95	79.95

Christian's Car Rentals

Modify your Christian's Car Rentals project from Chapter 2. Code the Rentals form using a WCF Service for the calculations.

Presentation Tier

The presentation tier should include data entry for the size of car: Economy, Mid size, or Luxury. Include text boxes for entering the renter's name, phone number, driver's license, credit card type, and credit card number. Use a combo box to select the credit card type. A group box should include the number of days rented, the beginning odometer reading, and the ending odometer reading.

Validate that the ending odometer reading is greater than the beginning odometer reading before allowing the data to be sent to the service component.

Make sure that an entry has been made for driver's license and that the number of days rented is greater than 0.

WCF Service

There is no mileage charge if the number of miles does not exceed an average of 100 miles per day rented.

Use the following rate table, which also appears in the Chapter 2 case study.

Car size	Daily rate	Mileage rate
Compact	26.95	.12
Mid size	32.95	.15
Luxury	50.95	.20

7

Web Applications

at the completion of this chapter, you will be able to . . .

1. Discuss concepts of Web-based applications.

2. Understand the types of files that make up a Web project.

3. Distinguish among the various types of button controls.

4. Understand the event structure used by Web applications.

5. Include hyperlinks and link buttons on a page.

6. Navigate from one Web page to another.

7. Design a consistent layout using ASP.NET master pages.

8. Create and apply cascading style sheets.

9. Validate Web input using the Validation controls.

10. Maintain state (data values) from one page to the next.

11. Incorporate Login controls for both new and existing users.

12. Use AJAX controls and perform partial-page updates.

In the previous chapters, you have worked with Windows Forms and created applications that run in a Windows environment. One of the most powerful features of .NET development is the ability to create applications that run on a variety of platforms. This chapter introduces you to the Web server controls and creating Web projects.

Important software note: Microsoft has a product for developing Web applications: Visual Web Developer 2008 Express Edition, which is a streamlined subset of Visual Studio. This chapter was created using Visual Studio Professional Edition, but the projects can be done using Visual Web Developer (VWD). The steps and screen captures may differ slightly if you are using VWD. If you are using the Express Edition of Visual Basic for your Windows applications, you will need to download and install Visual Web Developer for the Web applications.

Web Applications

Developing an application for the Internet is considerably different from creating a Windows program. Visual Studio makes it as easy as possible for you to transition from one development environment to another. But to be an effective Web developer, you must understand the differences.

Windows Forms allow you to develop applications that can run on any system with Windows operating systems; Web Forms are your gateway to cross-platform development. The first key difference that you will note is that a Web Form displays in a browser application such as Internet Explorer or Mozilla Firefox rather than on your desktop. The most common type of access is through the Web.

What is the Internet? Many people use the Internet on a regular basis but do not actually understand the basics. The Internet is really just an extremely large network of computers and the World Wide Web (WWW) is the system of hyperlinked documents that reside on the Internet. No one owns or controls the network. To use the network, a computer must have some type of connection. Typically, individuals get their connection from an Internet service provider (ISP) such as AOL, Earthlink, or MSN. Most phone companies and cable companies also provide service.

Client/Server Web Applications

Most Windows applications are stand-alone applications; Web applications require a server and a client. The Web **server** sends Web pages to the client, where the pages display inside a browser application (Figure 7.1).

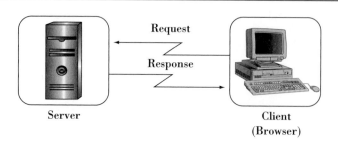

Server

Client
(Browser)

Figure 7.1

A server delivers Web pages to a client, where the pages display in a browser window. The server can be on a remote machine or on the same machine as the client.

Web Servers

To publish Web applications, you must either use a remote **Web server** or make your local machine a Web server. You can develop applications on a local machine and then publish them to a Web server at a later time. A common way to make the development machine a server is by installing Internet Information Services (IIS). IIS handles the Web server functions and the browser acts as the client. However, you do not need IIS to create Web projects; the Visual Studio IDE includes a development Web server and you also can use any available Web server that supports ASP.NET v3.5, such as Apache.

Web Clients

Browsers display pages written in hypertext markup language (HTML). The pages also may contain programming logic in the form of script, such as JavaScript, VBScript, or JScript, or as Java applets. The browser renders the page and displays it on the local system.

Likely you have seen Web pages that look different when displayed in different browsers or even in different versions of the same browser. Although many browser applications are available, the most common are Internet Explorer, Mozilla Firefox, Opera, Safari, and Netscape Navigator.

You may know which browser your users are using, such as when you are programming for a network within a company, called an *intranet*. Or you may develop applications that run on the Internet and might display in any browser. If your projects will run on different browsers, you should test and check the output on multiple browsers.

Browser Support

It's no secret that ASP.NET applications run best in Internet Explorer. However, you can run an application in any browser. An ASP.NET application is aware of the browser in which it is running. The HTML that it sends to the client is customized for the capabilities of the browser. For example, if the browser is capable of handling cascading style sheets, the font style information is formatted using styles; otherwise the font formatting is sent in another way, such as a Font tag.

Web Pages

One characteristic of HTML Web pages is that they are stateless. That is, a page does not store any information about its contents from one invocation to the next. Several techniques have been developed to get around this limitation, including storing "cookies" on the local machine and sending state information to the server as part of the page's address, called the uniform resource locator (URL). The server can then send the state information back with the next version of the page, if necessary. For more information on managing state, see "State Management" later in this chapter.

When a user requests a Web page, the browser (client) sends a request to the server. The server may send a preformatted HTML file, or a program on the server may dynamically generate the necessary HTML to render the page. One Microsoft technology for dynamically generating HTML pages is active server pages (ASP).

ASP.NET

The latest Web programming technology from Microsoft is ASP.NET 3.5, which represents major advances over the earlier ASP.NET and ASP. ASP.NET provides libraries, controls, and programming support that allow you to write programs that interact with the user, maintain state, render controls, display data, and generate appropriate HTML. When you use Web Forms in Visual Basic or Visual Web Developer, you are using ASP.NET 3.5.

Using VB and ASP.NET, you can create object-oriented event-driven Web applications. These programs can have multiple classes and can use inheritance.

Visual Basic and ASP.NET

Each Web Form that you design can have two distinct pieces: (1) the HTML and instructions needed to render the page and (2) the Visual Basic code. This separation is a big improvement over older methods that mix the HTML and programming logic (script or applets). The Web Form designer generates a file with an .aspx extension for the HTML and another file with an .aspx.vb extension for the Visual Basic code.

The HTML is generated automatically by the Visual Studio IDE. This is similar to the automatically generated code in Windows Forms. You can visually create the document using the IDE's designer; you can then view and modify the HTML tags in the Visual Studio editor.

The VB code contains the program logic to respond to events. This code file is called the "code-behind" file. The code looks just like the code you have been writing for Windows applications, but many of the events for the controls on Web Forms are different from those of Windows Forms. Another difference is that the VB code is not compiled into an executable (.exe) file as it is for Windows applications.

Types of Web Sites

Web applications are referred to as **Web sites** in Visual Studio. VS provides four types of Web sites, which you can see in the *Open Web Site* dialog box (Figure 7.2). Notice the options down the left side of the dialog box: File System, Local IIS, FTP Site, and Remote Site.

File System Web Sites

A File System Web site stores the Web pages and associated files in any folder on the local computer or other computer on the network. The Web pages are then tested using the Visual Studio Web server. The examples in this chapter all use File System sites.

Using File System sites and the Visual Studio Web server provides several advantages for Web developers over using IIS. The VS Web server does not expose the computer to security vulnerabilities and does not require administrative rights to create and debug a Web project. Also, the VS Web server can run on the Home Edition of Windows Vista or Windows XP, which some home users are running.

Use a File System Web site for development. You can use the *Copy Web Site* feature to convert to IIS or a remote server after you debug the application. ■

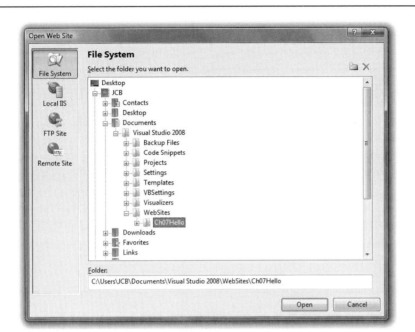

Figure 7.2

The four types of Web sites supported by Visual Studio and Visual Web Developer appear on the left edge of the Open Web Site *dialog box.*

IIS Web Sites

Internet Information Services (IIS) is Microsoft's production Web server and is part of the operating system in Windows 2000, XP Professional, Windows Vista, and Windows Server, but not in in Windows XP Home Edition. IIS includes a Web server, FTP server, e-mail server, and other services. When you run IIS on your local computer, you are hosting a Web server that you must take extra steps to secure.

You must have administrative rights on the computer to create IIS Web projects. If the security on your campus or corporate network does not allow the proper permissions, you cannot create IIS Web applications.

Remote Sites and FTP Sites

It is possible that your campus network will be set up for you to do development on a remote Web server. However, you must be granted administrative rights on the host computer. You cannot use an FTP site to create a new Web site; you only can open a previously created FTP Web site in Visual Studio.

Follow your instructor's directions for the type of site to use.

Creating Web Sites

You can create a new Web application in one of two ways, depending on the edition of the VB software you are using. For Visual Web Developer 2008 Express Edition, select *File / New Web Site*. If you are using Visual Studio 2008 Professional Edition, you can begin the same way, or you can choose to select *File / New Project* and then select *Web* for the project type and *ASP.NET Web Application* for the template. The following discussion focuses on the *New Web Site* technique since it can be used for either VWD or the Professional Edition.

In the *New Web Site* dialog box (Figure 7.3), you select *ASP.NET Web Site* for the template, *File System* for the location, and *Visual Basic* for the language. The *Location* field is set to a folder called Visual Studio 2008\WebSites, which is the suggested location for a File System site.

Figure 7.3

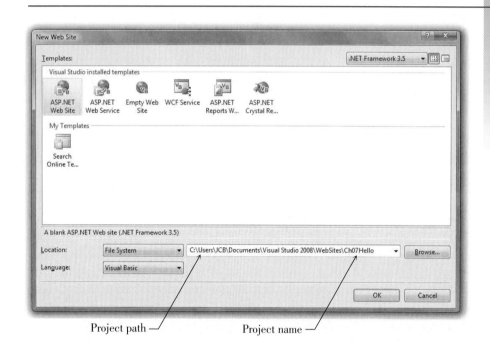

Project path — Project name —

Begin a new Web Forms project by selecting ASP.NET Web Site as the template from the New Web Site dialog box. Browse to the folder where you want to store the project and enter the name of the Web site at the end of the path.

The default for a File System Web site project location and name in Windows Vista is C:\Users\UserName\Documents\Visual Studio 2008\WebSites\WebSite1; in Windows XP it is C:\Documents and Settings\<username>\Visual Studio 2008\WebSites\WebSite1. You can browse to select a different folder if you wish. Give the project a name by changing the name (WebSite1) in the *Location* box.

Note: In a change from Visual Studio 2005, the 2008 edition has two models for Web applications. The *File / New Web Site* version, as described above, creates a folder for the Web site files but no project files. If you use the new *File / New Project / Web / ASP.NET Web Application* technique, you create a project structure, similar to a Windows application, with .sln, .suo, and .vbproj files. Also, the default name of a new project is WebApplication1, rather than WebSite1. All of the examples in this chapter use the Web Site model, rather than the Web Application project model. The Web Application model is similar to the technique used in Visual Studio 2003 but dropped in the 2005 edition.

IIS Note: The default for a local IIS project location and name is http://localhost/*ProjectName* (localhost is translated by IIS to your local virtual directory, usually C:\Inetpub\wwwroot).

Web Page Files

A new Web site automatically contains one Web page, called Default.aspx, which contains the visual representation of the page. A second file, Default. aspx.vb, the code-behind file, holds the VB code for the project. This model is very similar to a Windows project, which also keeps the visual elements separate from the code. But in the case of Web pages, the visual elements are created with HTML tags rather than VB code.

ASP.NET provides two models for managing controls and code. In addition to the **code separation model** described in the preceding paragraph, you also can use a **single-file model**, which combines the visible elements and the code in a single file. In early versions of ASP (before .NET), the single-file model was the only format available, so you may see old applications created in this style. We will use the code separation model for all programs in this text.

Web Forms in the Visual Studio IDE

As soon as you begin a Visual Basic Web application, you notice many differences from working on a Windows application. Instead of a Windows Form, you see a **Web Form**, also called a *Web page* or Web document.

The IDE allows you to view the *Design*, the *Source* (HTML and ASP.NET), or a *Split* window. Depending on the default setting, the Web Form may open showing the HTML source for the page (Figure 7.4). Click on the *Design* tab at the bottom of the window to display the page's design surface (Figure 7.5). To change the default behavior to always display the *Design* tab first, select *Tools / Options / Show all settings / HTML Designer / Start Pages in Design View.*

Figure 7.4

*The Visual Studio IDE with a new Web Form showing the HTML source for the page. If the page's **Source** tab is selected, click the **Design** tab.*

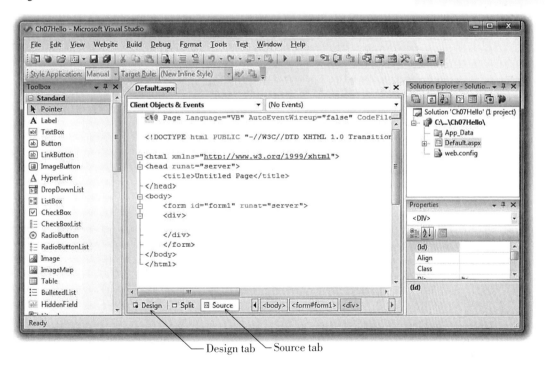

————— Design tab └─ Source tab

If you look closely at Figure 7.5, you will notice several other differences from Windows Forms. The toolbar is different, as is the list of files in the Solution Explorer. The toolbox has different controls, and even those that look the same, such as TextBoxes, Buttons, and Labels, are actually different from their Windows counterparts and have some different properties and events. For one example, Web controls have an ID property rather than a Name property.

When you look at the code for a Web Form (the .aspx.vb file), you see that the form inherits from System.Web.UI.Page. And in the Form Designer, you can see that a Button control inherits from System.Web.UI.WebControls.Button.

Figure 7.5

The Visual Studio IDE with a new Web Form showing the page's visual designer.

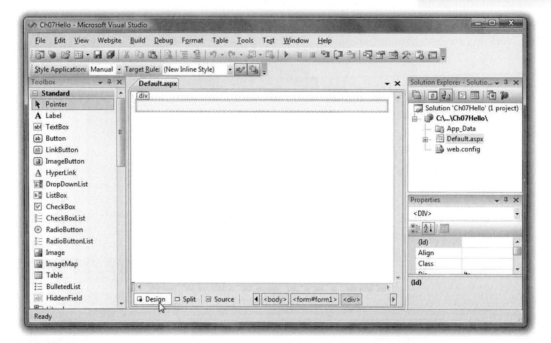

Naming a Web Form

In a new Web site, the first page is called Default.aspx. For most Web sites, the first page to display is called either *default* or *index*. For that reason, Microsoft has set the name of the first page as *Default*. As we add more pages and links to the site, we will give each page a meaningful name.

Opening an Existing Web Project

To open an existing Web site, first open the IDE and select *File / Open Web Site*. Browse to the folder that holds the Web page files and click *Open*.

Control Types

Several types of controls are available for Web Forms. You can mix the control types on a single form. Figure 7.6 shows the section tabs in the toolbox for Web

Figure 7.6

The toolbox for Web development has controls arranged into several groups.

Figure 7.7

The Standard section of the toolbox holds the ASP.NET server controls, which you will use primarily. Use the scroll bar to view the other sections of the toolbox.

Forms. For most of your work, you will use the controls in the *Standard* section of the toolbox, which is shown in Figure 7.7.

- *Standard (ASP.NET server controls).* These are the richest, most powerful controls provided by ASP.NET and the .NET Framework. Web server controls do not directly correspond to HTML controls but are rendered differently for different browsers in order to achieve the desired look and feel. Some of the special-purpose Web server controls are Calendar, CheckBox-List, AdRotator, and RadioButtonList.

- *Data.* This list of controls includes the GridView and DataList for displaying data.

- *Validation.* These controls are used to validate the data before they are sent to the server.

- *Navigation.* Includes a menu control.

- *Login.* The login controls and wizards, introduced in Visual Studio 2005, are covered later in this chapter and used in the hands-on project.

- *WebParts.* The WebParts set of components enables users to change the appearance and behavior of the interface from the browser.

- *AJAX Extensions.* This set of controls, new to Visual Studio 2008, allows you to create pages that do partial updates to speed page display.

- *HTML.* These controls are the standard HTML elements that operate only on the client. You cannot write any server-side programming logic for HTML controls. As you submit forms to the server, any HTML controls pass to the server and back as static text. You might want to use HTML controls if you have existing HTML pages that are working and you want to convert to ASP.NET for additional capabilities. You also will use the *HTML* tab to add <DIV> tags to your Web pages, to divide the page into divisions or sections.

- *Reporting.* This section, available in the Professional Edition and above, but not in Visual Web Developer, contains Microsoft ReportViewer and Crystal Reports controls.

You can see the available controls in the toolbox when a Web Form is in Design view. Generally, the *Standard* section is showing (refer to Figure 7.7). Try scrolling to the bottom of the toolbox and clicking on *Data*, *Validation*, *Navigation*, *Login*, *WebParts*, *AJAX Extensions*, and *HTML*.

In Design view, you can tell the difference between client-side HTML controls and server-side controls. Click on a control and a popup DataTip tells you the type of control and its ID (Name). Figure 7.8 shows two button controls, one an ASP.NET server control and the other an HTML control.

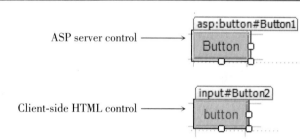

ASP server control   →

Client-side HTML control   →

Figure 7.8

The popup DataTip for each control identifies the type of control and its ID.

Event Handling

You write VB code for the events of Web controls in the same way that you write for Windows controls. The events may actually occur on either the client or the server, but the code is always executed on the server. The process of capturing an event, sending it to the server, and executing the required methods is all done for you automatically.

The events of Web Forms and controls are somewhat different from those of Windows Forms. For example, a Web Form has a Page_Load event rather than a Form_Load event. You can see the list of events for a control by clicking on the *Events* button in the Properties window for the control. You will see that a button still has a Click event, but the list of events is much shorter than it is for a Windows Forms button.

Some events may not occur and be handled as you would expect. All code executes on the server, but not all events are submitted to the server as they occur. A button click automatically triggers a **postback**, which is a round-trip to the server, but most other events do not. When an event is posted to the server, all events that have occurred since the last postback are processed. For example, the Change event of a text box and the SelectedIndexChanged event of a combo box do not trigger a postback to the server. The next time a button is clicked and the page is submitted to the server, the event handlers for those events execute. If you need to change that behavior and submit the event to the server immediately, you can set the AutoPostBack property of most controls to *true*, which forces a postback.

Button Controls

The Standard toolbox holds three types of button controls: **Button, LinkButton**, and **ImageButton** (Figure 7.9). The three work the same but differ in appearance. As the names imply, a LinkButton looks like a hyperlink but functions like a button and fires a Click event. An ImageButton can display a graphic image. Store a copy of the graphic in your Web site folder before adding it to a Web page.

In the Professional and higher editions, the Microsoft image library is located in the default installation folder: Program Files\Microsoft Visual Studio 9.0\Common7\VS2008ImageLibrary\1033\VS2008ImageLibrary.zip. You will need to extract the image files from the zipped file before you can use them.

Figure 7.9

Web server controls.

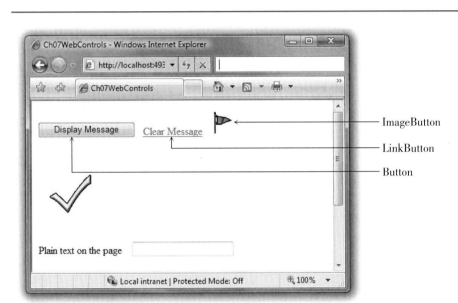

The code for the buttons is very similar to that in Windows Forms. Notice the event handlers for each type of button control.

```
'Project:      Ch07WebControls
'Programmer:   Bradley/Millspaugh
'Date:         June 2009
'Description:  Use different types of Web controls.

Partial Class _Default
    Inherits System.Web.UI.Page

    Protected Sub DisplayButton_Click(ByVal sender As Object, _
        ByVal e As System.EventArgs) Handles DisplayButton.Click
        ' Display a message using a button.

        MessageLabel.Text = "Welcome to Web Development"
    End Sub

    Protected Sub ClearLinkButton_Click(ByVal sender As Object, _
        ByVal e As System.EventArgs) Handles ClearLinkButton.Click
        ' Clear the message using a link button.

        MessageLabel.Text = ""
    End Sub
```

```
Protected Sub ActionImageButton_Click(ByVal sender As Object, _
    ByVal e As System.Web.UI.ImageClickEventArgs) _
    Handles ActionImageButton.Click
        ' Change the color of the label text.

        MessageLabel.ForeColor = Drawing.Color.Blue
    End Sub
End Class
```

Debugging

Running a Web application in the Visual Studio IDE is different from running a Windows application. The IDE does not automatically generate the code necessary for debugging a Web application. If you want to use the debugging tools, such as breakpoints and single-stepping, you must take steps to add debugging support to your project.

Run without Debugging

If you choose to run without debugging, you can choose *Debug / Start Without Debugging* or press Ctrl + F5. Production sites should not use the debugging feature; it is designed for the development and testing phases.

Run with Debugging

To add the necessary support for debugging, your project's **Web.config file** must contain the following line:

```
<compilation debug="true" />
```

TIP

Always remove debugging support before deploying an application. Debugging code slows the application considerably. ■

If you try to run with debugging (F5), you receive an error telling you that it can't start in debug mode because debugging is not enabled in the Web.config file (Figure 7.10). It gives you two options: modify the Web.config file to enable debugging or run without debugging (equivalent to Ctrl + F5).

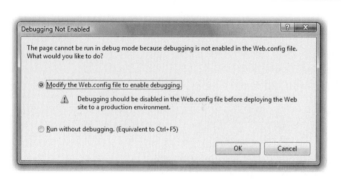

Figure 7.10

This dialog box appears if you attempt to run with debugging. Select Modify the Web.config file if you want to use the debugging tools; otherwise select Run without debugging.

After you allow modification of the Web.config file, you can set breakpoints, single-step execution, and display the contents of variables and properties. Try setting a breakpoint in the SubmitButton event procedure and rerun the program. The project compiles and displays in the browser. After you click on the button, the breakpoint halts execution and you can view the code and the values of properties, just as you can in Windows applications. Single-step execution using *Debug / Step Into* and view your objects and properties in the Locals window (in both Visual Web Developer and Visual Studio) or the Autos window (in Visual Studio only).

Note: Script debugging must be enabled in your browser to use the debugging tools.

The HyperLink Control

The **HyperLink control** looks just like a LinkButton but is used to navigate to another Web page. A hyperlink does not have a Click event; it is intended strictly for navigation. When the user clicks the hyperlink, the browser navigates to the page indicated in the **NavigateUrl property**. The page can be any valid HTML page or another Web Form.

You can set the navigation path (URL) value at design time or in code. To set the NavigateUrl property at design time, select the property and click on the Build button (the ellipsis). In the *Select URL* dialog box (Figure 7.11), you can select the page you want.

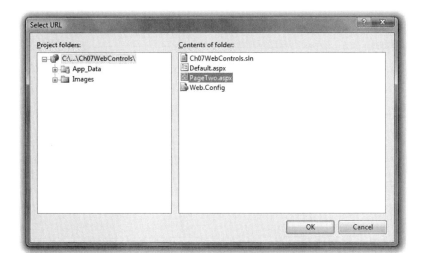

A hyperlink can appear as text or as an image, depending on the settings of the Text property and the ImageUrl property. If you set both properties, the image takes precedence and the text appears only when the image is not available.

It's easy to add a second Web Form to the Ch07WebControls project shown earlier. You don't need any code to navigate to the second form, but it's a good idea to include a link on the second form to return to the first. Of course, the user can use the *Back* button of the browser to return to the first page. Figure 7.12 shows a hyperlink on a page.

Choosing the Right Navigation Control

A hyperlink button and a link button look the same on the page. You can use either to navigate to another page. The hyperlink button has a NavigateUrl property, which holds the URL of the page to which to transfer. When the user clicks the button, a request is sent to the browser to retrieve the specified page.

If you need to perform any action before navigating to another page, use a link button. When the user clicks the link button, an event is fired and the page is submitted to the server. In the Click event handler, you can execute any necessary actions, such as saving the state of variables or controls, and then transfer to another page. Saving state is covered later in this chapter in the "State Management" section.

Figure 7.12

Navigate to another page using a hyperlink.

✓TIP

To test an individual page in a Web site that has multiple pages, right-click on the page in the Solution Explorer and select *View in Browser*. The selected page appears in the browser. ■

Linking to Another Page

To navigate to another Web page in code, you can use **Response.Redirect** or **Server.Transfer**. If you are transferring to another page on the same server (generally in the same application), use Server.Transfer. This method uses one less round-trip to the server than does Response.Redirect.

In both of these methods, you can specify the URL as absolute, with the complete path, or relative, which looks first in the current folder.

```
' Tells the browser (client) to request a new page.
Response.Redirect("http://www.microsoft.com/")

' The server loads the new page and begins processing without a request
' from the browser.
Server.Transfer("LoginPage.aspx")
```

Including Images on Web Pages

You can add graphics to a Web page using the Image control. The concept is similar to the PictureBox control on Windows Forms, but the graphic file is connected differently due to the nature of Web applications. Each Image control has an ImageUrl property that specifies the location of the graphic file.

To place an image on a Web page, you should first copy the graphic into the Web site folder. Although you can use graphics that are stored elsewhere, your project will be more self-contained and portable if you include graphics in the project folder. The best plan is to create a new Images folder in the project folder and store the images there. If the project is open in the IDE when you add the graphic files, click the *Refresh* button at the top of the Solution Explorer to make the files show up.

You can add an Image control directly on a Web page, inside a DIV element, or in a table cell. In the ImageUrl property, click on the Property button (...) to open the *Select Image* dialog box (Figure 7.13). If you have added the graphic to the project folder, it will appear in the *Contents of folder* pane.

Figure 7.13

You can set many properties of the Web page using the property settings for DOCUMENT. If you already have elements on the page, clicking on the page usually selects a `<DIV>` entry, rather than the page itself. The easiest way to set properties of the page is to drop down the *Object* list at the top of the Properties window and select *DOCUMENT*. You can set properties such as a background image and background color (BgColor).

Set the Title property of the Web page; that property determines the contents of the title bar in the browser. If you don't set the Title, the title bar displays "Untitled Page". ■

The Calendar Control

A handy Web control is the Calendar control (Figure 7.14), which displays a monthly calendar and allows the user to scroll to future dates and back to previous ones and select a date. You may want this control on your Web page for

Figure 7.14

selecting shipping dates, event dates, or any other time that you want a date to appear. After you add the control to your Web page, you can select *AutoFormat* from the smart tag to change the design.

The SelectedDate property holds the date selected on the calendar. You can set an initial value and/or retrieve the current setting. The control's SelectionChanged event fires when the user selects a new date.

```
'Program:       Ch07Calendar
'Programmer:    Bradley/Millspaugh
'Date:          June 2009
'Description:    Display and retrieve dates.

Partial Class _Default
    Inherits System.Web.UI.Page

    Private Sub Page_Load(ByVal sender As Object, _
      ByVal e As System.EventArgs) Handles Me.Load
        ' Set Calendar to today's date.

        Calendar1.SelectedDate = Now()
    End Sub

    Private Sub Calendar1_SelectionChanged(ByVal sender As System.Object, _
      ByVal e As System.EventArgs) Handles Calendar1.SelectionChanged
        ' Display selected date in the label.

        MessageLabel.Text = Calendar1.SelectedDate.ToShortDateString
    End Sub
End Class
```

▶ **Feedback 7.1**

1. Name some differences between a Windows Button control and a Web Button control.
2. Compare a HyperLink control and a LinkButton control: How do their appearances compare? How do their behaviors compare?
3. Write the statement(s) to navigate to About.aspx from the Click event of AboutLinkButton.
4. Code the statement to assign a date value from a text box to a calendar assuming that you know the value in the text box is a valid date format.

Layout and Design of Web Forms

You must always be aware that users may have different browsers, different screen sizes, and different screen resolutions. ASP.NET generates appropriate HTML to render the page in various browsers but cannot be aware of the screen size, resolution, window size, or user-selected font size on the target machine.

You can improve the basic layout of Web pages by using some of the features described in the following sections. Although ASP.NET allows you to use tables to control the layout of elements on the page, the recommended practice is to use styles to control layout. Using a master page, you can define the layout of menus, a company logo, and other static information that should appear on multiple pages. Using master pages and styles can make it easier to update a Web site because you can make a modification in a single location and the change is automatically carried through to all affected pages. As the number of pages becomes large, you also may want to consider creating a site map.

Current Standards for Page Layout

In the past, most programmers used tables to control placement of elements on a Web page and assigned style attributes, such as size, colors, and fonts, directly on the page. However, that practice is now discouraged in favor of using DIV elements and styles.

There are several reasons for the change in recommended practices. One important reason is based on accessibility by persons with disabilities. Special accessibility software, which can magnify sections of the page or convert text to voice, has difficulties with tables. Other reasons are based on performance and separation of the structure from the design.

Advantages of using DIV elements over using tables include

- Less HTML.

- Performance. The content is sent quicker and positioned on the page quicker. Also alternate devices, such as mobile devices, can retrieve the content quicker.

- Separation of structure from design. The DIV elements define the structure of the page only; the design elements are all contained in the CSS styles.

Although many Web programmers still use tables for layout, current recommendations are to use tables only for tabular data.

Cascading Style Sheets

One huge improvement in Visual Studio 2008 is the new tools for using styles in Web applications. These new tools, called *Expression Web*, expand, enhance, and simplify using **cascading style sheets (CSS)**. You can use cascading style sheets to create, modify, and apply styles to single elements on a page, one entire page, all pages of an application, or all applications of an organization.

Using Styles

Styles are rules that can specify page layout, position, font, color, alignment, margins, borders, background, and bullet and numbering formats. You can create and apply new styles within a page, attach an external .css file and apply the styles, and even save the styles in a page to an external .css file for use on other pages or Web sites.

You can define styles in several locations, including on the Web page for individual elements, called an *inline style*; in a *style* section of a Web page, called a *page style*; or in an external style sheet (.css file) that is linked or imported into the Web page. Generally, programmers use inline styles for elements that appear only once on a page, page styles for elements that may be used in more than one location on the page, and external style sheets for elements that may appear on more than one page of a Web site or in multiple Web sites.

The term "cascading" in cascading style sheets refers to the order of precedence of style rules. More locally created styles override the rules of the more globally created styles. For example, you might apply an h1 style from the style sheet (global) that sets the font, color, size, and alignment. And if you also apply a style defined in the page for the color and size, the local (page-defined) color and size take precedence, but the font and alignment of the style-sheet style are still in effect. And if you also apply an inline style for the size, the inline (more local) style will override the size but keep the color of the page-defined style and the font and alignment of the style-sheet style.

Types of Styles

In Visual Studio, you will use several new tools to define, apply, modify, and change the location of styles. The Apply Styles window and the Manage Styles window, both of which you will learn about in the next section, use the following icons in Table 7.1 to identify the various types of styles.

Cascading Style Sheet (CSS) Style Types   Table 7.1

Icon	Style type	How referenced
• (Red dot)	ID-based style; defined in a .css file. Applies to a specific element by ID.	Style name preceded by a pound sign. Example: `#footer`
• (Green dot)	Class-based style; defined in a .css file or the current page. Defines style properties that you want to apply to some, but not all, elements of a particular type, such as some (paragraph) elements.	Style name preceded by a period. Example: `.intro`
• (Blue dot)	Element-based style; defined in the style block of a page. Applies to all elements that use a particular tag, such as <p> (for paragraph) or <td> (for table cell).	Style name only. Example: `p {margin-left: 25px; margin-right: 25px}`
• (Yellow dot)	Inline style. Applies only to the specified item; will not be reused by another element.	In Design view, apply formatting such as font, size, and bold, from the *Format* menu or the formatting toolbar. In Source view, formatting appears using the style element of the opening tag. Example: `<p style="font-weight: bold; font-style: italic>`
◉ (Circled dot)	Indicates that the style is used on the current page.	A dot without a circle indicates that the style is defined but not used.
@ (At sign)	Indicates an imported external cascading style sheet.	

New Style Tools

The Visual Studio 2008 IDE and Visual Web Developer have new windows that make it easy to define, apply, and manage styles. The new windows—CSS Properties, Manage Styles, and Apply Styles—appear by default in the same area as the toolbox and are available from the *View* menu. Also, a new Style Application toolbar appears in the default layout of the IDE. Figure 7.15 shows the new tools.

The Style Application Toolbar

You can use the first drop-down list on the Style Application toolbar to select either *Manual* or *Auto* style application. The *Auto* selection disables the remaining

Figure 7.15

The new style windows and the Style Application toolbar.

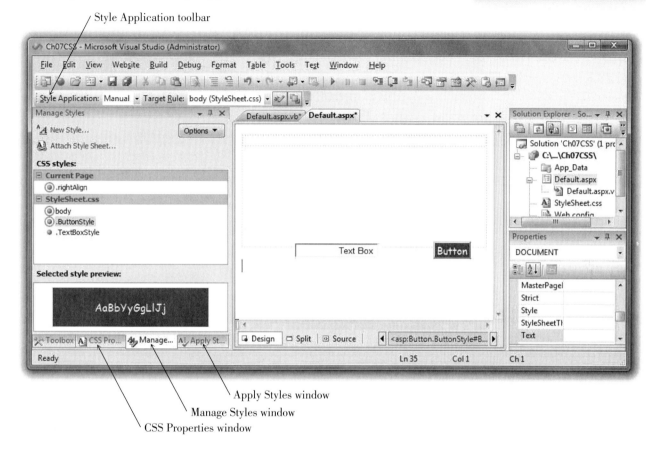

items in the toolbar and allows the software to determine where to place the CSS code. Select *Manual* to choose the location of the styles using the *Target Rule* drop-down list.

As an example, set the Style Application mode to *Manual* and drop down the *Target Rule* list. One option is *New Inline Style*, which places the style code directly into the HTML source code. You also can choose to create an external .css file that can be reused on multiple pages or projects. In this example, we will select the *Apply New Style* option, which will allow us to create a new style in a new or existing .css file.

Defining Styles

You define a new style in the *New Style* dialog box (Figure 7.16), which you can display from several locations. Choose *New Style* from the *Format* menu, or select *New Style* in either the Manage Styles window or the Apply Styles window. You also can right-click in the CSS Properties window and choose *New Style* from the context menu.

In the *New Style* dialog box, choose the category and then make settings. For example, click on *Font* in the *Category* list and set the font attributes; click on *Block* and set such attributes as text-align, text-indent, and vertical-align; click on *List* to set bullet and numbering attributes; and *Table* has settings for such attributes as borders and spacing.

Figure   7.16

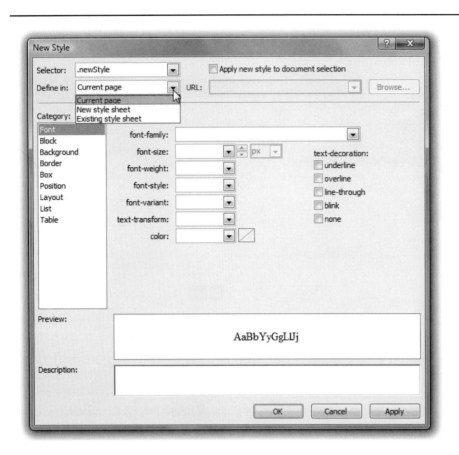

Define a new style in the New Style dialog box. Enter the name for the new style or choose the tag for an element type in the Selector box. The Define in box allows you to choose the location for the new style.

Managing Styles

In the Manage Styles window (refer to Figure 7.15), you can see a preview of each style. Hover the mouse pointer over a style name to display the code in the style. You also can see the settings for a given style in the CSS Properties window.

In the Manage Styles window, you can drag styles from one category to another to change the location of the style definition. For example, if you created a style in the current page and want to move it to the .css file so that you can use it in other pages, drag the style name from the Current Page pane to the StyleSheet.css (or other name of a .css file) pane. If you have more than one .css file attached to the page, you can choose the file to which to add a style.

Applying Styles

You can apply styles from several locations, including the Apply Styles window, the Manage Styles window, and the *New Style* dialog box. When you create a new style in the *New Style* dialog box, check the box for *Apply new style to document selection* (refer to Figure 7.16). Using the Apply Styles window, select the element on the page and click the desired style. To use the Manage Styles window, select the element on the page, then right-click the desired style name, and select *Apply Style* from the context menu.

Modifying Styles

You can change the attributes of a style from either the Apply Styles or Manage Styles window. Select the style name, right-click, and select *Modify Style* from

the context menu. You also can modify style attributes in the CSS Properties
window (Figure 7.17).

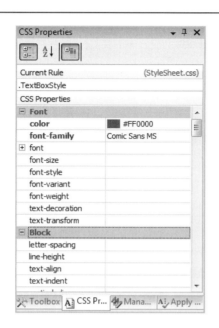

Figure 7.17

*View and modify style elements
in the CSS Properties window.*

Using DIV Elements to Lay Out a Web Page

A DIV element is a division or section of a page. You can add several DIV
elements to a page, give each a name, and create and apply styles for the elements. The DIV elements are considered the *structure* of the page; the styles
are the *design* and should be separated from the structure.

In the step-by-step exercise that follows, you will add four DIV elements to
a page, name each one, and create a style based on the name. In the style, you
will define all position, size, and font information.

Design View, Source View, and Split View

It would be nice if we could do all of our Web page layout in Design view, but,
in practice, that's pretty difficult. Many things are more easily accomplished in
Source view, by typing directly in the HTML. Using the new Split view makes
it much easier to add elements in Design view, see the results in the HTML,
and edit and move elements in Source view.

Creating a Page Layout—Step-by-Step

In this step-by-step exercise, you will create the Web page shown in Design
view in Figure 7.18. The page has four DIV sections: Header, LeftColumn,
MainContent, and Footer. The sizing and positioning are contained in four
styles: #Header, #LeftColumn, #MainContent, and #Footer. Note that styles
that are applied to named components begin with a pound sign and can be
stored in the page or an external style-sheet file. We will create a new style-
sheet file and store the styles there.

Make sure that you have available the graphics files from the text Web site
before you begin.

Figure 7.18

The completed step-by-step exercise. The page layout is created with four DIV elements and four styles.

Create a New Web Site

STEP 1: Create a new Web project based on the ASP.NET Web Site template. Name the site "Ch07DivLayout".

STEP 2: Click on the *Split* tab to view both the Source and Design panes. Notice the `<%@ Page` directive at the top of the page (Figure 7.19).

STEP 3: Scroll the top (Source) pane to see the HTML tags. Note that the `<div>` and `</div>` (beginning and end tags) are inside the `<form id="form1" runat="server">` (opening form tag) and `</form>` (closing form tag). See Figure 7.20.

STEP 4: In the Properties window, select the DOCUMENT object and change the Title property to "R 'n R Home Page". Press Enter and notice in the Source pane that the text between the `<title>` and `</title>` tags has changed. You can change the Title by typing directly in the HTML, if you wish.

Note that occasionally when you make the change in the Properties window, the change is not made in the HTML and the title is still "Untitled Page". It is actually more sure to make the change in the HTML.

Add Three More DIVs

This is one of the operations that is best done in the Source pane because you have much better control over the placement of elements.

STEP 1: Scroll the toolbox to the *HTML* tab, click on *Div*, drag to the Source pane, and drop it in front of the `</form>` tag. You also can drag the Div control from the toolbox to the Design pane, but it is not easy to drop it in exactly the right spot, before the ending `</form>` tag.

Figure 7.19

The Web page layout appears in both Source view and Design view in the Split tab.

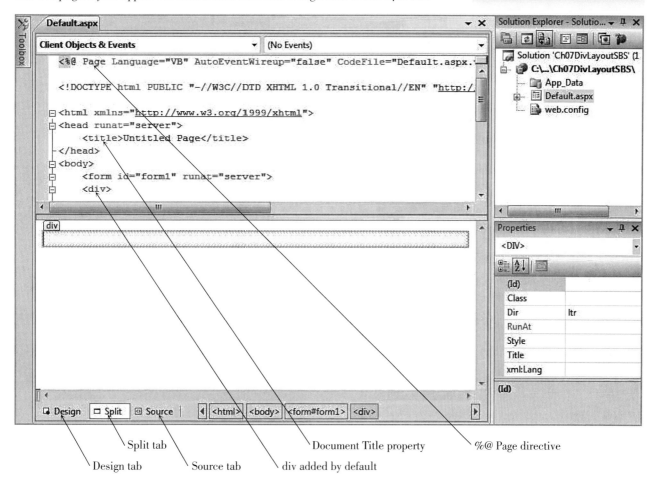

Split tab

Design tab   Source tab   div added by default

Document Title property   %@ Page directive

Figure 7.20

Examine the tags that make up the page.

Document title

body opening

form opening

div opening

div closing

form closing

body closing

STEP 2: Drag two more DIVs to the same location, before the </form> tag. If you drop a tag in the wrong location, it's easy to select it and drag to another spot.

STEP 3: Check the Source pane; you should have four sets of opening and closing DIV tags (<div> </div>) between the <form> and </form> tags.

It is possible to nest DIVs, but that's not what you want to do now, so make sure that you don't have one set inside another.

Name the DIVs

You can select a DIV in either the Source pane or the Design pane. In fact, when you select it in the Source pane, the DIV is highlighted in the Design pane.

STEP 1: Click inside the first DIV in either pane; the Properties window shows the properties for the DIV. Change the Id property to "Header" (without the quotes). Notice that the HTML for the DIV changed to reflect the new Id:

```
<div id="Header">
```

STEP 2: Change the Id of the second DIV to "LeftColumn" and note the change in the HTML.

Some programmers prefer to type the new Id directly into the HTML rather than use the Properties window.

STEP 3: Change the Id of the third DIV to "MainContent" and the Id of the fourth DIV to "Footer".

When you make changes in one pane or the other, the two panes can get out of sync. Whenever necessary, click on the notification bar to synchronize the two windows (Figure 7.21).

Figure 7.21

The completed Web form. Click on the notification bar to synchronize the two views.

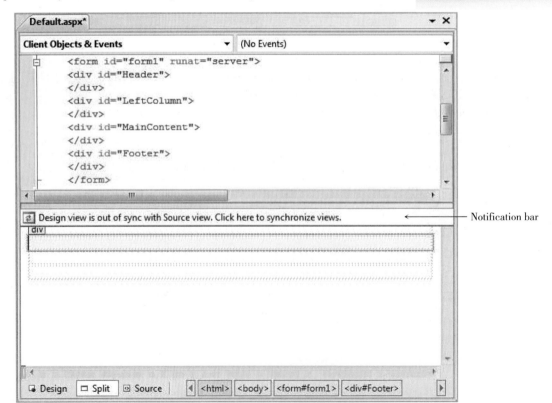

Set Up the Header Style

Now that the structure is defined, you will set up the design using styles.

STEP 1: If the CSS windows do not appear, you may need to open them from the *View* menu. Select *CSS Properties*, *Manage Styles*, and *Apply Styles*. You can perform most of the style tasks from any of these windows.

STEP 2: In the Manage Styles window, click on *New Style* (Figure 7.22).

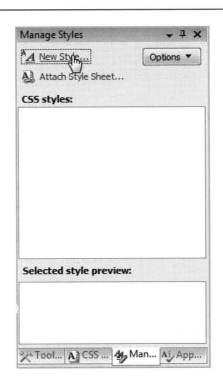

F i g u r e   7 . 2 2

The Manage Styles window. Click on New Style to add a new style.

STEP 3: In the *New Style* dialog box, enter "#Header" for *Selector*. Naming a style with the pound sign means that style will be applied to an element with that Id.

STEP 4: For *Define in*, select *New style sheet*. Notice that you also can choose to define the style in the current document or an existing style sheet.

STEP 5: In the URL text box, change the name of the style sheet to Div-Layout.css.

STEP 6: In the *Category* list, select *Block* and set *text-align* to *center* (Figure 7.23).

STEP 7: Click on the *Layout* category and set the *float* entry to *left*. This will make the DIV float to the left edge of the page.

STEP 8: Click on the *Position* category and set the *width* to *100%* (not 100 pixels). This will make the header extend all the way across the page, whatever its width or resolution.

STEP 9: Still in the *Position* category, set the *height* to *40px* (pixels).

 We plan to display a graphic in the header; the graphic is 36 pixels high.

Figure 7.23

Set text-align to Center in the New Style dialog box.

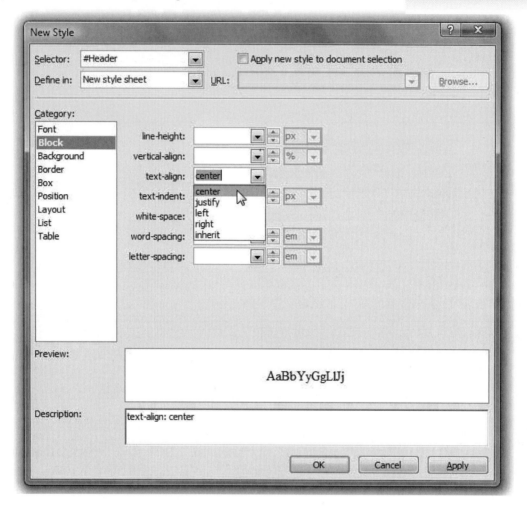

STEP 10: Press Enter, which adds the height entry to the *Description* pane at the bottom of the dialog box (Figure 7.24). Click *Yes* to the confirmation message "Do you want to attach the style sheet for the new style?"

STEP 11: Back in the IDE, notice that a new StyleSheet.css file appears in the Solution Explorer and a new `link` tag appears in the `head` section of the HTML; the `link` tag is required to use the styles from the external style-sheet file.

You also can attach a style-sheet file in the Manage Styles window or drag a style-sheet name from the Solution Explorer and drop it on the page; each of the techniques creates the new link tag.

Note: If you accidentally close the *New Style* dialog, you can right-click on the style name and select *Modify Style*.

Set Up the LeftColumn Style

STEP 1: Select the second DIV for "LeftColumn" and select *New Style* in the Manage Styles window. Name the new style "#LeftColumn" and choose to define it in *Existing style sheet*. The name of the style-sheet file should appear for *Url*.

Figure 7.24

The completed #Header style. Categories that have been modified are shown in bold.

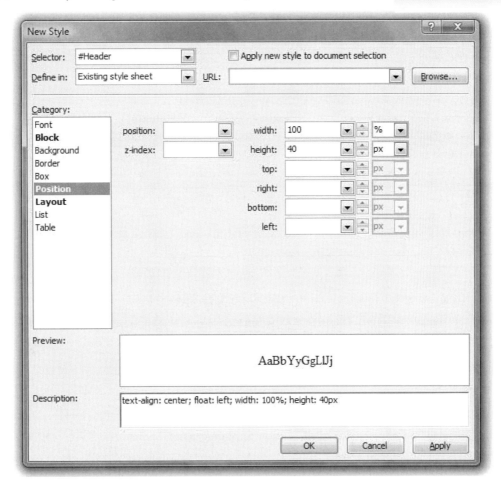

Notice that when you select the element before opening the *New Style* dialog box, the styles name appears automatically as soon as you type the pound sign.

STEP 2: For the *Font* category, select *Verdana* for *font-family* and *small* for *font-size*.

STEP 3: In the *Block* category, select *text-align: left.*

STEP 4: In the *Box* category, first uncheck the box for *padding, Same for all.* Then set the *top* padding to *20px,* which will make any text added to the DIV section move 20 pixels down from the top. Set *left padding* to *2%,* which will adjust the padding for the page size.

STEP 5: For the *Position* category, set the *width* to *18%* and the *height* to *250px.*

STEP 6: For *Layout,* set *float: left.* Click *OK.*

The description is: font-family: verdana; font-size: small; text-align: left; padding-top: 20px; padding-left: 2%; width: 18%; height: 250px; float: left

Set Up the MainContent Style

STEP 1: In either the Source or Design pane, select the MainContent DIV and select *New Style.*

STEP 2: Name the style "#MainContent" and define it in the existing style sheet.

STEP 3: Set the *font-family* to *Verdana* and *font-size* to medium.

STEP 4: Under *Box,* uncheck *Same for all* and set the top padding to *20px.*

STEP 5: For *Position*, set the *width* to *79%* and the *height* to *250px*.

STEP 6: For *Layout*, select *float: right*. This DIV will float to the right edge of the page.

Note that the width percentages do not add up to 100%.

LeftColumn padding:	2%
LeftColumn width:	18%
MainContent width:	79%

If you make the percentages add to 100%, the MainContent DIV will be forced down below the left column, instead of appearing next to it.

The description is: font-family: verdana; font-size: medium; padding: 20px; width: 79%; height: 250px; float: right.

Set Up the Footer Style

STEP 1: Select the Footer DIV and create a new style called "#Footer" in the existing style sheet.

STEP 2: Set the *font-family* to *Verdana*, *font-size* to *x-small*, and the *color* to *white*, which places *#FFFFFF* in the *color* text box.

STEP 3: Under *Background*, select *Navy* for *background-color*, which places *#000080* in the box.

STEP 4: For *Box*, uncheck *Same for all* and set the left padding to *20%*.

STEP 5: Under *Position*, set *width* to *79%* and *height* to *15px*.

STEP 6: For *Layout*, set *float: left*. Click *OK*.

The description is: font-family: verdana; font-size: x-small; color: #FFFFFF; background-color: #000080; padding-left: 20%; width: 79%; height: 15px; float: left.

Edit the StyleSheet File

STEP 1: Double-click on StyleSheet.css in the Solution Explorer, which opens the style-sheet file in the editor.

STEP 2: Select the body style, located at the top, which was added by default. Make sure to also select the opening and closing braces; then delete.

STEP 3: View your four new styles. You can edit the styles using the editor, which pops up the style attributes in full IntelliSense. If IntelliSense does not pop up automatically when you type a letter on a new line, press Ctrl + spacebar.

STEP 4: Close the *StyleSheet.css* tab and click *Yes* to the save question.

You also can edit styles in the CSS Properties window and the *Modify Style* dialog box. Right-click on a style name in the Manage Styles or Apply Styles window and select *Modify Style* from the context menu.

Examine the Page

STEP 1: Check the design. Your Design view should now resemble Figure 7.25. If it doesn't, review your styles and make any necessary modifications.

Add the Header Graphic

STEP 1: Right-click on the project name in the Solution Explorer and select *Add / New Folder*. Name the folder "Images".

STEP 2: Right-click on the new folder and select *Add / Existing Item*.

STEP 3: Browse to find the graphic files that came from the text Web site. Select RnRHeading.gif. Alternately, you can copy and paste the file into the folder, or drag it into the folder. With either of these two techniques, click the Solution Explorer's *Refresh* button to make the file show up.

Figure 7.25

The page layout with the styles created and applied.

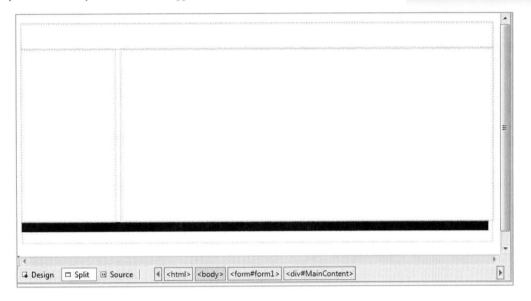

STEP 4: Click in the Header DIV in either the Source or Design pane. You are going to add an Image control to the Header DIV, which you can do in either the Source or Design pane.

STEP 5: Select the Image control from the *Standard* tab of the toolbox; add it to the Header DIV.

STEP 6: Select the new Image control and set its ImageUrl property to RnrHeading.gif from your project's Images folder.

The #Header style makes the image appear centered in the DIV.

Note: To add a different image, you may want to set the width and height properties of the image to fit in a specific DIV or location.

Add Links to the Left Column

STEP 1: Select the LeftColumn DIV in the Design pane and add a HyperLink control from the *Standard* tab of the toolbox. The #LeftColumn style defines the font and placement of the HyperLink.

STEP 2: Set the HyperLink's Text to "MSDN" and the NavigateUrl to "http://msdn.microsoft.com/".

STEP 3: Click after the HyperLink, press Enter, and add a second HyperLink control.

STEP 4: Set the Text to "Text Web Site" and the NavigateUrl to "http://mhhe.com/AdvBasic2008/".

Set Up the Main Content and Footer Areas

STEP 1: In the Design pane, click in MainContent, type "Contact Us:", and press Enter twice.

STEP 2: Press the spacebar four times, type a phone number, and press Enter twice.

STEP 3: Press the spacebar four times and type an e-mail address.

STEP 4: Click in the Footer DIV and type "Copyright 2009. All rights reserved."

STEP 5: Examine the Source and Design panes. Each of the items that you added and typed could be done in either pane.

Run the Application

STEP 1: Press F5 to run and select the option to modify the Web.config file to allow debugging. Your page should appear in a browser window.

STEP 2: Resize the width of the browser window (Figure 7.26). Because you used percentages for the width of each DIV, the text reflows to fit in the current width. If you wish, you can try changing the font size used by the browser to see how that will affect your page.

Figure 7.26

The completed page in a browser window.

Master Pages and Content Pages

A well-designed Web site should have a consistent look from page to page. **Master pages** provide the ability to define a standard layout and behavior that you use for all of the pages in an application. At run time, the individual **content pages** merge with the master page to produce the final layout for each page. A great advantage of using master pages is that you can make updates in a single location.

The master page is an ideal location to place the company logo and navigation controls for your site. A ContentPlaceHolder on the master page reserves a space for the content that changes from page to page. A single Web site can have multiple master pages and a given master page can have multiple content place holders.

When a Web site uses master pages, an extra step is required to display a content page. When a browser requests a content page, the content page is retrieved. ASP.NET then checks to see if the page has an associated master page. If so, the master page merges with the content page before the final Web page is rendered. The page's URL is the address of the content page.

To use a master page, you add a new Master Page item to the project. The page has an extension of *.master*.

It is possible to nest master pages. Using nested masters, you can define the look for the overall Web site and individual departments or groups can set their own look for their content.

To help visualize the size and location of DIV elements, temporarily turn on borders around each element in the element's style and turn them off again when finished. ∎

Creating Master Pages

To add a master page to a project, select the project in the Solution Explorer. Then you can either use the *Website* menu or right-click the project name and select from the context menu; select *Add New Item*. The default name is Master-Page.master, which you don't need to change. Always make sure that the *Place code in separate file* check box is checked.

When you view the HTML code for a master page, you will see

```
<%@ Master Language = "VB" CodeFile = "MasterPage.master.vb" Inherits="MasterPage" %>
```

Creating a Master Page—Step-by-Step

This step-by-step exercise creates a Web site with a master page and two content pages. Figure 7.27 shows the completed pages. Notice that the design of the master page is similar to the single page that you created in the previous step-by-step

Figure 7.27

Two content pages based on a master page for the completed step-by-step exercise.

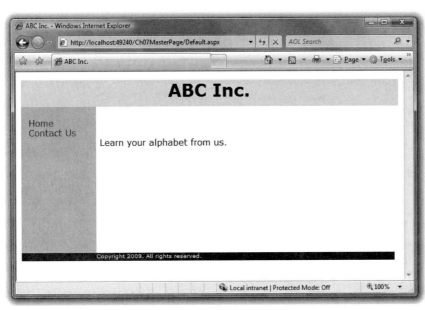

exercise, with a header area, left margin, main content, and footer. We will copy StyleSheet.css from the previous project and use it to format the master page.

Create the Web Site and Master Page

STEP 1: Create a new Web site project called Ch07MasterPage. Close the window for Default.aspx and delete the file in the Solution Explorer.

STEP 2: In the Solution Explorer, select the project name, right-click, and select *Add New Item*. Select the Master Page template. Leave the default name but make sure that the *Place code in separate file* check box is checked. Click *Add*.

STEP 3: Display the master page in the *Split* tab so that you can see both the Source and Design panes.

STEP 4: Change the DOCUMENT's Title property to "ABC Inc."

Set Up the Master Page DIV Elements

STEP 1: Notice the HTML code for the master page contains a pair of tags for a ContentPlaceHolder inside of the tags for a DIV.

```
<form id="form1" runat="server">
<div>
    <asp:ContentPlaceHolder id="ContentPlaceHolder1" runat="server">

    </asp:ContentPlaceHolder>
</div>
</form>
```

STEP 2: We need to place two DIVs above the existing one and one DIV below. The easiest way to do that is to place the insertion point in front of the opening `<div>` tag and press Enter to create a blank line. Then drag a Div element from the *HTML* tab of the toolbox to the blank line. Open up another blank line and drag a second Div element from the toolbox to the spot above the original DIV.

STEP 3: Create a blank line and add another Div from the toolbox to just below the original DIV. Your code should look like the following:

```
<body>
    <form id="form1" runat="server">
    <div>
    </div>
    <div>
    </div>
    <div>
        <asp:ContentPlaceHolder id="ContentPlaceHolder1" runat="server">

        </asp:ContentPlaceHolder>
    </div>
    <div>
    </div>
    </form>
</body>
```

STEP 4: Change the Id property of each of the DIVs, just as you did in the previous exercise. Name the first DIV "Header", the second one "LeftColumn", the third one (the one that contains the ContentPlaceHolder) "MainContent", and the fourth one "Footer". By using the same names, we will be able to use the same style sheet.

Import and Modify the Style Sheet

STEP 1: Right-click on the project name and select *Add Existing Item*. Browse to find StyleSheet.css in the Ch07DivLayout folder, which we created in the previous exercise. Click *Add*.

STEP 2: In the Manage Styles window, click *Attach Style Sheet*, select *StyleSheet.css*, and click *OK*.

> *Note*: To display the Manage Styles window, select *View / Manage Styles*.
>
> The Manage Styles window should now show the four styles, with each of the dots circled, indicating the styles used in the document. If any of the styles are not circled, check the Id property of the corresponding DIV. The names must match exactly for the styles to be applied automatically.

STEP 3: Display the CSS Properties window and click in the Footer DIV. The #Footer style elements display in the window, where you can view and modify them (Figure 7.28). Click on the *Summary* button to see only those elements that you have modified.

F i g u r e 7 . 2 8

The CSS Properties window showing the attributes of the #Footer style. a. The complete list and b. the summary.

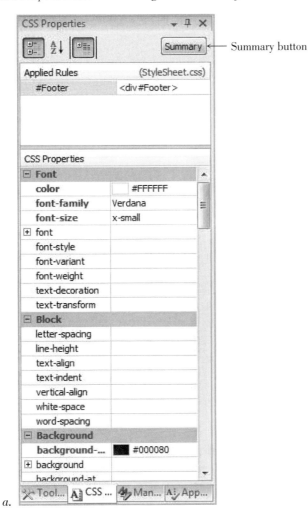

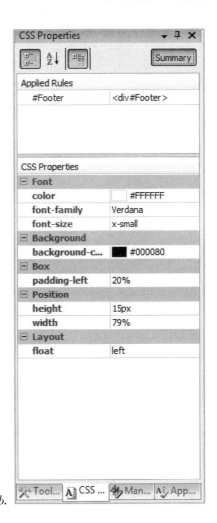

STEP 4: Change the height of the #Footer style to *30px*.

STEP 5: Display the Manage Styles window and point to the #Header style. The style attributes pop up for you to view (Figure 7.29).

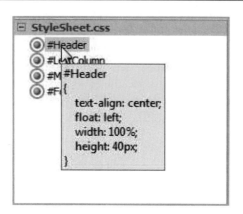

Figure 7.29

Hover the mouse pointer over a style name to pop up the attributes of the style.

STEP 6: Right-click on the #Header style and select *Modify Style*. The *Modify Style* dialog box appears, where you can make all of the same selections that you made for a new style. Select *Verdana* for *font-family*, *xx-large* for *font-size*, and *bold* for *font-weight* (Figure 7.30).

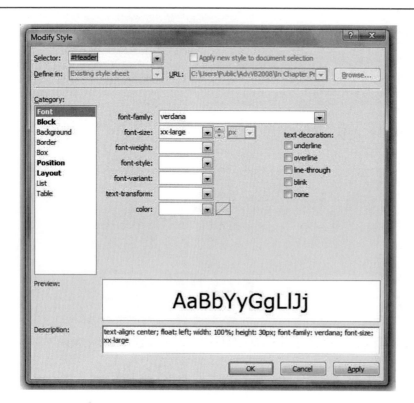

Figure 7.30

Modify styles in the Modify Styles dialog box.

STEP 7: Click on *Position* and set *height* to *50px*.

STEP 8: Click on *Background*, drop down the list for *background-color*, and click on *More Colors*. Click on the *Eyedropper* button and then move the Eyedropper cursor to a pale color anywhere on the screen. As you move the pointer around, you can see the selected color in the *New* box. Click on a spot when you like the color. Click *OK*.

STEP 9: Right-click the #LeftColumn style and select *Modify Style*. Change the *background-color* to another, somewhat darker shade. But beware, don't choose a very dark shade or the text will be difficult to read.

Set Up the Master Page Header and Left Side

STEP 1: Click in the Header DIV and type "ABC Inc."

STEP 2: Add a menu control from the *Navigation* section of the toolbox to the LeftColumn DIV. The easiest way to do this is to drag the control to the DIV in the Design pane, but you can also add it to the Source.

    Note: The default setting for the Orientation property is Vertical, which works for us. If you want the menu in the header area, you can change Orientation to Horizontal.

STEP 3: Using the menu control's smart tag, select *Edit Menu Items*.

STEP 4: In the *Menu Item Editor*, click on the button to *Add a root item*, which appears right under the word *Items*.

STEP 5: Set the Text property of the menu item to "Home" and the NavigateUrl to Default.aspx. Click *OK*.

STEP 6: And another root item; set its Text to "Contact Us" and its NavigateUrl to ContactInfo.aspx. Click *OK*.

Set Up the Master Page Footer

STEP 1: Click in the Footer DIV, and type "Copyright 2009. All rights reserved." (Figure 7.31).

    Note: If you want to include the copyright symbol (©), see "Including Special Characters on Web Pages" in Appendix B.

Figure 7.31

Type entries into the DIV elements.

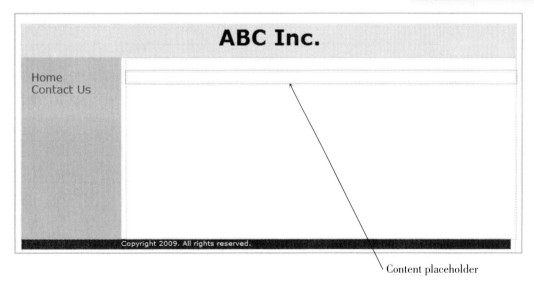

Content placeholder

Create the Default Content Page

STEP 1: Right-click the project name in the Solution Explorer and select *Add New Item*. Select the Web Form template.

STEP 2: On the *Add New Item* dialog, keep the name Default.aspx. Check the *Select master page* check box and make sure that *Place code in separate file* is selected (Figure 7.32). Click *Add*.

Figure 7.32

Check the option to Select master page when you create a new content page.

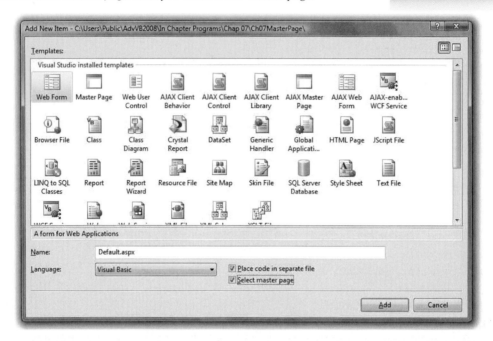

STEP 3: In the *Select a Master Page* dialog, select MasterPage.master from the *Contents of folder* list (Figure 7.33). Click *OK*.

Figure 7.33

Select the master page for the new content page.

STEP 4: Use the *Design* tab to view the new content page. Notice that the background from the master page is dimmed and you can modify only the Content area (Figure 7.34).

STEP 5: Change the Title property of the DOCUMENT from "Untitled Page" to "ABC Inc."

STEP 6: Click in the Content control, press Enter three times, type some text about the company, and press Enter. The Content control does not display unless it has some content.

Figure 7.34

The content page shows the master page elements dimmed. You can modify only the Content area.

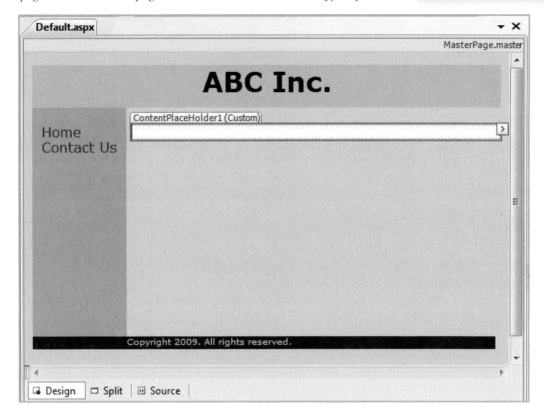

Add a Second Content Page

STEP 1: From the *Add New Item* dialog box, select the Web Form template. Name the page ContactInfo.aspx and make sure that the check box for *Select master page* is checked. Click *Add*.

STEP 2: In the *Select a Master Page* dialog, choose MasterPage.master. Click *OK*.

STEP 3: In the content area, type in a company phone number and an e-mail address for the Webmaster.

STEP 4: Set the page's Title property to "ABC Inc. Contact Information".

Run the Project

STEP 1: In the Solution Explorer, right-click on Default.aspx and select *Set As Start Page*.

STEP 2: Select Ctrl + F5 to run the project. Test the menu items and verify that the master page elements appear on both content pages.

Setting the Tab Order

Setting the tab order of controls is different for Web Forms than for Windows Forms. The *View / Tab Order* menu item is not available and you must manually change the TabIndex property of each control. By default, each control that is capable of receiving the focus has its TabIndex property set to zero. When the user presses the Tab key, the focus moves from one control to the next in the order the controls were added to the page. Set the TabIndex property of each control, beginning with 1 for the first; zero means that the TabIndex is not set. If multiple controls have the same TabIndex, the tab moves in the order the controls were added to the page.

Setting the Focus to a Control

You can set the focus to an ASP Web control using the Focus method of the control or the SetFocus method of the page. For example, to set the initial focus to QuantityTextBox, use either of these two statements in the Page_Load event handler:

```
QuantityTextBox.Focus()
```

or

```
SetFocus(QuantityTextBox)
```

Feedback 7.2

1. How is a master page created? How is a Web page assigned a master page?
2. In what order does the Tab key move the focus if you do not set the TabIndex property of any controls?
3. What steps must you take to create a cascading style sheet and apply it to a portion of a Web page?

Using the Validation Controls

ASP.NET provides several controls that can automatically validate input data. You add a **validation control**, attach it to an input control such as a text box, and set the error message. At run time, if the user enters bad data, the error message displays. Table 7.2 shows the ASP.NET validation controls.

The timing of the validation varies depending on the browser. For an uplevel browser (IE 5.5 or above), the validation is performed on the client without a postback to the server, so the page is not submitted with bad data. On a downlevel browser (all other browsers), the validation is performed on the server when the page is submitted. In an uplevel browser, the error message appears after the user inputs data and moves to another control; on a downlevel browser, any error messages display after the user clicks a button.

Note that a blank entry passes the validation for each of the controls except the RequiredFieldValidator. If you want to ensure that the field is not blank *and* that it passes a range check, for example, attach both a RangeValidator and a RequiredFieldValidator control to a field.

The following example validates data entry using validation controls; Figure 7.35 shows the form for the project. The validation controls appear in design time, showing the text that you set for the ErrorMessage property. At run time, the message does not appear unless the user violates the validation rule. Note that no code is required for the project to validate the data.

The ASP.NET Validation Controls

Table 7.2

Control	Purpose	Properties to set
RequiredFieldValidator	Requires that the user enter something into the field.	ControlToValidate ErrorMessage
CompareValidator	Compares the value in the field to the value in another control or to a constant value. You also can set the Type property to a numeric type and the CompareValidator will verify that the input value can be converted to the correct type.	ControlToValidate ControlToCompare *or* ValueToCompare Type (to force type checking) ErrorMessage
RangeValidator	Makes sure that the input value falls in the specified range.	ControlToValidate MinimumValue MaximumValue Type (to force type checking) ErrorMessage
RegularExpressionValidator	Validates against a regular expression, such as a required number of digits, or a formatted value, such as a telephone number or social security number. Use the Regular Expression Editor to select or edit expressions; open by selecting the ellipsis button on the ValidationExpression property.	ControlToValidate ValidationExpression ErrorMessage
ValidationSummary	Displays a summary of all of the messages from the other validation controls.	DisplayMode (Can be set to a bulleted list, list, or message box.)

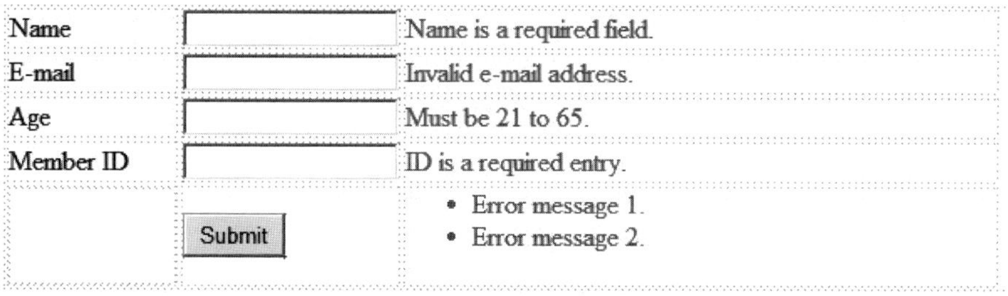

Figure 7.35

The Web Form for the validation controls example program.

The form in Figure 7.35 uses these validation controls:

Control	Validation control
NameTextBox	RequiredFieldValidator
EmailTextBox	RegularExpressionValidator
AgeTextBox	RangeValidator
MemberIDTextBox	RequiredFieldValidator
(Form)	ValidationSummary

Displaying Asterisks

You can set the behavior of the validation controls to match a common technique used on many Web sites. If the user enters invalid data or omits a required entry, you can display an asterisk next to the field in error and make the actual message appear in another location, such as at the bottom of the page. Set the validation control's ErrorMessage property exactly as described above, but set its Text property to an asterisk (or any other character that you want to display). At run time, the control doesn't display anything unless the associated control fails the validation; but when it fails, the asterisk displays next to the field in error. The ValidationSummary control will display the entire message defined in the validation control's ErrorMessage property.

If you use this technique, make sure that your error messages are descriptive and identify the field in error. Figure 7.36 shows the previous validation example modified to display the error messages only in the ValidationSummary control.

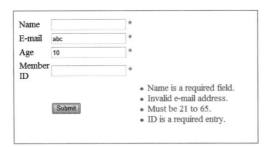

Figure 7.36

Display an asterisk next to the field in error and the complete error message in the Validation-Summary control.

Testing for Validity

You don't need any code to check validity using the validation controls. But at times you may need to check whether a single control or all controls on the page have passed validation. Each of the validation controls has an IsValid property that returns *true* if the control assigned to the validator passes. Also, the Page object has an IsValid property that is set to *true* when all controls on the page pass their validation.

```
If RequiredFieldValidator1.IsValid Then
    ' Perform some action.
End If

If Page.IsValid Then
    NavigateHyperlink.Enabled = True
End If
```

▶ Feedback 7.3

Describe how to validate a text box called QuantityTextBox using validation controls. A numeric entry is required, in the range 1 to 100. The field must not be blank.

The Web Application Objects

Your Web application has access to the server objects: Request, Response, Session, Application, and Server. These are intrinsic objects that you can use without creating an instance. A Request passes from the client to the server; a Response goes from the server to the client.

The **Request object** holds information about the current user, data entered by the user, and arguments to an HTTP request. You use the **Response object** to create cookies and the Request object to retrieve them. You will learn to handle cookies in the "Cookies" section later in this chapter.

The Response object sends the HTML to render a page to the browser. This example inserts text directly into the HTML stream:

```
Private Sub Page_Load(ByVal sender As System.Object, _
   ByVal e As System.EventArgs Handles MyBase.Load
      ' Print Hello World on the page.

      Response.Write("Hello World")
End Sub
```

The Session and Application objects are used to store state information in an ASP.NET application. These objects are covered in the "State Management" section that follows. You can use the Transfer method of the Server object to navigate to another Web page.

TIP Include the trailing slash when linking to a directory ("http://www.mysite.com/mydirectory/"); it saves one extra round-trip to the server. ■

State Management

As you know, traditional HTML pages are **stateless**, meaning that they do not retain values. Each time a Web page is rendered in a browser, all controls are re-created. Any values entered by the user, called the **state** of the page, are lost unless steps are taken to preserve the values. You may want to preserve state within a single page or to pass information from one page to another.

ASP.NET solves one of the problems of state management by maintaining the values in controls during a round-trip to the server or navigation to another page and back again. The values in all controls that have their EnableView-State property set to *true* are encrypted and stored in a property of a hidden control. When the page is redisplayed, the ViewState data are decrypted and used to fill the controls. You can see the tag for the hidden control, which is called __VIEWSTATE, if you view the source of a page in the browser. The following is an example of the ViewState for a form that has been submitted to the server and redisplayed. The control names and their values are compressed and encrypted into the single string and assigned to the Value property.

```
<input type="hidden" name="__VIEWSTATE"
   value="dDw5MTQ4NzEwMjE7Oz4tUQ/8e/xC31fa3oWMMe7CXP+ EAg==" />
```

If you want to maintain other data, such as to keep the User ID, a dataset, the values of objects or properties, or variables to share among multiple forms, you will need to implement state management. The following sections discuss some of the techniques for maintaining state, including storing values on the server and keeping values on the client.

Overview of State Management Techniques

ASP.NET has several tools for storing state information. The choices for maintaining state in .NET Web applications include:

Server Side

- *The Session and Application objects.* You can assign values to these objects, which are maintained on the server, and use them throughout an application. To use the Session object, the user must accept cookies or you must modify the Web.config file to specify cookieless operation.

- *Database fields.* You can write data into database fields and read them back when appropriate.

Client Side

- *Cookies.* You can create cookies in memory for temporary storage or on the user's hard drive for more permanent storage. This technique works only when the user's browser is set to accept cookies.

    Note: Malicious users can view cookies. Store information that can be used to look up a user; do not store sensitive user information.

- *Hidden fields.* You can create a hidden field and assign it a value; the value is passed to the server when the page is submitted, and replaced into the field when the page is re-created.

    Note: Malicious users can view and modify hidden fields. Do not use them to store sensitive information.

- *A string appended to the URL.* State information can be appended to the URL of a page to which to navigate and retrieved by the new page. Example: `http://localhost/Ch07Controls/Form1.aspx?user=Robert`.

    Note: Malicious users can access query strings. Do not use them to store sensitive information.
    To use a query string in code, append the query to a URL.

```
Server.Transfer("Page2.aspx?answer=" & AnswerTextBox.Text)
```

On the second page, use the `QueryString` method of the Request object and the name of the query string.

```
ATextBox.Text = Request.QueryString("answer")
```

- *The Web Form's ViewState property.* You can declare key/value pairs and assign them to the ViewState of a form; the values are available for subsequent posting of the page, but not to other pages.

- *Control State.* Allows you to keep property information for a control such as the current tab of a Tab control.

See "ASP.NET State Management Recommendations" in MSDN for more details regarding the advantages and disadvantages of each approach.

Application and Session Objects

The Application and Session objects are maintained on the server. You can use both to hold state information, but for applications with many users, this can be an inefficient technique.

The **Application object** stores information as long as the application is running. Only one copy exists for all users, so it is not a useful location to store information about users. The object is used sometimes to store information about the program, such as how many times the page has been hit or global values that are needed on multiple pages.

One instance of the **Session object** exists for each user, so you can use this object to store information about the user. Remember, though, that the information is stored on the server.

Each time the user accesses a site, the Session object is created and assigned a unique SessionID. The value is sent to the user through a dynamic cookie and is sent back to the server in the HTTP header when the user navigates to another page.

Session values are maintained as long as the session exists. A Session object usually ceases to exist when the session times out, which is 20 minutes by default (but can be modified). Some sites have a logout option in which the code can call the `Session.Abandon` method. Also, if the Internet service terminates, the Session objects are lost.

Session objects are easy to use, but you must be aware of some drawbacks. Because the information is stored on the server, storing large amounts of data for multiple users could bog down the server. Also, many Web sites split the server load among several systems, referred to as a **Web farm**. It is not uncommon for the user to be routed to a different server in the Web farm for each postback. In this case, the state information might not be on the correct server. This problem is handled in .NET by specifying the name of the machine that stores the session values in the Web.config file.

You use the Contents collection of the Session object to store values in code. Each item in the collection has a name and a value; you make up the name and assign a value to it. For example, this code assigns the value in NameTextBox to a session variable called "UserName".

> **✓TIP**
>
> If you know that you will not be using a Session object, set the document's EnableSession State property to *false* for improved efficiency. ■

```
Session("UserName") = NameTextBox.Text
```

The session variable is available in all forms of the application. You can retrieve the data using the same session variable name or an index number for the position of the variable within the collection.

If the session variable has not been created, an exception is thrown. You can either enclose the session variable in `Try` / `Catch` statements or test the value for `Nothing`.

```
Private Sub DisplayButton_Click(ByVal sender As System.Object, _
  ByVal e As System.EventArgs) Handles DisplayButton.Click
    ' Display a message.

    Try
        MessageLabel.Text = "Hello " & Session("UserName").ToString()
    Catch
        MessageLabel.Text = "Welcome to Web Development."
    End Try
End Sub
```

If you want the name to appear automatically when a page displays (or re-displays), place the code in your Page_Load event handler.

You can clear all session variables with the `Session.Clear()` method.

Cookieless Sessions

In normal operation, you cannot use the Session object if the user refuses to accept cookies or the browser cannot handle cookies. But ASP.NET includes a feature to work around this limitation. You can declare a session to be cookieless in the Web.config file.

In the system.web section of the Web.config file, add a sessionState tag and set `cookieless = "true"`. IntelliSense will assist in completing the tag.

```
<sessionState cookieless = "true"><\sessionState>
or
<sessionState cookieless = "AutoDetect"><\sessionState>
```

When running without cookies, an encrypted session ID is appended to the page's URL every time the page is posted to the server or the user navigates to another page.

Cookies

You can store state information as a cookie on the user's system. You can choose to store the value temporarily, for just the session, or store it on the user's hard drive for future trips to the Web site. You store the cookie using the Cookies property of the Response object and retrieve it using the Request object. The Expires property is used to make the value more permanent and set an expiration date. If you do not set the Expires property, the cookie expires when the current session ends. You cannot set either type of cookie if the user refuses to accept cookies.

A cookie is a string of text. Like session variables, you must assign a name and a value. This example stores the value from NameTextBox into a cookie called UserName.

Temporary Cookie Stored in RAM

```
' Save the cookie in memory for this session.
Response.Cookies("UserName").Value = NameTextBox.Text
or
Response.Cookies.Add(New System.Web.HttpCookie("UserName", NameTextBox.Text))
```

Permanent Cookie Stored on the Hard Drive

```
' Store the cookie for 3 years.
With Response.Cookies("UserName")
    .Value = NameTextBox.Text
    .Expires = Today.AddYears(3)
End With

' Retrieve the cookie.
MessageLabel.Text = "Hello " & Request.Cookies("UserName").Value
```

The ViewState

You can use **ViewState** to save and restore the state of ASP.NET controls and other values for a single page. The ViewState values are not retained when the user navigates to another page.

ViewState of Controls

Each ASP.NET control has an EnableViewState property, which is set to *true* by default. For each postback of a page, any control that has its EnableView-State set to *true* is automatically saved and restored.

The ViewState of a Web Form

You can store text values in the ViewState of the form. You may want to do this to maintain settings, values entered by the user, values of variables, or even a dataset. The ViewState information is passed to the server on each postback and returned with the form, but the data values are not maintained on the server. The values are available only to the current form, not to the entire application as are session and cookie values.

The ViewState property uses System.Web.UI.StateBag, which is a dictionary collection that holds names and values. Similar to the session and cookie techniques, you make up a name and assign a value to it.

```
' Store a value in ViewState.
ViewState("UserName") = NameTextBox.Text

' Retrieve a value from ViewState.
MessageLabel.Text = "Hello " & ViewState("UserName").ToString()
```

Although you cannot access the ViewState information on a different page, you can retrieve it when you reload the same page on subsequent trips to the server. The data for ViewState are actually stored in hidden controls on the Web Form. One disadvantage of using ViewState is that it increases the amount of information stored with a page, which can make the page take longer to load.

Note: If your application runs in a Web farm, you can assign one machine to handle all of the state management. To indicate this to the application, a change must be made to the `<sessionState>` element in the Web.config file by changing the mode from InProc to StateServer.

Retaining the Values of Variables

Local variables in a Web application work just like local variables in a Windows application: The variables are re-created each time the procedure begins. But module-level variables in Web applications do not work like the ones you are used to in Windows. Because the program is reloaded for each postback, the values of module-level variables are lost unless you take steps to save them. You can store the value of a module-level variable in a session variable, a ViewState variable, or a hidden control on the Web page; the control's EnableViewState property takes care of holding the value during postback.

Saving Module-Level Variables in Session Variables

To save a module-level variable in a session variable, declare the session variable and assign its value in code. All session variables are string, so you must convert any numeric variables to string before assigning their value. In the following example, Session("DiscountTotal") is a session variable and Discount-TotalDecimal is a module-level variable.

```vb
' Declare a module-level variable
Private DiscountTotalDecimal As Decimal

Private Sub SubmitButton_Click(ByVal sender As System.Object, _
  ByVal e As System.EventArgs) Handles SubmitButton.Click
    ' Perform calculations.
    Dim DiscountDecimal As Decimal

    ' Omitted code to convert input to numeric and calculate a discount.

    ' Add to the discount total.
    DiscountTotalDecimal += DiscountDecimal
      ' Save the discount total in a session variable.
    Session("DiscountTotal") = DiscountTotalDecimal.ToString()
End Sub
```

Checking for Postback

When an ASP.NET Web application loads, the Page_Load event occurs. But unlike Windows applications, the page is reloaded for each "round-trip" to the server (each postback). Therefore, the Page_Load event occurs many times in a Web application. The page's IsPostBack property is set to *false* for the initial page load and to *true* for all page loads following the first. If you want to perform an initialization task once, you can test for IsPostBack = False (or Not IsPostBack) in the Page_Load event handler. And if you want to make sure that you perform an action only on postback (not the initial page load), you can check for IsPostBack = True.

```vb
Private Sub Page_Load(ByVal sender As System.Object, _
  ByVal e As System.EventArgs) Handles MyBase.Load

    ' If a value exists for the discount total. . .
    If IsPostBack And (Session("DiscountTotal") IsNot Nothing) Then
        DiscountTotalDecimal = Decimal.Parse(Session("DiscountTotal").ToString)
    End If
```

Notice that the module-level variable, DiscountTotalDecimal, is assigned a value only on postback *and* if the session variable already has been assigned a value.

▶ Feedback 7.4

1. Write the statement to store the value in EmailTextBox to a Session object in a variable called *Email*.
2. What code is required to retrieve the value stored in the Session object Email and assign it to EmailLabel?
3. Write the code to send the Email value to a cookie on the client machine. Give the cookie an expiration of three years.
4. What technique(s) for state management allows you to share the values with other Web pages in the same application or session?

5. What technique(s) for state management allows you to maintain values for the current page only?
6. Why might it be necessary to check for a postback when writing Web applications?

Login Features

ASP.NET includes a group of controls for handling user login and managing passwords. A common function of Web sites is to have a user log in. To implement login, many other tasks are required, such as setting up a new user id and password and changing passwords. Microsoft recognized this need and created a set of controls for login procedures. A database maintains the membership and login information.

The Login Controls

With the **login controls**, you can have users log in or log out, as well as recover their passwords, without having to write any code. All validation is automatically included. The login controls appear in the *Login* section of the toolbox (Figure 7.37).

The Login control (Figure 7.38) allows the user to input the user name and the password. It also includes a check box to "Remember me next time" so that a user can store the login information on his or her own computer. The Login control has many useful properties. The DestinationPageUrl property allows you to set a page to which to link when a login is successfully completed. If you want to create a link for new users, you can set the CreateUserUrl to the page for new users and specify the wording to appear on a link using the Create-UserText property. You also can set the error messages that will display when the user enters an invalid user name or password.

Figure 7.37

The login controls appear in the Login *section of the toolbox.*

Figure 7.38

The Login control includes the properties and methods to allow the user to log in, validate the password, and link to other pages.

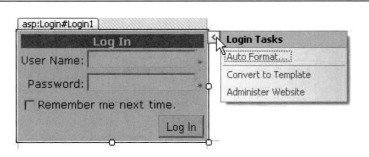

The CreateUserWizard (Figure 7.39) control provides the ability to enter information for a new member and add it to the database. The wizard requires a strong password, which must contain at least seven characters and at least one nonalphanumeric character. The control allows a user to enter a name, a password, password confirmation, e-mail address, and a security question and answer. The ContinueDestinationPageUrl property specifies the page to be displayed once the new user has been created.

Figure 7.39

The CreateUserWizard provides many functions for creating a new user account. The control is very customizable and includes validation.

Two other handy controls are the ChangePassword control and the PasswordRecovery control for existing users who would like to change their password or have forgotten their password. Figure 7.40 shows the two password controls.

Figure 7.40

The ChangePassword and PasswordRecovery controls can automate the task of managing passwords.

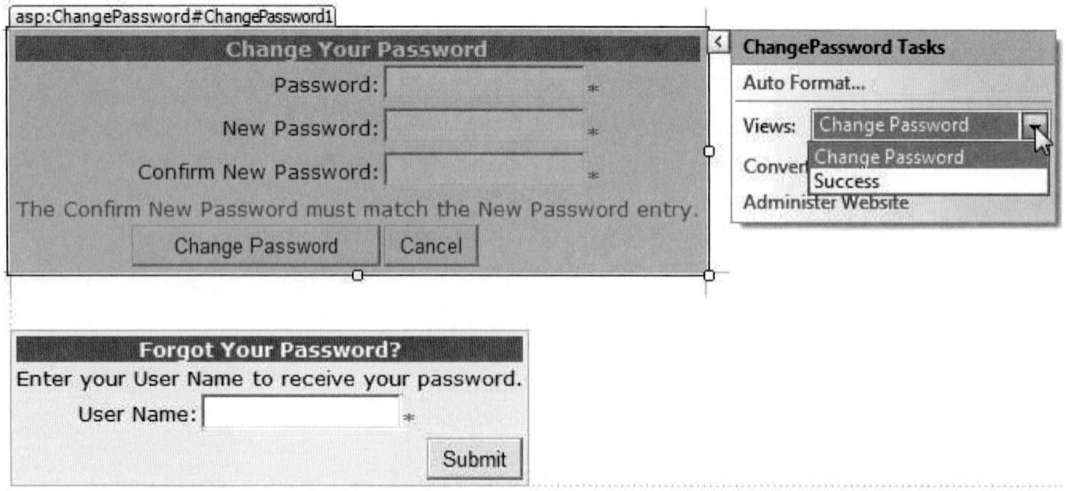

You can place a LoginStatus control on Web pages, which indicates whether the user is currently logged in and provides the link to either log in or log out. The control displays either text or an image, depending on the LoginImageUrl property. The default text is "Login" and "Logout," but you can set your own text by changing the LoginText and LogoutText properties. When the user clicks on *Login*, by default ASP.NET expects to transfer to a page named Login. aspx. You can change the login page name in the Web.config file by setting the loginUrl attribute of the forms element:

```
<authentication mode="Forms">
    <forms loginUrl="SignIn.aspx"
        defaultUrl="Index.aspx" />
</authentication>
```

The Logout property of the LoginStatus control specifies the action to take when the user logs out. The choices are to refresh the current page, transfer to the login page, or transfer to another page of your choosing. If you want to transfer to a specific page, set the LogoutAction property to Redirect and set the LogoutPageUrl property. In any case, logging out resets the IsAuthenticated property of the Page object's Request property and clears any cookies and session variables.

You can display the user's name using the LoginName control. Figure 7.41 shows two LoginStatus controls, one showing the LoginText and the other showing the LogoutText, and a LoginName control. Table 7.3 shows a summary of the available login controls.

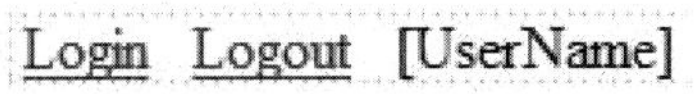

Figure 7.41

Login Logout [UserName]

Two LoginStatus controls and a LoginName control. You normally include only one LoginStatus control, which changes the text depending on whether the user is logged in or out.

The ASP.NET Login Controls   Table 7.3

Control	Function
CreateUserWizard	Collects information from a new user.
Login	A composite control with text boxes for the user name and password. Validates the user input.
LoginStatus	Toggles between a login and logout state depending on whether or not the user is logged in. Displays on the page and provides a link for logging in or out.
LoginName	Displays the user's login name when the user is logged in. With Windows Authentication, the control can display the user domain and account name.
LoginView	Templates that can vary content depending on the user status.
PasswordRecovery	Allows users to obtain their password through an e-mail address using a security question.
ChangePassword	A composite control that contains text boxes for the original password, new password, and confirmation for the new password.

Adding Login Controls to an Application

You can add the login controls by simply dragging and dropping them on a form. You may want your login form on the home page or you may want to have it on a separate page. It is common to have the password recovery and change password features available through a link. You will be able to control access to pages best if you have the login forms and public pages in the root directory of the Web site and maintain the member-only pages in a separate folder.

Using the Web Site Administration Tool

To set up user logins, you must use the ASP.NET Web Site Administration Tool (Figure 7.42). The Administration Tool is accessible from the *Website / ASP .NET Configuration* menu item, from the icon at the top of the Solution Explorer window, or from the smart tag of any login control.

Figure 7.42

Use the Web Site Administration Tool to set up user login. Click the How do I use this tool? link in the upper-right corner for detailed instructions on using the tool.

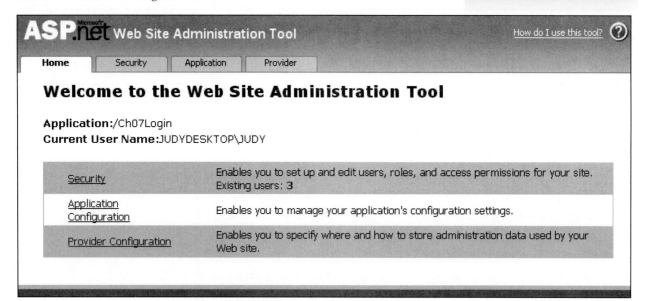

You will use the *Security* tab of the Administration Tool (Figure 7.43), which allows you to create and manage users, manage roles, and establish access rules. The *Roles* feature enables you to add groups (roles) that you can use to assign access privileges for groups of users. *Access Rules* determine which users or roles have access to individual folders.

You can create your first user from the *Security* tab if you wish, or you can add users from the CreateUserWizard control that you added to a Web page. Note that the information for the users is stored in a Microsoft SQL Server Express database by default. You can set a different database provider using the *Provider* tab of the Administration Tool.

Figure 7.43

In the Security tab of the Web Site Administration Tool, you can set up users, roles, and access rules.

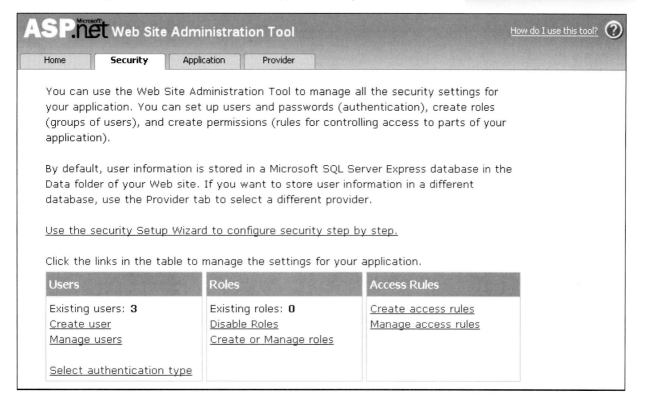

Required Entries

The Administration Tool provides many options that you can set. In order to make the login controls work, you *must* make two settings:

1. Authentication type: On the *Security* tab, click on *Select authentication type*. Select *From the internet* (Figure 7.44), which allows users to log on using a form.

2. Add an access rule: On the *Security* tab, click on *Create access rules*. Select your Members folder (which you must first create), select *Anonymous users* (to apply the rule to those that haven't logged in), and then select *Deny* (Figure 7.45). Click *OK*.

Setting Up a Login Application

To create a Web site that allows users to log in and display a page that exists in a Members folder, follow these general steps:

- Create the Web site and add a Login.aspx page and a NewUser.aspx page. Add a Members folder and create a page inside the folder. Include some text greeting the member on the members-only page.

- On the Default.aspx page, add two links for *Sign In* and *New User*. Link *Sign In* to Login.aspx and link *New User* to NewUser.aspx.

Select the option to allow users to log in from the Internet.

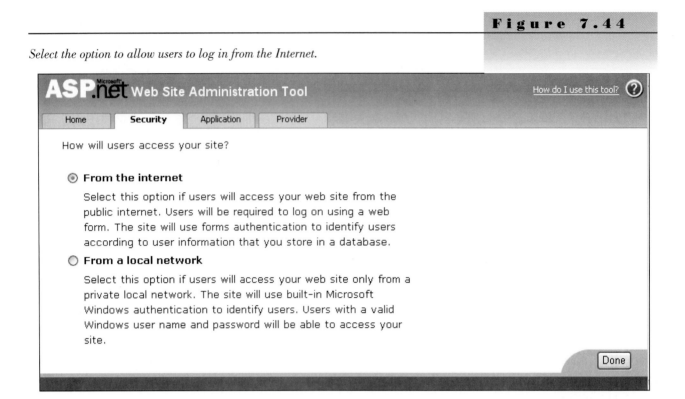

Set up an access rule for your Members folder.

Figure 7.46

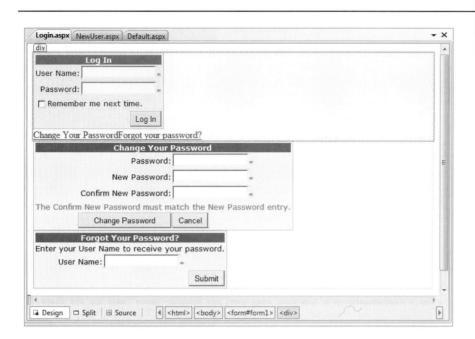

Set up the controls on Login.aspx.

- On Login.aspx, add a Login control, a ChangePassword control, and a Password Recovery control (Figure 7.46). Set the DestinationPageUrl to the members page in the Members folder.

- On NewUser.aspx, add a CreateUserWizard control and set the Continue-DestinationPageUrl to the page in the Members folder.

- Open the Web Site Administration Tool, click on the *Security* tab, click on *Select authentication type*, and select *From the internet* (and *Done*).

- Still on the *Security* tab, select *Create access rules* and set the two options for your Members folder for *All Users* and *Allow*.

Now run your program, add yourself as a user, and then try using the login.

You probably also noticed the option for e-mail. To set up e-mail accounts, you would need to use the SMTP settings on the *Application* tab. You may want to try it out if you have access to an SMTP server.

AJAX

One of the greatest recent advances in Web pages is the ability to use **Asynchronous JavaScript and XML (AJAX)** to create interactive Web applications. Visual Studio 2008 and ASP.NET 3.5 include the script manager for handling AJAX directly in the toolbox (Figure 7.47). Every AJAX application must have one (and only one) ScriptManager control. Later in this chapter, you will use the UpdatePanel control to control partial page updates.

Many AJAX controls are currently available and the number grows daily. You can freely download and use any controls that you find on Microsoft's community Web site: CodePlex.com. You also can create new controls and participate in the open-source community on CodePlex.com, which includes a sample

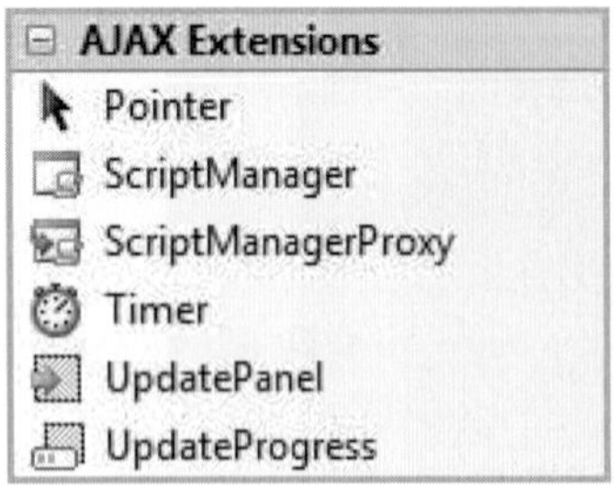

Figure 7.47

The AJAX controls in the toolbox. Every AJAX application must have a ScriptManager control.

AJAX Extensions
- Pointer
- ScriptManager
- ScriptManagerProxy
- Timer
- UpdatePanel
- UpdateProgress

Web site that demonstrates the controls and instructive walkthroughs about such topics as "Using Animations." At some point you will likely want to open the sample Web site and investigate the many items available. Many of the controls are called *extenders*; they add functionality to existing controls such as buttons and text boxes.

In the next section, you will download and use some of the available AJAX controls. You can find additional controls at www.codeplex.com/AtlasControlToolkit.

AJAX Control Toolkit

Before you can start using AJAX controls, you must download the AJAX toolkit and add controls to your toolbox. You will add the items to the toolbox during a step-by-step example that demonstrates extenders applied to a button control and a slide show extender added to an image control.

TIP

Always remember that a page using AJAX must contain one and only one ScriptManager control. ∎

Download and Use AJAX Controls—Step-by-Step

First you must download the AJAX toolkit zip file. Note that as of this writing, all URLs are correct, but they could change in the future.

Download the AJAX Control Toolkit

STEP 1: Go to www.asp.net/ajax/ and click on the *Downloads* link. Feel free to investigate the site and view any files that you'd like to see.

STEP 2: Click on the *Download the Control Toolkit* button. You may need to scroll down the page to see the actual link for AjaxControlToolkit-Framework3.5SP1.zip.

STEP 3: Click on the link for the AJAX control toolkit zip file and you will be given a license agreement to which you must agree if you want to continue.

STEP 4: Save the file in a convenient location, so that you can find it for the next step.

STEP 5: Extract all of the files in the zip files, again choosing an easily found location.

Create a New Web Site

STEP 1: Create a new Web site called Ch07AjaxControlToolkit.

Add the AJAX Controls to the Toolbox

STEP 1: Right-click on the toolbox in the IDE and select *Add Tab*, renaming the tab as AJAX Controls.

STEP 2: Select your new tab, right-click, and take the option *Choose Items*.

STEP 3: From the *Choose Toolbox Items* dialog box, browse to find the unzipped files for the AJAX toolkit. Open the SampleWebSite folder and then the Bin folder. Scroll to the bottom of the list and select the Ajax-ControlTookit.dll file and click *Open*. The *.NET Framework Components* tab now contains several highlighted and checked items from the AjaxControlToolkit namespace. Click *OK*. The new *AJAX Controls* toolbox tab should now contain many controls (Figure 7.48).

Figure 7.48

The new AJAX controls are added to the AJAX Controls tab of the toolbox.

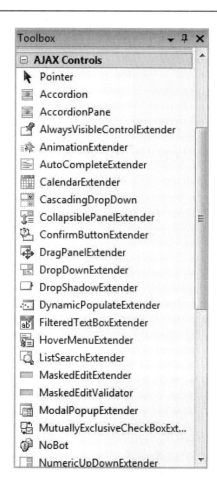

Add Controls to the Web Form

In this section, you will add a TextBox, Validator, and Extender controls.

STEP 1: From the *AJAX Extensions* tab of the toolbox, add a ScriptManager control to the form. If you double-click on the control in the toolbox, by default it is added below the DIV element on the form.

STEP 2: Click inside the DIV element and add a table with three rows and three columns. *Hint*: Select *Table / Insert Table*.

STEP 3: In the first cell of the first row, add the word "Name: ".

STEP 4: Add a NameTextBox in the second cell and a RequiredFieldValidator in the third cell.

STEP 5: Notice that the validator control has an arrow that looks like a smart tag. Select the arrow and the *Add Extender* option (Figure 7.49) to display the extenders that are associated with a validator control. Select the ValidatorCalloutExtender. You can always see a list or remove any of the applied extenders by selecting the *Remove Extender* option.

Figure 7.49

Select Add Extender from the validator control's smart tag.

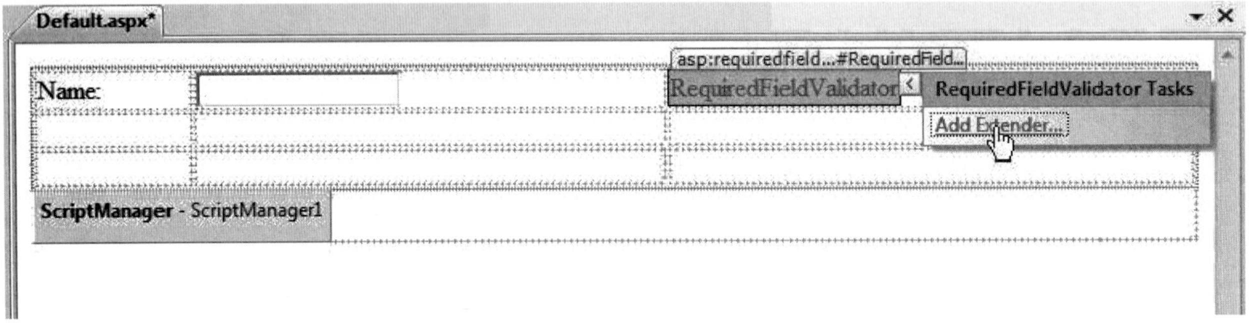

STEP 6: Set the ControlToValidate property of the RequiredFieldValidator1 to the NameTextBox.

STEP 7: Set the ErrorMessage property to "Name is required."

Add and Extend a Button Control

STEP 1: Next, add a *Submit* button so the page can be posted. Be sure to name the button and set the Text property.

STEP 2: Add a ConfirmButton extender and select *SubmitButton_ConfirmButtonExtender* from the drop-down *Object* list in the Properties window.

STEP 3: Set the ConfirmText property of the SubmitButton_ConfirmButtonExtender to "Confirm Extender causes this popup."

STEP 4: Run the application and click the *Submit* button, leaving the name blank. An annoying popup will occur when you click the button (Figure 7.50); the validator callout displays when you click the *OK* or *Cancel* button.

This example of the popup is useless but gives you an idea of some of the features that can be added with the AJAX control toolkit. You probably also noticed a lot of extenders for rounded corners and drop-down shadows. You may want to test these on your system; some do not run properly in IE8 on Vista.

Use a SlideShow Extender Control—Step-by-Step

The SlideShow Extender allows an image control to cycle through a series of pictures. It also provides the ability to add buttons to play, loop, or stop the slide show. In order to set up the multiple images, we will use a Web service.

Add and Set Up an Image Control

STEP 1: Add an image control to your Ch07AjaxControlToolkit default Web page.

Figure 7.50

Popups created by the ConfirmButtonExtender control; a. the message pops up in another window, b. the message appears in an icon on the form.

a.

b.

STEP 2: Add a folder called *Images* to your project and populate it with a few pictures. The sample program on the text Web site uses images that are installed by default with Windows Vista. The folder is *Vista Public Pictures / Sample Pictures.*

STEP 3: Set the ImageUrl property of the Image control to one of the pictures.

STEP 4: Set the Width property to 500.

STEP 5: Add the SlideShowExtender to your image. Set the AutoPlay and Loop properties to *true.*

Set up the Images

STEP 1: Right-click on the project name; select *Add New Item* and the Web Service template, naming it SlideService.asmx.

STEP 2: Under the App_Code folder, open the SlideService.vb file if it doesn't open automatically.

STEP 3: Add access to script services by uncommenting the following line:

```
<System.Web.Script.Services.ScriptService()> _
```

STEP 4: Write the Web method. The constructor for a slide requires three strings: the image path, the name of the image, and a description. We are going to use empty strings for the last two parameters. Substitute the filenames with the files that you added to the Images folder.

```
<WebMethod()> _
Public Function GetSlides() As AjaxControlToolkit.Slide()
    ' Create an array of slides.
    Dim Slides(3) As AjaxControlToolkit.Slide
    Slides(0) = New AjaxControlToolkit.Slide("images/Autumn Leaves.jpg", "", "")
    Slides(1) = New AjaxControlToolkit.Slide("images/Toco Toucan.jpg", "", "")
    Slides(2) = New AjaxControlToolkit.Slide("images/Waterfall.jpg", "", "")
    Return Slides
End Function
```

Connect the GetSlides Function to the Extender

STEP 1: In the Image1_SlideShowExtender properties, set the SlideShowServiceMethod to GetSlides.

STEP 2: Set the SlideShowServicePath property to SlideService.asmx.

STEP 3: Run the application. The images should appear, one at a time (Figure 7.51)

Figure 7.51

The images appear in an Image control. The SlideShowExtender and Web service cause the control to cycle through the images.

You can control the speed of the images by setting the PlayInterval property, which is set to three seconds by default (3000 milliseconds). You also may want to set the Description properties of the images; they can be displayed in a label by specifying the ImageDescriptionLabelID for the extender.

Partial Page Updates

AJAX allows you to reload only a portion of the Web page, rather than the entire page, on each postback. Often large portions of a Web page are unchanged for a postback. Using standard protocols, the entire page is redrawn every time. Using AJAX, the loading speed can increase dramatically by downloading and rendering only the portion that *does* change.

AJAX is an open and cross-platform technology that works on many operating systems. Because AJAX is included in Visual Studio 2008, you can use it on your Web pages. After you place the ScriptManager component on the page, you can add other controls, such as the UpdatePanel, which is a container for other controls.

Placing controls inside of an UpdatePanel determines what portion of the page updates on a postback. One fun way to test this is to place a label that contains the time inside the update panel and another outside the panel. When a *Submit* button posts back to the server, only the time inside the update panel changes. *Hint*: See "Retrieving the System Date and Time" in Appendix B for the methods to display the time.

In the following small program (Figure 7.52), the user enters a name in a text box and clicks the *Submit* button. The page then welcomes the user by name. The large image is outside the UpdatePanel so it does not redraw when the page posts back the response.

Figure 7.52

A Web page that uses AJAX must have a ScriptManager component. The UpdatePanel holds the controls that should be posted back to the server. The area outside the UpdatePanel remains unchanged.

```
Protected Sub SubmitButton_Click(ByVal sender As Object, _
  ByVal e As System.EventArgs) Handles SubmitButton.Click
    ' Concatenate Welcome to the name.

    WelcomeLabel.Text = "Welcome " & NameTextBox.Text
End Sub
```

Other AJAX Notes

When you add a new item to a Web site, you see two AJAX templates: an AJAX Master Page and an AJAX Web Form. These items are simply the Master Page and Web Form templates with a script manager already included.

There are some interesting extenders for a text box. The CalendarExtender changes a text box into a drop-down calendar when the user clicks on the box. You can control the format of the calendar by attaching a cascading style sheet. When the user selects a date, the date is entered in the text box. The Calendar-Extender allows you to control the date format. Another feature that is frequently used is a button that triggers the display of the calendar. In Ch07-AjaxControlToolkit, TextBox1 has a CalendarExtender with the PopupButtonID property set to image2, which contains a calendar. If you remove the Popup-ButtonID property, the calendar appears when the user clicks in the text box.

The FilteredTextBoxExtender lets you set the type of characters that are allowed or the ones that are not allowed in a text box.

If you are looking to learn more about AJAX development, check out the ASP.NET AJAX video series by Joe Stagner at www.asp.net/learn/ajax-videos/.

ASP.NET Page Life Cycle

To understand the logic on a Web page, it is important to understand how the page works behind the scenes. You know that a page renders each time it posts back. There are several steps that occur in addition to maintaining state. You also should understand when controls initialize and load.

Life cycle stage	Purpose
Page request	When user requests a page, ASP.NET determines if a cached page exists; if not, the page cycle begins.
Start	Determines if the request is a postback. The core properties of Request and Response initialize.
Page initialization	Controls are initialized but data are not yet loaded. Themes are applied.

Load	If it is a postback
	    Controls are filled with view state data.
	Else
	    Initial data binding occurs.
	Data values are loaded.

Validation	Validation controls call their Validate methods and the IsValid property is set.
Event handling	Event handling and page logic occur.
Unload	Response and Request properties are unloaded and cleanup is performed.

The page raises events during each of the stages of the life cycle. You can write your code in those event handlers.

Event	Purpose
PreInit	Set master page. Set theme. Set page culture (for internationalization).
Init or PreLoad	Set or check control properties.
Load	Perform initial data binding.
PreRender	Make any final changes to the page contents.
Unload	Close files, database connections.
Control Events	Save state of controls or page variables. Check IsValid property of validation controls as needed.

Managing Web Projects

Managing the files in a Web project is significantly different from handling Windows projects.

Location of Files

The Visual Studio IDE saves solution files in the default folder that you select in *Tools / Options / Projects and Solutions*. Even if you choose to store your Web site in the same location as solution files, two folders are created. For example, if you name your Web site Ch07Calendar and place it in the same folder specified for solutions, you will have one folder called Ch07Calendar and a second folder called Ch07Calendar(2). The solution files (.sln and .suo) are stored in the (2) folder. Although you may specify that you want to save the solution files in the same folder as the Web site, they are saved in the second folder. By selecting the solution name and selecting *File / Save SolutionName As*, you can browse and select the actual folder with the Web site, which makes it easier to open in the future.

Opening a Saved Web Site

If you have not saved the .sln and .suo files in the project folder, then you must open an existing Web site from inside the IDE. Select *File / Open Web Site* and browse to the folder that holds the Web files (not the solution files). With the folder selected, click *Open*.

Moving and Renaming a Web Project

If you have created your Web project as a File System project, you can easily move it from one location to another. You also can rename the project folder in the Windows Explorer when the project is not open. Unlike some previous editions of Visual Studio, no hard-coded complete paths are stored in the Web site files.

Moving and renaming an IIS Web site is considerably more complicated because you must use the Internet Information Services Manager to create a virtual directory. See Appendix C for additional information concerning IIS Web sites.

Copying and Publishing Web Sites

You can use the Copy Web tool to copy the current Web files to another Web site. You can copy files between any of the types of Web sites that you can use in Visual Studio, such as File System sites, IIS sites, remote Web sites, and FTP sites. It's best to develop Web sites as File System Web sites; when complete, you can copy them to an IIS site or other remote site.

Note: You must have sufficient permissions on the destination server to create and modify the site. To create or modify an IIS site, you must have administrative rights on the server.

Visual Studio provides both a Copy Web tool and a Publish Web utility. The Copy Web tool copies all files and can perform synchronization of the files in both locations. You can continue development of the site in either location. The Publish Web utility is for publishing a completed Web to a production Web site. The publish action performs a precompilation and strips the markup from the .aspx files. A published Web site will perform faster and be more secure than a copied site but cannot be used for further development. To make modifications to the site, you must work on the original files and republish when finished.

MSDN contains considerable information about the advantages and disadvantages of each method of deployment.

Your Hands-On Programming Example

Write a project for R 'n R—For Reading and Refreshment. Use a master page with the menu across the top. The menu will have links for home and contact information. Also include a Login link in the left column. Use your style sheet from the in-chapter programs; you will need to add a DIV for the menu immediately below the header.

The Login page should allow existing members to log in and recover or change their passwords, and allow a new user to create a new account.

The member page should show the current special and allow the member to order up to five products. Use a range validation to validate the quantity field.

Pages:

> MasterPage
> Default (home page)
> Login
> Create Account
> Contact Information
> Member Pages
>> Welcome
>> Thank you
>> Logged Out

The Login and CreateAccount pages hold the appropriate login controls. The Contact Information page displays the company phone for both inside and outside of the United States. The Logged Out page should simply display a message that the user is logged out.

Planning the Project

Sketch the forms (Figure 7.53*a* through *g*) that your users sign off as meeting their needs.

Figure 7.53

The planning sketches for the hands-on programming example: a. the Default (home page) form; b. the Login form; c. the Create Account form; d. the Contact Information form; e. the Welcome form; f. the Thank You form; and g. The Logged Out form.

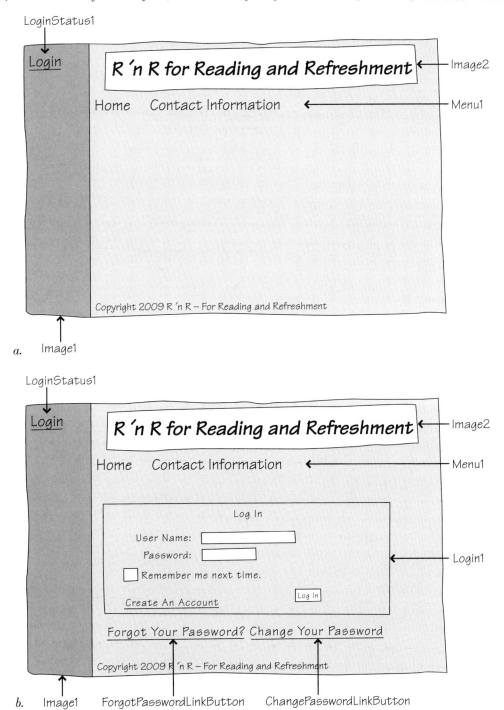

LoginStatus1

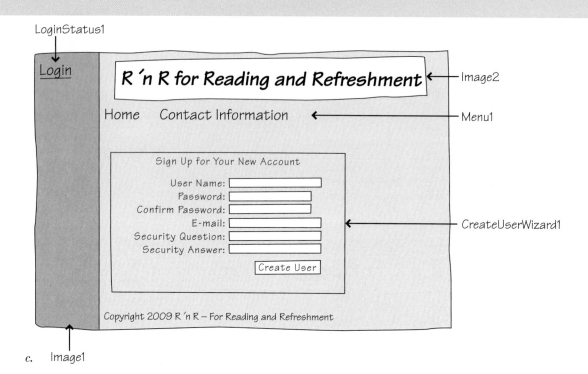

c. Image1

LoginStatus1

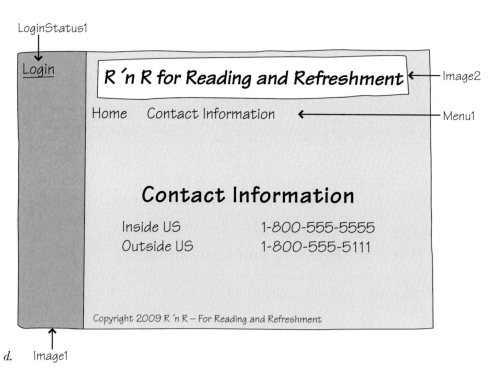

d. Image1

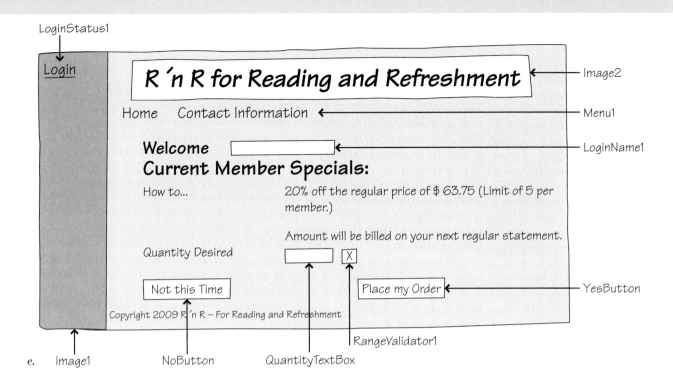

LoginStatus1

Login

R 'n R for Reading and Refreshment ← Image2

Home   Contact Information ← Menu1

Welcome [   ] ← LoginName1

Current Member Specials:

How to...   20% off the regular price of $ 63.75 (Limit of 5 per member.)

Amount will be billed on your next regular statement.

Quantity Desired   [   ] [X]

[Not this Time]   [Place my Order] ← YesButton

Copyright 2009 R 'n R – For Reading and Refreshment

RangeValidator1

e.   Image1   NoButton   QuantityTextBox

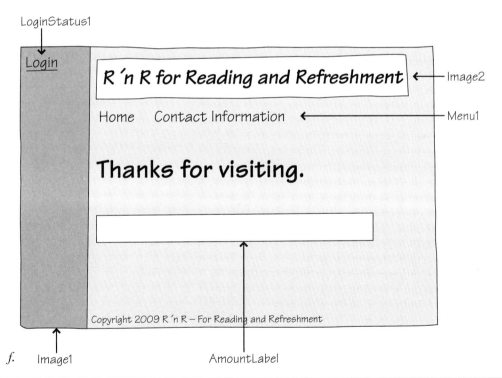

LoginStatus1

Login

R 'n R for Reading and Refreshment ← Image2

Home   Contact Information ← Menu1

Thanks for visiting.

[   ]

Copyright 2009 R 'n R – For Reading and Refreshment

f.   Image1   AmountLabel

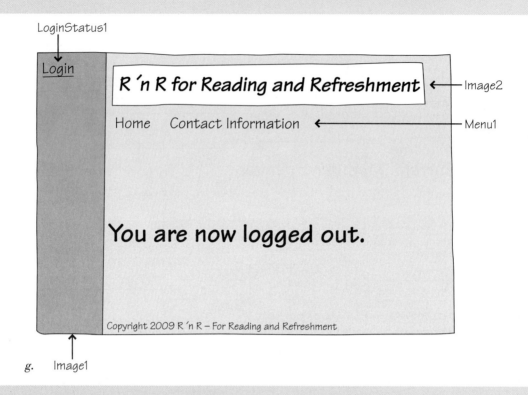

g.

Plan the Objects, Properties, and Methods Plan the objects and property settings for the master page, the seven forms, and their controls.

The MasterPage

Object	Property	Setting
Site1.Master	Title	R 'n R
	Style:background-color	LightCyan (or other light color of your choice)
Layout	DIV/StyleSheet	
Menu	Items	Home
		NavigateUrl: Default.aspx
		Contact Us
		NavigateUrl: ContactInformation.aspx
	Font	Underline
LoginStatus	LogoutPageUrl	LoggedOut
	Logout Action	Redirect
	Font	Underline
Header	Image1	ImageUrl: BlueHills.jpg
	Image2	RnRHeading.gif
		(Add the files from the StudentData folder to the project's Images folder before setting the property.)
ContentPlaceHolder	Name	ContentPlaceHolder1
Footer	Text	Copyright 2009 R 'n R — For Reading and Refreshment

The Default Page

Object	Property	Setting
Default.aspx	Title	R 'n R Home Page
	MasterPageFile	Site1.Master

The Login Page

Object	Property	Setting
Login.aspx	Title	Welcome to R 'n R
	MasterPageFile	Site1.Master
Login	CreateUserText	Create an Account
	CreateUserUrl	CreateAccount.aspx
	DestinationPageUrl	MemberPages/Welcome.aspx
PasswordRecovery1	Visible	False
ChangePassword1	Visible	False
ForgotPasswordLinkButton	Text	Forgot Your Password?
ChangeYourPasswordLinkButton	Text	Change Your Password?

Methods	Actions—Pseudocode
ForgotPasswordLinkButton_Click	Make the password recovery control visible.
ChangeYourPasswordLinkButton_Click	Make the change password control visible.
Login1_LoggedIn	Transfer to MemberPages/Welcome.aspx

The CreateAccount Page

Object	Property	Setting
CreateAccount.aspx	Title	R 'n R Create a New Account
	MasterPageFile	Site1.Master
CreateUserWizard	CreateUserText	Create an Account
	ContinueDestinationPageUrl	MemberPages/Welcome

The Contact Information Page

Object	Property	Setting
ContactInformation.aspx	Title	R 'n R Contact Information
	MasterPageFile	Site 1.Master
Coments	Text	Contact Information
	Text	Inside US
	Text	1-800-555-5555
	Text	Outside US
	Text	1-888-555-5111

The Welcome Page (Member Page)

Object	Property	Setting
Welcome.aspx	Title	Welcome to R 'n R
	MasterPageFile	Site1.Master
Table contents (10 by 3 table)		
LoginName		
	Merged cells	Current Member Specials:
	Center Column	How to…
	Right Column	20% off the regular price of $63.75. (Limit of 5 per member.)
	Center	Quantity Desired
	Right	QuantityTextBox
	Center	NoButton
	Right	YesButton
RangeValidator1	ControlToValidate	QuantityTextBox
	MinimumValue	0
	MaximumValue	5
	Text	*
	Type	Integer
	ToolTip	Must be integer 0–5.

Methods	Actions—Pseudocode
YesButton	Calculate amount.
	Append result to query string.
	Transfer to Thank You page
NoButton	Transfer to Thank You page.

The Thank You Page (Member Page)

Object	Property	Setting
ThankYou.aspx	Title	R 'n R Thank You
	MasterPageFile	Site1.Master
AmountLabel		

Methods	Actions—Pseudocode
Page_Load	If the query string contains a value
	If amount > 0
	Display the amount in AmountLabel.

The Logged Out Page (Member Page)

Object	Property	Setting
LoggedOut.aspx	Title	R 'n R Logged Out
	MasterPageFile	Site1.Master

Write the Project Following the sketches in Figure 7.53, create the forms. Figure 7.54 shows the completed forms.

- Set the properties of each of the form objects, according to your plans.

- Write the code for the forms. Working from the pseudocode, write each event handler.

- When you complete the code, test the operation several times. Test the validation routines and navigate back and forth between the forms. Sign out and make sure that you can sign in again and navigate correctly.

Figure 7.54

The forms for the hands-on programming example: a. the Default (home page) form; b. the Login form; c. the Create Account form; d. the Contact Information form; e. the Welcome form; f. the Thank You form; and g. The Logged Out form.

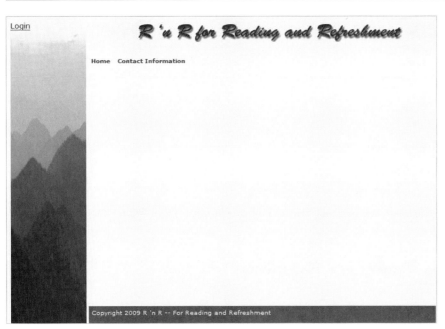

a.

b.

Figure 7.54

(Continued)

c.

d.

Figure 7.54

(Continued)

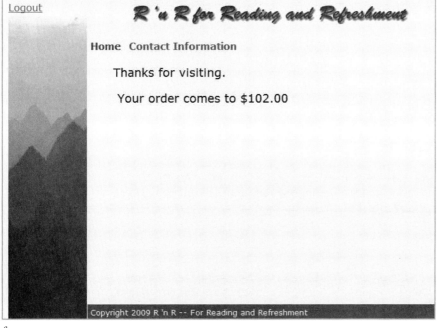

e.

f.

Figure 7.54

(Concluded)

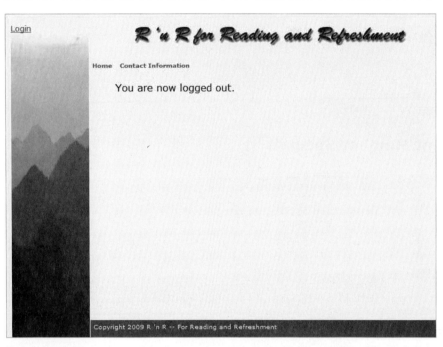

g.

The Project Coding Solution

The Default Page No code.

The Login Page

```
'Project:      Ch07HandsOn
'Programmer:   Bradley/Millspaugh
'Date:         June 2009
'Description:  Login information for R 'n R.

Partial Class Login
    Inherits System.Web.UI.Page

    Protected Sub ForgotPasswordLinkButton_Click(ByVal sender As Object, _
      ByVal e As System.EventArgs) Handles ForgotPasswordLinkButton.Click
        ' Display the Password Recovery control.

        PasswordRecovery1.Visible = True
    End Sub

    Protected Sub ChangePasswordLinkButton_Click(ByVal sender As Object, _
      ByVal e As System.EventArgs) Handles ChangePasswordLinkButton.Click
        ' Display the ChangePassword control.

        ChangePassword1.Visible = True
    End Sub

    Protected Sub Login1_LoggedIn(ByVal sender As Object, _
      ByVal e As System.EventArgs) Handles Login1.LoggedIn
        ' Successful login. Transfer to Welcome page.

        Response.Redirect("MemberPages/Welcome.aspx")
    End Sub
End Class
```

The CreateAccount Page No code.

The Contact Information Page No code.

The Welcome Page

```
'Project:      Ch07HandsOn
'Programmer:   Bradley/Millspaugh
'Date:         June 2009
'Description:  Display Welcome page for R 'n R.

Partial Class Welcome
    Inherits System.Web.UI.Page

    Protected Sub YesButton_Click(ByVal sender As Object, _
      ByVal e As System.EventArgs) Handles YesButton.Click
      ' Calculate amount and link to Thank You page.

      Dim AmountDecimal As Decimal = 63.75D * _
        Decimal.Parse(QuantityTextBox.Text) * 0.8D
        Server.Transfer("ThankYou.aspx?amount=" & AmountDecimal.ToString("C"))
    End Sub

    Protected Sub NoButton_Click(ByVal sender As Object, _
      ByVal e As System.EventArgs) Handles NoButton.Click
        ' Link to Thank You page.

        Server.Transfer("ThankYou.aspx")
    End Sub
End Class
```

The Thank You Page

```
'Project:      Ch07HandsOn
'Programmer:   Bradley/Millspaugh
'Date:         June 2009
'Description:  Display Thank you page for R 'n R.

Partial Public Class ThankYou
    Inherits System.Web.UI.Page

    Protected Sub Page_Load(ByVal sender As Object, _
      ByVal e As System.EventArgs) Handles Me.Load
        ' Display the amount if it exists.

        If Request.QueryString("amount") IsNot Nothing Then
            Dim AmountString As String = Request.QueryString("amount")
            AmountLabel.Text = "Your order comes to " & AmountString
        End If
    End Sub

End Class
```

Summary

1. A Web application resides on a server and displays in the client's browser application.
2. A network within a company is called an intranet.

3. ASP.NET can send the correct code for any browser. Different code is sent for uplevel browsers and downlevel browsers.

4. HTML Web pages do not store information from one access to the next. To store information from Web pages, you must use one of the state management techniques.

5. Web programming in Visual Studio uses ASP.NET 3.5, which is the newest Web programming technology from Microsoft.

6. The .aspx file contains the specifications for the user interface. The VB code is contained in the .aspx.vb file, which is called the "code-behind" file.

7. The controls for Web Forms are not the same controls as for Windows Forms. Many of the controls are designed to work similarly to their Windows counterparts. Controls may be HTML controls or ASP.NET server controls.

8. Click events of buttons cause a postback to the server; most other events are not processed as they occur but are held until the next postback.

9. The LinkButton acts like a button and looks like a hyperlink. Use a LinkButton rather than a HyperLink control if you need to perform some action before navigating to the next page.

10. Use the Image control to include graphics on a Web page; the ImageUrl property points to the location of the graphic file.

11. The Calendar control allows the user to enter or select a date that you can then display or use in the program.

12. Setting the tab order differs from a Windows application. By default, all controls have their TabIndex property set to zero, which means that it is unset. You must manually set the TabIndex properties of controls that you want to appear in the tab sequence.

13. The layout of the page is easier using a cascading style sheet.

14. A master page can define the layout of a page for a consistent look for menus and the company logo. A content page has its MasterPageFile property set to the name of the master page.

15. The validation controls can validate input data on the client machine before being transmitted to the server when using an uplevel browser. The controls include the RequiredFieldValidator, CompareValidator, RangeValidator, RegularExpressionValidator, and the ValidationSummary. On a downlevel browser, the validation is performed on the server.

16. The `Response.Redirect` method can navigate to any other Web page. The `Server.Transfer` method can navigate to any other page on the same server and is more efficient than `Response.Redirect` because it requires one less round-trip to the server.

17. An ASP.NET project can use the Request, Response, Session, Application, and Server objects.

18. HTML pages do not maintain data values, called the state, from one access to another or from one page to another. Using the ViewState, ASP.NET can restore the contents of controls for a postback within a single page.

19. State management may be handled on the server side or the client side. Techniques include Application and Session objects, cookies, and the form's ViewState property.

20. A set of login controls can automatically handle user login/logout and manage passwords.

21. AJAX controls provide the capability of partial page updates as well as the ability to add interactivity to a Web page.

22. You can copy a Web site to another location using the Copy Web tool. The copied Web site will be available for further development. You also can publish a Web site to deploy it for use; the published site is in a precompiled state and cannot be modified by development tools.

Key Terms

Application object *317*

Asynchronous JavaScript and XML (AJAX) *327*

Button *285*

cascading style sheet (CSS) *291*

code separation model *281*

content page *304*

HyperLink control *287*

ImageButton *285*

intranet *277*

LinkButton *285*

login controls *321*

master page *304*

NavigateUrl property *287*

postback *284*

Request object *315*

Response object *315*

`Response.Redirect` *288*

server *276*

`Server.Transfer` *288*

Session object *317*

single-file model *281*

state *315*

stateless *315*

validation control *312*

ViewState *319*

Web farm *317*

Web Form *281*

Web page *281*

Web server *277*

Web site *278*

Web.config file *286*

Review Questions

1. What are uplevel browsers and downlevel browsers? How are ASP.NET programs handled differently for the two levels of browsers?
2. Describe the purpose of these Web project files: .aspx, .aspx.vb, .css, Web.config, .master.
3. What are the three types of button controls available for Web Forms?
4. Explain the differences between a LinkButton and a HyperLink control.
5. What methods can you use to navigate to another page? How do they differ?
6. What is the purpose of a master page? How is it created? implemented?
7. List the validation controls. Give an example for using each type.
8. What techniques are available for state management on the server side?
9. List four methods of state management and give the advantages and disadvantages of each.
10. What is the purpose of the LoginStatus control? How is it used?
11. What control must be added to a Web page to allow AJAX functionality?

Programming Exercises

7.1 Create a Web site for Tricia's Travels. Include an appropriate logo. Use login controls for existing and new users. On the members page, include links for "Land" special and "Cruise" deal of the week. Use a master page for the layout of your site. On the specials pages, include a *Submit* button and allow the user to enter the number of travelers (a required field). Users should be able to navigate home through a menu or link without pressing the *Submit* button.

7.2 Modify Exercise 7.1 to include another page that requires calculations and uses at least one validation control. Display the result of the calculation on another page.

7.3 Create a personal Web site. The first page should include your name and a favorite image. Include links to pages describing your hobbies, education, and employment. Include links to other Web sites if you wish. Use a cascading style sheet, a master page, or both.

7.4 Create a Web site for your company (you may invent any products and/or company names that you wish). Include fields that require validation on the home page and links to at least three other pages. Use a master page and/or a cascading style sheet.

7.5 Expand Exercise 7.4 to include login controls and only allow access to some pages for those that have signed in.

7.6 Expand Exercise 7.5 to include a page that has calculations and another page that displays the result of the calculations. Use at least one validation control.

Case Studies

Claytor's Cottages

Design and create a Web site for Claytor's Cottages. Set up a master page for the layouts and use a cascading style sheet for the font styles. The company logo (and optional image) should appear on every page along with the copyright information. Include a menu with links for Home, Contact Us, Rewards Members, and Reservations.

The Rewards Members page requires a login page that allows existing members to log in and new users to create an account.

Set up pages for each of the menu items. The reservations page will be an "under construction" page. You will modify this page in the Chapter 8 case study.

The login should take members to a Members page, which describes the current promotion: "Come enjoy the season with us." Promote the season of your choice and include a description of the bonus "evening wine and cheese events." Include a page to indicate that the user has logged out.

Christian's Car Rentals

Design and create a Web site for Christian's Car Rentals. Set up a master page for the layouts and use a cascading style sheet for the font styles. The company logo (and optional image) should appear on every page along with the copyright information. Include a menu with links for Home, Contact Us, Star Program, and Reservations.

The Star Program page requires a login page that allows existing members to log in and new users to create an account.

Set up pages for each of the menu items. The Reservations page will be an "under construction" page. You will modify this page in the Chapter 8 case study.

The login should take members to the Current Promotions page. Include a promotion using promotion code RALC41 that gives an extra day for every four rental days; or include a promotion of your choice. Include a Logout page.

Use the following for the Contact Information page or make up your own information:

By Mail   Christian's Car Rentals Customer Support
              1000 W. 14th Street
              Los Angeles, CA 92333
By E-mail   CustomerSupport@ChristiansCars.com
By Phone   1-800-555-1234

8

Web Database Applications

at the completion of this chapter, you will be able to . . .

1. Display and update database files in Web applications.

2. Access data with a data source control.

3. Display data using the grid, details, and/or a form view.

4. Select records from a list box by using a parameterized query.

5. Display data from related tables.

6. Determine when to use a data reader rather than a dataset.

7. Set up a multitier Web application.

8. Maintain state for data in a multipage application.

The previous chapter introduced you to Web Forms. In this chapter, you will expand your knowledge of Web applications by incorporating database access. You also will use components to create multitier Web projects.

Data Access in ASP.NET

More and more applications are written for execution on the Web. And the majority of those applications access data in some form. Many examples quickly come to mind, such as looking up reference data; online ordering; companies that store all customer, product, and employee information in a database with Web access; user IDs and passwords; and even bill paying and online banking.

Adding database access to a Web project is significantly different from accessing data in a Windows application. ASP.NET database controls differ from those used in Windows. You must add a data source control to the Web Form and configure it for data access. And ASP.NET does not provide support for dragging fields to the form for automatically creating data-bound controls.

Binding fields to data on a Web Form does not automatically provide for two-way data binding. By default, a Web page *displays* data from bound fields but does not pass changes back to the data source. Later in this chapter, you will learn how to specify data updating.

Data Source Controls

Data source controls handle all of the database access for a Web page including selecting records for display and inserting, deleting, and editing records for database updates. The data source control automatically opens a connection, executes commands, and closes the connection. On your Web page, you can place data-bound controls that connect to the data source control.

The toolbox contains several types of data source controls in the *Data* section (Figure 8.1). You can use the **SqlDataSource control** for every type of database or choose a specific type for your specific database. For example, the AccessDataSource inherits from the SqlDataSource, but it has some settings

Figure 8.1

The Data section of the toolbox holds the data source controls and controls for displaying data on a Web page.

default to those needed by Microsoft Access. Since we are using SQL Server, we will use the SqlDataSource. And later in this chapter, you will use the **ObjectDataSource control** for multitier applications.

Adding Data to a Web Project

To make it easier to work on projects in the classroom and at home, we include the database in the project folder. Recognize that for a production job in industry, your final application would connect to the database server. After you create a new Web site project, right-click the App_Data folder and select *Add Existing Item* from the context menu. Browse to find the database and add it to your project. You should do this step before configuring a data source.

Adding a SqlDataSource Control

When you drag a SqlDataSource control to a Web page, you see the control on the page. It appears at design time but not at run time. Open the smart tag and select *Configure Data Source* (Figure 8.2).

The Configure Data Source wizard will look familiar to you (Figure 8.3). Select *New Connection* and browse to the database file in the App_Data folder for your project. Choose the option to save the connection to the application configuration file.

A SqlDataSource control on a Web Form; select Configure Data Source to set up the database access.

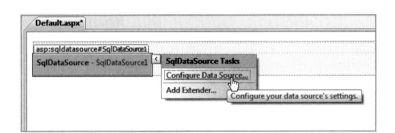

In the familiar Configure Data Source wizard, you can set up a new connection for the data source.

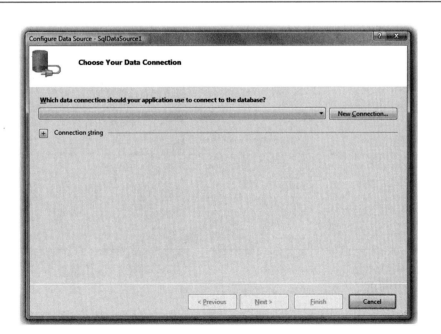

The next page of the wizard asks you to configure the Select statement. You have options for specifying a custom SQL statement or stored procedure and an option to select the columns from a table or view (Figure 8.4). Also notice the check box that specifies returning only unique rows and the *WHERE* and *ORDER BY* buttons for customizing the SQL statement. You can drop down the *Name* list to choose any single table in the database file. Note that selecting the option to specify a custom SQL statement or stored procedure gives you the opportunity to open the standard Query Designer that you have used in the past.

Figure 8.4

The Configure Data Source wizard can help you set up the SQL SELECT *statement.*

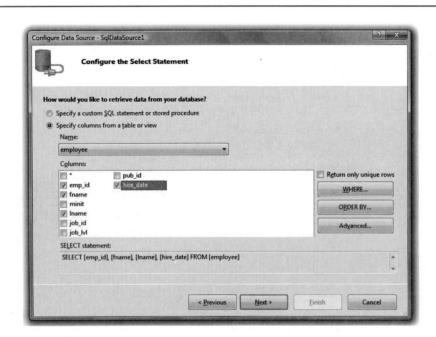

Making the Connection String Dynamic

The connection string is automatically created and placed in the Web.config file with a hard-coded path to your directory:

```
connectionString="Data Source=.\SQLEXPRESS;AttachDbFilename=&quot;
C:\Documents and Settings\UserName\Desktop\pubs.MDF&quot;;Integrated Security=True;
User Instance=True" providerName="System.Data.SqlClient"
```

To make your project portable, delete the absolute path name and substitute "|DataDirectory|" (typing the vertical bars but not the quotes). This convention indicates that the database is in the project's App_Data folder.

```
<connectionStrings>
    <add name="pubsConnectionString"
    connectionString="Data Source=.\SQLEXPRESS;AttachDbFilename=
    &quot;|DataDirectory|pubs.MDF&quot;;Integrated Security=True;User Instance=True"
    providerName="System.Data.SqlClient" />
</connectionStrings>
```

Displaying Data on a Form with a Data Source

It is very simple to display data on a Web page; you need only a data source and a control to display the information. The next few sections illustrate using a DataGrid, a DetailsView, a FormView, and a DropDownList control.

Displaying Data in a GridView Control

You can display data in a **GridView control**, which is similar to the Windows DataGridView. The smart tag on the GridView allows you to set an auto format as well as choose a data source. You do not need to write any code (Figure 8.5).

Figure 8.5

A simple database application that displays the stores table in a grid without writing any code.

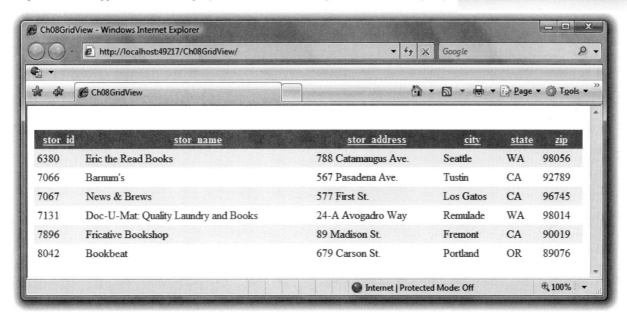

The smart tag for the grid also offers options for pagination and sorting. When you select sorting, the grid displays with column headings in a link style format. Clicking on a header causes the grid to display in ascending order for that column.

Very often, the selected data produce more rows than fit on a screen. As you know, scroll bars appear automatically, but many users prefer to view just one page at a time. Selecting the smart tag check box for pagination automatically adds pagination to a grid.

Notice in Figure 8.5 that the header text is underlined. These "links" allow the user to sort by that column. Clicking the heading once sorts the data in ascending sequence; clicking again sorts in descending order. The grid's AllowSorting property is a Boolean value that determines whether the user can perform sorting. By default, AllowSorting is set to *true*.

It is usually preferable to set the width of the grid in percents rather than pixels. By default, the Width property of each of the data controls is set in pixels. For best display on a Web form, set the grid's Width property to a percent, including the sign, such as "80%" (without the quotes). You can test this on a Web page by resizing the browser window; the grid and its columns all resize and the data in the cells wrap when necessary for display.

When you drag a table from the Server Explorer and drop it on a Web Form, a GridView and SqlData-Source automatically generate. ■

Displaying Data in a DetailsView Control

Another alternative for displaying the data is one record at a time, using the **DetailsView control**. Once again, there is no code to write; you simply add a data source and a detail control. Configure the data source and assign a data source to the detail data control.

As with the grid, the column names are used by default for field labels on a DetailsView control (Figure 8.6). Selecting *Enable Paging* on the smart tag provides links to other records, which you would want only for a very small table.

Figure 8.6

A DetailsView control displays individual records without writing any code. The links for other records are provided by the Enable Paging option on the smart tag.

You can customize the display of data by selecting *Edit Fields* from the DetailsView's smart tag. To manually set the headers, select a field from the *BoundField* list; the properties for the field appear, where you can set the Header-Text property (Figure 8.7). You also can reorder the fields and add and remove fields from the display. Select a field in the *Selected Fields* list and click the

Figure 8.7

Set properties of the bound fields, including the Header-Text, in the Fields dialog box. You also can reorder the fields and add and remove fields.

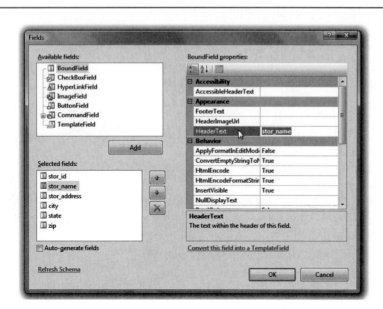

Delete button to remove it from the display. Both the *Fields* dialog box and the control's smart tag have an option to add a new field.

Similar to the GridView, you can set the Width property of the DetailsView control to a percent, such as 80%.

Displaying Data on a FormView Control

Another option for displaying data in individual fields is the **FormView control**. Similar to a DetailsView, a FormView displays one record at a time, but you have more control of the layout of the fields.

To use a FormView control, first add and configure your data source and then add the FormView control. When you set a FormView object to a data source, a template that contains the bound fields is automatically generated. To modify the layout, you must edit the template. Notice the links to additional records in Figure 8.8; that option is created by selecting *Enable Pagination* on the control's smart tag.

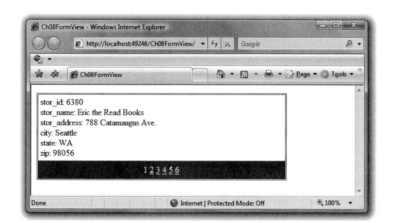

Figure 8.8

Bound data are displayed in a FormView control. The links are provided by the Enable Pagination option.

To modify the layout of a FormView, select *Edit Templates* from the smart tag. With **ItemTemplate** selected (Figure 8.9), you can type text directly in the template on the form. Modify the headings by selecting and editing the displayed template. You can change the order of the fields, delete fields, change the text in the labels, or change the type of controls. When you finish making changes, return to the smart tag and select *End Template Editing*.

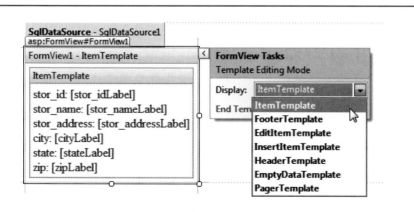

Figure 8.9

You can select the option to edit the item template or several other templates when you select Edit Templates from the FormView's smart tag.

To see an example of improved formatting in a FormView, look at Ch08Bindings in Design view (Figure 8.10). The heading "Publishing Contact Details" was added and formatted with the H1 html block format. In order to align the labels and fields of data, a table was added to the item template, the controls were moved into the table cells, and the identifying labels for the fields were edited. Notice that the City, State, and Zip fields appear on one line with a comma after the city. The output looks great and there is still no code.

Figure 8.10

To format the template for the FormView, you can add a table, add text, and apply formatting.

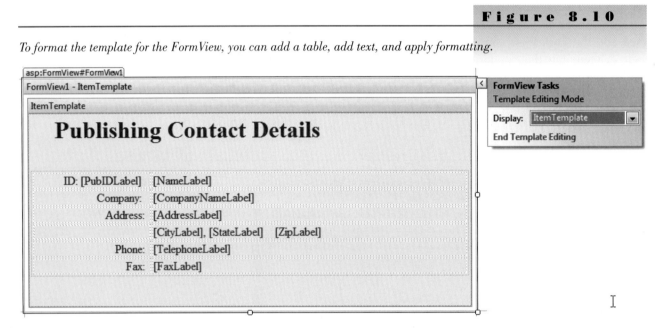

Examining the Data Bindings

The actual data bindings for Web applications are very different from the Windows version. To view the bindings, open Ch08Bindings, select the smart tag on the FormView control, and select *Edit Templates*. Next, click on the PubID-Label control and select *Edit DataBindings* from its smart tag. Notice that the PubIDLabel uses Text as the bindable property (Figure 8.11). The *Binding for Text* specifies that the field is bound to PubID in the data source.

Figure 8.11

The data binding for the Text property of PubIDLabel is accomplished with the selection for Binding for Text.

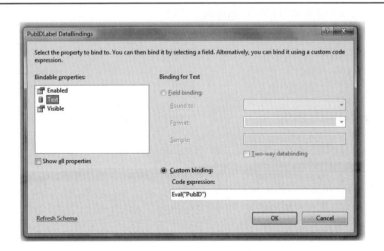

You may want to check the *Show all properties* box to see how many different properties can be used for binding. You generally use the Text property because you want the data to display.

Displaying Data in a Drop-Down List

You can use several of the controls from the *Standard* section of the toolbox for displaying bound data. Any control that has a DataSource property can be bound to data. The DropDownList control can be bound to data and used for selecting a record, in a manner similar to the combo box selection in Windows applications. However, you must use a parameterized query to display the result of the selection.

The following step-by-step exercise uses a data-bound drop-down list for selecting records. The ViewState property of the DropDownList control maintains the contents of the list from one invocation to the next. However, if the application has multiple pages and the user can navigate between the pages, you must take steps to maintain the list contents. See "Maintaining the State of List Boxes" later in this chapter.

Creating a Parameterized Query—Step-by-Step

The steps for displaying a selection from a drop-drown list in a Web application are different from the Windows version. The following step-by-step exercise takes you through setting up the controls and writing a parameterized query to retrieve the matching record for a selection.

Set Up the Database Access

STEP 1: Create a new Web site project called Ch08DropDownList. Select the solution name and save the solution file in the project folder.

STEP 2: Set the DOCUMENT's Title property to "Ch08DropDownList".

STEP 3: Select the App_Data folder, right-click, and select *Add Existing Item*. Add the Pubs.mdf file.

STEP 4: Add a SqlDataSource control from the *Data* tab of the toolbox. Name the control StoresSqlDataSource. Configure it to connect to the stores table in the Pubs database in the project's App_Data folder. Select only the stor_id and stor_name fields.

STEP 5: Edit the Web.config file to make the project portable: Remove the entire hard-coded path from the connection string and replace it with "|DataDirectory|\Pubs.mdf". The AttachDbFilename attribute should look like this:

```
AttachDbFilename=|DataDirectory|\Pubs.mdf;
```

Add and Configure the Drop-Down List

STEP 1: Place a DropDownList control on the form and name it StoreName-DropDownList.

STEP 2: In the control's smart tag, select *Choose Data Source*. In the Data Source Configuration Wizard (Figure 8.12), set the data source to StoresSqlDataSource, with stor_name displaying and stor_id as the data field for the value. The value is used for the parameterized query, to retrieve the matching data for the selected store. Click *OK*. *Note:* If the display and value lists are not populated, click on the *Refresh Schema* link on the *Choose a Data Source* dialog box.

Figure 8.12

Set the data source for the drop-down list. Set the field to display and the field for the value, which will be used to look up the correct detail record.

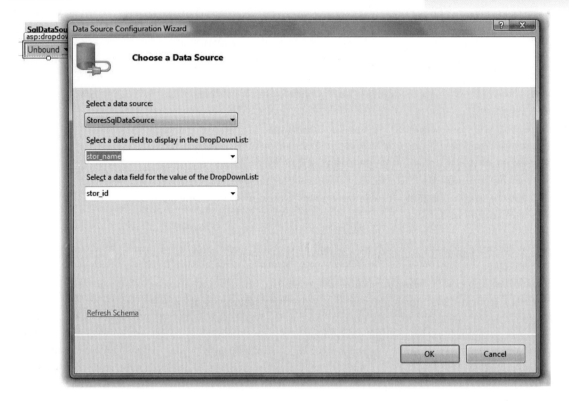

STEP 3: In the smart tag for the DropDownList control, select the *Enable-AutoPostBack* check box, so that a new selection by the user triggers a postback to the server.

STEP 4: Set the Width property of the control to "50%".

Add a Second Data Source Control

STEP 1: Add a second SqlDataSource control, naming it SingleStoreSqlData-Source.

STEP 2: When you configure the data source, for the connection select the PubsConnectionString, rather than create a new connection.

STEP 3: Select all fields in the sales table and click on the *WHERE* button. For *Column*, select stor_id. Set the *Source* to *Control*. Then set the *ControlID* to StoreNameDropDownList (Figure 8.13). Click on *Add* to generate the WHERE clause. Click on *OK*.

STEP 4: In the Configure Data Source Wizard, notice that the SELECT statement now includes the WHERE clause. Click *Next* and *Finish*.

Add a FormView Control for the Store Data

STEP 1: Click in the Web Form after the second data source control and press Enter two or three times for spacing.

STEP 2: Add a FormView control from the Data section of the toolbox. Set the control's Width property to "80%".

TIP

When adding a second data source from the same database, select the existing connection string rather than create a new connection. ■

Figure 8.13

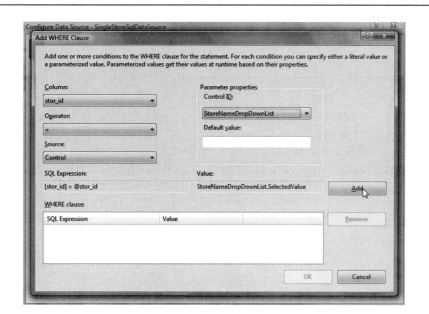

In the Add WHERE Clause *dialog box, select the column from the new data source and the control whose value you want to use for the selection criterion.* When *you click* Add, *the* WHERE *clause is automatically generated.*

STEP 3: In the control's smart tag, set the data source to SingleStoreSqlDataSource.

STEP 4: Run the program. Try selecting a new store from the drop-down list. The store's data should appear in the FormView. But it's pretty ugly. Stop execution.

TIP

If you get an error reconfiguring a data source, it is sometimes quicker to delete the control and add a new one than to try to debug the old one. ∎

Format the FormView Data in a Table

STEP 1: Select *Edit Templates* from the FormView smart tag.

STEP 2: Click after the last data line in the template and select *Table / Insert Table*. Add a table with six rows and two columns. Click *OK*.

STEP 3: Widen the FromView control and the new table. Then drag each of the data fields to a cell in the second column of the table. Type new, meaningful identifying labels in the first column. Although you could cut and paste the field names into the cells, the field names are too cryptic to show the user. Delete the field names (Figure 8.14).

Figure 8.14

Lay out the bound controls and identifying labels in a table.

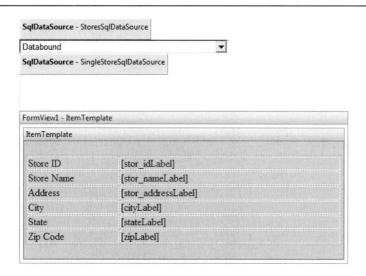

STEP 4: On the smart tag, select *End Template Editing*.

STEP 5: Select *Auto Format* and choose a format from the list.

STEP 6: Run again. Do you like what you see? If not, reformat some more. Don't forget to choose *End Template Editing* each time you finish editing, before you run the program again. Figure 8.15 shows one version of the finished application.

Figure 8.15

The completed selection application for the step-by-step exercise.

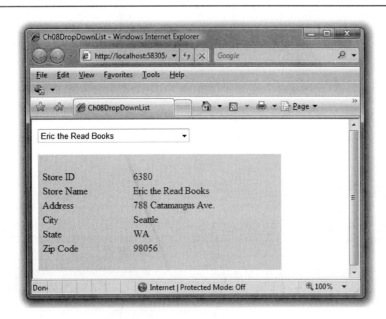

Displaying Data from Related Tables

Adding a bit of complexity to the drop-down list program that you just completed, the next step is to add a grid with related records. The following step-by-step exercise builds on the Ch08DropDownList program to create Ch08RelatedTables. Figure 8.16 shows the completed form, which displays the sales for a selected store.

Figure 8.16

The completed Ch08Related-Tables program, which adds to the previous step-by-step exercise.

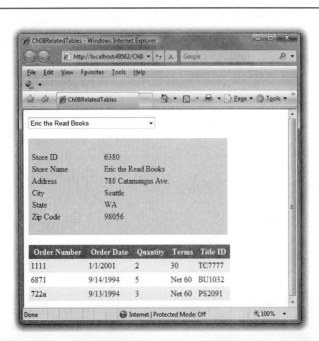

Adding Related Tables—Step-by-Step

This exercise is a continuation of the previous step-by-step exercise. However, we want to keep the two projects separate.

Make a Copy of the Project Folder

STEP 1: Make sure that the project from the previous step-by-step exercise is closed and make a copy of the entire folder, using Windows Explorer. Rename the project folder to Ch08RelatedTables.

STEP 2: Open the Ch08RelatedTables project.

STEP 3: Change the solution name and the DOCUMENT's Title property to "Ch08RelatedTables".

Add a Third Data Source

STEP 1: Add another SqlDataSource to the form, naming it SalesSqlDataSource. Note that the data source can appear anywhere on the form. You might want to drag all three data source controls to the top of the page.

STEP 2: Configure the SalesSqlDataSource to select all fields from the sales table. Set up the WHERE clause as you did in Step 3 of "Add a Second Data Source Control" in the preceding exercise (refer to Figure 8.13). This will add a WHERE clause that matches the selected stor_id from the drop-down list.

Add a GridView Control to Display the Sales Data

STEP 1: Add a blank line for spacing following the FormView.

STEP 2: Add a GridView control from the Data section of the toolbox.

STEP 3: Set the GridView's data source to SalesSqlDataSource.

STEP 4: You can run it now, if you wish. However, we prefer to do some formatting first.

Format the Grid

STEP 1: In the grid's smart tag, select *Edit Columns*.

STEP 2: Click on the stor_id field in the *Selected fields* box and click the *Delete* button. There's no need to display the store ID for each sale.

STEP 3: Select each field in the *Selected fields* box and change the HeaderText property to a better heading. (You can refer to Figure 8.16 for our idea of better headings.)

STEP 4: Select the Order Date field and scroll the Properties list to find the DataFormatString. Click in the settings box and notice the suggested formats shown below (Figure 8.17). Type "{0:d}" (without the quotes) to format the date as a short date. Click *OK*.

STEP 5: Select an auto format from the smart tag.

STEP 6: Set the grid's Width property to "80%".

STEP 7: *Now* run the project. Test the drop-down list to make sure that the grid fills with the sales for the selected store.

Once again there is no code. How hard was that?

Figure 8.17

Set the DataFormatString to display the order date as a short date.

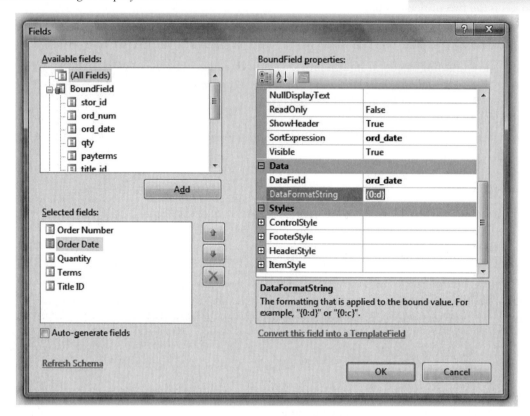

Displaying Related Data on Multiple Pages

In the next example, we are going to display the related information from the stores and sales tables using multiple pages. This approach uses a hyperlink field from the first table to navigate to a second page (Figure 8.18).

When you edit the columns of the data controls, one of the options is a HyperLinkField. You will set three properties for the hyperlink: Text, DataNavigateUrlFields, and DataNavigateUrlFormatString. The key of the selected store passes between the two pages using the DataNavigateUrl-FormatString. The Text property is the value that displays for the link and the DataNavigateUrlFields indicates the field in the table for the lookup value.

Property	Purpose	Example
DataNavigateUrlFields	Column of table for lookup value.	stor_id
DataNavigateUrlFormat-String	Navigation link that passes a query string to the second page.	Sales.aspx?stor_id={0}
Text	Text to display for the link.	Sales

Figure 8.18

The user can click the hyperlink field to view the data from the related table. a. The Default.aspx page and b. the Sales.aspx page with the sales for the selected store.

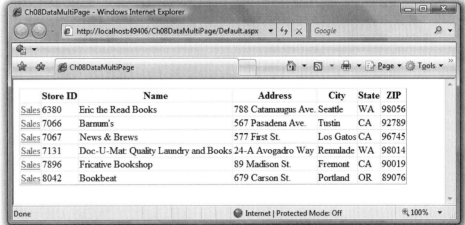

a.

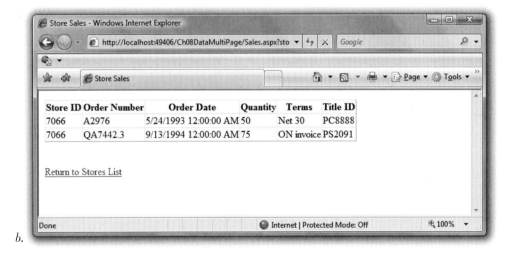

b.

Creating Multiple Pages—Step-by-Step

This exercise creates the two forms shown in Figure 8.18.

Create the Project

STEP 1: Create a Web site called Ch08DataMultiPage and save the solution file in the project folder.

STEP 2: Copy the Pubs database into the App_Data folder.

STEP 3: Set the Title property to "Ch08DataMultiPage".

Set Up the Data Source

STEP 1: Add a SqlDataSource to the Default.aspx page; select all fields in the stores table of the Pubs database.

STEP 2: For portability, edit the hard-coded path in the Web.config connection string to "|DataDirectory|\Pubs.mdf".

Design the First Page

STEP 1: Add a GridView to the page and set the data source to the one you created.

STEP 2: From the smart tag of the GridView, select *Edit Columns*.

STEP 3: Scroll down the *Available fields* list, click on HyperLinkField, and click the *Add* button.

STEP 4: In the *Selected fields* list, move your hyperlink field to the top of the list.

STEP 5: Set the following properties for the hyperlink:

Text:	Sales
DataNavigateUrlFields:	stor_id
DataNavigateUrlFormatString:	Sales.aspx?stor_id={0}

STEP 6: Set the HeaderText property of each field to something meaningful.

STEP 7: Click *OK* to close the dialog box.

Set Up the Second Page

STEP 1: Add another Web Form to the Web site; name the form Sales.aspx and set the Title to "Store Sales".

STEP 2: Place a GridView on the form.

STEP 3: From *Choose Data Source*, select *<New data source>*.

STEP 4: Click on the database icon and click *OK*.

STEP 5: Drop down the list of connections and select *PubsConnectionString*. Click *Next*.

STEP 6: Select all fields from the sales table.

STEP 7: Click on the *WHERE* button and use the following values:

Column:	stor_id
Source:	QueryString
QueryString field:	stor_id

STEP 8: Click on *Add*. Click on *OK*. Then click *Next* and *Finish* in the wizard.

STEP 9: Add a HyperLink control from the *Standard* tab of the toolbox. Set the Text and NavigateUrl properties to provide a return to the stores page.

Test the Project

STEP 1: Right-click on Default.aspx in the Solution Explorer and set it as the startup page.

STEP 2: Run the program. Click on the Sales link for any row. The second page should appear with the sales for the selected store.

Format

STEP 1: Add any formatting that you think will improve the display. The grid in Figure 8.18 has the HeaderText property set for each field in the grid.

Selecting Data in a GridView

You can display a *Select* button in the rows of a GridView, which the user can use to select a row. You can choose to display the *Select* button as a link, a button, or an image. In Figure 8.19, the *Select* button displays as a button, but in Figure 8.20, the *Select* button is configured with its ButtonType set to Link, its SelectText set to "View Info", and the button moved to the right end of the grid.

Figure 8.19

	Name	Telephone
Select	ACM	212-869-7440
Select	Addison-Wesley	617-944-3700
Select	Apt	212-697-0887
Select	Bantam Books	800-223-6834
Select	Benjamin/Cummings	800-950-2665
Select	Beta V	206-556-9205

Choose Enable Selection from the grid's smart tag to create a Select button in the rows of the grid.

Figure 8.20

Name	Telephone	
ACM	212-869-7440	View Info
Addison-Wesley	617-944-3700	View Info
Apt	212-697-0887	View Info
Bantam Books	800-223-6834	View Info
Benjamin/Cummings	800-950-2665	View Info
Beta V	206-556-9205	View Info

This Select button is configured as a Link, with its Select-Text property set to "View Info" and the button moved to the last position of the grid.

To create a *Select* button in the rows of a GridView, select *Enable Selection* in the grid's smart tag. You can modify the style, position, and text of the button by selecting *Edit Columns*. In the *Fields* dialog box (Figure 8.21), choose the *Select* entry in the *Selected fields* list to set the properties of the button.

Figure 8.21

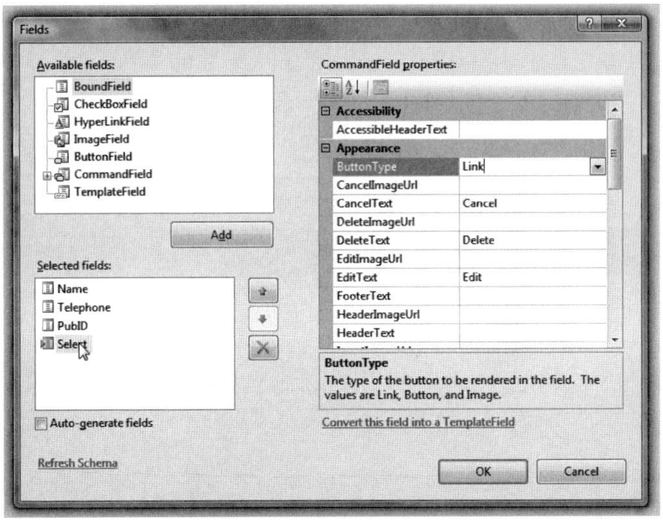

Select Edit Columns to display the Fields dialog box. The entry labeled Select is the new Select button; click on it to modify its properties and reorder the list of fields.

You respond to a *Select* button click in the GridView's SelectedIndex-Changed event handler. You can refer to the cells in the selected row as Grid-View1.SelectedRow.Cells(*index*). The index of the first column is zero.

```
Protected Sub GridView1_SelectedIndexChanged(ByVal sender As Object, _
  ByVal e As System.EventArgs) Handles GridView1.SelectedIndexChanged
    ' Save the selected items.

    Dim Row As GridViewRow = GridView1.SelectedRow
    Session("Name") = Row.Cells(0).Text
    Session("Phone") = Row.Cells(1).Text
    Server.Transfer("InfoPage.aspx")
End Sub
```

Data Readers versus Datasets

So far, all of your database projects have used a dataset, the default return value from a SqlDataSource. Another choice is a data reader. A **DataReader object** provides a forward-only result set from a data source. The forward-only feature means that access is fast—sometimes called the "fire-hose" connection. However, it also means that a data reader is not suitable for doing file updates. The sorting capability is also disabled when you use a data reader.

For a Web application, you want to keep the connection time to the database as short as possible. A data reader often provides the quickest method for loading a list box or retrieving other small amounts of information that are not subject to change while the Web page displays. If you are displaying larger amounts of data or want to work with related tables, a dataset is the proper choice. Often a single application may contain both a data reader and a dataset.

The DataSourceMethod property of the SQLDataSource control allows you to choose whether the file access uses a dataset or a data reader. Try running a program and changing the data source method. With a small file, the difference may not be noticeable. If you or your campus has downloaded the AdventureWorks sample database file from Microsoft, you can use it to test the difference.

Caching

The SqlDataSource control has the ability to cache data to improve performance for your applications. The EnableCaching property is not set by default, but you can set the value to *true*. You also can set the CacheDuration property. A different cache is kept for each connection and set of parameters.

When you are using the caching feature, you can set the FilterExpression property of the data source control. The filter expression allows you to filter the data in the cache without submitting a new request to the database.

▶ ### Feedback 8.1

1. What is the difference between a DetailsView and a FormView control?
2. Give an example where multiple data source controls would be needed.
3. When would it be best to use a data reader instead of a dataset?

Updating a Database

All of the Web database projects to this point have only displayed data, which is the most common operation for Web applications. However, sometimes Web applications also allow updates to the database. For example, an online shopping application allows the user to browse the products, which is a display operation. But when the user adds something to a shopping cart, the information must be saved.

Web applications do not automatically configure data binding for updates. Allowing updates requires a change in the configuration of the data source. In the *Configure the Select Statement* page of the Data Source Configuration Wizard, you can click on the *Advanced* button (Figure 8.22), which enables you to generate INSERT, UPDATE, and DELETE SQL statements for the data source (Figure 8.23).

Figure 8.22

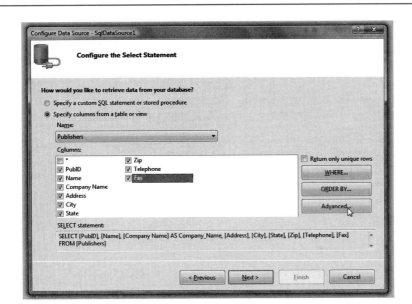

Figure 8.23

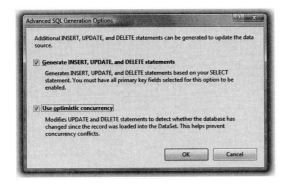

Another choice on the *Advanced SQL Generation Options* dialog box is optimistic concurrency. If there is any chance that multiple users may be updating the database at the same time, select this option. The concurrency setting performs a check when saving modified data to make sure that no changes have been made to the original data source since the dataset was filled.

Updating with a Data Source Control

Adding basic update features does not require coding. Once the data source is set to the appropriate SQL update statements, the smart tag for the GridView, DetailsView, and FormView controls have extra check boxes that allow you to enable editing and deleting.

Updating in a GridView

When you are configuring a GridView, you can select *Enable Editing* and *Enable Deleting* on the smart tag. Making these two selections adds a new column to the grid with *Edit* and *Delete* link buttons (Figure 8.24). Later you will see how to customize the links for updating.

The basic operation of the updating works quite well, as long as the user is careful not to violate any constraints. When you run the application, the grid

If you don't see *Enable Editing* and *Enable Deleting*, it means that you haven't configured the UPDATE, INSERT and DELETE statements (see Figre 8.23). ■

Figure 8.24

Select Enable Editing *and* Enable Deleting *to allow updating to the data in a GridView. Selecting the two options creates a new column in the grid with* Edit *and* Delete *links.*

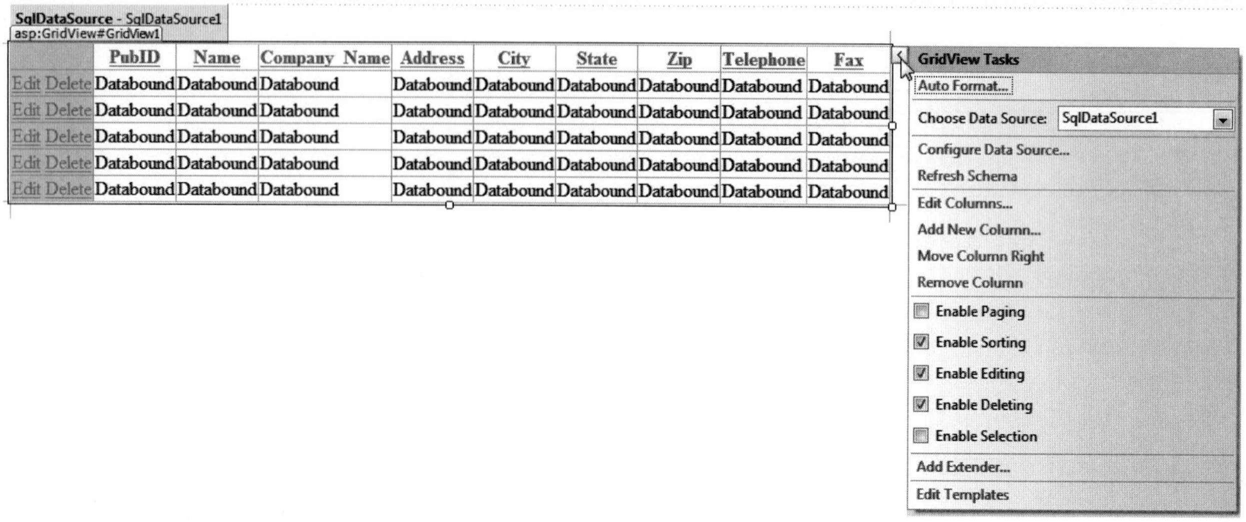

appears with the action link buttons (Figure 8.25). The user cannot make any changes to data until clicking the *Edit* link button, at which time the two link buttons for that row change to *Update* and *Cancel*. If the user clicks on the *Delete* button, the current record is deleted from the database without confirmation. And unlike Windows applications, the changes are immediately saved back to the original data source (the copy you added to the project).

Figure 8.25

The user can click on the Edit *or* Delete *link button for a given row to update the data for that row. For the* Edit *option, the two buttons change to* Update *and* Cancel; *for* Delete, *the record is deleted from the database.*

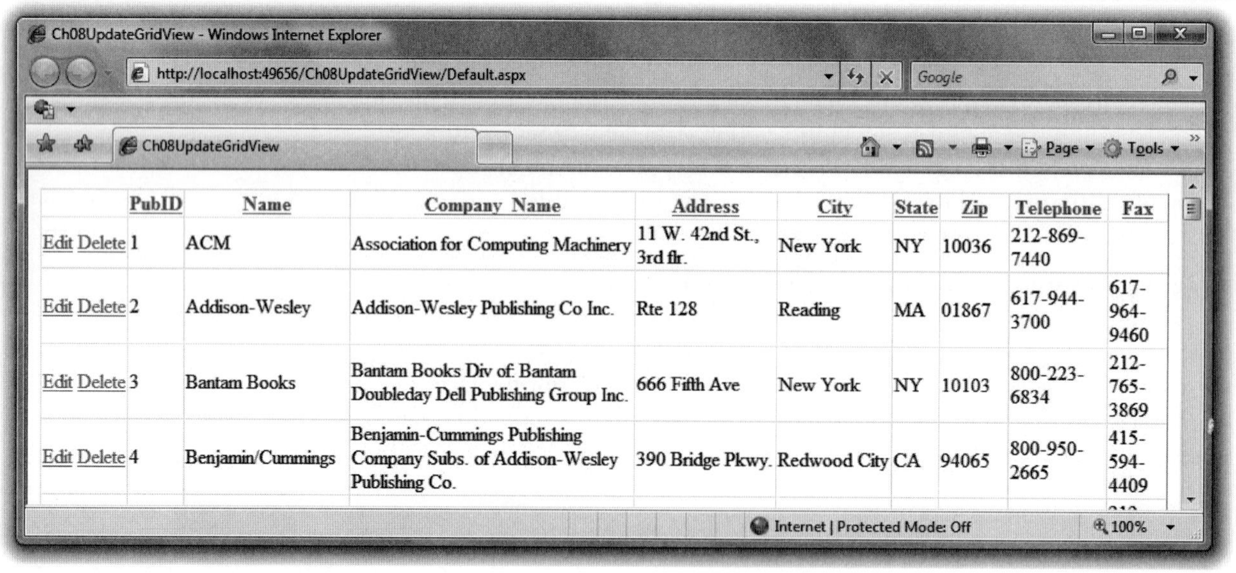

Allow Selection of Grid Rows　You can customize the update application by setting additional properties. On the grid's smart tag, you can check *Enable Selection* (refer to Figure 8.24), which creates a third action link button labeled

Select. When you choose the option to *Edit Fields*, you can change many properties of the action buttons. A new CommandField was added to the Selected fields list; this is the field that holds the link buttons (Figure 8.26). You can set the text of the buttons, the header text for the column, and the ButtonType property to Button, Link, or Image.

Figure 8.26

Set the ButtonType and modify the text to display in the Fields dialog box.

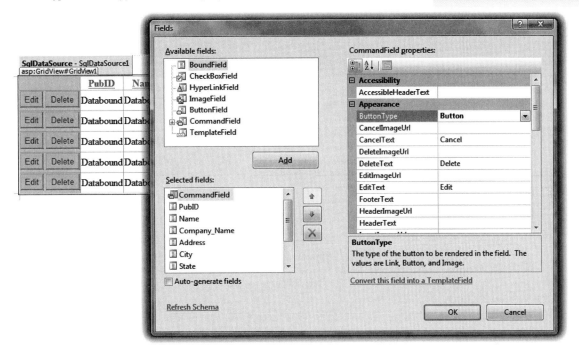

Add a Drop-Down List to a Grid Cell When the user clicks the *Edit* button for a grid row, the controls in the row change to text boxes to allow editing. You can change the control for each cell, such as provide a drop-down list for selection. You can fill the list with the fields from the data source used for the grid or declare another data source that holds the list items.

Follow these steps to add a drop-down list to a grid update program. You can see the finished result (Figure 8.27) in Ch08UpdateGridViewEnhanced.

- Select *Edit Columns* from the GridView's smart tag.

- In the *Fields* dialog box, select the field and click on *Convert this field into a TemplateField.* Close the dialog box.

- Use the smart tag of the GridView to select *Edit Templates.* You will see that there are several templates available.

- Choose *EditItemTemplate* and the cell for the one column appears.

- Delete the text box.

- Drag a DropDownList into the cell.

- From the smart tag of the drop-down list, choose the data source and assign the display and value fields.

- Return to the GridView smart tag and select *End Template Editing.*

- Make sure that *Enable Editing* is checked.

- Run the program and click on the *Edit* link. A drop-down list should appear in the cell.

Figure 8.27

In Editing mode, a drop-down list appears for the State column, to allow the user to make a selection from the list.

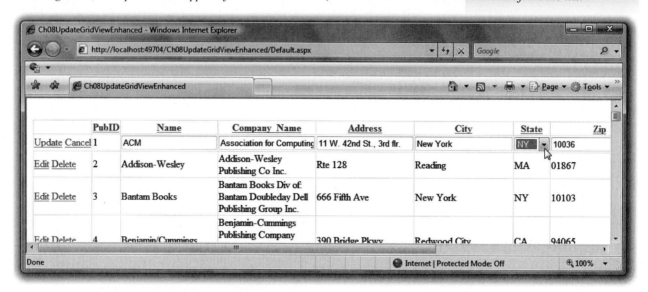

Updating in a DetailsView or a FormView

You may choose to update in a GridView, a DetailsView, or a FormView. The GridView does not have an *Insert* option; however, a *New / Insert* option is available for the DetailsView and FormView. Both of these controls display a single record at a time, so you must make sure to turn on *Enable Paging* to allow navigation.

Figure 8.28 shows updating in a DetailsView control; Figure 8.29 shows the DetailsView *Edit* option (what the user sees after clicking the *Edit* button);

Figure 8.28

When you choose to update in a DetailsView control, Edit, Delete, and New buttons are created when you select Enable Editing, Enable Deleting, and Enable Inserting on the control's smart tag.

Figure 8.29

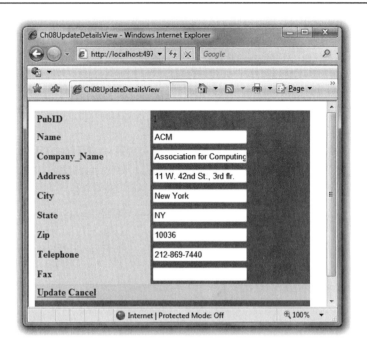

The Edit form that displays when the user selects Edit in a DetailsView. Notice that the two buttons are now Update and Cancel.

and Figure 8.30 shows the DetailsView *Insert* option that appears to the user after clicking the *New* button. The DetailsView control in the figure was formatted with an *Auto Format* option.

Figure 8.30

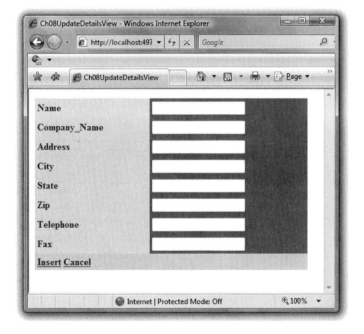

The form for adding a new record that displays when the user selects New in a DetailsView. Notice that the two buttons are now Insert and Cancel.

Updating in a FormView control is similar to a DetailsView control. The DetailsView is automatically formatted in a table layout, but for the FormView, you must edit the templates if you want to align the columns. For updating in a FormView, you must edit the ItemTemplate for navigation and display, modify the EditItemTemplate to determine how the data appear during an *Edit* operation, and change the InsertItemTemplate for the *Insert* operation.

Figure 8.31 shows updating in a FormView control; Figure 8.32 shows the FormView during an *Edit* operation; and Figure 8.33 shows the FormView during an *Insert* operation. The ItemTemplate has been formatted with a table, but the EditItemTemplate and InsertItemTemplate have not been modified so that you can see the default layout. Note that you apply only one *Auto Format* option to the control, which displays somewhat different for the *Edit* and *Insert* modes.

Figure 8.31

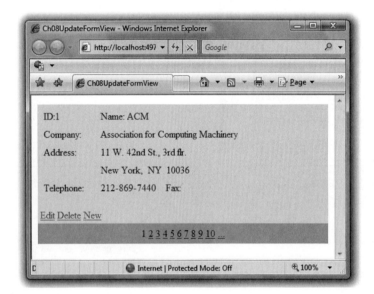

Updating in a FormView control, Edit, Delete, and New buttons are created when you select Enable Editing, Enable Deleting, and Enable Inserting on the control's smart tag.

Figure 8.32

The Edit form that displays when the user selects Edit in a FormView. The EditItemTemplate controls the format during an Edit operation; this example was not changed from the default layout. An Auto Format option was applied to the FormView control; the Edit option shows a variation of the format.

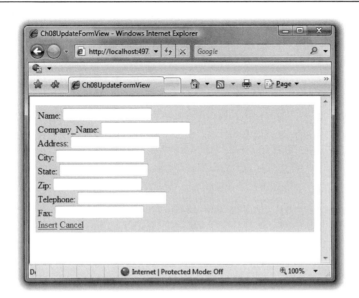

Figure 8.33

The Insert form for adding a new record that displays when the user selects New in a FormView. The InsertItem-Template controls the layout during an Insert operation; this is the unmodified default layout displayed with the Auto Format option applied to the FormView control.

Updating Using a Drop-Down List for Navigation

You can allow updates to the database that uses a drop-down list for navigation (Figure 8.34), but you must write some code to keep the list box contents up-to-date. Each time a record is added, modified, or deleted, you must rebind the drop-down list so that the contents are kept in sync with the database. For each event that could change the contents of the list, you should call the **DataBind method** of the drop-down list.

You can find the code for this example in Ch08UpdateDetailsView-ListBox.

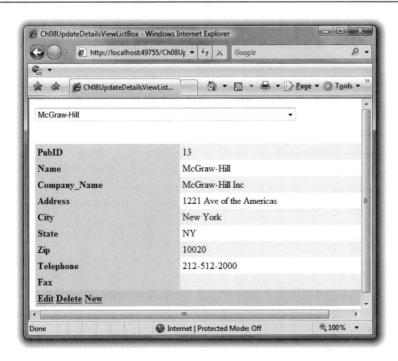

Figure 8.34

In an update program that uses a drop-down list for navigation, you must write code to keep the list updated to match the data.

You can easily create the event handlers for the events of the Details-View control. Select the control and click on the *Events* button in the Properties window. Double-click on an event name to create the event handler. You will need event handlers for the ItemInserted, ItemUpdated, and Item-Deleted events.

```
Protected Sub DetailsView1_ItemInserted(ByVal sender As Object, _
  ByVal e As System.Web.UI.WebControls.DetailsViewInsertedEventArgs) _
  Handles DetailsView1.ItemInserted
    ' Update the list.

    DropDownList1.DataBind()
End Sub

Protected Sub DetailsView1_ItemUpdated(ByVal sender As Object, _
  ByVal e As System.Web.UI.WebControls.DetailsViewUpdatedEventArgs) _
  Handles DetailsView1.ItemUpdated
    ' Update the list.

    DropDownList1.DataBind()
End Sub

Protected Sub DetailsView1_ItemDeleted(ByVal sender As Object, _
  ByVal e As System.Web.UI.WebControls.DetailsViewDeletedEventArgs) _
  Handles DetailsView1.ItemDeleted
    ' Update the list.

    DropDownList1.DataBind()
End Sub
```

When the data in a DetailsView control change, an event fires. The code in the event handler causes the drop-down list to rebind to the database, thus refreshing the contents. Note that in the example program, Ch08UpdateDetails-ViewListBox, the data source is sorted by the Name field, so each time the list is rebound, the list appears in alphabetic order.

Another little trick that you may want to try is to display the details only after an item is selected. You want the DetailsView control to appear only on a postback. Add the following code to the Page_Load event handler:

```
Protected Sub Page_Load(ByVal sender As Object, _
  ByVal e As System.EventArgs) Handles Me.Load
    ' Display the details only when a title is selected.

    If IsPostBack Then
        DetailsView1.Visible = True
    Else
        DetailsView1.Visible = False
    End If
End Sub
```

You can add a new line to the beginning of the list box to give the user instructions. However, you want to do this only once, the first time the list is bound. For this, you need to use two techniques: (1) executing a statement only once when the program does not maintain the values of variables and (2) adding an instruction line to the top of the list.

The easiest way to make sure that you execute a statement only once is to add a hidden field to the form and give it an initial value. In code, check the value; if it hasn't changed, execute the statement and change the value of the hidden field. The hidden field's EnableViewState, which is *true* by default, keeps its state for multiple trips to the server.

You can add a line to the top of the drop-down list in the list's DataBound event handler. This event fires when the control has been bound to its data source. Select the DropDownList control, click on the *Events* button in the Properties window, and double-click the DataBound event to create the event handler.

```
Protected Sub DropDownList1_DataBound(ByVal sender As Object, _
  ByVal e As System.EventArgs) Handles DropDownList1.DataBound
    ' Add instructions as the first entry in the list.

    If RunOnceHiddenField.Value <> "True" Then
        DropDownList1.Items.Insert(0, "(Select a Name)")
        RunOnceHiddenField.Value = "True"
    End If
End Sub
```

You also may want to remove the "(Select a Name)" item from the top of the list after the first selection. Check for its existence in the Page_Load event handler.

```
Protected Sub Page_Load(ByVal sender As Object, _
  ByVal e As System.EventArgs) Handles Me.Load
    ' Display the details only when a title has been selected.

    If IsPostBack Then
        DetailsView1.Visible = True
        If DropDownList1.Items(0).Text = "(Select a Name)" Then
            DropDownList1.Items.RemoveAt(0)
        End If
    Else
        DetailsView1.Visible = False
    End If
End Sub
```

Note: These techniques for maintaining state work for a single-page application because the ViewState property of a control returns the value from one invocation to the next. But for a multipage application, you must use session or application variables to maintain state.

The HTML Code for the Data Source Control

It is interesting to take a look at the HTML code that generates automatically for your data source control. Even if you can't write HTML, you can probably read it and get a pretty good idea of what is going on. Examine the following code for the update procedures. Notice the SQL statements.

TIP

If the Properties window does not display for a data control, make sure that you are not currently in the *Edit Template* mode. ∎

```
<asp:SqlDataSource ID="nameSqlDataSource" runat="server" ConnectionString=" <% $
ConnectionStrings:ContactsConnectionString %> "
    SelectCommand="SELECT [PubID], [Name] FROM [Publishers] ORDER BY [Name]">
</asp:SqlDataSource><asp:SqlDataSource ID="infoSqlDataSource" runat="server"
ConnectionString=" <% $ ConnectionStrings:ContactsConnectionString %> "
    DeleteCommand="DELETE FROM [Publishers] WHERE [PubID] = @original_PubID"
InsertCommand="INSERT INTO [Publishers] ([Name], [Company Name], [Address], [City],
[State], [Zip], [Telephone], [Fax]) VALUES (@Name, @Company_Name, @Address, @City,
@State, @Zip, @Telephone, @Fax)"
    SelectCommand="SELECT [PubID], [Name], [Company Name] AS Company_Name, [Address],
[City], [State], [Zip], [Telephone], [Fax] FROM [Publishers] WHERE ([PubID] = @PubID)"
    UpdateCommand="UPDATE [Publishers] SET [Name] = @Name, [Company Name] =
@Company_Name, [Address] = @Address, [City] = @City, [State] = @State, [Zip] = @Zip,
[Telephone] = @Telephone, [Fax] = @Fax WHERE [PubID] = @original_PubID">
    <SelectParameters>
        <asp:ControlParameter ControlID="DropDownList1" Name="PubID" PropertyName=
        "SelectedValue"
            Type="Int32" />
    </SelectParameters>
    <DeleteParameters>
        <asp:Parameter Name="original_PubID" Type="Int32" />
    </DeleteParameters>
    <UpdateParameters>
        <asp:Parameter Name="Name" Type="String" />
        <asp:Parameter Name="Company_Name" Type="String" />
        <asp:Parameter Name="Address" Type="String" />
        <asp:Parameter Name="City" Type="String" />
        <asp:Parameter Name="State" Type="String" />
        <asp:Parameter Name="Zip" Type="String" />
        <asp:Parameter Name="Telephone" Type="String" />
        <asp:Parameter Name="Fax" Type="String" />
        <asp:Parameter Name="original_PubID" Type="Int32" />
    </UpdateParameters>
    <InsertParameters>
        <asp:Parameter Name="Name" Type="String" />
        <asp:Parameter Name="Company_Name" Type="String" />
        <asp:Parameter Name="Address" Type="String" />
        <asp:Parameter Name="City" Type="String" />
        <asp:Parameter Name="State" Type="String" />
        <asp:Parameter Name="Zip" Type="String" />
        <asp:Parameter Name="Telephone" Type="String" />
        <asp:Parameter Name="Fax" Type="String" />
    </InsertParameters>
</asp:SqlDataSource>
```

Exception Handling

When you perform updates without writing any code, you cannot handle the exceptions. Many things can go wrong when the user adds and edits data. Often database constraints, such as a duplicate primary key and referential integrity violations, will cause exceptions. Bad input data and null fields also can cause exceptions.

Catching Constraint Violations

The SqlDataSource control and the various data display controls have events for which you can write code. To catch exceptions for constraint violations, you should write code in the event handlers for the SqlDataSource. Note that the control has a set of "ing" events and a set of "ed" events. For example, the Deleting, Inserting, and Updating events are fired just before the action is taken, and the Deleted, Inserted, and Updated events occur immediately following the action. To catch constraint violations, you need to place the code in the "completed" event handlers.

The e argument of the event handlers, SqlDataSourceStatusEventArgs, has an Exception object, with a Message property and an ExceptionHandled property. You can check for the existence of an exception, display the error message, and set ExceptionHandled to *true* so that the program can continue after you have handled the error. The following code checks for a successful Updated event; you also will need to write similar code in the Deleted and Inserted event handlers.

```vb
Protected Sub SqlDataSource1_Updated(ByVal sender As Object, _
  ByVal e As System.Web.UI.WebControls.SqlDataSourceStatusEventArgs) _
  Handles SqlDataSource1.Updated
    ' Check for successful update.

    If e.Exception Is Nothing Then
        MessageLabel.Visible = False
    Else
        MessageLabel.Text = "Unable to save the edited data." & _
        "</br> </br>" & e.Exception.Message
        e.ExceptionHandled = True
    End If
End Sub
```

Validating Input Data

The types of input validation you should perform depend on the requirements of the data fields. Most of the updating programs in this chapter are based on the Contacts database, which does not have any constraints. The program for this section is based on the sales table of the Pubs database, which has *many* constraints. The duplicate key and referential integrity constraints will be caught by the code in the previous section, but the user sees only the "Unable to complete" message and is not given a chance to make corrections. For missing and invalid data, it would be much better to catch the error, show a helpful message, allow the user to make a correction, and continue.

To catch bad input before the update action, you should use the "ing" events of the data display control, such as the DetailsView control. Each of the data display controls has ItemUpdating, ItemInserting, and ItemDeleting events, as well as corresponding "ed" events.

In the event handler arguments, you can access the data values. For ItemUpdating, the e argument (DetailsViewUpdateEventArgs) has both a NewValues collection and an OldValues collection. The values are stored as key/value pairs that you access with the field names. For example, e.NewValues. Item("ord_date") holds the value that the user entered for the ord_date field.

The sales table that we are updating does not allow null fields in the ord_date, qty, or payterms fields. In addition, the ord_date must be a valid date and qty must be an integer. The following code tests for non-null fields;

For payterms, it sets the value to an empty string; for qty, it sets the value to zero; but for the ord_date (which is part of the primary key), a value is required, so the user is prompted for the value. When the value cannot be corrected in code, the program displays a message and sets e.Cancel = True, which holds the screen for the user to make corrections.

```vb
Protected Sub DetailsView1_ItemUpdating(ByVal sender As Object, _
    ByVal e As System.Web.UI.WebControls.DetailsViewUpdateEventArgs) _
    Handles DetailsView1.ItemUpdating
    ' Perform validation before the update is saved.
    ' Validate the order date.
    If e.NewValues.Item("ord_date") Is Nothing Then
        ' Empty field. Must be entered.
        MessageLabel.Text = "Date is a required field."
        MessageLabel.Visible = True
        e.Cancel = True
    Else
        Dim TestDate As DateTime
        Dim TestDateString As String = e.NewValues.Item("ord_date").ToString
        If DateTime.TryParse(TestDateString, TestDate) Then
            ' Passed validation.
        Else
            ' Failed validation.
            MessageLabel.Text = "Invalid date format for Order Date"
            MessageLabel.Visible = True
            e.Cancel = True
        End If
    End If

    ' Validate the quantity.
    If e.NewValues.Item("qty") Is Nothing Then
        ' Convert null value to zero.
        e.NewValues.Item("qty") = 0
    Else
        Dim TestInteger As Integer
        Dim TestQtyString As String = e.NewValues.Item("qty").ToString
        If Integer.TryParse(TestQtyString, TestInteger) Then
            ' Passed validation.
        Else
            ' Failed validation.
            MessageLabel.Text = "Quantity must be valid integer."
            MessageLabel.Visible = True
            e.Cancel = True
        End If
    End If

    ' Validate pay terms.
    If e.NewValues.Item("payterms") Is Nothing Then
        ' Convert null value to empty string.
        e.NewValues.Item("payterms") = String.Empty
    End If
End Sub
```

Similar code is required for the ItemInserting event handler, but the e event argument has a Values collection, as opposed to the NewValues collection of the ItemUpdating event.

You can see the complete program with both input validation and exception handling in Ch08CatchExceptions.

▶ **Feedback 8.2**

1. How do you specify that you want the data source to contain the SQL statements for updating?
2. What action must you take to make a GridView have a column that holds *Edit* and *Delete* buttons?
3. How do you specify the layout for inserting and updating in a FormView control?
4. When using a drop-down list and a details view for updates, what code is required to keep the list up-to-date? Where should the code be placed?
5. Where is exception handling for an *Insert* performed?
6. In what event handler(s) should you place input validation?

Multiple Tiers

If it makes sense to separate a Windows application into multiple tiers, it makes twice as much sense for a Web application. In a Web application, it's best to include the data access components in a separate data access component, preferably as a WCF Service component.

Using an ObjectDataSource

The ObjectDataSource is designed to connect to any type of object; you will use one to connect data from a WCF Service to a data control on a Web page.

Creating a Service for Database Updating—Step-by-Step

The following multitier application uses a WCF Service to provide the data for a Web database. The technique for the service is similar to that in Chapter 6, except this service will provide methods for updating the database.

Create an Empty Solution

STEP 1: Create a new project by selecting *File / New Web Site*. Select the Empty Web Site template and name it Ch08MultipleTier.

STEP 2: In the Solution Explorer, select the solution name and *File / Save Ch08MultipleTiers.sln As*. Browse to the location where you want to store the multiproject solution and click on the *New Folder* button. Create a new folder and save the .sln file there.

Add a WCF Service

STEP 1: Select the solution name in the Solution Explorer and select *Add / New Web Site* from the *File* menu or right-click on the solution name in the Solution Explorer.

STEP 2: Select the WCF Service template.

STEP 3: Browse to select the folder that you created in the previous step and add back the default name "\WCFService1" to the end of the path. Click *OK*.

STEP 4: Add the Contacts.mdf database to the App_Data folder.

Rename the WCF Service

STEP 1: In the Solution Explorer, rename the Service.vb file to "Contacts-Service.vb".

STEP 2: Open the ContactsService.vb file and change the name of the service's class to ContactsService.

```
Public Class ContactsService
```

STEP 3: Open the Service.svc file and change the service attribute to

```
service="ContactsService"
```

STEP 4: Open the Web.config file and scroll down to near the bottom and find the `<system.serviceModel>` tag. Under `<services>` change to:

```
<service name="ContactsService" behaviorConfiguration="ServiceBehavior">
```

STEP 5: In the Solution Explorer, rename the IService.vb file to IContacts-Service.vb.

STEP 6: Open the IContactsService.vb file and change the name to IContactsService:

```
Public Interface IContactsService
```

STEP 7: In the ContactsService.vb code file, change the `Implements` statement:

```
Public Class ContactsService
    Implements IContactsService
```

STEP 8: In the Web.config file, change the contract name in the endpoint tag, which appears below the line that you changed previously.

```
<endpoint address="" binding="wsHttBinding" contract="IContactsService">
```

STEP 9: Save all and close the various files.

Create the Dataset

STEP 1: Right-click on the App_Code folder in the Solution Explorer; select *Add New Item* and select the DataSet template. Name it ContactsDataSet.xsd.

STEP 2: Display the Database Explorer (*View / Database Explorer*) in Visual Web Developer Express, or the Server Explorer (*View / Server Explorer*) in Visual Studio.

STEP 3: Expand Contacts.mdf and drag the publishers table to the DataSet Designer.

STEP 4: Right-click on the PublishersTableAdapter and select *Configure*. The configuration settings should all be correct, but viewing them helps to understand the existing queries. The SQL `SELECT` should select all fields from the publishers table.

STEP 5: Click the *Advanced Options* button and confirm that the check box generates INSERT, UPDATE, and DELETE statements. Click *OK* and then *Next*.

STEP 6: You can uncheck the *Return a DataTable* box but make sure that the check box to *Create methods to send updates directly to the database* is checked (Figure 8.35). Click *Next* and *Finish*.

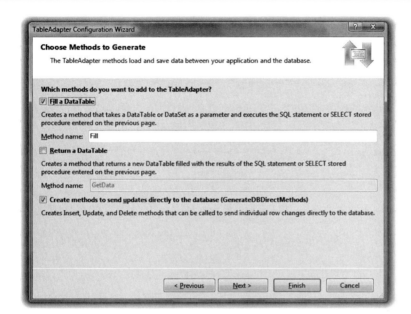

Figure 8.35

If you want to be able to update the database using a WCF Service, you must select Create methods to send updates directly to the database *(GenerateDBDirectMethods).*

STEP 7: In the DataSet Designer, click on PubID and change the ReadOnly property to *false* in the Properties window.

Write Contracts and Methods in the Service

You will need four Web methods: GetContacts, UpdateContacts, Delete-Contact, and InsertContact. The arguments needed by the Web methods are dictated by the corresponding DataSet methods, which you will call in your code.

STEP 1: Build the solution, so that IntelliSense can help you with the code.

The GetContacts method is similar to the one you wrote in Chapter 6. You will need to provide the contract code in the IContacts-Service.vb and the method in the ContactsService.vb.

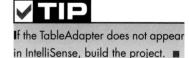

If the TableAdapter does not appear in IntelliSense, build the project. ■

STEP 2: Open the IContactsService.vb file, delete the two existing operation contracts, and add the GetContacts contract:

```
<OperationContract()> _
Function GetContacts() As ContactsDataSet
```

STEP 3: Open the ContactsService.vb file, delete the two existing functions, and write the GetContacts function:

```
Public Function GetContacts() As ContactsDataSet _
    Implements IContactsService.GetContacts
        ' Return the dataset.

    Try
        Dim ContactsTableAdapter As New _
            ContactsDataSetTableAdapters.PublishersTableAdapter
        Dim AContactsDataSet As New ContactsDataSet
        ContactsTableAdapter.Fill(AContactsDataSet.Publishers)

        Return AContactsDataSet
    Catch ex As Exception
        Throw ex
    End Try
End Function
```

STEP 4: In order to pass the individual fields for the update, you must declare each field as a parameter. You can see the list required by the TableAdapter's `Update` method and make sure to include each of those parameters (Figure 8.36).

Figure 8.36

Type the TableAdapter's Update *method and IntelliSense shows you the list and order of the required parameters.*

```
Dim ContactsTableAdapter As New _
    ContactsDataSetTableAdapters.PublishersTableAdapter
ContactsTableAdapter.Update (|
```
> ▲ 5 of 5 ▼ Update (**Name As String**, CompanyName As String, Address As String, City As String, State As String, Zip As String, Telephone As String, Fax As String, Original_PubID As Integer) As Integer

STEP 5: Create the `UpdateContacts` contract and function.

IContactsService:

```
<OperationContract()> _
Function UpdateContacts(ByVal Name As String, _
  ByVal CompanyName As String, _
  ByVal Address As String, ByVal City As String, _
  ByVal State As String, ByVal Zip As String, _
  ByVal Telephone As String, ByVal Fax As String, _
  ByVal Original_PubID As Integer) As Integer
```

ContactsService:

```
Public Function UpdateContacts(ByVal Name As String, _
  ByVal CompanyName As String, _
  ByVal Address As String, ByVal City As String, _
  ByVal State As String, ByVal Zip As String, _
  ByVal Telephone As String, ByVal Fax As String, _
  ByVal Original_PubID As Integer) As Integer _
  Implements IContactsService.UpdateContacts
    ' Update the dataset.
```

```
        Try
            Dim ContactsTableAdapter As New _
              ContactsDataSetTableAdapters.PublishersTableAdapter
            ContactsTableAdapter.Update(Name, CompanyName, Address, _
              City, State, Zip, Telephone, _
              Fax, Original_PubID)
        Catch ex As Exception
            Throw ex
        End Try
    End Function
```

STEP 6: Write the DeleteContact contract and function. The TableAdapter's Delete method requires only the key of the record to be deleted.

IContactsService:

```
<OperationContract()> _
Sub DeleteContact(ByVal PubID As Integer)
```

ContactsService:

```
Public Sub DeleteContact(ByVal PubID As Integer) _
  Implements IContactsService.DeleteContact
    ' Delete a row from the Contacts DataSet.

    Try
        Dim ContactsTableAdapter As New _
          ContactsDataSetTableAdapters.PublishersTableAdapter
        ContactsTableAdapter.Delete(PubID)
    Catch Ex As Exception
        Throw Ex
    End Try
End Sub
```

STEP 7: Write the InsertContact contract and method. You may wonder why the record key (PubID) is not included as a parameter, but you may recall that this field is an identity field, which is automatically generated by the database.

IContactsService:

```
<OperationContract()> _
Sub InsertContact(ByVal Name As String, ByVal CompanyName As String, _
  ByVal Address As String, ByVal City As String, _
  ByVal State As String, ByVal Zip As String, _
  ByVal Telephone As String, ByVal Fax As String)
```

ContactsService:

```
Public Sub InsertContact(ByVal Name As String, _
  ByVal CompanyName As String, _
  ByVal Address As String, ByVal City As String, _
  ByVal State As String, ByVal Zip As String, _
  ByVal Telephone As String, ByVal Fax As String) _
  Implements IContactsService.InsertContact
    ' Insert a row into the Contacts DataSet.
```

```
        Try
            Dim ContactsTableAdapter As New _
                ContactsDataSetTableAdapters.PublishersTableAdapter
            ContactsTableAdapter.Insert(Name, CompanyName, Address, City, _
                State, Zip, Telephone, Fax)
        Catch Ex As Exception
            Throw Ex
        End Try
    End Sub
```

STEP 8: Build (compile) the solution.

Set Up the Project to Consume the Data Service

STEP 1: Right-click on the name of the solution and choose *Add / New Web Site*. Select the ASP.NET Web Site template, make sure that it is going into the Ch08MultipleTier folder, and name it DisplayContacts.

STEP 2: Build the solution.

Note: If you receive an error message saying that you cannot use a section registered as `allowDefinition='MachineToApplication'`..., right-click on the Web.config file for the DisplayContacts project (not the Web.config in the WCF Service project) and select *Exclude from project*. Build again; the error message should disappear. This message is due to a conflict between the two Web.config files.

STEP 3: Right-click the DisplayContacts project in the Solution Explorer and set it as the startup project.

STEP 4: Right-click on the DisplayContacts project again and choose the option to add a service reference. Discover and add the reference to ContactsService, setting the namespace to ContactsDataService.

STEP 5: Build the solution.

Add Controls to the Default Web Page

STEP 1: Add an ObjectDataSource control to the Default.aspx page. The ObjectDataSource control can connect to a service, a data component, or other class.

STEP 2: Select *Configure Data Source* from the smart tag. Select ContactsDataService.ContactsServiceClient and click *Next*.

STEP 3: You must choose a method for each of the tabs. For the *SELECT* tab, drop down the method list and select *GetContacts*, the method you wrote that returns a DataSet.

STEP 4: Click on the *UPDATE* tab and select *UpdateContacts*, which contains the parameter list that you created in the service. Then switch to the *INSERT* tab and select *InsertContact*; on the *DELETE* tab, select *DeleteContact*. After you have chosen a method for all four tabs, click *Finish*.

Note: If the *Finish* button is not enabled, confirm that you are selecting the methods that you created.

STEP 5: Place a DetailsView control on the page.

STEP 6: On the smart tag, set the data source to ObjectDataSource1. Select the four check boxes for *Enable Paging*, *Enable Inserting*, *Enable Editing*, and *Enable Deleting*. Choose one of the formats from *Auto Format* and set the Width property of the DetailsView control to "80%".

STEP 7: On the smart tag, select *Edit Fields*. In the *Fields* dialog box, click on PubID in the *Selected fields* list and set the ReadOnly property to *false*.

STEP 8: Set the Title property of the Default page to DisplayContacts. Save all.

Test the Project

STEP 1: Press Ctrl + F5 to run the project. Test each of the options.

   Remember: If you make any modifications to the WCF Service, you must rebuild the solution and then select *Update Web References* for the project that consumes the WCF Service.

STEP 2: You can view the database in the DataSet Designer. Right-click on the table name and select *Preview data*. You should be able to see all of the changes to the database.

Feedback 8.3

1. List the steps to get the data from the Northwind Employees database using a data service.
2. What code would be needed for an Update method in the data service class?

Maintaining the State of List Boxes

As you know, the ViewState property can maintain the state of controls for multiple displays of a single page. But as the user navigates between pages, you must maintain the state, generally in a session variable. For labels and text boxes, the process is straightforward, but maintaining state of a list box is a little more complicated.

Maintaining the Selection of a Drop-Down List

If you want the form to "remember" which selection the user made from a drop-down list, you can save the SelectedIndex property in a session variable:

```
' Save the SelectedIndex in a session variable.
Session("CardType") = CreditCardDropDownList.SelectedIndex
```

Because you are saving the SelectedIndex, which is an integer, use this code to restore the selection:

```
' Restore the SelectedIndex from the session variable.
CreditCardDropDownList.SelectedIndex = CType(Session("CardType"), Integer)
```

Maintaining the List in a Dynamic List Box

If you want to maintain state for a list box that has items added at run time, you must save the Items collection in a session variable:

```
' Save the Items collection in a session variable.
Session("Titles") = TitlesListBox.Items
```

Saving the Items collection is easier than restoring it. You must declare a variable of type ListItemCollection and another variable to hold a single item as type ListItem. Assign the session variable to the collection variable, loop through the collection, and add each item to the list.

```
' Restore the Items collection from a session variable.
Dim TitleListItemCollection As ListItemCollection
Dim TitleListItem As ListItem

TitleListItemCollection = CType(Session("Titles"), ListItemCollection)
For Each TitleListItem In TitleListItemCollection
    ShoppingCartListBox.Items.Add(TitleListItem.ToString())
Next
```

Unbound Controls

Sometimes you need to write data from controls that are not bound to a database. Consider making online reservations for travel. When you log on to the airline's Web site, you would not expect (or want) to see the entire reservations file. Therefore, it would be incorrect to bind detail controls to the database. After the user enters the data for a flight and confirms a reservation, that information must be transferred from the text boxes or other controls to a file.

Using Unbound Controls with a SqlDataSource

In the following example, which you can see in Ch08UnboundControls, the user enters data into unbound text boxes (Figure 8.37). The *Submit* button calls the Insert method of the SqlDataSource, which inserts the data from the text boxes into a new record in the database.

Figure 8.37

The user enters data for a new record into unbound text boxes.

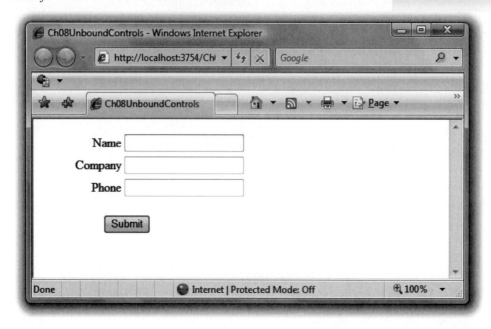

The data source controls include a very helpful feature to help you set up the database queries for unbound controls. For each of the SQL queries (SELECT, INSERT, UPDATE, and DELETE), you can display a *Command and Parameter Editor* dialog. For example, to display the dialog for the INSERT command, select the data source control and click on the build button for the InsertQuery property in the Properties window (Figure 8.38).

Figure 8.39 shows the dialog for an INSERT command. Notice the INSERT command at the top of the window includes a parameter for each field of data. In the *Parameters* list, you can see that Name is connected to NameTextBox. Text. Each parameter can connect to a parameter source. When you want to connect to a control, select *Control* from the *Parameter source* drop-down list and select the control to which to connect from the *ControlID* drop-down list.

Select the control to use for each parameter in the Command and Parameter Editor dialog.

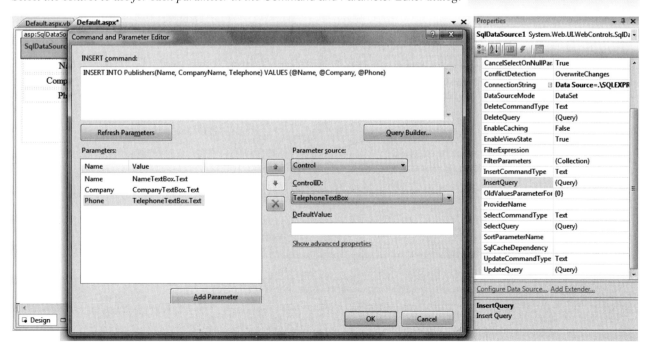

The UPDATE, DELETE, and SELECT SQL statements have similar dialogs, so you can set up the parameters for each of those statements.

To create a project that connects to unbound controls:

- Create a Web page that contains the fields for input.

- Add your database into the App_Data folder for your project.

    Note: It isn't necessary for the database to be inside the project folder; if it is elsewhere, you must add a connection to the database in the Server Explorer window and allow the Insert query parameters to generate later in this process.

- Add a data source control to the page.

- When configuring the data source:

    - If not already selected, select the option to *Specify columns from a table or view to retrieve data.*

    - Select all fields (*).

    - Click on the *Advanced* button and check the option to *Generate INSERT, UPDATE, and DELETE statements.*

    - Complete the configuration wizard as usual.

- From the Properties window of the DataSource control, select the build button for the InsertQuery property.

    For each control:

    - Select the parameter from the *Parameters* list.

    - Set the *Parameter source* to *Control.*

    - Select the ControlID from the drop-down list.

Using Unbound Controls with an ObjectDataSource

You also can use unbound controls with an ObjectDataSource, which you use for a multitier application. The concepts for attaching parameters to form controls is the same as for a SqlDataSource, but the dialogs are somewhat different. For the ObjectDataSource, you must set up the **Parameters collection** for each of the SQL commands that you want to use. For example, you can set the SelectParameters, the InsertParameters, the UpdateParameters, and the DeleteParameters (Figure 8.40). In the *Parameter Collection Editor* dialog, you select the parameter from the *Parameters* list, select *Control* from the *Parameter source* drop-down list, and select the control to which to attach from the *ControlID* dropdown list. Figure 8.41 shows setting the parameters for the Insert command.

Setting Up a WCF Service

Earlier in this chapter, we used a WCF Service to supply the data for bound controls. You also can use a WCF Service to handle the data for unbound controls. The service contains methods for each of the queries that you need. If you want to insert records in a database using a service, you must have an Insert method. And every data source requires at least a Select method.

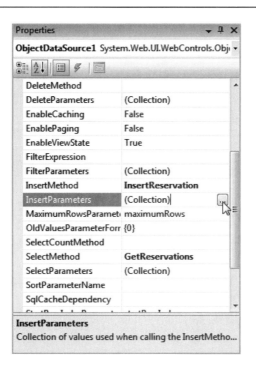

Figure 8.40

Select the InsertParameters property to enter the parameters for the Insert *command.*

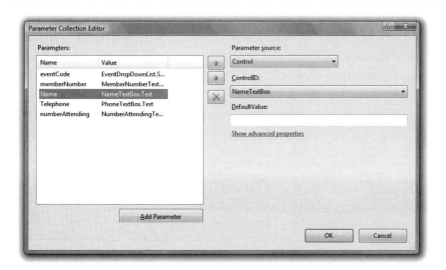

Figure 8.41

In the Parameter Collection Editor *dialog, select the parameter and the control to which to connect.*

Adding a Table from the IDE

If you need a new table in a database, you can add one from the Server Explorer (or Database Explorer in Visual Web Developer Express). This is similar to the process of adding a new stored procedure. Select the *Tables* node for the database, right-click, and select *Add New Table* from the context menu (Figure 8.42). The entry screen allows you to enter the new column names and the data types; a check box determines if the field allows nulls. You can set other column properties in the Properties window.

Figure 8.42

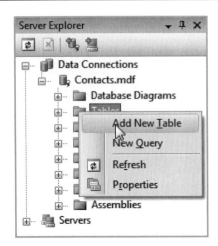

Viewing Data

When you are testing your application, you can view your inserted record from several locations in the IDE. You can select the database from the Server Explorer or double-click on the database icon in the Solution Explorer. Select the table and choose *Show Table Data*. You also can display the table data from the DataSet Designer, as you did in the step-by-step exercise. Your new record should display at the end of the table.

Feedback 8.4

1. Write the code to save the items collection from the CompanyName list box in a session variable.
2. Assuming that a data source generates an `Insert` query, how can you associate the parameter list of the query to text boxes on the Web page?

Creating Custom Error Pages

When you work with a database, it is especially important to control what the user is allowed to see. If you allow the application to generate a default error screen, that can show the user field names and stack information, which can provide an unscrupulous user with the tools to hack the application and compromise the database.

One way of protecting your program is by using a custom error page, which you can display instead of the default error message. To set up a custom error page, you first create the page and then set the Web.config file to indicate the page to use. In fact, you can set up multiple pages and specify the page to use for specific error conditions. The default Web.config file contains a section, which is commented out, that refers to these error pages.

```
<!--
    The <customErrors> section enables configuration
    of what to do if/when an unhandled error occurs
    during the execution of a request. Specifically,
    it enables developers to configure html error pages
    to be displayed in place of an error stack trace.

    <customErrors mode="RemoteOnly" defaultRedirect="GenericErrorPage.htm">
        <error statusCode="403" redirect="NoAccess.htm"/>
        <error statusCode="404" redirect="FileNotFound.htm"/>
    </customErrors>
-->
```

First, create some form of error page. In most cases, something generic is just fine. Then modify the Web.config file. Move the tag for the end of comments (-->) to just above the <customErrors> tag. Change the mode to "On" and indicate which page to use for errors. If you do not have specific pages for the 403 and 404 status codes, you may remove them.

```
-->
<customErrors mode= "On" defaultRedirect= "ErrorPage.aspx" >
</customErrors>
```

Note: Wait to set the Web.config entry for a custom error page until your project is working correctly. Otherwise, your custom error page will display for any errors, including compiler errors.

Using Validation Controls

Although you cannot use the validation controls for the GridView, DetailsView, and FormView controls, you *can* use them for validation of individual controls. And you may need to turn validation on and off during program execution. For example, in a shopping cart application, the user may display the page with customer information many times, but the personal information is required only when checking out. You can turn off the validation controls by setting their Enabled property to *false*. Set the Enabled property to *true* to turn on validation. After you set the property to *true*, use the `Page.Validate` method to force a validation.

```
' Validate the customer information.
CustomerRequiredValidator.Enabled = True
CityRequiredValidator.Enabled = True
AccountNumberRangeValidator.Enabled = True
Page.Validate()     ' Force a validation.

If Page.IsValid Then
    Server.Transfer("Confirmation.aspx")
End If
```

Note: The complete shopping cart program is on the text Web site.

Your Hands-On Programming Example

Create a project for Katali Club for reservations for its upcoming events. The reservations page should have a drop-down list that contains the names of the events. The user should be able to indicate the member number, name, phone number, and the number of guests. Use validation controls to require that an entry is made for each of the text boxes.

Use a WCF Service including an `Insert` method for the reservations table in the KataliClub database (available in the StudentData folder on the text Web site).

Store the event pricing and perform the calculations in a separate class for the business tier.

Pricing

Wine Tasting	55.00
Day at the Races	37.50
Jazz under the Stars	42.75
President's Ball	99.00

Include a custom error page and modify Web.config to use your page.

Planning the Project

Sketch the forms (Figure 8.43) that your users sign off as meeting their needs.

Figure 8.43

The planning sketches of the hands-on programming example: a. the default page and b. the error page.

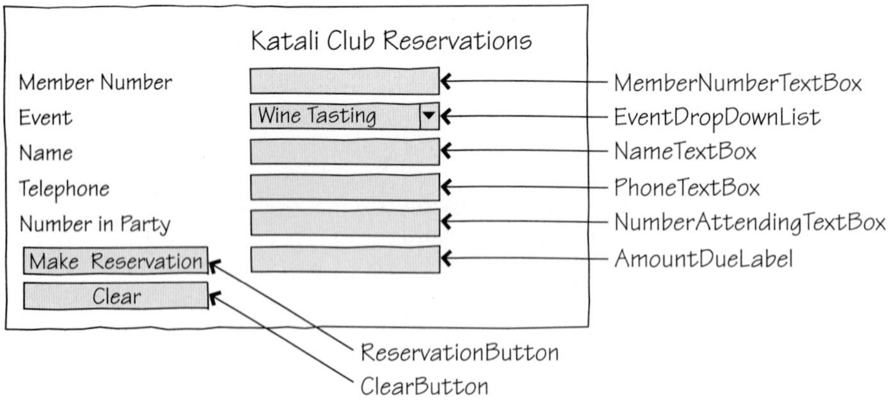

Plan the Objects, Properties, and Methods **Plan the two tiers.** Determine the objects and property settings for the forms and their controls, and for the data-tier component.

Presentation Tier

Default Page

Object	Property	Setting
ObjectDataSource1	Data source	ReservationsService.DataServiceClient (your WCF Service name)
MemberNumberTextBox		
EventDropDownList	Items (collection)	Wine Tasting Day at the Races Jazz under the Stars President's Ball
NameTextBox		
PhoneTextBox		
NumberAttendingTextBox		
ReservationButton	Text	Make a Reservation
ClearButton	Text	Clear
AmountDueLabel	Text	(blank)
MemberNumberRequiredFieldValidator	ErrorMessage ControlToValidate	Required field MemberNumberTextBox
NameRequiredFieldValidator	ErrorMessage ControlToValidate	Required field NameTextBox
PhoneRequiredFieldValidator	ErrorMessage ControlToValidate	Required field PhoneTextBox
NumberRequiredFieldValidator	ErrorMessage ControlToValidate	Required field NumberAttendingTextBox

Event handlers/methods	Actions—Pseudocode
ReservationButton_Click	Insert a record in the reservations table. Call the business tier to calculate the amount due. Display the amount due.
ClearButton_Click	Clear the text boxes and label.

Error Page

Object	Property	Setting
Text on the page	Centered 16pt Red Black	"Application Error" "Unable to complete the requested operation."

Business Tier

EventPricing

Event handlers/methods	Actions—Pseudocode
Constructor	Find price for event. Calculate amount due.
Amount property	Return the amount due.

Data Tier

ClubDataService

Object	Property	Setting
KaliClubDataSet	Connection	KataliClub.mdf
	Table	Reservations
	Fields	All
	Method to Generate	Fill

Methods	Actions—Pseudocode
GetReservations	Create a dataset that holds the Reservations table. Return the dataset.
InsertReservation	Insert a record, using the Insert method of the table adapter.

Write the Project Following the sketches in Figure 8.43, create the forms. Figure 8.44 shows the Default form at design time and Figure 8.45 shows the completed forms.

- Make sure to create a folder that contains two distinct projects, the WCF Service and the Web site.

- Create the WCF Service, adding the objects from your plan.

- Write the methods for the service, following the pseudocode.

- Create each of the Web pages, setting the properties according to your plans.

- Write the code for the default form. Working from the pseudocode, write each event handler.

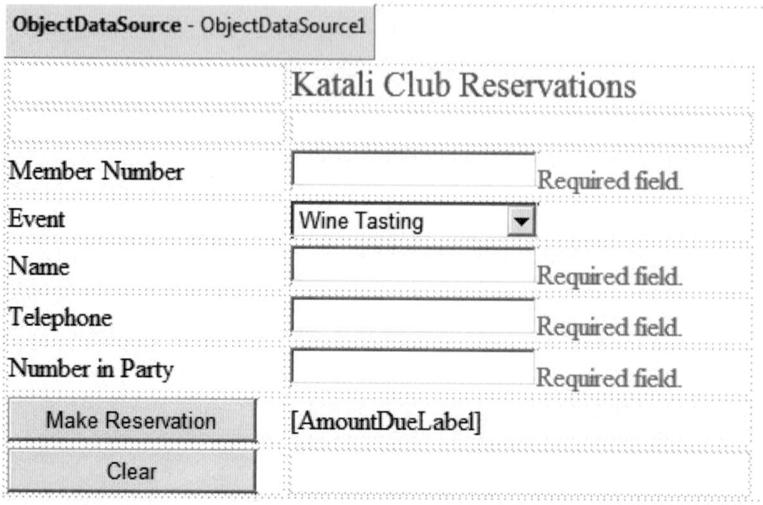

Figure 8.44

The Default form in design view.

Figure 8.45

The forms for the hands-on programming example: a. the default page and b. the error page.

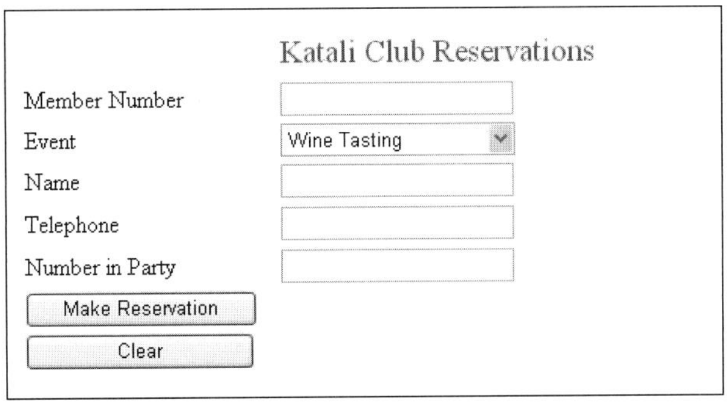

a.

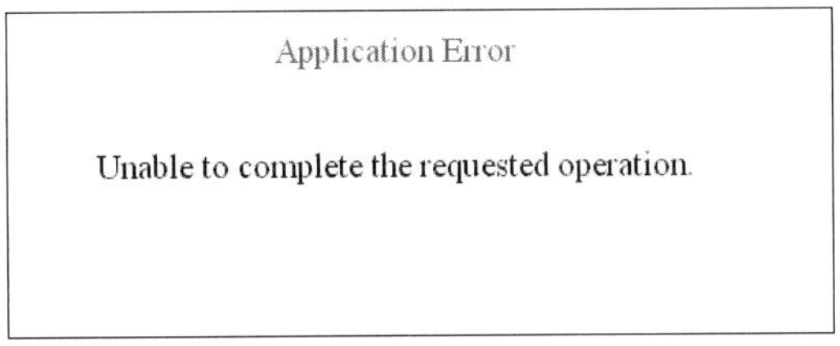

b.

- When you complete the code, test the operation multiple times. View inserted records and make sure that all test data were correctly written to the file.

- When the program is working correctly, modify the Web.config to provide for custom errors.

The Project Coding Solution

The User Interface

```
'Program:    Ch08HandsOn
'Class:      Default
'Programmer: Bradley/Millspaugh
'Date:       June 2009
'Description: Save a reservation in the club database.

Partial Class _Default
    Inherits System.Web.UI.Page

    Protected Sub ReservationButton_Click(ByVal sender As Object, _
      ByVal e As System.EventArgs) Handles ReservationButton.Click
        ' Insert a record in the reservations table.

        Try
            ' Display amount for billing.
            ObjectDataSource1.Insert()
            Dim AmountDue As New _
              EventPricing(Integer.Parse(NumberAttendingTextBox.Text), _
              EventDropDownList.SelectedIndex)
            AmountDueLabel.Text = "Charged to your account: " _
              & AmountDue.Amount.ToString("C")
        Catch Ex As Exception
            Server.Transfer("ErrorPage.aspx")
        End Try
    End Sub
End Sub
```

```vbnet
    Protected Sub ClearButton_Click(ByVal sender As Object, _
      ByVal e As System.EventArgs) Handles ClearButton.Click
        ' Clear the form controls.

        MemberNumberTextBox.Text = String.Empty
        EventDropDownList.SelectedIndex = -1
        NameTextBox.Text = String.Empty
        PhoneTextBox.Text = String.Empty
        NumberAttendingTextBox.Text = String.Empty
        AmountDueLabel.Text = String.Empty
    End Sub
End Class
```

The Error Page No code.

The Data Tier

EventPricing

```vbnet
'Program:      Ch08HandsOn
'Class:        EventPricing
'Programmer:   Bradley/Millspaugh
'Date:         June 2009
'Description:  The business tier to calculate a reservation price.

Public Class EventPricing
    Private WINE_TASTINGDecimal As Decimal = 55D
    Private JAZZ_UNDER_STARSDecimal As Decimal = 37.5D
    Private DAY_RACESDecimal As Decimal = 42.75D
    Private PRESIDENTS_BALLDecimal As Decimal = 99D

    Private TotalAmount As Decimal

    Sub New(ByVal NumberInteger As Integer, ByVal EventInteger As Integer)
        ' Calculate the amount due.
        Dim PriceDecimal As Decimal

        Select Case EventInteger
            Case 0
                PriceDecimal = WINE_TASTINGDecimal
            Case 1
                PriceDecimal = DAY_RACESDecimal
            Case 2
                PriceDecimal = JAZZ_UNDER_STARSDecimal
            Case 3
                PriceDecimal = PRESIDENTS_BALLDecimal
        End Select
        TotalAmount = PriceDecimal * NumberInteger
    End Sub

    Public ReadOnly Property Amount() As Decimal
        Get
            Return TotalAmount
        End Get
    End Property
End Class
```

The Data Tier
KataliClubDataService

```vb
'Program:    Ch08HandsOn
'Class:      DataService
'Programmer: Bradley/Millspaugh
'Date:       June 2009
'Description: Defines methods to return data and
'                insert a reservation.

Public Class DataService
    Implements IDataService

    Public Sub New()
    End Sub

    Public Function GetReservations() As System.Data.DataSet _
      Implements IDataService.GetReservations
        ' Retrieve the dataset.

        Try
            Dim ClubDataSet As New KataliClubDataSet
            Dim ReservationsTableAdapter As _
              New KataliClubDataSetTableAdapters.ReservationsTableAdapter
            ReservationsTableAdapter.Fill(ClubDataSet.Reservations)
            Return ClubDataSet
        Catch Ex As Exception
            Throw Ex
        End Try
    End Function

    Public Sub InsertReservation(ByVal EventCode As String, _
      ByVal MemberNumber As String, _
      ByVal Name As String, ByVal Telephone As String, _
      ByVal NumberAttending As Integer) _
      Implements IDataService.InsertReservation
        ' Insert a reservation into the reservation table.

        Try
            Dim ReservationsTableAdapter As New _
              KataliClubDataSetTableAdapters.ReservationsTableAdapter
            ReservationsTableAdapter.Insert(EventCode, MemberNumber, Name, _
              Telephone, NumberAttending)
        Catch Ex As Exception
            Throw Ex
        End Try
    End Sub
End Class
```

Summary

1. By default, data binding on a Web Form is for display only.
2. Visual Studio provides several types of data source controls, including a SqlDataSource, AccessDataSource, and ObjectDataSource.
3. To add data access to a Web Form, add a data source control and configure the data source. You can then bind individual fields to the data source control.

4. A connection's ConnectionString can be set as a dynamic property, which is stored in Web.config. Modify the connection string to use "|Data-Directory|" instead of the absolute path to make your project portable.

5. A GridView control displays bound data in a grid; the DetailsView and FormView controls display one record at a time. A DetailsView displays fields in rows and columns; a FormView is more free form and you can modify the layout of the data by editing the item template.

6. Any controls in the *Standard* section of the toolbox that have a DataSource property can be bound to data.

7. To use a DropDownList for record selection, you must create a parameterized query to retrieve the record matching the selection.

8. You can add a hyperlink field column to a GridView and allow the user to navigate to another page, passing a string that can be used for a query on the second page.

9. A data reader provides a forward-only connection to a database for quick access of data. It is appropriate for small amounts of data that are not to be updated or for loading information into a control. You can specify using a data reader instead of a dataset when you configure the data source control.

10. You can specify caching when you configure a data source, which can improve performance of a Web-based data application.

11. To allow updating, you must configure the data source to generate the appropriate SQL statements. After the data source is properly configured for updates, you must enable editing, inserting, and deleting for the data control.

12. Concurrency checking is for applications that have multiple concurrent users, to prevent multiple saves of the same record.

13. For updating in a FormView control, you must configure the templates for each of the editing modes.

14. An update application that uses a drop-down list for navigation must include code to keep the list's Items collection synchronized with the database.

15. You can ensure that a given statement executes only once for a Web page by assigning a value to a hidden field and allowing the ViewState setting to keep the value. If the user can navigate to a different page and back again, you must use another technique for state management, such as session or application variables.

16. To catch and handle exceptions for constraint violations, write code in the event handlers for the Deleted, Inserted, and Updated events of the data source control.

17. To validate user input, write code in the event handlers for the Item-Updating, ItemInserting, and ItemDeleting events of the control used to display the data. You can catch any bad data, display a message, and allow the user to make a correction.

18. With Web pages the use of multitier design is even more important than in Windows applications. You can create a data-tier component using the same techniques as in a Windows application or use a WCF Service for the data tier.

19. To maintain the state of a list box, you can store the SelectedIndex property in a session variable.

20. Maintaining the state for items that have been added to a list box requires that you save the Items collection in a session variable and restore the list by looping through the ListItemCollection to add each saved ListItem to the list.

21. Connect unbound controls to a data source using the dialogs for *Insert* or *Update*. The `Insert` and `Update` methods of the data source object call the SQL statement to execute.

22. The ObjectDataSource contains parameter collections that allow unbound controls to be connected to the SQL statement parameters.

23. You can use the Server Explorer to add tables to a database and view table contents in the IDE.

24. To turn off the action of validation controls, set their Enabled property to *false*. After enabling the controls, force a validation with the `Page .Validate` method.

25. Custom error pages provide a measure of security by keeping secure information from being displayed in a stack trace or error message.

Key Terms

data source control *352*
`DataBind` method *375*
DataReader object *368*
DetailsView control *356*
FormView control *357*

GridView control *355*
ItemTemplate *357*
ObjectDataSource control *353*
Parameters collection *390*
SqlDataSource control *352*

Review Questions

1. What is a data source control and how is it used?
2. Explain the similarities and differences among the GridView, DetailsView, and FormView controls.
3. How can you include a database file in a Web project and make that project portable?
4. What is the purpose of the FormView's ItemTemplate? How can you modify the template?
5. Which controls in the `Standard` section of the toolbox can be bound to database data?
6. Explain how to use a drop-down list for record selection and display the selected record in a DetailsView or FormView control.
7. Explain the differences between a data reader and a dataset. When is it best to use a data reader instead of a dataset?
8. What actions must you take to allow updating of a database from a Web Form? to the data source? to the data control(s)?
9. Explain how to store and retrieve the state for a dynamic list, which holds items that have been added during the program run.
10. Explain how to store and retrieve the state for a drop-down list in a multi-page application.
11. Discuss the concept of updating a database using unbound controls.
12. How can you force the validation controls to ignore the validation until you are ready to validate?
13. How are custom error pages implemented in a Web application? Why would you want custom pages?

Programming Exercises

8.1 Create a Web site that displays the Products table in the Northwind database. Use a DetailsView with pagination.

8.2 Modify Exercise 8.1 to retrieve the data from a WCF Service.

8.3 Modify Exercise 8.1 or 8.2 to allow the user to update the data in the products table. *Hint*: The products table has constraints. Include error handling as shown on page 379.

8.4 Create a Web site that displays the book information from the books table of the RnR Books database. Use a drop-down list for selecting the title and a DetailsView for all the fields.

8.5 Modify Exercise 8.4 to allow updates to the data in the books table.

8.6 Modify Exercise 8.4 or 8.5 to use a WCF Service for the database.

8.7 Create a Web site that allows the user to display customer and order information from the Northwind database. When the user selects a customer name from a list, the rest of the information about the customer should display. Include a link called *Orders* to a second page that displays a grid of orders for the selected customer.

8.8 Display the Suppliers table from the Northwind database in a data grid. Allow the grid to be sorted by Supplier ID, Company Name, or Postal Code and Country. Include pagination. Select a formatting style for the grid and use appropriate headers for the columns; that is, use Supplier ID with a space, not the default SupplierID.

8.9 Using the Ch08ShoppingCart project from the text Web site, add the code to insert the customer information into the database. In Server Explorer, create a table called OnlinePurchase with the fields on the customer page.

Case Studies

Claytor's Cottages

Complete the Reservations function of the Web site for Claytor's Cottages. Display the room information. Allow the user to enter his or her name, phone number, credit card type, card number, expiration date, room, arrival date, and the number of days.

Optional: Enter arrival and departure dates using a Calendar control.

Challenge: Validate that the days are available.

Christian's Car Rentals

Complete the Reservations function of the Web site for Christian's Car Rentals. The user must select the size of car and enter the number of days, his or her name, phone number, and credit card information (card type, number, and expiration date).

Generate a string Confirmation ID, which is used as the primary key in the reservation table.

Optional: Enter pickup and drop-off dates using a MonthCalendar control.

Challenge: Validate that there are vehicles remaining in the size category assuming that the company has 20 in each category.

Use a service for the database access.

9

Reports

at the completion of this chapter, you will be able to . . .

1. Create a Crystal Reports template and display the report from a Windows Form or a Web Form.

2. Use advanced reporting features, such as numeric functions, grouping, sorting, and special fields.

3. Base a report on a data file or a dataset.

4. Display a report at run time based on a user request.

Writing Reports

Writing and printing reports is an extremely important topic for most business applications. Visual Studio offers several options for reporting applications, which are not available in Visual Basic Express Edition. The *New Project* dialog box includes a Reporting option, which contains templates for a Crystal Reports application and a Microsoft Reports application. Reporting templates are also available for Web applications.

By far, the most popular reporting tool for Visual Studio applications is the report designer called **Crystal Reports**, which is owned by Business Objects, a SAP company. The Crystal Report Gallery contains wizards to guide you in creating standard reports, forms, and even mailing labels, or you can use an existing report or generate a new one. You can display a report from a Windows Form or a Web Form.

Visual Studio 2008 (Professional Edition and above) includes Crystal Reports 2008 Basic. Note that Business Objects sells a version of Crystal Reports with more features than the one included in Visual Studio. As of this writing, the newest version is Crystal Reports 2008, which is compatible with VS 2008.

Creating and Displaying a Crystal Reports

In this section, you will learn to create a Crystal Reports report template and display the report from a Windows application. Crystal Reports can connect to several types of data, including SQL Server, Access, Excel, and many others, including an ADO.NET DataSet, which can be based on many different types of objects, including business objects and collections.

Creating a Grouped Report—Step-by-Step

This exercise walks you through the steps for creating a Crystal Report template in a Windows Form application. Figure 9.1 shows the completed report, which is based on the products and categories tables of the Northwind SQL Server database.

Create the Project

STEP 1: Create a new Windows Forms application project called Ch09-DatasetSBS.

STEP 2: Rename the form to ReportForm.

STEP 3: Change the form's Text property to "Northwind Product Report".

STEP 4: Add Northwind Database as a new data source, selecting the products and categories tables. Save all.

Begin the Report

STEP 1: In the Solution Explorer, right-click on the project name and select *Add / New Item* from the context menu. Select the *Crystal Report* template from the *Reporting* category.

STEP 2: Type the name "Products.rpt" and click on the *Add* button (Figure 9.2).
    Note: The first time that you create a Crystal Report template, you must accept its license agreement.

Figure 9.1

The completed report for the step-by-step exercise.

Northwind Products

6/1/2009   Your Name

Product ID	Product Name	Unit Price	Units In Stock	Extended Price
Beverages				
1	Chai	18.00	39	702.00
2	Chang	19.00	17	323.00
39	Chartreuse verte	18.00	69	1,242.00
38	Côte de Blaye	263.50	17	4,479.50
24	Guaraná Fantástica	4.50	20	90.00
43	Ipoh Coffee	46.00	17	782.00
76	Lakkalikööri	18.00	57	1,026.00
67	Laughing Lumberjack Lager	14.00	52	728.00
70	Outback Lager	15.00	15	225.00
75	Rhönbräu Klosterbier	7.75	125	968.75
34	Sasquatch Ale	14.00	111	1,554.00
35	Steeleye Stout	18.00	20	360.00
Beverages			**559.00**	**12,480.25**
Condiments				
3	Aniseed Syrup	10.00	13	130.00
4	Chef Anton's Cajun Seasoning	22.00	53	1,166.00
5			0	

Figure 9.2

Select the Crystal Report template and give the new report a name in the Add New Item dialog box.

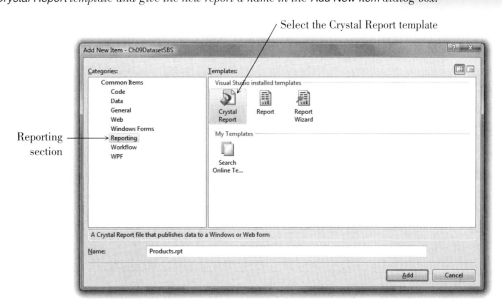

STEP 3: In the *Crystal Reports Gallery*, which opens automatically, make sure the option for *Using the Report Wizard* and the Standard report type are selected (Figure 9.3). Click *OK*.

Figure 9.3

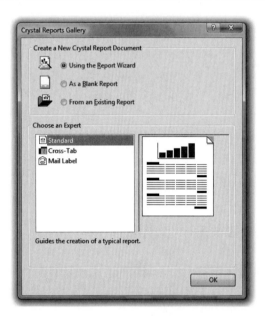

Set Up the Report

STEP 1: In the Available Data Sources pane, expand the Project Data node, then expand the ADO.NET DataSets node, and select the Northwind-DataSet. Click on the double-arrow button to add both tables to the Selected Tables pane (Figure 9.4).

Figure 9.4

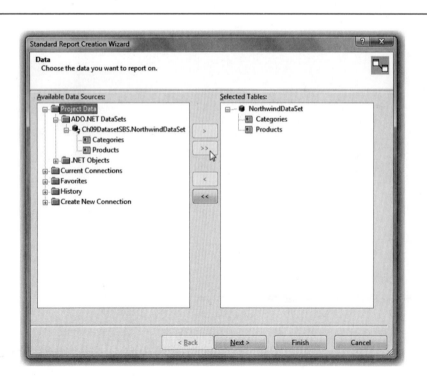

STEP 2: Click *Next*, which takes you to the *Link* page of the wizard. On this page, the wizard attempts to determine the fields that link the related tables. When the fields have identical names, as do the CategoryID fields in these tables, the wizard has no problem determining the links (Figure 9.5). The link line indicates the fields that link the two tables.

When key fields are not identically named, you must manually connect the fields on this screen to show the links.

Figure 9.5

The Link page shows how the two tables are linked.

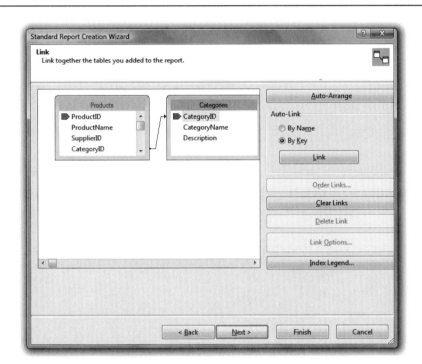

STEP 3: Click *Next* to display the *Fields* page. On this page, you select the fields that you want to display on the detail lines of the report. Select the field names from the list on the left and add them to the list on the right. You can either click the field name and click the arrow button or double-click the field name.

STEP 4: From the products table, add these fields: ProductID, ProductName, UnitPrice, and UnitsInStock (Figure 9.6).

STEP 5: Click *Next* to view the *Grouping* page. You use this page to choose the field on which to sort and group the report. You must sort on any field that you want to use for group breaks (subtotals). Click *CategoryName* and > to add the CategoryName field to the *Group By* box. Notice the sort order selected below the list (Figure 9.7).

STEP 6: Click *Next* to display the *Summaries* page. On this page, you select the fields that you want to subtotal and total. The wizard automatically includes all fields defined as numeric. But it doesn't make sense to calculate totals on some numeric fields, such as the ProductID and UnitPrice fields.

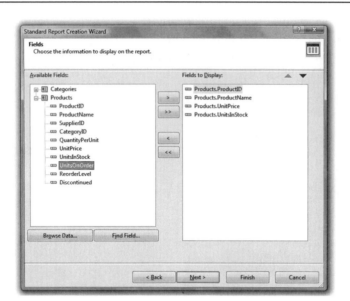

Figure 9.7

Select the field to use for grouping the report.

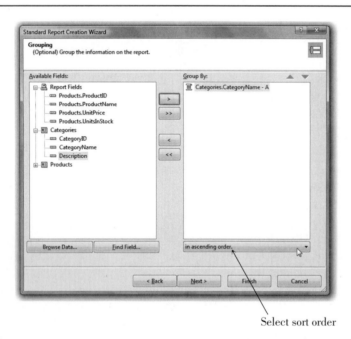

Select sort order

Remove the ProductID and UnitPrice fields from the *Summarized Fields* list. Also, drop down the list box below the summarized fields to see all the choices. You must have the Sum of Products.UnitsInStock selected to enable the drop-down list. Make sure to leave *Sum* selected (Figure 9.8). Click *Next*.

STEP 7: On the *Group Sorting*, *Chart*, and *Record Selection* screens, just press *Next*.

STEP 8: For *Report Style*, click on each of the entries in the *Available Styles* box to see the possibilities. Then click on *Standard* and click *Finish*.

The report designer appears with the entries that you selected (Figure 9.9).

Figure 9.8

Allow the wizard to summarize only the UnitsInStock field.

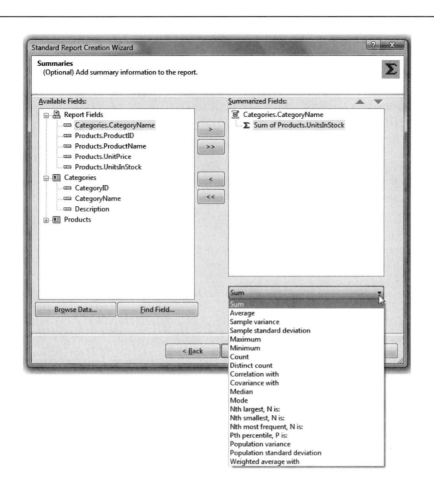

Figure 9.9

The Crystal Reports report designer with the selected options.

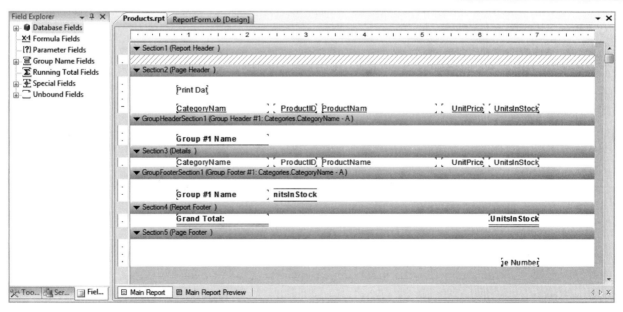

At this point, the report template is complete. However, you will make lots of adjustments and changes to the content and format. The various parts of the report layout screen are covered in the section "Modifying the Products Report—Step-by-Step."

STEP 9: Preview the report by selecting the *Main Report Preview* tab at the bottom of the Document window. The preview is designed to show layout; it cannot show the actual data because you must write code to fill the dataset.

Displaying a Report from a Windows Form—Step-by-Step

To see the actual report, you need to display it from a form.

Set Up the Form

STEP 1: Return to the Form Designer window and widen the form.

STEP 2: Drag a CrystalReportViewer control from the *Crystal Reports* section of the toolbox to the form.

By default, the Dock property of the report viewer control is set to fill the form. To resize the form and control, click on the form's title bar, which selects the form instead of the control. With the form selected, you can resize both the form and control. You also can change the Dock property of the control, if you wish.

STEP 3: From the smart tag for the report viewer, select *Choose a Crystal Report* (Figure 9.10). Drop down the list and select Products.rpt. Click *OK*.

Figure 9.10

Enlarge the form and the CrystalReportViewer control. Select Choose a Crystal Report *from the control's smart tag.*

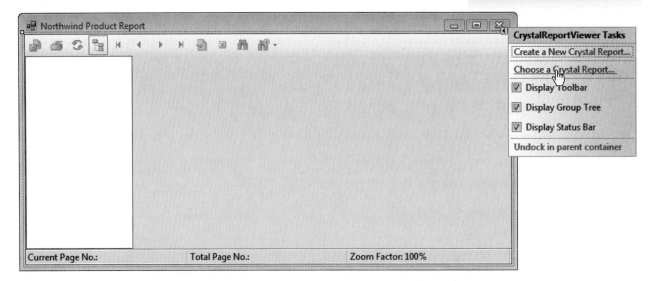

Write Code to Fill the Dataset

STEP 1: Double-click on the form's title bar to open the Editor window and create a Form_Load event procedure.

STEP 2: At the top of the file, declare module-level variables for the dataset and the two table adapters. Although you could declare them inside the Form_Load event procedure, it's better programming to declare them at the module level, and later you may decide to display the report from a user option.

```
Private ADataSet As NorthwindDataSet
Private ACategoriesTableAdapter _
  As NorthwindDataSetTableAdapters.CategoriesTableAdapter
Private AProductsTableAdapter _
  As NorthwindDataSetTableAdapters.ProductsTableAdapter
```

STEP 3: Write the code to instantiate and fill the table adapters and dataset, and assign the dataset to the report in the Form_Load event procedure:

```
' Fill the dataset and set up the report.

Try
    ' Fill the dataset.
    ADataSet = New NorthwindDataSet
    AProductsTableAdapter = _
      New NorthwindDataSetTableAdapters.ProductsTableAdapter
    ACategoriesTableAdapter = _
      New NorthwindDataSetTableAdapters.CategoriesTableAdapter
    AProductsTableAdapter.Fill(ADataSet.Products)
    ACategoriesTableAdapter.Fill(ADataSet.Categories)

    ' Set up the report.
    Dim ProductReport As New Products
    ProductReport.SetDataSource(ADataSet)

    ' Set the report viewer.
    CrystalReportViewer1.ReportSource = ProductReport

Catch Ex As Exception
    MessageBox.Show("Error encountered: " & Ex.Message)
End Try
```

Run the Project

STEP 1: Run the project. The report should appear with the data you selected. Maximize the form to see the entire report.

STEP 2: Click on the *Toggle Group Tree* button in the toolbar of the report viewer.
Note: You can turn off the display of the group tree by setting the report viewer control's DisplayGroupTree property to *false*.

Notice that the wizard automatically included the category name on the detail lines, which we will remedy soon. Take note of the spacing and formatting to see if there is anything else you'd like to change (like maybe the date?).

STEP 3: Close the form to return to design mode. You will make some adjustments to the report layout in the section "Modifying the Products Report—Step-by-Step."

You can switch to the report designer at any time by double-clicking on the .rpt file in the Solution Explorer or by clicking on the .rpt tab in the main document window.

Using the Report Designer

When the Crystal Reports report designer displays, you have many options. You can see a separate section in the toolbox (Figure 9.11) and a **Field Explorer** window (Figure 9.12), which appears as a separate tab in the Toolbox window.

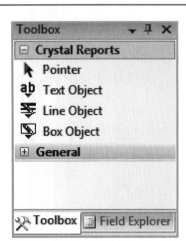

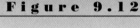

Figure 9.12

The Crystal Reports Field Explorer is a separate window.

You can use the Field Explorer to add new fields to your report. Use the items in the toolbox to add elements such as lines, boxes, or additional text that is not bound to a data field, such as explanations or additional title lines.

Note: If the Field Explorer window does not appear, select *View / Other Windows / Document Outline*. You must be viewing the report designer, not the preview.

You also can display toolbars specific to Crystal Reports when designing a report. Right-click in the menu/toolbar area of the main IDE window and select *Crystal Reports - Main* and *Crystal Reports - Insert* to see the extra toolbars.

The report template contains several bands for information. Refer to Figure 9.9.

* The **Report Header** appears one time at the beginning of the report. You can place any item in this band that you want to appear on only the first page of a multipage report.

* The **Page Header** appears at the top of each page. Generally, the Page Header section holds the report title and column headings.

- The **Group Header** band appears when you select grouping for your report. This band appears in the report each time the field contents change in the field that you selected for grouping.

- The **Details** band holds the data for the body of the report. Here you place the fields that you want to appear on each line of the report. Generally, these are the data from each record.

- The **Group Footer** band appears when you select grouping for your report. This band appears at the end of each group and generally displays subtotals.

- The **Report Footer** appears once at the end of the report. If your report has totals, they appear in this band.

- The **Page Footer** appears at the bottom of each page. By default, page numbers appear in this band.

Modifying a Report Design

You can move, resize, and reformat the fields in the designer. Click on any field and resize using the sizing handles, or drag the control to move it. To reformat a field, right-click and select *Format Object* from the context menu.

Modifying the Products Report—Step-by-Step

The default settings for the Products report need some modifications.

Set Up the Report Header

STEP 1: Right-click on the top gray band labeled "Section1 (Report Header)" and select *Don't Suppress*. This removes the diagonal lines in the Report Header section, indicating that the section is suppressed.

STEP 2: Add a Text Object from the toolbox to the Report Header band (the white strip below the gray Report Header band).

STEP 3: Double-click inside the new object to set the insertion point. Type "Northwind Products" and click outside the object.

STEP 4: Right-click on the new object and select *Format Object*. Click on the *Font* tab and set the size to 14.

STEP 5: Resize the object as needed. You also can resize the Report Header band. You may need to click outside of the object and then reselect it to resize, move, or enter data.

Fix the Date and Eliminate the Repeating Category Names

STEP 1: In the Page Header band, widen the Print Date field to display the entire date. Remember, you can switch back and forth between the report design and report preview at any time using the tabs at the bottom of the window.

STEP 2: In the Details section, select and delete the CategoryName field.

STEP 3: In the Group Footer band, move the group Units in Stock field to line up with the one in the Details band.

Set the Page Margins

STEP 1: In the report designer, right-click on a blank area and choose *Design / Page Setup* from the context menu.

STEP 2: Increase the top margin to 1.0 inch. You also can increase the left and right margins if your printer is one of those that cannot print closer than one-third inch from the edge of the page. Click *OK*.

Sort the Report

STEP 1: Right-click on the report design to display the context menu. Select *Report / Record Sort Expert*. Currently the report is sorted by the CategoryName field; we want to sort by product name within each category group.

STEP 2: Add Product.ProductName to the list. Notice the *Sort Direction* defaults to *Ascending*. Click *OK*.

STEP 3: Run your program again. This time the report should be sorted by product name within categories, with a larger top margin.

Look carefully at the column headings and data in the fields. Many are cut off and should be fixed. Stop the program and return to design view so you can further modify and beautify the report.

Add a Calculated Field

STEP 1: Display and examine the Field Explorer (Figure 9.13). Notice that you can expand the nodes for the database fields to see which fields are included in the report or used in a formula. The selected fields appear with a check mark.

F i g u r e   9 . 1 3

The Field Explorer shows the fields that are included in the report and can be used to add new fields.

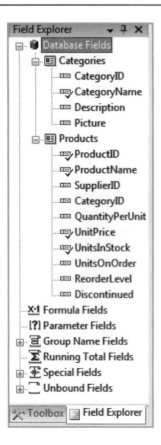

STEP 2: Right-click on *Formula Fields* and select *New* from the context menu.

STEP 3: Enter ExtendedPrice for the formula name and click *Use Editor*. The Formula Workshop - Formula Editor opens to help you create a new formula (Figure 9.14).

Figure 9.14

Use the Formula Editor to create or edit formulas.

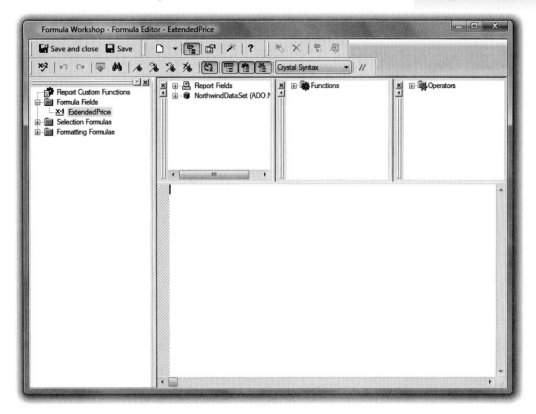

STEP 4: Before creating the new formula, examine the Formula Editor. Expand the nodes to see the functions and operations that you can select. You will use the editor to create a very simple formula.

STEP 5: Make sure that ExtendedPrice is still showing in the title bar at the top of the editor. Then, in the *Report Fields* list, select *Products .UnitPrice.* Double-click on the field name and see that it is added to the large box at the bottom of the wizard.

STEP 6: In the list on the right side, expand the *Operators* and *Arithmetic* nodes and double-click on *Multiply.* An asterisk is added to the formula you are building. Note that you also can just type the asterisk, if you wish.

STEP 7: Double-click on *Products.UnitsInStock* in the *Report Fields* list; your formula should be complete (see Figure 9.15).

   Notice the drop-down list, which has two selections: *Crystal Syntax* and *Basic Syntax.* If you want to type a formula directly in the Formula pane, you will want to switch to *Basic Syntax,* which is Visual Basic syntax. *Crystal Syntax* is the proprietary syntax used by Crystal Reports and is similar to C or Java syntax.

STEP 8: Click on the Editor's *Save and close* button.

STEP 9: In the Field Explorer, expand the *Formula Fields* node to see your new ExtendedPrice field.

   Now you will add the new ExtendedPrice field to the Details section of your report.

STEP 10: You must be able to see the right side of the report design; you can scroll the Designer window or close your Solution Explorer and Properties window to view the right end of the lines.

TIP

Click on the *X-2* toolbar button to check your formula for syntax errors before closing the *Formula Workshop* dialog box. ■

Figure 9.15

Create the new formula for the ExtendedPrice formula field by making selections in the Formula Editor.

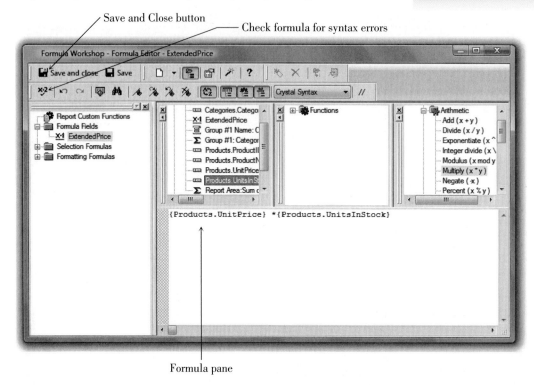

Formula pane

STEP 11: Drag the ExtendedPrice field from the Field Explorer and drop it at the
right end of the Details section of the report (Figure 9.16). You may have
to adjust the field size and/or spacing to allow room for the new field.

Figure 9.16

Drag the new field to the right end of the Details line.

▼ Section1 (Report Header)

Northwind Products

▼ Section2 (Page Header)

Print Date

ProductID ProductName   UnitPrice UnitsInStock

▼ GroupHeaderSection1 (Group Header #1: Categories.CategoryName - A)

Group #1 Name

▼ Section3 (Details)

ProductID ProductName   UnitPrice UnitsInStock

▼ GroupFooterSection1 (Group Footer #1: Categories.CategoryName - A)

Group #1 Name   nitsIn Stock

▼ Section4 (Report Footer)

Grand Total: UnitsIn Stock

▼ Section5 (Page Footer)

je Number

When you drop the outline of the field, you will see the new field appear in the Details section and the new column heading appear in the Page Header band of the report.

STEP 12: Right-click the new ExtendedPrice field in the Details band and choose *Insert / Summary*. In the *Insert Summary* dialog box (Figure 9.17), you can specify where the subtotal should appear. Drop down the *Summary location* list and select *Group #1: Categories.CategoryName - A*. Click *OK* to see the new field in the Group Footer band.

Figure   9.17

Specify that the subtotal should appear for each group.

STEP 13: Again right-click the ExtendedPrice field in the Details band and select *Insert / Summary*. This time accept the location *Grand Total (Report Footer)* and click *OK*. You should now have ExtendedPrice fields in the Detail, Group Footer, and Report Footer bands, but the spacing must be adjusted (Figure 9.18).

Figure   9.18

The ExtendedPrice field has a subtotal in the Group Footer section and a grand total in the Report Footer section.

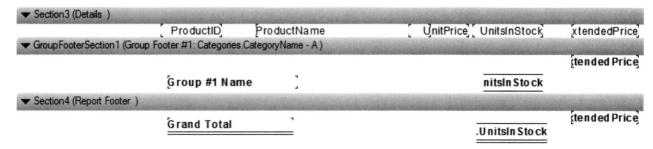

Add a Special Field

STEP 1: In the Field Explorer, expand the *Special Fields* node and notice all of the predefined fields that you can add to a report.

STEP 2: Drag the *Page N of M* field to the Page Footer section. Delete the existing Page field, resize the new field, and move it to the bottom-right corner of the section.

STEP 3: Add the File Author field to the Page Header section, to the right of the Print Date field. You will likely want to resize and adjust the File Author field after you view the report.

You can create highly intelligent reports by programming nearly every element of a report. See the Crystal Decisions Web site for many examples. ■

STEP 4: Right-click in any white area of the report design and select *Report / Summary Info*. Enter your name into the *Author* text box so that your name will appear in the File Author special field. Notice that you can enter other properties of the report, which you also can display using special fields. Check out the *Statistics* tab while you're here; then click *OK*.

Fix the Field Spacing, Alignment, and Column Headings

As you make the following changes, you can view the report design and/or re-run the project as often as you like to view the result of your modifications and see what else must be done. You may want to run the application and set the form's WindowState property to Maximized to more easily view the entire report. Refer back to Figure 9.1 for help as you work through the following steps.

STEP 1: Look at the report. It needs lots of formatting changes. Notice that the report date may be cut off, that the left margin is much larger than the right margin (due to the new field that you added), that the headings should be reformatted and aligned, that the group totals should be formatted alike and aligned, and that the report totals should be formatted alike and aligned.

STEP 2: Also check the placement of the two special fields that you added: Author and Page N of M. Do you need to make any changes to those?

STEP 3: Select all of the column headings, the fields in the Details band, the subtotals, and the grand totals. You can do this with Shift-click or Ctrl-click, or by dragging a selection box around the fields using the mouse pointer. When all of the fields are selected, drag left about one-half or three-fourths inch. Your goal is to make the left and right margins approximately equal. If you don't like the result, you can *Undo*, or make individual adjustments.

STEP 4: In the Group Footer band, select both subtotal fields (you may have to deselect the rest of the report fields first). With the two fields selected, right-click and select *Format Multiple Objects*. Set the top and bottom border style of both objects to be the same. Click *OK* in the dialog box and display the context menu again. This time select *Align / Baseline*.

   Note: If the *Align* option is not on the context menu, make sure that you still have both objects selected.

STEP 5: Format and align both grand total fields in the Report Footer section. Next you will modify the column headings. You don't have to keep the field names as column headings—you can write headings that are more meaningful and friendlier to a user. You also can make the headings appear on multiple lines.

STEP 6: Point to the dividing line between the Page Header and Group Header bands. Drag downward to increase the size of the Page Header band.

STEP 7: Select the ProductID header and drag a bottom handle downward to allow for two lines of text.

STEP 8: Double-click on ProductID in the Page Header to begin edit mode; the selection handles will disappear and the border will change so that you can make modifications. Click between the two words and press the Enter key to make the heading appear on two lines.

TIP

You can select one or more objects and use the keyboard arrow keys to move the objects a small amount in the desired direction. ∎

STEP 9:   If you are still in edit mode, click on a white area of the report design
to return to design mode. Right-click on the Product ID in the Page
Header and select *Format Object*. Examine your many choices for formatting. Then on the *Font* tab, select *Bold* and, on the *Paragraph* tab,
select *Centered* for *Alignment*. You also can select the alignment from
the Crystal Reports toolbar, if you displayed it earlier.

STEP 10: Modify each of the other column headings to have multiple words appearing on two lines.

STEP 11: Select multiple headings, right-click, and select *Format Multiple
Objects*. Bold and center each of the headings.

STEP 12: Select all of the headings, right-click, and align the tops of the headings. You also can drag the headings as a group.

STEP 13: Check the preview to examine the alignment and spacing. Make note
of any fields that should be moved or realigned or have data cut off.
Then return to design mode and finish up the report layout. The
report should now look like Figure 9.1.

Displaying a Report from a Web Form

You can display reports from Web Forms, but there are a few differences from
Windows Forms. Just as with all controls, the Web version of a CrystalReport-
Viewer control is different from a Windows version.

You first add a CrystalReportSource control from the *Reporting* section of
the toolbox to the Web page. In the smart tag for the control, select *Configure
Report Source* and select the name of the .rpt file. Then add a CrystalReport-
Viewer control to the page and set its ReportSource to the CrystalReportSource
that you just added.

You can display the report that you designed in the previous step-by-step
exercise from a Web Form. Begin a new Web site project and copy the two files
for the report, Products.rpt and Products.vb, into the project's folder. Add the
.rpt file to the project using *WebSite / Add Existing Item* or the shortcut menu in
Solution Explorer. After you add the report files to the project folder, the report
name appears in the configuration for the CrystalReportSource control.

When your report is based on a dataset, as in the step-by-step exercise,
you must write additional code in the Web page to fill the dataset and set the
data source for the report. Include `Imports CrystalDecisions.Crystal-
Reports.Engine` at the top of the file.

```
'Project        Ch09DisplayReport
'Programmer     Bradley/Millspaugh
'Date           June 2009
'Description     Display a Crystal Report on a Web page.

Imports CrystalDecisions.CrystalReports.Engine

Partial Class _Default
    Inherits System.Web.UI.Page
    Private ADataSet As NorthwindDataset
    Private ACategoriesTableAdapter _
       As NorthwindDatasetTableAdapters.CategoriesTableAdapter
    Private AProductsTableAdapter _
       As NorthwindDatasetTableAdapters.ProductsTableAdapter
```

```
    Protected Sub Page_Load(ByVal sender As Object, _
      ByVal e As System.EventArgs) Handles Me.Load

        ' Fill the dataset and set up the report.

        ' Fill the dataset.
        ADataSet = New NorthwindDataset
        AProductsTableAdapter = _
          New NorthwindDatasetTableAdapters.ProductsTableAdapter
        ACategoriesTableAdapter = _
          New NorthwindDatasetTableAdapters.CategoriesTableAdapter
        AProductsTableAdapter.Fill(ADataSet.Products)
        ACategoriesTableAdapter.Fill(ADataSet.Categories)

        ' Set up the report data source.
        Dim Report As New ReportDocument
        Report.Load(Request.PhysicalApplicationPath & "Products.rpt")
        Report.SetDataSource(ADataSet)
        CrystalReportViewer1.ReportSource = Report
    End Sub
End Class
```

Selecting from Multiple Reports

In this section, you will allow the user to select the desired report and display the report on a second form. In order to pass the selection to the second form, you will set up a property of the form and set up an enum to assist in the selection. The example has a MainForm, with menu selections to print one of two reports. When the user selects one of the menu items, the event handler must pass the selection to the second form—ReportsForm. On ReportsForm, a single CrystalReportViewer control can display the selected report.

Creating a Property of the Form

The MainForm menu commands must pass data to ReportsForm indicating the report to display. The best way to do this is to add a property to Reports-Form.

```
' Module-level property declaration.
' SelectedReport property of the form.

Private SelectedReportType As ReportType
WriteOnly Property SelectedReport() As ReportType
    ' Set SelectedReport property using the ReportType enum.
    Set(ByVal Value As ReportType)
        SelectedReportType = Value
    End Set
End Property
```

Notice that the SelectedReport property is declared as ReportType. Although you could set up the property as integer, string, or Boolean, there is a real advantage in using an enumeration for the available choices. In Reports-Form, in addition to creating the SelectedReport property, we'll create an enum to indicate the possible choices.

```
' Selection for report type.
Public Enum ReportType
    SalesByType
    SalesByTitle
End Enum
```

To refer to one of the elements of the enum, use Name.Element: `Report-Type.SalesByType` or `ReportType.SalesByTitle`. If you are referring to an enum in a different class, include the class name: `ReportsForm.ReportType.SalesByTitle`.

In MainForm, the user can select a particular report from a menu choice. The menu item's event handler can set ReportsForm's property using the enum values.

```
' MainForm
Private Sub SalesByTypeToolStripMenuItem_Click(ByVal sender _
  As System.Object, ByVal e As System.EventArgs) _
  Handles SalesByTypeToolStripMenuItem.Click
    ' Display the sales by type report.
    Dim ReportForm As New ReportsForm

    With ReportForm
        .SelectedReport = ReportsForm.ReportType.SalesByTitle
        .Show()
    End With
End Sub
```

In ReportsForm, the code can check the value of the property by using the enum values:

```
If SelectedReportType = ReportType.SalesByTitle Then
    ' Code to display the SalesByTitle report.
Else
    ' Code to display the other report.
End If
```

Your Hands-On Programming Example

Write a project to display one of two reports. On the main form, the user can select the report from menu choices. When a selection is made, display the report on a second form.

Use the titles table from the Pubs database. Create a WCF Service to fill the dataset. The report fields are title ID, title, type, price, year-to-date sales, and the publication date. Display the sum and the average year-to-date sales. Use the report footer to display the summary information. Set the format of the publication date to month and year, such as June 2009.

Main Form Menu
File
 Reports
  Sales by Type
  Sales by Title
 Exit

Reports Form Menu
File
  Close

Note that you should display the reports in the Report form's Form_Activated method, rather than the Form_Load method. The Form_Load event occurs only the first time a form is loaded; the Form_Activated occurs every time a form displays.

Planning the Project

Sketch the forms (Figure 9.19) that your users sign off as meeting their needs. Also sketch the two reports (Figure 9.20), which the users must sign off.

Plan the Objects, Properties, and Methods   Plan the objects and property settings for the two forms and their controls. Figure 9.21 shows the diagram of the program components.

Figure 9.19

The planning sketches for the hands-on programming example: a. the main form; b. the reports form.

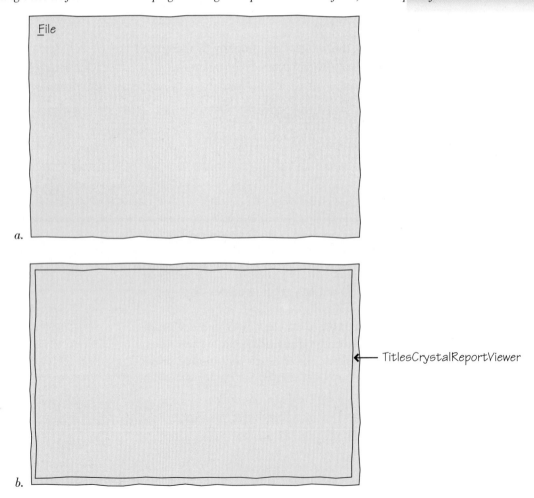

Figure 9.20

The two reports to display: a. the Sales by Type; b. the Sales by Title.

6/1/2009	Book Sales by Type			
Title ID	**Title**	**Price**	**YTD Sales**	**Date Published**
Business				
BU1111	Cooking with Computers: Surreptitious	11.95	3,876	June 1991
BU1032	The Busy Executive's Database Guide	19.99	4,095	June 1991
BU7832	Straight Talk About Computers	19.99	4,095	June 1991
BU2075	You Can Combat Computer Stress!	2.99	18,722	June 1991
Business			30,788.00	
Mod_Cook				
MC2222	Silicon Valley Gastronomic Treats	19.99	2,032	June 1991
MC3021	The Gourmet Microwave	2.99	22,246	June 1991
Mod_Cook			24,278.00	
Comp				

a.

6/1/2009	Year to Date Sales by Title			
Title ID	**Title**	**Price**	**YTD Sales**	**Date Published**
PC1035	But Is It User Friendly?	22.95	8,780	June 1991
PS1372	Computer Phobic AND Non-Phob	21.59	375	October 1991
BU1111	Cooking with Computers: Surrept	11.95	3,876	June 1991
PS7777	Emotional Security: A New Algorit	7.99	3,336	June 1991
TC4203	Fifty Years in Buckingham Palace	11.95	15,096	June 1991
PS2091	Is Anger the Enemy?	10.95	2,045	June 1991
PS2106	Life Without Fear	7.00	111	October 1991
PC9999	Net Etiquette			May 2002
TC3218	Onions, Leeks, and Garlic: Cookii	20.95	375	October 1991
PS3333	Prolonged Data Deprivation: Four	19.99	4,072	June 1991
PC8888	Secrets of Silicon Valley	20.00	4,095	June 1994
MC2222	Silicon Valley Gastronomic Treats	19.99	2,032	June 1991
BU7832	Straight Talk About C			Jur

b.

Figure 9.21

The components for the hands-on programming example.

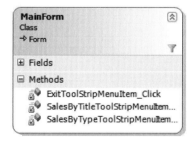

Main Form

Object	Property	Setting
MainForm	Name	MainForm
	Text	Report Selection
FileToolStripMenuItem	Text	&File
ReportsToolStripMenuItem	Text	&Reports
SalesByTypeToolStripMenuItem	Text	Sales by &Type
SalesByTitleToolStripMenuItem	Text	&Sales by Title
ExitToolStripMenuItem	Text	E&xit

Event handlers/methods	Actions—Pseudocode
SalesByTypeToolStripMenuItem_Click	Set ReportsForm.SelectedReport to SalesByType. Display ReportsForm.
SalesByTitleToolStripMenuItem_Click	Set ReportsForm.SelectedReport to SalesByTitle. Display ReportsForm.
ExitToolStripMenuItem_Click	Close the form.

Reports Form

Object	Property	Setting
FileToolStripMenuItem	Text	&File
CloseToolStripMenuItem	Text	&Close
TitlesCrystalReportViewer	Name	TitlesCrystalReportViewer
	DisplayGroupTree	False
Enum	ReportType	SalesByType
		SalesByTitle

Event handlers/methods	Actions—Pseudocode

Activated	If SelectedReport = SalesByTitle
	    Instantiate correct report object.
	    Assign the dataset to the report source.
	    Assign the report to the viewer control.
	Else
	    Instantiate correct report object.
	    Assign the dataset to the report source.
	    Assign the report to the viewer control.

CloseToolStipMenuItem_Click	Close the form.
SelectedReport Property Set	Set the value of the property.

WcfDataService

Event handlers/methods	Actions—Pseudocode
GetData	Instantiate a dataset and TableAdapter. Fill the dataset. Return the dataset.

Write the Project Create the application following the sketches in Figures 9.19 and 9.20. Figure 9.22 shows the completed Windows forms.

- Create a project with the two forms.

- Set the properties of each of the form objects according to your plans.

- Set up the data source.

- Create the WCF Service that returns a dataset.

- Add the two Crystal Reports components, basing the reports on the dataset.

- Write the code for the forms. Working from the pseudocode, write each event handler.

- When you complete the code, test the operation multiple times. The program should be able to display either report, multiple times, in any sequence.

Figure 9.22

The forms for the hands-on programming example: a. the main form; b. the reports form.

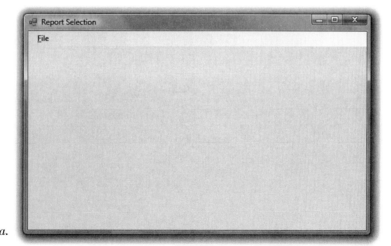

a.

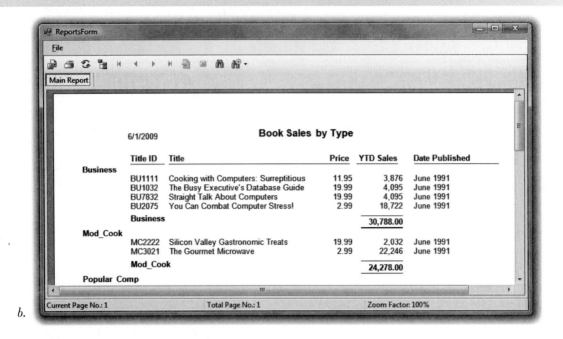

b.

The Project Coding Solution

MainForm

```
'Project:      Ch09HandsOn
'Programmer:   Bradley/Millspaugh
'Date:         June 2009
'Description:  Main form allows user to select report to display.

Public Class MainForm

    Private Sub SalesByTypeToolStripMenuItem_Click(ByVal sender _
        As System.Object, ByVal e As System.EventArgs) _
        Handles SalesByTypeToolStripMenuItem.Click
          ' Display the titles by publication date report.
        Dim ReportForm As New ReportsForm

        With ReportForm
            .SelectedReport = ReportsForm.ReportType.SalesByType
            .Show()
        End With
    End Sub

    Private Sub SalesByTitleToolStripMenuItem_Click(ByVal sender As Object, _
        ByVal e As System.EventArgs) _
        Handles SalesByTitleToolStripMenuItem.Click
          ' Display the titles by name report.
        Dim ReportForm As New ReportsForm

        With ReportForm
            .SelectedReport = ReportsForm.ReportType.SalesByTitle
            .Show()
        End With
    End Sub
End Class
```

```vb
        Private Sub ExitToolStripMenuItem_Click(ByVal sender As Object, _
          ByVal e As System.EventArgs) Handles ExitToolStripMenuItem.Click
            ' Close the program.

            Me.Close()
        End Sub
    End Class
End Class
```

ReportsForm

```vb
'Project:      Ch09HandsOn
'Programmer:   Bradley/Millspaugh
'Date:         June 2009
'Description:  Display the report.

Public Class ReportsForm

    ' SelectedReport property of the form.
    Private SelectedReportType As ReportType

    ' Selection for report type.
    Public Enum ReportType
        SalesByType
        SalesByTitle
    End Enum

    WriteOnly Property SelectedReport() As ReportType
        ' Set the SelectedReport property by using the ReportType enum.
        Set(ByVal Value As ReportType)
            SelectedReportType = Value
        End Set
    End Property

    Private Sub CloseToolStripMenuItem_Click(ByVal sender As Object, _
      ByVal e As System.EventArgs) Handles CloseToolStripMenuItem.Click
        ' Close the form.
        Me.Close()
    End Sub

    Private Sub ReportsForm_Activated(ByVal sender As Object, _
      ByVal e As System.EventArgs) Handles Me.Activated
        ' Display the selected report.
        Dim DataService As New WcfDataService.DataServiceClient()

        Try
            If SelectedReportType = ReportType.SalesByTitle Then
                Dim TitlesReport As New TitlesReport
                TitlesReport.SetDataSource(DataService.GetData)
                TitlesCrystalReportViewer.ReportSource = TitlesReport
            Else
                Dim TypeReport As New TypeReport
                TypeReport.SetDataSource(DataService.GetData)
                TitlesCrystalReportViewer.ReportSource = TypeReport
            End If
        Catch Ex As Exception
            Throw Ex
        End Try
    End Sub
End Class
```

WcfDataService

```
'Project          Ch09HandsOn
'Programmer       Bradley/Millspaugh
'Date             June 2009
'Class            IDataService
'Description       Main form allows user to select report to display.

<ServiceContract()> _
Public Interface IDataService

    <OperationContract()> _
    Function GetData() As PubsDataSet

End Interface

'Project          Ch09HandsOn
'Programmer       Bradley/Millspaugh
'Date             June 2009
'Class            DataService
'Description       Retrieves the data.

Public Class DataService
    Implements IDataService

    Public Sub New()
    End Sub

    Public Function GetData() As PubsDataSet _
      Implements IDataService.GetData
        ' Fill the dataset.
        Dim APubsDataSet As New PubsDataSet
        Dim TitlesTableAdapter As New _
            PubsDataSetTableAdapters.titlesTableAdapter
        TitlesTableAdapter.Fill(APubsDataSet.titles)

        Return APubsDataSet
    End Function
End Class
```

Summary

1. Crystal Reports is a tool for producing reports from database files.
2. You add a Crystal Reports report designer to a project, use the Report Wizard to design the report, add a CrystalReportViewer control to a form, and assign the viewer's ReportSource property to the report.
3. You can select the data for a report from SQL Server or from a dataset defined in the project.
4. The Field Explorer holds elements that can be added to a report.
5. The report designer is organized into bands, called the Report Header, Page Header, Group Header, Details, Group Footer, Page Footer, and Report Footer.

6. The *Special Fields* node in the Field Explorer holds many predefined fields that can be added to a report.
7. You can write code to instantiate a report and display it at run time.
8. If you move a Crystal Reports project from one location to another, you must reset the data source unless the report is based on a dataset that is instantiated and filled in code or an available SQL Server instance.

Key Terms

Crystal Reports   *404*   Page Footer   *413*
Details   *413*   Page Header   *412*
Field Explorer   *412*   Report Footer   *413*
Group Footer   *413*   Report Header   *412*
Group Header   *413*

Review Questions

1. Why use Crystal Reports instead of the printing feature of VB?
2. What is the function of the .rpt file? the CrystalReportViewer control?
3. Explain the concept of bands in report design. What bands are available for a report?
4. Explain where these bands appear in a finished report: Report Header, Page Header, Details.
5. Name some examples of special fields that can be added to a report.

Programming Exercises

9.1   Add a report to one of your previous projects. Make the report show data related to the application.

9.2   Create an application to display a report of the authors in the Pubs database. Include the last name, first name, city, and phone fields. The project can be a Web Form or a Windows Form.

9.3   Write a Windows application to display a report based on the Northwind database. The report should show employees by territory. Use the Employees, EmployeeTerritories, and Territories tables and group by territory. Make sure to display the territory name rather than the ID.

9.4   Write a Windows or a Web application to display a selected report. Include two reports and allow the user to select during program execution. Make one report display the store name and address information from the Pubs database. Make the second report show sales by store, with group totals by store.

Case Studies

Claytor's Cottages

Modify the Guests page of the Claytor's Cottages case study project. Add a button or a menu item to display a report that shows the guest information.

Christian's Car Rentals

Modify the Customers page of your Christian's Car Rentals case study project. Add a button or a menu item to display a report that shows the customer information.

C H A P T E R

10

Collections

at the completion of this chapter, you will be able to . . .

1. Declare and reference collections.

2. Determine the proper collection type for a specific situation.

3. Understand various data structures.

4. Create a collection of objects and add and remove items in the collection.

5. Add objects to the Items collection of a list box, control the display, and retrieve selected objects.

6. Understand generics and be able to create generic procedures.

7. Create a generic collection of objects.

Throughout your programming, you have used a series of collections. List boxes have a collection of items. Tables have a collection of rows and of columns and datasets have collections of tables. In this chapter, you will examine various types of collections such as stacks, queues, dictionaries, hash tables, sorted lists, and array lists. A collection may consist of a group of individual data items or a collection of objects (remember that a data item is an object).

You will find that programmers and programming documentation often use the words *collection*, *list*, and *data structure* interchangeably. For most of the references in this chapter, you can substitute one term for another.

With generics, you create a strongly typed object, such as a procedure or a class, but the type is not defined until the object is instantiated or the procedure called. You will code a generic procedure and create a generic collection class.

Referencing Collection Items

You have referenced some of the built-in collections of VB all along. You can refer to the individual elements of most collections by either a key (a string value) or an index (the numeric position). For example, to reference an individual table in the Tables collection of a DataSet object:

```
' The Stores table.
PubsDataSet.Tables("Stores")
```

or

```
' Also refers to the Stores table, assuming that it is the first table.
PubsDataSet.Tables(0)
```

or

```
' Also refers to the Stores table by using the bang notation.
PubsDataSet.Tables!Stores
```

System.Collections Namespace

A collection is a group of objects. The **System.Collections namespace** provides classes for several different types of collections. When you need to create a collection, you should be aware of the different types available and the strengths and weaknesses of each type. You may need to inherit from a list class or simply select the type of collection that is best for a specific situation. An understanding of the types of collections can make the task easier and the program more efficient.

Some types of collections are based on the way the items are handled. For example, a **queue** is like a line: the first item in should be the first one out (**FIFO**—first in, first out). Compare this to a **stack**: the last one in is the first one out (**LIFO**—last in, first out). We often use these terms in conversation; for example, when you refer to a stack of dishes at the end of the buffet line, it is a collection of dishes in which the last one in the stack should be the first one removed. And hopefully the first person in the queue (in line) is the first one served.

Several types of collections are of the dictionary type. A **dictionary** consists of a key and value pair, similar to a word and its corresponding definition in a language dictionary. Two types of dictionary lists are the Hashtable and the SortedList.

Collection class	Purpose
ArrayList	A collection that is similar to an array. The size of the list is dynamically increased to accommodate the elements added. Provides some useful methods, such as `Contains`, `Insert`, `RemoveAt`, and `Sort`.
BitArray	A collection that holds Boolean values.
CollectionBase	The parent class for creating strongly typed collections. An abstract class used only for inheritance.
DictionaryBase	The parent class for creating dictionary-type collections with pairs of keys and values. An abstract class, used only for inheritance.
Hashtable	A dictionary-type collection of keys and values. Sorted by the keys, which are hash codes of the values.
Queue	An unsorted collection in which the first element in is the first out (FIFO).
SortedList	A dictionary-type collection of keys and values sorted by the keys. Keys may be based on hash codes or other values.
Stack	An unsorted collection in which the last element in is the first element out (LIFO).

Because all of the collection classes inherit from the same base, they share many properties and methods. A good example is the Count property, which contains the number of elements in the list.

The following examples are based on a program in which an array of strings is used to add and remove items from the different types of collections. Figure 10.1

Figure 10.1

The form used for the collection examples, Ch10Lists. The user can choose to create a stack, queue, sorted list, or hash table and add and remove items in the collections.

shows the program with the original list, which is loaded from the `LanguageString` array with this definition:

```
Private LanguageString As String() = {"English", "Spanish", "Chinese", _
    "Italian", "German", "French", "Tagalog"}
```

Each of the collections is declared at the class level:

```
Private ASortedList As SortedList
Private AHashtable As Hashtable
Private AStack As Stack
Private AQueue As Queue
```

Using Stacks

The Stack class provides an unsorted list in which the last item added is the first one removed. The terms *push* and *pop* are used to refer to adding and deleting from a stack. Use the **Push method** to add an item to the list and a **Pop method** to remove an item.

```
' Add an item to the stack.
AStack.Push(ItemString)
```

The `Pop` method removes the last item from the list. If you want to look at the last item without removing it, use the **Peek method**.

```
' View the last item without removing it.
ItemString = AStack.Peek()

' Remove the last item from the list.
AStack.Pop()
```

Because stacks are unsorted, they are not the best type of list if you must perform searches. Items in a stack appear in the reverse order of entry. Figure 10.2 shows the example program with the elements added to a stack.

Figure 10.2

The elements in a stack appear in reverse order from original entry.

Using Queues

The Queue class provides an unsorted list of items in which the first item added to the list is the first one to be removed. You use the **Enqueue method** to add items to the queue and the **Dequeue method** to remove items.

```
' Add an item to the queue.
AQueue.Enqueue(ItemString)
```

A queue, like a stack, provides a `Peek` method for viewing the next item to be removed without actually removing it.

```
' View the next item to be removed without removing it.
ItemString = AQueue.Peek()

' Remove the first item from the list.
AQueue.Dequeue()
```

Queues share several characteristics with stacks: both are unsorted and slow for searching. Do not use either a stack or a queue if you will be performing many searches on your list.

A queue appears in the same order as the original data. Figure 10.3 shows the example program with the elements added to a queue.

Figure 10.3

The elements in a queue appear in the same order as the original entry.

Using Hash Tables

The Hashtable class provides a dictionary-type collection that is based on key/value pairs. **Hash tables** are the fastest type of list for searching. The keys of a hash table are calculated using an algorithm, which must produce a unique key for each entry and produce the same key every time the calculation is made. You can write your own code for creating hash codes, or use the `GetHashCode` method to calculate the key. Add items to a hash table using the `Add` method and remove an item using the `Remove` method.

```
' Calculate the hash code for the key.
KeyString = ItemString.GetHashCode.ToString()
' Add an item to the hash table.
AHashtable.Add(KeyString, ItemString)

' Calculate the hash code of a selected item.
ItemString = LanguagesList.SelectedItem.ToString()
KeyString = ItemString.GetHashCode.ToString()
' Remove the selected item by key.
AHashtable.Remove(KeyString)
```

A hash table is not a good choice when you need the data in a specific order or when you need to add elements at a specific position. You do not control where the hash table inserts new elements. Hash tables require that each key be unique, so it's not a good choice if there could be duplicate keys.

When you refer to the collection of items in a hash table, you must specify the Values property:

```
' Reload the list from the hash table collection.
LanguagesListBox.Items.Clear()
For Each ItemString In AHashtable.Values
    LanguagesListBox.Items.Add(ItemString)
Next
```

Sorted Lists

As the name implies, a SortedList is a collection that is arranged in sorted order. The list consists of key and value pairs and is automatically sorted by the keys. New items are placed in the proper sequence based on the key. Sorted lists use the Add, Remove, and RemoveAt methods. The example program uses the first three letters of the item as the key.

Sorted lists combine many of the features of a hash table and an array list. You can access an element of a sorted list by key, by value, or by index. The keys that you assign must be unique and may be created from a hash code calculation.

```
' Create the key.
KeyString = ItemString.Substring(0, 3)
' Add the key and item to the sorted list.
ASortedList.Add(KeyString, ItemString)
```

Sorted lists work well when you need to search for items or remove items from anywhere in the list.

```
' Retrieve the selected item to be removed.
ItemString = LanguagesListBox.SelectedItem.ToString
' Set the key as the first three characters of the item.
KeyString = ItemString.Substring(0, 3)
' Remove the item by key.
ASortedList.Remove(KeyString)
```

You also can remove an item from a sorted list by its index. But you must be careful because the indexes of items change as elements are added or removed from the list.

```
' Remove the item by index.
ASortedList.RemoveAt(IndexInteger)
```

When you refer to the collection of items in a sorted list, you must specify the Values property.

```
' Reload the list from the sorted list collection.
LanguagesListBox.Items.Clear()
For Each ItemString In ASortedList.Values
    LanguagesListBox.Items.Add(ItemString)
Next
```

The values of a sorted list appear in sorted order. Figure 10.4 shows the example program with the elements added to a sorted list.

Figure 10.4

The elements in a sorted list appear in alphabetic order.

Using the Example Program

The example program loads a string array with languages and allows the user to select the collection type. The user can then add an element to the collection or remove an element. Each time the collection changes, the Items property of the list box is cleared and reloaded with the contents of the collection. Refer to Figures 10.2, 10.3, and 10.4 for the completed form.

```
'Project:      Ch10Lists
'Programmer:   Bradley/Millspaugh/Price
'Date:         June 2009
'Description:  Store an array of strings in various collection types.

Public Class ListsForm
    ' Define class-level variables first.
    Private LanguageStrings As String() = {"English", "Spanish", "Chinese", _
        "Italian", "German", "French", "Tagalog"}
    Private ListTypeString As String
    Private IndexInteger As Integer

    Private ASortedList As SortedList
    Private AHashtable As Hashtable
    Private AStack As Stack
    Private AQueue As Queue

    Private Sub StyleComboBox_SelectedIndexChanged(ByVal sender As Object, _
      ByVal e As System.EventArgs) Handles StyleComboBox.SelectedIndexChanged
        ' Create a new collection based on the selected collection type.

        IndexInteger = 0
        LanguagesListBox.Items.Clear()
        ListTypeString = StyleComboBox.SelectedItem.ToString
        Select Case ListTypeString
            Case "Original"
                DisplayOriginal()
            Case "Hashtable"
                AHashtable = New Hashtable()
            Case "Stack"
                AStack = New Stack()
            Case "Queue"
                AQueue = New Queue()
```

```vb
            Case "Sorted List"
                ASortedList = New SortedList()
        End Select
    End Sub

    Private Sub DisplayOriginal()
        Dim ItemString As String

        ' Display the array in its original order.

        LanguagesListBox.Items.Clear()
        For Each ItemString In LanguageStrings
            LanguagesListBox.Items.Add(ItemString)
        Next
    End Sub

    Private Sub AddButton_Click(ByVal sender As System.Object, _
      ByVal e As System.EventArgs) Handles AddButton.Click
        Dim KeyString As String
        Dim ItemString As String

        ' Add the next element to the selected collection.

        If IndexInteger <= LanguageStrings.GetUpperBound(O) Then ' End of array.
            ItemString = LanguageStrings(IndexInteger)
            Select Case ListTypeString
                Case "Original"
                    MessageBox.Show("Cannot add to the original list.")
                Case "Hashtable"
                    KeyString = ItemString.GetHashCode.ToString
                    AHashtable.Add(KeyString, ItemString)
                    ' Reload the list from the hash table collection.
                    LanguagesListBox.Items.Clear()
                    For Each ItemString In AHashtable.Values
                        LanguagesListBox.Items.Add(ItemString)
                    Next
                Case "Stack"
                    AStack.Push(ItemString)
                    ' Reload the list from the stack.
                    LanguagesListBox.Items.Clear()
                    For Each ItemString In AStack
                        LanguagesListBox.Items.Add(ItemString)
                    Next
                Case "Queue"
                    AQueue.Enqueue(ItemString)
                    ' Reload the list from the queue.
                    LanguagesListBox.Items.Clear()
                    For Each ItemString In AQueue
                        LanguagesListBox.Items.Add(ItemString)
                    Next
                Case "Sorted List"
                    KeyString = ItemString.Substring(O, 3)
                    ASortedList.Add(KeyString, ItemString)
                    ' Reload the list from the sorted list collection.
                    LanguagesListBox.Items.Clear()
                    For Each ItemString In ASortedList.Values
                        LanguagesListBox.Items.Add(ItemString)
                    Next
            End Select
```

```vbnet
            IndexInteger += 1               ' Move to the next array element.
        Else
            MessageBox.Show("No more items for the list.")
        End If
    End Sub

    Private Sub RemoveButton_Click(ByVal sender As System.Object, _
        ByVal e As System.EventArgs) Handles RemoveButton.Click
        Dim KeyString As String
        Dim ItemString As String

        ' Remove an item from the collection.

        Select Case ListTypeString
            Case "Original"
                MessageBox.Show("Cannot remove from the original list.")
            Case "Hashtable"
                If LanguagesListBox.SelectedIndex <> -1 Then
                    ItemString = LanguagesListBox.SelectedItem.ToString
                    KeyString = ItemString.GetHashCode.ToString
                    AHashtable.Remove(KeyString)
                    ' Reload the list from the hash table collection.
                    LanguagesListBox.Items.Clear()
                    For Each ItemString In AHashtable.Values
                        LanguagesListBox.Items.Add(ItemString)
                    Next
                Else
                    MessageBox.Show("Select the item to remove.")
                End If
            Case "Stack"
                AStack.Pop()
                ' Reload the list from the stack.
                LanguagesListBox.Items.Clear()
                For Each ItemString In AStack
                    LanguagesListBox.Items.Add(ItemString)
                Next
            Case "Queue"
                AQueue.Dequeue()
                ' Reload the list from the stack.
                LanguagesListBox.Items.Clear()
                For Each ItemString In AQueue
                    LanguagesListBox.Items.Add(ItemString)
                Next
            Case "Sorted List"
                If LanguagesListBox.SelectedIndex <> -1 Then
                    ItemString = LanguagesListBox.SelectedItem.ToString
                    KeyString = ItemString.Substring(0, 3)
                    ASortedList.Remove(KeyString)
                    ' Reload the list from the sorted list collection.
                    LanguagesListBox.Items.Clear()
                    For Each ItemString In ASortedList.Values
                        LanguagesListBox.Items.Add(ItemString)
                    Next
                Else
                    MessageBox.Show("Select the item to remove.")
                End If
        End Select
    End Sub
End Class
```

Using Array Lists

An ArrayList can dynamically increase in size as new elements are added. You can use the **Capacity property** to set the size of the list. However, if additional elements are added, the capacity is automatically increased in chunks. You can use the **TrimToSize method** to set the capacity of the collection to the actual number of elements.

An array list is similar to an array in many respects but provides more properties and methods to make array programming much easier. Here is a list of some of the most useful properties and methods of an array list:

Array list properties and methods	Purpose
Capacity	Holds the number of elements that the collection can contain.
Count	Holds the actual number of elements in the collection.
IsFixedSize	Determines whether the collection is a fixed size.
IsReadOnly	Determines whether the collection is read only.
Item	The value stored at the specified index.
Add	Add an element to the end of the collection.
AddRange	Add the contents of a collection to the end of the collection.
Clear	Remove all elements from the collection.
Contains	Searches for a specific value in the collection.
CopyTo	Copy elements into an existing array.
RemoveAt	Remove the element at the specified location.
RemoveRange	Remove a series of elements.
ToArray	Copy the elements to a new array.
TrimToSize	Set the capacity to the actual number of elements.

► Feedback 10.1

Write the code to add ElementString to the following:

Class	Object name
1. Hashtable	AHashTable
2. SortedList	ASortedList
3. Stack	AStack
4. Queue	AQueue

Creating a Collection of Objects

When you create your own business class, such as Product, Book, Person, or Employee, you usually need more than one of each object type. One Product or Book object is not very useful—you likely will need to define multiple items. You can accomplish this by creating a collection class and adding objects to the collection. You can choose from the various types of collection classes, depending on your needs for speed, sorting, retrieval by value, index, or key.

You can refer to the members of a collection in two different ways depending on the type of collection. Like an array, you can specify an index number, which is the object's position in the collection. This technique is convenient only if the order of the members does not change. Alternately, you can give each object a string key that uniquely identifies the object, and can store and retrieve the objects in the collection by their keys. Sometimes objects already have a field that is unique and can be used as a key, such as a personal identification number (PIN), a customer number, or an account number. Or you can use a hashing algorithm to create a unique key based on the name or some other unique value. When you remove objects from a collection, the indexes for the remaining objects change to reflect their new position, but the key fields never change.

A Collection of Student Objects

The following examples create and access a collection of Student objects. The project has a Student class with properties for Name and GPA. In the form (Figure 10.5), the user can enter a student's name and GPA and add to the collection, remove a selected student from the collection, or display the GPA for a selected student. A list box on the form displays the current contents of the collection after each addition or deletion, and a label on the form displays the Count property of the collection.

Figure 10.5

Add or remove students from a collection, or display the GPA for a selected student.

Declaring a Collection

You can declare and instantiate the collection at the class level. Select the best collection type for your application. This example uses a sorted list and a hash code of the name as the key.

```
' Declare class-level variables.
Private StudentsHashtable As Hashtable
```

Adding Objects to a Collection

After the user enters the name and GPA and clicks the *Add* button, create the key using the GetHashCode method, which performs a calculation on the name and produces an integer. Because the key must be string, convert the hashed key to a string.

```
' Declare and instantiate a new Student.
Dim AStudent As New Student(NameTextBox.Text, _
  Decimal.Parse(GpaTextBox.Text))
' Calculate a key.
KeyString = AStudent.Name.GetHashCode.ToString
' Add to the collection.
StudentsHashtable.Add(KeyString, AStudent)
```

Removing an Element from a Collection

Many collection types have both Remove and RemoveAt methods. The Remove method generally deletes an element by key and the RemoveAt method removes by index. For a keyless collection, such as an ArrayList, the Remove method removes the specified object from the collection and the RemoveAt deletes by index.

The example Hashtable program uses the Remove method. It retrieves the selected name from the list box, calculates the key using GetHashCode, and removes the element by key.

```
' Get the key from the selected student name.
Dim KeyString As String = StudentsListBox.SelectedItem.GetHashCode.ToString
StudentsHashtable.Remove(KeyString)
```

Retrieving an Element from a Collection

You can retrieve an object that has been placed in a collection using the Item property.

```
' Get the key for the selected name.
Dim KeyString As String = StudentsListBox.SelectedItem.GetHashCode.ToString
' Get the selected student item from the collection.
Dim AStudent As Student = CType(StudentsHashtable.Item(KeyString), Student)
```

For most collection types, the Item property is defined as the default property of the collection. You can leave out the word "Item" from statements:

```
AStudent = CType(StudentsHashtable(KeyString), Student)
```

Using For Each / Next

When you want to access each object in a collection, you can use a For Each / Next structure. Dictionary-type collections, such as sorted lists and hash tables, return an object of **DictionaryEntry data type**. Therefore, you must cast the element to the object type that you need.

```
Dim AStudent As Student
Dim StudentDictionaryEntry As DictionaryEntry

' Loop through the collection and display the items in a list box.
StudentsListBox.Items.Clear()
For Each StudentDictionaryEntry In StudentsHashtable
    AStudent = CType(StudentDictionaryEntry.Value, Student)
    StudentsListBox.Items.Add(AStudent.Name)
Next
```

The Completed Program

Here is the complete Student collection application. It has a Student class and
a form, which appears in Figure 10.5.

The Student Class

```
'Project:       Ch10StudentCollection
'Module:        StudentClass.vb
'Programmer:    Bradley/Millspaugh/Price
'Date:          June 2009
'Description:   Create a Student class.

Public Class Student

    ' Private property variables.
    Private NameString As String
    Private GpaDecimal As Decimal

    ' Property procedures.
    Public Property Name() As String
        Get
            Return NameString
        End Get
        Set(ByVal Value As String)
            NameString = Value
        End Set
    End Property

    Public Property GPA() As Decimal
        Get
            Return GpaDecimal
        End Get
        Set(ByVal Value As Decimal)
            GpaDecimal = Value
        End Set
    End Property

    ' Class constructor.
    Public Sub New(ByVal NameString As String, _
        ByVal GpaDecimal As Decimal)
        ' Create a Student object.

        Name = NameString
        GPA = GpaDecimal
    End Sub
End Class
```

The Form Class

```
'Project:        Ch10StudentCollection
'Module:         StudentCollectionForm
'Programmer:     Bradley/Millspaugh/Price
'Date:           June 2009
'Description:    A form for entering and viewing Student objects
'                in a Students collection. Uses a Hashtable collection.

Public Class CollectionsForm

    ' Declare class-level variables.
    Private StudentsHashtable As Hashtable

    Private Sub AddButton_Click(ByVal sender As System.Object, _
      ByVal e As System.EventArgs) Handles AddButton.Click
        Dim KeyString As String

        ' Create a Student object and add it to the collection.
        If NameTextBox.Text <> "" Then
            Try
                ' Declare and instantiate a new Student.
                Dim AStudent As New Student(NameTextBox.Text, _
                  Decimal.Parse(GpaTextBox.Text))
                ' Calculate a key.
                KeyString = AStudent.Name.GetHashCode.ToString
                ' Add to the collection.
                StudentsHashtable.Add(KeyString, AStudent)
                DisplayList()
                ' Clear the text boxes.
                With NameTextBox
                    .Clear()
                    .Focus()
                End With
                GpaTextBox.Clear()
            Catch err As FormatException
                With GpaTextBox
                    .SelectAll()
                    .Focus()
                End With
                MessageBox.Show("Numeric GPA required." & _
                  ControlChars.NewLine & NameTextBox.Text & _
                  " Not Added.", "A Collection of Students")
            Catch err As Exception
                With NameTextBox
                    .SelectAll()
                    .Focus()
                End With
                MessageBox.Show("Duplicate student name." & _
                  ControlChars.NewLine & NameTextBox.Text & _
                  " Not Added." & err.Message, "A Collection of Students")
            End Try
        Else
            With NameTextBox
                .SelectAll()
                .Focus()
            End With
```

```vbnet
            MessageBox.Show("Please enter a name.", _
                "A Collection of Students")
        End If
End Sub

Private Sub RemoveButton_Click(ByVal sender As System.Object, _
    ByVal e As System.EventArgs) Handles RemoveButton.Click
    ' Remove selected item from the collection.

    With StudentsListBox
        If .SelectedIndex <> -1 Then
            ' Get the key from the selected student name.
            Dim KeyString As String = .SelectedItem.GetHashCode.ToString
            StudentsHashtable.Remove(KeyString)
            DisplayList()
        Else
            MessageBox.Show("Select a student from the list.", _
                "A Collection of Students")
        End If
    End With
End Sub

Private Sub DisplayButton_Click(ByVal sender As System.Object, _
  ByVal e As System.EventArgs) Handles DisplayButton.Click
    ' Display the GPA for the selected student.
    Dim AStudent As Student

    With StudentsListBox
        If .SelectedIndex <> -1 Then
            ' Get the key for the selected name.
            Dim KeyString As String = .SelectedItem.GetHashCode.ToString
            ' Get the selected student item from the collection.
            AStudent = CType(StudentsHashtable.Item(KeyString), Student)
            MessageBox.Show("The GPA for " & AStudent.Name & " is " & _
                AStudent.GPA.ToString, "A Collection of Students")
        Else
            MessageBox.Show("Select a student from the list.", _
                "A Collection of Students")
        End If
    End With
End Sub

Private Sub DisplayList()
    ' Display the collection items in a list box.
    Dim AStudent As Student
    Dim StudentDictionaryEntry As DictionaryEntry

    With StudentsListBox
        .Items.Clear()
        ' Loop through the collection and add each item to a list box.
        For Each StudentDictionaryEntry In StudentsHashtable
            AStudent = CType(StudentDictionaryEntry.Value, Student)
            .Items.Add(AStudent.Name)
        Next
        ' Display the count.
        countLabel.Text = StudentsHashtable.Count.ToString
    End With
End Sub
```

```
      Private Sub CollectionsForm_Load(ByVal sender As System.Object, _
          ByVal e As System.EventArgs) Handles MyBase.Load
           ' Instantiate the collection.

          StudentsHashtable = New Hashtable
      End Sub
End Class
```

Feedback 10.2

1. Write the code to refer to a single item in a collection of the Persons class. The collection is a hash table with hash codes of the person's name as the key.
2. Which property of a collection class is usually the default property?
3. Write the code to remove an object from the Persons collection.
4. Write the code to retrieve a Person object from the collection.

Using an Items Collection

The **Items collection** of a list box or combo box is actually a collection of objects, not just strings. You can add objects to the Items collection and retrieve the complete object in the Item property.

When you add an object to the Items collection, what displays in the list? The answer is whatever is returned by the object's ToString method. You can write your own ToString method in the object's class, which must override the base class ToString method. Add this function to the StudentClass:

```
' Procedure in the Student class to override the ToString function.
Public Overrides Function ToString() As String
    ' Return the Name property for this object's ToString method.

    Return NameString
End Function
```

In the form, you can add an instantiated Student object directly to a list box Items collection:

```
' Add the Student object to the collection.
StudentsListBox.Items.Add(AStudent)
```

Since the ToString function is overridden in the Student class, the name displays in the list box, just like it did in the earlier example but with a lot less code.

You can retrieve the Item property from the list, convert to the correct type, and reference the individual properties of the object.

```
With StudentsListBox
    If .SelectedIndex <> -1 Then
        ' Get the selected student item from the collection.
        AStudent = CType(.Items.Item(.SelectedIndex), Student)
        MessageBox.Show("The GPA for " & AStudent.Name & " is " & _
            AStudent.GPA, "A Collection of Students")
    Else
        MessageBox.Show("Select a student from the list.", _
            "A Collection of Students")
    End If
End With
```

Here is the complete Student Collection application's form code that uses the modified class with the overridden **ToString** function. Compare this one with the first version to see all the code that could be removed.

```
'Project        Ch10StudentCollection#2
'Module         StudentCollectionForm
'Programmer     Bradley/Millspaugh/Price
'Date           June 2009
'Description     A form for entering and viewing Student objects
'                in a Students collection. Uses a ListBox collection.

Public Class CollectionsForm

    Private Sub AddButton_Click(ByVal sender As System.Object, _
        ByVal e As System.EventArgs) Handles AddButton.Click
        ' Create a Student object and add it to the collection.

        If NameTextBox.Text <> "" Then
            Try
                ' Declare and instantiate a new Student.
                Dim AStudent As New Student(NameTextBox.Text, _
                    Decimal.Parse(GpaTextBox.Text))
                ' Add the Student object to the collection.
                StudentsListBox.Items.Add(AStudent)
                ' Display the count.
                CountLabel.Text = StudentsListBox.Items.Count.ToString
                ' Clear the text boxes.
                With NameTextBox
                    .Clear()
                    .Focus()
                End With
                GpaTextBox.Clear()
            Catch err As FormatException
                With GpaTextBox
                    .SelectAll()
                    .Focus()
                End With
                MessageBox.Show("Numeric GPA required." & _
                    ControlChars.NewLine & NameTextBox.Text & _
                    " Not Added.", "A Collection of Students")
```

```vb
            Catch err As Exception
                With NameTextBox
                    .SelectAll()
                    .Focus()
                End With
                MessageBox.Show("Duplicate student record." & _
                    ControlChars.NewLine & NameTextBox.Text & _
                    " Not Added." & err.Message, "A Collection of Students")
            End Try
        Else
            NameTextBox.Focus()
            MessageBox.Show("Please enter a name.", _
                "A Collection of Students")
        End If
    End Sub

    Private Sub RemoveButton_Click(ByVal sender As System.Object, _
        ByVal e As System.EventArgs) Handles RemoveButton.Click
        ' Remove selected item from the collection.

        With StudentsListBox
            If .SelectedIndex <> -1 Then
                .Items.RemoveAt(.SelectedIndex)
                ' Display the count.
                CountLabel.Text = .Items.Count.ToString
            Else
                MessageBox.Show("Select a student from the list.", _
                    "A Collection of Students")
            End If
        End With
    End Sub

    Private Sub DisplayButton_Click(ByVal sender As System.Object, _
        ByVal e As System.EventArgs) Handles DisplayButton.Click
        ' Display the GPA for the selected student.
        Dim AStudent As Student

        With StudentsListBox
            If .SelectedIndex <> -1 Then
                ' Get the selected student item from the collection.
                AStudent = CType(.Items.Item(.SelectedIndex), Student)
                MessageBox.Show("The GPA for " & AStudent.Name & " is " & _
                    AStudent.GPA.ToString, "A Collection of Students")
            Else
                MessageBox.Show("Select a student from the list.", _
                    "A Collection of Students")
            End If
        End With
    End Sub
End Class
```

Feedback 10.3

1. If you add an object to the Items collection of a list box or combo box, what displays in the list?
2. How can you specify which property of your object should appear in the list?

Generics

One of the great things about object-oriented programming is the ability to re-use the objects you create, but one of the difficulties is creating objects that are generic enough to be used in many programming situations. Let's take a look at a procedure that will swap two variables:

```
Public Sub Swap(ByRef Item1Integer As Integer, ByRef Item2Integer As Integer)
    Dim TempInteger As Integer

    TempInteger = Item1Integer
    Item1Integer = Item2Integer
    Item2Integer = TempInteger
End Sub
```

This procedure will swap two integers. Using the `ByRef` causes the procedure to swap the values in the original memory location, not copies (`ByVal`) sent to the procedure.

But what if you want to swap Longs, or Strings, or Dates? You could use Object variable types instead, but there are more overhead and performance hits for using this type of variable. As you know, you can create overridden procedures, but then you have to have one procedure for each variable type you want to handle.

Generics provide a way to define strongly typed procedures or classes where the object type is not declared until you use the procedure or instantiate the class. With generics, you don't have to specify what type of variable object you are going to use until you use it. Let's take a look at that same Swap procedure using generics:

```
Public Sub Swap (Of GenericType) (ByRef Item1Type As GenericType, _
   ByRef Item2Type As GenericType)
    Dim TempType As GenericType

    TempType = Item1Type
    Item1Type = Item2Type
    Item2Type = TempType
End Sub
```

The key to this procedure is the references to `GenericType`. `GenericType` is replaced by the type of variable that you pass in. Once you've defined your new procedure, you can use it by defining two variables of the same type and calling the procedure. To call the procedure to swap two integers:

```
Dim Number1Integer As Integer = 111
Dim Number2Integer As Integer = 222

Swap(Number1Integer, Number2Integer)    ' Swaps '111' with '222'.
```

Or we could call the procedure passing it two strings:

```
Dim Name1String as String = "John"
Dim Name2String as String = "Mary"

Swap(Name1String, Name2String)    ' Swaps 'John' with 'Mary'.
```

More examples of calling our new Swap procedure would be (assume that all the variables have already been declared):

```
Swap(ALong, BLong)            ' Swaps the two longs.
Swap(FirstDate, SecondDate)   ' Swaps the two dates.
' The next statement produces a compiler error because both
' parameters must be of the same type.
Swap(ALong, FirstDate)        ' Compiler Error!
```

Generic Classes

Generic classes allow you to instantiate strongly typed classes while maintaining a high degree of reusability. Let's take a look at the Swap procedure as it is declared in a class. You can code this class in two different ways. The first is to specify `GenericType` in the class header so the entire class will be of that type. The second is to define the methods in the classes with `GenericType` (just as in the previous Swap procedure header). The first example using the class header is:

```
Class GenericClass(Of GenericType)
    Public Sub Swap(ByRef Item1Type As GenericType, _
      ByRef Item2Type As GenericType)
        Dim TempType As GenericType

        TempType = Item1Type
        Item1Type = Item2Type
        Item2Type = TempType
    End Sub
End Class
```

To use this new class, you instantiate it and then call the method of the class:

```
Dim Number1Integer As Integer = 333
Dim Number2Integer As Integer = 444

' Instantiate the generic class.
Dim SwapIntegersGenericClass As New GenericClass(Of Integer)

' Swaps '333' with '444'.
SwapIntegersGenericClass.Swap(Number1Integer, Number2Integer)
```

You'll notice that the IDE is smart enough to know that when you have instantiated the class with a type of Integer, coding the method call prompts you for integers (Figure 10.6).

The second class example, with the methods defined as `GenericType`, is:

```
Class GenericClass
    Public Sub Swap (Of GenericType)(ByRef Item1Type As GenericType, _
      ByRef Item2Type As GenericType)
        Dim TempType As GenericType

        TempType = Item1Type
        Item1Type = Item2Type
        Item2Type = TempType
    End Sub
End Class
```

F i g u r e   1 0 . 6

The smart IDE prompts for the data type specified in the declaration.

```
      Private Sub CalculateButton_Click(ByVal sender As System.Object, _
        ByVal e As System.EventArgs) Handles CalculateButton.Click
              ' Swap integers using the generic class.
              Dim Number1Integer As Integer = 333
              Dim Number2Integer As Integer = 444

              ' Instantiate the generic class.
              Dim SwapIntegersGenericClass As New GenericClass(Of Integer)

              SwapIntegersGenericClass.Swap(
              Swap (ByRef Item1Type As Integer, ByRef Item2Type As Integer)
```

| AcceptButton |
| AccessibleDescription |
| AccessViolationException |
| ActivationContext |
| AddressOf |
| Aggregate |
| AllowTransparency |
| Anchor |
| AppDomain |
| AppDomainManagerInitializationOptions |

| Common | All |

```
      End Sub
End Class
```

The Entire Program

```
'Project        Ch10Generics
'Programmer     Bradley/Millspaugh/Price
'Date           June 2009
'Description     A form for entering two values to
'                be swapped using a generic swap routine.
'                Two different generic class types are contained in
'                this example. One example, including the instantiation
'                and method calls, is commented out.

Public Class GenericsForm

    Private Sub SwapButton_Click(ByVal sender As System.Object, _
      ByVal e As System.EventArgs) Handles SwapButton.Click
        ' Instantiate the generic class and test using string or numeric types.
        Dim FirstValueDecimal, SecondValueDecimal As Decimal
        ' Dim SwapClass As New GenericClass

        Dim FirstEntryString As String = FirstValueTextBox.Text
        Dim SecondEntryString As String = SecondValueTextBox.Text
        Try
            FirstValueDecimal = Decimal.Parse(FirstEntryString)
            SecondValueDecimal = Decimal.Parse(SecondEntryString)
            ' Both fields are numeric.
            Dim SwapDecimalsClass As New GenericClass(Of Decimal)
            SwapDecimalsClass.Swap(FirstValueDecimal, SecondValueDecimal)
            ' SwapClass.Swap(FirstValueDecimal, SecondValueDecimal)
            MessageBox.Show("First value is " & FirstValueDecimal)
        Catch ex As Exception
            ' Swap two text values.
            Dim SwapStringsClass As New GenericClass(Of String)
            SwapStringsClass.Swap(FirstEntryString, SecondEntryString)
            ' SwapClass.Swap(FirstEntryString, SecondEntryString)
            MessageBox.Show("First value is " & FirstEntryString)
        End Try
    End Sub
End Class
```

```
' This is a generic class.
Class GenericClass(Of GenericType)
    Public Sub Swap(ByRef Item1Type As GenericType, _
       ByRef Item2Type As GenericType)
        ' Swap two values using a temporary location.
        Dim TempType As GenericType

        TempType = Item1Type
        Item1Type = Item2Type
        Item2Type = TempType
    End Sub
End Class
```

Generic Collections

Collections are a great way to store your variables and keep them together. One of the drawbacks with collections is that all items are stored as object type variables, so a collection can store a string, an integer, and a class object all in the same collection without any problem. Usually that is not what you want, as your collection will probably contain objects of the same object type. You can write a "generic" wrapper around the class, which guarantees that all objects in the collection are the same type.

Generic collections provide a way to define strongly typed collections where the collection type is not declared until you instantiate the class. By using generics, you will have a strongly typed collection class that can be used with any object type that you want. Just instantiate the generic collection class, specifying the type you want to use. And from then on, that collection is "locked in" to the specified type.

Just as we did earlier with generic classes, we will define our generic collection class using the "Of Type" specifier.

```
Public Class GenericCollection(Of GenericType)
    Inherits CollectionBase

    ' Code goes here . . .
End Class
```

Inheriting from a CollectionBase class gives our new collection class some inherited properties and methods, such as Count and Clear.

A collection class will need Add, Remove, and Item methods that utilize GenericType. The complete class code listing looks like this:

```
Public Class GenericCollection(Of GenericType)
    Inherits CollectionBase

    Public Function Add(ByVal Value As GenericType) As Integer
        ' Add the passed "Value" to the inherited List.

        Return List.Add(Value)
    End Function
```

```
    Public Sub Remove(ByVal Value As GenericType)
        ' Remove the passed "Value" from the inherited List.

        List.Remove(Value)
    End Sub

    Public ReadOnly Property Item(ByVal IndexInteger As Integer) As GenericType
        Get
            ' Cast the List object to the correct type and return it.

            Return CType(List.Item(IndexInteger), GenericType)
        End Get
    End Property
End Class
```

Remember that some properties, like Count, were inherited from CollectionBase, so there is no need to duplicate them here.

Once you instantiate the GenericCollection class and specify a type, using GenericType, you have imposed a restriction on the class that it must use that type in its methods—wherever you use GenericType. The following code is an example of how you might use this class.

```
' Create the GenericCollection instance, and specify a type
' (in this case, String).
Dim StringCollection As New GenericCollection(Of String)

' Add two strings.
StringCollection.Add("The sky is blue.")
StringCollection.Add("The car is green.")

' The next statement will cause a compiler error (with Option Strict On).
' because it must be a String since that is how StringCollection
' was declared (in the instantiation of the GenericCollection class).
StringCollection.Add(123)
Debug.WriteLine("Our List contains " & StringCollection.Count.ToString & _
    " items.")
```

While our generic collection example is useful, there may not be any need to create them yourself since Visual Studio includes a number of generic collections in the Systems.Collections.Generic namespace:

- List—A basic generic collection, like the GenericCollection example, using an array whose size is dynamically increased as required.

- Dictionary—A name/value collection that indexes each item with a key.

- LinkedList—A doubly linked list, where each item points to the next item in the chain.

- Queue—A first-in, first-out (FIFO) collection of objects.

- ReadOnlyCollection—A collection with a fixed set of items that can't be changed once it's created.

- Stack—A last-in, first-out (LIFO) collection.

- SortedDictionary—A key/value collection that's kept in perpetually sorted order by the key.

- SortedList—A collection of key/value pairs that are sorted by key based on the IComparer setting.

See the System.Collections.Generic namespace in Help for the complete list of collection classes, interfaces, and structures.

To create a collection of your class, specify the generic type to be used in the declaration:

```
Private StudentsDictionary As Dictionary(Of String, Student)
```

In a Dictionary collection, the key and the value are required. In this example, the key is a string and the collection is of Student objects. Notice that the DisplayList procedure differs when using the generic class. This same code could be used for other key/value combinations such as a SortedList.

```
'Project:        Ch10GenericStudentCollection
'Module:         StudentCollectionForm
'Programmer:     Bradley/Millspaugh/Price
'Date:           June 2009
'Description:    A form for entering and viewing Student objects
'                in a Students collection. Uses a Dictionary collection.

Imports System.Collections.Generic

Public Class CollectionsForm

    ' Declare class-level variables.
    Private StudentsDictionary As Dictionary(Of String, Student)

    Private Sub AddButton_Click(ByVal sender As System.Object, _
      ByVal e As System.EventArgs) Handles AddButton.Click
        Dim KeyString As String

        ' Create a Student object and add it to the collection.
        If NameTextBox.Text <> "" Then
            Try
                ' Declare and instantiate a new Student.
                Dim AStudent As New Student(NameTextBox.Text, _
                  Decimal.Parse(GpaTextBox.Text))
                ' Calculate a key.
                KeyString = AStudent.Name.GetHashCode.ToString
                ' Add to the collection.
                StudentsDictionary.Add(KeyString, AStudent)
                DisplayList()
                ' Clear the text boxes.
                With NameTextBox
                    .Clear()
                    .Focus()
                End With
                GpaTextBox.Clear()
            Catch err As FormatException
                With GpaTextBox
                    .SelectAll()
                    .Focus()
```

```vbnet
            End With
            MessageBox.Show("Numeric GPA required." & _
                ControlChars.NewLine & NameTextBox.Text & _
                " Not Added.", "A Collection of Students")
        Catch err As Exception
            With NameTextBox
                .SelectAll()
                .Focus()
            End With
            MessageBox.Show("Duplicate student name." & _
                ControlChars.NewLine & NameTextBox.Text & _
                " Not Added." & err.Message, "A Collection of Students")
        End Try
    Else
        NameTextBox.Focus()
        MessageBox.Show("Please enter a name.", _
            "A Collection of Students")
    End If
End Sub

Private Sub RemoveButton_Click(ByVal sender As System.Object, _
    ByVal e As System.EventArgs) Handles RemoveButton.Click
    ' Remove selected item from the collection.

    With StudentsListBox
        If .SelectedIndex <> -1 Then
            ' Get the key from the selected student name.
            Dim KeyString As String = .SelectedItem.GetHashCode.ToString
            StudentsDictionary.Remove(KeyString)
            DisplayList()
        Else
            MessageBox.Show("Select a student from the list.", _
                "A Collection of Students")
        End If
    End With
End Sub

Private Sub DisplayButton_Click(ByVal sender As System.Object, _
    ByVal e As System.EventArgs) Handles displayButton.Click
    Dim AStudent As Student

    ' Display the GPA for the selected student.

    With StudentsListBox
        If .SelectedIndex <> -1 Then
            ' Get the key for the selected name.
            Dim KeyString As String = .SelectedItem.GetHashCode.ToString
            ' Get the selected student item from the collection.
            AStudent = CType(StudentsDictionary.Item(KeyString), Student)
            MessageBox.Show("The GPA for " & AStudent.Name & " is " & _
                AStudent.GPA, "A Collection of Students")
        Else
            MessageBox.Show("Select a student from the list.", _
                "A Collection of Students")
        End If
    End With
End Sub
```

```
    Private Sub DisplayList()
        ' Loop through the collection and display the items in a list box.
        Dim AStudent As Student
        With StudentsListBox
            .Items.Clear()
            For Each Pair As KeyValuePair(Of String, Student) In _
              StudentsDictionary
                AStudent = CType(Pair.Value, Student)
                .Items.Add(AStudent.Name)
            Next
            ' Display the count.
            CountLabel.Text = StudentsDictionary.Count.ToString
        End With
    End Sub

    Private Sub CollectionsForm_Load(ByVal sender As System.Object, _
      ByVal e As System.EventArgs) Handles MyBase.Load
        ' Instantiate the collection.

        StudentsDictionary = New Dictionary(Of String, Student)
    End Sub
End Class
```

Feedback 10.4

1. What must be done to change a regular method into a generic method? a generic class?
2. What type of objects can be used with generics?
3. List and describe at least three types of generic collections.

Your Hands-On Programming Example

Create a program that maintains a collection of generic Client objects. The Client class should have properties for Name, PhoneNumber, and AccountNumber. Make the Name and PhoneNumber strings, but make the AccountNumber generic. Use the list box Items collection to store the instantiated Client class objects. Demonstrate in your code that you can code both Longs and Strings for the AccountNumber (not at the same time; just remark out the working code for either the Long or the String, similar to the treatment in the Ch10Generics example program earlier in this chapter).

On the form, allow the user to add new clients using text boxes for Name, Account Number, and Phone Number. The list box should show the client names. Allow the user to add new clients, remove clients, and display the information (name, account number, and phone number) for a selected client. Display the current count of the number of clients in the collection. Maintain the list in sorted order.

The program must create a Client object and add it to the list box collection, which must display the client names. Do not allow missing data or a missing selection to cancel the program.

Planning the Project

Sketch the form (Figure 10.7) that your users sign off as meeting their needs.

Figure 10.7

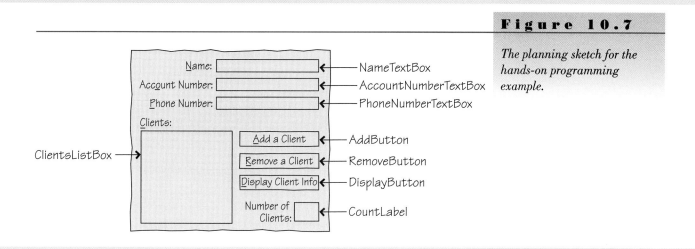

The planning sketch for the hands-on programming example.

Plan the Objects, Properties, and Methods Plan the objects and properties for the Client class and for the form and its controls. Figure 10.8 shows the diagram of the program components.

Figure 10.8

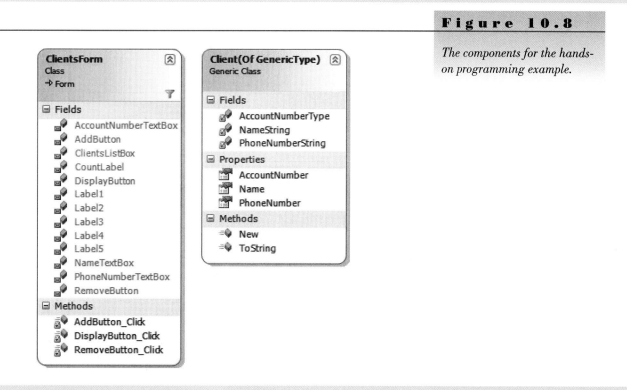

The components for the hands-on programming example.

The Form

Object	Property	Setting
ClientsForm	Name	ClientsForm
	AcceptButton	AddButton
	Text	A Collection of Clients
Label1	Text	&Name:
	TextAlign	TopRight
Label2	Text	Acc&ount Number:
	TextAlign	TopRight
Label3	Text	&Phone Number:
	TextAlign	TopRight
Label4	Text	&Clients:
NameTextBox	Text	(blank)
AccountNumberTextBox	Text	(blank)
PhoneNumberTextBox	Text	(blank)
ClientsListBox	Name	ClientsListBox
	Sorted	True
AddButton	Text	&Add a Client
RemoveButton	Text	&Remove a Client
DisplayButton	Text	&Display Client Info
Label5	Text	Number of Clients:
	TextAlign	MiddleRight
CountLabel	Text	(blank)
	BorderStyle	Fixed3D
	TextAlign	MiddleCenter

Event handlers/methods	Actions—Pseudocode
AddButton.Click	If Name is present
	If Account Number is present
	Create a new Client object.
	Add the Client to the collection.
	Add the Client object to the list box.
	Display the collection count.
	Clear the text boxes and set the focus.
	Else
	Display error message for missing Account Number.
	Else
	Display error message for missing Name.
RemoveButton.Click	If a selection is made from the list
	Remove the selected Client from the collection by the
	selected index.
	Display the collection count.
	Else
	Display error message for a missing selection.

DisplayButton.Click	If a selection is made from the list
	Retrieve the selected Client object.
	Set up the string with all client information.
	Display the information in a message box.
	Else
	Display error message for missing selection.

Client Class

Public properties	Private property variables
Name	NameString
PhoneNumber	PhoneNumberString
AccountNumber	AccountNumberType

Procedures/methods	Actions—Pseudocode
New	Instantiate a Client object with the three properties.
ToString	Return NameString.
Property Get and Set	Name.
Property Get and Set	AccountNumber.
Property Get and Set	PhoneNumber.

Write the Project Create the application following the sketch in Figure 10.7. Figure 10.9 shows the completed Windows form.

- Create a project with a Windows Form.

- Set the properties of each of the form objects, according to your plans.

- Create and code the Client class, following your plans.

- Write the code for the form. Working from the pseudocode, write each event procedure.

- When you complete the code, test the operation multiple times. The program should be able to add, remove, and display client information in any order and keep the count current at all times.

Figure 10.9

The form for the hands-on programming example.

The Project Coding Solution
The Clients Form

```
'Project:        Ch10HandsOn
'Class:          ClientsForm
'Programmer:     Bradley/Millspaugh/Price
'Date:           June 2009
'Description:    Collect and display client information.
'                Uses generic Client class objects and stores those
'                objects in the Items collection of a list box.

Public Class ClientsForm
    Private Sub AddButton_Click(ByVal sender As System.Object, _
      ByVal e As System.EventArgs) Handles AddButton.Click
        ' Dim AClient As Client(Of Long)
        Dim AClient As Client(Of String)

        ' Create a Client object and add it to the collection.
        If NameTextBox.Text <> "" Then
            If AccountNumberTextBox.Text <> "" Then
                ' Declare and instantiate a new Client.
                'AClient = New Client(Of Long)(NameTextBox.Text, _
                '  PhoneNumberTextBox.Text, _
                '  Long.Parse(AccountNumberTextBox.Text))
                AClient = New Client(Of String)(NameTextBox.Text, _
                  PhoneNumberTextBox.Text, AccountNumberTextBox.Text)
                ' Add the client to the list box.
                ClientsListBox.Items.Add(AClient)
                ' Display the count.
                CountLabel.Text = ClientsListBox.Items.Count.ToString
                ' Clear the text boxes.
                With NameTextBox
                    .Clear()
                    .Focus()
                End With
                PhoneNumberTextBox.Clear()
                AccountNumberTextBox.Clear()
            Else
                ' Missing account number.
                MessageBox.Show("Please enter the account number.", _
                  "Clients", MessageBoxButtons.OK, _
                  MessageBoxIcon.Exclamation)
                AccountNumberTextBox.Focus()
            End If
        Else
            ' Missing name.
            MessageBox.Show("Please enter a name.", "Clients", _
              MessageBoxButtons.OK, MessageBoxIcon.Exclamation)
            NameTextBox.Focus()
        End If
    End Sub

    Private Sub RemoveButton_Click(ByVal sender As System.Object, _
      ByVal e As System.EventArgs) Handles RemoveButton.Click
        ' Remove the selected client from the collection.

        With ClientsListBox
            If .SelectedIndex <> -1 Then
                ' Remove the Client object from the listbox.
                .Items.RemoveAt(.SelectedIndex)
                CountLabel.Text = .Items.Count.ToString
```

```vbnet
            Else
                ' No selection made from the list.
                MessageBox.Show("Select an item from the list.", "Clients", _
                    MessageBoxButtons.OK, MessageBoxIcon.Exclamation)
            End If
        End With
    End Sub

    Private Sub DisplayButton_Click(ByVal sender As System.Object, _
      ByVal e As System.EventArgs) Handles DisplayButton.Click
        ' Dim AClient As Client(Of Long)
        Dim AClient As Client(Of String)
        Dim InfoString As String

        ' Display the information for one client.

        With ClientsListBox
            If .SelectedIndex <> -1 Then
                ' Retrieve the selected Client object from the list.
                ' AClient = CType(.Items(.SelectedIndex), Client(Of Long))
                AClient = CType(.Items(.SelectedIndex), Client(Of String))
                InfoString = "Client:    " & AClient.Name & _
                    ControlChars.NewLine & _
                    "Account Number: " & AClient.AccountNumber & _
                    ControlChars.NewLine & _
                    "Phone Number:    " & AClient.PhoneNumber
                MessageBox.Show(InfoString, "Selected Client Information", _
                    MessageBoxButtons.OK, MessageBoxIcon.Information)
            Else
                ' No selection made from the list.
                MessageBox.Show("Select a client name from the list.", _
                    "Clients", MessageBoxButtons.OK, MessageBoxIcon.Exclamation)
            End If
        End With
    End Sub
End Class
```

The Client Class

```vbnet
'Project:       Ch10HandsOn
'Class:         Client
'Programmer:    Bradley/Millspaugh/Price
'Date:          June 2009
'Description:   Create a client object using generics.

Public Class Client(Of GenericType)
    ' Private class-level variables.
    Private NameString As String
    Private PhoneNumberString As String
    Private AccountNumberType As GenericType

    Public Property Name() As String
        Get
            Return NameString
        End Get
        Set(ByVal Value As String)
            NameString = Value
        End Set
    End Property
```

```
    Public Property PhoneNumber() As String
        Get
            Return PhoneNumberString
        End Get
        Set(ByVal Value As String)
            PhoneNumberString = Value
        End Set
    End Property

    Public Property AccountNumber() As GenericType
        Get
            Return AccountNumberType
        End Get
        Set(ByVal Value As GenericType)
            AccountNumberType = Value
        End Set
    End Property

    Public Sub New(ByVal NameString As String, _
      ByVal PhoneNumberString As String, _
      ByVal AccountNumberType As GenericType)
        ' Set the properties of a newly instantiated Client object.

        Name = NameString
        PhoneNumber = PhoneNumberString
        AccountNumber = AccountNumberType
    End Sub

    Public Overrides Function ToString() As String
        ' Return the Name property for this object's ToString method.

        Return NameString
    End Function
End Class
```

Summary

1. Items in a collection may be referenced by their key, their value, or their index, depending on the type of collection.
2. The .NET System.Collections namespace contains several types of collection classes with differing characteristics, advantages, and disadvantages.
3. A queue is first-in, first-out (FIFO); stacks are last-in, first-out (LIFO).
4. A dictionary style of list contains key and value pairs; examples include the hash table and the sorted list.
5. Stacks use `Push` and `Pop` for adding to and removing from a collection; queues use `Enqueue` and `Dequeue` for adding and removing. Both have a `Peek` method to allow you to view the next element without removing it.
6. A hash table is a dictionary-type collection and is the quickest list type for searching. The keys of hash tables may be based on a hash code of some unique value. Use the `Add` and `Remove` methods for hash tables.
7. A sorted list is a dictionary-type collection that you can access by key, value, or index. Use the `Add`, `Remove`, and `RemoveAt` methods for adding and removing items. The keys must be unique and may be based on hash codes.
8. An ArrayList can be resized at run time. This collection type has many useful methods that can simplify array handling.

9. An element of the Items collection of a dictionary-type collection has a data type of DictionaryEntry.
10. `For Each / Next` loops are used to iterate through a collection.
11. You can add objects to the Items collection of a list box or combo box; the list displays the value returned by the object's `ToString` method. You can retrieve a selected object from the list and access the individual properties of the object by casting the Item property from a DictionaryEntry to an object of the correct type.
12. Generics provide a way to define strongly typed procedures or classes where the object type is not declared until you use the procedure or instantiate the class.
13. VS includes several types of predefined generic collections.

Key Terms

Capacity property *440*	hash table *435*
collection *432*	Items collection *446*
data structure *432*	LIFO *432*
`Dequeue` method *434*	list *432*
dictionary *433*	`Peek` method *434*
DictionaryEntry data type *442*	`Pop` method *434*
`Enqueue` method *434*	`Push` method *434*
FIFO *432*	queue *432*
generic classes *450*	stack *432*
generic collections *452*	System.Collections namespace *432*
generics *449*	`TrimToSize` method *440*

Review Questions

1. Describe each of the following collection styles:
   a. Dictionary
   b. Hash table
   c. Stack
   d. Queue
   e. Sorted list
2. What is an ArrayList?
3. What are the advantages of using a collection instead of an array?
4. What are the advantages of using a hash table over a sorted list? the disadvantages?
5. What is the data type of an item from the Items collection of a dictionary-type collection?
6. What displays in a list box or combo box if you add an object to the list?
7. What are generics? Give an example of how generics can be used.
8. How is a generic collection more useful than a regular collection?

Programming Exercises

10.1 Create a project that maintains a collection of vendors. Each vendor should have properties for company name, phone, contact person, and e-mail. Allow the user to add a vendor, display the list of vendors, display a single vendor, or remove a vendor. Display the vendor names in a list box. As each vendor is added to the collection, add the name to the list. When a vendor is removed from the collection, remove the name from the list. Allow the user to select a vendor from the list and display the vendor's properties in a message box. Use a hash code of the company name for the key.

10.2 Following the specifications for Exercise 10.1, use the Items collection of a ListBox to store the Vendor objects. Override the `ToString` method to allow the name of the vendor to display in the ListBox.

10.3 Write an application that maintains a collection of customers. Each Customer object should have properties for Last Name, First Name, PIN (the key), Phone Number, Cell Phone Number, and FAX Number. The user can add customers, remove customers, and display the complete information for a selected customer. Store the concatenated first and last names in a list box, to show the current contents of the collection and allow the user to select a customer to remove or display.

Display the customer information in a message box, or consider using a second form. If you use a second form, you will need to create a property of the form that holds a Customer object so you can pass the selected object to the form.

10.4 Following the specifications for Exercise 10.3, use the Items collection of a ListBox to store the Customer objects. Override the `ToString` method to use the Last Name and First Name (i.e., Doe, Jane), which will display in the ListBox.

10.5 Expand either Exercise 10.1 or 10.2 to use generics in the Vendor class. In your code, demonstrate that you can instantiate it using different data types.

10.6 Expand either Exercise 10.3 or 10.4 to use generics in the Customer class. In your code, demonstrate that you can instantiate it using different data types.

Case Studies

Claytor's Cottages

Create a project that maintains a generic collection of customers. Each Customer object should contain Customer Name, Customer Number (key if a collection is used), and Phone Number. Allow options for adding and removing objects. Use a list box to display the customer names, giving the user the option to display a selected customer.

Christian's Car Rentals

Create a project that maintains a generic collection of advertisers. Each Advertiser object should contain Company Name, Number (key if a collection is used), and Account Representative's Name. Allow options for adding and removing Advertiser objects. Use a list box to display the company name, giving the user the option to display a selected advertiser.

11

User Controls

at the completion of this chapter, you will be able to . . .

1. Create a Windows user control using inheritance from an existing control type.

2. Add a new user control to a form.

3. Add properties to a user control.

4. Raise an event in a control class and write code to handle the event in a form.

5. Create a new composite control by combining preexisting controls.

6. Create a Web user control and add it to a Web page.

You can create your own controls to use on Windows Forms or Web Forms. You may want to modify or combine existing controls, called **user controls**, or write your own controls from scratch, called *custom controls*. Because of the object-oriented nature of .NET, you can inherit from existing controls and modify their behavior, such as creating a text box with validation or a self-loading list box.

This chapter shows you how to create user controls for both Windows and the Web. Just as for built-in controls, Windows controls are completely different from Web controls, so they are covered in separate sections of the chapter.

Windows User Controls

When you want to modify the behavior of an existing control or combine controls to use in multiple situations, you can create your own user control. Sometimes you find yourself using a certain set of controls in many situations, such as text boxes for name and address, or maybe a combination of text and graphics for a company logo. You can create your own user control that is made up of the individual controls. The new user control is called a **composite control**, and the controls that you combine are called **constituent controls**. You can add the new user control to the toolbox and use it in other Windows projects.

In VB you can inherit a new control from an existing control. The first example in this chapter uses inheritance to create a new control, and later you will create a composite control.

The Control Author versus the Developer

The distinction between a control's author and the **developer** who uses the control is much more important with user controls than any of the other project types. The **author** creates the control (and tests and compiles it) and the control appears in the toolbox. When you author a control, you must plan for the design-time behavior of your control as well as its run-time behavior.

Creating a New Control

Generally you create a new control by beginning a new project based on the Windows Forms Control Library template. The controls that you create in this type of project can be used in multiple Windows projects. You also can choose to add a new UserControl to an existing project, which is the technique that you use if you want to use the control in only the current project. In both techniques, the new UserControl object appears as a design surface, similar to a form, in a Designer window (Figure 11.1).

Note: The Windows Forms Control Library template is not available in the Express Edition of Visual Basic.

You design the visual interface for a composite control in the Designer window by dragging the constituent controls to the design surface. For an inherited control, you do not see the visual representation of your control in the designer; instead you use the designer to add nonvisual components.

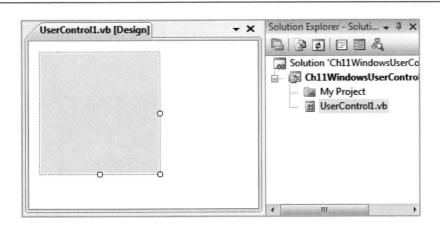

Figure 11.1

Use the design surface of a UserControl to create a new user control.

In the Code Editor window, you can view and modify the class that is created for the control. The class automatically inherits from the UserControl class, which you can see in the UserControl.Designer.vb file.

Inheriting from an Existing Control

The easiest way to create a user control is to inherit from an existing control. You can inherit from most of the Windows Forms controls except the Progress Bar. For example, you can create your own Label control that has the font, size, color, and text alignment set as you want it; or create a new TextBox control that validates in a certain way, that only accepts numeric keystrokes, always selects the entry when it gets the focus, or has a particular font or alignment. Your new control will have all of the properties, methods, and events of the base class, unless you write code to override the behaviors. And you can add new properties, methods, and events for your derived control.

To create your customized control, follow these general steps. The step-by-step exercise that follows gives the detailed instructions.

- Create a project based on the Windows Forms Control Library template.

- Modify the class name and the `Inherits` clause in the Designer.vb file to inherit from the base class that you want to use, such as TextBox, Label, or Button.

- Add any additional functionality that you want.

- Build the DLL. After you create the DLL, you will need to create a Windows project to test the new control.

Creating an Inherited User Control—Step-by-Step

In this step-by-step exercise, you will create a new UserControl that inherits from a TextBox control. The new control, called ValidDateTextBox, will look exactly like all other text boxes, but it will validate the entry for a valid date in the control's Validating event handler. If the entry is not a valid date, it will appear highlighted (selected) and the Cancel argument is set to *true*, so that the focus remains in the control. This essentially forces the user to fix the entry before moving to the next control. Later you will learn to raise an event for invalid entries, for which you can write code in the form. You should *not* display a message box to the user from the control; that task should be left to the form's code.

Create a New Project

STEP 1: Begin a new Windows project called *Ch11ValidDate* using the Windows Forms Control Library template (Figure 11.2).

Figure 11.2

Create a new project using the Windows Forms Control Library template.

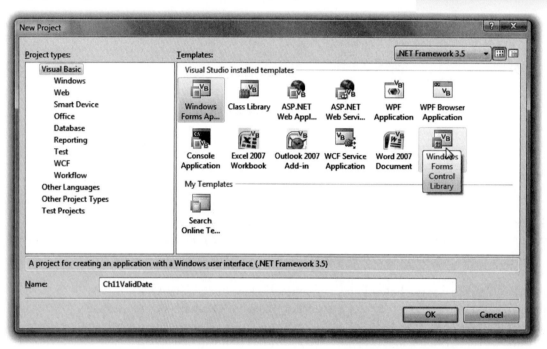

STEP 2: Save all and make sure to check the check box for *Create directory for solution*. This solution will have multiple projects.

STEP 3: Name the file for the new control *ValidDateTextBox.vb* (Figure 11.3).

Figure 11.3

Add a new UserControl called ValidDateTextBox.vb.

STEP 4: Change the Name property in the Properties window to "ValidDate-TextBox".

STEP 5: Close the Designer window. Show all files and open the ValidDate-TextBox.Designer.vb file in the Editor window. Check the class name and modify the `Inherits` clause to inherit from TextBox instead of UserControl:

☑**TIP**

Keep the control's Designer window closed at all times unless you need to add a component, and then close it again. Having the Designer window open when you compile can cause the control to not compile correctly and may remove it from the toolbox. ∎

```
Partial Class ValidDateTextBox
    Inherits System.Windows.Forms.TextBox
```

STEP 6: Delete the `Me.AutoScaleMode` statement in the InitializeComponent sub procedure. A TextBox control does not have autoscaling.

STEP 7: Close the Editor window for ValidDateTextBox.Designer.vb and save all.

STEP 8: Open the ValidDateTextBox.vb file in the editor and add opening comments.

```
'Project:        Ch11ValidDate
'Programmer:     Your Name
'Date:           Today's date
'Description:    An inherited user control to extend the functionality of
'                a text box. Checks for a valid date format.
```

Add an Event Handler

STEP 1: Drop down the *Class* list and select *(ValidDateTextBox Events)*. This step gives you access to all of the events for the TextBox class. Alternately, you can click the *Events* button in the Properties window.

STEP 2: From the *Events* list, select *Validating*.

STEP 3: Type the code to test for a valid date. The code tests for a valid date; if the date is invalid, it highlights the text and keeps the focus in the field. Notice that you use the `Me` keyword to refer to the current class, or this control itself.

```
Private Sub ValidDateTextBox_Validating(ByVal sender As Object, _
    ByVal e As System.ComponentModel.CancelEventArgs) _
    Handles MyBase.Validating
      ' Test for a valid date.
      Dim TestDate As Date

      If Not DateTime.TryParse(Me.Text, TestDate) Then
          Me.SelectAll()
          e.Cancel = True
      End If
End Sub
```

Build the Project

STEP 1: Build the solution. This step should place .dll, .xml, and .pdb files in the project's bin\Debug or bin\Release folder. You can choose *Show All Files* to see these files. The .dll file holds the new control; the .xml file holds configuration information; and the .pdb file holds debugging information. For production jobs, when debugging is complete, you no longer create or need debugging files.

Test the User Control in a Form

To test the control, you need a form. Although you can create a new solution, the easiest method is to add another project to this solution.

STEP 1: From the *File* menu, select *Add / New Project* and make sure to change the selected template to *Windows Forms Application*. (*Alternative*: Right-click the solution in the Solution Explorer and select *Add / New Project*.)

STEP 2: Name the new project *Ch11TestUserControl* and browse to create the project in the same solution as the user control. Note that it isn't necessary to place the two projects in the same solution but doing so makes your project more portable.

STEP 3: Name the form file *TestDateForm.vb*.

STEP 4: Right-click on the Ch11TestUserControl project in the Solution Explorer and set it as the startup project.

STEP 5: Set the Text property of the form to "Test ValidDateTextBox Control".

Note: Later in the chapter, we will discuss accessing the control from a separate solution.

Add Controls to the Form

The new user control appears in the *Ch11ValidDate Components* section of the toolbox (Figure 11.4).

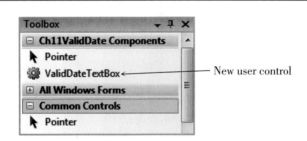 — New user control

Figure 11.4

The new user control appears in the toolbox.

STEP 1: Add two labels, a ValidDateTextBox control, and a text box to the form, changing the following properties. Figure 11.5 shows the completed form.

Control	Property	Setting
Label1	Text	&Date
Label2	Text	&Name
ValidDateTextBox1	Name	HireDateValidDateTextBox
TextBox1	Name	NameTextBox

✓ TIP

Specify a bitmap to be displayed in the toolbox by adding the ToolBox-BitmapAttribute. For example,

```
<ToolboxBitmap("C:\" & _
  "Ch11ValidDate\" & _
  "ToolBoxImage.bmp")> _
  Public Class _
  ValidDateTextBox
```

Figure 11.5

The completed form to test the ValidDateTextBox control.

Run the Project

STEP 1: Run the project. Your form should appear.

STEP 2: Type in some bad data in the Date text box and press the Tab key. The text should appear highlighted and the focus should remain in the control. Try various good and bad data and tab to the next control.

STEP 3: Close the form.

> *Note*: If the control contains bad data, you won't be able to close the form using the Close box. Enter good data in the text box or return to the VS IDE and click the *Stop Debugging* button.

If you change the name of your user control, you must rebuild the project, close the solution, and reopen to update the toolbox. ■

Adding Properties to a Control

You can set up new properties of a control class, just as you do for other classes. Declare a module-level private variable to hold the property and create Property procedures. The properties that you create for a control class appear in the Properties window when the developer adds an instance of the control to a form.

Setting Default Values for Properties

You can set a property variable to an initial value, which gives the property a default value. When the developer adds an instance of the control to a form, the default value appears in the Properties window. If the developer changes the value of the property, the new value is retained in the property. That is, the control is initialized only once, when it is added to the form. Any changes made at design time are retained. This behavior matches the design-time behavior of all controls that you add to a form.

If you create a ReadOnly property, the developer cannot change its value. However, the code for the control can change the value.

You cannot name a property procedure and a private variable with the same name. ■

Add Two Properties to the Control

STEP 1: Open ValidDateTextBox.vb in the editor and add code for Minimum-Date and MaximumDate properties. By performing validation in the Property procedure, you can prevent the developer from setting an invalid date in the Properties window.

```
' Store the property values.
Private MinDate As Date = Now.Date
Private MaxDate As Date = Now.Date.AddYears(1)

Public Property MaximumDate() As Date
    Get
        Return MaxDate
    End Get
    Set(ByVal value As Date)
        ' Make sure that the MaximumDate property is set.
        If value >= MinDate Then
            MaxDate = value
        Else
            Throw New ArgumentOutOfRangeException("MaximumDate", _
                "The maximum date must be greater than the minimum date.")
        End If
    End Set
End Property
```

```
Public ReadOnly Property MinimumDate() As Date
    Get
        Return MinDate
    End Get
End Property
```

After you rebuild the project, the new properties are automatically exposed to the developer in the Properties window. Read-only properties appear grayed and are available only in code (Figure 11.6).

Figure 11.6

The new MaximumDate and MinimumDate properties appear in the Properties window. The read-only MinimumDate property is grayed.

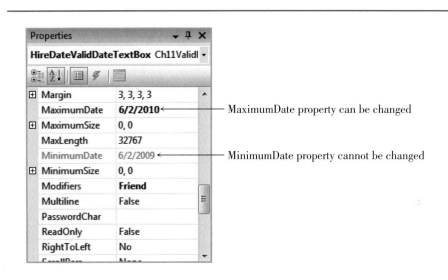

MaximumDate property can be changed

MinimumDate property cannot be changed

Adding Events to a Control

Most objects can generate events, also called *raising events* or *firing events*. The controls on the user interface raise events, such as Click, DoubleClick, MouseUp, and Move. The form (the container of the control) can respond to each event with code, or ignore an event. Events are often caused by user action, such as a click or mouse move, but some events are generated by the system, such as a timer firing or events such as Form_Load.

The objects that you create from your classes or user controls can generate events; the form can respond to those events (or ignore them). For example, if a condition exists in an object and the user should be notified, your object *should not* display a message to the user; the user interface must display the message. Your object must either raise an event or throw an exception, to which the form module can respond.

First, we need a little terminology: An object that generates or raises an event is called the **event source** or the **event provider**. The object that responds to an event is called an **event sink** or an **event consumer**. For example, when the user clicks a command button and the form's OkButton_Click event handler executes, the command button is the event source and the form is the event sink.

Raising Events

Two things are needed for your control class to generate events:

1. Declare the event in the Declaration section of the class, including any arguments that you intend to pass.

```
Public Event InvalidDate(ByVal Message As String)
```

2. Raise the event in code. When a condition occurs that should trigger the event, use the RaiseEvent statement.

```
If Not DateTime.TryParse(Me.Text, TestDate) Then
    ' Invalid date format, raise an event.
    RaiseEvent InvalidDate("Invalid date.")
End If
```

The Event and RaiseEvent Statements—General Form

```
[Public] Event EventName([Arguments])
RaiseEvent EventName[(Arguments)]
```

An **Event statement** must appear at the module level and is public by default.

The Event and RaiseEvent Statements—Examples

```
' Module-level declarations.
Event QuantityBelowReorderPoint(BelowQuantityInteger As Integer)
' In program logic.
RaiseEvent QuantityBelowReorderPoint(QuantityInteger)

' Module-level declarations.
Event TaskComplete()
' In program logic.
RaiseEvent TaskComplete
```

The **RaiseEvent statement** must appear in the same class as the Event declaration.

Responding to Events

Any class can be an event sink and respond to the events raised by your event source. You, as the application developer, can write code to respond to the control's events. After you add a user control to a form, the new event will be available. Drop down the *Methods* list in the Editor window and your event will appear on the list. You can select the event to create the code template (Sub and End Sub statements) for the event handler and write the code that you want to execute when the event fires.

```
Private Sub HireDateValidDateTextBox_InvalidDate(ByVal Message As String) _
  Handles HireDateValidDateTextBox.InvalidDate
    ' Display the validation error message.

    MessageBox.Show(Message)
End Sub
```

For this example, the form responds to the event by displaying a message to the user. Remember, the user interface should handle all interaction with the user—the control should never display messages.

Putting It All Together

Now that you have seen the individual elements of creating properties and generating events, it's time to put it all together. This code shows the completed control that you began in the step-by-step exercise. The ValidDate control tests for a valid date format as well as a date within the selected range: between the MinimumDate and MaximumDate properties. If the Text property fails either test, an event is raised, with an appropriate error message.

The User Control

```
'Project:      Ch11ValidDate
'Module:       ValidDateTextBox.vb
'Programmer:   Bradley/Millspaugh
'Date:         June 2009
'Description:  An inherited user control to extend the functionality of
'              a text box. Validates for a valid date format and
'              validates for a valid date entry within a given range.

Public Class ValidDateTextBox
    ' Module-level declarations.

    ' Declare the event.
    Public Event InvalidDate(ByVal Message As String)

    ' Store the property values.
    '   Initial values provide the default values that appear in
    '   the Properties window for the control.
    Private MinDate As Date = Now.Date
    Private MaxDate As Date = Now.Date.AddYears(1)

    Private Sub ValidDateTextBox_Validating(ByVal sender As Object, _
        ByVal e As System.ComponentModel.CancelEventArgs) _
        Handles Me.Validating
        ' Test for a valid date.
        Dim TestDate As Date

        If Not Date.TryParse(Me.Text, TestDate) Then
            ' Invalid date format; raise an event.
            RaiseEvent InvalidDate("Invalid date.")
            Me.SelectAll()
            e.Cancel = True
        Else
            ' Check the date range.
            If TestDate < MinDate Or TestDate > MaxDate Then
                RaiseEvent InvalidDate("Date out of range.")
                Me.SelectAll()
                e.Cancel = True
            End If
        End If
    End Sub

    Public Property MaximumDate() As Date
        Get
            ' Make sure that the MaximumDate property is set.
            If value >= MinDate Then
                MaxDate = value
```

```
                Else
                    Throw New ArgumentOutOfRangeException("MaximumDate", _
                        "The maximum date must be greater than the minimum date.")
                End If
            End Get
            Set(ByVal value As Date)
                MaxDate = value
            End Set
        End Property

        Public ReadOnly Property MinimumDate() As Date
            Get
                Return MinDate
            End Get
        End Property
End Class
```

The Form for Testing the User Control

```
'Project:      Ch11TestUserControl
'Programmer:   Bradley/Millspaugh
'Date:         June 2009
'Description:  Test the ValidDateTextBox user control, which extends
'              the functionality of a text box to validate for a valid
'              date entry within a given range.

Public Class TestDateForm

    Private Sub HireDateValidDateTextBox_InvalidDate(ByVal Message As String) _
        Handles HireDateValidDateTextBox.InvalidDate
        ' Display the validation error message.

        With HireDateValidDateTextBox
            MessageBox.Show(Message & " Range: " & _
                .MinimumDate.ToShortDateString() & " to " & _
                .MaximumDate.ToShortDateString(),"Invalid date")
        End With
    End Sub

    Private Sub TestDateForm_FormClosing(ByVal sender As Object, _
        ByVal e As System.Windows.Forms.FormClosingEventArgs) _
        Handles Me.FormClosing
        ' Cancel date validation if the form is closing.

        e.Cancel = False
    End Sub
End Class
```

Creating a Composite User Control

Another common reason for creating a user control is to combine multiple controls into a single user control. You may want to do this to avoid adding the same type of labels and text boxes repeatedly or perhaps you have a consistent combination of company logo and sign-in boxes for multiple forms.

This example creates a new composite control that combines the ValidDateTextBox control with a label. The label will have a default Text property that can be modified by the application developer.

Create a New Composite User Control

The steps for creating the composite control are similar to those already covered. Begin a new Windows project based on the Windows Forms Control Library template but do not change the inheritance; leave it as a UserControl. You will use the control's visual designer (Figure 11.7), which you can treat just like a form. It is a container that can contain as many controls as you need. You can name the constituent controls and refer to them as you would in any application.

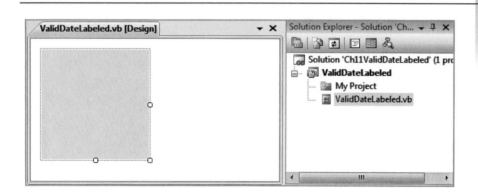

Adding a Control to the Toolbox

Controls that have already been developed are not automatically added to the toolbox, but it's easy to add them yourself. In this case, we are beginning a new project to create a new user control that has our ValidDateTextBox control as one of the constituent controls, so ValidDateTextBox must be added to the toolbox. First select the tab of the toolbox that you want to use, then right-click on the toolbox and select *Choose Items*. In the *Choose Toolbox Items* dialog box (Figure 11.8) on the *.NET Framework Components* tab, click on the *Browse* button. Browse to find your control's .dll file in its bin\Debug (or bin\Release) folder and select it; the control will then appear selected on the *.NET Framework Components* tab. When you close the dialog box, the control appears in the toolbox (Figure 11.9).

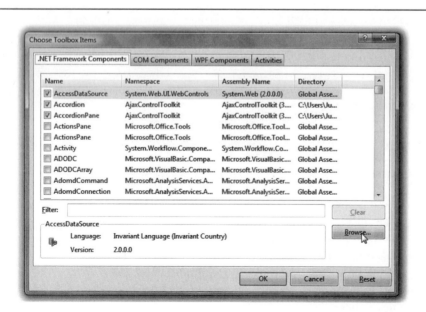

Figure 11.9

You can use the *Choose Toolbox Items* dialog box to add many other controls. Any controls that you add will appear on the toolbox tab that is active at the time of the addition.

Adding Constituent Controls

You can add any controls or components from the toolbox to the design surface of your composite control. Figure 11.10 shows adding a label and a ValidDate-TextBox control. Notice also that the label's Text property has been set to a default value and the text alignment has been changed from the default.

Usually it's best to resize the composite control to not have extra space around the edges (Figure 11.11). Also, if you set the constituent controls to anchor to all four edges of the user control, the interior controls will resize when the developer resizes the user control. Otherwise, the sizes of the interior controls will remain fixed when the composite control is resized in the final application.

Figure 11.10

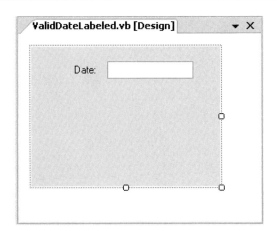

Figure 11.11

Resize the composite control to remove the extra space around the edge and anchor the constituent controls to all four edges of the control.

Exposing Properties of Constituent Controls

The properties of the constituent controls are available inside the composite control, but not to the application developer. You, as the control author, determine which properties of the constituent controls to expose to the application developer.

In the example shown in Figures 11.9 and 11.10, you want to allow the developer to modify the Text property of the label and the Text property of the ValidDateTextBox control. So, in this case, we'll create new properties called LabelText and DateText that will be tied to the Text properties of the constituent controls. For the LabelText property, we'll give it a default value of "Date: ". For the DateText property, we will allow it to default to an empty string.

```
'Project:        Ch11ValidDateLabeled
'Programmer:     Bradley/Millspaugh
'Date:           June 2009
'Description:    A composite user control that combines a ValidDate control
'                and a label.

Public Class ValidDateLabeled
    ' Composite user control properties.
    Private DateString As String
    Private LabelTextString As String = "Date: "  ' Default value.

    ' Declare the event.
    Public Event InvalidDate(ByVal Message As String)

    Property DateText() As String
        Get
            Return DateString
        End Get
        Set(ByVal Value As String)
            DateString = value
            ValidDateTextBox1.Text = DateString
        End Set
    End Property

    Property LabelText() As String
        Get
            Return LabelTextString
        End Get
        Set(ByVal Value As String)
            LabelTextString = Value
            DateLabel.Text = LabelTextString
            ' Move the text box 4 pixels to the right of the label.
            ValidDateTextBox1.Left = DateLabel.Right + 4
        End Set
    End Property
```

```
      Private Sub ValidDateTextBox1_InvalidDate(ByVal Message As String) _
         Handles ValidDateTextBox1.InvalidDate
            ' Pass the event up to the calling class.

            Message &= " Date range: " & ValidDateTextBox1.MinimumDate & " to " & _
               ValidDateTextBox1.MaximumDate
            RaiseEvent InvalidDate(Message)
      End Sub
End Class
```

Notice the `Property Set` procedure for the LabelText property in the preceding code. If not for the following code (also shown in the code above), which moves the text box four pixels to the right of the label each time the Text property of the label changes, when the developer changes the label's Text property, the label could overlap the ValidDateTextBox:

```
' Move the text box 4 pixels to the right of the label.
ValidDateTextBox1.Left = DateLabel.Right + 4
```

Exposing the Events of the Constituent Controls

Any events of the constituent controls are available in the code of the composite control, but the events are not available to the form on which the control is placed. If you want the events of the control to be available, you must declare the event in the composite control and pass the event along.

```
' Declare the event at the module level.
Public Event InvalidDate(ByVal Message As String)
```

Write code in the event handler for the constituent control. You can simply raise the event or write additional code. In the following example for ValidDateLabeled, the message is expanded upon to display the valid date range.

```
Private Sub ValidDateTextBox1_InvalidDate(ByVal Message As String) _
   Handles ValidDateTextBox1.InvalidDate
      ' Pass the event up to the calling class.

      Message &= " Date range: " & ValidDateTextBox1.MinimumDate & " to " & _
         ValidDateTextBox1.MaximumDate
      RaiseEvent InvalidDate(Message)
End Sub
```

Using the Composite Control

After you create the composite control, you can test it in a form, in the same way that you tested the inherited control. Add a new project for the test form, add a reference to the project that holds the composite control, and add the control to the form. If the new control does not appear in the toolbox, use the *Choose Items* command, as described earlier.

As you test the new control, you may decide to make modifications to the user control. Make sure to close the user control's designer before rebuilding. Rebuild the solution and re-add the control to the form to get the updated control.

> ## Feedback 11.1

1. Write the statements necessary to raise an event called WillSoundAlarm in a class module. Where will each statement appear?
2. What steps are necessary to respond to the WillSoundAlarm event in a form, assuming that the associated control is called Alarm?

Web User Controls

Web user controls work differently from Windows user controls. You can think of a Web user control as a "mini-page" that you can display on many other pages. You can create reusable pieces of your interface that contain HTML controls, server controls, and any needed code in a code-behind module. You create the user control and drag it to one or more Web pages. Create Web user controls by creating a project using the ASP.NET Web Site template and then adding a WebUserControl to the project.

You have undoubtedly seen several controls for credit card information on Web sites with a shopping cart. The following example creates a Web User Control that contains drop-down lists for the type of card, the expiration month, and expiration year as well as a text box for the card number.

Creating a Web User Control—Step-by-Step

Create the Project

STEP 1: Open a new Web site project using the ASP.NET Web Site template and name it *Ch11WebUserControls*.

STEP 2: From the *Website* menu, select *Add New Item* and select the Web User Control template. Name the control *CreditCardWebUserControl* and click *Add*.

   If the *Source* tab is displaying, click on the *Design* tab.

Design the User Interface

STEP 1: Type "Card Type: " and press the spacebar about five times.

STEP 2: Add a drop-down list. Click on *Edit Items* in the smart tag and add items in the ListItem Collection Editor (Figure 11.12). Add the credit card types: Mastercard, Visa, American Express, and Discover.

STEP 3: Name the control CardTypeDropDownList.

STEP 4: Press Enter to go the next line and type "Expiration Month: ".

STEP 5: Add a drop-down list that contains the numbers 1 to 12. Name the list ExpirationMonthDropDownList.

STEP 6: Type "Year: " and add a drop-down list named YearDropDownList.

STEP 7: In the Page_Load event handler, type the code to fill the drop-down list.

```
Dim ThisYear as Integer = Now.Year
For CountInteger As Integer = 0 to 9
    YearDropDownList.Items.Add(ThisYear + CountInteger)
Next
```

Figure 11.12

Add the credit card types in the ListItem Collection Editor. Click the Add button and type the text value in the Text property of each item.

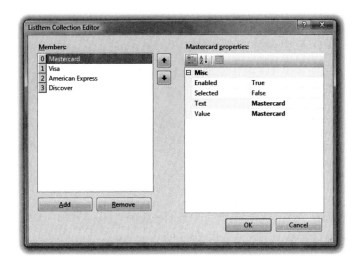

STEP 8: On the user interface, press Enter to go to the next line.

STEP 9: Add the text "Card Number: " and a text box called CardNumber-TextBox.

Expose Properties of the Control

To allow the Web page to retrieve the values that the user enters, you must set up properties of the user control. You can make the properties read only, unless the Web page must be able to set initial values.

When the value from a control holds the property, it isn't necessary to declare module-level variables to hold the property values.

STEP 1: Add the property procedures for CreditCardType, ExpirationMonth, ExpirationYear, and CreditCardNumber.

```
ReadOnly Property CreditCardType() As String
    Get
        If CardTypeDropDownList.SelectedIndex <> -1 Then
            Return CardTypeDropDownList.SelectedItem.ToString
        Else
            Return String.Empty
        End If
    End Get
End Property

ReadOnly Property ExpirationMonth() As String
    Get
        If ExpirationMonthDropDownList.SelectedIndex <> -1 Then
            Return ExpirationMonthDropDownList.SelectedValue
        Else
            Return String.Empty
        End If
    End Get
End Property

ReadOnly Property ExpirationYear() As String
    Get
        If YearDropDownList.SelectedIndex <> -1 Then
            Return YearDropDownList.SelectedValue
```

```
                  Else
                        Return String.Empty
                  End If
            End Get
      End Property

      ReadOnly Property CreditCardNumber() As String
            Get
                  Return CardNumberTextBox.Text
            End Get
      End Property
```

Compile the Control

STEP 1: Build the solution.

Test the Control

STEP 1: Switch to Default.aspx.

STEP 2: Drag the user control file, CreditCardWebUserControl.ascx, from the Solution Explorer to the form's design surface (Figure 11.13).

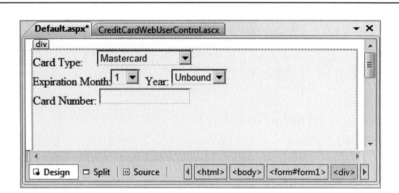

Figure 11.13

Drag the user control to the Web page.

STEP 3: Run the project. You can test the user interface, but to use the property values, you must write some code.

STEP 4: To retrieve and display the values entered into the constituent controls of the user control, add a button and a large label to the form. Of course, in an application, you would retrieve the properties for further processing. Name the button SubmitButton and the label DisplayLabel.

```
Protected Sub SubmitButton_Click(ByVal sender As Object, _
   ByVal e As System.EventArgs) Handles SubmitButton.Click
      ' Check the values in the control properties.

      DisplayLabel.Text = "Card type: " & _
         CreditCardWebUserControl1.CreditCardType & _
         "<br>Exp. Month: " & _
         CreditCardWebUserControl1.ExpirationMonth & _
         "<br>Exp. Year: " & _
         CreditCardWebUserControl1.ExpirationYear & _
         "<br>Credit Card #: " & _
         CreditCardWebUserControl1.CreditCardNumber.Substring( _
         CreditCardWebUserControl1.CreditCardNumber.Length - 4, 4)
End Sub
```

STEP 5: As a further enhancement, change DisplayLabel.Text to display only the last four digits of the credit card number.

Hint: Use Substring(*StartIndex*,*CharactersToPrint*).

▶ Feedback 11.2

1. Explain how to create a new Web user control.
2. How do you add a Web user control to a form?

Your Hands-On Programming Example

Create a Windows user control that contains the labels and text boxes for data entry of First Name, Last Name, Street Address, City, and State. Use masked text boxes for the ZIP Code and Telephone. Add a project to test the control. For testing purposes, display the values from the controls in a MessageBox from the test form.

This control must make the data entered available to the form, which means that properties must be exposed. The control could either expose each text box as a separate property or create one property that returns a data structure holding all of the values. In this program, we will expose a PersonText property, which is based on a Person structure.

To share a Person structure between the control and the form, make sure that the Person structure is declared as `Public`. You can refer to it by the full namespace such as `Ch11HandsOn.PersonInfo.Person`.

You will declare the Person structure in the user control's module and expose a property based on the structure. The form can declare a variable of type Person to retrieve the property of the control.

Planning the Project

Sketch the control (Figure 11.14) and a form (Figure 11.15) that your users sign off as meeting their needs.

Plan the Objects, Properties, and Methods Plan the objects and properties for the user control and for the form and its controls. Figure 11.16 shows the diagram of the program components.

Figure 11.14

A planning sketch of the user control for the hands-on programming example.

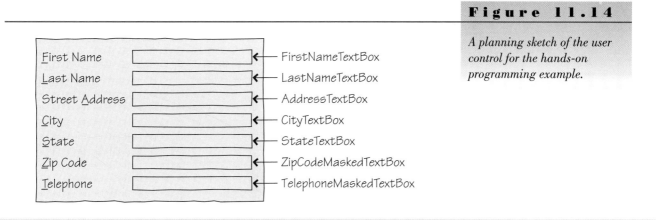

Figure 11.15

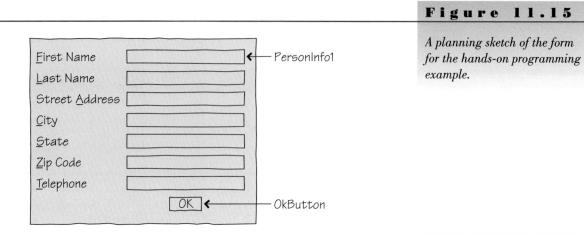

Figure 11.16

The User Control Project

Object	Property	Setting
UserControl	Name	PersonInfo
Label1	Text	&First Name
	TabOrder	0
Label2	Text	&Last Name
	TabOrder	2
Label3	Text	Street &Address
	TabOrder	4
Label4	Text	&City
	TabOrder	6
Label5	Text	&State
	TabOrder	8
Label6	Text	&Zip Code
	TabOrder	10
Label7	Text	&Telephone
	TabOrder	12
FirstNameTextBox	Text	(blank)
	TabOrder	1

LastNameTextBox	Text	(blank)
	TabOrder	3
AddressTextBox	Text	(blank)
	TabOrder	5
CityTextBox	Text	(blank)
	TabOrder	7
StateTextBox	Text	(blank)
	TabOrder	9
ZipCodeMaskedTextBox	Text	(blank)
	Mask	Zip Code
	TabOrder	11
TelephoneMaskedTextBox	Text	(blank)
	Mask	Phone number
	TabOrder	13

Event handlers/methods	Actions—Pseudocode
ReadOnly Property Get PersonText	Set up the Person structure. Return the Person structure.

The Person Structure

Name	Elements
Person	FirstName As String LastName As String Address As String City As String State As String ZIP As String Telephone As String

The Form Project

Object	Property	Setting
DataEntryForm	Name	DataEntryForm
	Text	Consume the User Control
	AcceptButton	OkButton
UserControl	Name	PersonInfo
OkButton	Name	OkButton
	Text	&OK

Event handlers/methods	Actions—Pseudocode
OkButton_Click	Retrieve the PersonText property from the control. Display the fields in a message box.

Write the Project Create the application following the sketches in Figures 11.14 and 11.15. Figure 11.17 shows the completed Windows form.

- Create a project based on the Windows Forms Control Library. Name the project Ch11HandsOn.

- Create and code the control, following your plans.

- Add a Windows project for the form, calling the project Ch11HandsOnApp. Set the properties of each of the form objects, according to your plans.

- Write the code for the form. Working from the pseudocode, write the event handler.

- When you complete the code, test the operation.

Figure 11.17

The completed form for the hands-on programming example.

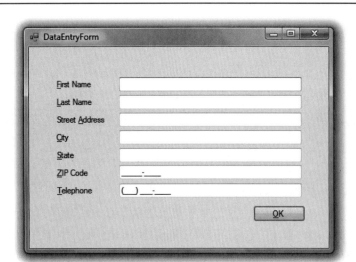

The Project Coding Solution
The PersonInfo User Control

```
'Project:      Ch11HandsOn
'Programmer:   Bradley/Millspaugh
'Module:       PersonInfo
'Date:         June 2009
'Description:  A user control for entering name and address information.

Public Class PersonInfo

    Public Structure Person
        Dim FirstName As String
        Dim LastName As String
        Dim Address As String
        Dim City As String
        Dim State As String
        Dim ZIP As String
        Dim Telephone As String
    End Structure
```

```
      Private APerson As Person

      Public ReadOnly Property PersonText() As Person
          Get
              APerson.FirstName = FirstNameTextBox.Text
              APerson.LastName = LastNameTextBox.Text
              APerson.Address = AddressTextBox.Text
              APerson.City = CityTextBox.Text
              APerson.State = StateTextBox.Text
              APerson.ZIP = ZipCodeMaskedTextBox.Text
              APerson.Telephone = TelephoneMaskedTextBox.Text
              Return APerson
          End Get
      End Property
End Class
```

The Form

```
'Project:      Ch11HandsOn
'Module:       DataEntryForm
'Programmer:   Bradley/Millspaugh
'Date:         June 2009
'Description:  Consume the control for name and address entry.


Public Class DataEntryForm

    Private Sub OkButton_Click(ByVal sender As System.Object, _
      ByVal e As System.EventArgs) Handles OkButton.Click
        ' Retrieve the entered information.

        With PersonInfo1.PersonText
            MessageBox.Show( _
              .FirstName & " " & _
              .LastName & ControlChars.NewLine & _
              .Address & ControlChars.NewLine & _
              .City & ", " & .State & " " & _
              .ZIP & ControlChars.NewLine & _
              .Telephone & ControlChars.NewLine, _
              "Display Entered Information")
        End With

        '' Alternate code, using a Person class.
        'Dim APerson As PersonInfoControl.PersonInfo.Person
        'APerson = PersonInfo1.PersonText
        'With APerson
        '    MessageBox.Show( _
        '      .FirstName & " " & _
        '      .LastName & ControlChars.NewLine & _
        '      .Address & ControlChars.NewLine & _
        '      .City & ", " & .State & " " & _
        '      .ZIP & ControlChars.NewLine & _
        '      .Telephone & ControlChars.NewLine, _
        '      "Display Entered Information")
        'End With
    End Sub
End Class
```

Summary

1. A user control provides the ability to create a composite control consisting of other constituent controls or to inherit and modify the functionality of an existing control type.

2. The control's author and the developer are two distinct roles. The author must plan for the design-time behavior of the control as well as the run-time behavior. The developer uses the controls created by the author.

3. Windows user controls are created by using the Windows Forms Control Library template.

4. To create a new control that inherits from an existing control, modify the `Inherits` clause in the new control's Designer.vb file.

5. Properties are added to user controls in the same fashion as in other classes. The public properties are automatically exposed in the Properties window. Properties may have default values set.

6. It takes two steps to raise events from a user control: (1) Declare the event using the `Event` statement in the Declarations section of the class; (2) fire the event in the program logic using the `RaiseEvent` method.

7. A class that raises an event is called an *event source* or *event provider*; the class that responds to the event is called an *event sink* or *event consumer*.

8. The application developer writes event handlers for the events of user controls in the same fashion as for other control events.

9. Web user controls are created by adding a Web User Control object to an ASP.NET Web application. Create the user control using a Web User Control template. Drag the completed control to the design surface of a Web page.

10. To declare and use a structure or a class in more than one project, make the structure public and give the full namespace when referring to it.

Key Terms

author *466*
composite control *466*
constituent control *466*
developer *466*
event consumer *472*
event provider *472*

event sink *472*
event source *472*
`Event` statement *473*
`RaiseEvent` statement *473*
user control *466*

Review Questions

1. Discuss the differences in the inheritance when creating a composite control compared to expanding the functionality of an existing control.
2. Differentiate between the terms *developer* and *author* when discussing user controls. What different tasks must be done by each?
3. What project type is used when creating a Windows user control?
4. Explain how to expose properties for a user control.
5. What is an event? How is one added to a user control? How is the event accessed and used by the developer?
6. How can a user control be added to a form?
7. How can a Web user control be added to a Web form?

Programming Exercises

11.1 Create a Web user control that has text boxes and labels for

First Name
Last Name
Address
City
State
ZIP Code
E-mail

Expose the fields as properties, either as individual properties or as a single property based on a structure or a class.

Create a Web site for ordering products that uses the control. The Web page also should include text boxes for the ship-to address. Include a check box on the page asking if the shipping address is the same. If the answer is yes, copy the information from the control to the shipping text boxes.

11.2 Create a Windows user control that consists of a text box that accepts only a given range of numeric values. Allow properties to set the minimum and the maximum values. Test the control for the range of 0 to 100 and for 1 to 10. Create a form to test the control's operation.

11.3 Create a Web user control that provides the functions described in Exercise 11.2. Test the control on a Web page.

11.4 Create a Windows user control that allows the user to select dates from two DateTimePicker controls, one for arrival date and one for departure date. Display the number of days between the two dates. Create a form to test the control's operation.

11.5 Create a Web user control that provides the functions described for Exercise 11.4 and test the control on a Web page.

Case Studies

Claytor's Cottages

Create a control that holds a graphic and text for a company logo. Place the control on your About form and at least one other form.

Christian's Car Rentals

Create a control that holds a graphic and text for a company logo. Place the control on your About form and at least one other form.

C H A P T E R

12

Help Files

at the completion of this chapter, you will be able to . . .

1. Create the necessary files to set up HTML Help.

2. Use the HTML Help Workshop to create a Help file with a table of contents, index, and display pages.

3. Connect the Help file to a VB application.

4. Set up and display F1 context-sensitive Help.

5. Display and activate the title bar **Help** button.

6. Add Help references to a MessageBox.

Windows applications support the use of HTML Help files. HTML Help files have a browser look and feel. Using HTML Help you can display Help to your user in several different formats, including a Help facility with topics, an index, and a table of contents. You also can implement context-sensitive Help (F1) and popup Help.

Note: A new SDK (software development kit) is available for Windows Vista Help, but Microsoft currently recommends using the HTML Help 1.4 SDK.

Several companies sell third-party Help authoring tools that can be used for creating Help files for your applications.

HTML Help Workshop

HTML Help Workshop is a separate application from Visual Studio. You use the program to organize and assemble your pages and then compile the various files into one compiled Help file with an extension of .chm.

HTML Help Workshop also includes the Microsoft **HTML Help Image Editor** for creating screen shots and working with images, an HTML editor, and an *HTML Help ActiveX control* that you can use to add navigation to an HTML page. The **Help Viewer** provides a three-paned window for displaying online Help topics, many Help screens, and an extensive reference to HTML tags, attributes, character sets, and style sheets.

The download for HTML Help is at http://msdn.microsoft.com/en-us/library/ms669985(VS.85).aspx. Although the download page indicates it is Htmlhelp 1.4, the install dialogs show 1.3. You can download the HelpDocs.zip further down the same page.

One great feature of HTML Help is that the size of the files is not limited. The Workshop condenses the files as it compiles, reducing storage requirements. Many enhancements have been made to the security for Help files; it is important to have the latest version to minimize security risks.

Setting Up Help

The first step in setting up a Help system is to plan its organization. Decide on the main subject headers and the topics beneath each header. Each page that you display is a separate HTML file, which you organize and connect together using HTML Help Workshop.

A Help Facility

Figure 12.1 shows a Help screen for HTML Help Workshop, which illustrates how your Help pages will appear. The left pane holds tabs for *Contents* and *Index* (also *Search* and *Favorites* tabs, which this chapter doesn't cover). Each of the book icons represents a heading, and each page icon represents an HTML page.

To get a better idea of the look and feel of Help, take a closer look at the *Contents* tab of Visual Studio Help (Figure 12.2), which is just a very large application of Help. Each header can display open or closed. Beneath each header are topics and/or additional headers, creating a hierarchy of headers

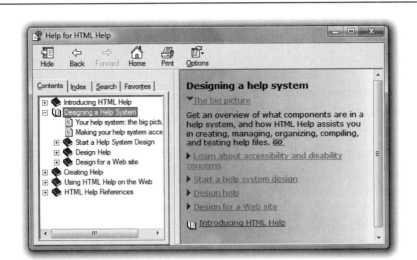

Figure 12.1

A window displaying HTML Help.

Figure 12.2

A screen from Visual Studio Help.

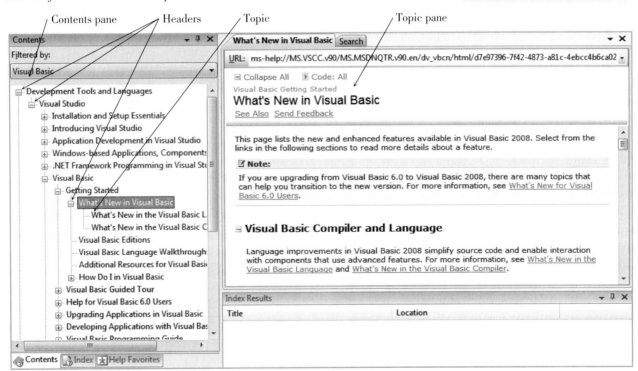

and topics. Notice too that if you select a header and display it in the Contents window, a screen appears that usually has some introductory information and links to the topics beneath the header.

Every screen that displays in the Contents pane is called a ***Help topic*** and is a separate HTML file. So your first step is to design the header pages, topic pages, and any extra pages that you want to display from links. You also may think of Help topics that you want to display only from context-sensitive Help. Plan the links that you want to include on each page before you begin creating the pages. Although you can add links later, you'll save yourself considerable time by entering the links when you create the pages. You must create all of the pages as HTML documents (file extension .htm). You can use Word, Visual Studio, or any HTML editor to create the pages.

Save yourself some trouble and first create a folder for the .htm files. Place any graphics, sounds, and multimedia files that you want to use in the folder. When you create links to any files or other documents, link to the file in the folder but do not include a path as part of the link. For example, if a PageA.htm requires a link to PageB.htm, do not allow the editor to specify "C:\MyProject-Folder\HTMLHelpFiles\PageB.htm". Instead make the link say simply "PageB.htm" (no backslashes). Later you will be able to move or rename the folder without changing the links. And if no path is provided, the current folder is searched first.

This text is not intended to be a tutorial on creating HTML pages. The chapter illustrations assume that you already have created the HTML files.

File Types

An HTML Help project consists of several files. Some you create yourself, using a text editor; others are created as you work in HTML Help Workshop.

File type	File extension	Purpose
Project Header file	.hhp	Holds references to the rest of the files in the project. Similar to the project file in a VB project. The Workshop creates this file when you begin a new project.
Topic files	.htm	Holds the pages to display in the Help Contents pane, one file for each screen. These are in HTML (Web page) format. You create these files using an HTML editor or text editor.
Graphic and multimedia files	.jpeg, .gif, .png, .wav, .midi, .avi, and others	Images, sounds, and videos for which you supply links on HTML pages. You supply these files.
Table of Contents file	.hhc	Stores the headings and organization for the *Contents* tab. Created by the Workshop when you define the table of contents.
Index file	.hhk	Holds the entries for the searchable index. Created by the Workshop when you define the index.
Compiled Help file	.chm	Holds the compiled Help project. The Workshop creates this file when you compile the project.

Creating the Files

Before you begin using HTML Help Workshop, you should first plan your Help system and create the HTML files. Here are the general steps for creating Help files; detailed instructions follow in the step-by-step exercise.

1. Plan the topics to include.
2. Create HTML pages for each topic.

3. Using HTML Help Workshop:

- Add the HTML files.

- Create the Table of Contents.

- Create the Index.

- Compile the Help file.

4. Connect the compiled Help file to the application.

Creating a Help Facility

The following step-by-step exercise creates a Help facility using HTML pages that are already created. For this exercise, you can design and create your own HTML pages or use the ones supplied on the text Web site in the folder *Ch12SBS/HTML*.

Before you begin the exercise, make sure that you have HTML Help Workshop on your system. If not, refer to "HTML Help Workshop" earlier in this chapter.

Creating a Help Facility—Step-by-Step

Figure 12.3 shows the completed Help facility, and Figure 12.4 shows the Hours of Operation topic page with two additional links.

Figure 12.3

The completed Help facility for the step-by-step exercise.

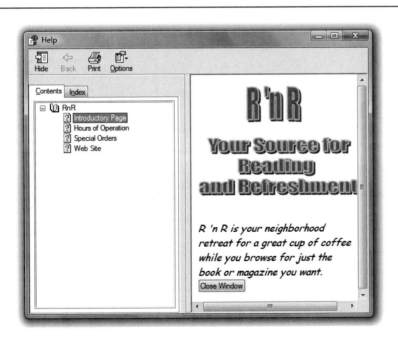

Begin the Exercise

STEP 1:   Locate the Ch12SBSHelp folder on the text Web site; copy it to your working folder. Examine the files. You should have a VB solution, project, and form files, and an HTML folder holding six .htm files and a subfolder called RnR_files. You will use the HTML files to create the Help facility and later connect it to the VB project.

Figure 12.4

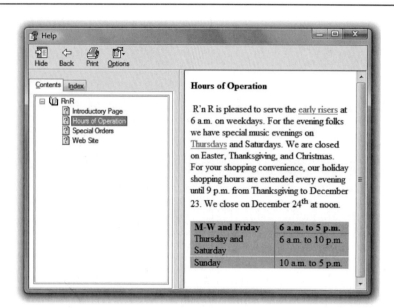

A topic page that has links to two additional pages. These linked pages are included in the Help project but do not appear in the Contents.

Begin a Project in the Workshop

STEP 1: Open *HTML Help Workshop*.

STEP 2: Select *New* from the *File* menu. Notice that several components are listed; choose *Project*. Click *OK*.

STEP 3: On the first wizard screen, click *Next*.

STEP 4: On the *New Project Destination* page, use the *Browse* button to locate and open the HTML folder beneath your project folder and name the file *RnRHelp*. (The wizard will add the extension .hhp.) Click *Open*; then click *Next*.

STEP 5: On the *Existing Files* page, select *HTML files (.htm)*. Click *Next*.

   Note: We are going to add the files now, with the wizard. You also can add files later.

STEP 6: On the *HTML Files* page, click *Add*. You can add all of the .htm files at once: Use your mouse to select all files or click on the first file-name, Shift-click on the last one (to select them all), and click *Open*. Back on the *HTML Files* page, you should see all six files. Click *Next*.

STEP 7: On the final wizard screen, click *Finish*. You will see a listing of the beginnings of your project file.

STEP 8: Take a look at the menus and buttons (Figure 12.5). The buttons down the left edge of the window change, depending on which tab is displayed. You will see this later as we create *Contents* and *Index* tabs.

Change Project Options

STEP 1: Click on the *Change Project Options* button to display the *Options* dialog box.

STEP 2: On the *General* tab, drop down the list for *Default File* and select RnR.htm.

STEP 3: On the *Files* tab, change the compiled file to *RnRHelp.chm* (delete the hard-coded path). Click *OK*.

Figure 12.5

The HTML Help Workshop window, showing the entries in the project file.

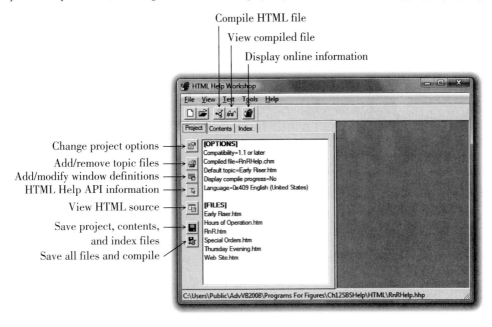

Create the Table of Contents

STEP 1: Switch to the *Contents* tab. On the next dialog, select the option to create a new contents file and accept the default name: Table of Contents. hhc. Click *Save*.

STEP 2: Notice that a different set of buttons displays. Figure 12.6 shows the completed *Contents* tab, which you will create in the next few steps.

STEP 3: Click on the *Contents properties* button and view the *General* tab.

STEP 4: Deselect the option to *Use folders instead of books* (if it is selected). Notice also that you can supply your own images—one for the closed state and one for the open state. Click *OK*.

Figure 12.6

Create the Table of Contents on the Contents tab.

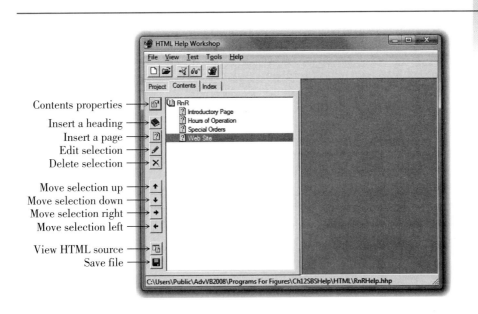

STEP 5: Click on *Insert a heading* and enter the title that you want to display for the first heading icon: *RnR*. Click on *Add* and select the topic "R 'n R—For Reading and Refreshment", which is the RnR.htm file. Click *OK*, and *OK* again to return to the *Contents* tab.

In the next few steps, if you get the dialog box asking if you want this entry at the beginning, answer *No*.

STEP 6: Click on *Insert a page*. Enter *Introductory Page* and add the *RnR.htm* topic. Click *OK*.

STEP 7: Add an entry for *Hours of Operation*, selecting the *Hours of Operation* topic.

STEP 8: Add an entry for *Special Orders*, selecting the *Special Orders* topic.

STEP 9: Add an entry for *Web Site*, selecting the *Web Site* topic.

The Table of Contents should be complete.

Create the Index

The index takes some planning. You should select words that a person would be apt to search for. Since our minds don't all work the same way, it sometimes takes a little creativity to think of topics that people might enter. However, you don't want to clutter the index by including every word in the Help file. Certainly one page may have multiple entries in the index.

STEP 1: Click on the *Index* tab and select the option to create a new index file. Accept the default name *Index.hhk*. Notice that the buttons have changed for the *Index* tab.

STEP 2: Click on *Insert a keyword* and enter the word *hours*, which will display in the index. Click on the *Add* button and select the *Hours of Operation* topic file. Click *OK* and *OK* again to get back to the *Index* tab.

STEP 3: The *Hours* topic could use some more keywords in the index: Add *holidays* referring to *Hours of Operation*.

Note that the order of entry is not important. The Workshop knows how to sort. You will sort the index when it is complete.

STEP 4: Add the keyword *custom orders* that refers to the *Special Orders* topic.

STEP 5: Add the keyword *special orders* that refers to the *Special Orders* topic.

STEP 6: Add the keyword *special*. With the *Add* button, add three pages: *Special Orders*, *Come Join the Fun Every Thursday Evening*, and *Early Riser's Special*.

STEP 7: Add the keyword *online* that refers to the *Web Site* topic.

STEP 8: Add the keyword *home page* that refers to the *Web Site* topic.

STEP 9: Examine the buttons and notice that you can edit or delete an entry, as well as move an entry up, down, left, or right (Figure 12.7), which you can use to create hierarchical relationships.

STEP 10: Click the *Sort* button to sort in alphabetic order.

The index should be finished now. You can always add more entries later.

Compile the Help Project

STEP 1: Switch back to the *Project* tab and click the *Save all files and compile* button at the bottom left. The Workshop compiles the file and displays statistics in the right pane (Figure 12.8). You may want to widen the pane a little to view the results. If the compiler detects any problems with missing or misspelled files or links, it displays error diagnostics

Figure 12.7

The index keywords in the Index tab.

Index properties →
Insert a keyword →
Edit selection →
Delete selection →
Move selection up →
Move selection down →
Move selection right →
Move selection left →
Sort keywords alphabetically →
View HTML source →
Save file →

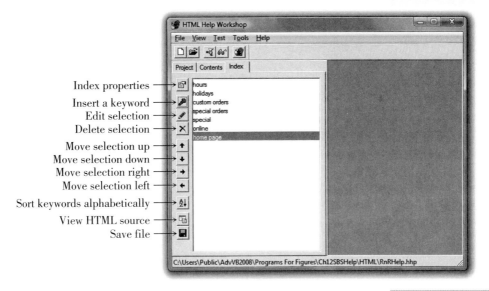

Figure 12.8

The compiler displays any error diagnostic messages and statistics.

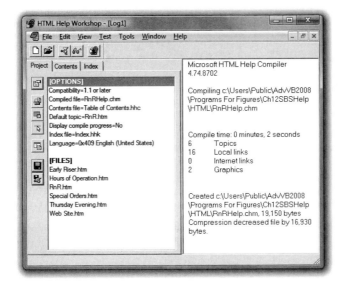

in the right pane. No error diagnostics means a clean compile and we are ready to connect this file to the VB project.

If you have any error diagnostic messages, you must locate them, fix them, and recompile. When you do, you will be prompted to save the Log file. Accept the defaults.

View and Test the Help File

STEP 1: Click on the *View compiled file* toolbar button (the glasses) or select *View / Compiled Help File*. You may have to browse for your file, called *RnRHelp.chm*. Click *View* to display your Help file in a new window.

STEP 2: Test the entries in the *Contents* tab and the *Index* tab. Test the two links on the Hours of Operation page to make sure that they work.

If a link doesn't work, you may have to return to the HTML editor and correct a page. Any time you change a page or any entry, *you must recompile the Help project*.

When you are finished, close the Help Viewer window and return to the main window with the *Project* tab displayed.

Add Navigation Using the ActiveX Control

The HTML Help Workshop comes with a control, called the *HTML Help ActiveX control*, that you can add to Web pages.

STEP 1: In the *[Files]* section on the *Project* tab, double-click on RnR.htm, which opens the page in the HTML editor.

STEP 2: Look at the tags and text and scroll down to the bottom of the file.

STEP 3: Click just before the closing `</body>` tag and verify that you have an insertion point rather than selected text.

STEP 4: Click on the *HTML Help ActiveX Control* button on the toolbar (the wizard's cap), which starts a wizard. Drop down the list for commands and notice that there are many choices. Select *Close Window* and click *Next*.

STEP 5: Select *As a button* and click *Next*.

STEP 6: On the *Button Options* page, choose to display text on the button and enter *Close Window* for the text. Click *Next*; then *Finish*.

STEP 7: Notice in the HTML editor window that code has been added for an object. Save and compile again. (Any time you change *anything*, you must recompile.)

STEP 8: View your compiled Help file again. After you are sure that everything else works, test the new button on the introductory page.

STEP 9: Close the HTML Help Workshop.

Connecting the HTML Help File to an Application

To add Help to your VB project, all you have to do is drag a **HelpProvider component** to your form and set the **HelpNamespace property** to the Help's .chm file. Adding a HelpProvider component has some similarities with adding a ToolTip component—new properties are added to the other controls on the form. For example, if you add a HelpProvider component named HelpProvider1, the form and each button will have new properties for **HelpKeyword** on HelpProvider1, **HelpNavigator** on HelpProvider1, and HelpString on HelpProvider1.

Property	Purpose
HelpKeyword	Used to specify the exact topic to display. Use the HTML filename. The HelpNavigator property must be set to *Topic* for this to work. Example: Hours of Operation.htm
HelpNavigator	Determines the page to display, such as Table of Contents, Index, or Topic.
HelpString	An actual string of text to display for popup Help.

Continuing the Step-by-Step Exercise

It's time to add the compiled Help file to a VB project.

Open the Project

STEP 1: Open the solution file in the Ch12SBSHelp folder.

STEP 2: Display the form in the designer.

Connect the Help File for F1 Help

STEP 1: Add a HelpProvider component from the Components section of the toolbox to the form.

STEP 2: Set the HelpNamespace property of HelpProvider1 to your Help file (RnRHelp.chm). You can browse to select the file, which should be in the HTML folder.

STEP 3: Set the form's ShowHelp on HelpProvider1 property to *true*.

STEP 4: Set the form's HelpNavigator on HelpProvider1 property to TableOf-Contents.

STEP 5: Run the program and press F1. Your Help screen should pop up with the Table of Contents displayed.

STEP 6: Close the form.

Adding Help to a Menu

You can use two methods of the Help object to display Help in code: the **ShowHelp method** and the **ShowHelpIndex method**.

ShowHelp Method—General Forms

```
Help.ShowHelp(control, helpfile)
Help.ShowHelp(control, helpfile, HelpNavigatorSetting)
Help.ShowHelp(control, helpfile, string for keyword to display)
Help.ShowHelp(control, helpfile, HelpNavigatorSetting, TopicID)
```

The various options allow you to specify whether the Index, Table of Contents, or a specific topic should display.

ShowHelp Method—Examples

```
Help.ShowHelp(Me, "RnRHelp.chm")
Help.ShowHelp(Me, "C:\My Documents\RnRHelp.chm")
```

Notice that you can use the full path for the Help file, but for development, it works best to place a copy of the .chm file in the bin\Debug folder for the project and specify the filename as a string without the path.

The ShowHelpIndex method is similar to the ShowHelp, but it always displays the *Index* tab of the Help file.

ShowHelpIndex Method—Example

Example

```
Help.ShowHelpIndex(Me, "RnRHelp.chm")
```

Display the Help File from Menu Items

STEP 1: Move a copy of RnRHelp.chm to the project's bin\Debug folder.

STEP 2: Modify the HelpProvider1 component's HelpNamespace property to remove the path. Without the path, the program will search in the bin\Debug folder for the file.

STEP 3: Write the code for the two *Help* menu items: ContentsToolStripMenuItem and IndexToolStripMenuItem.

```vb
'Project:       Ch12SBSHelp
'Programmer:    Your Name
'Date:          Today's Date
'Description:   Incorporates F1 help, help from a menu, _
'               and a Help Button

Public Class MainForm

    Private Sub ExitToolStripMenuItem_Click(ByVal sender As System.Object, _
      ByVal e As System.EventArgs) Handles ExitToolStripMenuItem.Click
        ' End the program.

        Me.Close()
    End Sub

    Private Sub ContentsToolStripMenuItem_Click(ByVal sender As System.Object, _
      ByVal e As System.EventArgs) Handles ContentsToolStripMenuItem.Click
        ' Display the Help Contents.

        Help.ShowHelp(Me, "RnRHelp.chm")
    End Sub

    Private Sub IndexToolStripMenuItem_Click(ByVal sender As System.Object, _
      ByVal e As System.EventArgs) Handles IndexToolStripMenuItem.Click
        ' Display the Index contents.

        Help.ShowHelpIndex(Me, "RnRHelp.chm")
    End Sub
End Class
```

STEP 4: Test it all!

Modifying Help Files

You can modify the Help Web pages, add pages to Help, and change the organization of the Help project. You must always remember to recompile after any change. The compiled Help .chm file holds all of the HTML pages in compressed form. When Help displays, it uses only those compressed pages, not the individual HTML pages. When you distribute an application, only the .chm file is needed, not the many files that make up the Help project.

TIP

Close the Help project in HTML Help Workshop when you are working on a VB project and close the VB project when you are working in the Workshop. One application cannot work on the file if the other is using it. ∎

Connecting Context-Sensitive Help Topics to Controls

If you have gotten this far in developing applications, you have probably used **context-sensitive Help**. You place the cursor on an element, press F1, and a Help topic (hopefully about the element you selected) pops up.

You can implement context-sensitive Help in your VB applications by setting the HelpKeyword and HelpNavigator for each element. The control must be able to receive the focus, so although labels and picture boxes have the appropriate properties, they cannot respond to F1 Help. Set the control's HelpNavigator property to *Topic* and the HelpKeyword property to the name of an HTML file.

Continue the Example Program?

You can test context-sensitive Help: Open the Ch12SBSHelp project and add two or three buttons. For each control, set the HelpNavigator property to *Topic* and HelpKeyword property to one of these values: *RnR.htm*, *Hours of Operation.htm*, *Special Orders.htm*, *Web Site.htm*, *Early Riser.htm*, or *Thursday Evening.htm*.

Adding a Help Button to a Message Box

You may want to offer the user a *Help* button when an error occurs (Figure 12.9). Several of the signatures for the Show method of a message box allow you to include the name of a Help file. You can include the name of your Help file and a *Help* button is added to the message box. See MSDN Help on message boxes for more details.

Figure 12.9

Display a Help button on a message box.

```
MessageBox.Show("Simulating an error", "Error Condition", _
    MessageBoxButtons.OK, MessageBoxIcon.Error, _
    MessageBoxDefaultButton.Button1, 0, "RnRHelp.chm")
```

The Help Button

A Windows application that has a *Help* button on the title bar can provide popup Help while the user is working. When the user clicks the *Help* button, the pointer changes into the question mark (Figure 12.10). Then the user can click on an element and a Help topic pops up (Figure 12.11). Unlike F1 Help, you can assign popup Help to controls that cannot receive the focus, such as labels and picture boxes.

Figure 12.10

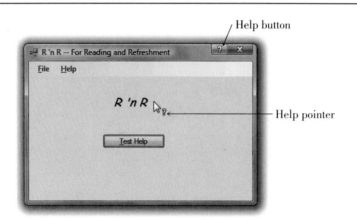

Help button

Help pointer

Figure 12.11

This is an application to give lots of help to RnR users.

A popup Help topic pops up on top of the selected element.

You can create popup Help by setting the form's HelpButton property to *true* and both the MaximizeBox and MinimizeBox properties to *false*. For each control that should display popup Help, you set the **HelpString property** to the text to show in a ToolTip-style box.

Other Forms of User Assistance

Good programs provide assistance to the user. In this chapter, you learned about providing Help, context-sensitive Help, and popup Help. You also can provide helpful information using ToolTips and status bars. You might consider showing the formula for a calculation in a ToolTip as well as instructions for data entry. Instructions in status bars can be very useful and unobtrusive. It's a good idea to use the MouseOver event of controls to change the message in a status bar; then use the MouseOver event of the form to reset the status-bar text.

Feedback 12.1

1. Give the file type and purpose of each of the following file extensions.
   a. .hhk
   b. .hhc
   c. .chm
   d. .jpeg
   e. .avi
   f. .htm
2. List five types of user assistance that can be added to an application.

Summary

1. Windows supports Help files in HTML Help.
2. The HTML Help Workshop is a separate application that combines topic files (HTML pages), graphics and multimedia files, contents files, and index files into a Help project. The compiled file has the extension .chm.
3. The HelpFile can be assigned to the VB project at design time or run time. At run time, use the `ShowHelp` or `ShowHelpIndex` method.
4. Adding a HelpProvider component to a form adds properties to the other controls on the form. Set the HelpKeyword, HelpNavigator, and HelpString properties to determine how Help is displayed for each control.
5. For context-sensitive Help, set the HelpNavigator property of a control to *Topic* and the HelpKeyword property to the name of an HTML file.
6. You can display a *Help* button on a message box using one of several overloaded signatures for the `MessageBox.Show` method.
7. To display the *Help* button on the title bar of a form, set the form's HelpButton property to *true* and the MaximizeBox and MinimizeBox properties to *false*. For each control, set the HelpString property to the text that you want to display.
8. ToolTips and status bars also can be considered a part of the Help supplied by an application.

Key Terms

context-sensitive Help   *503*
Help topic   *493*
Help Viewer   *492*
HelpKeyword property   *500*
HelpNamespace property   *500*
HelpNavigator property   *500*
HelpProvider component   *500*

HelpString property   *504*
HTML Help ActiveX control   *492*
HTML Help Image Editor   *492*
HTML Help Workshop   *492*
`ShowHelp` method   *501*
`ShowHelpIndex` method   *501*

Review Questions

1. How is each Help topic defined in HTML Help?
2. How is the Help file connected to a VB project for F1 Help?
3. How do you connect individual forms and controls to specific Help topics?
4. What Help file(s) must be distributed with a VB application?
5. How do you display Help in code from a menu item?
6. How can you display a *Help* button on a message box?
7. What is popup Help?

Programming Exercises

12.1 Use Word, Visual Studio 2008, or any HTML editor to create Web pages about your favorite hobbies or sports. Include at least one image.

Assemble and compile the file using HTML Help Workshop.

Add the Help to a small VB project.

12.2 Add Help to any of your VB projects.

Case Studies

Claytor's Cottages

Add Help to your Claytor's Cottages case study project.

Christian's Car Rentals

Add Help to your Christian's Car Rentals case study project.

13

Additional Topics in Visual Basic

at the completion of this chapter, you will be able to . . .

1. Write Windows applications that run on mobile devices.

2. Display database information on a mobile device.

3. Create interfaces with Windows Presentation Foundation (WPF).

4. Query a variety of data sources using Language-Integrated Queries (LINQ).

5. Understand and apply the concepts of localization.

6. Use threading in an application using the BackgroundWorker component.

This final chapter introduces you to some of the additional features of programming. As more mobile devices appear on the market, it becomes more important to have a scalable development environment. Visual Studio fills the bill; you can program for mobile devices using the same tools that you already know.

Another topic in this chapter, localization, also deals with the increased worldwide use of communication devices. When you are creating applications that can be viewed in many countries, you should consider the needs of the users in each country.

The chapter also deals with running processes in the background (asynchronously) to improve performance for time-consuming tasks.

WPF provides developers with tools for creating state-of-the-art interfaces. The programming remains consistent with previous Visual Basic application. This chapter demonstrates the use of WPF with Windows applications.

LINQ is the final topic in this chapter, providing a consistent language for querying many types of data.

Device Applications

Creating output for PDAs, cell phones, and pagers requires different protocols, but you can use Visual Basic to develop applications for these mobile devices. The Visual Studio IDE has features for creating solutions that deploy to Smart Devices. **Smart Devices** are those mobile devices that run compact and mobile versions of Windows.

Using Emulators

When you use VS to develop Smart Device applications, you can view the output in a regular window or in an **emulator**. An emulator displays an image of the device on the computer screen, which gives a better visual concept of the final output. As you can imagine, the screen appears much different on a phone device than it does on a device like the Pocket PC or SmartPhone. Visual Studio Professional Edition installs with target platforms for Windows Mobile 5.0 Pocket PC SDK, Pocket PC 2003, Windows CE, and Windows Mobile 5.0 Smartphone SDK. The automatically installed emulators differ depending on the version of Windows that you select. You can download additional emulators for other SDKs such as Windows Mobile 6.0. Figure 13.1 shows an application displaying in a device emulator.

Smart Device Applications

When you begin a new project for a Smart Device, you select *Smart Device* for the *Project type* and the Smart Device Project template (Figure 13.2) rather than the Windows Application template. The toolbar and toolbox look similar to those for a Windows application, but the device controls are a different set from the Windows set. You will find that the device controls have far fewer properties than their Windows counterparts.

Figure 13.1

A Smart Device application displaying in an emulator.

Figure 13.2

Begin a new Smart Device application by selecting the Device Application template.

A First Smart Device Application—Step-by-Step

It's time for another Hello World application.

Create the Project

STEP 1: Create a new project and select the Smart Device project type and the Smart Device Project template. Name the project *Ch13HelloWorldSmartDevice*.

STEP 2: After you click *OK*, you will get another dialog with a drop-down box for *Target platform*. Select *Windows Mobile 5.0 Smartphone SDK* and the Device Application template (Figure 13.3).

Figure 13.3

Select the type of mobile device.

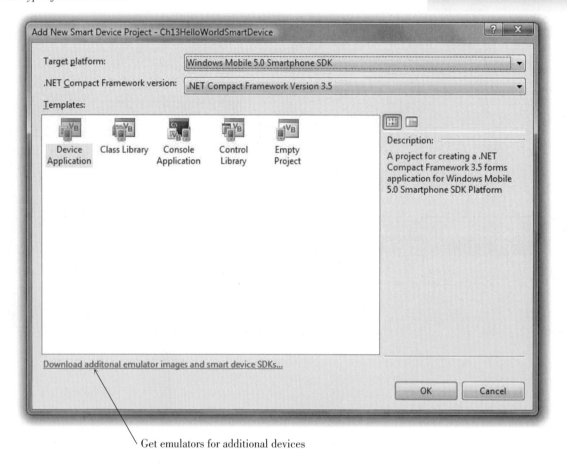

Get emulators for additional devices

STEP 3: Notice that the form displays in an emulator (Figure 13.4). You can choose to show or hide the emulator image in *Tools / Options / Device Tools / Show skin in Windows Forms Designer*.

STEP 4: Name your form *HelloWorldForm* and set the Text property to Hello World.

Figure 13.4

The form for new Smart Device project displays in an emulator by default.

STEP 5: Add a NameTextBox with a label prompting "Name:". Add a Hello-Label with its Text property deleted (Figure 13.5).

Add Menu Items

STEP 1: By default, a new device form has a MainMenu control, which appears along the bottom of the form and in the component tray. Click on either the menu bar or the component and use the menu editor to add a *File* menu with a *Display* and an *Exit* menu item. Notice that the menu item appears *above* the menu name, rather than below as in Windows applications.

STEP 2: Name the *Display* menu item as *DisplayMenuItem* and the *Exit* menu item *ExitMenuItem*. Note that the Smart Device menus are a different type of menu control and the editor does not automatically name the items.

Figure 13.5

Add controls to the form for the Device application.

Write the Code

STEP 1: Write the code for the menu item to display the name in the text box.

```
Private Sub DisplayMenuItem_Click(ByVal sender As System.Object, _
    ByVal e As System.EventArgs) Handles DisplayMenuItem.Click
        ' Display the Hello World message.

        HelloLabel.Text = "Hello " & NameTextBox.Text
End Sub
```

STEP 2: Write the code for the *Exit* menu item.

```
Private Sub ExitMenuItem_Click(ByVal sender As System.Object, _
    ByVal e As System.EventArgs) Handles ExitMenuItem.Click
        ' Exit the application.

        Me.Close()
End Sub
```

Run the Application

STEP 1: Run the program and select any of the device emulators (Figure 13.6). Click *Deploy*. Note that if you have a real device to attach, you can select a choice that is not an emulator.

Figure 13.6

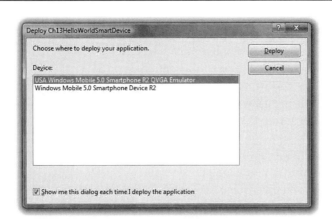

Choose the emulator to use when you run the program.

STEP 2: And wait a while. Your project will take a little time to load, but you must remember that this is a full device emulator.

At first you will see the emulator display with fake data. When the application actually loads, you will see your Hello World screen. At your leisure, you may want to play with many of the features of the emulator. Right now you want to type in a name and click on the *Display* menu item (Figure 13.7). To display the menu, click on the left silver button below the emulator screen.

Figure 13.7

The Hello World application running in a device emulator.

STEP 3: After you test the application, you can close it by closing the emulator's window or by switching back to the IDE and selecting the option to stop debugging. If you choose to save the state of the emulator, the next run will load faster.

A Database Application

Smart Devices also can access database files. SQL Server Compact 3.5 creates files with an .sdf extension that you can use in a Smart Device application. The Ch13SmartDeviceDataBase project uses the Northwind.sdf file available on the text Web site. The file also can be found in the Visual Studio files. The default installation path is C:\Program Files\Microsoft SQL Server Compact Edition\v3.5\Samples.

Adding database access to a Smart Device application is similar to the techniques that you use in Windows. You can add a new data source using the Data Sources window or the *Data* menu, and you can drag a table or fields from the Data Sources window to the form to create bound controls. As in Windows development, you have the option of including the database in your project.

When you add a data source to your project, you must change the *Data Source* to Microsoft SQL Server Compact 3.5 (Figure 13.8).

Figure 13.8

In the Data Source Configuration Wizard, change the data source for a mobile application.

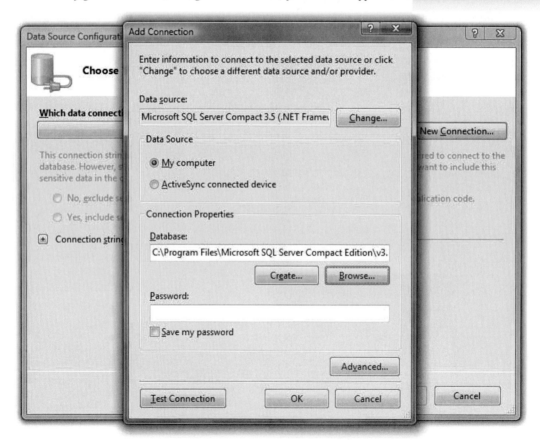

Run the Ch13SmartDeviceDataBase project using the Windows Mobile 5.0 Pocket PC R2 emulator. Refer to Figure 13.1 for the output.

Changing Column Styles

The formatting for the columns of a data grid is different from the familiar Windows DataGridView. The data grid contains a TableStyles property, which is a collection. From the DataGridTableStyle Collection Editor, select the Grid-ColumnStyles collection. In the DataGridColumnStyle Collection Editor (Figure 13.9), you can change the width or header text of the individual columns.

TIP

Select the option to save the emulator state; your project will load faster on subsequent executions. ■

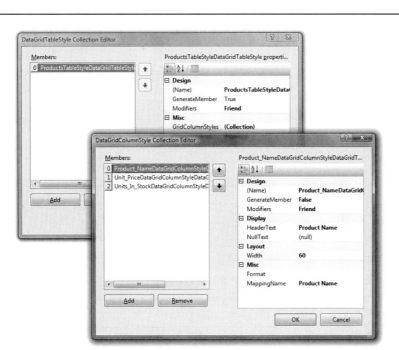

Figure 13.9

Change the column styles of the grid's columns in the DataGridColumnStyle Collection Editor.

Creating a Data Form

The smart tag of the data grid gives you the option to *Generate Data Forms.* When you select the item, you generate a form as well as a *New* menu item on your form, which would be used for adding a new item to the database. You can delete the *New* menu item and the associated code if you are not creating a database update program.

After you add a data form to a data grid application, you can double-click on a row in the data grid and the single record displays on the data form (Figure 13.10).

Updating a Database

It is difficult to test a database update program using an emulator because the emulator does not retain the database from one run to the next without some advanced configuration. If you have an actual Smart Device cradled to your computer, you can transfer the database file to the device and actually test the update process.

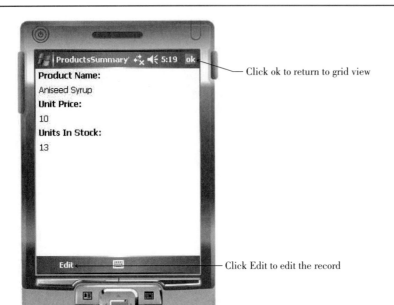

— Click ok to return to grid view

— Click Edit to edit the record

Displaying Records in Details View

As with a Windows project, the Data Sources window allows you to drag the table for a data grid or for a details view. One difference that you notice immediately is the lack of a binding navigator.

The Ch13ProductDetails program displays the Product ID, Product Name, Unit Price, Units In Stock, and the Discontinued fields. As you can see in Figure 13.11, Product Name is in a combo box, which is used to select the record to which to navigate.

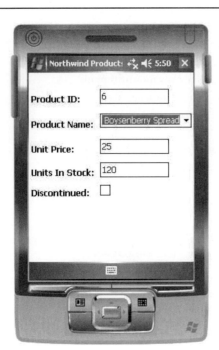

Setting the data binding properties of the combo box is similar to a Windows control. In the smart tag, set the DataSource and DisplayMember properties. Then scroll to the top of the Properties window, expand the *(DataBindings)* entry, select *(Advanced)*, and set the *Data Source Update Mode* to Never.

Feedback 13.1

What is a Smart Device application?

Windows Presentation Foundation (WPF)

Interface design is changing considerably and the tools also are changing. Using **Windows Presentation Foundation (WPF)**, a great new feature included in Visual Studio 2008, you can create the special effects that you see in Windows Vista applications. You can write WPF applications for both Windows XP and Windows Vista, but the special effects do not appear in XP unless you install a plug-in on a machine running XP SP2.

Microsoft has announced to developers that they are phasing out Windows Forms in favor of WPF. For that reason, you may choose to write all of your Windows applications using WPF rather than Windows Forms; the programming is basically the same. At this time, Windows XP and Windows Forms are much more prevalent than Vista and WPF applications, but you can look for that to change in the next few years.

WPF includes development platforms for both Windows and Web applications. You can write stand-alone WPF Windows applications, applications that run in a browser, and programs that display XPS documents, such as those generated from Office 2007. You can see various examples of WPF designs at http://windowsclient.net/community/showcase.aspx.

Silverlight is a related technology that has some of the features of WPF but has the ability to run on multiple browser platforms. The browser applications created through Visual Studio require .NET components to be installed on the client machine and only run in Internet Explorer. This restriction makes Silverlight a more universal development option, outside of a local intranet where the administrator has control over machine configuration.

The Roles of Designer and Programmer

The new user interfaces, which include so many special effects, often include a role for a designer as well as a programmer. And the new tools make it easy to separate the design from the programming.

WPF development is available in both Visual Studio and the Expression Interactive Designer. Programmers generally use Visual Studio and designers prefer Expression Interactive Designer. A programmer can create a window in Visual Studio and the same window.xaml file can be opened and modified in Expression. For example, a programmer may place a button on a window and then the designer can transform the button to a flashy design feature: The programming behind the button is still created by the programmer, who writes in VB or C#, just as in a Windows Forms application.

WPF applications contain two basic files: the Window.xaml file and the Application.xaml file. The design code is written in **Extensible Application Markup Language (XAML)** (pronounced "zammel"). The XAML browser applications are referred to as **XBAPs (XAML browser applications)**.

WPF Features

The feature set for WPF applications includes the layouts and controls. The controls are very similar to Windows Forms such as buttons, labels, radio buttons, check boxes, and list boxes. The layout is set up in a panel. The most commonly used layout is the grid, which, as the name implies, allows you to lay out the controls in rows and columns. Other layouts include a DockPanel, which places controls along the edge of the panel; a Canvas that is a freestyle layout; and a StackPanel.

The XAML style element provides the same type of functionality as a cascading style sheet in an HTML environment. WPF also uses templates, including a data template and a control template.

WPF has considerable flexibility for including multimedia. You can include text or documents, images, video and audio (the MediaElement control), 2D graphics such as a line or ellipse, and 3D graphics, using Direct3D. Transformations and effects include rotation and resizing objects using Rotate-Transform and ScaleTransform. A Storyboard class for animation may contain one or more timelines. WPF also includes data binding and interface automation.

WPF stand-alone applications have full trust from a security standpoint. Therefore, they are capable of using Windows Communication Foundation (WCF). Both the browser and stand-alone applications use ClickOnce for deployment.

At this time WPF does not support MDI, such as in Excel, but does use a multiple-instance SDI, like Word 2007. Some programmers have created their own MDI applications in WPF using classes. See www.codeproject.com/KB/WPF/mwiwpf.aspx for more information. However, these techniques are written in XAML and beyond the scope of this book. Some developers recommend creating multiple "screens" using the TabControl or by having a collapsible panel.

The new technology also allows us to create hybrid applications. You can add WPF features to your Windows Forms applications, and the Windows controls that you have learned about can be added to a WPF page.

Creating a WPF Project

You will find several differences in developing WPF applications from Windows Forms applications. The first is very obvious: For the project template (Figure 13.12), you select WPF Application (or WPF Browser Application). The Properties window (Figure 13.13) is a little different; the Name property is set at the top of the window. Also, a Search box allows you to find a property quickly. Labels have a Content property instead of a Text property; a Window has a Title property; and a text box has a Text property.

Changing the name of a form can be very challenging. You must change the name of the file in the Solution Explorer, but that does not change the name of

Figure 13.12

Select the template for a WPF application from the New Project dialog box.

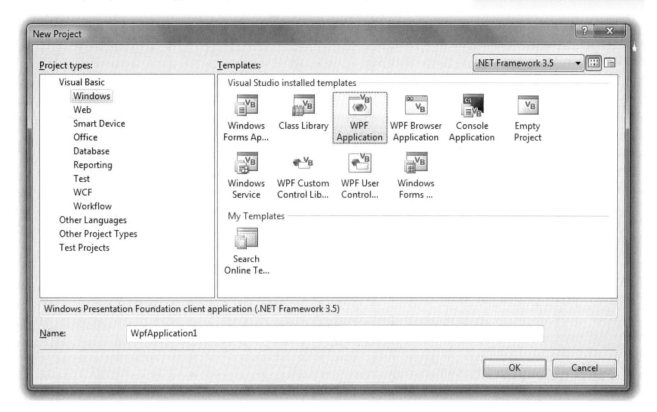

Figure 13.13

The Properties window for a WPF window.

the class. Use *Refactor / Rename* in the context menu to change the name of the class, to assure that all references are changed. If you change the name of the startup form, you also must open the Project Designer (double-click on *My Project* in the Solution Explorer) to set the Startup URI from the drop-down box; it does not change automatically. Remember, this is the first release of this product and some of the automatic changes will likely come with future releases.

A WPF Calculation Example

The following example uses the same basic controls as Windows Forms to create a calculation application (Figure 13.14). Set the button's IsDefault property to make it the accept button.

Figure 13.14

A WPF calculation application.

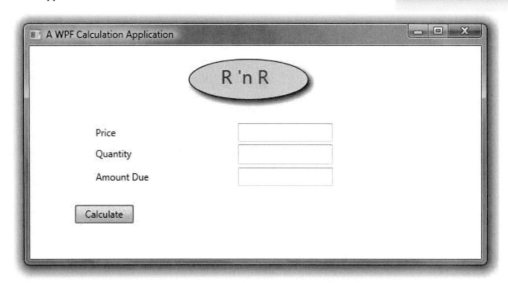

```
'Project      Ch13WpfCalculations
'Programmer   Bradley/Millspaugh
'Date         June 2009
'Description   Uses WPF to perform a calculation.

Class Window1

    Private Sub CalculateButton_Click(ByVal sender As System.Object, _
        ByVal e As System.Windows.RoutedEventArgs) Handles CalculateButton.Click
        ' Calculate the amount due.
        Try
            AmountDueTextBox.Text = (Decimal.Parse(PriceTextBox.Text) * _
                Integer.Parse(QuantityTextBox.Text)).ToString("C")
        Catch
            MessageBox.Show("Price and Decimal must contain numeric values.")
        End Try
    End Sub
End Class
```

A Multiple-Window Example

You can add extra windows to a WPF application by selecting *New Window* from the *Project* menu. Use the same techniques to show and hide windows as you do with Windows Forms.

```
'Project       Ch13WpfMultipleWindows
'Programmer    Bradley/Millspaugh
'Date          June 2009
'Description    Main window.

Class MainWindow

    Private Sub ChildButton_Click(ByVal sender As System.Object, _
      ByVal e As System.Windows.RoutedEventArgs) Handles ChildButton.Click
        ' Display the child window.

        Dim AChildWindow As New ChildWindow
        AChildWindow.Show()   ' ShowDialog also available.
    End Sub

    Private Sub ExitButton_Click(ByVal sender As Object, _
      ByVal e As System.Windows.RoutedEventArgs) Handles ExitButton.Click
        ' Close the project.

        Me.Close()
    End Sub
End Class

'Project       WpfMultipleWindows
'Programmer    Bradley/Millspaugh
'Date          June 2009
'Description    Child window.

Partial Public Class ChildWindow

    Private Sub CloseButton_Click(ByVal sender As System.Object, _
      ByVal e As System.Windows.RoutedEventArgs) Handles CloseButton.Click
        ' Close this window.

        Me.Close()
        ' Me.Hide is also available.
    End Sub
End Class
```

Interoperability

Another feature that Visual Studio 2008 allows you to implement features WPF in a Windows Form application project. The toolbox for windows applications contains a category called *WPF Interoperability* that contains an ElementHost control, which is a container that allows you to add WPF controls to a Windows Form. You can add other WPF controls to the toolbox or add the controls in code. You may want to add a grid panel inside an ElementHost control to help lay out multiple controls

Right-click on the toolbox, select *Choose Items*, and click on the *WPF components* tab to see the possibilities. Adding an Imports for System.Windows. Controls allows you to add controls in code. A WPF button appears the same on a Windows Form as it does on the XAML window, but the coding becomes

much more complex. See http://msdn.microsoft.com/en-us/library/ms742215
.aspx for a walkthrough on "Hosting a Windows Presentation Foundation
Control in Windows Forms."

The following application uses two element hosts:

```
'Project        Ch13WindowsWpfInteroperability
'Programmer     Bradley/Millspaugh
'Date           June 2009
'Description     Uses an Element Host to access WPF Expander Control.

Imports System.Windows.Controls

Public Class WPFInteropForm

    Private Sub WPFInteropForm_Load(ByVal sender As System.Object, _
        ByVal e As System.EventArgs) Handles MyBase.Load
        Dim MoreExpander As New Expander

        With MoreExpander
            .Header = "More Information"
            .Content = "In this section you can display additional inf"
        End With

        ExpanderElementHost.Child = MoreExpander

        Dim WpfButton As New System.Windows.Controls.Button
        WpfButton.Content = "WPF Button"
        ButtonElementHost.Child = WpfButton
    End Sub
End Class
```

▶ **Feedback 13.2**

1. What property is used to display information on a WPF button?
2. Where is the name of an object specified for a WPF control or form?
3. What is the purpose of the ElementHost control?

LINQ

A great enhancement to Visual Studio is the introduction of **Language-Integrated Queries (LINQ)**. LINQ gives the developer a standard language that can be used to query any data source that is defined as an object, a database, or as XML. This includes arrays, collections, database, flat files, and XML. This section presents several of the LINQ keywords and demonstrates applications that query a variety of data sources.

In addition to the hard-coded LINQ queries discussed in this chapter, you also can create dynamic LINQ. See msdn.microsoft.com/en-us/vbasic/bb964686.aspx.

LINQ Keywords

A LINQ query is written using operators that are standard regardless of the source of the data. The primary operators in a query (Table 13.1) are From, In, Where, and Select.

Primary LINQ Operators

Table 13.1

Operator	Purpose	Example
From	Name of a single element.	`From AnItem`
In	Specifies the source of the data (all of the elements to query).	`In AmountDecimal`
Where	A Boolean expression that specifies the condition for the query.	`Where AnItem < 100D`
Select	Execute the query. The identifier determines the type of data element(s) that will be returned from the query.	`Select AnItem`

The LINQ Query—General Form

```
Dim VariableName = From ItemName In Object Where Condition Select ListOfFields/Items
```

The *VariableName* in the format does not need a data type assigned. In Visual Studio 2008, if the data type is not specified, the compiler can assign a type in a process called *type inference*. To see an example of type inference, type `Dim Amount = 5` and then hover the mouse over the variable; it would show you that, through type inference, Amount is presumed to be of type Integer. Change the value to 5.5 and hover over Amount and the type will be Double. Although it is not wise to use type inference when the type is known, the feature was introduced to allow some of the operators in LINQ (`Order By`, `Where`) to be used on unspecified data types.

The result of the query is retrieved from the object represented by *VariableName*.

The LINQ Query—Example

```
Dim BelowMinimumQuery =
    From AnItem In AmountDecimal
    Where AnItem < 100D
    Select AnItem
```

In this example, AmountDecimal is an array and AnItem is a single element that is not declared elsewhere. The query is similar to a `For Each`—it steps through the array, assigns each element to AnItem, and performs the comparison. Use BelowMinimumQuery to retrieve the result of the query.

A First Look at LINQ

For our first look at LINQ, we are going to query an array. The array contains a series of decimal values.

```
Dim AmountDecimal() As Decimal = {100D, 50D, 35.75D, 123.1D, 12.4D}
```

For the query, our `In` clause will address the name of the array, Amount Decimal. The `In` clause always refers to the name of the object, which could be an array or even an Items collection from a list box such as SchoolsListBox. Items. The `From` is one element in the collection and does not need to be declared. Think of the `From` object as the same as a single element in a `For Each` loop.

The query is called BelowMinimumQuery. Using type inference, your `Dim` statement becomes

```
Dim BelowMinimumQuery = _
  From AnItem In AmountDecimal _
  Where AnItem < 100D _
  Select AnItem
```

The `Where` clause allows us to provide a condition; if we want all records in a collection, just omit the `Where` clause. Notice that this `Where` checks to see if an item is less than one hundred. The `Select` clause then executes the query giving us a result set in BelowMinimumQuery. You may then use the query results as a new collection. In this example, we are going to display the items in a list box using the `ToList` method of the query object.

```
'Project       Ch13LinqArray
'Programmer    Bradley/Millspaugh
'Date          June 2009
'Description    Use LINQ to query an array.

Public Class LinqForm

    Private Sub Form1_Load(ByVal sender As System.Object, _
      ByVal e As System.EventArgs) Handles MyBase.Load
        ' Display the amounts below the minimum of 100.
        Dim AmountDecimal() As Decimal = {100D, 50D, 35.75D, 123.1D, 12.4D}

        Dim BelowMinimumQuery = _
            From AnItem In AmountDecimal _
            Where AnItem < 100D _
            Select AnItem

        BelowMinimumListBox.DataSource = BelowMinimumQuery.ToList()
    End Sub
End Class
```

Additional LINQ Keywords

Many other operators are available for LINQ queries (see Table 13.2), including sorting and grouping. The aggregate operators include `Average`, `Count`, `Max`, `Min`, and `Sum`, giving you a lot of power for finding summary information from a table through a query.

LINQ to SQL

You can apply a LINQ query to a relational database, even though the database's language is not based on objects. To use LINQ with a database, you need to add a new item to a database project called the LINQ to SQL Classes template. In a project that already has a form and data source defined, select *Project / Add New Item* and select *LINQ TO SQL Classes* from the *Templates* list.

Operator
OrderBy/ThenBy
Reverse
GroupBy
Distinct
ToList
ToArray
ToLookup
Any
All
Contains
Count (LongCount)
Min
Sum
Max
Aggregate
Average

When you add the LINQ to SQL template to a project, you create a strongly typed DataContext class. You set up the object database model using a new design surface with two panes, called the Object Relational (O/R) Designer, which appears in the main Document window (Figure 13.15). Using the O/R Designer, you can simply drag database tables from the Server Explorer (or the Database Explorer in the Express Edition) to the design surface. The tables that you add to the left pane are referred to as *entities*; the right pane holds optional stored procedures or methods. Figure 13.16 shows the design surface with the Employee class. You may notice that Visual Studio changes the plural table name to singular when it creates a class; the titles table became the Title class.

When writing the code, you refer to the DataContext. The titles table is a member of the Pubs database. The corresponding DataContext is automatically called the PubsDataContext. Once you have created the DataContext class, you can create a DataContext object in code. You can then query the database using the same LINQ operators that you saw in the previous sections.

```
' Query the titles table.
Dim PubsData As New PubsDataContext()
Dim SalesQuery = _
  From ATitle In PubsData.titles _
  Select ATitle.title, ATitle.ytd_sales
```

Figure 13.15

Adding the LINQ to SQL Classes template to a database project creates a new design surface for visualizing your data.

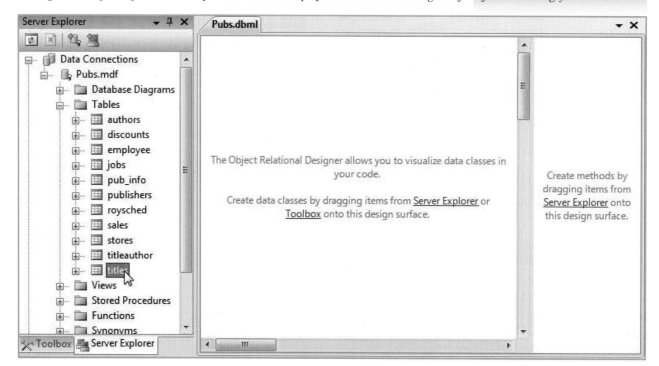

Figure 13.16

The new Title class, based on the titles table of the Pubs database.

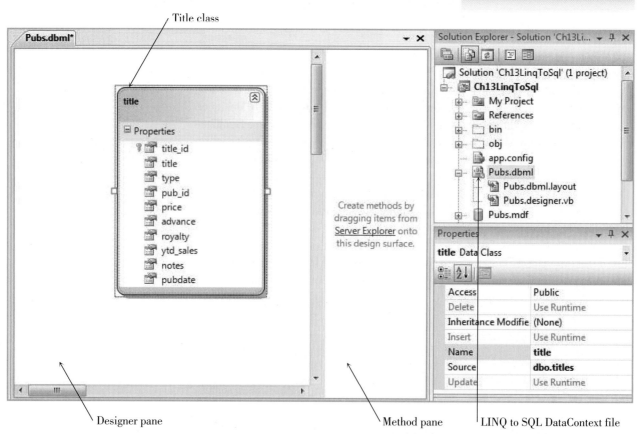

If you assign the results of this query to output, you probably want to format the numeric field, which is ytd_sales in this example. For a DataGridView, you can format each of the columns:

```
With TitlesDataGridView
    .DataSource = SalesQuery.ToList
    .Columns(0).HeaderText = "Title"
    With Columns(1)
        .HeaderText = "YTD Sales"
        .DefaultCellStyle.Format = "n2"
        .DefaultCellStyle.Alignment = DataGridViewContentAlignment.MiddleRight
    End With
End With
```

When you assign the result of a query to a text box, the ToString method from the query does not allow the arguments for formatting in the current release. You can use the VB format functions to solve this problem. Hopefully, the ToString method will be overloaded on future releases to allow the same type of formatting we are accustomed to.

```
TotalSalesTextBox.Text = FormatCurrency(TotalSalesQuery.ToString())
```

It is simple to find the total from a field in the database. The following code finds the sum of the year-to-date sales from the titles table in Pubs. Figure 13.17 shows the output of this program.

```
Dim TotalSalesQuery = _
    Aggregate ATitle In PubsData.titles _
    Into Sum(ATitle.ytd_sales)
TotalSalesTextBox.Text = FormatCurrency(TotalSalesQuery.ToString())
```

Figure 13.17

The LINQ to SQL program output.

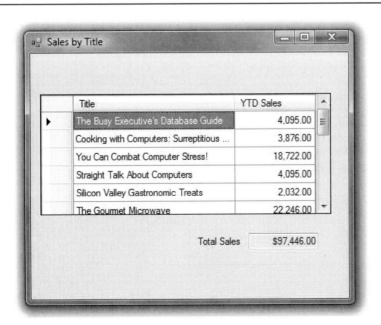

LINQ to XML

You can use LINQ to XML to retrieve data elements from an XElement or XDocument object. You can refer to the elements in an XElement object on the In clause of LINQ as well as in the Select clause. *Note*: You can refer to the authors' beginning text, "Programming in Visual Basic 2008", or to Appendix B for more information about the XElement and XDocument objects.

Our example will use the books.xml file.

```xml
<?xml version='1.0'?>
<!-- This file represents a fragment of a book store inventory database -->
<bookstore>
  <book genre="autobiography" publicationdate="1981" ISBN="1-861003-11-0">
    <title>The Autobiography of Benjamin Franklin</title>
    <author>
      <first-name>Benjamin</first-name>
      <last-name>Franklin</last-name>
    </author>
    <price>8.99</price>
  </book>
  <book genre="novel" publicationdate="1967" ISBN="0-201-63361-2">
    <title>The Confidence Man</title>
    <author>
      <first-name>Herman</first-name>
      <last-name>Melville</last-name>
    </author>
    <price>11.99</price>
  </book>
  <book genre="philosophy" publicationdate="1991" ISBN="1-861001-57-6">
    <title>The Gorgias</title>
    <author>
      <name>Plato</name>
    </author>
    <price>9.99</price>
  </book>
</bookstore>
```

An XElement object loads the file for use by your program.

```vb
Dim BookData = XElement.Load("books.xml")
```

VB includes a new feature called ***XML literals***, which simplifies referring to child elements, attributes, and descendants (Figure 13.18). Table 13.3 shows examples of using the XML literals.

The child element book in the file is then referred to as ABook.<book>. The attribute uses @ notation such as ABook.@ISBN while the descendant fields use an ellipsis ABook...<price>.

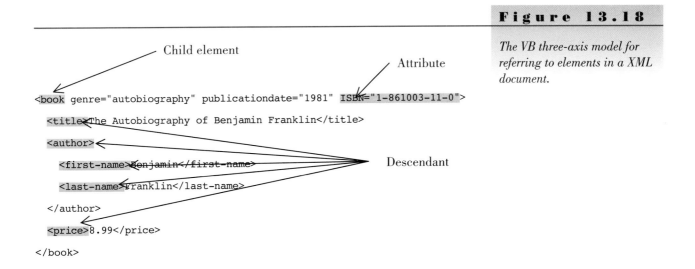

The XML literals that you can use to refer to XML elements.

Table 13.3

XML element	XML literal	Example within a query
Child element	<element name>	ABook.<book>
Attribute	@attribute name	ABook.@ISBN
Descendant	...<descendant name>	ABook...<price>

The code to fill a list box in alphabetic order is

```
' Retrieve the book data.
Dim BookQuery = _
  From ABook In BookData.<book> _
  Order By ABook...<title>.Value _
  Select ABook...<title>.Value
TitlesListBox.DataSource = BookQuery.ToList()
```

You can use the results as you would any other data. You also can do a further query on the result of the first query. Use a `Where` clause to "query the query" to find information about the book selected from the list box.

```
Dim SelectedBookQuery = _
  From SelectedBook In BookQuery _
  Where (SelectedBook...<title>.Value.ToString = _
    TitlesListBox.SelectedItem.ToString) _
  Select SelectedBook.<author>.Value, _
    SelectedBook.@ISBN, SelectedBook...<price>.Value
```

The Complete LINQ to XML Program Listing

```
' Project:       Ch13LinqToXML
' Programmer:    Bradley/Millspaugh
' Date:          June 2009
' Description:   Read an XML file into an XDocument and use
'                LINQ to XML to extract the titles and display
'                in a list box, Details show for selected book.

Public Class XmlListForm
    Private BookData As XElement

    Private Sub XmlListForm_Load(ByVal sender As System.Object, _
        ByVal e As System.EventArgs) Handles MyBase.Load
        ' Read the XML file into an XElement and use LINQ to query the data.
        BookData = XElement.Load("books.xml")

        'Retrieve the book data.
        Dim BookQuery = From ABook In BookData.<book> _
            Order By ABook...<title>.Value _
            Select ABook...<title>.Value
        TitlesListBox.DataSource = BookQuery.ToList()
    End Sub

    Private Sub TitlesListBox_SelectedIndexChanged(ByVal sender _
        As System.Object, ByVal e As System.EventArgs) _
        Handles TitlesListBox.SelectedIndexChanged
        ' Display the detail information for the selected book.

        ' Retrieve the book data.
        Dim BookQuery = _
            From ABook In BookData.<book> _
            Select ABook
        Dim SelectedBookQuery = _
            From SelectedBook In BookQuery _
            Where (SelectedBook...<title>.Value.ToString = _
                TitlesListBox.SelectedItem.ToString) _
            Select SelectedBook.<author>.Value, _
                SelectedBook.@ISBN, SelectedBook...<price>.Value

        BooksDataGridView.DataSource = SelectedBookQuery.ToList
    End Sub
End Class
```

If you want to refer to individual attributes in the results of any query, or manipulate the output in some way, you can use a For Each statement.

Feedback 13.3

1. What is LINQ?
2. What types of queries are available in LINQ?
3. Explain what is meant by type inference.
4. Describe the notations available with XML literals.

World-Ready Programs

There was a time when the term *localization* meant that you had to create a separate version of an application for each specific language or country. This was an after-the-fact approach. Today's approach is the opposite. The planning of applications that will be used in different countries, languages, and cultures should be part of the design and original development stages.

Globalization, Localizability, and Localization

Making your programs "world-ready" is a three-part process: globalization, localizability, and localization. **Globalization** is the process of designing your program for multiple cultures and locations. The user interface as well as the output should allow for multiple languages. This is implemented through a set of rules and data for a specific language called a ***culture/locale***. A culture/locale contains information about character sets, formatting, currency and measurement rules, and methods of sorting.

Localizability determines whether an object can be localized. The resources that must change are separated from the rest of the code, resulting in one set of code that can change and another set that does not change.

The final step is **localization**, the actual process of translating the interface for a culture/locale. By setting the form's Localizable property to *true*, you can set different Text values for each control for each language. The form has a Language property that is set to *(Default)*, the current language set by the operating system. You can select a different language by dropping down the list for the Language property (Figure 13.19). When you change the form's Language

Figure 13.19

Drop down the list for the form's Language property to select a language for development.

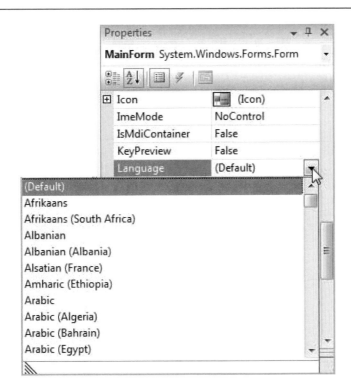

property to a different language, you can enter the Text property of each control in the current language. A separate resource file is created for each language that you select (Figure 13.20).

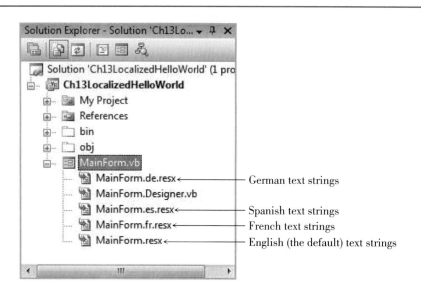

Figure 13.20

A resource file is created for each language. The .resx file holds the text strings for the Text properties of each control.

— German text strings
— Spanish text strings
— French text strings
— English (the default) text strings

The **CultureInfo class** contains an associated language, sublanguage, calendar, and access to cultural conventions for number formatting, date formatting, and comparisons of strings. Table 13.4 shows a partial list of the choices; see the Help files for *CultureInfo Class* for a complete listing of all of the culture/locale values. To use the CultureInfo class in a program, you must import the System.Globalization namespace.

A Partial Listing of the Values for the CultureInfo Class

Table 13.4

CultureInfo value	Language—Country/region
af	Afrikaans
af-ZA	Afrikaans—South Africa
ca	Catalan
zh-HK	Chinese—Hong Kong SAR
zh-CHS	Chinese (Simplified)
en-CA	English—Canada
en-GB	English—United Kingdom
en-US	English—United States
fr-FR	French—France
es-ES	Spanish—Spain
es-MX	Spanish—Mexico
de-DE	German—Germany

Normally, the language set in the operating system is the language that displays on the user interface. You also can set the language for testing purposes by modifying the class constructor using the My.Application object.

```
Public Sub New()
    ' Set the UI culture to German (Germany)
    My.Application.ChangeUICulture("de-DE")

    ' This call is required by the Windows Form Designer.
    InitializeComponent()
End Sub
```

Note: This example is for a standard Windows application. Setting the culture at run time is not supported for mobile devices.

Writing a Localized Hello World—Step-by-Step

STEP 1:   Create a new Windows Forms application project called *Ch13LocalizedHelloWorld*.

STEP 2:   Name the form and change or delete the Text property.

STEP 3:   Set the form's Localizable property to *true*.

STEP 4:   Add a Label and change its Font property to a larger size, such as 14 or 16 points.
   Note: If you change the font before you change languages, the font change applies to all languages unless you specifically override the font for a given language.

STEP 5:   Set the Text property of the label to *Hello*.

STEP 6:   Change the form's Language property to French.

STEP 7:   Set the Text property of the label to *Bonjour*.

STEP 8:   Change the form's Language property to Spanish.

STEP 9:   Set the Text property of the label to *Hola*.

STEP 10: Change the form's Language property to German.

STEP 11: Set the Text property of the label to *Hallo*.

STEP 12: Show all files in the Solution Explorer and examine the .resx files for the Form.

STEP 13: Switch to the form's code, type Sub New, and add the following lines before the InitializeComponent() call.

```
' Set the UI culture to German (Germany).
My.Application.ChangeUICulture("de-DE")
```

STEP 14: Test the program. Try changing the CultureInfo argument to see the French and Spanish texts.

► Feedback 13.4

1. Write the statement to test the Hello application for French.
2. Where should the statement be placed?

Threading

You can use the **BackgroundWorker** component to execute a long-running task. The concept of doing work in the background is frequently referred to as a *thread*. A **thread** is a separate execution path that allows a program to do more than one thing at a time. To make your application access data or process information while doing some other task at the same time, you can set up a BackgroundWorker to execute the time-consuming operations **asynchronously**, "in the background."

What actually happens is that a thread runs for a short time and suspends operation (goes to sleep) so the program can switch to another thread. Each thread has its own code to execute the desired operations, and the computer switches rapidly from one to the next, so it appears that all are executing simultaneously.

You should be aware of the differences between the terms *multitasking* and *multithreading*. Multitasking allows your computer to appear as though it is running several programs at once. Actually, each program, called a *process*, gets a share of the processor time. Each process executes in a separate area of memory and requires substantial computer resources. A process requires a complete copy of a program's code and data. However, within a single program, you may have multiple tasks to perform. Each of the tasks in the one program can be set up as a thread. A thread uses fewer resources than a process because the thread does not require its own copy of the code and all data. However, the programmer must be very careful about what each thread is doing and with which data items.

You may want to have multiple threads for several reasons. If you want your application to display animation and also have the user enter information and perform other processing, you can place each task in a separate thread. Some methods, such as connecting to a network or a database, may have to wait for a response. Methods that wait for a response are called *blocking methods*. Often a blocking method is placed in a separate thread so that if a problem occurs with the connection, you can interrupt just the thread rather than the entire application. You can use multithreading to take full advantage of multiple-core processors, and also to load several database tables at the same time.

Background Workers

To use a background worker, add a BackgroundWorker component from the *Components* section of the toolbox. In code, you specify which procedure to execute in the background and then call the component's `RunWorkerAsync` method to run the thread. Your calling thread continues to run normally and the worker runs asynchronously. The `RunWorkerAsync` method can handle parameters.

The `DoWork` method of the BackgroundWorker does the processing for the time-consuming operation. You can start the background work while executing any procedure; the following example uses a *Start* button and a *Cancel* button to control the processing. The code requires an `Imports` statement for System.ComponentModel to access the BackgroundWorker class in code.

The objects and methods for the typical background processing are

Object	Event/method	Explanation
StartButton	Click	Calls the RunWorkerAsync event handler.
CancelButton	Click	Calls the CancelAsync event handler.
	General procedure that you write	Handles all of the background processing. May return a value; can accept arguments.
BackgroundWorker	`DoWork`	Starts the background operation and gets results if appropriate. Checks if operation is canceled.
BackgroundWorker	`RunWorkerCompleted`	Executes when asynchronous operation is completed or canceled.

Two interesting Boolean properties of the BackgroundWorker class are the WorkerReportsProgress and the WorkerSupportsCancellation.

A BackgroundWorker Program

The form for this Windows program has only a *Start* and *Cancel* button. For an actual program, you would have other processing occurring on the form.

```
'Program:      Ch13BackgroundWorker
'Programmer:   Bradley/Millspaugh
'Date:         June 2009
'Description:  Run a time-consuming task in the background.

Imports System.ComponentModel

Public Class BackgroundWorkerForm

    Private Sub BackgroundWorker1_DoWork(ByVal sender As System.Object, _
      ByVal e As System.ComponentModel.DoWorkEventArgs) _
      Handles BackgroundWorker1.DoWork
        ' Create a reference to the worker.
        Dim Worker As BackgroundWorker = CType(sender, BackgroundWorker)

        ' Get any arguments using e.Argument such as:
        ' Dim CountInteger As Integer = Fix(e.Argument)

        ' Start the time-consuming process.
        ' TaskForBackgroundWork() for a sub procedure.
        e.Result = TaskForBackgroundWork() ' If you have a function.

        ' Check for cancel.
        If Worker.CancellationPending Then
            e.Cancel = True
        End If
    End Sub
```

```vb
Private Function TaskForBackgroundWork() As Long
    ' Private Sub TaskForBackgroundWork()
    ' You can set this as a sub procedure or function procedure depending
    ' on the tasks that need to be accomplished. Of course, you can name
    ' this procedure anything you want.
    Dim TotalLong As Long

    Try
        For CountInteger As Long = 1 To 1000000000
            TotalLong + = CountInteger
        Next
        Return TotalLong
    Catch
        ' Can throw an exception during the asynchronous operation.
    End Try
End Function

Private Sub StartButton_Click(ByVal sender As System.Object, _
    ByVal e As System.EventArgs) Handles StartButton.Click
    ' Start the background work.

    BackgroundWorker1.RunWorkerAsync()

End Sub

Private Sub CancelBackgroundButton_Click(ByVal sender As Object, _
    ByVal e As System.EventArgs) Handles CancelBackgroundButton.Click
    ' Cancel the background work.

    BackgroundWorker1.CancelAsync()
End Sub

Private Sub BackgroundWorker1_RunWorkerCompleted(ByVal sender As Object, _
    ByVal e As System.ComponentModel.RunWorkerCompletedEventArgs) _
    Handles BackgroundWorker1.RunWorkerCompleted
    ' Executes when the background work is complete or cancelled.

    If e.Cancelled Then
        ' Operation cancelled by user.
        MessageBox.Show("Cancelled", "Background Worker")
    ElseIf Not (e.Error Is Nothing) Then
        ' Error occurred during the operation.
        MessageBox.Show("Error " & e.Error.Message)
    Else
        ' MessageBox.Show("Background Work complete")
        MessageBox.Show("Total is " & e.Result.ToString())
    End If
End Sub
End Class
```

Feedback 13.5

1. Where does the code for background processing belong?
2. Write the code to start execution of your background work.
3. What steps are needed to cancel a background operation?

Your Hands-On Programming Example

Create a Smart Device application to display customer contact information.
Use the Northwind.sdf customers table to test your application.

Planning the Project

Figure 13.21 shows the completed layout, which the users sign off as meeting
their needs.

Figure 13.21

The layout for the Smart Device application to display customer information.

CustomerForm

Object	Property	Setting
CustomerForm	Name	CustomerForm
	Text	Northwind Customers
Company_NameLabel	Text	Company:
Contact_NameLabel	Text	Contact:
Contact_TitleLabel	Text	Title:
PhoneLabel	Text	Phone:
FaxLabel	Text	Fax:
Company_NameComboBox	DataSource	CustomersBindingSource
	DisplayMember	Company Name
Contact_NameTextBox	Bound field	Contact Name
Contact_TitleTextBox	Bound field	Contact Title
PhoneTextBox	Bound field	Phone
FaxTextBox	Bound field	Fax

Event handlers/methods	Actions—Pseudocode
Form_Load	Fill the dataset.

Write the Project

- Create the Smart Device application.

- Add the data source and configure the SELECT statement to sort by Company Name.

- Set the properties of the form objects, according to your plans.

- Write the code, according to your plans.

- Test the operation several times.

The Project Coding Solution

CustomerForm

```
'Project:      Ch13HandsOn
'Programmer:   Bradley/Millspaugh
'Date:         June 2009
'Description:  A Smart Device application to display customer information
'              from a database.

Public Class CustomerForm

    Private Sub CustomerForm_Load(ByVal sender As System.Object, _
        ByVal e As System.EventArgs) Handles MyBase.Load
        ' Fill the dataset.
        ' (Automatically generated code.)
        If NorthwindDataSetUtil.DesignerUtil.IsRunTime Then
            Me.CustomersTableAdapter.Fill(Me.NorthwindDataSet.Customers)
        End If
    End Sub
End Class
```

Summary

1. Visual Studio includes tools for creating applications for Smart Devices and mobile Web devices.
2. Emulators allow testing for output to many specific devices.
3. The Visual Basic code for mobile applications is the same as for Web Forms and Windows Forms.
4. Data can be accessed on a mobile device using SQL Server Compact 3.5.
5. Windows Presentation Foundation (WPF) can be used to create rich user interfaces, such as those in Windows Vista.
6. A WPF user interface is coded in XAML; a XAML browser application is called XBAP.
7. WPF applications are similar to Web applications in that they are created as two files: one for the user interface and one for the programming logic.
8. LINQ is a query language that can query object data types.
9. You can use a LINQ to XML query to select data elements using a three-axis model to specify the individual items. The axes are child elements, attribute elements, and descendant elements.

10. Applications can be world-ready through globalization, localizability, and localization.
11. The CultureInfo class contains many language/region combinations for localization of applications.
12. Localization applies formatting and language modifications to applications to customize them for a specific country or region.
13. The BackgroundWorker component allows multiple actions (threads) to occur simultaneously, sharing the processing time for an application.

Key Terms

asynchronous   *534*
BackgroundWorker   *534*
culture/locale   *531*
CultureInfo class   *532*
emulator   *508*
Extensible Application Markup
   Language (XAML)   *518*
globalization   *531*
Language-Integrated Queries
   (LINQ)   *522*

localizability   *531*
localization   *531*
Smart Device   *508*
thread   *534*
Windows Presentation Foundation
   (WPF)   *517*
XAML browser application
   (XBAP)   *518*
XML literals   *528*

Review Questions

1. List three devices and emulators available for mobile application development.
2. Discuss accessing data for display on a mobile device.
3. What is WPF? How does it apply to Windows and Web applications?
4. What is the purpose of LINQ? Name three operators.
5. Define each of the following:
   a. Globalization.
   b. Localizability.
   c. Localization.
   d. Culture/locale.
6. Using Help files, list three countries or locales for each of the following languages:
   a. English.
   b. Spanish.
   c. Arabic.
7. List the steps to create a Button control with different Text properties for multiple languages.
8. Explain the purpose and significance of multithreading in applications.

Programming Exercises

13.1 Write a mobile application that displays the company name, address, and hours of operation. Use your own information or use the following:

Tricia's Travels
1101 Main Place
Tustin Hills, AZ
Open M–F 9–5 and Saturdays 10–2

13.2 Create a mobile application for converting miles into kilometers. Use a text box to enter the miles and display the result in kilometers. Include a menu item labeled *Calculate*.

13.3 Write a Smart Device application to display the employee table of Northwind.sdf. Display the employees in a grid, sorted by employee last name. Allow the user to double-click a row of the grid and display the current record in a separate form. Do not display an Edit form.

13.4 Write a Smart Device application to display the employee table of Northwind.sdf. Display the employees in details view, with a concatenated employee name in a combo box for navigation.

13.5 Localize one of your previous programs to at least one other language.

13.6 Convert one of your previous programs to a WPF application. Add features for the buttons. Note that some of the features will not work in WPF, such as keyboard access and printing.

13.7 Create an application that uses LINQ to fill a data grid view with the products from the Northwind database. Display the product name, product id, and supplier for those products that have less than 20 units in stock and do not have any units on order. List the products in alphabetic order.

Case Studies

Claytor's Cottages

Localize one of your previous programs to at least one other language.

Christian's Car Rentals

Localize one of your previous programs to at least one other language.

Answers to Feedback Questions

➤ Feedback 1.1

1. A set of classes for developing and running Windows applications, Web applications, and WCF services written in multiple languages on multiple platforms.
2. What are the meaning and function of each of these terms?
   a. CLR: Common Language Runtime, an environment that manages the execution of code during run time, including security and memory management.
   b. CLS: Common Language Specification, standards that specify how a language that interacts with the CLR should behave.
   c. MSIL: Microsoft Intermediate Language, the result of a compile of a .NET source language.
   d. PE: Portable executable file, combines the MSIL with metadata.
3. Each value type variable has its own memory location; reference type variables refer to an object. If you assign one reference type variable to another, both variables refer to the same object in memory.

➤ Feedback 1.2

```
CopyrightLabel.Text = My.Application.Info.Copyright
```

➤ Feedback 1.3

Use one of the time methods of the Now object. A timer is necessary to update the time.

```
Private Sub Timer1_Tick(ByVal sender As System.Object, _
  ByVal e As System.EventArgs) Handles Timer1.Tick
    ' Update the time in the status bar.

    CurrentTimeStatusStripLabel.Text = Now.ToShortTimeString
End Sub
```

➤ Feedback 1.4

```
Dim AnAboutForm As New AboutForm
With AnAboutForm
    .MdiParent = Me
    .Show()          ' Modeless.
'   .ShowDialog()   ' Modal.
End With
```

▶ Feedback 2.1

1. Validation, calculations, business logic, and enforcing business rules.
2. Data entry using visual controls such as radio buttons, check boxes, and list boxes.
   User event handling with buttons and menu selections.
   Sending user input to the business tier.
   Doing form-level validation such as checking for null values.
   Formatting input and output.
   Displaying the forms requested by the user.

▶ Feedback 2.2

1. Property procedures allow the private properties in your class to be accessed under control of your code through `Gets` and `Sets`.
2. Each class needs to be in charge of its own data. If the properties are not declared as `Private`, the objects of other classes have access to those variables; the property values are no longer hidden (not encapsulated).
3.
```
Sub New(ByVal LastNameString As String, ByVal FirstNameString As String,
    ByVal BirthDate As Date)
    ' . . .
End Sub
```
4.
```
Dim AStudent As New Student(FirstNameTextBox.Text, LastNameTextBox.Text, _
    Date.Parse(DateTextBox.Text))
```
5. An exception should be thrown in the business tier and a message should appear in the presentation tier, telling the user what error has occurred and what can be done to fix it.

▶ Feedback 2.3

1. Module level; can be used by all procedures.
2. When the class is destroyed the variable is destroyed; generally when the project ends.
3. Private.
4. No. To make it visible, change the access level to Protected.

▶ Feedback 3.1

1. A *row* contains all of the fields that make up a record about one friend.
   A *column* will contain one piece of information, such as a name or phone number.
   A *record* contains all of the information about a single friend.
   A *field* contains one piece of information, such as a name or a phone number.
   A *primary key field* contains a piece of information that uniquely identifies each friend. In this case, it's likely the name.

2. XML data are stored as text, which will allow them to pass through firewalls and over the Internet.

▶ Feedback 3.2

1. *TableAdapter*: Communicates with the data source; contains the SQL statements.
   DataSet: Contains the data; is not directly connected to the data source.
   BindingSource: Maintains the record position within the table; can be used to filter or sort the database.
   BindingNavigator: A toolbar that contains buttons for navigation and update.
2. First select either DataGrid or Details for the table name in the Data Sources window; then drag the table to the form.

▶ Feedback 3.3

1. The ZIP code field may be sorted using the Sort property of the binding source or by using the ORDER BY SQL clause in the Query Builder.
2. Using the DataSet Designer, add a new column to the table.
   In the Properties window for the new column, set the Expression property to contain the concatenated fields:

```
City + ', ' + State + ' ' + ZIP
```

▶ Feedback 3.4

1. The binding source and the TableAdapter can be declared at the class level but should be loaded when needed. The assignment from the data tier frequently occurs in the Form_Load event handler.
2. The return type must be DataSet.
3. `FirstNameLabel.DataBindings.Add("Text", CustomersBindingSource, "FirstName")`

▶ Feedback 4.1

1. 1:1: Each user has one ID and each ID is associated with only one user.
   1:M: Each customer may have many orders. Each order can only belong to one customer.
   M:N An ingredient may be in many recipes and a recipe may have many ingredients.

2. The Categories table is the one table and the Products table is the many table.
   The primary key field is CategoryID from the Category table and the foreign key field is CategoryID in the Products table.
3. The Categories table is the parent table and the Products table is the child table.

➤ Feedback 4.2

1.
```
CustomersTableAdapter.Fill(NorthwindDataSet.Customers)
OrdersTableAdapter.Fill(NorthwindDataSet.Orders)
```
2. Open the DataSet Designer and examine the line connecting the tables. You can right-click and select *Edit relationship* to view the settings in a dialog box.
3. Drag the job description field as a combo box. Drag the employee table from the Data Sources window and drop it on the description field. Change the DropDownStyle to Simple.

➤ Feedback 4.3

1.
```
' Filter an existing DataSet based on a combo box selection.
    SelectionString = StoresComboBox.SelectedValue.ToString
    With StoresBindingSource
        .DataMember = "stores"
        .Filter = "stor_id = '" & SelectionString & "'"
    End With
```
2.
```
Dim ProductInteger As Integer
    Dim ProductDataRow As Data.DataRow
    Dim CategoryDataRow As Data.DataRow

    ' Find the data row for the selected product.
    ProductInteger = Convert.ToInt32(ProductListBox.SelectedValue)
    ProductDataRow = ProductsDataSet.products.FindByproduct_id( _
      ProductInteger)
    ' Find the matching row from the categories table.
    CategoryDataRow = ProductDataRow.GetParentRow( _
      "ProductsToCategoriesRelation")
    CategoryLabel.Text = CategoryDataRow!CategoryID.ToString
```
3.
```
Dim CategoryInteger As Integer
Dim CategoryDataRow As Data.DataRow
Dim ProductDataRow As Data.DataRow
Dim ProductDataRows As Data.DataRow()

    ' Get the selected category ID.
    CategoryInteger = Convert.ToInt32(CategoryComboBox.SelectedValue)
    ' Find the row from the category table for the selected category.
    CategoryDataRow = ProductsDataSet.categories.FindByCategoryID( _
      CategoryInteger)
```

```
' Fill an array of product rows for the selected category.
ProductDataRows = CategoryDataRow.GetChildRows( _
    "ProductsToCategoriesRelation")
' Fill a list box with the array of products.
ProductsListBox.Clear()
For Each ProductDataRow in ProductDataRows
    ProductsListBox.Items.Add( _
        ProductDataRow!CategoryName.ToString)
Next
```

Feedback 4.4

1. This represents an M:N relationship between the Orders table and the Products table. The OrderDetails table is the junction table, which creates two 1:M relationships, joining the two tables. The Orders-to-OrderDetails relationship is a 1:M with the Orders table as the parent and the Order-Details table as the child. The Products-to-OrderDetails relationship is a 1:M with the Products table as the parent and the OrderDetails table as the child.
2. You would first retrieve all of the ProductIDs from the OrderDetails table based on the OrderID. Then you would retrieve the ProductName for each of those ProductIDs from the Products table.

Feedback 5.1

```
NorthwindTableAdapter.Update(CustomerDataSet)
```

Feedback 5.2

```
1. With CustomersBindingSource
       If .Position = 0 Then
           .MoveLast()
       Else
           .MovePrevious()
       End If
   End With
2. With CustomersBindingSource
       ToolStripStatusLabel1.Text = "Record " & _
           (.Position + 1).ToString() & " of " & .Count.ToString()
   End With
```

Feedback 5.3

1. Yes.
2. Clear the text boxes.
   Set the focus to the first text box.

Disable navigation.
Set the text boxes' ReadOnly property to *False*.
Set up the buttons for an Add:
    Change the Text of the *Add* button to "Save".
    Change the Text of the *Delete* button to "Cancel".
    Disable the *Edit* button.
    Display "Adding" in the status bar.

▶ Feedback 6.1

1. XML and SOAP.
2. Web service specifications.
3. Address, binding, and contract.

▶ Feedback 6.2

1. `<OperationContract()>`
2. The IService file specifies the names of the procedures used in a contract.
   The Service.vb file contains the actual procedures and the code to fulfill
   the contract.

▶ Feedback 6.3

```
Dim InventoryWebService As New InventoryServiceReference.InventoryServiceClient
```

▶ Feedback 7.1

1. A Windows Button has a Name property and a Web Button has an ID property.
   A Windows Button has a BackgroundImage property. A Web Forms Button
   has a BorderColor property.
2. The HyperLink control and the LinkButton control look the same. However,
   the LinkButton has a click event and the HyperLink has a NavigateUrl
   property.
3. `Server.Transfer("About.aspx")`
4. `Calendar1.SelectedDate = DateTextBox.Text`

▶ Feedback 7.2

1. Add a MasterPage item to the project. When a new Web page is added, a
   check box allows selection for an associated master page.
2. The default tab order is the order in which the controls were added to
   the page.

3. You can create a new .css file and add styles to it, or you can create the styles first and select the option to create a new .css file. You can apply the styles by using the Apply Styles window.

Feedback 7.3

1. Add a RequiredFieldValidator and RangeValidator to your document.
2. Set the ControlToValidate property for all three validators to Quantity-TextBox.
3. Set the RequiredFieldValidator's Enabled property to *true*.
4. Set the RangeValidator's MinimumValue property to 1 and its Maximum-Value to 100.
5. Finally, set the RangeValidator's Type property to a numeric type (Integer or Double).

► Feedback 7.4

```
1. Session("Email") = EmailTextBox.Text
2. EmailLabel.Text = Session("Email").ToString()
3. With Response.Cookies("Email")
       .Value = Session("Email").ToString()
       .Expires = Today.AddYears(3)
   End With
```

4. Use the Session object or store the state values in a cookie on the client machine.
5. Using the ViewState property allows you to maintain values for only the current page.
6. The Page_Load event occurs for every round-trip to the server. Initialization steps should be executed only for the first display of the page (`Not IsPostBack`); retrieving session variables should occur only when it is a postback (`IsPostBack`).

► Feedback 8.1

1. Both a FormView and a DetailsView display one record at a time, but you have more control over the layout with a FormView control by designing a template.
2. Multiple data source controls are needed when a filter is required. When you have a list box, one data source control populates the list with all of the records and a different data source control is used to filter the dataset.
3. A data reader is best when there are no updates.

▶ Feedback 8.2

1. In the *Configure the Select Statement* page of the Data Source Configuration Wizard, you can click on the *Advanced* button, which enables you to generate INSERT, UPDATE, and DELETE SQL statements for the data source.
2. The *EnableEditing* and *EnableDeleting* check boxes on the smart tag cause the rows of a GridView to contain *Edit* and *Delete* buttons.
3. The FormView contains separate templates for both inserts and updates.
4. The list must be rebound in one of the "ed" event handlers such as ItemDeleted.
5. The Inserted event handler.
6. The ItemInserting event handler contains the validation. Use the Values collection of the e event argument.

▶ Feedback 8.3

1. Assuming that the service returns a dataset, the application must contain a service reference to the service. It is also necessary to instantiate a WCF Service object. The object is used to call the methods within the service.
2. The TableAdapter must call the Update method.

▶ Feedback 8.4

1. `Session("Companies") = CompanyNameListBox.Items`
2. In the *Parameter Collection Editor* dialog, select the parameter from the *Parameters* list, select *Control* from the *Parameter source* drop-down list, and select the control to which to attach from the *ControlID* drop-down list.

▶ Feedback 10.1

1. `KeyString = ElementString.GetHashCode.ToString`
   `AHashTable.Add(KeyString, ElementString)`
2. `ASortedList.Add(KeyString, ElementString)`
3. `AStack.Push(ElementString)`
4. `AQueue.Enqueue(ElementString)`

▶ Feedback 10.2

1. `PersonsHashTable.Item(KeyString)`
2. The Item property of a collection is usually the default property.
3. `PersonsHashTable.RemoveAt(KeyString)`
4. `APerson = CType(PersonsHashTable.Item(KeyString), Person)`

▶ Feedback 10.3

1. Whatever is returned by that object's `ToString` method.
2. You can write your own `ToString` method, which must override the base class `ToString` method.

▶ Feedback 10.4

1. a. For the datatype use GenericType.

   ```
   Public Sub Swap (Of GenericType) (ByRef Item1Type As GenericType, _
       ByRef Item2Type As GenericType)
       Dim TempType As GenericType
   ```

   b. ```
   Public Class GenericCollection (Of GenericType) _
       Inherits CollectionBase
   ```

2. Any type of object may be used with a generics class, but all objects within a single collection must be of the same type.
3. List, Dictionary, LinkedList, Queue, ReadOnlyCollection, Stack, Sorted-Dictionary, SortedList.

# ▶ Feedback 11.1

1. `Event WillSoundAlarm()`—must appear at the module level (in the Declarations section).
   `RaiseEvent WillSoundAlarm()`—appears in the program logic.
2. An instance of the Alarm control contains a WillSoundAlarm event; code it as you would an event for any other object.

# ▶ Feedback 11.2

1. Use the ASP.NET Web Site template and add a WebUserControl to the project.
2. Create your control; then drag the control file from the Solution Explorer onto a Web form.
   ```

▶ Feedback 12.1

1.
- a. .hhk is an index file that holds entries for the searchable index.
- b. .hhc is the Table of Contents file, which stores the headings and organization for the *Contents* tab.
- c. .chm is a compiled help file, which holds the compiled Help project.
- d. .jpeg is a graphic file used to hold an image.
- e. .avi is a multimedia file used to store a movie.
- f. .htm is a topic file that holds the screens to display in the Help Contents pane.
2. Context-sensitive help
   Pop-up help
   ToolTips
   Status bars
   Help menu

▶ Feedback 13.1

A Smart Device application runs on a device using a Windows operating system.

▶ Feedback 13.2

1. Content property.
2. The Properties window contains a text box in the heading area for entering object names.
3. The ElementHost control provides the ability to add WPF controls to a Windows Form application.

▶ Feedback 13.3

1. Language integrated queries (LINQ) is a standard language to query data.
2. LINQ is commonly used for collections of data such as an array, for XML, and for SQL datasets converted to objects using the LINQ to SQL template.
3. With type inference, the data type is determined by the usage of the field.
4. Child .<fieldname> Attribute .@fieldname Descendant …<fieldname>

▶ Feedback 13.4

1. `My.Application.ChangeUICulture("fr-FR")`
2. The statement should be placed in the Sub New() procedure.

▶ Feedback 13.5

1. The code for background processing may be placed in any procedure.
2. `BackgroundWorker1.RunWorkerAsync()`
3. Use the BackgroundWorker CancellationPending method in the DoWork event handler. Call the CancelAsync method to cancel the operation in the event handler for the *Cancel* button. In the RunWorkerCompleted event handler, check for e.Cancelled.

B

Review of Introductory VB Concepts

This appendix is intended as a review of VB topics generally covered in an introductory course. You should always treat the MSDN Help files as your primary reference and look there when you need more explanation about any of these topics.

Microsoft's Visual Studio

The latest version of Microsoft's Visual Studio, called Visual Studio 2008, includes Visual Basic, Visual C++, C# (C sharp), and the .NET Framework version 3.5. Visual Studio 2008 is sometimes referred to as Visual Studio Version 9.

The .NET Framework

The programming languages in Visual Studio run in the .NET Framework. The Framework provides for easier development of Web-based and Windows-based applications, allows objects from different languages to operate together, and standardizes how the languages refer to data and objects. Many third-party vendors have produced versions of other languages to run in the .NET Framework, including FORTRAN, COBOL, and Java.

The .NET languages all compile to a common machine language, called Microsoft Intermediate Language (MSIL). The MSIL code, called *managed code*, runs in the Common Language Runtime (CLR), which is part of the .NET Framework.

Microsoft includes the .NET Framework as part of the Windows operating system. When a person installs any available updates for their operating system, the .NET Framework is included.

Visual Studio

Visual Studio (VS) is a collection of products from Microsoft. The package comes with the Visual Studio integrated development environment (IDE) and Visual Basic, C++, and C# programming languages. All of the languages share the same IDE, so it should be relatively easy for a programmer to switch from one language to another. Visual Studio comes in several versions with varying capabilities and prices. In Help you can see a matrix showing the features of the Express Edition, Professional Edition, and Team Developer Edition.

Visual Studio runs on Windows XP and Windows Vista.

Namespaces

Namespaces are used to organize and reference groups of classes in the .NET Framework. No two classes can have the same name within a namespace. The classes in the Framework are organized into namespaces such as

System
System.Data

System.Drawing
System.Windows.Forms

Multiple files can be in the same namespace, and one file can hold more than one namespace. Some businesses use namespaces to organize their classes by application area.

By default, a new VB project includes references for certain namespaces. If you want to use the classes in other namespaces, you can add an `Imports` statement. For example, to write data in a StreamWriter (which replaces a sequential file for VB), you must declare an object of the StreamWriter data type, which is in the System.IO namespace (not included in the default references). You can use either of the following two approaches:

1. Use an `Imports` statement:

```
' This statement appears at the top of the file, before the Class statement:
Imports System.IO
----
' This statement appears inside the class, either at the module level or inside a
' procedure:
Dim BooksStreamWriter As StreamWriter
```

2. Do not use an `Imports` statement but qualify every reference by including the namespace:

```
' This statement appears inside the class, either at the module level or inside a
' procedure:
Dim BooksStreamWriter As System.IO.StreamWriter
```

If you examine the code automatically generated by the designers, you will see that every reference is completely qualified.

Visual Basic Solutions and Projects

A VB solution consists of one or more projects and a project consists of several files. The Visual Studio IDE automatically creates a folder for a new solution; all files in the solution should be stored in that folder.

The Solution File

The VB solution file is a text file that stores the names of the projects and configuration information for the solution. The file can be edited with a text editor and has an extension of .sln. The companion .suo file stores information about the screen layout of the environment and is *not* a text file, so it cannot be edited. However, you can delete the .suo file; the next time you open the solution, the .suo file is rebuilt.

By default, VS 2008 does not automatically show the solution file in the Solution Explorer. Select *Tools / Options / Projects and Solutions / Always show solution* to show the solution files. You need to display the solution file to rename it or add another project to the solution.

Project Files

VB project files, which have the extension .vbproj and .vbproj.user, are text files that store configuration settings, the names of the files needed for the project, and references to library routines needed by the project. You can examine and modify the project file with a text editor (very carefully).

VB Files

All VB code, including general classes, Windows Form classes, and code files, are stored in files with a .vb extension. A .vb file is sometimes referred to as a *module*, although, technically speaking, a module in VB is defined by `Module / End Module` statements.

A single .vb file can hold one or more classes. Or a file can consist only of sub procedures and functions to be called by classes defined in other files.

A .vb file that is used to define a Windows Form has a companion resource file with an extension of .resx and a .Designer.vb file that contains the Windows designer-generated code. The resource file holds strings of text and any graphics or other resources needed to render the form on the screen.

For a Web application, the form files have the extension .aspx. The .aspx file is used to create the form and controls, which will be rendered with HTML. The companion file, the .aspx.vb file, holds the VB code for the form. This code file is called the *code-behind* file.

By default, some of the files in a solution are not shown in the Solution Explorer. You can display all files by clicking on the *Show All Files* button at the top of the Solution Explorer window.

Data Types, Variables, and Constants

The data values that you use in a VB project may be variables or constants. They may be stored and manipulated as one of the intrinsic data types, a structure, or an object based on one of the built-in classes or classes that you write. The intrinsic data types in VB are based on classes and have properties and methods. You can see these by typing a variable name and a period—IntelliSense will pop up with the list of properties and methods.

Data Types

Data type	Use for	Storage size in bytes
Boolean	True or False values.	2
Byte	0 to 255, binary data	1
Char	Single Unicode character	2
Date	1/1/0001 through 12/31/9999	8
Decimal	Decimal fractions, such as dollars and cents.	16

continued

Data type	Use for	Storage size in bytes
Single	Single-precision floating-point numbers with six digits of accuracy.	4
Double	Double-precision floating-point numbers with 14 digits of accuracy.	8
Short	Small integer in the range –32,768 to 32,767	2
Integer	Whole numbers in the range –2,147,483,648 to +2,147,483,647	4
Long	Larger whole numbers.	8
String	Alphanumeric data: letters, digits, and other characters.	varies
Object	Any type of data	4

Selecting the Data Type

Use String data type for text characters; also for numbers that are used for identification, such as part numbers, social security numbers, and ID numbers. As a general rule, do not use numeric data types for numbers unless you plan to calculate with the numbers. In VB, strings are immutable, which means that once created, they cannot be changed. Each time that your code makes changes to a string, behind the scenes a new string is created for the new value. You also can use Char for single-character text fields.

When dealing with whole numbers, use Integer for any values that you don't expect to surpass the range limit (see table above). For example, make counters and ages Integer. Use Long for whole numbers that may be larger than the limit. Use Byte only for compatibility with routines that require it, such as reading byte data from a file.

For fractional values, you can choose Single, Double, or Decimal. Single and Double are stored as floating-point numbers, which can have some rounding errors when working with decimal fractions, such as dollars and cents. Use Decimal for dollar amounts as well as other values stored in tenths and hundredths, such as interest rates or temperatures.

Variables

You declare variables using the `Dim` statement (for dimension), or one of the other declaration statements that define the accessibility of the variable, such as `Public`, `Private`, `Friend`, or `Static`. A variable name (identifier) can be as long as you like (up to 16,383 characters); may consist of letters, digits, and underscores; cannot contain any spaces or periods; cannot be a VB keyword, and must begin with a letter.

```
{Dim|Public|Private|Static} VariableName As DataType
```

You can assign an initial value to a variable as you declare it, and you can declare multiple variables on one statement and all will have the assigned data type.

Examples

```
Dim NameString As String
Public TotalDecimal As Decimal
Private CountInteger As Integer = 1
Dim MyForm As Form
Static EventCountInteger As Integer
Dim CountInteger, IndexInteger As Integer    ' Two Integer variables.
Dim CompanyNameString As String = "Amalgamated Programming, Inc."
```

Naming Conventions

Good programming practice dictates that variable names should always be meaningful. Include the data type or class in the name. Use Pascal casing, starting the name with an uppercase letter and each word with a capital letter.

Examples
AllDoneBoolean
SalesAmountDecimal
FirstNameString
NameTextBox
VideosComboBox

Constants

Declare a constant for a value that will not change during program execution. The naming rules for constants are the same as for variables. However, this text uses the widely used naming convention of all uppercase names with underscores to separate words.

```
Const COMPANY_NAME_String As String = "R 'n R -- For Reading and Refreshment"
Const TYPE_ONE_Integer As Integer = 1
```

Declaring Numeric Constants

VB is a strongly typed programming language. Although you can choose to ignore the typing (see "Option Explicit and Option Strict" later in this appendix), you should always be aware of the data type. When you declare a numeric constant, such as 100 or 125.59, VB assigns a data type. By default, any whole number is created as Integer and any fractional value is created as Double. If you want the constant to be another data type, add a type-definition character to the right end of the number. For example: 125.5D for Decimal data type or

125.5F for Single (the *F* stands for floating point). The type-declaration characters are

Decimal	D
Double	R
Integer	I
Long	L
Short	S
Single	F

Intrinsic Constants

Intrinsic constants are system-defined constants that reside in the .NET class library. You must specify the class or group name to use the constants. Some examples of helpful constants are Color.Red, Color.Blue, Color.Orange (and dozens more); ControlChars.NewLine; ControlChars.LineFeed; MessageBox-Buttons.YesNoCancel; and MessageBoxIcons.Question. IntelliSense is a great help; just type the group name and a period, and all of the available choices pop up for your selection.

Scope and Lifetime

See Chapter 2 for a review of scope and lifetime. The scope of variables and constants has changed from VB 6.

VB scope may be block-level, local (procedure-level), module-level, or namespace-level.

Public, Private, and Static Variables

The form for a `Dim` statement is

```
{Dim|Public|Private|Friend|Protected|Protected Friend|Static} VariableName As DataType
```

The default is Private, so if you use either the `Dim` or `Private` keyword, the variable is Private. Public variables are available to any other object and can violate encapsulation rules. Private variables are available only to the class in which they are declared; Protected variables are available to the current class and any classes that inherit from the current class. Friend variables are available to any classes in the current application. Protected Friend variables are a combination of Protected and Friend—they are available to any classes that inherit from the current class in the current application.

Static variables are local variables with a lifetime that matches the module rather than the procedure. If you declare a variable as Static, it is not destroyed each time the procedure exits. Instead, the variable is created once the first time the procedure executes and retains its value for the life of the module. You can use a static variable to maintain a running count or total, as well as keep track of whether a procedure has executed previously.

```
Static DoneOnceBoolean As Boolean ' Boolean variables are initialized as False.
If DoneOnceBoolean Then
    Exit Sub                        ' Already been here before.
Else
    ' Coding that you want to do one time only.
    DoneOnceBoolean = True
End If
```

Option Explicit and Option Strict

Option Explicit and Option Strict can significantly change the behavior of the editor and compiler. Turning the options off can make coding somewhat easier but provide opportunities for hard-to-find errors and very sloppy programming.

Option Explicit

When Option Explicit is turned off, you can use any variable name without first declaring it. The first time you use a variable name, VB allocates a new variable of Object data type. This is a throwback to very old versions of Basic that did not require variable declaration and caused countless hours of debugging programs that just had a small misspelling or typo in a variable name.

   You should always program with Option Explicit turned on. In VB, the option is turned on by default for all new projects.

Option Strict

Option Strict is a newer option introduced in VB. This option makes VB more like other strongly typed languages, such as C++, Java, and C#. Option Strict does not allow any implicit (automatic) conversions from a wider data type to a narrower one, or between String and numeric data types.

   With Option Strict turned on, you must use the conversion methods, such as `Integer.Parse` and `Decimal.Parse` to convert to the desired data type from String or from a wider data type to a narrower type, such as from Decimal to Integer.

   The best practice is to always turn on Option Strict, which can save you from developing poor programming habits and likely save hours of debugging time. By default, Option Strict is turned off. You can turn it on through *Tools / Options*. Expand *Projects and Solutions* and select *VB Defaults*.

   Note: Option Strict includes all of the requirements of Option Explicit. If Option Strict is turned on, variables must be declared, regardless of the setting of Option Explicit.

Conversion between Data Types

With Option Strict turned on, you must explicitly convert data to the correct type. Each of the following methods converts a string expression to the named data type. To convert between numeric data types, use the methods of the Convert class or the `CType` function. The Convert class has methods that begin with "To" for each of the data types: `ToDecimal`, `ToSingle`, and `ToDouble`. However, there is no ToInteger; you must specify the integer data types using their .NET class names (Int16, Int32, and Int64), rather than the VB data types.

Method	Return type	Example
Boolean.Parse(*String*)	Boolean	ResultBoolean = Boolean.Parse("False")
Date.Parse(*String*)	Date	ResultDate = Date.Parse(DateTextBox.Text)
Double.Parse(*String*)	Double	AnswerDouble = Double.Parse("1234.5678")
Decimal.Parse(*String*)	Decimal	NumberDecimal = Decimal.Parse(NumberTextBox.Text)
Integer.Parse(*String*)	Integer	NumberInteger = Integer.Parse(QuantityTextBox.Text)
Single.Parse(*String*)	Single	NumberSingle = Single.Parse(QuantityTextBox.Text)
Long.Parse(*String*)	Long	NumberLong = Long.Parse(NumberTextBox.Text)
Short.Parse(*String*)	Short	NumberShort = Short.Parse(NumberTextBox.Text)
Convert.ToDecimal (*Expression*)	Decimal	NumberDecimal = Convert.ToDecimal(NumberSingle)
Convert.ToInt32 (*Expression*)	Integer	ValueInteger = Convert.ToInt32(ValueDouble)
Convert.ToSingle (*Expression*)	Single	AmountSingle = Convert.ToSingle(AmountDecimal)
(*Expression*).ToString	String	IdNumberString = IdNumberInteger.ToString()
CType(*Object*, *Type*)	Specific type	PubsDataSet = CType(DataInput, DataSet) NumberInteger = CType(NumberTextBox.Text, Integer)

Formatting Numeric Values

Use the format specifier codes with the ToString method to format data.

```
BalanceTextBox.Text = BalanceDecimal.ToString("C")
```

Format specifier code	Name	Description
C or c	Currency	Formats with a dollar sign, commas, and two decimal places. Negative values are enclosed in parentheses.
F or f	Fixed-point	Formats as a string of numeric digits, no commas, two decimal places, and a minus sign at the left for negative values.
N or n	Number	Formats with commas, two decimal places, and a minus sign at the left for negative values.
D or d	Digits	Use only for *integer* data types. Formats with a left minus sign for negative values. Usually used to force a specified number of digits to display.
P or p	Percent	Multiplies the value by 100, adds a space and a percent sign, rounds to two decimal places; negative values have a minus sign at the left.

Calculations

Calculations are performed according to the hierarchy of operations:

1. All operations within parentheses. Nested parentheses (parentheses inside parentheses) are performed first. Multiple operations within the parentheses are performed according to the rules of precedence (described in the following steps).
2. All exponentiation, using the ^ operator. Multiple exponentiation operations are performed from left to right.
3. All multiplication and division (* /). Multiple operations are performed from left to right.
4. All addition and subtraction (+ −) are performed from left to right.

There are no implied operations in VB. For example, the algebra expression 2Y must be written as 2 * Y in VB.

Arrays

You can establish arrays using any of the declaration statements: `Dim`, `Public`, `Private`, `Protected`, `Friend`, `Protected Friend`, or `Static`. You declare the array name and data type, and you can choose to either specify the upper bound of the array *or* assign initial values to the array. The upper bound of the array is the highest subscript allowed and is 1 less than the number of elements in the array, since all arrays are zero based. For example, the statement

```
Dim NameString(10) As String
```

declares an array of 11 elements, with subscripts from 0 to 10.

Alternately, you can assign initial values to the array, in which case you do not specify the upper bound but you use empty parentheses to indicate that it is an array. Use brackets around the initial values. For example, the statement

```
Dim NameString() As String = {"Sue", "Lee", "Tony", "Ann", "Leslie", "Sammy", _
    "Terry", "Laura", "Theresa", "Richard", "Dennis"}
```

also declares an array of 11 elements with subscripts from 0 to 10.

All of the array elements are the same data type. If you omit the data type, just as with single variables, the type defaults to Object, unless Option Strict is turned on, in which case an error message is generated.

Example Array Declarations

```
Dim BalanceDecimal(10) As Decimal
Dim ProductString(99) As String
Dim ValueInteger() As Integer = {1, 5, 12, 18, 20}
Dim DepartmentsString() As String = {"Accounting", "Marketing", "Human Relations"}
Private CategoryString(10) As String
Public IdNumberString(5) As String
Private QuestionInteger(5, 100) As Integer     ' Two-dimensional array.
Static AnswerString(100, 25, 5) As String      ' Three-dimensional array.
```

To declare a multidimensional array, specify the upper bounds of each of the dimensions, separated by commas (as in the last two declarations in the previous examples). Use brackets around groups when assigning initial values to a multidimensional array:

```
Dim NameString(,) As String = {{"Sue", "Lee", "Juliana", "Tony"}, _
                               {"Ann", "Leslie", "Michael", "Sammy"}, _
                               {"Terry", "Laura", "Salvatore", "Theresa"}}
```

Collections

A collection is similar to an array but much more powerful. Collections have an Items property, which contains the references to all elements of the collection. You can add elements using the `Items.Add` method, remove elements using the `Items.Remove` or `Items.RemoveAt` method, and access the `Count` property.

Retrieve a single element of the collection by using the Item property. You can specify the element using an index, as in an array, or by a key, which is a unique string.

VB has many built-in collections, such as the DataTable collection of a DataSet and the DataRow collection of a DataTable. The preferred method of traversing all elements of a collection is to use the `For Each` loop. See the topic "For Each / Next" for further information.

Chapter 10 covers creating and using collections of various types.

Structures

You can use the `Structure` and `End Structure` statements to combine multiple fields of related data. For example, an Employee structure may contain last name, first name, social security number, street, city, state, ZIP code, date of hire, and pay code. A Product structure might contain a description, product number, quantity, and price.

```
[Public | Private] Structure NameOfStructure
    Dim FirstField As Datatype
    Dim SecondField As Datatype
    ...
End Structure
```

The `Structure` declaration cannot go inside a procedure. You generally place the `Structure` statement at the top of a module with the module-level declarations. You also can place a `Structure` in a separate file.

```
Structure Employee
    Dim LastNameString As String
    Dim FirstNameString As String
    Dim SSNString As String
    Dim StreetString As String
    Dim CityString As String
    Dim StateString As String
    Dim ZipString As String
    Dim HireDate As Date
    Dim PayCodeInteger As Integer
End Structure
```

```
Public Structure Product
    Dim DescriptionString As String
    Dim ProductNumberString As String
    Dim QuantityInteger As Integer
    Dim PriceDecimal As Decimal
End Structure

Structure SalesDetail
    Dim SaleDecimal() As Decimal
End Structure
```

By default, a structure is Public. If you include an array inside a structure, you cannot specify the number of elements. You must use a `ReDim` statement in code to declare the number of elements.

In many ways, a structure is similar to defining a new data type.

Declaring Variables Based on a Structure

Once you have created a structure, you can declare variables of the structure, just as if it were another data type.

```
Dim OfficeEmployee As Employee
Dim WarehouseEmployee As Employee
Dim WidgetProduct As Product
Dim InventoryProduct(100) As Product
Dim HousewaresSalesDetail As SalesDetail
Dim HomeFurnishingsSalesDetail As SalesDetail
```

Accessing the Elements in a Structure Variable

Each field of data in a variable declared as a structure is referred to as an *element* of the structure. To access elements, use the dot notation similar to that used for objects: Specify *Variable.Element*.

```
OfficeEmployee.LastNameString
OfficeEmployee.HireDate
WarehouseEmployee.LastNameString
WidgetProduct.DescriptionString
WidgetProduct.QuantityInteger
WidgetProduct.PriceDecimal
InventoryProduct(IndexInteger).DescriptionString
InventoryProduct(IndexInteger).QuantityInteger
InventoryProduct(IndexInteger).PriceDecimal
```

Notice the use of indexes in the preceding examples. Each example was taken from the preceding `Structure` and `Dim` statements. A variable that is not an array, such as WidgetProduct, does not need an index. However, for InventoryProduct, which was dimensioned as an array of 101 elements, you must specify not only the InventoryProduct item but also the element within the structure.

Including an Array in a Structure

To declare an array in a structure (see the SalesDetail structure shown earlier), use the `ReDim` statement inside a procedure to give the array a size.

```
' Module-level declarations.
Structure SalesDetail
    Dim SaleDecimal() As Decimal
End Structure

Dim HousewaresSalesDetail As SalesDetail

' Inside a procedure (such as the Form_Load):
' Establish the number of elements in the array.
ReDim HousewaresSalesDetail.SaleDecimal(6)

' In processing:
HousewaresSalesDetail.SaleDecimal(DayIndexInteger) = TodaysSalesDecimal
```

Exception Handling

Run-time errors are called *exceptions*. Exceptions can occur when you try to use a conversion method, such as `Single.Parse` or `Decimal.Parse`, and the user has entered nonnumeric data or left a text box blank. When an operation fails, the CLR throws an exception, which you can trap and handle using .NET's structured exception handling.

Try / Catch Blocks

To trap or catch exceptions, enclose any statement(s) that might cause an error in a `Try` / `Catch` block. If an exception occurs while the statements in the `Try` block are executing, program control transfers to the `Catch` block; if a `Finally` statement is included, the code in that section executes last, whether or not an exception occurred.

```
Try
    ' Statements that may cause error.
Catch [VariableName As ExceptionType]
    ' Statements for action when exception occurs.
[Finally
    ' Statements that always execute before exit of Try block]
End Try

Try
    QuantityInteger = Integer.Parse(QuantityTextBox.Text)
    QuantityLabel.Text = QuantityInteger.ToString()
Catch
    MessageLabel.Text = "Error in input data."
End Try
```

The `Catch` as it appears in the preceding example will catch any exception. You also can specify the type of exception that you want to catch, and even have several `Catch` statements, each to catch a different type of exception. To specify a particular type of exception to catch, use one of the predefined exception classes, which are all based on, or derived from, the System.Exception class. View a complete list of system exception classes by selecting *Debug / Exceptions*.

To catch bad input data that cannot be converted to numeric, write this `Catch` statement:

```
Catch Err As InvalidCastException
    MessageLabel.Text = "Error in input data."
```

The Exception Class

Each exception is an instance of the Exception class. The properties of this class allow you to determine the code source of the error, the type of error, and the cause. The Message property contains a text message about the error and the Source property contains the name of the object causing the error.

You can include the text message associated with the type of exception by specifying the Message property of the Exception object, as declared by the variable you named on the `Catch` statement.

```
Catch AnErr As InvalidCastException
    MessageLabel.Text = "Error in input data: " & AnErr.Message
```

Handling Multiple Exceptions

Include multiple `Catch` blocks (handlers) to trap for different kinds of errors. When an exception occurs, the `Catch` statements are checked in sequence. The first one with a matching exception type is used.

```
Catch AnErr As InvalidCastException
    ' Statements for nonnumeric data.
Catch AnErr As ArithmeticException
    ' Statements for calculation problem.
Catch AnErr As Exception
    ' Statements for any other exception.
```

The last `Catch` will handle any exceptions that do not match the first two exception types. Note that it is acceptable to use the same variable name for multiple `Catch` statements; the variable you declare on a `Catch` statement has block-level scope, so it is visible only inside that single `Catch`.

Catching Errors with TryParse

Catching exceptions is a very resource-consuming operation. A more efficient approach is to perform conversions using the `TryParse` methods. `TryParse` attempts the conversion and returns Boolean *true* if successful and *false* if unsuccessful. The converted value is available in an argument of the method. Just as with the `Parse` methods, `TryParse` works on string data only.

```
' Convert input to integer.
Dim ConvertedInteger As Integer
If Integer.TryParse(NumberTextBox.Text, ConvertedInteger) Then
    ' Successful conversion; perform calculation with ConvertedInteger.
Else
    ' Unsuccessful conversion.
    MessageBox.Show("Invalid input data.")
End If
```

The `Integer.TryParse` method returns *true* and places the converted value into the second argument (ConvertedInteger in the preceding example). For an unsuccessful conversion, the method returns *false* and the ConvertedInteger argument holds zero.

Method	Returns	Example
`Short.TryParse(`*`String,`* *`VariableShort`*`)`	Short	`If Short.TryParse(NumTextBox.Text,` `VarShort) Then`
`Integer.TryParse(`*`String,`* *`VariableInteger`*`)`	Integer	`If Integer.TryParse(NumTextBox.Text,` `VarInteger) Then`
`Long.TryParse(`*`String,`* *`VariableLong`*`)`	Long	`If Long.TryParse(NumTextBox.Text,` `VarLong) Then`
`Decimal.TryParse(`*`String,`* *`VariableDecimal`*`)`	Decimal	`If Decimal.TryParse(NumTextBox.Text,` `VarDecimal) Then`
`Single.TryParse(`*`String,`* *`VariableSingle`*`)`	Single	`If Single.TryParse(NumTextBox.Text,` `VarSingle) Then`
`Double.TryParse(`*`String,`* *`VariableDouble`*`)`	Double	`If Double.TryParse(NumTextBox.Text,` `VarDouble) Then`
`DateTime.TryParse(`*`String,`* *`VariableDateTime`*`)` *or* `Date.TryParse(`*`String,`* *`VariableDate`*`)`	Date	`If DateTime.TryParse(DateTextBox.Text,` `VarDate) Then` `If Date.TryParse(DateTextBox.Text,` `VarDate) Then`
`Boolean.TryParse(`*`String,`* *`VariableBoolean`*`)`	Boolean	`If Boolean.TryParse(TrueFalseTextBox.Text,` `VarBoolean) Then`

Control Structures

You use control structures to modify the sequence of the logic flow in a program. Each of the control structures tests expressions to determine the path to take.

Boolean Expressions

You test a Boolean expression for *true* or *false*. An expression may be based on the value of a Boolean variable or on the relationship of two or more values. You can form an expression using the six relational operators and the logical operators.

Relational operators	Logical operators
> (greater than)	`And`
< (less than)	`Or`
= (equal to)	`Not`
>= (greater than or equal to)	`AndAlso`
<= (less than or equal to)	`OrElse`
<> (not equal to)	

Comparisons must be on like types, and may compare strings and/or numeric values.

If / Then / Else

Although you will see examples of the single-line If statement, the block If statement is the recommended form.

The Single-Line If Statement

```
If Expression Then ActionToTakeWhenTrue Else ActionToTakeWhenFalse
```

Example

```
If CountInteger > 0 Then DisplayTheCount
```

The Block If Statement

```
If Expression Then
    Action(s)ToTakeWhenTrue
[ElseIf Expression Then
    Action(s)ToTake]
[Else
    Action(s)ToTake]
End If
```

Examples

```
If FirstTimeBoolean Then
    InitializeVariables()
    FirstTimeBoolean = False
End If

If NameTextBox.Text <> "Smith" Then
    ' Take some action.
Else
    MessageBox.Show("Hello Ms. Smith")
End If
```

Nested If Statements

You can nest one or more block If statements completely inside another block If statement. Indenting each level of If helps to visualize the logic but isn't a requirement. By default, the IDE automatically indents code for you. You can turn that feature off by deselecting *Tools / Options / Text Editor / Basic / VB Specific / Pretty listing (reformatting) of code* and changing *Indenting* to *None* on the *Editor* page.

```
If Expression Then
    If Expression Then
        Action(s)ToTake
    Else
        Action(s)ToTake
    End If
```

```
Else
    If Expression Then
        Action(s)ToTake
    Else
        Action(s)ToTake
    End If
End If
```

Select Case

The `Select Case` structure can test for several values and is easier to read and debug than a deeply nested `If` statement. The data type of the expression to test must match the type of the constants. For the constants, you can use a combination of relational operators, constant ranges, and multiple constants.

- When using a relational operator (e.g., `Is >= 100`), the word `Is` must be used.

- To indicate a range of constants, use the word `To` (e.g., `80 To 99`).

- Multiple constants should be separated by commas.

The elements used for the constant list may have any of these forms:

```
Is relational-operator constant        Case Is < 10
constant To constant                    Case 25 To 50
constant [, constant...]                Case 2, 5, 9
```

When you want to test for a string value, you must include quotation marks around the literals. It is best to convert the string value to uppercase (or lowercase) so that a match does not depend on an exact case match.

```
Select Case Expression
    Case ConstantList
        Statement(s)ToExecute
    [Case ConstantList
        Statement(s)ToExecute]
    ...
    [Case Else]
        [Statement(s)ToExecute]
End Select
```

Examples

```
Select Case ListIndexInteger
    Case 0
        HandleItemZero()
    Case 1, 2, 3
        HandleItems()
    Case Else
        HandleNoSelection()
End Select
```

```
Select Case TeamNameTextBox.Text.ToUpper()
    Case "TIGERS"
        ' (Code for Tigers)
    Case "LEOPARDS"
        ' (Code for Leopards)
    Case "COUGARS", "PANTHERS"
        ' (Code for Cougars and Panthers)
    Case Else
        ' (Code for any nonmatch)
End Select
```

If the `Case Else` clause is omitted and none of the `Case` expressions is *true*, the program continues execution at the statement following the `End Select`. If more than one `Case` value is matched by the expression, only the statements in the *first* matched `Case` clause execute.

Loops

A loop repeats program statements and checks a condition to determine when to exit the loop. VB has several constructs for forming loops, including the `For / Next`, `Do / Loop`, and `For Each / Next`.

Each time execution passes through a loop, it is called one *iteration*.

For / Next

A `For / Next` is the preferred looping construct when you know ahead of time how many iterations you need. You must declare a variable to use as the loop index, which can be any of the numeric data types. The initial value, test value, and step may be constants, variables, numeric property values, or expressions.

```
For LoopIndex [As NumericDataType] = InitialValue To TestValue [Step Increment]
    ' Statement(s) to execute inside the loop.
Next [LoopIndex]
```

When `Step` is omitted, the increment defaults to 1.

```
For IndexInteger = 1 To 10
    Debug.WriteLine(IndexInteger)
Next IndexInteger
```

The loop index is compared to the test value. If the loop index is *greater than* the test value, control passes to the statement following the `Next` statement. Otherwise, the statement(s) inside the loop are executed. At the `Next` statement, the loop index is incremented and tested again.

You also can use a negative increment. In this case, the test is made for *less than* the test value.

```
For IndexInteger = 10 To 1 Step −1
    Debug.WriteLine(IndexInteger)
Next IndexInteger
```

You can define the loop index variable in the `For / Next` statement, which declares it as a block variable. The scope of the variable is only within the For block (until the Next), so it will not be in scope after completion of the loop.

```
For IndexInteger As Integer = 1 To 10
    ' IndexInteger can be used here.
Next IndexInteger
' IndexInteger is out of scope here.
```

Do Loops

Do Loops begin with the Do keyword and end with the Loop keyword. You can test a condition at the top of the loop, which might prevent the statements within the loop from executing even once, or at the bottom of the loop. You can form the condition for ending the loop with either the While or Until keyword. The While continues execution of the loop as long as an expression evaluates *true*; the Until continues execution until the expression evaluates *true*.

```
Do {While | Until} Expression
    ' Statement(s) to execute inside the loop.
Loop
```

or

```
Do
    ' Statement(s) to execute inside the loop.
Loop {While | Until} Expression
```

Examples

```
Do While CountDownInteger > 0
    ' Statements inside the loop.
    CountDownInteger -= 1
Loop
```

```
Do
    ' Statements to check for a match.
    If InputTextBox.Text = SearchValueString Then
        FoundBoolean = True
    End If
Loop Until FoundBoolean
```

For Each / Next

The For Each / Next loop is the preferred construct for stepping through all elements of an array or a collection. When Option Strict is on, you must declare a single variable of the same type as the array elements or the members of the collection. Inside the loop, the variable holds the current object or array element, which is read only. The array or collection elements cannot be altered inside the loop.

One great advantage of using the For Each / Next is that you don't have to manipulate indexes or test for the number of elements.

```
For Each VariableName [As DataType] In {ArrayName | CollectionName}
    ' Statements to execute inside the loop.
Next
```

Examples

```
Dim ItemString As String
For Each ItemString In ItemStringArray
    Debug.WriteLine(ItemString)
Next
```

```
' Same as above code, but using a block variable.
For Each ItemString As String In ItemStringArray
    Debug.WriteLine(ItemString)
Next
```

```
Dim EmployeeArrayDataRow As DataRow()    ' Array of data rows.
Dim EmployeeDataRow As DataRow           ' A single data row.
' Code here to fill the EmployeeArrayDataRow array with rows (found in Chapter 4).
For Each EmployeeDataRow In EmployeeArrayDataRow
    Debug.WriteLine("Employee First Name = " & EmployeeDataRow.Item("fname"))
    Debug.WriteLine("Employee Last Name = " & EmployeeDataRow.Item("lname"))
Next
```

See Chapter 10 for many examples of using For Each with various types of collections, including the Items collection of a list box.

Early Exit

In each of the loop constructs, you can exit early, before the test condition is *true*. Although many structured-programming purists advise against this practice, it is widely used in programming.

Use the Exit For or Exit Do, depending on the type of loop you are using.

```
Do
    If InputTextBox.Text = "END" Then
        Exit Do
    End If
    ' Process some more...
Loop Until NumberProcessed = 10
```

```
For IndexInteger = 1 To 10
    Debug.WriteLine(IndexInteger)
    If IndexInteger = MatchInteger Then
        Exit For
    End If
Next IndexInteger
```

Continue

Use the Continue statement to skip the rest of the statements inside the loop. This transfers control to the last statement in the loop and retests the loop exit condition. Use Continue For or Continue Do, depending on the type of loop construct.

```
For LoopInteger As Integer = 0 To NameListBox.Items.Count - 1
    If NameListBox.Items(LoopInteger).ToString() = String.Empty Then
        Continue For
    End If
    ' Code to do something with the name found.
Next
```

```
LoopInteger = -1
Do Until LoopInteger = NameListBox.Items.Count - 1
    LoopInteger += 1
    If NameListBox.Items(LoopInteger).ToString() = String.Empty Then
        Continue Do
    End If
    ' Code to do something with the name found.
Loop
```

Message Boxes

You can display a message to the user in a message box, which is a predefined
instance of the MessageBox class. The overloaded Show method of the MessageBox object allows you to specify the message, an optional icon, title bar
text, and button(s).

```
MessageBox.Show(TextMessage)
MessageBox.Show(TextMessage, TitlebarText)
MessageBox.Show(TextMessage, TitlebarText, MessageBoxButtons)
MessageBox.Show(TextMessage, TitlebarText, MessageBoxButtons, MessageBoxIcon)
```

Examples

```
MessageBox.Show("Enter numeric data.")
```

```
MessageBox.Show("Try again.", "Data Entry Error")
```

```
MessageBox.Show("This is a message.", "This is a title bar", MessageBoxButtons.OK)
```

```
Try
    QuantityInteger = Integer.Parse(QuantityTextBox.Text)
    QuantityLabel.Text = QuantityInteger
Catch err As InvalidCastException
    MessageBox.Show("Nonnumeric Data.", "Error", MessageBoxButtons.OK, _
        MessageBoxIcon.Exclamation)
End Try
```

The message string that you display may be a string literal enclosed in
quotes or it may be a string variable. If the message is too long for one line,
Visual Basic wraps it to the next line. You can control the line breaks by
concatenating ControlChars.NewLine characters into the string.

The string that you specify for TitlebarText will appear in the title bar of the message box. If you choose the first form of the Show method, without the TitlebarText, the title bar will appear empty.

You specify the buttons to display using the MessageBoxButtons constants from the MessageBox class. The choices are OK, OKCancel, RetryCancel, YesNo, YesNoCancel, and AbortRetryIgnore. The default for the Show method is OK, so unless you specify otherwise, you will get only the OK button. The Show method returns a DialogResult object that you can check to see which button the user clicked.

The easy way to select the icon to display is to select from IntelliSense, which pops up with the complete list. The actual appearance of the icons varies from one operating system to another. You can see a description of the icons in Help under the "MessageBoxIcon Enumeration" topic.

Declaring an Object Variable for the Method Return

To capture the information about the outcome of the Show method, declare a variable to hold an instance of the DialogResult type.

```
Dim ResponseDialogResult As DialogResult

ResponseDialogResult = MessageBox.Show("Clear the current order figures?", _
   "Clear Order", MessageBoxButtons.YesNo, MessageBoxIcon.Question)
```

The next step is to check the value of the return, comparing to the Dialog-Result constants, such as Yes, No, OK, Retry, Abort, and Cancel.

```
If ResponseDialogResult = Windows.Forms.DialogResult.Yes Then
    ' Code to clear the order.
End If
```

Specifying a Default Button and Options

Two additional signatures for the MessageBox.Show method are

```
MessageBox.Show(TextMessage, TitlebarText, MessageBoxButtons, MessageBoxIcons, _
   MessageBoxDefaultButton)
MessageBox.Show(TextMessage, TitlebarText, MessageBoxButtons, MessageBoxIcons, _
   MessageBoxDefaultButton, MessageBoxOptions)
```

To make the second button (the *No* button) the default, use this statement:

```
ResponseDialogResult = MessageBox.Show("Clear the current order figures?", _
   "Clear Order", MessageBoxButtons.YesNo, MessageBoxIcon.Question, _
   MessageBoxDefaultButton.Button2)
```

You can make the message appear right-aligned in the message box by setting the MessageBoxOptions argument:

```
ResponseDialogResult = MessageBox.Show("Clear the current order figures?", _
   "Clear Order", MessageBoxButtons.YesNo, MessageBoxIcon.Question, _
   MessageBoxDefaultButton.Button2, MessageBoxOptions.RightAlign)
```

Sub and Function Procedures

Programs are made up of a series of procedures, which are the building blocks of programming. In VB, you *must* write event handlers to respond to the events caused by the user. You also can create *general* procedures, which are not associated with any event but are called from other procedures.

You can write sub procedures, function procedures, and property procedures. A sub procedure is a block of code that does not return a value. A function procedure (or just *function*) is a block of code that returns a value. Property procedures are used to get or set the values of properties in class modules and form modules.

Calling Procedures

You can call a sub procedure with or without the optional word `Call`. Assuming that you have written a sub procedure named PrintHeadings that requires an ending date as an argument, you call it with this statement:

```
[Call] PrintHeadings(EndingDate)
```

To call a sub procedure that does not require arguments, use empty parentheses:

```
[Call] DisplayTheDate()
```

You call a function procedure by using it in an expression, just like calling one of VB's built-in functions. Assuming that you have written a function called *AverageCost* that requires three Decimal arguments and returns a Decimal result, call the function like this:

```
AverageDecimal = AverageCost(FirstDecimal, SecondDecimal, ThirdDecimal)
```

Passing Arguments

The values that you pass to procedures are called *arguments*. You absolutely *must* supply the arguments in the correct order and in the correct data type. The names of the variables are not passed to the called procedure, only a copy of the data (`ByVal`) or the address of the data value (`ByRef`). (Refer to the "ByRef and ByVal" topic.)

When you write sub procedures and functions, you must specify the values to be passed. Inside the procedures, those values are referred to as *parameters*. (The calling code passes *arguments*; the called procedure receives those values and calls them *parameters*.)

Writing Sub Procedures

To write a new procedure, place the insertion point on a blank line between procedures and type the procedure header (without the parentheses). For example, you can type `Private Sub PrintHeadings` and press Enter. VB adds the parentheses and the `End Sub` statement.

```
Private Sub PrintHeadings()

End Sub
```

Of course, you also can type the parameter list and the parentheses, if you wish.

```
Private Sub PrintHeadings(ByVal EndingDate As Date)
```

The parameter passed to the PrintHeadings sub procedure is a local variable inside the procedure. Call the PrintHeadings sub procedure in any of these ways:

```
PrintHeadings(Today)            ' Pass today's date.
PrintHeadings(MyFavoriteDate)
PrintHeadings(#2/2/2009#)
```

The PrintHeadings sub procedure uses the EndingDate parameter inside the procedure to reference the value passed for the parameter.

```
Private Sub PrintHeadings(ByVal EndingDate As Date)
    ' Print the date.

    Debug.WriteLine(EndingDate.ToShortDateString())
End Sub
```

Writing Function Procedures

Functions return a value, so a function procedure must have a data type for the return value. The procedure header for a function looks like this:

```
[{Public|Private|Protected|Friend|Protected Friend}] _
  Function FunctionName(ParameterList) As DataType
```

Somewhere inside the function procedure, before exiting, you must return a value. You can use the Return statement (the preferred technique) or assign a value to the function name (which was the technique used in VB 6). That value is returned to the calling statement.

```
Private Function AverageCost(ByVal FirstCostDecimal As Decimal, _
  ByVal SecondCostDecimal As Decimal, _
  ByVal ThirdCostDecimal As Decimal) As Decimal
    ' Calculate the average of three numbers.

    ' Preferred Return statement:
    Return (FirstCostDecimal + SecondCostDecimal + ThirdCostDecimal) / 3D

    ' Alternate Return statement:
    ' AverageCost = (FirstCostDecimal + SecondCostDecimal + ThirdCostDecimal) / 3D
End Function
```

ByRef and ByVal

By default, arguments are passed ByVal (by value), which is a change from VB 6. ByVal forces VB to make a copy of the data and pass the copy. If the called procedure makes any changes to the argument, it has no effect on the original variable that you passed. By contrast, passing an argument `ByRef` (by reference) means that the address of your program variable is passed to the procedure. Therefore, if the called procedure makes any changes to the parameter's value, the change will be made to the original variable. To protect your variables and provide better separation of program tasks, you should specify that an argument be passed `ByVal`, unless you have a very good reason for allowing the called procedure to modify the original variable.

Public, Private, Protected, Friend, or Protected Friend

Just as for variable declarations, you can declare sub procedures and functions to be Public, Private, Protected, Friend, or Protected Friend. The accessibility of procedures matches that of similarly declared variables. If you omit the accessibility keyword when writing a procedure, the default is Public.

VB Functions and Methods

VB provides many intrinsic functions and methods for math operations, financial calculations, string manipulation, and date/time processing.

IntelliSense helps you type the arguments of functions and methods. When you type the parentheses, the arguments pop up, showing the correct order. The argument to enter is shown in bold. The order of the arguments is important because the function uses the values based on their position in the argument list. If the arguments are supplied in the incorrect order, the result is wrong. And if the data types are incorrect, a compile error occurs.

Methods may have overloaded parameter lists, which means that there is more than one way to call the method. When you enter the arguments, you must match one of the parameter lists exactly. Note that VB does allow implicit widening conversions, so a supplied argument may be of a wider data type than that specified in the parameter.

Working with Dates

You can use the methods of the DateTime structure to retrieve the system date, break down a date into component parts, test whether the contents of a field are compatible with the Date data type, and convert other data types to a Date.

The DateTime Structure

When you declare a variable of Date data type in VB, the .NET Common Language Runtime uses the DateTime structure, which has an extensive list of properties and methods. You can use the shared members of the DateTime structure (identified by a yellow "S" in the MSDN Help lists) without declaring an instance of Date or DateTime. For example, to use the Now property:

```
TodaysDate = Now
```

To use the nonshared members, you must reference an instance of a DateTime structure, such as a variable of Date type:

```
TimeLabel.Text = TodaysDate.ToShortTimeString()
```

Here is a partial list of some useful properties and methods of the Date-Time structure:

Property or method	Purpose
Date	Date component.
Day	Integer day of month; 1–31.
DayOfWeek	Integer day; 0 = Sunday.
DayOfYear	Integer day; 1–366.
Hour	Integer hour; 0–23.
Minute	Integer minutes; 0–59.
Second	Integer seconds; 0–59.
Month	Integer month; 1 = January.
Now (shared)	Retrieve system date and time.
Today (shared)	Retrieve system date.
Year	Year component.
`ToLongDateString`	Date formatted as long date.
`ToLongTimeString`	Date formatted as long time.
`ToShortDateString`	Date formatted as short date.
`ToShortTimeString`	Date formatted as short time.

Retrieving the System Date and Time

You can retrieve the system date and time from your computer's clock using the Now property or the Today property. Now retrieves both the date and time; Today retrieves only the date.

```
Dim DateAndTimeDate As Date
DateAndTimeDate = Now

Dim TodaysDate As Date
TodaysDate = Today
```

To display the values formatted:

```
DateTimeLabel.Text = DateAndTimeDate.ToLongDateString()
DateLabel.Text = TodaysDate.ToShortDateString()
```

Date Variables

The Date data type may hold values of many forms that represent a date. Examples could be May 26, 2009 or 5/26/09 or 5-26-2009. When you assign a literal value to a Date variable, enclose it in # signs:

```
Dim TheDate as Date = #5/26/2009#
```

Converting Values to a Date Format

If you want to store values in a Date data type, you need to convert the value to a Date type. Use `DateTime.Parse` or `Date.Parse` to convert a string value to a Date type; it will throw an exception if it is unable to create a valid date from the argument. You also can use the `DateTime.TryParse` or `Date.TryParse` to do the conversion, which returns a Boolean *false* for an invalid date. The converted date is placed in the string argument.

```
' Convert using Parse.
Dim TheDate As Date
Try
    TheDate = DateTime.Parse(DateTextBox.Text)
Catch
    MessageBox.Show("Invalid date.")
End Try
```

```
' Convert using TryParse.
Dim TheDate As Date
If (Date.TryParse(DateTextBox.Text, TheDate)) Then
    ' Good date, use TheDate.
Else
    MessageBox.Show("Invalid date.")
End If
```

Financial Functions

Visual Basic provides functions for many types of financial and accounting calculations, such as payment amount, depreciation, future value, and present value. When you use these functions, you eliminate the need to know and code the actual formulas yourself. Each financial function returns a value that you can assign to a variable, or to a property of a control.

Category	Purpose	Function
Depreciation	Double-declining balance.	DDB
	Straight line.	SLN
	Sum-of-the-years' digits.	SYD
Payments	Payment.	Pmt
	Interest payment.	IPmt
	Principal payment.	PPmt
Return	Internal rate of return.	IRR
	Rate of return when payments and receipts are at different rates.	MIRR
Rate	Interest rate.	Rate
Future value	Future value of an annuity.	FV
Present value	Present value.	PV
	Present value when values are not constant.	NPV
Number of periods	Number of periods for an annuity. (Number of payments)	NPer

You must supply each function with the necessary arguments in the correct sequence and data type. For example, the following `Pmt` function has three parameters: the interest rate, number of periods, and amount of loan. If you supply the values in a different order, the `Pmt` function will calculate incorrectly.

The PMT Function

You can use the `Pmt` function to find the amount of each payment on a loan if the interest rate, the number of periods, and the amount borrowed are known.

```
Pmt(InterestRatePerPeriodDouble, NumberOfPeriodsDouble, AmountOfLoanDouble)
```

The interest rate must be specified as Double and adjusted to the interest rate per period. For example, if the loan is made with an annual rate of 12 percent and monthly payments, the interest rate must be converted to the monthly rate of 1 percent. Convert the annual rate to the monthly rate by dividing by the number of months in a year (AnnualPercentageRate / 12).

The number of periods for the loan is the total number of payments. If you want to know the monthly payment for a five-year loan, you must convert the number of years to the number of months. Multiply the number of years by 12 months per year (NumberOfYears * 12).

The `Pmt` function requires Double arguments and returns a Double value.

```
Try
    MonthlyRateDouble = Double.Parse(RateTextBox.Text) / 12.0
    MonthsDouble = Double.Parse(YearsTextBox.Text) * 12.0
    AmountDouble = Double.Parse(AmountTextBox.Text)
    MonthlyPaymentDouble = -Pmt(MonthlyRateDouble, MonthsDouble, AmountDouble)
    PaymentLabel.Text = MonthlyPaymentDouble.ToString("C")
Catch
    MessageBox.Show("Invalid data.")
End Try
```

Notice the minus sign when using the `Pmt` function. When an amount is borrowed or payments made, that is considered a negative amount. You need the minus sign to reverse the sign and make a positive answer.

The Rate Function

You can use the `Rate` function to determine the interest rate per period when the number of periods, the payment per period, and the original amount of the loan are known.

```
Rate(NumberOfPeriodsDouble, PaymentPerPeriodDouble, LoanAmountDouble)
```

The `Rate` function requires Double arguments and returns a Double value.

```
Try
    MonthDouble = Double.Parse(YearsTextBox.Text) * 12.0
    PaymentDouble = Double.Parse(PaymentTextBox.Text)
```

```
    AmountDouble = Double.Parse(LoanAmtTextBox.Text)
    PeriodicRateDouble = Rate(MonthDouble, -PaymentDouble, AmountDouble)
    AnnualRateDouble = PeriodicRateDouble * 12.0
    YearlyRateLabel.Text = AnnualRateDouble.ToString("P")
Catch
    MessageBox.Show("Invalid data.")
End Try
```

Notice that the `Rate` function, like the `Pmt` function, needs a minus sign on one of its arguments to produce a positive result.

Functions to Calculate Depreciation

If you need to calculate the depreciation of an asset in a business, Visual Basic provides three functions: the double-declining-balance method, the straight-line method, and the sum-of-the-years'-digits method.

The `DDB` function calculates the depreciation for a specific period within the life of the asset, using the double-declining-balance method formula. Once again, you do not need to know the formula but only the order in which to enter the arguments.

```
DDB(OriginalCostDouble, SalvageValueDouble, LifeOfTheAssetDouble, PeriodDouble)
```

The `DDB` function returns a Double value and requires Double arguments.

```
Try
    CostDouble = Double.Parse(CostTextBox.Text)
    SalvageDouble = Double.Parse(SalvageTextBox.Text)
    YearsDouble = Double.Parse(YearsTextBox.Text)
    PeriodDouble = Double.Parse(PeriodTextBox.Text)
    DepreciationLabel.Text = DDB(CostDouble, SalvageDouble, YearsDouble, _
        PeriodDouble).ToString("C")
Catch
    MessageBox.Show("Invalid data.")
End Try
```

The other financial functions work in a similar manner. You can use Help to find the argument list, an explanation, and an example.

Mathematical Functions

In Visual Basic, the mathematical functions are included as methods in the System.Math class. To use the methods, you must either import System.Math or refer to each method with the Math namespace.

For example, to use the `Abs` (absolute value) method, you can use either of these techniques:

```
AnswerDouble = Math.Abs(ArgumentDouble)
```

or

```
Imports System.Math              ' At the top of the module.
AnswerDouble = Abs(ArgumentDouble)  ' Inside a procedure.
```

A few functions are not methods of the Math class but are Visual Basic functions. These functions, such as `Fix`, `Int`, and `Rnd`, cannot specify the Math namespace.

A good way to see the list of math methods is to type "Math." in the editor; IntelliSense will pop up with the complete list. The following is a partial list of the Math methods:

Method	Returns	Argument data type	Return data type
`Abs(x)`	The absolute value of x. $\|x\| = x$ if $x \geq 0$ $\|x\| = -x$ if $x < 0$	Overloaded: All types allowed.	Return matches argument type.
`Atan(x)`	The angle in radians whose tangent is x.	Double	Double
`Cos(x)`	The cosine of x where x is in radians.	Double	Double
`Exp(x)`	The value of e raised to the power of x.	Double	Double
`Log(x)`	The natural logarithm of x, where $x \geq 0$.	Double	Double
`Max(x1, x2)`	The larger of the two arguments	Overloaded: All types allowed. Both arguments must be the same type.	Return matches argument type
`Min(x1, x2)`	The smaller of the two arguments	Overloaded: All types allowed. Both arguments must be the same type.	Return matches argument type
`Round(x)` `Round(x, DecimalPlaces)`	The rounded value of x, rounded to the specified number of decimal positions. *Note:* .5 rounds to the nearest even number.	Overloaded: Double or Decimal; Integer DecimalPlaces	Return matches argument type
`Sign(x)`	The sign of x. -1 if $x < 0$ 0 if $x = 0$ 1 if $x > 0$	Overloaded: All types allowed.	Return matches argument type
`Sin(x)`	The sine of x where x is in radians.	Double	Double
`Sqrt(x)`	The square root of x where x must be ≥ 0.	Double	Double
`Tan(x)`	The tangent of x where x is in radians.	Double	Double

Here are some useful VB functions:

Function	Returns	Argument data type	Return data type
`Fix(x)`	The integer portion of x (truncated).	Any numeric expression	Integer
`Int(x)`	The largest integer $\leq x$.	Any numeric expression	Integer
`Rnd()`	A random number in the range 0–1 (exclusive).		Single

Working with Strings

Visual Basic provides many methods for working with text strings. Strings in Visual Studio are immutable, which means that once a string is created, it cannot be changed. Although many programs in this text seem to modify a string, actually a new string is created and the old string is discarded.

For string handling, you can use any of the many methods of the String class. You also can use the StringBuilder class, which is more efficient if you are building or modifying strings, since the string *can* be changed in memory. In other words, a StringBuilder is *mutable* (changeable) and a String is *immutable*.

Here is a partial list of the methods in the String class. For shared methods, you don't need to specify a String instance; for nonshared methods, you must attach the method to the String instance. For example:

Shared Method

```
If Compare(AString, BString) > 0 Then
    ' . . .
```

Nonshared Method

```
If MyString.EndsWith("ed") Then
    ' . . .
```

Method	Returns

Compare(*AString, BString*)
(Shared)
	Integer:
	   Negative if AString < BString
	   Zero if AString = BString
	   Positive if AString > BString

Compare(*AString, BString,*
  IgnoreCaseBoolean)
(Shared)
	Case insensitive if IgnoreCaseBoolean is *True.*
	Integer:
	   Negative if AString < BString
	   Zero if AString = BString
	   Positive if AString > BString

Compare(*AString, AStartInteger,*
  BString, BStartInteger, LengthInteger)
(Shared)
	Compare substrings; start position indicates beginning character to compare for a length of LengthInteger.
	Integer:
	   Negative if AString < BString
	   Zero if AString = BString
	   Positive if AString > BString

Compare(*AString, AStartInteger,*
  BString, BStartInteger, LengthInteger,
  IgnoreCaseBoolean)
(Shared)
	Case insensitive if IgnoreCaseBoolean is *True.*
	Compare substrings; start position indicates beginning character to compare for a length of LengthInteger.
	Integer:
	   Negative if AString < BString
	   Zero if AString = BString
	   Positive if AString > BString

continued

Method	Returns
EndsWith(*AString*)	Boolean. *True* if the String instance ends with AString. Case sensitive.
Equals(*AString*)	Boolean. *True* if the String instance has the same value as AString. Case sensitive.
IndexOf(*AString*)	Integer. Index position in String instance that AString is found. Positive: String found at this position. Negative: String not found.
IndexOf(*AString, StartPositionInteger*)	Integer. Index position in String instance that AString is found, starting at StartPositionInteger. Positive: String found at this position. Negative: String not found.
IndexOf(*AString, StartPositionInteger, NumberCharactersInteger*)	Integer. Index position in String instance that AString is found, starting at StartPositionInteger, for a length of Number-CharactersInteger. Positive: String found at this position. Negative: String not found.
Insert(*StartIndexInteger, AString*)	New string with AString inserted in the String instance, beginning at StartIndexInteger.
LastIndexOf(*AString*)	Integer: Index position of AString within String instance, searching from the right end.
LastIndexOf(*AString, StartPositionInteger*)	Integer: Index position of AString within String instance, searching leftward, beginning at StartPositionInteger.
LastIndexOf(*AString, StartPositionInteger, NumberCharactersInteger*)	Integer: Index position of AString within String instance, searching leftward, beginning at StartPositionInteger, for a length of NumberCharactersInteger.
PadLeft(*TotalLengthInteger*)	New String with String instance right justified; padded on left with spaces for a total length of TotalLengthInteger.
PadLeft(*TotalLengthInteger, PadChar*)	New String with String instance right justified; padded on left with the specified character for a total length of TotalLength-Integer.
PadRight(*TotalLengthInteger*)	New String with String instance left justified; padded on right with spaces for a total length of TotalLengthInteger.
PadRight(*TotalLengthInteger, PadChar*)	New String with String instance left justified; padded on right with the specified character for a total length of TotalLength-Integer.
Remove(*StartPositionInteger, NumberCharactersInteger*)	New String with characters removed from String instance, beginning with StartPositionInteger for a length of Number-CharactersInteger.
Replace(*OldValueString, NewValueString*)	New String with all occurrences of the old value replaced by the new value.
StartsWith(*AString*)	Boolean. *True* if the String instance starts with AString. Case sensitive.

continued

Method	Returns
Substring(*StartPositionInteger*)	New String that is a substring of String instance; beginning at StartPositionInteger, including all characters to the right.
Substring(*StartPositionInteger, NumberCharactersInteger*)	New String; a substring of String instance, beginning at StartPositionInteger for a length of NumberCharactersInteger.
ToLower()	New String; the String instance converted to lowercase.
ToUpper()	New String; the String instance converted to uppercase.
Trim()	New String; the String instance with all white-space characters removed from the left and right ends.
TrimEnd()	New String; the String instance with all white-space characters removed from the right end.
TrimStart()	New String; the String instance with all white-space characters removed from the left end.

Functions for Determining the Data Type

At times you may need to determine the data type of a value.

Function	Return/purpose
IsArray(*VariableName*)	*True* or *false*, depending on whether the variable is an array.
IsDate(*Expression*)	*True* or *false*, depending on whether the expression is a valid date or time value.
IsNumeric(*Expression*)	*True* or *false*, depending on whether the expression evaluates to a numeric value.
IsObject(*VariableName*)	*True* or *false*, depending on whether the variable represents an object.
Is Nothing	*True* or *false*, depending on whether an object variable is set to Nothing. Example: `If MyObject Is Nothing Then`

TypeOf	Checks the type of an object variable. This special syntax can only be used in a logical expression:
	`If TypeOf ObjectVariable Is ObjectType Then`
	Example:
	`If TypeOf MyControl Is TextBox Then`

TypeName(*VariableName*)	Returns the data type of a nonobject variable. Example: `Debug.WriteLine(TypeName(ValueVariable))`

Windows Forms

A Windows project can have one or more forms. Each form is a separate class that has a visible user interface plus code. Because a form is a class, you can add properties to the form by declaring a module-level variable and Property procedures.

The Startup Object

When a project begins execution, the startup form is loaded into memory. Set the startup form in *Project / ProjectName Properties.*

Declaring and Showing Forms

To show a form, you instantiate an object of the form's class and show it.

```
Dim ProgramSummaryForm As New SummaryForm
ProgramSummaryForm.Show()
```

or

```
ProgramSummaryForm.ShowDialog()
```

The `Show` method shows the form as a regular window, called a *modeless* window. The `ShowDialog` method displays the form as a modal window (dialog box), which means that the user must respond to the dialog box before switching to another window in the application.

VB also provides a default instance of each form in a project, so it isn't necessary to declare and instantiate a form before showing it.

```
SummaryForm.Show()
```

Closing Forms

Use `Me.Close()` to close the current form, or *NamedForm*`.Close()` to close any other form. The keyword `Me` refers to the current class and is assumed if omitted, so you can close the current form with just `Close()`.

Form Properties

The two properties of a form that you always set are the Name and Text. You also can choose whether to display minimize and maximize buttons, a close button, and a control box (the system menu that pops up at the left end of the title bar). If you want to display a form with no title bar, you must set Control Box to *false* and Text to an empty string.

Size and Location Properties

When a form is first displayed, it uses several properties to determine the location and size. Set the StartPosition to set its position on the screen. WindowState determines whether the form displays in the size you created it or maximized or minimized.

The Location property determines the form's placement in its container, and the Size property sets the size in pixels.

Set the IsMdiContainer property to *true* for a parent form that will hold child forms. To create a child form, you cannot set a property at design time; instead you must set the parent in code:

```
Dim FirstChildForm As New FirstChildForm()
FirstChildForm.MdiParent = Me
FirstChildForm.Show()
```

Accept and Cancel Buttons

One of the buttons on a form should be the *accept button* and one should be the *cancel button*. When a user types information on a form, generally he or she wants to press the Enter key when finished, rather than pick up the mouse and click a button. Set the form's AcceptButton to the button that should activate when the user presses Enter; set the CancelButton to the button to activate when the user presses the Escape key. Good programmers make sure to set an accept button on every form and a cancel button when appropriate.

Form Events

These events occur in this order when a form first loads into memory:

New	The constructor. Occurs once when the form is instantiated.
Load	Occurs once before the first time the form is displayed. The controls on a form are not available during the Load event; therefore, you cannot set the focus in this event handler. This procedure is the location most programmers use for initialization tasks.
Activate	Occurs when a form becomes the active window. During a project with multiple forms, the Activate event occurs each time the user switches from one form to another. The Deactivate event occurs for the form losing active status.

These events occur as a form's life ends.

Deactivate	Occurs when the form loses focus to another form in the project. It does not occur if the user switches to another application, the application closes, or the form closes.
Closing	Occurs just before the Closed event. This gives the programmer a chance to cancel the close process if necessary.
Closed	Occurs after the form is closed. Most programmers place cleanup code in this event handler.

Using Multiple Forms

A project can show and hide multiple forms. Each form is a class and can have Public and Private members. You can access the Public members (variables and procedures) of one form from another. However, this is considered poor form as it violates rules of encapsulation. Note that members declared with the `Friend` keyword are public to any other forms in the project.

You can share data between forms by setting properties of the form. If you need to pass data between forms, create a property of the form, write Property Set / Get procedures, and set the properties as needed.

Controls

The .NET intrinsic (built-in) controls appear in the toolbox, and you can add more controls to the toolbox by right-clicking on the toolbox and selecting *Choose Items*.

Create an instance of a control class on a form by clicking on the control's icon and drawing the control on the form or by double-clicking the control's icon, which creates a control of default size. You can create multiple controls of one class by Ctrl-clicking on the icon—the pointer remains a crossbar as long as you keep the Ctrl key pressed and you can create as many controls of that type as you wish. Release the Ctrl key when you are finished drawing that control type.

You can select multiple controls using Ctrl-click or Shift-click, or by drawing a selection box around the controls with the mouse pointer. The selected controls are treated as a group and you can move them, delete them, or change their common properties.

Common .NET Controls

The majority of VB programming is performed using just a few controls: Label, TextBox, CheckBox, RadioButton, ListBox, ComboBox, and Button.

The Label Control

Use a Label control for the words and instructions on the form as well as program output that you don't want the user to be able to modify. Set the Text property for the words that you want to appear. You also can set the font and size and change its style with the BorderStyle and BackColor properties. A Label cannot receive the focus.

The TextBox Control

Use a TextBox for user input. The Text property holds the contents of the Text-Box. You can enable/disable a TextBox by setting its Enabled property to *true* or *false*. You also can use a TextBox for program output. Set its ReadOnly property to *true* for output that you don't want the user to be able to change. This allows the user to still select the output and copy it to the clipboard for pasting in another location.

The CheckBox Control

Use a CheckBox for options the user can select or deselect. Each CheckBox operates independently, so any number of check boxes may be selected.

The Checked property of a CheckBox holds its current state and may be *true* or *false*. You can test and set the Checked property in code.

```
If TheCheckBox.Checked Then
    ' Take some action.
    TheCheckBox.Checked = False
End If
```

The Radio Button Control

Radio buttons, formerly called *option buttons*, appear in groups. Only one radio button in a group can be selected at one time. A group is defined as all of the buttons that belong to one container. A container can be a form or a GroupBox.

The Checked property of a radio button holds its state and can be *true* or *false*. The Text property determines the words next to the button. You can test or change the Checked property in code. The best way to reset radio buttons is to set the default button's Checked property to *true*, which sets the other buttons in the group to *false*.

```
If ARadioButton.Checked Then
    ' Take action for the selected button.
    DefaultRadioButton.Checked = True
End If
```

List Boxes and Combo Boxes

ListBoxes and ComboBoxes are very similar. A ListBox appears on the form in the size that you create it; a ComboBox can be made to appear small and drop down when the user clicks on the down arrow. You can set the DropDownStyle property of a ComboBox control to Simple, Dropdown, or DropdownList. A Simple and Dropdown both have a text box, which allows the user to make an entry as well as select from the list. A DropdownList does not have a text box, so the user can make a selection from the list but cannot add any entries.

List controls have an Items property that holds the elements that appear in the list. You can set the Items property at design time or add elements at run time using the `Items.Add` method.

```
NamesComboBox.Items.Add("John")
```

You can remove items from the list using the `Items.Remove` method to remove a particular item and `Items.RemoveAt` to remove an element by index. Clear the list using the `Items.Clear` method.

Each item in the list can be referenced by an index (zero-based). The SelectedIndex property holds the index of the currently selected list element and is −1 if nothing is selected. The Items.Count property holds a count of the number of elements in the list. Setting the list's Sorted property to *true* causes the list to remain sorted in alphabetic order.

The elements in the Items collection are actually objects that can have multiple properties. See "Using the Items Collection" in Chapter 10 to store and use objects.

The Button Control

Buttons typically carry out the actions of a program. Set the button's Name property before writing any code for its Click event and set its Text property for the words that you want to appear on the button.

Buttons should be accessible from the keyboard, so set their Text properties with a keyboard access key, also called *hotkeys* or *shortcut keys*. Place an ampersand in front of the letter that you want to be the access key. For example, set the Text to *&Print* in order to display *Print*. To actually display an ampersand, use two ampersands: *Name && &Address* to display *Name & Address*.

Setting the Tab Order

When the user presses the Tab key, the focus should move from one control to the next, in sequence. Each of the controls on the form has a TabIndex property and most have a TabStop property. The TabIndexes determine the order that the focus moves using the Tab key.

Labels do not have a TabStop property since they cannot receive the focus. But labels *do* have a TabIndex property. This allows you to use a label to set up keyboard access keys for the text boxes that accompany the labels. For example, set a label's Text to *&Name* and its TabIndex property to 0. Then set the corresponding text box's TabIndex to 1 (one higher than the TabIndex for its label). When the user enters the access key (Alt + N in this case), the focus attempts to go to the label and instead goes to the next higher TabIndex for a control that *can* receive the focus.

You can manually set the TabIndex property of each control or use the IDE's tool: With the Form Designer window active, select *View / Tab Order*. Click the crosshair mouse pointer on each control, in sequence, to set the tab order.

Using the Validate Event and CausesValidation Property

Use the Validate event and CausesValidation property for field-level validation on a form. You can check the validity of each field in its Validating event handler.

Each control on the form has a CausesValidation property that is set to *true* by default. When the user finishes an entry and presses Tab or clicks on another control, the Validating event occurs for the control just left. That is, the event occurs if the CausesValidation property of the *new* control is set to *true*. You can leave the CausesValidation property of most controls set to *true* so that validation occurs. Set CausesValidation to *false* on a control such as Cancel or Exit to give the user a way to bypass the validation if he or she doesn't want to complete the transaction.

The Timer Component

Programmers often use a Timer component to animate an image or keep the current time displayed on the screen. A Timer can fire events at a predetermined interval. Add a Timer component to a form, where it appears in the component tray. Set the Interval property to the length of time to wait before firing a Tick event. The interval is measured in milliseconds, so set it to 1000 for a one-second delay. The Enabled property turns the Timer on or off, much like turning on or off an alarm clock. You can set the Enabled property at design time or run time.

Write code in the Timer's Tick event handler, such as moving an image or displaying the current time.

Menus

It's easy to create menus using the MenuStrip control. Add a MenuStrip control from the toolbox; the component appears in the component tray below the form. The words *Type Here* appear at the top of the form so that you can enter the text for your first menu item. After you type the text for the first menu, the words *Type Here* appear both below the menu item and to the right of the menu item. You can choose to next enter menu items below the first menu or type the words for the second menu. As you type the words for menu names and menu items, you are entering the Text property of individual controls. You can use the default names that are assigned to each menu item.

Printing

VB is designed to create programs with a graphical user interface. It is not designed to create nicely formatted reports. Crystal Reports is a nice feature if you want to print a report from a database, but it doesn't help much for program output unless you create a dataset from the output. Many third-party vendors sell products that can create reports from a VB program.

That said, you *can* print from VB, but printing is not easy to format well. Use the PrintDocument and PrintPreviewDialog classes to produce output for the printer and also preview on the screen.

Note: You can see a complete print/print preview program in the ApxB-Printing folder in the InChapterPrograms folder on the text Web site.

The PrintDocument Control

You set up output for the printer using the methods and events of the Print-Document component. Add a PrintDocument component to a form; it appears in the component tray.

You write the code to set up the lines to print in the PrintDocument's Print-Page event handler. The PrintPage event is fired once for each page to be printed. This technique is referred to as a *callback*, in which the object notifies the program that it needs to do something or that a situation exists that the program needs to handle. The object notifies the program of the situation by firing an event.

To start printing output, you execute the `Print` method of the PrintDocument component. This code belongs in the Click event handler for the *Print* button or menu item that the user selects to begin printing.

```
Private Sub PrintButton_Click(ByVal sender As System.Object, _
  ByVal e As System.EventArgs) Handles PrintButton.Click
    ' Print output on the printer.

    PrintDocument1.Print()        ' Start the print process.
End Sub
```

```
Private Sub PrintDocument1_PrintPage(ByVal sender As Object, _
  ByVal e As System.Drawing.Printing.PrintPageEventArgs) _
  Handles PrintDocument1.PrintPage
    ' Set up actual output to print.

End Sub
```

Notice the argument: e As System.Drawing.Printing.PrintPageEvent-Args. You can use some of the properties and methods of the PrintPageEvent-Args argument for such things as determining the page margins and sending a string of text to the page.

The Graphics Page

You set up a graphics page in memory and then the page is sent to the printer. The graphics page can contain strings of text as well as graphic elements.

You must specify the exact location on the graphics page for each element that you want to print. You can specify the upper-left corner of any element by giving its X and Y coordinates, or by using a Point structure or a Rectangle structure.

Using the DrawString Method

You use the DrawString method to send a line of text to the graphics page. The DrawString method belongs to the Graphics object of the PrintPageEvent-Args argument (refer back to the procedure header for the PrintPage event handler).

The DrawString method is overloaded. The format presented here is the least complicated and requires that page coordinates be given in X and Y format.

```
DrawString(StringToPrint, Font, Brush, XCoordinate, YCoordinate)
```

Examples

```
e.Graphics.DrawString(PrintLineString, PrintFont, Brushes.Black, XSingle, YSingle)
e.Graphics.DrawString("My text string", MyFont, Brushes.Black, 100F, 100F)
e.Graphics.DrawString(NameTextBox.Text, New Font("Arial", 10), Brushes.Red, _
    LeftMarginString, CurrentLineSingle)
```

Before you execute the DrawString method, you should set up the font that you want to use and the X and Y coordinates.

Setting the X and Y Coordinates

For each line that you want to print, you must specify the X and Y coordinates. It is helpful to set up some variables for setting these values, which should be declared as Single data type.

```
Dim XSingle As Single
Dim YSingle As Single
```

The PrintPageEventArgs argument has several useful properties, such as MarginBounds, PageBounds, and PageSettings. You can use these properties to determine present settings. For example, you may want to set the X coordinate to the current left margin and the Y coordinate to the top margin.

```
XSingle = e.MarginBounds.Left
YSingle = e.MarginBounds.Top
```

To send multiple lines to the print page, you must increment the Y coordinate. You can add the height of a line to the previous Y coordinate to calculate the next line's Y coordinate.

```
' Declarations at the top of the procedure.
Dim PrintFont As New Font("Arial", 12)
' Make the line 2 pixels higher than the font:
Dim LineHeightSingle As Single = PrintFont.GetHeight + 2
' . . . more declarations here.


' Print a line.
e.Graphics.DrawString(PrintLineString, PrintFont, Brushes.Black, XSingle, _
   YSingle)
' Increment the Y position for the next line.
YSingle += LineHeightSingle
```

Aligning Decimal Columns

Alignment of the decimal points in numeric output can be tricky with proportional fonts, where the width of each character varies. The best approach is to format each number as you want it to print and then measure the length of the formatted string. You need an object declared as a SizeF structure, which has a Width property, and you need to use the `MeasureString` method of the Graphics class. Both the SizeF structure and `MeasureString` method work with pixels, which is the same unit of measure used for the X and Y coordinates of the `DrawString` method.

The following example prints a left-aligned literal at position 200 on the line and right-aligns a formatted number at position 500. (Assume that all variables are properly declared.)

```
Dim StringSize As New SizeF()      ' SizeF structure for font size info.

' Set X for left-aligned column.
XSingle = 200F
' Set ending position for right-aligned column.
ColumnEndSingle = 500F

' Format the number.
FormattedOutputString = AmountDecimal.ToString("C")

' Calculate the X position of the amount.
' Measure string in this font:
StringSize = e.Graphics.MeasureString(FormattedOutputString, PrintFont)
' Subtract width of string from the column position.
ColumnXSingle = ColumnEndSingle — StringSize.Width
' Set up the line--each element separately.
e.Graphics.DrawString("The Amount = ", PrintFont, Brushes.Black, _
   XSingle, YSingle)
e.Graphics.DrawString(FormattedOutputString, PrintFont, Brushes.Black, _
   ColumnXSingle, YSingle)
' Increment line for next line.
YSingle += LineHeightSingle
```

Note: To see a program that creates right-aligned output, see ApxBSomePrintingExtras on the text Web site. The sample program also shows how to create multiple-page output.

Displaying a Print Preview

A really great feature of the printing model is *print preview*. You can view the printer's output on the screen and then choose to print or cancel, thus saving paper while testing your programs.

Add a PrintPreviewDialog component to your form's component tray; then write two lines of code in the event handler for the button or menu item where the user selects the print preview option. The PrintPreviewDialog class uses the same PrintDocument component that you declared for printer output. You assign the PrintDocument to the Document property of the PrintPreviewDialog and execute the `ShowDialog` method. The same PrintPage event handler executes as for the PrintDocument.

```
Private Sub PrintPreviewButton_Click(ByVal sender As System.Object, _
    ByVal e As System.EventArgs) Handles PrintPreviewButton.Click
        ' Print the list to the print preview dialog.

    PrintPreviewDialog.Document = PrintDocument
    PrintPreviewDialog.ShowDialog()
End Sub
```

Web Applications

Chapter 7 of this text reviews the elementary topics for creating Web applications.

Including Special Characters on Web Pages

If you want to display special characters such as ©, ®, or ™ on a Web page, you can use one of these techniques:

1. Switch to Source view and place the insertion point where you want the symbol to appear. For the copyright symbol, type "©" without the quotes. (That's ampersand, "copy", and a semicolon, with no spaces.) This must be in the HTML source.
2. In Design view, place the insertion point where you want the symbol to appear, hold down the Alt key, type "0169" on the numeric keypad, and release the Alt key. Again, do not type the quotes.
3. You also can use the numeric code in the HTML source: Enter "©" for the copyright symbol in Source view.

Other Codes
® is "®" or Alt + 0174
™ is "™" or Alt + 0153

Data Files

Visual Studio handles data files using streams, which are objects designed to transfer a series of bytes from one location to another. The various stream objects are found in the System.IO namespace, which you should import at the top of the file.

A simple way to read and write small amounts of data is to use the Stream-Reader and StreamWriter objects. Generally, you write the StreamWriter code first, to create the data file. Then you can write the StreamReader code to read the file that you just created.

Writing Data

To write data to a file, you first have the user input the data into text boxes and then write the data to the disk. The steps for writing data are

- Declare a new StreamWriter object, which also declares the name of the data file. Instantiating a new StreamWriter object opens the file. The file must be open before you can write in the file. If the file does not already exist, a new one is created. The default location for the file is the directory from which the .exe is running. If you are running from the IDE in Debug mode, the default directory is the bin\Debug directory beneath the folder for the current project. You also can specify the complete path of the file. Set the BooleanAppend argument to *true* to specify that you want to append data to an existing file.

- Use the StreamWriter's `WriteLine` method to copy the data to a buffer in memory. (A buffer is just a temporary storage location.)

- Call the StreamWriter's `Close` method, which transfers the data from the buffer to the file and releases the system resources used by the stream. After you write a file, you can view it using a text editor or the VS IDE.

Instantiating a StreamWriter Object

```
Dim ObjectName As New StreamWriter("FileName")
Dim ObjectName As New StreamWriter("FileName", BooleanAppend)
```

Examples

```
Dim PhoneStreamWriter As New StreamWriter("Phone.txt")
Dim NamesStreamWriter As New StreamWriter("C:\MyFiles\Names.txt")
Dim LogFileStreamWriter As New StreamWriter("C:\MyFiles\LogFile.txt", True)
```

The StreamWriter object has both a `Write` and a `WriteLine` method. The difference between the two is that the `WriteLine` method places a carriage-return character at the end of the elements for each execution of the method.

The WriteLine Method

```
ObjectName.WriteLine(DataToWrite)
```

The DataToWrite argument may be string or numeric. The `WriteLine` method converts any numeric data to string and actually writes string data in the file.

Examples

```
PhoneStreamWriter.WriteLine(NameTextBox.Text)
PhoneStreamWriter.WriteLine(PhoneTextBox.Text)

NamesStreamWriter.WriteLine("Sammy")

BankBalanceStreamWriter.WriteLine(BalanceDecimal.ToString)
```

Closing a File

Use the StreamWriter's `Close` method when finished writing the data.

Reading Files

Use the StreamReader class to read the data from a file that you created with a StreamWriter.

The steps for reading the data from a file are

- Declare an object of the StreamReader class. The constructor declares the filename and optional path. Instantiating the object opens the file so that you can read from it. However, if no such file exists, an exception occurs. For this reason, you should declare the StreamReader object in a procedure so that you can enclose it in a `Try` / `Catch` block.

- Use the `ReadLine` method to read the data. You may need to use a loop to retrieve multiple records.

- When finished, close the stream using the StreamReader's `Close` method.

Instantiating a StreamReader Object

```
Dim ObjectName As New StreamReader("FileName")
```

Examples

```
Try
    Dim NamesStreamReader As New StreamReader("C:\MyFiles\Names.txt")
Catch
    MessageBox.Show("File does not exist")
End Try
```

```
' In declarations section, to create a module-level variable.
Private PhoneStreamReader As StreamReader
' In a procedure, to catch an exception for a missing file.
Try
    PhoneStreamReader = New StreamReader("Phone.txt")
Catch
    MessageBox.Show("File does not exist")
End Try
```

The ReadLine Method

The StreamReader's `ReadLine` method, which has no arguments, reads the next line from the file. Assign the data read to the desired location, such as a label, a text box, or a string variable.

```
NameLabel.Text = PhoneStreamReader.ReadLine()
```

Checking for the End of the File

The StreamReader's `Peek` method looks at the next element without really reading it. The value returned when you peek beyond the last element is negative 1 (−1).

```
If PhoneStreamReader.Peek <> −1 Then
    NameLabel.Text = PhoneStreamReader.ReadLine()
    PhoneLabel.Text = PhoneStreamReader.ReadLine()
End If
```

The `ReadLine` method does not throw an exception when you attempt to read past the end of the file.

Project Resources

Graphic and sound files used by a project are stored in the Resources folder. You can add files to the Resources folder when you set the Image property of a PictureBox control or display the *Resource* tab of the Project Designer (*Project / ProjectName Properties*). After you have added a file to the Resources folder, you can easily refer to it using the new My object.

`My.Resources.Ding` (refers to the sound file Ding.wav, stored in the Resources folder).

`My.Resources.Logo` (refers to the graphic file Logo.gif, stored in the Resources folder).

Playing a Sound

To play a sound file that is stored in the Resources folder, use

```
My.Computer.Audio.Play(My.Resources.Ding, AudioPlayMode.WaitToComplete)
```

XML Files

More and more documents are being stored as XML files. In Chapter 13 we discussed XML as a part of database files. The same format also is used for word processing and other types of office files.

There are many advantages to using XML rather than other file formats. XML is a platform-independent format that is not tied to a specific language or vendor. Because it is text based, you can view and edit the file contents with text-edit tools. It is easy to make changes, such as adding fields. XML is Unicode compliant and can be used internationally.

The authors' beginning VB text contains more information on XML files, including writing and reading XML files.

Nodes, Elements, and Attributes

The first things you notice when looking at an XML file are the tags. The tags delineate elements of the file. The basic structure is a tree, starting with the root node (a file can have only one) and branching out in child nodes. A child also can contain child nodes. Nodes that are at the same level are referred to as siblings.

XML File Terminology   Table B.1

Term	Meaning	Example from books.xml
<> </>	Start tag and end tag.	`<price> 5.99 </price>` `<emptyNode></emptyNode>` *or* `<emptyNode/>`

Element	Contents within a set of tags.	`<title>The Gorgias</title>`
		`<author>`
		`        <name>Plato</name>`
		`</author>`

Node	A branch on the tree; the root node is the most outside with the child nodes inside.	`Root node <bookstore>`
		Child nodes `<book>`
		`<title>` and `<author>` are child nodes of `<book>`

Sibling	Nodes at the same level.	`<title>` and `<author>`
Attribute	Name values embedded within an element; the name of the attribute is assigned a value enclosed in either single or double quotes.	`<book genre="autobiography"` `publicationdate="1981" ISBN="1-861003-11-0">`
Text	Value placed within tags.	`<first-name>Benjamin</first-name>`
Comment	Used for remarks only.	`<!-- This file represents a fragment of a` `book store inventory database -->`

A node may have additional attributes with values assigned. The value may be placed in either single quotes or double quotes. In the following line, genre, publicationdate, and ISBN are attributes.

```
<book genre="autobiography" publicationdate="1981" ISBN="1-861003-11-0">
```

VB includes XDocument and XElement classes for working with xml files.

Loading an XML File into an XDocument Object

You can use the Load method of an XDocument to read an XML file. For the Filename entry, you can specify a complete path or a URI; otherwise the Load method looks in the current directory, which is bin\Debug in your VB project.

```
Dim BookXDocument = XDocument.Load("books.xml")
Private CustomerXDocument As XDocument = XDocument.Load("C:\Data\customers.xml")
Dim InventoryDocument = XDocument.Load(CurDir() & "\inventory.xml")
```

Loading an XML File into an XElement Object

In addition to using an XDocument, you also can load an XML file into an XElement object. The difference between the two is that the XDocument contains the information about the document from the top of the file, while the root node is the first item in an XElement object.

```
Dim BookData = XElement.Load("books.xml")
```

C

Deployment

Deploying Windows Applications

Deployment refers to the process of distributing an application to users. You can choose from the two older methods of deployment—XCopy and Windows Installer—or use the newer ClickOnce deployment introduced with Visual Studio 2005. Many third-party tools are also available for deploying applications.

XCopy deployment simply means to copy the executable file to the destination computer, which must have .NET installed. XCopy is acceptable for only the simplest application. No entries are made in the registry or the *Programs* menu, and conflicts with component versions are possible.

Using Windows Installer, you can create a Setup application and distribute a program on CD. The user runs the Setup wizard to install the program. When you update the program, you must create a new installation CD and the user must reinstall the entire application.

ClickOnce Deployment

ClickOnce deployment is the current deployment tool from Microsoft. Using ClickOnce, you can distribute applications through a Web page, a network file share, or media such as a CD. You can set up the deployment so that the application automatically checks for updates and the user does not have to reinstall the entire application.

ClickOnce overcomes the basic problems found with Windows Installer deployment. A user no longer needs to reinstall an entire application; updates can be made for only those portions that have changes. Installing an application does not require Administrative privileges; ClickOnce provides the ability to grant Code Access Security permissions for an application. Another advantage is that applications deployed with ClickOnce do not share components, which does away with the version conflicts of shared components when installing or uninstalling programs.

Using the Publish Tab

To use ClickOnce deployment, first open the application in the VS IDE, open the Project Designer (*Project / Properties*), and click on the *Publish* tab.

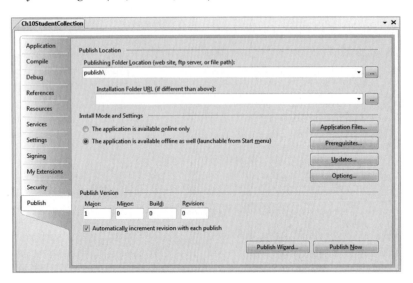

Notice that you can select from a Web site, an FTP server, or a file path as the location to publish the application. Options are available to publish offline or only online. When the application is available offline, a shortcut appears on the *Start* menu and the user can uninstall the application by using the *Add or Remove programs* option of the Control Panel.

If you click on the *Application Files* button, you will see a list that includes the .exe file for the project. You can click on *Show all files* to see other options.

Many settings are available on the *Publish Options* dialog that displays when you select the *Options* button. You may find it interesting to note that the check box for *CD installations* includes the ability to automatically start Setup when the CD is inserted.

Update Strategies

The developer can decide the strategy and timing for checking for updates. By default, an application checks for an update in the background while the application is running. The next time the program executes, the user receives a prompt if an update is available. The other choices are to have the application check for an update during the application startup or to have a user interface for updates.

Click on the *Updates* button to see the *Application Updates* dialog. When you select the *After the application starts* radio button, you enable the radio buttons that specify the frequency.

Using the Publish Wizard

To use the wizard, you must first enter the publish location. Then click the *Publish Wizard* button, which displays the first page of the wizard.

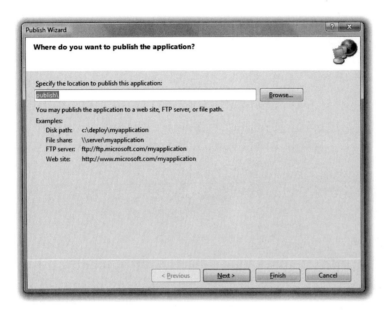

Enter the location and click *Next*.

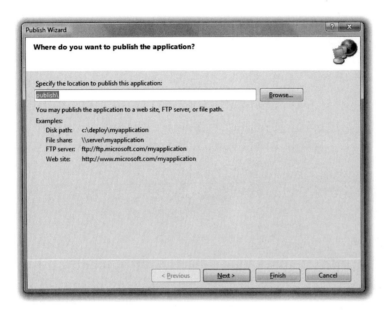

If you have a Web site or a file share path, you can enter that. Other-wise, select the option for CD-ROM or DVD. Note that you will have to use a utility to actually burn the CD or DVD after the wizard completes. Click *Next*.

If the installed application will check for updates, select that option and additional choices will appear for the timing of the check. Click *Next*.

Click *Finish* and the necessary files will be created in the location that you chose. If you specified a CD or DVD, you must burn the files yourself. Running the Setup.exe file installs the application and adds a shortcut on the *Start* menu.

Deploying Web Projects

Visual Studio offers two methods for transferring files to a Web server. You can use the Copy Web Site tool or the Publish Web Site utility. Note that the Publish Web Site utility is not available in Visual Web Developer Express Edition.

Using the Copy Web Site Tool

Using Visual Studio 2008, you can create local Web Sites, IIS Web Sites, FTP sites, or remote sites. The Copy Web Site tool allows you to copy files between any of the Web Site types created with Visual Studio using an FTP-style utility.

To run the Copy Web Site tool, right-click the project name in the Solution Explorer or open the *Website* menu, then select *Copy Web Site*. The Copy Web Site tool opens in the VS IDE main document window with the *Source Web Site* list populated with the files from the open Web site. Select the remote site from the *Connections* list or click *Connect* to browse for the site.

The Source Web site is the one that is currently open in the IDE; the Remote Web site is the one to which you want to copy the files. Even though you use the designations for the source and remote sites, it is possible to transfer files in either direction. In other words, you can copy a file *from* the remote site *into* the IDE site.

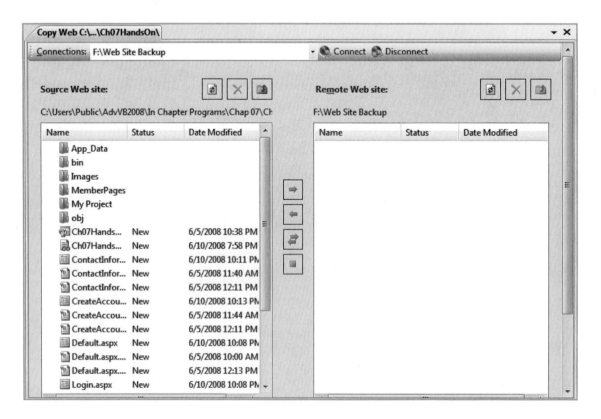

An excellent feature of the tool is the ability to synchronize the files between the sites. The synchronize file status may be unchanged, changed, new, or deleted. The tool compares the time stamps on the files at each site to determine the status. The synchronization feature does not allow merging. If two files have the same name, you are prompted to select the file to keep. A check box allows you to show the deleted files since the last copy operation.

See "*How to: Copy Web Site Files with the Copy Web Site Tool*" in MSDN for steps to copy all files at once, copy files individually, or synchronize files.

Publishing a Web Site

The Publish Web Site utility precompiles the Web pages and code content. The compilation process removes the source code from the files and leaves only stub files and compiled assemblies for the pages. You can specify the output location as either a directory or a server location.

Precompiling the Web pages offers a couple of advantages over just copying the pages. One advantage is response speed. When pages are just copied to a site, they must compile when a request is made for the page. Not having the source code on the site also provides some security. During the publish process, you have the option of having markup protection, which does not allow for later updates to the pages. If you opt to not have the files updatable, the code in single-file pages is deployed as source code rather than being compiled into an assembly.

The Build process within the IDE is for testing purposes. When you are ready to deploy, your Web site project is precompiled and the output is files that you can deploy to a production server. Publishing compiles the files in the App_Code, App_GlobalResources, App_LocalResources, and App_Themes folders. The output includes only the files within the project and not the Machine.config file. As a result, the configuration on the target server may differ from that of the development server.

Access the *Publish Web Site* option from the *Build* menu or the project's context menu. The first box allows you to specify the publish location, which can be a folder on the current machine, a network share, an ftp server, or an http server that you specify with a URL. Note that you must have Create and Write permissions in the target location. A check box gives the option of allowing the precompiled site to be updatable.

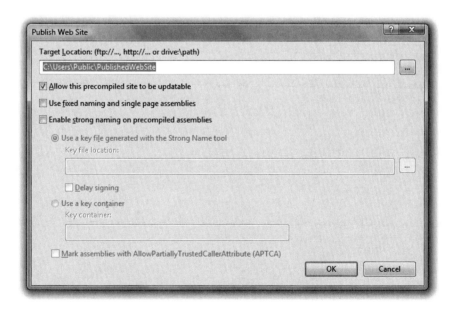

After you publish a Web site, you can examine the files. You can open the .aspx file with Notepad only to find that it does not contain the markup language code. The file is on the site as a placeholder for use as part of the URL. The bin folder contains the compiled files for the pages and the .dll files with the executable code for the Web site.

Although you can test publishing a Web site, you must be running IIS on your computer to be able to open the page in your browser using *http://localhost/foldername/Default.aspx.*

D

Tips and Shortcuts for Mastering the Environment

Set Up the Screen for Your Convenience

As you work in the Visual Studio integrated development environment (IDE), you will find many ways to save time. Here are some tips and shortcuts that you can use to become more proficient in using the IDE to design, code, and run your projects.

Close or Hide Extra Windows

Arrange your screen for best advantage. While you are entering and editing code in the Editor window, you don't need the toolbox, the Solution Explorer window, the Properties window, or any other extra windows. You can hide or close the extra windows and quickly and easily redisplay each window when you need it.

Hiding and Displaying Windows

You can use AutoHide on each of the windows in the IDE. Each window except the Document window in the center of the screen has a pushpin icon that you can use to AutoHide the window or "tack" it into place.

You can AutoHide each window separately, or select *Window / Auto Hide All*. In this screen, all extra windows are hidden.

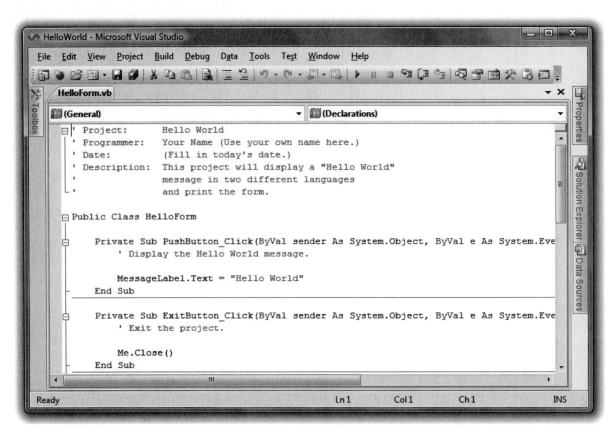

Point to the icon for one of the hidden windows to display it. In the next example, notice the mouse pointer on the Solution Explorer icon, which opens the Solution Explorer window temporarily. When you move the mouse pointer out of the window, it hides again.

Mouse pointer

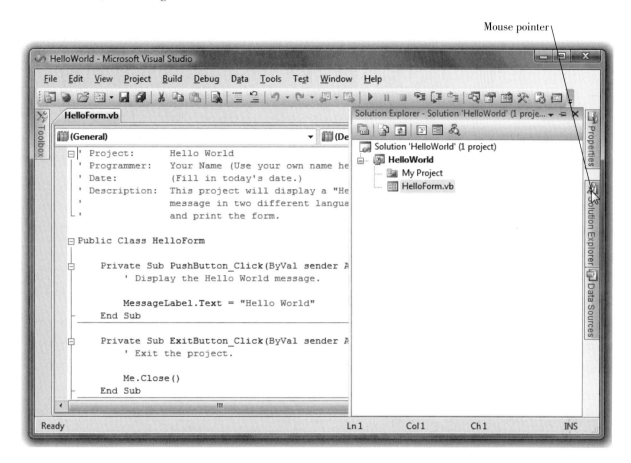

To undo the AutoHide feature, display a window and click its pushpin icon.

Each of the IDE windows that has an AutoHide feature also has a drop-down menu from which you can choose to float, dock, AutoHide, hide, or make into a tabbed window. The tabbed window option is interesting: it makes the window tabbed in the center Document window.

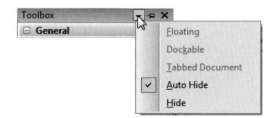

Closing Windows

You can close any window by clicking its *Close* button. You also can close any extra tabs in the Document window; each document has its own *Close* button.

Displaying Windows

You can quickly and easily open each window when you need it. Each window is listed on the *View* menu, or use the buttons on the Standard toolbar.

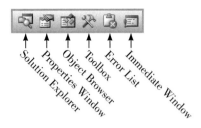

Display Windows Using Keyboard Shortcuts

Solution Explorer window	Ctrl + Alt + L
Properties window	F4
Toolbox	Ctrl + Alt + X

Display the keyboard shortcuts as part of the popup ToolTips: select *Tools / Customize / Show shortcut keys in ScreenTips.*

Switch between Documents When you have several tabs open in the Document window, you can switch by clicking on their tabs or use keyboard shortcuts. Note that these keyboard shortcuts are for VB keyboard settings; other keyboard settings differ.

Editor window for form's code	F7
Form Designer	Shift + F7
Cycle through open document tabs	Ctrl + F6
Cycle through all open windows	Ctrl + Tab

Visual Studio displays only as many tabs as fit in the current size of the document window. If you have more documents open than displayed tabs, you can use the new drop-down list of open documents.

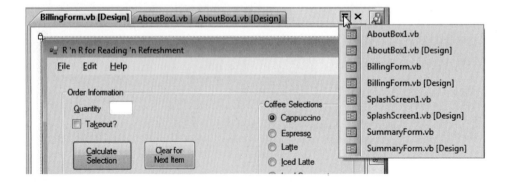

Use the Full Screen

When you are designing a form or editing code, you can work in full-screen mode. This gives you maximum screen space by getting rid of all extra windows. Unfortunately, it also hides all toolbars (the Text Editor toolbar can be a great timesaver while editing code). Select *View / Full Screen* to display in full-screen mode. A small *Full Screen* button appears on the menu, which you can use to switch back to regular display. You also can press Shift + Alt + Enter or select *View / Full Screen* a second time to toggle back. If you want to display the Text Editor toolbar while in full-screen mode, select *View / Toolbars / Text Editor*.

Modify the Screen Layout

For most operations, the Visual Studio tabbed Document window layout works very well and is an improvement over the older VB 6 environment. However, if you prefer, you can switch to MDI (multiple document interface), which is similar to the style used in VB 6. Set this option in *Tools / Options / Environment / General / Multiple Documents*.

Each of the windows in the IDE is considered either a Tool window or a Document window. The Document windows generally display in the center of the screen with tabs. The rest of the windows—Solution Explorer, Properties window, Task List, Output, Server Explorer, and others—are Tool windows and share many characteristics. You can float each of the Tool windows, tab-dock them in groups, and move and resize individual windows or groups of windows.

Dock Windows Using the Guide Diamonds

Guide diamonds are an improvement added to VS 2005. When you start dragging a dockable tool window, the diamonds appear to give you visual cues to help dock to the desired location. As you drag toward one of the edges, the corresponding arrow darkens. To tab-dock a window, you need to make the center of the diamond darken. Experiment!

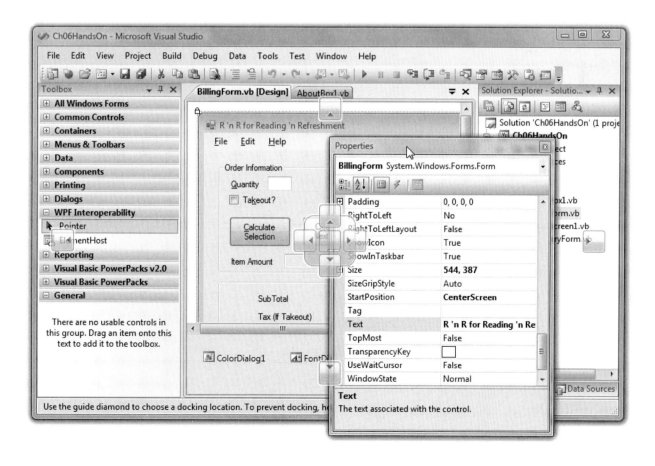

Split the Screen Vertically

You can view the Editor window and the form design at the same time. With at least two tabs open, select *Window / New Vertical Tab Group*. You may want to close the extra windows to allow more room for the two large windows.

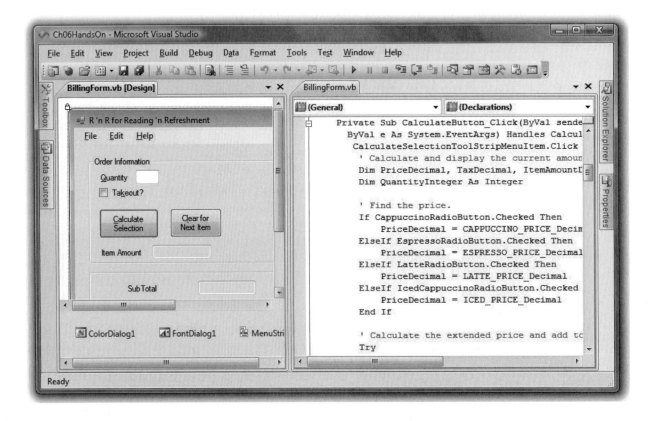

Reset the IDE Layout

To reset the IDE windows to their default locations, select *Window / Reset Window Layout.*

Set Options for Your Work

You can change many options in the VS IDE. Choose *Tools / Options* to display the *Options* dialog box. You may want to click on each of the categories to see the options that you can select.

    Note: If you are working in a shared lab, check with the instructor or lab technician before changing options.

Projects and Solutions: Set the default folder for your projects. It's best to leave the *Build* and *Run* options to automatically save changes, but you may prefer to have a prompt or save them yourself.

Text Editor: You can set options for all languages or for Basic, which is Visual Basic. The following presumes that you first select Basic and that *Show all settings* is selected.

General: Make sure that *Auto list members* is selected and *Hide advanced members* is deselected. You may want to turn on *Word wrap*, so that long lines wrap to the next line instead of extending beyond the right edge of the screen.

Tabs: Choose *Smart* indenting; *Tab size* and *Indent size* should both be set to 4.

VB Specific: All options should be selected.

Use Shortcuts in the Form Designer

You can save time while creating the user interface in the Form Designer by using shortcuts.

Use the Layout Toolbar

The Layout toolbar is great for working with multiple controls. You must have more than one control selected to enable many of the buttons. The same options are available from the *Format* menu.

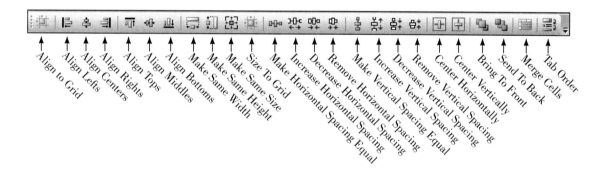

Nudge Controls into Place

Sometimes it is difficult to place controls exactly where you want them. Of course, you can use the alignment options of the *Format* menu or the Layout toolbar. You also can nudge controls in any direction by holding down the Ctrl key and pressing one of the arrow keys. Nudging moves a control one pixel in the direction you specify. For example, Ctrl + Right arrow moves a selected control one pixel to the right.

Use Snap Lines to Help Align Controls

As you create or move controls on a form, snap lines pop up to help you align the controls, which can be a great help in creating professional-looking forms. Blue snap lines appear to align tops, bottoms, lefts, or rights of controls.

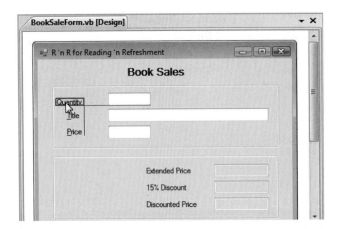

When you see a red line toward the lower edge of controls, that means that the baselines of the text within the controls are aligned.

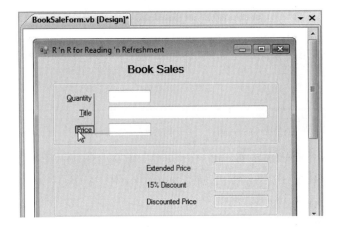

The snap lines also can help you to standardize the vertical spacing between controls. As you drag a control up or down near another control, a small dotted line appears to indicate that the controls are the recommended distance apart.

Dotted line

Use Shortcuts in the Editor

Several features of the Editor can save you time while editing code. These are summarized in the following sections.

Comment and Uncomment Selected Lines

Use the *Comment Selected Lines* command when you want to convert some code to comments, especially while you are testing and debugging projects. You can remove some lines from execution to test the effect without actually removing them. Select the lines and click the *Comment Selected Lines* button; each line will have an apostrophe appended at the left end.

Use the *Uncomment Selected Lines* command to undo the *Comment Selected Lines* command. Select some comment lines and click the button; the apostrophes at the beginning of the lines are deleted.

Use the Text Editor Toolbar

By default, the Text Editor toolbar displays when the Editor window is open. You also can open the toolbar yourself from the *View / Toolbars* menu item.

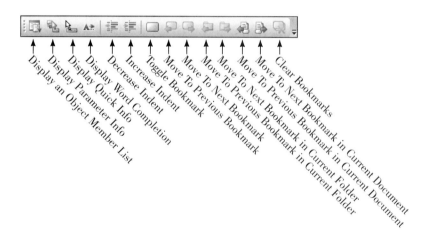

You can save yourself considerable time and trouble if you become familiar with and use some of these shortcuts.

- *Toggle Bookmark.* This button sets and unsets individual bookmarks. Bookmarks are useful when you are jumping around in the Editor window. Set a bookmark on any line by clicking in the line and clicking the *Toggle Bookmark* button; you will see a mark in the gray margin area to the left of the marked line. You may want to set bookmarks in several procedures where you are editing and testing code.

- *Jump to Next Bookmark* and *Jump to Previous Bookmark.* Use these buttons to quickly jump to the next or previous bookmark in the code.

- *Clear All Bookmarks.* You can clear individual bookmarks with the *Toggle Bookmark* button or clear all bookmarks using this button.

Use Keyboard Shortcuts When Editing Code

While you are editing code, save yourself time by using keyboard shortcuts. Note that these shortcuts are based on the default Visual Basic keyboard mapping. See *Tools / Options* and select *Show all settings*. Then select *Environment / Keyboard / Keyboard mapping scheme*. Drop down the list and select *Visual Basic 6*, if it isn't already selected.

Task	Shortcut
Delete from the insertion point left to the beginning of the word.	Ctrl + Backspace
Delete from the insertion point right to the end of the word.	Ctrl + Delete
Complete the word.	Ctrl + Spacebar *or* Alt + Right arrow
Create an empty line above the current line. Insertion point can be anywhere in the line.	Ctrl + Enter
Create an empty line below the current line. Insertion point can be anywhere in the line.	Ctrl + Shift + Enter
Swap the two characters on either side of the insertion point (transpose character). Note that this shortcut does not work in VB Express.	Ctrl + T
Swap the current word with the word on its right (transpose word). Insertion point can be anywhere in the word.	Ctrl + Shift + T
Swap the current line with the next line (transpose line). Insertion point can be anywhere in the line.	Ctrl + Alt + T
Cut the current line to the clipboard with the insertion point anywhere in the line.	Ctrl + Y (*VS Prof. default keyboard*) Ctrl + L (*VB Express default keyboard*)
Jump to a procedure (insertion point on procedure name). Use this shortcut while working on the sub procedures and functions that you write. For example, when writing a call to a function, you might want to check the coding in the function. Point to the procedure name in the `Call` and press F12. If you want to return to the original position, set a bookmark before the jump.	F12
Jump to the top of the current code file.	Ctrl + Home
Jump to the bottom of the current file.	Ctrl + End
View the form's Designer window.	Shift + F7
Return to the Editor window.	F7

You can display the keyboard shortcuts as part of the popup ToolTips; select *Tools / Customize / Show shortcut keys in ScreenTips.*

Most of the editing and selecting keyboard shortcuts for Microsoft Word also work in the VS Editor window.

Split the Editor Window

You can view more than one section of code at a time by splitting the Editor window. Point to the Split bar at the top of the vertical scroll bar and drag the bar down to the desired location. To remove the split, you can either drag the split bar back to the top or double-click the split bar.

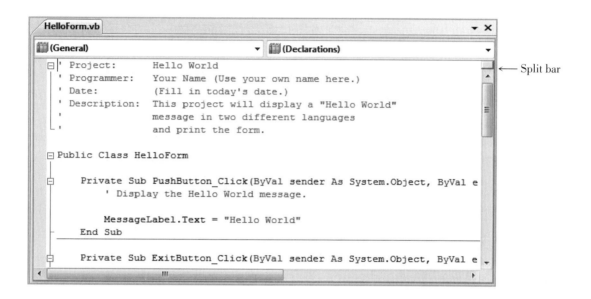

Use Drag-and-Drop Editing

You can use drag-and-drop to move or copy text to another location in the Editor window or to another project. To move code, select the text, point to the selection, and drag it to a new location. You can copy text (rather than move it) by holding down the Ctrl key as you drag.

Use the Task List

The Task List displays error messages after your program is compiled. This makes sense—your tasks are to fix each of the errors. You also can add items to the task list as a reminder to yourself, so that you don't forget to do something. A very easy way to add items to the Task List is to write a comment in your code with the TODO keyword.

```
' TODO Come back here and write this code.
' TODO Check on this.
```

You also can add tasks to the Task List by clicking on the *Create User Task* button at the top of the list; this creates a new line where you can enter text.

Drag Commonly Used Code to the Toolbox

When you have some lines of code that you use frequently, you can select the text and drag it to the toolbox. Then when you need to insert the code, drag it from the toolbox to the Editor window. The text appears in the toolbox when the Editor window is open, but not when a form is in design mode.

Caution: This shortcut should not be used on shared computers in a classroom or lab, as the text remains in the toolbox. Use it only on your own computer. You can delete previously stored text from the toolbox by right-clicking and selecting *Delete* from the context menu.

For another, newer, way to handle small pieces of code you reuse often, see "Use Code Snippets and Samples" later in this appendix.

Rename Variables and Objects

Use the rename feature to automatically rename variables and objects. In the Editor window, right-click on a variable name or an object name and select *Rename*. In the *Rename* dialog box, you can enter the new name and the item is renamed everywhere in that form. For a multiform project, the *Rename* dialog box offers the choice of renaming in only the current form or all forms. This feature, called Symbol Rename, is part of a more robust feature called **refactoring**, which is available in some of the .NET languages (but not VB). Refactoring allows the programmer to modify the name and class of variables and objects.

Use Context-Sensitive Help

The quickest way to get Help is to use context-sensitive Help. Click on a control or a line of code and press F1; Help displays the closest matching item it can locate. You also can get help on the IDE elements: Click in any area of the IDE and press Shift + F1; the Help explanation will be about using the current window or IDE element, rather than about the objects and language.

Use the Debugging Tools

The VS IDE provides many tools to help you debug programs. The most helpful techniques are to examine the values of variables during program execution and to single-step through the program and watch what happens.

The Debug Toolbar and Menu

You can use the *Debug* menu or the tools on the Debug toolbar for debugging. The Debug toolbar appears automatically during run time, or you can display the toolbar by right-clicking any toolbar and selecting *Debug*. The most useful items for debugging your programs are shown in the following table.

Menu command or toolbar button	Purpose	Keyboard shortcut
Start	Begin debug execution.	F5
Continue	Continue execution. (Available at break time only.)	F5
Start Without Debugging	Begin execution without invoking the debugger. This option can make a program run sometimes when it won't run with *Start*.	Ctrl + F5
Stop Debugging	Stop execution of a program.	Shift + F5
Step Into	Execute the next statement; steps into any called sub procedures or functions. (Available at break time only.)	F8
Step Over	Execute the next statement; rapidly executes any calls to sub procedures or functions without stepping. (Available at break time only.)	Shift + F8
Step Out	Rapidly finish the current procedure; reenter break time when the procedure finishes.	Ctrl + Shift + F8

The function keys for Step Into, Step Over, and Step Out apply to the VB keyboard settings. If you are using general development settings, the applicable keys are F11, F10, and Shift + F11.

Set Breakpoints

You can set breakpoints in code, which cause execution to halt on the marked statement. After setting a breakpoint, begin execution as usual. When the breakpoint line becomes current, the program halts, enters break time, and displays the code with the current line highlighted (as the *next* statement to execute).

To set a breakpoint, use the *Debug* menu, the Debug toolbar, a keyboard shortcut (F9), or the easiest way: Place the mouse pointer in the gray margin indicator area at the left edge of the Editor window and click; the line will be highlighted in red and a large red dot will display in the margin indicator.

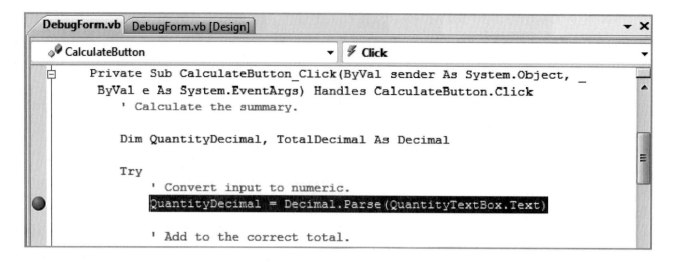

View the Contents of Expressions

At break time, you can view the current values of expressions in several ways. The three most useful techniques are

1. Display the value in a DataTip, which is a ToolTip-like popup in the Editor window. Point to the variable or expression that you want to view and pause; the current value pops up in a DataTip.

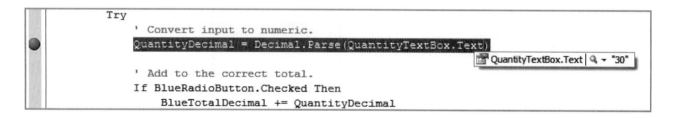

2. Use the Locals window, which displays all objects and variables that are within scope at break time. You can also expand the Me entry to see the state of the form's controls.

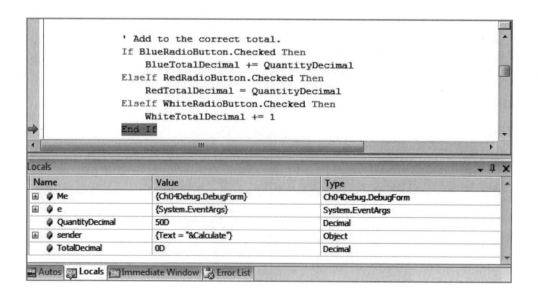

3. Use the Autos window, which "automatically" displays all variables and control contents that are referenced in the current statement and three statements on either side of the current one. Note that the Autos window is not available in the Express Edition.

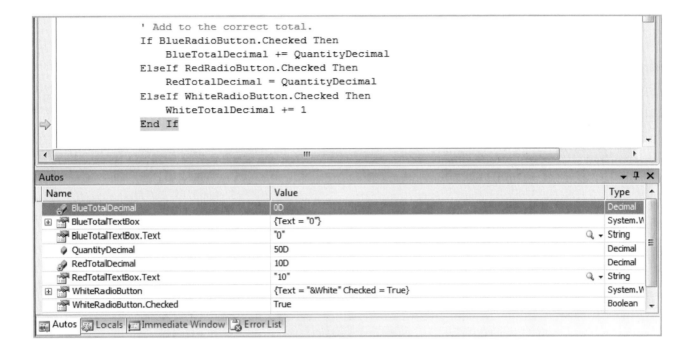

Single-Step through Code

The best way to debug a project is to thoroughly understand what the project is doing every step of the way. Use the Visual Studio stepping tools to trace program execution line by line and see the progression of the program as it executes through your code.

You step through code at break time. Set a breakpoint or choose one of the stepping commands at design time; the program will begin running and immediately transfer to break time.

The three stepping commands are *Step Into*, *Step Over*, and *Step Out*. These commands force the project to execute a single line at a time and to display the Editor window with the current statement highlighted. As you execute the project, by pressing a button, for example, the Click event occurs. Execution transfers to the Click event handler, the Editor window for that procedure appears on the screen, and you can follow line-by-line execution.

Most likely you will use the *Step Into* command more than the other two stepping commands. When you choose *Step Into*, the next line of code executes and the program pauses again in break time. If the line of code is a call to another procedure, the first line of code of the other procedure displays.

To continue stepping through your program execution, continue choosing the *Step Into* command. When a procedure is completed, your form will display again, awaiting an event. You can click on one of the form's buttons to continue stepping through code in an event handler. If you want to continue execution without stepping, choose the *Continue* command.

The *Step Over* command also executes one line of code at a time. But when your code calls another procedure, *Step Over* displays only the lines of code in the current procedure being analyzed; it does not display lines of code in the called procedures.

You use the *Step Out* command when you are stepping through a called procedure. It continues rapid execution until the called procedure completes, and then returns to break mode at the statement following the `Call`.

When you have seen what you want to see, continue rapid execution by choosing the *Continue* command (F5). If you want to restart execution from the beginning, choose the *Restart* command (Ctrl + Shift + F5).

Write to the Output Window

You can place a `Debug.WriteLine` method in your code. In the argument, you can specify a message to write or an object that you want tracked.

```
Debug.WriteLine(TextString)
Debug.WriteLine(Object)
```

Examples

```
Debug.WriteLine("calculateButton event handler entered.")
Debug.WriteLine(quantityTextBox.Text)
```

When the `Debug.WriteLine` method executes, its output appears in the Output window. You can clear the Output window: Right-click in the window and choose *Clear All*.

An advantage of using `WriteLine` rather than the other debugging techniques is that you do not have to break program execution.

Copy and Move Projects

In a programming class, you often must move projects from one computer to another and must base one project on another one. To create a new project based on a previous one, you should copy the project folder. Then you can move and rename it as necessary.

Copy and Move a Project

You can copy an entire project folder from one location to another using My Computer. Make sure that the project is not open in Visual Studio and copy the entire folder.

To base one project on a previous project, take the following steps:

- Make sure the project is not open. *Note*: This is *extremely* important.

- Copy the folder to a new location using the Windows Explorer.

- Rename the new folder for the new project name, still using the Explorer.

- Open the new project (the copy) in the Visual Studio IDE.

- In the IDE's Solution Explorer, rename the solution and the project. The best way to do this is to right-click on the name and choose the *Rename* command from the shortcut menu. To rename the solution, you must display the solution name. Select *Tools / Options / Projects and Solutions / General / Always show solution.*

- Rename the forms, if desired. If you rename the startup form, you must open the Project Designer (*Project / ProjectName Properties*) and set the Startup Object.

- Open the *Project Properties* dialog and change the assembly name to match your new project name.

Warning: Do not try to copy a project that is open using the *Save As* command, attempting to place a copy in a new location.

Refresh the Database in an Update Program

When you write a database update program, you must test all options, including adding records, deleting records, and modifying records. With a little caution, you can delete the modified version of the database and replace it with an unchanged version.

How Windows Applications Handle the Database File

When you set up a new data source, the wizard asks whether you want to add the database file to the project folder. To make your projects portable, you should always say Yes. But when you run the application, *another* copy is made, into the bin\Debug (or bin\Release) folder. Your program actually updates the copy in bin\Debug.

The version of the file that you retrieve for each program run depends on a property of the database file. Select the file in the Solution Explorer and set the property for *Copy to Output Directory* to *Copy if newer.* By default, the property is set to *Copy always,* which means that, for every program run, you get a new, fresh copy of the file and cannot see changes made on the last program run. With the *Copy if newer* setting, each time you run the application, VS checks the timestamp on the two copies of the database: if they are the same or the file in bin\Debug is newer, no copy is performed. But if the file in bin\Debug is older or no file exists in bin\Debug, then the file from the project folder is copied as the application begins to run.

You can easily return to the original version of the data file by deleting the copy in bin\Debug. In addition to the .mdf file (the main database file), you also must delete the log.ldf file, which holds the index and timestamp information.

You may not be able to see the database files in the Solution Explorer initially. Select *Show All Files* and click the *Refresh* button; then expand the bin\Debug folder nodes to see the .mdf and log.ldf files. You can delete the files directly in the Solution Explorer by right-clicking and selecting *Delete.*

Use Code Snippets and Samples

Code Snippets

Code snippets are small samples of code that can show you how to accomplish many programming tasks. The *Insert Snippet* menu option is available on the context menu (right-click) of the Editor window.

When you select a snippet type, the editor places the code right in your program, where you can study it and/or modify and use it. You can learn many useful techniques by opening snippets.

Sample Projects

Visual Studio includes many sample projects (all editions except the Express Edition) that you can use to learn new techniques. From the *Help* menu, select *Contents*. Expand the nodes for *Development Tools and Languages / Visual Studio / Visual Basic* to find the *Samples* node.

The walkthroughs in Help are another avenue for pursuing your study of VB. These tutorials give step-by-step introductions to many techniques and controls.

Glossary

A

abstract class   Used only to create derived classes; cannot have an object instantiated from the class.

abstraction   A model of an object, for the purpose of determining the characteristics (properties) and the behaviors (methods) of the object.

AcceptChanges method Resets a dataset to indicate that no changes have been made. Usually used after an Update method, which commits the changes to the original data source.

accessibility (classes, variables, and procedures) Used to determine which classes can use the element. Examples: Public, Private, Protected, Friend, and Protected Friend.

accessibility (software) Program design that allows a disabled person to use your application.

Active Server Pages (ASP) A platform for developing server-based Web applications.

ActiveX Data Objects (ADO) .NET   A standard set of objects that Visual Studio programmers can use to retrieve and modify data from any source.

AddNew method   Used to begin the Add operation for adding a new record to a dataset.

AdRotator control   A Web control that randomly selects from a collection of advertisements each time the page is displayed.

AJAX (Asynchronous JavaScript and XML)   Tools for creating interactive Web pages that can rapidly update part of a page.

AllowPaging property Adds pagination to a DataGrid Web control.

AllowSorting property Allows the user to sort the data grid by clicking on a column heading.

Application object   Stores state information as long as the application is running.

assembly   A basic unit of code that may be a single PE file or multiple files; built and deployed as a single implementation unit.

assembly information Information about a program stored in the AssemblyInfo.vb file.

assembly manifest   A file that contains metadata about the version, a table describing all of the files needed by the assembly, and a reference list that specifies all of the external files needed, such as DLLs created by someone else.

asynchronous   Task or operation running independently in the background.

attributes   A keywordlike tag used to add information about elements.

author   The programmer that creates the control used by the developer.

B

BackGroundWorker   Class for instantiating thread objects for asynchronous processing.

base class   The parent class of the current class, from which the current class is inherited.

BeginEdit method   Binding source method that starts the edit process.

BindingNavigator   Toolbar in a database application with buttons for navigation and updating.

BindingSource object   An object that controls binding controls to a form; handles currency management, navigation, sorting, filtering, and updating.

block-level scope   A variable that is visible and accessible only within the block of code in which it is declared.

business rules   The logic performed by an application, including validation, calculations, and updating rules.

business services tier   One segment of a multitier application; the class or classes that perform the business rules.

Button A control that the user can click to perform an action. Windows Button control: fires a Click event; Web Button control: fires a Click event and causes a postback to occur.

C

CancelEdit method Cancels the current edit or add and returns to the original version of the data.

Capacity property Sets or retrieves the size of an ArrayList.

cascading deletes When you delete a parent record, all child records for that parent are automatically deleted.

cascading style sheet (CSS) A file that holds formatting information for fonts, color, and spacing in Web documents.

cascading updates Updates all related child records when the primary key field of the parent is modified.

CheckBoxList control A Web control that displays a group of check boxes in a ListBox.

child class An inherited class. Also called a *subclass* or *derived class*.

child form An MDI form that displays inside of a parent form. All child forms are closed when the parent form closes.

child table The "many" table in a 1:M relationship in a relational database.

class diagram A diagram generated by the IDE that shows the members of a class.

client A program that uses (consumes) a service or accesses a user control.

code separation model Web page code design that separates the VB code into a separate file from the HTML.

collection An object used to hold and manage the references to a group of related objects.

column Used to store a single element of a row in a table. Also called a *field*.

common language runtime (CLR) Manages the execution of managed code developed for the .NET Framework.

Common Language Specification (CLS) Standards that specify how a language that interacts with the CLR should be formed and should behave.

component A nonvisual object on a form; appears in the component tray.

composite control New user control created by combining individual controls.

concurrency An issue that arises when more than one user can update the same file.

concurrency control The process of handling conflicts in updates by multiple users.

constituent control The individual controls that are used to create a composite control.

constructor A method that automatically executes when an object is instantiated; the New method.

consumed Calling a WCF Service or a user control.

content page Web page based on a master page.

context-sensitive Help Displays the Help topic that concerns the current element; triggered by placing the pointer on or clicking in an element and pressing F1.

ContextMenuStrip component A menu component used to create context (right-mouse) menus.

Count property Retrieves the number of elements in a table or collection.

criteria The condition used in the WHERE clause of a SQL statement to specify which rows should be retrieved or modified; also used for the RowFilter property of a DataView.

Crystal Reports A feature included in VS that allows you to easily generate database reports.

culture/locale A set of rules that contains information about a specific language and culture; includes specifications for numeric formatting. Used for localization.

CultureInfo class Provides access to culture-specific information.

Current property A property of the binding source that returns the current row.

CurrentChanged event Combo box or list box event that fires when a change has been made to the list.

D

data access tier The component in a multitier database project that holds the table adapters.

data entity The component in a multitier database project that holds the dataset and validation code.

data source The location from which data are retrieved; may be a database, spreadsheet, or other type of file.

data source control
ASP.NET 3.5 control that provides access to data from a Web page.

Data Sources window
Portion of IDE used for adding data sources to a project and for dragging data tables and fields to the form.

data structure A grouping of related variables; declared with `Structure / End Structure` statements.

data table A collection of related records or rows.

data tier One segment of a multitier application; the class or classes that retrieve and store the data in a database.

DataBind method Required by Web projects to fill bound controls.

DataBindings object The property of a control that will bind that control to a single data field.

DataBindings.Add method Method that binds a control to a data source.

DataGrid control A Web control that displays data in rows and columns; provides features such as pagination and sorting.

DataGridView control A Windows control that displays bound data in a grid.

DataReader Provides a forward-only result set from a data source.

DataRelation object An object that describes the relationship between the tables in a relational database.

DataRow object A row of data within a data table, typically represents a single record.

DataSet Designer Displays the XML schema for a database. Shows relationships; can be used to modify the dataset, such as adding new columns.

DataSet object Holds a copy of the data in memory, disconnected from the data source. May contain multiple tables, relationships, and constraints.

DataSource property Used for binding to connect a control to a dataset.

DateTime structure A structure from the DateTime class; provides properties and methods for working with time measurements.

deployment Distributing an application to the user.

Dequeue method Used to remove an item from a Queue list.

derived class An inherited class. Also called a *subclass* or *child class*.

design pattern Time-tested solutions to common programming situations.

destructor A method that automatically executes when an object is destroyed. In VB, the `Dispose` method is the destructor, which executes at an indeterminate time, whenever garbage collection occurs.

detail table The child table in a master/detail or parent/child relationship in a relational database.

Details The section of a Crystal Reports object that holds the data for the individual lines in the body of the report.

DetailsView control Web database control used to display a single record.

developer The programmer who writes an application that incorporates controls; as opposed to the author that creates the controls.

dictionary A type of collection that consists of key and value pairs.

DictionaryEntry data type The type of a single entry in a dictionary collection.

DisplayMember property For the various list controls, determines the field name for the data to display in the list.

.dll file Dynamic link library file, which holds executable code; used for Web projects.

E

emulator A software simulation of a physical device. Many emulators are available for mobile application development.

encapsulation The combination of characteristics of an object along with its behaviors.

endpoint A WCF Service contract item; indicates an address to which a message can be sent and the binding used.

EndEdit method Ends the current edit for a grid control.

Enqueue method Used to add items to a Queue list.

enum The key word used to create an enumeration.

enumeration A list of constant values, which must be one of the integer data types.

ErrorProvider component Tool for displaying error messages on individual fields; useful for field-level validation.

event consumer The object that responds to a raised event. Also called *event sink*.

event handler   A procedure that executes automatically when an event occurs.

event provider   An object that generates or raises an event. Also called *event source*.

event sink   The object that responds to a raised event. Also called *event consumer*.

event source   An object that generates or raises an event. Also called *event provider*.

Event statement   Must appear at the module level in order for your class to raise an event.

Extensible Application Markup Language (XAML)   Source code language used to create a WPF application.

F

Field Explorer   A section of the toolbox that displays while Crystal Reports is active; holds elements that can be added to a report.

fields   The elements represented in columns of a table; also used to refer to variables.

FIFO   First-in, first-out. The organization used to store items in a queue.

filter   Criteria used to select specific records.

flexibility   The ability of an application to adapt to changes in the database or user interface; a feature facilitated by mulitier applications.

foreign key   The field in a child table that links a record to the corresponding record in the parent table.

foreign-key constraints   Ensures that if the primary key in the parent table is modified or deleted, the corresponding record(s) in the child table are modified to match.

FormView control   Web database control used to display a single record; provides for flexible layout by using a template.

G

garbage collection   The process in which the .NET Framework destroys unused objects and reclaims memory.

generic class   A class that contains methods that can be instantiated using different data types.

generic collection   A collection with a single type of object that is declared at design time.

generics   Ability to create code, methods, or classes, without specifying the data type.

GetChanges method   Used to retrieve only the rows with the specified row state.

GetChildRows method   Retrieves an array of rows that are linked to the parent row.

GetParentRow method   Retrieves the parent row of a child row.

globalization   Designing your application for multiple languages, cultures, and locations.

GridView control   Web database control for displaying records in rows and columns.

Group Footer   A section of a Crystal Reports object that appears at the end of each group and generally displays subtotals.

Group Header   A section of a Crystal Reports object that appears in the report at the top of a new group, based on the field that you selected for grouping.

H

HasChanges method   Used to determine if any changes have been made to a dataset.

hash table   The fastest type of collection for searching. Based on a key/value pair where the key is calculated using an algorithm.

Help topic   A single HTML page in HTML Help; each screen that displays in the Contents pane.

Help Viewer   Part of the HTML Help Workshop that provides a way to view Help topics, screens, and HTML references.

HelpKeyword property   A property of a control that appears when a HelpProvider is added to the form; used to specify the exact topic to display.

HelpNamespace property   A property of a HelpProvider control; specifies the path and name of the Help file.

HelpNavigator property   A property of a control that appears when a HelpProvider is added to the form; used to specify the page to display, such as Table of Contents, Index, or Topic.

HelpProvider component   Used to display Help files in your application. Adding the component to a form adds new Help properties to the controls on the form.

HelpString property   An actual string of text to display for popup Help.

HTML Help ActiveX control   Used for adding navigation to an HTML page. Add the control to a page in the HTML Help Workshop.

HTML Help Image Editor A separate application used for creating screen shots and working with images.

HTML Help Workshop A separate application used to create Help files for an application.

Hyperlink control A Web control used to navigate to another Web page.

I

identifier The name for a variable, field, object, or procedure; supplied by the programmer.

ImageButton A Web button control that can display a graphic.

inheritance Derive a new class from an existing class. The new class has all of the public and protected properties and methods of the existing class.

instance member A class variable or property that is not shared by multiple instances of the class. Includes instance properties and instance variables.

instance property A class property that is not shared by multiple instances of the class. Each instance has its own copy of the property.

instance variable A class variable that is not shared by multiple instances of the class. Each instance has its own copy of the variable.

intranet A network within a company.

IsMdiContainer property Used to determine if a form is the parent for an MDI application.

Items collection The collection of related objects in a single object or control such as a ListBox.

ItemTemplate Determines how the data for each row should appear in a DataList or FormView.

J

junction table A third table used to link two tables in a many-to-many relationship.

L

LayoutMdi method A method that determines the layout of the child windows within an MDI parent.

lifetime The period of time that a variable remains in scope.

LIFO Last-in, first-out; the technique used to store items in a stack.

LinkButton A Web control that looks like a hyperlink but functions like a button and fires a Click event.

Language-Integrated Query (LINQ) A standard language for querying any data source.

list A collection of related objects.

ListItem object A single object from the Items collection of a Web list box control.

localizability A setting of a form that allows an application to be localized; the resources that must be localized are separated from the code that does not change.

localization The actual process of translating the interface for a culture/locale.

login controls A set of controls to automate the sign-on procedure for a Web application.

lookup Logic for locating an item within an array or list of elements.

M

managed code Code that is compiled to run in the CLR.

managed data Data that are managed by the CLR during run time.

many-to-many relationships A relationship between tables in a relational database in which multiple records in one table can be related to multiple records in the second table.

master page A Web page that provides a template for the layout for any related content pages. A Web site may have multiple master pages.

master table The primary table in a relational database. The "one side" of a one-to-many relationship. Also called the *parent table*.

MdiParent property Property to set the parent of a form; used for MDI applications.

MenuStrip component Component for creating menus for a Windows Form.

metadata Data that describe data. For example, attributes that describe an application, such as <WebService> or <WebMethod>.

Microsoft intermediate language (MSIL) A platform-independent set of compiled instructions that is combined with the metadata to form a file called a portable executable (PE) file.

module-level scope A Private variable that is declared inside any class, structure, or module but outside of any sub procedure or function. Can be used in any procedure of the current class or module.

multiple document interface (MDI)   An application in which a user can open multiple child windows inside a parent window.

multitier application   An application that separates the functions of an application into multiple classes; separating the user interface from the business logic from the database access.

My   An object in Visual Basic used to access information about the user, system, application, and resources; replaces API calls.

N

namespace   A way of organizing classes, interfaces, and structures into groups. Any Public class or identifier in any one namespace must be unique. To qualify the name of an item, include the complete namespace designation, such as System.Web.UI.WebControls.

namespace scope   A variable, constant, class, or structure declared with the *Public* modifier. The identifier can be used in any procedure within the namespace, usually the entire application.

NavigateUrl property   A property of a Web control that determines the address of the page to navigate to when the user clicks on the control.

.NET Framework   A set of class library files that provides for developing and running Windows applications, Web applications, and XML Web Services written in multiple languages on multiple platforms.

.NET Framework class library   The files that hold the classes and interfaces that form the .NET Framework.

Now property   Returns the current date and time.

O

ObjectDataSource control   Data source control that can connect to many types of objects, including a Web service.

one-to-many relationship   In a relational database, one record in the parent table may be related to many records in a child table.

one-to-one relationship   In a relational database, one record in the parent table relates to only one record in the child table.

operation contract   The methods declared in an Interface that must be coded in a class that implements the Interface.

overloading   When two methods have the same name but a different argument list.

Overridable   The keyword used to allow a method in a derived class to override (replace) the method from the superclass.

override   A method in a derived class that is used instead of the method in the base class that has the same name. An overriding method must have the same argument list as the method in the base class.

P

Page Footer   A section of a Crystal Reports object that will appear at the bottom of each page of a report and generally contains the page number.

Page Header   A section of a Crystal Reports object that will appear at the top of each page and generally holds the report title and column headings.

parameterized constructor   A constructor that requires arguments.

parameterized query   A query in which a wild card is used in place of hard-coded criteria so that the value can be specified at run time.

Parameters collection   Set of criteria for database queries.

parent class   The original class that can be inherited to create a child class. Also called a *superclass* or *base class*.

parent form   The container form in an MDI application.

parent table   The primary table in a relational database. The "one side" of a one-to-many relationship. Also called a *master table*.

partial class   In Visual Studio, a class can be split over multiple files; each file contains a partial class.

partial type   Refers to a partial class.

Peek method   Used to look at the last item in a stack list without removing it.

polymorphism   Refers to method names having identical names but different implementations depending on the current object or the arguments supplied.

Pop method   Removes an item from a stack list.

populate   Fill a DataSet object with data from a data source.

Position property   A property of the binding source of a form that holds the current row number.

PositionChanged event   An event of the binding source; fires when a user navigates to another record.

postback A Web form is sent to the server and returned to the browser. Also called a *round-trip* to the server.

presentation tier The segment of a multitier application that provides the user interface.

primary key field The field (or combination of fields) that uniquely identifies each record.

procedure-level scope The scope of any variable that you declare inside a procedure or function, but not within a block. The variable can be used only inside that procedure.

Project Designer A tabbed dialog that appears in the main document window of the IDE; provides a location for viewing and setting project properties and resources.

property procedure Public procedures that expose the private properties of a class; contains `Get` and `Set` procedures.

Push method Used to add an item to a stack list.

Q

Query Builder Database window used to design SQL statements.

queue An unsorted collection in which the first element in is the first out (FIFO).

R

RaiseEvent statement Raises (or fires) an event; must appear in the same module as the `Event` declaration in order for your control class to raise an event.

ReadOnly The modifier used in a property procedure to create a ReadOnly property.

record The data for one item, person, or transaction. Also known as a *row*.

refactoring A feature of some programming languages that allows the programmer to change the name and class of objects.

reference object An object used to connect a Visual Basic project to external components. Found in the References node of the Solution Explorer.

reference type An identifier that refers to an object, such as a form. The identifier holds the address of the object; as opposed to a value type, which holds the actual value, such as a numeric variable.

referential integrity In a relational database, a constraint that requires that the keys of the records in a child table match keys in the parent table. If a record in the parent table is modified or deleted, the changes also must apply to the corresponding record(s) in the child table.

RejectChanges method Rolls back all changes that have been made to a dataset since it was created or the last `AcceptChanges` method executed.

RemoveAt method Deletes an item from a collection by index number.

RemoveCurrent method Deletes the current record from a data source.

Report Footer In Crystal Reports, the section of the report that appears once at the end of the report.

Report Header In Crystal Reports, the section of the report that appears one time at the beginning of the report.

Request object An object sent by the browser to the server; holds information about the current user, data entered by the user, and arguments to an HTTP request.

Response object An object returned by the server to the browser in an HTML page. Can be used to retrieve the cookies being held in the Request object.

Response.Redirect The method used to navigate to another Web page in code.

reusability The ability to reuse or obtain the functionality from one class of object when you have another similar situation; writing applications in components that can be used in more than one situation.

root namespace The primary namespace used by an application. By default, named the same as the application, but can be overridden with `Namespace` directives.

row The data for one item, person, or transaction. Also known as a *record*.

RowState property A property of a DataRow; indicates whether any changes have been made to the row.

S

scalability The ability of an application to handle an increase or decrease in the number of users and the number of servers.

scope The area of the program that can "see" and reference a variable, constant, or method. May be namespace-level, module-level, procedure-level, or block-level.

selection queries Queries that select data from a database and return the selected data to your program.

server   Web applications: formats and sends Web pages to the client system.

Server.Transfer   The method used to transfer to another Web page that is located on the same server.

service   Software routine that can be provided on one system and accessed from another application or from a remote system; see *Windows Communication Foundation*.

service reference   A reference added to a project that specifies a service component that must be loaded.

Session object   An object used for managing state in a Web application; holds data for the current user.

shadow   Replaces the base-class method in the derived class, but not in any new classes derived from that class. A shadowing method need not have the same argument list as the base-class method.

shared member   A member of a class that exists once for all instances of the class. Includes shared properties and shared variables.

shared property   A property of a class that exists once for all instances of the class. All instances access the same copy of the property.

shared variable   A variable of a class that exists once for all instances of the class; often used to accumulate totals. All instances access the same copy of the variable.

ShowHelp method   Displays a Help topic page from code.

ShowHelpIndex method   Displays the Help files with the *Index* tab selected.

Simple Object Access Protocol (SOAP)   Establishes a protocol for handling requests and responses including class names, method names, and parameters. Used to standardize object creation and calling sequences across platforms.

single document interface (SDI)   A Windows application that contains a form or forms that each stands alone; does not contain parent and child forms.

single-file model   Web page design that includes VB code embedded within the HTML used for page design.

singleton pattern   Design pattern that ensures that only a single instance can be created of a class.

Smart Device   Mobile device that runs the Windows operating system.

splash screen   A form that displays first, while the rest of the application loads.

SQL Server Express Edition   Version of SQL Server that automatically installs with Visual Studio. Used to access a database on a single computer.

SqlDataSource control   An ASP.NET control for connecting database data to the application.

stack   An unsorted collection in which the last element in is the first element out (LIFO).

state   The current values of all variables and controls in a Web page.

stateless   The state of the page is not saved. By default, HTML pages are stateless and techniques must be used to save the state.

StatusStrip component   Used to create a status bar on a form; frequently used to display application status, error messages, date, and time.

stored procedure   A set of SQL commands stored within the SQLServer database for later execution.

Structured Query Language (SQL)   A standardized language for creating, querying, and maintaining databases.

subclass   An inherited class. Also called a *child class* or *derived class*.

superclass   May be inherited to create a subclass. Also called a *base class* or *parent class*.

System.Collections namespace   Provides classes for several different types of collections.

T

table   Data stored in rows and columns or records and fields.

TableAdapter   Database object that communicates with the data source; uses SQL.

thread   A separate path of execution that allows a program to do more than one thing at a time.

throw an exception   Generate an exception object to indicate that an error has occurred.

Throw statement   Sends or "throws" an exception. A Throw statement in a Catch block sends any caught exceptions up a level.

Timer component   A Windows component that can fire an event at a specified interval.

ToolStrip component   Used to create a flexible toolbar that can contain combo boxes, text boxes, as well as buttons.

TrimToSize method Used to reduce the size of an ArrayList to the number of elements that actually hold data.

TryParse method Allows a value to be tested outside of the Try/Catch process; uses less system resources.

U

unbound controls A control for displaying data that are not directly bound to the data source.

unique constraint In a relational database, a constraint that specifies that a specific column cannot contain duplicate entries.

uniform resource identifier (URI) Uniquely identifies a resource on the Web.

Update method A method of a TableAdapter to transfer all changes in the dataset to the data source.

UpdateAll method A method of the TableAdapterManager that sequences updates for related tables.

user control A new control developed by combining or inheriting existing controls.

V

Validating event Event used for testing the contents of a field.

validation control Controls for Web applications that can validate user input on the client side.

Value keyword In a Property Set procedure, used to refer to the incoming value for the property.

value type An identifier that holds the actual value of the object; as opposed to a reference type, which holds the address of an object.

ValueMember property A property of a bound Windows ListBox or ComboBox control; holds the field name of the data to return for a selected item. For example, the DisplayMember holds the data that display in the list (such as a string of text) and the ValueMember holds the record key that corresponds to the DisplayMember.

ViewState An ASP.NET server control feature for storing state with the Web page.

W

WCF Service Windows Communication Foundation; a software routine accessed remotely as a service.

Web document See *Web Form.*

Web farm Many servers sharing the load to host Web sites.

Web Form Used to create the user interface for a Web application. Also called *Web page.*

Web page An HTML representation of a display page for Web applications; used to create the user interface for a Web application.

Web server The computer/ software needed to format and send HTML pages to a browser.

Web site A collection of Web forms.

Web.config file Contains configuration settings for a Web application. Can be used to set security and permissions as well as dynamic properties such as connection strings.

Windows Communication Foundation (WCF) Microsoft technology for distributed computing.

Windows Presentation Foundation (WPF) Application template to write a WPF application, or use a WPF Browser template to create a browser application.

WithEvents Keyword used in the declaration of an object that specifies that the object generates events to which the program can respond.

WriteOnly The modifier used in a property procedure to create a property that can be set but not returned.

X

XAML See *Extensible Application Markup Language.*

XAML browser application (XBAP) A WPF application that runs in a browser. The user interface is created using XAML.

XML Extensible markup language. An industry-standard format for storing and transferring data as text using identifying tags.

XML literals Shortcut notation for referencing child, attribute, and descendant elements of an XML file.

Index

SYMBOLS

\# (pound sign)
    beginning styles, 295
    enclosing literal date values, 578
& (ampersand), before keyboard access key
    letters, 589
* * (asterisks), in validation controls, 314
… (ellipsis), in a descendant, 528, 529
@ (at sign) icon, 292
@ (at sign) notation, in an attribute, 528, 529
<> (brackets)
    enclosing attribute names in WCF, 250
    in an XML file, 598
^ (exponentiation) operator, 562
\+ (addition) operator, 562
< (less than) operator, 163, 567
< = (less than or equal to) operator, 567
<> (not equal to) relational operator, 567
= (equal to) operator, 163, 567
> (greater than) operator, 163, 567
> = (greater than or equal to) operator, 567
/ (division) operator, 562
* (multiplication) operator, 562
− (minus sign)
    with Pmt function, 580
    with Rate function, 581
− (subtraction) operator, 562
'(apostrophes), indicating commented lines, 615
1:1 relationship. *See* one-to-one (1:1)
    relationship
1:M relationships. *See* one-to-many (1:M)
    relationships

A

Abandon method, 317
abc, of a WCF Service, 250
About Box template, 31
Abs (absolute value) method, 581, 582
absolute URL, 288
abstract class, 51–52
abstraction, 50
.accdb files, 107
accept button, on a form, 587
AcceptChanges method, 191, 193
Access (software), 111, 200
access code, in data-tier projects, 266–267
access rules, 324, 325, 326
AccessDataSource control, 352–353
accessibility, of a variable or class, 76–77
accessibility keywords, for procedures, 577
accessibility modifiers, 74, 75
accessibility software, 291
action buttons, in GridView, 371
Activate event, 587
active server pages. *See* ASP

ActiveX control, 500
ActiveX Data Objects (ADO) .NET, 106, 110
Add button
    allowing changes after clicking, 225
    code for, 202–203
    in a DataGridView object, 188
Add Class option, 77
Add Column dialog box, 226, 227
Add Component option, 77
Add method
    of an array list, 440
    of DataBindings, 136–137, 210
    of a generic collection class, 452–453
    for a hash table, 435
    of Items, 563, 589
    of a sorted list, 436
Add New Data Source, 112
Add New Item dialog box, 309–310, 405
    Splash Screen template, 31
Add New Smart Device Project dialog, 510
Add New Stored Procedure option, 131
Add New Table option, 391–392
Add operation, 201, 202
Add Service Reference dialog box, 257
Add WHERE Clause dialog box, 361
addition (+) operator, 562
AddNew method, 191, 197, 202
AddRange method, 440
Administrative privileges, ClickOnce
    installation and, 600
ADO.NET, 3, 106, 110
Advanced Options dialog, in TableAdapter
    Configuration Wizard, 130
Advanced SQL Generation Options dialog
    box, 369
aggregate operators, in LINQ, 524, 525
AJAX (Asynchronous JavaScript and XML),
    327–328
    control toolkit, 328
    downloading and using controls,
    328–330
    templates, 334
AJAX Controls toolbox tab, 329
AJAX Extensions list of controls, for Web
    Forms, 283
AJAX Master Page, 334
AJAX Web Form, 334
Alias field, 146
alignment
    of decimal points in numeric output, 593
    fixing in reports, 418–419
All operator, in LINQ, 525
AllowDBNull property, 212, 229
AllowSorting property, 355
AllowUserTo * properties, 115

ampersand (&), before keyboard access key
    letters, 589
And logical operator, 567
AndAlso logical operator, 567
Any operator, in LINQ, 525
apostrophes (' '), indicating commented lines, 615
App_Data folder, 354
application(s)
    connecting HTML Help files to, 500–504
    deploying, 600–603
    hybrid, 518
    multitier, 53–54
    separating into multiple classes, 178
Application Files button, 601
Application object, 315, 316, 317
Application tab, in Project Designer, 12
Application Updates dialog, 602
ApplicationException class, 61
Application.xaml file, 518
Apply New Style option, 293
Apply new style to document selection
    check box, 294
Apply Styles window, 292, 293
    applying styles from, 294
    icons in, 292
    modifying styles from, 294–295
arguments
    assigning to properties, 57–58
    constructor requiring, 57
    order of, 577
    passing, 575
    passing ByRef and ByVal, 576–577
array lists, 440
ArrayList collection class, 433
arrays, 562–563
    including in structures, 564–565
    querying using LINQ, 523–524
ASP (active server pages), 6, 277
ASP server control, 284
ASP.NET, 6, 278
    data access in, 352–368
    Internet Explorer and, 277
    login controls, 323
    models for managing controls and
    code, 281
    page life cycle, 334–335
    state management, 315
    validation controls, 312, 313
    Web Site Administration Tool, 324–325
    Web Site template, 280, 480
.aspx extension, 278, 556
.aspx files, 336, 556
aspx.vb extension, 278
.aspx.vb file, 556
assemblies, 5

assembly information
retrieving, 16
setting, 14–15
Assembly Information dialog box, 14, 16
assembly manifest, 5
assembly reference list, 5
AssemblyInfo.vb file, 9, 15
asterisks (* *), in validation controls, 314
asynchronous execution of time-consuming operations, 534
Asynchronous JavaScript and XML. *See* AJAX
At sign (@) icon, for styles, 292
Atan method, 582
attributes, 5
using XML literals, 528, 529
viewing in Windows Explorer, 17
in XML files, 598
author, of a control, 466
Author text box, 418
Auto style application, 292–293
AutoHide, using on windows, 608
AutoPostBack property, 284
Autos window, 621
Average operator, in LINQ, 525

B

background processing, 535
Background workers, 534–535
BackgroundImage property, 31
BackgroundWorker component, 534
BackgroundWorker object, 535
BackgroundWorker program, 535–536
bad input, catching, 379, 566
bang (!) notation
changing binding at run time, 210
referring to individual fields, 168
base class, 51, 79–80
Basic Syntax, in the Formula Editor, 415, 416
BeginEdit method, 193
bin folder, 9–10
bin\Debug folder
copying the database file to, 189–190
database file copy in, 623
deleting a file in, 224
binary, data stored in, 109
Binding for Text, 358
BindingNavigator bar, 113
BindingNavigator class, 188
BindingSource class
DataError event, 218
events for, 198
navigation methods of, 196–197
properties and methods of, 191, 196
sorting with, 127
BindingSource objects, 109
binding form controls, 135
editing methods of, 197–198
managed by the BindingSource object, 195–198
method calls from, 189
properties and methods of, 196
BitArray collection class, 433
bitmap, in the toolbox, 470
blank fields, validation of, 312
block If statement, 568
block-level scope, 75–76

blocking methods, 534
blocks. *See also* classes
breaking programs into, 50
blue dot icon, for styles, 292
blue snap lines, 8
books.xml file, 528
Boolean data type, 556
Boolean expressions, testing, 567–568
BooleanAppend argument, 595
BorderStyle property, 588
bound controls, updating datasets in, 199–211
bound data, formatting, 120–123
bound fields, setting properties of, 356
bound table data, managing, 195–198
bound text box, formatting of, 120
brackets ()
enclosing attribute names in WCF, 250
in an XML file, 598
break time, stepping through code at, 621
breakpoints, setting, 286, 619–620
browser window, resizing width of, 304
browsers, 277
Build process, within the IDE, 605
Builder button, of a property, 31
building-block concept, 53
built-in collection, 563
business class
building a basic, 58–60
modifying, 68–72
business rules, 53
business services tier, 53, 54, 58–59
Button control, 285, 589
button controls
adding and extending, 330
for Web Forms, 285–286
buttons
adding to the ToolStrip container, 22
changing for update selections, 201
specifying for message boxes, 574
ByRef modifier, 577
Byte data type, 556, 557
ByVal modifier, 57, 576–577

C

C (currency) format specifier code, 561
caching, 368
calculated fields, 414–417
calculation application, in WPF, 520
calculations
hierarchy of operations for, 562
performing in WCF Services, 259–260
Calendar control, 289–290
CalendarExtender, in AJAX, 334
Call optional word, 575
callback, 591
called procedures, stepping through, 622
calling, procedures, 575
camel casing, 119
Cancel button
CausesValidation property, 213, 214
code for, 204–205
on a form, 587
CancelButton object, 535
CancelEdit method, 191, 193, 197
CancelEventArgs argument, 64
CancelNew method, 191, 197

Canvas layout, for WPF applications, 518
Capacity property, of an array list, 440
captions, for database fields, 119
Cascade constant, 27
cascading deletes, 219, 220
cascading style sheets (CSS), 291, 292
cascading updates, 219, 220
Case Else clause, 570
Catch blocks, 565, 566. *See also* Try/Catch blocks
catching, exceptions, 60
category names, eliminating repeating, 413
CausesValidation property
of a control, 213, 214
of each control on a form, 63
field-level validation of a form, 590
turning on, 64
.cd extension, 32
Cell Style Builder dialog box, 121, 122
ChangePassword control, 322, 323, 327
Char data type, 556, 557
CheckBox control, 588
Checked property
of CheckBox, 588
of a Label control, 588
passing from a check box, 81
of a radio button, 589
child class, 51
child elements, using XML literals, 528, 529
child forms, 25, 26, 586. *See also* child windows
child nodes, in XML, 598
child records
adding after parent, 223
deleting first, 219
child rows
finding, 169, 174
retrieving related, 170–172
child table, 150
child windows. *See also* child forms
layout options for, 27
listing open, 26–27
.chm extension, 492, 494
Choose a Crystal Report, 410
Choose Toolbox Items dialog box, 329, 476, 477
circled dot icon, for styles, 292
class-based style, 292
class code, for a two-tier application, 59–60
Class Details toolbar, 32
Class Details window, 32, 33, 34
class diagrams, 31
creating, 31–32
customizing, 32–34
class files, 11, 77
class level, collection at, 441
class-level scope. *See* module-level scope
class-level variables, 138
class library, 2–4
classes, 50
adding for data tiers, 138
allowing properties to be accessed, 55
creating, 54–73
creating a hierarchy of, 51
creating inherited, 77–80
declaring as Public, 74
designing, 54
instantiating strongly typed, 450
reusing, 52

Clear All Bookmarks button, 615
Clear method
   of an array list, 440
   of ErrorProvider, 65
   of a generic collection class, 452–453
   of Items, 589
ClickOnce deployment, 600–603
client
   in client/server Web applications, 276
   for a WCF service, 260
client application, in WCF, 250
client code, for a WCF service, 264
client/server Web applications, 276–278
client-side HTML controls, 284
client user interface, 264
Close button, for a window, 609
Close method
   for a form, 586
   of StreamReader, 596
   of StreamWriter, 596
Closed event, 587
Closing event, 587
CLR (Common Language Runtime), 2, 554
CLS (Common Language Specification), 3
COBOL, 554
code
   converting to comments, 615
   dragging to the toolbox, 618
   for forms, 140
   modifying in Data Designer, 222–223
   single-stepping through, 621–622
   for a Smart Device application, 512
Code Access Security permissions, 600
code-behind file, 278, 280, 556
code blocks, declaring variables inside, 75
Code Editor window, 467
code separation model, 281
code snippets, 624
CodePlex.com, 327–328
CollectionBase collection class, 433
collections, 563. *See also* data structures; lists
   adding objects to, 442
   classes for different types of, 432
   creating, 441–446
   declaring, 441
   defining strongly typed, 452
   example program, 437–439
   referring to individual elements of, 432
   removing elements from, 442
   retrieving elements from, 442
   types of, 432
Collections namespace, 3
Collections.Generic namespace, 453–454
Color enumeration, 81
column(s)
   adding new, 226, 227
   checking all in a table, 230–231
   in a data table, 107
   selecting for selection criteria, 361
   setting properties of new, 228
   sorting by in a grid, 355
column headings
   changing, 114–115
   fixing in reports, 418–419
column styles, in a Smart Device application, 515
ColumnChanged event, 215, 216, 229

COM objects, 5
combo box selection, navigating from, 210–211
combo boxes
   adding for selection, 124–125
   binding table data to, 135–137
   DropDownStyle property of, 158
   populating with data, 123–124
   properties of, 158, 165
   in a Smart Device application, 516–517
   sorting data for, 127–130
   state of, 210–211
ComboBox control, 129, 589
Command and Parameter Editor dialog, 389
CommandField properties, 371
Comment Selected Lines command, 615
comments, in XML files, 598
common language runtime (CLR), 2, 554
Common Language Specification (CLS), 3
company logo, placing in a master page, 304
Compare methods, 583
CompareValidator control, 313
compartments, of a class diagram, 33
Compile tab, 12
Compiled Help file, 494
compiling, a Help project, 498–499
components, throwing exceptions from, 62
composite controls, 466
   creating, 475–479
   declaring events in, 479
   designing the visual interface, 466
   resizing, 477
concatenation, 126
concurrency
   problems, 199
   setting, 369
Configure Data Source wizard, 353–354
ConfirmButtonExtender control, 330, 331
conflicts, in updates, 199
connection strings, 354
constant values, assigning, 82
constants, 556, 558–559
   scope of, 74–76, 559
   in a Select Case structure, 569
constituent controls, 466
   adding, 477–478
   code in event handlers for, 479
   dragging to the design surface, 466
   exposing events of, 479
   exposing properties of, 478–479
Constraint objects, 108
constraint violations, catching, 378–379
constraints, 152, 379
Constraints collection, 108
constructors, 56
   creating, 78
   overloading, 57
   for slides, 332
consumer application, for a WCF service, 260
consumption of services, 251
ContactsService.vb file, 383
container, 589
Contains method, 440
Contains operator, in LINQ, 525
content pages, 304, 311
Content property, for WPF labels, 518
Contents collection, of the Session object, 317

contents file, for Help, 497–498
Contents tab, 492–494, 497–498
context menus, 21–22
context-sensitive Help, 503, 618
ContextMenuStrip component, 19, 21–22
Continue command, 619, 621, 622
Continue statement, 572–573
ContinueDestinationPageUrl property, 322
contracts, in WCF, 250
control(s), 588–590
   adding events to, 472–473
   adding properties to, 471–472
   adding to forms, 139, 470
   adding to the toolbox, 476–477
   adding to Web Forms, 329–330
   aligning using snap lines, 613–614
   assigning properties to resources, 10
   binding data to, 188
   common .NET, 588–589
   connecting context-sensitive Help
     topics, 503
   creating, 466–467
   inheriting from existing, 467
   nudging into place, 613
   popup DataTips, 284
   selecting for database fields, 118–119
   setting tab order for Web Forms, 311–312
   types of, 282–284
   validation of individual, 393
   ViewState property of, 319
   for WPF applications, 518
control class
   creating an instance of, 588
   generating events, 472–473
Control Events event, 335
control structures, 567–573
control types, selecting for Details view,
    118–119
ControlBox property, 30
conversion, between data types, 560–561
Convert class, To methods, 560
Convert this field into a TemplateField, 371
cookieless sessions, 318
cookies, 316, 318
Cookies property, 318
&copy, for the copyright symbol, 594
Copy always setting, 623
Copy if newer setting, 623
Copy to Output Directory property, 189–190, 623
Copy Web Site tool, 604–605
Copy Web tool, 336
copyright symbol, displaying, 594
CopyTo method, 440
CopyToOutputDirectory property, 221
Cos method, 582
Count (LongCount) operator, in LINQ, 525
Count property
   of an array list, 440
   of BindingSource, 191, 196
   of a collection, 441
   of collection classes, 433
   of a generic collection class, 452–453
   of Items, 589
Create access rules, 325, 326
Create directory for solution check box, 252,
    253, 261, 468

Create methods to send updates directly to the database, 383
Create User Task button, 618
CreateUserText property, 321
CreateUserUrl property, 321
CreateUserWizard control, 322, 323, 327
credit card information, controls for, 480
criteria, for a SQL query, 160
cross-language programming, 2
Crystal Report template, 405
Crystal Reports, 404
    controls, 284
    creating a report template, 404–410
    toolbars specific to, 412
Crystal Reports Gallery, 404, 406
Crystal Syntax, in the Formula Editor, 415, 416
CrystalReportViewer control, 410, 419
CSS. *See* cascading style sheets
.css files, 291
CSS Properties window, 292, 293
    editing styles in, 302
    modifying style attributes in, 295
    modifying the Footer DIV, 307
CSS windows, opening, 299
Ctrl-clicking, 588
culture/locale, 531
CultureInfo class, 532–533
currency, 109
Current property, 191, 196
CurrentChanged event, 198
custom controls, 466
custom error pages, 392–393
customized controls, 467
CyrstalReportSource control, 419

D

D (Decimal) type declaration character, 559
D (digits) format specifier code, 561
data
    accessing in the .NET Framework,
        107–109
    adding to Web projects, 353
    binding from stored procedures, 137
    binding to controls, 188
    caching, 368
    displaying from related tables, 362
    displaying in a DetailsView control,
        356–357
    displaying in a grid, 113–114
    displaying in individual fields, 117–118
    displaying on a form with a data source,
        355–359
    displaying on multiple Web pages, 364–365
    formatting in a TextBox, 120–121
    handling, 106
    helping users to enter valid, 224–225
    hiding, 50
    populating combo boxes with, 123–124
    retrieving using stored procedures, 132
    selecting in a GridView control, 366–367
    sorting for ComboBox, 129
    viewing in the IDE, 392
    writing, 595–596
data access
    in ASP.NET, 352–368
    splitting from the dataset, 267

data access layer, 108, 263
data access tier, 261
data binding properties, of combo boxes, 517
data bindings, for Web applications, 358–359
data-bound controls, 110–111, 164, 221–222
data-bound drop-down list, 359
data component, as a separate tier, 133
data entity tier, 261
data exceptions. *See also* exception(s)
    handling, 217–218
data fields. *See also* field(s)
    binding to form controls, 135–137
    unbound, 166–172
data files, 594–597
data form, for a Smart Device application,
    515, 516
Data list of controls, 283
Data namespace, 3
data objects, 189, 191–195. *See also* objects
data readers, versus DataSets, 368
data relationships. *See also* relationships
    among tables, 150–153
Data section, of the toolbox, 352–353
data service
    instantiating, 264
    setting up a project to consume, 386
data source(s), 107
    adding, 112–113, 138, 262–263,
        363, 514
    configuring, 263
    displaying data on a form with, 355–359
    setting for drop-down lists, 359, 360
Data Source Configuration Wizard,
        112, 153, 154
    Advanced button, 368–369
    changing the data source for a mobile
        application, 514
    displaying, 132
    setting the data source, 359, 360
data source controls, 352–354
    adding, 360
    HTML code for, 377–378
    updating with, 369–378
Data Source Update Mode, 125
Data Sources window, 110–111
    creating data-bound controls, 221–222
    displaying, 112
    selecting a database field in, 118
data storage, 2
data streams, types for reading and writing, 3
data structures, 432. *See also* collections; lists;
        structures
data table, 107. *See also* table(s)
data tier, 53, 54
    adding a class for, 138
    components, 262
    creating, 137–140
    dividing into separate projects, 261
    projects, 266–267
Data Tier class, 176–177
data-tier component
    code to instantiate, 134–135
    creating, 133–134
data types, 556–557
    for array elements, 562
    conversion between, 560–561

functions for determining, 585
    selecting, 557
data WCF service, 261–265
DataAdapters. *See* TableAdapter objects
database(s)
    copying for development and testing, 112
    larger-scale, 106
    security considerations for, 232
    terminology, 107
    updating, 368–380, 381–387, 515, 623
    viewing changes to, 387
database access, setting up, 359
database applications
    creating, 106, 111–123
    for Smart Devices, 514–517
Database Explorer, 110, 212
database fields
    setting the captions for, 119
    storing state information, 316
database files
    copy behavior of, 189–190
    designing and maintaining, 111–112
    local, 112
database handling, 189–191
database objects, coding a form's, 134–135
database queries, for unbound controls, 389
DataBind method, 375
DataBound event handler, 377
DataColumn collection, 108
DataContext class, 525
DataError events
    of BindingSource, 218
    in DataGridView, 217–218
    handling, 225–226
DataGridColumnStyle Collection Editor, 515
DataGridTableStyle Collection Editor, 515
DataGridView control
    binding to a DataSet, 135
    DataError event, 217–218
    error icons, 216–217
    on a form, 114
    formatting, 121, 122, 123, 178
    properties of, 115
    single table in, 188
DataGridView icon, 113
DataGridView program, 215–217
DataManager class, 267
DataNavigateUrlFormatString property, 364
DataReader objects, 368
DataRelation object, 108, 157
DataRow collection, 108
DataRow objects, 167–168, 193
DataRows collection, 167–168
DataRowState enumeration, 192
DataSet classes
    filtering, 162–166
    Merge method, 266
    properties and methods, 191
    writing validation code inside, 215
DataSet Designer, 115–117
    accessing, 111
    adding a relationship in, 157
    changing field captions in, 119
    code automatically generated by, 134
    displaying Query Builder from, 127, 128
    displaying table data from, 392

DataSet Designer—*Cont.*
　　displaying tables in, 167
　　new expressions in, 125–126
　　opening, 126, 218, 219, 221
　　Properties window, 266
　　viewing a table definition, 213
　　viewing code generated by, 117
　　viewing or creating a relationship, 157
DataSet object model, 108, 109
DataSet objects, 107–108
　　declaring, 134
　　holding one or more tables, 108
　　methods returning, 139
DataSet Project property, 262
datasets, 189
　　adding and viewing, 111
　　adding validation to, 229–232
　　assigning to reports, 411
　　changing captions assigned to fields, 119
　　creating, 153, 154, 382–383
　　disconnected, 106
　　displaying in DataGridView, 114
　　filtering, 164–166
　　generating with multiple tables, 153, 154
　　modifying properties of, 116
　　previewing data, 116
　　updating, 188–189, 198–199
　　updating in bound controls, 199–211
　　writing code to fill, 410–411
Dataset.xsd file, 268
DataSource property
　　of a combo box, 123, 158
　　of a control, 359
　　setting to BindingSource, 135
　　of a table, 228
DataSourceMethod property, 368
DataSourceUpdateMode, 210
DataTable collection, 108
DataTable objects, 108
DataTips, 620
date(s)
　　displaying in a report, 413
　　working with, 577–579
Date data type, 556
date formats
　　converting values to, 579
　　for the DateTimePicker control, 120
Date property, 578
Date Time formats, 121
Date variables, 578
Date.Parse method, 579
DateText property, 478–479
DateTime structure, 24, 577–578
DateTime.Parse method, 579
DateTimePicker control, 120
DateTime.TryParse method, 579
Date.TryParse method, 579
Day property, 578
DayOfWeek property, 578
DayOfYear property, 578
DBNull, 213, 229
DDB (double-declining balance) function, 579
Deactivate event, 587
Debug folders, 9
Debug menu, 619
Debug toolbar, 619

debugging, in Web Forms, 286–287
Debugging Not Enabled dialog, 286
debugging tools, 618–622
decimal columns, aligning, 593
Decimal data type, 556, 557
decimal fractions, working with, 557
decimal positions, setting, 120
default buttons, in messages boxes, 574
default Web page, adding controls to, 386
Default.aspx.vb file, 280
DefaultValue property, 213
Delete button
　　becoming the Cancel button, 204
　　code for, 204–205
　　in a DataGridView object, 188–189
Delete method, of TableAdapter, 385
DELETE statement, 198, 199, 368–369
DeleteContact contract and function, 385
DeleteContact Web method, 386
DeleteParameters, 390, 391
deploying, Windows applications, 13
deployment, 600
depreciation functions, 579, 581
Dequeue method, 434–435
derived classes, 51, 52
descendants, 528, 529
design
　　separating from programming, 517
　　of a Web page, 295
Design pane, selecting a DIV in, 298
design patterns, 28
design surface
　　adding constituent controls, 476
　　of a composite user control, 477
　　of a UserControl, 466, 467
　　for a Web page, 281, 282
Design tab, 310
Design view, 295, 296
designer-generated code, 11
Designer window, 466
designers, 18, 517–518
Designer.vb file, 51, 556
DestinationPageUrl property, 321
destructors, 56
detail table, 150
Details band, in Crystal Reports, 413
Details view
　　converting to, 117–118
　　displaying records in, 516–517
　　selecting the control type for, 118–119
Details view program, 213–215
DetailsView control
　　changing data firing an event, 376
　　displaying data in, 356–357
　　updating in, 372–373
developer, of a control, 466
developer-written code, 11
development, selecting a language for, 531
Device Application template, 509, 510
device applications, 508–517
device controls, 508
device emulators. *See* emulators
DialogResult constants, 574
DialogResult type, 574
Dictionary collection, 453, 454–456
dictionary lists, types of, 433

dictionary-type collection, 435
DictionaryBase collection class, 433
DictionaryEntry data type, 442
Dim statement, 557
disabilities, accessibility by persons with, 291
Display menu item, 511
DisplayContacts project, 386
DisplayMember property, 165
　　of a combo box, 158
　　setting for a combo box, 123
DisplayStyle, setting to Nothing, 228
Dispose destructor, 56
Dispose method, 56
Distinct operator, in LINQ, 525
DIV elements, 295
　　adding, 296–298
　　advantages of using, 291
　　laying out a Web page, 295
　　naming, 298
　　setting up for a master page, 306
　　typing entries into, 309
DIV sections, in a Web page, 295
<DIV> tags, adding to Web pages, 284
division (/) operator, 562
.dll extension, 5
.dll file, 469, 476
DLLs (dynamic link libraries), 5
Do Loops, 571
Dock property, 410
docking, windows using guide diamonds, 611
DockPanel layout, 518
DOCUMENT object, selecting, 296
Document windows
　　in the IDE, 611
　　switching between open tabs, 610
documents, 610
dot notation, accessing elements in structures, 564
Double data type, 557, 558
double-declining-balance method, 581
downlevel browsers, validation in, 312
DoWork method, 534, 535
drag-and-drop editing, 617
Drawing namespace, 3
DrawString method, 592–593
drop-down lists
　　adding and configuring, 359–360
　　adding to grid cells, 371–372
　　displaying data in, 359
　　maintaining the selection of, 387
　　rebinding, 375
　　updating for navigation, 375–377
Dropdown style, 589
DropDownItems collection, 20
DropDownItems property, 20
DropDownList control, 359
DropdownList style, 589
DropDownStyle property, 158, 211, 589
dynamic link libraries (DLLs), 5

E

e argument, of event handlers, 379
e.Cancel, setting, 64
"ed" events, of a control, 379
Edit and Delete links, 369–370
Edit button, code for, 206
Edit Columns dialog box, 114–115, 121, 122, 228

Edit Columns option, 226
Edit Data Source with Designer button, 127
Edit form, in DetailsView, 373
edit logic, 205–206
edit methods, 193
Edit operation
    buttons displayed during, 201
    in FormView, 374
Edit Templates, 357
Editor, shortcuts in, 614–618
Editor window, 617, 618
element-based style, 292
ElementHost control, 521
elements
    removing from collections, 442
    retrieving from collections, 442
    of structures, 564
    in XML files, 598
ellipsis (…), in a descendant, 528, 529
Else clause, 63
e-mail accounts, for SMTP settings, 327
empty string, as default value, 213
empty value, testing, 229
Empty Web Site template, 381
emulators, 508, 509
    automatically installed, 508
    deploying to, 513
    Smart Device project displaying, 510, 511
    using, 508, 509
Enable Deleting, in GridView, 369–370
Enable Editing, in GridView, 369–370
Enable Pagination option, 357
Enable Paging option, 356, 372
Enable Selection, in GridView, 370–371
EnableCaching property, 368
Enabled property
    of check boxes, 205
    of TextBox, 588
    of a Timer component, 590
    of validation controls, 393
EnableViewState property
    of ASP.NET controls, 319
    of controls, 315
    of a hidden field, 377
encapsulation, 50–51, 54, 73
End Structure statement, 563
End Template Editing, 357
EndEdit method, 193
    of BindingSource, 191, 197
    of TableAdapterManager, 189
EndingDate parameter, 576
endpoints, in WCF, 250
EndsWith method, 584
Enqueue method, 434
entities, in O/R Designer, 525
enum, in ReportsForm, 420–421
Enum statement, 81–83
enumeration, 81–83
environment options, 7–8
equal to (=) operator, 163, 567
Equals method, 584
error diagnostic messages and statistics, 499
error icons, in DataGridView, 216–217
error indicators, 64–66
error messages
    displaying after compilation, 617

displaying custom instead of default,
    392–393
displaying in popups, 65
field names in, 232
including when throwing exceptions, 62
turning off left over, 226
error pages, creating custom, 392–393
ErrorMessage property, 314
ErrorProvider component, 63, 64–65
ErrorProvider control, 213, 214
errors, catching with TryParse methods, 566–567
Escape key
    activating CancelButton, 587
    handling, 211, 217
    steps necessary for, 214, 215
event(s)
    adding to controls, 472–473
    for BindingSource, 198
    of forms, 587
    generating, 472
    raised in each life cycle stage, 335
    raising, 472–473
    responding to, 473
event consumer, 472
event handlers, assigning, 21–22
event handling
    life cycle stage, 334
    for Web controls, 284
event provider, 472
event sink, 472
event source, 472
Event statement, 473
exception(s), 565. See also data exceptions
    catching for constraint violations, 378–379
    guidelines for throwing, 62
    handling multiple, 566
    passing additional information in, 61–62
    throwing and catching, 60–62
    throwing up a level, 62
Exception class, 61, 566
exception classes
    in .NET Framework, 61
    predefined, 565
exception handling, 565–566
    adding, 225–226
    alternatives to, 62–63
    for database updates, 378–379
exclamation mark (! or bang), 168
.exe extension, 5
.exe file, 10
Execute Query button, 128, 129
Existing Files page, 496
Exit Do statement, 572
Exit For statement, 572
Exit menu item, 511, 512
Exp method, 582
Expand option, from the Class Diagram menu, 33
Expires property, of a cookie, 318
Express Edition, of Visual Studio, 554
expression fields, 129
Expression Interactive Designer, 517
Expression Web, 291
expressions, 125–126, 620–621
extenders, 328, 330
Extensible Application Markup Language
    (XAML), 518

external style sheet (.css file), 291
Eyedropper cursor, 308

F

F (fixed-point) format specifier code, 561
F (Single) type declaration character, 559
F1, 618
F1 Help, 501
field(s). See also data fields
    adding concatenated, 126
    adding expressions to concatenate,
        125–126
    adding to reports, 412
    allowing nulls, 212–213
    in a data table, 107
    declaring as parameters, 384
    displaying data in individual, 117–118
    dragging into the Details section, 416–417
    hidden, 316
    referring to, 167–168
    retrieving specific, 169
Field Explorer, 414
Field Explorer window, 412
field-level validation
    code using, 66–68
    on a form, 590
    performing, 63–68
field names, 168
field spacing, in reports, 418–419
Fields dialog box, 356–357
    in GridView, 371
    Select entry, 367
Fields page, of the report wizard, 407, 408
FIFO (first in, first out), 432–433
file(s). See also data files; database files; Help
        files; XML files
    adding for a class, 77
    appending data to existing, 595
    compiling in App_* folders, 605
    reading, 596–597
    synchronizing with Copy Web Site,
        604–605
    types for reading and writing, 3
File Author special field, 417
File menu, 19, 511
File System Web sites
    developing Web sites as, 336
    for development, 278, 279
    project location and name, 280
FileToolStripMenuItem, 19–20
Fill method
    in the Form_Load event handler, 132
    for a table, 116
    of TableAdapter, 127, 191, 266
Fill methods, 156, 222
Filter column, 161
Filter icon, in a class diagram, 33, 34
Filter method, 162
filter string, 163
FilteredTextBoxExtender, 334
FilterExpression property, 368
filtering, DataSets, 164–166
filters
    rules for creating, 163
    selecting DataSet rows, 162
    selecting records, 159, 160

Finally statement, 565
financial functions, 579–581
Find Children program, 171–172
Find Parent program, 170
FindBy method, 169, 174
fire-hose connection, 368
firing, events, 472
Fix VB function, 582
flexibility, of multitier applications, 106
Focus method, 64
Font property, changing, 533
Footer DIV, 303, 309
Footer style, 302
For Each loop, 563
For Each statement, 530
For Each/Next loop, 571–572
For Each/Next structure, 442–443
For/Next looping construct, 570–571
foreign key, 108, 150
ForeignKey constraints, 108, 152
form(s)
    adding controls to, 139, 470
    assigning context menus to, 21
    closing, 586
    coding, 140
    declaring and showing, 586
    displaying from the main form, 72–73
    events of, 587
    making into a parent, 26
    properties of, 420–421, 586–587
    sharing data between, 588
    testing user controls in, 469–470
    using multiple, 587–588
form controls, binding data fields to, 135–137
Form Designer, 135, 613–614
Form_Load event, 222
Format property, of DateTimePicker, 120
format specifier codes, of the ToString method, 561
Format String Dialog, 121, 123
Formatting and Advanced Binding dialog box,
    120–121, 125
FormBorderStyle property, 30
FormClosing event, 31
FormClosing event handler, 195, 214–215
Formula Workshop—Formula Editor, 414–416
formulas, in reports, 415
FormView control
    adding for store data, 360–361
    Auto Format option applied to, 375
    displaying data on, 357–358
    formatting data in a table, 361–362
    formatting in, 358
    modifying the layout of, 357
    updating in, 372–373
FormView object, 357
FORTRAN, 554
forward-only result set, 368
Framework. *See* .NET Framework
Friend keyword, 77, 577, 587
Friend variables, 559
From object, in LINQ, 524
From operator, in LINQ, 523
FTP Web sites, 279
full device emulator. *See* emulators
full screen, using, 610–611
function procedures. *See* functions

functions, 575, 582
    calling, 79, 575
    determining data types, 585
    financial, 579–581
    intrinsic in VB, 577
    mathematical, 581–582
    writing, 576
FV (future value of annuity) function, 579

G

garbage collection, 2, 83–84
GDI+ graphics, namespace for, 3
general procedures, 575
Generate Data Forms option, 515
Generate Insert, Update and Delete statements
    option, 130
generated code, modifying, 222–223
generic classes, 450–452, 454
generic collection class, 452
generic collections, 452–456
Generic namespace, generic collections in,
    453–454
generic type, specifying, 454
GenericCollection class, 453
generics, 432, 449–456
GenericType, 449, 450
Get blocks, 55
Get method, 266
GetChanges method, 191, 193
GetChildRows method, 170, 174
GetContacts contract, 383
GetContacts function, 383–384
GetContacts Web method, 383, 386
GetData method, 116
GetHashCode method, 435, 442
GetParentRow method, 169, 174
GetSlides function, 332
global variables, 75
globalization, 531
Globalization namespace, 532
GotFocus event procedure, 223
grand total, in a Report Footer section, 417
graphic and multimedia files, in Help, 494
graphic files, storing, 597
graphical user interface, 591
graphics. *See* image(s)
graphics files, 10
graphics page, 592
greater than (>) operator, 163, 567
greater than or equal to (> =) operator, 567
green dot icon, for styles, 292
grid
    displaying data in, 113–114
    displaying on Windows Forms, 8
    formatting, 363–364
    setting the width of, 355
grid layout, for WPF applications, 518
grid properties, 115
grid rows, allowing selection of, 370–371
GridView control
    adding, 363
    displaying data in, 355
    selecting data in, 366–367
    updating in, 369–372
Group Footer band, 413
Group Header band, 413

group tree, 411
GroupBy operator, in LINQ, 525
grouped reports, 404–410
Grouping page, of the report wizard, 407, 408
guide diamonds, 611

H

H2 html block format, in FormView, 358
hard drive, cookie stored on, 318
HasChanges method
    calling, 192
    of DataSet, 191
    return value for, 195
HasErrors property, 191
hash tables, 435–436
Hashtable class, 435
Hashtable collection class, 433
Header DIV, for a master page, 309
header graphic, adding to a Web page,
    302–303
#Header style, completed, 301
header style, for Web pages, 299–300
HeaderText property, 115, 356
Hello World application, for a Smart Device,
    510–514
Hello World program, localized, 533
Hello World service
    completed form consuming, 259
    creating, 252–254
Help button, 503–504
Help .chm file, 502
Help facility, creating, 495–500
Help files. *See also* HTML Help files
    creating, 494–495
    displaying from menu items, 502
    modifying, 502
    types of, 494
    viewing and testing, 499–500
Help menu items, 502
Help project
    compiling, 498–499
    recompiling, 500
Help screen, for HTML Help Workshop,
    492, 493
Help system, planning, 492, 494
Help topics, in the Contents pane, 493–494
Help Viewer, 492
HelpButton property, of a form, 504
helper classes, declaring, 77
HelpKeyword property, 500, 503
HelpNamespace property, 500
HelpNavigator property, 500, 503
HelpProvider component, 500
HelpString property, 500, 504
.hhc extension, 494
.hhk extension, 494
.hhp extension, 494
hidden fields, storing state information, 316
Hide box, in the Class Details window, 33
hierarchical update program, 220–232
hierarchical updates, 220
HierarchicalUpdate property, 194, 218
hotkeys, for buttons, 589
Hour property, 578
.htm extension, 494
.htm files, folder for, 494

HTML (hypertext markup language)
 browser pages written in, 277
 generated by Visual Studio IDE, 278
 tags, 109
HTML code
 for a data source control, 377–378
 for a master page, 305
HTML documents, Help pages as, 494
HTML Files page, 496
HTML Help ActiveX control, 492, 500
HTML Help files, 492, 500–504. *See also*
 Help files
HTML Help Image Editor, 492
HTML Help project, 494
HTML Help Workshop, 492–495
 beginning a project in, 496
 Contents tab, 497–498
 Index tab, 498, 499
 window, 497
HTML list of controls, for Web Forms,
 283–284
HTML pages, as stateless, 315
HTML source, for a Web page, 281
HTML tags, in a Web page, 296, 297
HTTP, as a transport protocol, 252
hybrid applications, 518
hyperlink, 287, 288
HyperLink control, 287–288, 303
hyperlink field, 364, 365, 366
hypertext markup language. *See* HTML

I

I (Integer) type declaration character, 559
icons, in message boxes, 574
IContactsService.vb file, 383
ID-based style, 292
IDE (integrated development environment), 2
 adding a table from, 391–392
 elements, 618
 indenting code automatically, 568
 layout, 612
If statements, 568–569
IIS (Internet Information Services), 277, 279
IIS Web sites, 279, 336
IL. *See* MSIL
image(s)
 Description properties of, 333
 including on Web pages, 288–289
 placing on buttons, 22
Image control, 288
 adding and setting up, 330–331
 adding to the Header DIV, 303
image files, 10–11
image library, 285
Image property, 597
ImageButton control, 285
ImageUrl property, 288, 289, 303
immutable strings, 557, 583
implicit (automatic) conversions, of
 data types, 560
implicit empty constructor, 78
implied operations, 562
Imports statement, 534, 555
In clause, in LINQ, 524
In operator, in LINQ, 523
indentation, of code by the IDE, 568

index
 creating for Help, 498, 499
 of a list, 589
 referencing collection elements, 432
 of a sorted list, 436
Index file, in Help, 494
index number, 441
index position, 168
Index tab
 for a Help file, 501
 of a Help page, 492
IndexOf methods
 of BindingSource, 191
 of String, 584
infinity symbol, 166, 167
"ing" events, of a control, 379
inheritance, 51, 80
inherited classes, 77–80
inherited user controls, 467–471
Inherits clause
 in the Designer.vb file, 467
 following the Class declaration, 77
 modifying, 468
Init event, 335
inline style, 291, 292
input data, validating, 379–380
Insert a heading button, 498
Insert a keyword button, 498, 499
Insert a page button, 498
INSERT command. *See also* INSERT statement
 dialog for, 389
 parameters for, 390, 391
Insert method
 of BindingSource, 191, 197
 of SqlDataSource, 388
 of String, 584
Insert operation, in FormView, 374, 375
Insert option, in DetailsView, 373
Insert Snippet menu option, 624
INSERT statement, 198, 199, 368–369.
 See also INSERT command
Insert Summary dialog box, 417
InsertContact contract and method, 385–386
InsertParameters property, 390, 391
InsertQuery property, 389, 390
instance members. *See* instance variables
instance properties, 69
instance variables, 69
Int VB function, 582
Integer data type, 557, 558
integers, 81
Integrated Development Environment. *See* IDE
IntelliSense
 arguments of functions and methods, 577
 discovering available objects, 13
 displaying methods in a Web service, 258
 icons for message boxes, 574
interface, in WCF, 250
Internet, basics of, 276
Internet Information Services. *See* IIS
Internet service providers (ISPs), 276
interoperability, of WPF with Windows Forms,
 521–522
Interval property, of a Timer component, 24, 590
intranet, 277
intrinsic constants, 559

intrinsic functions, 577
IO namespace, 3
IPmt (interest payment) function, 579
IRR (internal rate of return) function, 579
is a relationship, 51
Is Nothing function, 585
IsArray function, 585
IsDate function, 585
IService.vb, 250, 251
IsFixedSize property, 440
IsMdiContainer property, 26, 586
IsNotNothing condition, 4
IsNumeric function, 585
IsObject function, 585
IsPostBack property, 320
ISPs (Internet service providers), 276
IsReadOnly property, 440
IsValid property, 314
Item method, 452–453
Item property, 440, 442
ItemDeleted event handler, 376
ItemInserted event handler, 376
ItemInserting event handler, 380
Items collection
 of ContextMenuStrip, 21
 of a list box or combo box, 446–448
 saving in a session variable, 387–388
Items Collection Editor, 19, 20
Items property
 of a collection, 563
 of ListBox, 589
ItemTemplate, 357
ItemUpdated event handler, 376
ItemUpdating event handler, 379
iteration, of a loop, 570

J

Java, 554
JIT (just-in-time) compiler, 5
Jump to Next Bookmark button, 615
Jump to Previous Bookmark button, 615
junction table, 150, 172–173

K

key(s)
 of a hash table, 435
 referencing collection elements, 432
keyboard access keys, for buttons, 589
keyboard shortcuts, 610, 616–617
keys, uniquely identifying objects, 441
KeyUp event handler, 217

L

L (Long) type declaration character, 559
Label control, 588
LabelText property, 478–479
Language-Integrated Queries. *See* LINQ
Language property, of a form, 531–532
last in wins concurrency control, 199
LastIndexOf methods, 584
layers, applications in, 53
layout options, for child windows, 27
Layout toolbar, for multiple controls, 613
LayoutMdi method, 27
layouts, for WPF applications, 518
.ldf file, deleting, 191

LeftColumn DIV, 303
LeftColumn style, 300–301
less than (<) operator, 163, 567
less than or equal to (< =) operator, 567
lifetime, of a variable, 76
LIFO (last in, first out), 432–433
Like (pattern match) operator, 163
line breaks, in a message box, 573
lines, commenting and uncommenting, 615
Link, configuring a Select button as, 367
link button, 287
Link page, of the report wizard, 407
LinkButton control, 285
LinkedList generic collection, 453
LINQ (Language-Integrated Queries), 522–530
    example query, 523–524
    form of queries, 523
    keywords, 522–523, 524, 525
Linq namespace, 3
LINQ query, 524–527
LINQ to SQL Classes template, 524–526
LINQ to XML program listing, 530
list boxes
    binding table data to, 135–137
    displaying items in, 524
    filling in alphabetic order, 529
    filling with data, 123
    maintaining a list in dynamic, 387–388
    maintaining the state of, 387–388
    properties of, 165
    sorting data for, 127–130
List generic collection, 453
ListBox control, 589
ListItem Collection Editor, 480, 481
lists, 432. *See also* collections; data structures
    binding at run time, 163–164
    selecting records from, 123–126
    sorted, 436–437
Load event, 335, 587
Load event handler, 140
load life cycle stage, 334
Load method, of an XDocument, 598
local database files, 112
local scope. *See* procedure-level scope
local variables, 319
localizability, 531
Localizable property, 531, 533
localization, 531
localized Hello World, 533
Locals window, 620
Location property, of a form, 586
Log method, 582
logic, of update programs, 200–201
logical operators, 567
login, 321–327
login applications, 325, 327
login controls, 321–323, 324
Login list of controls, for Web Forms, 283
Login section, of the toolbox, 321
Login.aspx page, 325, 327
LoginName control, 323
LoginStatus control, 322–323
LoginView control, 323
log.ldf file, deleting, 623
logo, placing in a master page, 304
Logout property, of the LoginStatus control, 323

Long data type, 557
lookup operation, 157–159
loop index, 570
loops, forming, 570–573

M

main content area, 303
Main Report Preview tab, 410
MainContent style, 301–302
MainForm, 420, 421
Manage Styles window, 292, 293, 294
    applying styles from, 294
    Attach Style Sheet, 307
    clicking on New Style, 299
    icons in, 292
    modifying styles from, 294–295
    viewing style attributes, 308
managed code, 2, 554
managed data, 2
managed providers, 106
Manual style application, 292–293
many-to-many relationships (M:N), 150–151,
        152, 172–177
masked text box, 118
master/detail records, 153–157
Master Page item, 304
Master Page template, 306
master pages, 304
    creating, 305–309
    nesting, 304
    selecting for contents pages, 310
    setting up DIV elements, 306
    using to control layout, 290–291
master table, 150
Math class, methods in, 581
mathematical functions, 581–582
Max method, 582
Max operator, in LINQ, 525
MaxDate property, 120
MaximizeBox property, 504
MaximumDate property, 471–472
MaximumInputLength property, 225
MaxLength property, 224
.mdb files, 107
.mdf files, 107
    deleting, 191, 623
MDI (multiple document interface), 25, 611
MDI applications, in WPF, 518
MDI project, 26
MdiParent property, 26
MDIWindowListItem property, 27
Me entry, expanding, 620
Me keyword, 586
    referring to a property or method, 80
    referring to the current class, 57, 469
MeasureString method, 593
Me.Close, 586
MediaElement control, 518
Members folder, access rules for, 325, 326
Members list, in the Items Collection Editor,
        19–20
menu bar, properties for, 19
Menu Item Editor, 309
menu items, 19
    adding to a Smart Device application,
        511–512

designating as the Window menu, 27
    editing individual, 21
menus, 590–591
    adding help options to, 501–502
    creating, 18–20, 590–591
Menus & Toolbars section, of the toolbox, 18
MenuStrip control, 590–591
MenuStrips, 18–20, 22
Merge methods, 266, 268
message boxes, 573–574
    adding Help buttons to, 503
    replacing with ErrorProviders, 65
Message property, 566
MessageBox class, 573
MessageBoxButtons constants, 574
MessageBoxOptions argument, 574
messages. *See also* error messages
    changing in status bars, 504
    right-aligned in a message box, 574
metadata, 2, 5
methods
    of the base class, 79
    blocking, 534
    defining with GenericType, 450
    inheriting, 78–79
    with overloaded parameter lists, 577
    overloading, 52
    in VB, 577
Microsoft image library, 285
Microsoft Intermediate Language. *See* MSIL
Microsoft Jet Engine, 111
Microsoft .NET Framework Software
        Development Kit (SDK), 2
Microsoft Report Viewer controls, 284
Microsoft Visual Database Tools, 128
Microsoft Windows Installer, 13
milliseconds, 590
Min method, 582
Min operator, in LINQ, 525
MinDate property, 120
MinimizeBox property, 504
MinimumDate property, 471–472
minus sign (−)
    with Pmt function, 580
    with Rate function, 581
Minute property, 578
MIRR function, 579
M:N (many-to-many relationships), 150–151,
        152, 172–177
mobile devices
    culture at run time not supported, 533
    developing applications for, 508–517
    programming for, 508
    selecting the type of, 510
modal window (dialog box), 586
modeless window, 586
Modify Style dialog box, 302, 308
Module / End Module construct, 75
module-level scope, 75
module-level variables, 76, 319
modules. *See also* .vb files
    in previous VB versions, 75
Month property, 578
monthly calendar, 289–290
MouseOver event, 504
MoveFirst method, 191

MoveLast method, 191
MoveNext method, 191
MovePrevious method, 191
.msi files, 13
MSIL (Microsoft Intermediate Language)
    code, 554
    compiling to, 4–5
multidimensional arrays, 563
multiple document interface. *See* MDI
multiple forms, 587–588
multiple reports, selecting, 420–421
multiple tiers, 133–140, 381–387
multiple variables, 558
multiplication (*) operator, 562
MultiSelect property, 115
multitasking, 534
multithreaded programming, classes for, 3
multithreading, 534
multitier applications, 53–54
    considerations, 178
    M:N program written as, 175
MustInherit, in the class header, 51
mutable strings, in StringBuilder, 583
My objects, 13–14, 597
My.Application object, 533
My.Application.Info object, 16, 17
MyBase keyword, 78, 79
My.Computer.Info object, 14
My.Resources object, 10

N

N (number) format specifier code, 561
Name property
    of a button, 589
    of a form, 586
    of a splash form, 30
    for a WPF application, 518
named constants, 74, 81
namespace-level variables, 76
namespace scope, 74–75
Namespace statements, 74
namespaces, 2–3, 74, 554–555
NameTextBox, 511, 512
naming
    conventions for variables, 558
    DIV elements, 298
    projects, 14
    properties, 55
    rules for constants, 558
    variables, 557
    Web Forms, 282
NavigateUrl property, 287
navigation
    from a combo box selection, 210–211
    disabling and enabling, 203
navigation bar, 188
navigation controls, in a master page, 304
Navigation list of controls, for Web Forms, 283
navigation methods, of BindingSource,
        196–197
nested If statements, 568–569
nested parentheses, 562
.NET Framework, 554
    accessing data in, 107–109
    class library, 2–4
    classes organized into namespaces, 554–555

composition of, 2–6
    parts of, 2
.NET Framework Redistributable, 13
New constructors, overloaded, 78
New event, in a form, 587
New Inline Style option, 293
NewLine character, 573
New procedure, 56
New Project Destination page, 496
New Project dialog box, 404, 519
New Style dialog box, 293–294, 299–300, 301
New Web Site dialog box, 280
NewUser.aspx page, 325
NewValues collection, 379
nodes, in XML files, 598
non-null fields, testing for, 379–380
nonshared members, of the DateTime
        structure, 577
nonshared methods, of the String class, 583
NorthwindDataSet, 406
Northwind.sdf file, 514
not equal to (<>) operator, 567
Not logical operator, 567
Nothing, testing a value for, 317
Now property, 24, 578
NPer (number of periods) function, 579
NPV function, 579
n-tier applications, 53
nudging, controls into place, 613
nulls, checking for, 212–213
NullValue property, 213
number of periods function, 579
numeric constants, declaring, 558–559
numeric data types. *See also* value types
    converting between, 560
    using, 557
numeric values, formatting, 561

O

OASIS, Web site, 250
obj folder, 9–10
Object data type, 557
object-oriented programming. *See* OOP
Object Relational (O/R) Designer, 525, 526
object variables. *See* reference types
ObjectDataSource control, 353
    adding to Default.aspx, 386
    unbound controls with, 390–391
    using, 381
objects. *See also* data objects
    adding to collections, 442
    creating a collection of, 441–446
    instantiating, 76
    renaming, 618
    reusable, 53
Of Type specifier, 450, 452
OldValues collection, 379
one-to-many (1:M) relationships, 150, 151
    "one side" of, 157, 166
one-to-one (1:1) relationship, 150, 151, 152
OOP (object-oriented programming), 50–54
    terminology of, 50–52
Open Table Definition, 212
Open Web Site dialog box, 278, 279
operation contract
    creating, 254

in WCF, 251
    writing, 264
OperationContract attribute, 250
operations, canceling, 204
operators
    available for LINQ queries, 524, 525
    in LINQ, 522–523
    listing of, 163
optimistic concurrency control, 199, 369
option buttons, 589
Option Explicit, 560
    altering settings for, 12
    setting to on, 8
Option Strict, 560
    altering settings for, 12
    setting to on, 8
    turning on, 560
Options button, on the Publish tab, 601
Options dialog box, 6, 7
    changing the default control type in, 119
    displaying, 612
O/R Designer, 525, 526
Or logical operator, 567
ORDER BY clause, 129
OrderBy/ThenBy operator, in LINQ, 525
OrElse, 229, 567
Organization for the Advancement of Structure
        Information Standards. *See* OASIS
Original version, of a DataRow object, 193
output, for the printer, 591
Output window, writing to, 622
overloaded methods, 52
overloading, constructors, 57
overridable methods, 78
Overrides keyword, 78
overriding methods, in the base class, 52

P

P (percent) format specifier code, 561
padding, 301
PadLeft methods, 584
PadRight methods, 584
Page Footer band, 413
Page Header band, 412
page initialization life cycle stage, 334
page layout, standards for, 291
Page_Load event, 320
page margins, in a report, 413–414
Page N of M field, 417
page request life cycle stage, 334
page style, 291
pagination, adding to a grid, 355
parameterized constructor, 57
parameterized query, 159, 160
    creating, 160–162, 359–362
parameters
    inside procedures, 575
    for parameterized queries, 160
Parameters Collection Editor dialog, 390, 391
Parameters list, for INSERT, 389
parent and child relationship, in MDI, 25
parent class, 51
parent form, 25, 26
parent records, 219, 223
parent rows, 168–170, 174
parent table, 150

parentheses, calculation operations within, 562
partial classes, 11
partial types. *See* partial classes
partial Web page updates, 333–334
Pascal casing, 119, 558
passing, arguments, 575
PasswordRecovery control, 322, 323, 327
passwords
    automating the management of, 322
    managing, 321
    strong, 322
pattern match (Like) operator, 163
payments functions, 579
payroll application, creating, 58
Payroll class
    adding shared variables, 69
    completed, 70–72
    modifying, 69
.pdb file, 10, 469
Peek method
    of a queue, 435
    of a stack, 434
    of StreamReader, 597
permissions, base classes for, 3
pessimistic concurrency control, 199
Place code in separate file check box, 305, 306,
    309, 310
PlayInterval property, 333
Pmt (payment) function, 579, 580
polymorphism, 52
Pop method, 434
popup, displaying a message in, 65
popup Help, 503–504
popup tooltips, 617
portable executable (PE) file, 2, 5
Position property, 191, 196
PositionChanged event, 198
postback
    checking for, 320
    DetailsView control appearing on, 376
    forcing, 284
    triggering, 284
pound sign (#), in styles applied to named
    components, 295
PPmt (principal payment) function, 579
precompiling, Web pages, 605
PreInit event, 335
PreLoad event, 335
PreRender event, 335
present value functions, 579
presentation (or user interface) tier, 53.
    See also user interface
    separating from the data tier, 133
    summary form in, 69
    of the Titles Authors M:N program,
    175–176
    of a two-tier payroll application, 58
Preview button, previewing DataSet data, 116
primary key, 150
primary key field, 107
primary table, 150
Print method, 591
print page, 593
print preview, 594
PrintDocument component, 591
PrintDocument control, 591–592

printing, 591–594
PrintPage event handler, 591
PrintPageEventArgs argument, 592
PrintPreviewDialog class, 594
Private keyword, 50, 77, 577
private variables, 54, 559
procedure header, for a function, 576
procedure-level scope, 75
procedure-level variables, lifetime of, 76
procedures, 575
processes, in multitasking, 534
Professional Edition, of Visual Studio, 554
programmers, role of, 517–518
programming, separating from design, 517
programming languages, integrating, 2
programs, world-ready, 531–533
project(s)
    copying and moving, 622–623
    creating, 6–7, 256–257
    declaring namespaces, 74
    including references for
      namespaces, 555
    naming, 14
    options for, 612
    saving, 6
    separating into multiple tiers, 133–140
Project Designer, 12–13
    adding references, 9
    Publish tab, 600–601
    selecting the splash screen form in, 30
    tabs, 12
project files, 7, 556
project folder, copying, 363, 622–623
Project Header file, in Help, 494
Project Properties dialog box. *See* Project
    Designer
project resources, 10, 597
project scope, 74
project-to-project reference, 5
properties. *See also* variables
    adding to controls, 471–472
    adding to ReportsForm, 420–421
    assigning arguments to, 57–58
    of the base class, 79
    for binding, 359
    of combo boxes, 158
    of constituent controls, 478–479
    creating in a class, 54–56
    of dataset fields, 268
    default values for control, 471–472
    exposing in Web controls, 481–482
    of forms, 586–587
    for a menu bar, 19
    naming, 55
    for a Web page, 289
Properties window
    of DataSet Designer, 219, 221
    read-only properties grayed in, 472
    for a WPF application, 518, 519
property procedures, 55–56, 575
Property Set procedure, 479
Proposed version, of a DataRow
    object, 193
Protected Friend keyword, 77, 577
Protected keyword, 56, 77, 577
Protected variables, 559

Provider tab, of the Web Site Administration
    Tool, 324, 325
public function, 254, 264
public Get methods, 69–70
Public keyword, 77
    not legal inside a procedure, 75
    Sub New procedure as, 56
    sub procedures and functions as, 577
    use of, 50
Public members, accessing a form's, 587
Public modifier, 74
public variables, 54, 559
publish location, 605
Publish Options dialog, 601
Publish tab
    for ClickOnce deployment, 600–601
    in Project Designer, 13
Publish Web Site utility, 605–606
Publish Web utility, 336
Publish Wizard, 602–603
Pubs database, stored procedures in, 131
Pubs.mdf database file, 112
Push method, 434
pushpin icon, on IDE windows, 608
PV (present value) function, 579

Q

Query Builder
    displaying, 127–128
    generating SQL, 160–162
    with a sort and an added expression, 129
    using, 128
Query Designer, 129, 354
QueryString method, 316
question mark pointer, 503, 504
Queue class, 434
Queue collection class, 433
Queue generic collection, 453
queues, 432–435QuickStarts, tutorials, 624

R

R (Double) type declaration character, 559
radio buttons, 589
RadioButton control, 589
RaiseEvent statement, 472–473
raising, events, 472–473
RAM, temporary cookie stored in, 318
RangeValidator control, 313
Rate function, 579, 580–581
read-only properties, 56, 472
reading, files, 596–597
ReadLine method, 596, 597
ReadOnly property
    changing the value of, 471
    setting for text boxes, 204
    of text boxes, 205, 588
ReadOnlyCollection collection, 453
record count, displaying, 198
record number, displaying, 196, 198
records
    adding, 188, 202
    in a data table, 107
    deleting, 188–189, 204
    displaying in DetailsView, 356, 516–517
    editing, 200
    referring to, 167–168

saving added or edited, 202
    selecting for a DataSet, 160
    selecting from a list, 123–126
red dot icon, for styles, 292
ReDim statement, 564–565
Redistributable file, 13
refactoring, 618
reference objects, 5
reference types, 3–4
references, adding, 9
References tab, in Project Designer, 12
referential integrity, 152, 219
reflection, 5
Refresh button, in Solution Explorer, 288
RegularExpressionValidator control, 313
RejectChanges method, 191, 193
related table update program, 220–232
related tables, 153–159
    adding, 363–364
    displaying data from, 362
    updating, 218–232
Relation dialog box, 155, 157, 167
relational operators, 567
relationships. *See also* data relationships
    viewing and modifying, 167
    viewing or setting for tables, 157
relative URL, 288
Release folders, 9
Remember me next time check box, 321
remote sites, 279
Remote Web site, 604
Remove method
    for a collection, 442
    of a generic collection class, 452–453
    for a hash table, 435
    of Items, 563, 589
    of a sorted list, 436
    of String, 584
RemoveAt method
    of an array list, 440
    of BindingSource, 197
    for a collection, 442
    of Items, 563, 589
    of a sorted list, 436
RemoveCurrent method, 191, 197–198, 204
RemoveRange method, 440
Rename command, 623
Rename dialog box, 618
Replace method, of String, 584
report(s)
    adding special fields to, 417–418
    assigning datasets to, 411
    creating grouped, 404–410
    displaying from Web Forms, 419–420
    displaying from Windows forms, 410–411
    fixing, 418–419
    formatting, 418
    modifying, 413–419
    previewing, 410
    selecting multiple, 420–421
    setting up, 406–410
    sorting, 414
    writing, 404
report design, modifying, 413
report designer
    in Crystal Reports, 408, 409

switching to, 411
    using, 412–413
Report Fields list, 415, 416
Report Footer band, 413
Report Header band, 412, 413
Report list of controls, 284
report template
    creating in Crystal Reports, 404–410
    information bands, 412–413
report types, selecting, 406
Report Wizard, 406
ReportsForm, 420
Request object, 315
RequiredFieldValidator control, 312, 313
resource files, creating, 532
resources, adding, 10
Resources folder, 10–11, 597
Resources tab, 12, 597
Response object, 315
Response.Redirect method, 288
Restart command, 622
.resx extension, 10, 556
.resx files, 10, 532
return functions, 579
Return statement, in a function, 576
reusability, 51
reusable objects, 53
Reverse operator, in LINQ, 525
right-aligned output, 593
RightToLeft property, 23
Rnd VB function, 582
Roles feature, 324, 325
rolldown button, 33
rollup button, 33
root namespace, 74
Round method, 582
RowHeadersVisible property, 115
rows
    in a data table, 107
    retrieving an array of, 170–172
    retrieving matching, 173–174
    selecting from an existing DataSet, 162
RowState property, 192
    of DataRow, 192
    of DataSet, 191
    of table rows, 198
run time, binding a list at, 163–164
RunWorkerAsync method, 534
RunWorkerCompleted method, 535

S

S (Short) type declaration character, 559
sample projects, in Visual Studio, 624
Save all files and compile button, 498
Save button
    for both Adds and Edits, 202
    code for, 202–203
    modifying the event handler for exit, 223–224
    user clicking on, 189
Save new projects when created option, 6
save query, adding for exit, 223–224
SaveItem event, 189
scalability, of multitier applications, 106
scalable development environment, 508
schema, of a typed DataSet, 107, 110
scope, of variables and constants, 74–76, 559

screen
    setting up in the IDE, 608–613
    splitting vertically, 612
    using the full, 610–611
screen fields, filling with summary data, 73
script, 277
ScriptManager component, 333
ScriptManager control, in AJAX, 327, 328
.sdf extension, 514
SDI (single document interface), 25
SDK (.NET Framework Software
    Development Kit), 2
Second property, 578
security, for databases, 232
Security namespace, 3
Security tab
    in Project Designer, 13
    of the Web Site Administration Tool,
    324–325
Select a Master Page dialog, 310, 311
"(Select a Name)" item, removing from the top
    of a list, 377
Select authentication type, 325, 326, 327
Select button, in GridView, 366
Select Case structure, 569–570
Select clause, in a LINQ query, 524
Select Image dialog box, 288–289
Select link button, in GridView, 371
Select master page check box, 309, 310
Select method, 52
Select operator, in LINQ, 523
Select statement. *See* SQL SELECT statement
Select URL dialog box, 287
Selected Tables pane, 406
SelectedDate property, 290
SelectedIndex property, 387, 589
SelectedIndexChanged event, 165–166
SelectedIndexChanged event handler, 367
SelectedValue property, 165
SelectionChangeCommitted event, 165–166, 169
SelectionChangeCommitted event handler, 174
SelectionChanged event, 290
SelectParameters, 390, 391
separator bar, in a menu, 19
server. *See* Web servers
Server Explorer
    adding a new table to a database, 392
    creating stored procedures, 131
    viewing, 212
    in the VS IDE, 110
server objects, Web application access to, 315
server-side controls, 284
Server.Transfer method, 288
service application, in WCF, 250
service reference, 257, 264, 265, 386
ServiceContract attribute, 250
services, in a WCF Service, 251–252
Service.svc, 255
Service.vb file, 250, 251, 253–254
Session object, 315, 317
    drawbacks of, 317
    storing state information, 316
session variables
    clearing all, 318
    enclosing in Try/Catch statements, 317
    saving module-level variables in, 319–320

<sessionState> element, in the Web.config file, 319
Set portion, of a property procedure, 56
Set statement, 55
SetColumnError method, 229
SetError method, 65–66
Setup application, for deployment, 600
Setup wizard, 600
shadowing, a base class method, 78–79
Shadows keyword, 79
shared components, version conflicts of, 600
shared members. *See also* shared variables
   of the DateTime structure, 577
shared methods
   of the Payroll class, 73
   of the String class, 583
shared properties. *See also* shared variables
   from the Payroll class, 73
   Payroll class calculating, 70–72
   retrieving, 69–70
shared variables. *See also* shared members; shared properties
   versus instance variables, 69
Shift-click, selecting multiple controls, 588
Short data type, 557
shortcut keys, for buttons, 589
shortcuts, in the Editor, 614–618
Show All Files button, 8–9, 11, 556
Show all settings option, 7
Show method
   for a form, 586
   information about the outcome of, 574
   of a message box, 503
   of the MessageBox object, 573
   using prior to Focus, 29
Show Table Data option, 392
ShowDialog method, 586, 594
ShowHelp method, 501
ShowHelpIndex method, 501–502
siblings, in XML files, 598
Sign method, 582
Signing tab, in Project Designer, 13
Silverlight, 517
Simple style, of a combo box, 589
Sin method, 582
Single data type, 557
single document interface (SDI), 25
single-file model, 281
single-line If statement, 568
single-step execution, for Web applications, 286
singleton design pattern, 28–29
singleton form, 29
SizeF structure, 593
Sleep method, 45
SlideShow Extender, 330
SLN (straight line) function, 579
.sln extension, 555
.sln files, 335
Smart Device applications, 508–514
   displaying an emulator, 509
   running, 513–514
Smart Device project, 510–511, 512
Smart Device Project template, 508, 509
Smart Devices, 508, 514
Smart indenting, 613

smart tags
   of MenuStrip, 19
   opening, 18
snap lines, aligning controls, 8, 613–614
snap-to-grid method. *See* snap lines
SnapToGrid option, 8
Snippet categories, 624
SOAP (Simple Object Access Protocol), 250, 252
Solution Explorer, 8–11
   displaying service references in, 257, 258
   View Class Diagram button, 31, 32
solution files, 335, 555
solution name, displaying, 9
solutions, 555
   options for, 612
   renaming, 623
Sort method, 127
Sort property, 137
sorted lists, 436–437
Sorted property, 589
SortedDictionary generic collection, 454
SortedList collection class, 433
SortedList generic collection, 454
sorting, reports, 414
sound files, storing, 597
sounds, playing, 597
Source pane, 296, 298
Source property
   of ApplicationException, 61
   of Exception, 566
Source view, Web page layout in, 295
Source Web site, 604
special characters, on Web pages, 594
special effects, in WPF, 517
special fields, adding to reports, 417–418
Splash Screen template, 31
splash screens
   creating, 29–30
   displaying, 31
   setting, 30
Split bar, 617
Split tab, 296, 297, 306
Split view, 295
Split window, for Web Forms, 281
Spring property, 23
SPROC. *See* stored procedures
SQL (Structured Query Language), 127
SQL injections, 131
SQL JOIN statements, 153
SQL queries, 130
SQL SELECT statement, 127–129, 160, 354
SQL Server, 111, 126
SQL Server 2008 Express Edition, 111–112
SQL Server Compact 3.5, 514
SQL Server database, updating, 200
SQL Server Express, data sources, 107
SQL Server stored procedures. *See* stored procedures
SQL statements, 128, 198–199
SqlDataSource control, 352, 353
   adding, 353–354, 359, 363
   caching data, 368
   event handlers for, 379
   unbound controls with, 388–390
Sqrt method, 582

Stack class, 434
Stack collection class, 433
Stack generic collection, 453
StackPanel layout, 518
stacks, 432–433
   compared to queues, 435
   using, 434
Standard (ASP.NET server controls) section, of the toolbox, 283–284, 359
Standard Report Creation Wizard, 406–409
Standard toolbar, window buttons on, 609–610
Start command, 619
start life cycle stage, 334
Start Without Debugging command, 619
StartButton object, 535
StartPosition property
   of a form, 586
   of a splash form, 30
StartsWith method, 584
startup form, 586
Startup URI, 520
state
   information, storing, 316
   maintaining for list boxes, 387–388
   management of, 315–320
   of a page, 315
stateless characteristic
   of HTML pages, 315
   of HTML Web pages, 277
statements, executing only once, 377
Static keyword, 76
Static variables, 559–560
status bars, 23–24, 504
StatusLabel objects, 23
StatusStrip component, 23–24
Step Into command, 117, 619, 621
Step Out command, 619, 621, 622
Step Over command, 619, 621, 622
stepping commands, 621
stepping tools, 621
sticky control, 213
sticky text box, 64
Stop Debugging command, 619
stored procedures
   binding data from, 137
   creating in the VS IDE, 131–132
   example of empty, 132
   retrieving data using, 132
   using, 131–132
Storyboard class, in WPF, 518
straight-line method, 581
StreamReader class, 596
StreamReader object, 596
streams, 594–595
StreamWriter object, 595
String class, 583
String data type, 119, 557
string value, testing for, 569
StringBuilder class, 583
strings
   appended to URLs, 316
   working with, 583–585
strong password, 322
Structure statement, 563
structure variables, 564
Structured Query Language. *See* SQL

structures, 563–565. *See also* data structures
  declaring as Public, 74
  including arrays in, 564–565
  separating from design, 291
  of Web pages, 295
Student Collection application
  complete, 443–446
  complete form code, 447–448
Student objects, creating a collection of, 441
style(s)
  applying from several locations, 294
  applying named components, 295
  controlling layout, 290–291
  defining, 293–294
  locations for defining, 291
  managing, 294
  modifying, 294–295
  types of, 292
  using, 291–292
  in Web applications, 291
Style Application toolbar, 292–293
style name, 294
style rules, order of precedence of, 292
style section, of a Web page, 291
style sheets, importing and modifying, 307–309
stylesheet file, editing, 302
Sub New procedure, 56
sub procedures, 575–576
subclasses, 51, 52
Substring methods, 585
subtotals, for reports, 417
subtraction (−) operator, 562
sum-of-the-years'-digits method, 579, 581
Sum operator, in LINQ, 525
Summaries page, of the report wizard,
  407–408, 409
summary data, displaying, 72–73
.suo files, 335, 555
superclass, 51
svcutil.exe, 255, 256
swap procedure, using generics, 449–452
SYD (sum-of-the-years' digits) function, 579, 581
Symbol Rename, 618
synchronization feature, of Copy Web Site,
  604–605
system date and time, 578
System namespace, 3, 74
System.ApplicationException class, 61
System.Collections namespace, 432
System.Exception class, 61, 565
System.Globalization namespace, 532
System.IO namespace, 594
System.Math class, 581
System.Web.UI.StateBag dictionary
  collection, 319

T

tab-docking, windows, 611
tab order, setting, 311–312, 590
tabbed windows, 609
TabIndex property, 311, 312, 590
table(s). *See also* data table
  adding from the IDE, 391–392
  adding related, 363–364
  displaying data from related, 362
  joining multiple, 153

  modifying the relationship of, 221
  related, 153–159
  relationships among, 150–153
  updating related, 218–232
  viewing or setting relationships for, 157
  viewing the relation between, 154–155
table data, binding, 135–137
table definition, viewing and modifying,
  212–213
table lookup, 157–159
table lookup column, 226–228
Table of Contents, for Help, 497–498
Table of Contents file, in Help, 494
TableAdapter class, 191
TableAdapter Configuration Wizard,
  130, 199, 383
TableAdapter objects, 108, 189
  declaring at the class level, 134
  holding multiple queries, 160
  separating from the DataSet, 261
  for tables, 116
  Update method, 218
TableAdapterManager component, 218
TableAdapterManager object, 189, 194
TableNewRow event, 215, 216, 229
TableNewRow event handler, 230
tabs, options for, 613
TabStop property, 590
tags, in XML, 109–110, 597–598
Tan method, 582
Task List, 617–618
Team Developer Edition, of Visual
  Studio, 554
temporary projects, 6–7
test program, 16–17
text
  displaying on a status bar, 23
  typing onto a form template, 357
  in XML files, 251, 598
text binding, for a combo box, 210
text boxes
  AJAX extender for, 334
  assigning results of LINQ queries to, 527
  converting to combo boxes, 124
  formatting data in, 120–121
  inserting data from, 388
  making sticky, 64
  unbound, 168
  Validating event of, 63–64
text controls, assigning context
  menus to, 21
Text Editor, options for, 613
Text Editor toolbar, 611, 615
text fields, MaxLength property, 224
text format, of XML, 251
Text property
  as bindable, 358
  of a button, 589
  of a form, 586
  for a hyperlink field, 364
  of a Label control, 588
  of a radio button, 589
  of a splash form, 30
  of TextBox, 588
  of a validation control, 314
  for WPF text boxes, 518

TextBox control, 467, 588
TextBox control type, 119
threading, 534–536
Threading namespace, 3
threads, 31, 534
three-tier application, 53
Throw keyword, 61–62, 134
throwing, exceptions, 60
Tickevent handler, 590
tiers
  creating applications in, 53
  multiple, 133–140, 381–387
TileHorizontal constant, 27
TileVertical constant, 27
Timer component, 24, 590
title bar, hiding a form's, 29
title class, in O/R Designer, 525, 526
Title property, for a WPF window, 518
Titles Authors M:N program, 175–177
ToArray method, 440
ToArray operator, in LINQ, 525
Today property, 578
TODO keyword, 617
Toggle Bookmark button, 615
Toggle Group Tree button, 411
ToList method, 524
ToList operator, in LINQ, 525
ToLongDateString method, 24, 578
ToLongTimeString method, 24, 578
ToLookup operator, in LINQ, 525
ToLower method, 585
Tool windows, in the IDE, 611
toolbars
  creating with ToolStrips, 22–23
  specific to Crystal Reports, 412
toolbox
  adding AJAX controls to, 329
  adding user controls to, 476–477
  Data section of, 352–353
  dragging code to, 618
  Login section of, 321
  Menus & Toolbars section, 18
  new user control appearing in, 470
  for Web Forms, 282–283
Toolbox window, Crystal Reports
  section, 412
ToolBoxBitmapAttribute, 470
toolkit, AJAX, 328
ToolStrip components, 22–23
ToolTip text, for a button, 22–23
ToolTips, 504, 617
topic files, in Help, 494
TopMost property, of a splash form, 30
ToShortDateString method, 24, 578
ToShortTimeString method, 24, 578
ToString method
  codes for formatting, 136
  format specifier codes, 561
  in a LINQ query, 527
  of an object, 446
ToUpper method, 585
Transfer method, 315
Trim method, 585
TrimEnd method, 585
TrimStart method, 585
TrimToSize method, 440

Try/Catch blocks, 565–566
    adding in the Save button's event
      handler, 225
    creating objects inside, 76
    enclosing code in, 60–61
Try/Catch/Finally/End Try blocks, 75–76
TryParse method
    catching errors, 566–567
    code using, 66–68
    of the numeric classes, 62–63
tutorials, QuickStart, 624
two-tier application, calculating
      prices, 80–81
type-definition characters, 558–559
type inference, in LINQ, 523
typed DataSets, 107, 110
TypeName function, 585
TypeOf function, 585
types, 3

U

unbound controls, 166
    creating a project connecting to, 390
    with an ObjectDataSource, 390–391
    with a SqlDataSource, 388–390
unbound data fields, 166–172
unbound text boxes, 168
Uncomment Selected Lines command, 615
uniform resource locator. See URL
unique constraints, 108, 152
Universal Resource Identifiers (URIs), 252
Unload event, 335
unload life cycle stage, 334
unmanaged code, 2
Until keyword, 571
Update method
    calling, 200
    parameters required by, 384
    of TableAdapter, 189, 191, 193,
      194–195, 218
update methods, 194, 197–198
update process, testing, 515
update programs
    code for complete, 206–210
    logic of, 200–201
    for related tables, 220–232
    summary of sample, 200
    testing, 199
UPDATE statement, 198, 199, 368–369
update strategies, in ClickOnce deployment,
    601–602
UpdateAll method, 189, 191, 193, 194–195,
    219, 220
UpdateContacts contract and
    function, 384–385
Updated event, checking for, 379
UpdatePanel, 333
UpdateParameters, 390, 391
updates
    allowing for databases, 368–380
    user options during, 201–204
updating, DataSets, 188–189
uplevel browsers, validation in, 312
    bound, of an array, 562
    se names, for constants, 558
    niform Resource Identifiers), 252

URL (uniform resource locator), 252, 277
    selecting for a Web page, 287
    specifying as absolute or relative, 288
    string appended to, 316
user controls, 466
    code for, 474–475
    creating composite, 475–479
    creating inherited, 467–471
    dragging to Web pages, 482
    form for testing, 475
    making modifications to, 479
    testing in forms, 469–470
    Web, 480–483
    in Windows, 466–479
user input data, validating, 212–217
user interface, 58. See also presentation
    (or user interface) tier
    controls raising events, 472
    designing, 480–481
    displaying a summary form, 69
    separating from data access, 133
    for theater ticket purchases, 80
    validating at the field level, 63–68
user logins, handling, 321
user options, during an update, 201–204
users
    allowing to select dates, 289–290
    helping to enter valid data, 224–225
    providing assistance to, 504

V

valid data, code testing for, 469
Validate event, 590
Validate method, 393
Validating event
    of bound controls, 213
    canceling, 64
    of a text box, 63–64
Validating event handler
    If statement turning ErrorProvider on or
      off, 66
    procedure header for, 64
    testing for the ClosingBoolean variable, 215
validation
    adding to a Details view program, 213–215
    adding to datasets, 229–232
    forcing, 393
    of input data, 379–380
    placing in data tier projects, 266–267
    timing of, 312
    of user input data, 212–217
    writing code for WCF, 267–268
    writing inside the dataset, 215
validation controls, 312–314, 393
validation life cycle stage, 334
Validation list of controls, 283
ValidationSummary control, 313, 314
ValidDate control, 474–475
ValidDateTextBox control
    adding, 470
    adding to the toolbox, 476
    combining with a label, 475
ValidDateTextBox.vb control, 468
ValidDateTextBox.vb file, 469
validity, testing for, 314
Value keyword, 55

value types, 3–4. See also numeric data types
ValueMember property, 158, 165
values
    assigning to arrays, 562
    assigning to properties, 54–55
Values collection, 380
Values property
    for a hash table, 436
    of a sorted list, 436–437
variables, 556, 557–558. See also properties
    declaring, 74, 564
    defining private, 54
    inheriting, 78–79
    lifetime of, 76
    naming, 557
    private, 559
    public, 559
    renaming, 618
    retaining the values of, 319–320
    scope of, 74–76, 559
    static, 559–560
VB. See Visual Basic (VB)
.vb extension, 77, 556
.vb files, 556
VB functions. See functions
VB project files. See project files
VB projects. See projects
VB solutions. See solutions
.vbproj extension, 556
.vbproj.user extension, 556
vertical spacing, between controls, 614
View Class Diagram button, 31, 32
View compiled file toolbar button
    (the glasses), 499
ViewState data, 315
ViewState property
    of the DropDownList control, 359
    maintaining state of a single page, 387
    saving and restoring state of ASP.NET
      controls, 319
    of a Web Form, 316
Visible property, of a column, 228
Visual Basic (VB)
    ASP.NET and, 278
    as an object-oriented language, 50
    printing from, 591
    program development for, 2
    referring to elements in XML
      documents, 529
Visual Basic code, in Web Forms, 278
Visual Basic Development Settings, 7
Visual Basic Language option, in Snippet
    categories, 624
visual designer, of a control, 476
Visual Studio 2008, 6, 554–555
Visual Studio designer, 130
Visual Studio IDE, 2, 6–13, 554
    changing options in, 7–8, 612–613
    creating stored procedures in, 131–132
    database handling in, 189–191
    developing database applications,
      110–111
    Development settings, 7
    setting up the screen in, 608–613
    Web Forms in, 281–282
Visual Studio Professional Edition, 279

Visual Studio projects location, 7
Visual Studio Query Builder. *See* Query Builder
Visual Studio Version 9. *See* Visual
    Studio 2008
Visual Studio Web server, 278
Visual Web Developer 2008 Express Edition,
    276, 279
Visual Web Developer (VWD), 276
VS. *See* Visual Studio
VS (Visual Studio .NET) IDE. *See* Visual
    Studio IDE
VS 2008. *See* Visual Studio 2008
VWD (Visual Web Developer), 276

W

WCF (Windows Communication Foundation),
    250, 518
WCF Service
    accessing data through, 261–268
    adding, 253
    coding, 254, 263–264
    consuming, 256–259
    creating, 252–256, 381–387
    files, 250–251
    form using, 260
    Library project, 261
    Library template, 262, 263
    making modifications to, 387
    performing calculations in, 259–260
    renaming, 253–254, 382
    services included in, 251–252
    setting up for unbound controls, 390
    testing, 255–256
Web Application project model, 280
Web applications. *See also* Web sites
    access to server objects, 315
    adding login controls, 324
    creating, 327–328, 594
    data bindings for, 358
    developing, 6, 276–278
    models for, 280
    running, 286, 304
    selections from a drop-down list, 359
    separating into multiple tiers, 381–387
Web clients, 277
Web controls
    compiling, 482–483
    event handling, 284
    exposing properties of, 481–482
Web documents. *See* Web pages
Web farm, 317
Web Form template, 309
Web Forms, 281. *See also* Web pages
    adding controls to, 329–330
    control types for, 282
    cross-platform development, 276
    displaying reports from, 419–420
    layout and design of, 290–312
    naming, 282
    pieces of, 278
    setting tab order for controls, 311–312
    toolbox for, 282–283
    for validation controls, 312
    ViewState property of, 319
    in the Visual Studio IDE, 281–282
Web methods, for Web services, 383

Web page layout
    creating, 295–304
    with styles created and applied, 303
Web pages, 277, 281. *See also* Web Forms
    adding controls to default, 386
    adding HTML Help ActiveX control to, 500
    creating multiple, 365–366
    database access for, 352
    displaying data on, 355
    displaying related data on multiple,
        364–365
    images on, 288–289
    improving the layout of, 290
    layout out using DIV elements, 295
    layout standards, 291
    life cycle in ASP.NET, 334–335
    LoginStatus control on, 322–323
    navigating to another, 287–288
    partial updates, 333–334
    precompiling, 605
    setting properties, 289
    special characters on, 594
Web projects
    adding data to, 353
    adding database access to, 352
    deploying, 604–606
    making portable, 354
    managing, 335–336
    moving and renaming, 335–336
    opening existing, 282
    running, 286
Web server controls, 283
Web servers, 276–277
    transferring files to, 604
Web Service specifications (WS-*), 250
Web services
    classes for building and using, 3
    writing contracts and methods in, 383–386
Web Services Description Language
    (WSDL), 252
Web Site Administration Tool, 324–325
Web site project, 306
Web Site types, 604
Web sites. *See also* Web applications
    copying and publishing, 336
    creating, 279–290, 296
    opening saved, 335
    publishing, 605–606
    types of, 278–279
    using master pages, 304
Web user controls, 480–483
Web.Config file
    adding support for debugging, 286
    conflict between two, 386
    connection string in, 354
    custom error pages in, 392–393
    editing to make a project portable, 359
    WCF code added to, 250
WebParts list of controls, 283
Web.Services namespace, 3
Where clause, in LINQ, 524, 529
WHERE clauses
    generating, 361
    in SELECT statements, 160
Where operator, in LINQ, 523
While keyword, in a Do loop, 571

Width property
    of the DetailsView control, 357
    of a grid, 355
    of the SizeF structure, 593
wildcard, in a WHERE clause, 160
Window menu
    adding, 26–27
    in MDI, 25
windows
    adding to WPF applications, 521
    closing, 609
    closing or hiding extra, 608–610
    displaying, 609–610
    displaying hidden, 609
    docking, 611
    hiding and displaying, 608–609
    for managing styles, 292, 293
    tabbed, 609
Windows
    user controls, 466–479
    version of, 554
Windows applications
    deploying, 13, 600–603
    handling a database file, 623
    using WCF Service methods, 256–259
Windows Class Library template, 262
Windows Communication Foundation.
    See WCF
Windows database applications, 112–117
Windows Explorer, 17
Windows Form application, Crystal Report
    template in, 404–410
Windows Forms
    accessing and displaying database data
        on, 106
    compared to Web Forms, 281
    developing applications running on any
        system, 276
    displaying a report from, 410–411
    displaying the grid on, 8
    events compared to Web Forms, 284
    interoperability with WPF, 521–522
    phasing out in favor of WPF, 517
Windows Forms Control Library template, 466,
    467, 468
Windows Forms controls, 467
Windows Installer, 13, 600
Windows operating environment, graphical
    components for programs, 3
Windows Presentation Foundation. *See* WPF
Windows projects, forms in, 585–588
Windows.Forms namespace, 3
WindowToolStripMenuItem, 27
Window.xaml file, 518
word wrap, turning on, 613
WorkerReportsProgress property, 535
WorkerSupportsCancellation property, 535
world-ready programs, 531–533
World Wide Web Consortium (W3C), 109, 250
World Wide Web (WWW), 276
WPF (Windows Presentation Foundation),
    517–522
    development platforms, 517
    examples of designs, 517
    including multimedia, 518
    stand-alone applications, 518

WPF applications
    adding extra windows to, 521
    feature set of, 518
    files in, 518
    selecting for the project template,
      518, 519
WPF Interoperability category, 521
WPF project, 518–520
Write method, 595
write-only property, 56
WriteLine method, 595–596
    of Debug, 622
    of StreamWriter, 595
WriteOnly modifier, 56
WS-ReliableMessaging, 250
WS-Security, 250
WSDL (Web Services Description Language), 252

X

X and Y coordinates, 592–593
XAML (Extensible Application Markup
    Language), 518
Xaml style element, 518
XBAPs (XAML browser
    applications), 518
XCopy deployment, 13, 600
XDocument object, 528–530, 598
XElement object, 528–530, 598
XML, 109
    advantages of using, 597
    data stored in, 109–110
    files, 597–598
    literals, 528
    namespace, 3

    processing, 3
    specifications for, 109
    Web Services, 250
    for Web services, 251
.xml file, 469
.xsd file, 115

Y

Year property, 578
yellow dot icon, for styles, 292